TERRIBLE
MAGNIFICENT
SOCIOLOGY

W. W. NORTON & COMPANY

Independent Publishers Since 1923

TERRIBLE
MAGNIFICENT
SOCIOLOGY

LISA WADE

Tulane University

W. W. NORTON & COMPANY

Independent Publishers Since 1923

W. W. NORTON & COMPANY has been independent since its founding in 1923, when William Warder Norton and Mary D. Herter Norton first published lectures delivered at the People's Institute, the adult education division of New York City's Cooper Union. The firm soon expanded its program beyond the Institute, publishing books by celebrated academics from America and abroad. By midcentury, the two major pillars of Norton's publishing program—trade books and college texts—were firmly established. In the 1950s, the Norton family transferred control of the company to its employees, and today—with a staff of five hundred and hundreds of trade, college, and professional titles published each year—W. W. Norton & Company stands as the largest and oldest publishing house owned wholly by its employees.

Editor: Sasha Levitt
Assistant Editor: Erika Nakagawa
Project Editor: Laura Dragonette
Managing Editor, College: Marian Johnson
Managing Editor, College Digital Media: Kim Yi
Associate Director of Production, College: Benjamin Reynolds
Media Editor: Eileen Connell
Associate Media Editor: Ariel Eaton
Media Editorial Assistant: Alexandra Park
Media Project Editor: Danielle Belfiore

Marketing Research and Strategy Director: Julia Hall
Design Director, College: Rubina Yeh
Text Design: Marisa Nakasone
Photo Editor: Catherine Abelman
Photo Researcher: Dena Digilio Betz
Director of College Permissions: Megan Schindel
Permissions Manager: Bethany Salminen
Text Permissions Specialist: Josh Garvin
Composition: Graphic World, Inc. / Sunil Kumar, Project Manager
Manufacturing: Transcontinental — Beauceville, QC

Permission to use copyrighted material is included in the credits section of this book, which begins on page C-1.

ISBN: 978-0-393-26530-9

W. W. Norton & Company, Inc., 500 Fifth Avenue, New York, N.Y. 10110
    www.wwnorton.com
W. W. Norton & Company Ltd., 15 Carlisle Street, London W1D 3BS

1 2 3 4 5 6 7 8 9 0

ABOUT THE **AUTHOR**

LISA WADE, PHD, is an Associate Professor at Tulane University with appointments in Sociology, the Gender and Sexuality Studies Program, and the Newcomb Institute. An accomplished scholar, award-winning teacher, and public sociologist, she has become well known for delivering conversational yet compelling translations of sociological theory and research. She's the author of *American Hookup: The New Culture of Sex on Campus* and, with Myra Marx Ferree, *Gender: Ideas, Interactions, Institutions*.

BRIEF CONTENTS

CONTENTS

12

OUR FUTURE ON EARTH 312

CONCLUSION The Sociological Imagination 342

PREFACE

When I was a child, I did not live in so-called good school districts. I never took an AP class; if I was "gifted," nobody in my high school much noticed. I took the SAT but didn't know I was supposed to study for it. Though I applied to a handful of colleges, I was only admitted to one. And when I arrived for move-in day, it was the first time I'd ever set foot on a college campus. I never could have imagined that someday I would write a book like this.

Sociology has given me so much: a career, peers, even friends. It has given me a platform from which to contribute meaningfully to public debate. But more than anything, it's given me purpose. Sociology helps us see the social forces that transcend the individual and, with that lens, it empowers us to try to make the world a better place. To teach sociology is to give people the tools they need to remake their societies. And while I've had the opportunity to share sociology with many different kinds of people in myriad ways, this book is among the most incredible opportunities I've ever been afforded.

First and foremost, I wanted the book to be a good read. I devoted myself to writing crisply and engagingly. I looked for rich examples and clear statistics. I steered into rather than away from emotions, knowing that sociology not only can, but *should*, inspire curiosity, awe, intrigue, and delight, as well as disappointment, frustration, and even righteous anger. There is no excuse for sociology to be anything but riveting.

I did my best to do justice to the diversity of voices that have contributed to sociological thought, both in the past and today. That meant not only being inclusive but placing this wide array of scholars shoulder to shoulder with those who have historically been lifted up as our "founding fathers." To do this, I was determined to be inclusive far beyond the central sociological concerns with race, class, and gender, and their intersections. Without diminishing the importance of these axes of identity, this book is also attentive to sexual orientation, disability, age, body size, citizenship status, the rural/urban divide, and more. I teach expressly about the value of standpoint, while modeling what it means to take diversity of viewpoint seriously. I hope readers will see themselves reflected not just in what sociologists study but in who sociologists are.

My vision also included a somewhat different approach to the lay of the sociological land. I start with an innovative chapter on the self. Most readers have grown up with the tradition of American individualism, an ideology that sits uncomfortably alongside sociology's basic premise: that there are social forces that transcend individuals. I tackle this problem head-on. In Chapter 1, I show that the individual self is, paradoxically, itself a social fact. Prepped with this astounding idea, readers are better able to accept the role of social facts in shaping other features of daily life.

I also felt it was important to include a chapter that theorizes social organizations, institutions, and structures. These are challenging ideas that deserve careful explication, especially if readers are to fully comprehend the nature of social inequality. This book takes the time to fully introduce them. Likewise, I include a chapter on elite power. All too often we focus on the disadvantages that accrue to some but fail to shine a light on the advantages that accrue to others—and the work they do to preserve those advantages. Elites do not go unexamined here.

I introduce historical figures and sociological research methods throughout the text instead of at the beginning. I do not expect readers to care about the modes of data collection for findings they have not yet encountered and the history of a field they have not yet studied. So, these things are introduced when they become relevant to the book's overall intellectual trajectory. Comprehensive discussions of both sociological history and research methods are also included as appendices.

Roughly speaking, the book is organized in such a way as to introduce core theoretical concepts, address the complex phenomena of social inequality, and explore the potential for social change. Instead of sending readers off with just a few inspiring words, each of the final three chapters is aimed at empowering people to become not just sociological thinkers but engaged and efficacious members of their communities, both large and small. The book ends optimistically, without downplaying the real challenges we face or laying all the responsibility for social change on the next generation.

There is so much more to tell about the earnest care that's been poured into this text. We agonized over punctuation, obsessed over prose, carefully unwrapped concepts, and made harmony out of the whole. Suffice to say,

Terrible Magnificent Sociology comes out of a deep respect for sociology, a true love of writing, and genuine hope for the future.

None of this would have been possible without the help, support, and encouragement of dozens of others. Most notably, Dr. Myra Marx Ferree. In 2006, as I was finishing up graduate school, Myra changed my life, and not for the first time. Long story short, she asked if I wanted to coauthor a sociology of gender textbook that W. W. Norton had been nagging her to write for quite some time. Of course, I said yes! Seven years later, we released *Gender: Ideas, Interactions, Institutions.* That experience gave me the confidence to write *American Hookup: The New Culture of Sex on Campus*, a book that was released to the general public. Academics aren't always well-suited to writing such books, so I am forever indebted to Nathaniel Jacks and Alane Mason for taking a chance on me. *American Hookup* presented me with an opportunity to become a better writer, and I grasped it. Only then, with that and *Gender* under my belt, did I think I could write a textbook like this one.

To all of you at Norton, thank you from the bottom of my heart. As an employee-owned company, you stand proudly behind the texts you publish. You've placed great trust in me. Even now, I remain surprised and delighted at your willingness to support my vision. You gave me free rein to write this book as I pleased; I hope it doesn't disappoint. Thank you specifically to the entire team that has supported its development and launch, including assistant editor Erika Nakagawa, project editor Laura Dragonette, designer Marisa Nakasone, photo editor Catherine Abelman, text permissions specialist Josh Garvin, copy editor Laura Sewell, and production manager Ben Reynolds. A big thank you also to media editor Eileen Connell, associate media editor Ariel Eaton, and media editorial assistant Alexandra Park for your work in creating a thoughtful, cohesive, and engaging digital support package.

Above all, I am grateful to my editor, Sasha Levitt. As a solo author, I leaned heavily on Sasha's expertise. She was my most attentive sounding board, a generous reader of early and all drafts, and an inspirational critic. She steered me off more than one bad path and set me on countless good ones. Alongside practical support, she has offered endless enthusiasm. After four books together, we have become a fantastic team, and good friends too. I hope we continue to write books together for a very, very long time.

Over the years, I've subjected many unsuspecting students to drafts of this book. Thank you to the Occidental College Sociology 101 students who read rough chapters in class. I hope the free textbook was worth it! And thank you to Aaron Hammonds, Claire Krelitz, Sean Ransom, Naomi Schiller, and Carrie Wade for your careful and thoughtful feedback. I am grateful, also, to the *Terrible Magnificent Sociology* Book Club: Alejandra Arroyo, Allen Chen, Taylor Gorretta, Matthew Hao, Kailey Hecht, Anna Lipton, Estephany Lopez, Claudia Oppermann, Megan Purdome, and Michaela Smith-Simmons. Long before the book had its improbable name, these students went over each draft chapter with a fine-tooth comb, looking for opportunities to improve the writing, pedagogy, and narrative. Their fingerprints are all over this text, and it is immeasurably better for their contributions.

As the book reached maturity, it benefited tremendously from the feedback provided by the following reviewers:

REVIEWERS

Alison Better, Kingsborough Community College, CUNY
Marni A. Brown, Georgia Gwinnett College
Kelsy Burke, University of Nebraska
Jennifer Chernega, Winona State University
Elizabeth Clifford, Towson University
Brianne Dávila, California Polytechnic State University, Pomona
Sarah Epplen, Minnesota State University, Mankato
Amanda Fehlbaum, Youngstown State University
Kjerstin Gruys, University of Nevada, Reno
Eileen Huey, Texas A&M University
Sahan Savas Karatasli, University of North Carolina, Greensboro
Kyle Knight, University of Alabama in Huntsville
Michele Lee Kozimor, Elizabethtown College
Joseph Kremer, Washington State University
Elizabeth Legerski, University of North Dakota
Sara Lopus, California Polytechnic State University, San Luis Obispo
Juan Martinez, Northeastern Illinois University
Naomi McCool, Chaffey College
Geoffrey Moss, Temple University
Schneur Zalman Newfield, Borough of Manhattan Community College
Holly Ningard, Ohio University
Tracy E. Ore, St. Cloud State University
Carla A. Pfeffer, University of South Carolina
Sarah M. Pitcher, San Diego City College
Chelsea Platt, Park University
C. Brady Potts, Occidental College
Barbara Prince, Lebanon Valley College
Kayla Pritchard, South Dakota School of Mines and Technology
Anna Sanders-Bonelli, Durham Technical Community College
Paromita Sanyal, Florida State University
Emily Shafer, Portland State University
Jennifer Simmers, University of California, Riverside
David Springer, University of Illinois at Chicago
Tara Tober, University of California, Santa Barbara
Jason S. Ulsperger, Arkansas Tech University
Alicia Walker, Missouri State University
J. Alison Watts, Community College of Philadelphia

I am eternally grateful for their willingness to donate their finite time and energy to this project. These reviewers helped strengthen all the chapters, particularly those for which I had the weakest preparation. Sasha and I took none of their feedback for granted. As a result, the text is more comprehensive, sophisticated, and exacting than it would be otherwise.

And with that, dear book, you are released into the world. We wish so much for you! May you inspire students to read for class every day. May you enliven discussion and make your instructors' workload light. May students genuinely like you; may they sometimes decide to keep you! May you help students discover their own identities as sociologists and a pathway to graduation and beyond. And may you spark a lifelong love for sociology in all who encounter you.

Lisa Wade
Tulane University

TERRIBLE
MAGNIFICENT
SOCIOLOGY

W. W. NORTON & COMPANY

Independent Publishers Since 1923

THE SCIENCE OF SOCIAL FACTS

Some 70,000 years ago, humans began migrating out of Africa. This migration would lead us to settle the farthest reaches of vast continents. We came to live alongside ice caps in the Arctic and under the hot sun of the equator, in underground caves and on the peaks of mountains, in the desert and in the swamp, on plains and in jungles. We crossed oceans to reach the most remote of islands. Today, we live on checkerboards of cultivated crops and in landscapes made of concrete, glass, and steel. We've been to the moon. Someday we might live on Mars.

What is it about us that has enabled this? We're vulnerable to heat and cold. We don't have much in the way of teeth, horns, or claws. We're not particularly fast and have limited ability to climb or dig. We can't even growl. Even our closest relatives are more impressive physically. Chimpanzees are stronger and more nimble, with fur coats, formidable fangs, and big toes like thumbs. If a human and a chimpanzee found themselves alone on a desert island, which one would be more likely to survive? Honestly, probably the chimpanzee.

Put a thousand chimpanzees up against as many humans, though, and it'd be smarter to place your bet on us. "All the huge achievements of humankind throughout history," writes the Israeli historian Yuval Noah Harari, "have been based on this ability to cooperate flexibly and in large numbers."[1] *That* is what makes us special. We have a remarkable ability to tolerate one another, even when we're strangers and even under duress. Try putting 400 chimpanzees shoulder to shoulder and knee to seat in an airplane on its way from New York to Los Angeles. It would be a bloodbath. But humans do this easily. We cooperate. We organize. We share. We're really, really good at working together.

In fact, we've evolved to work together. We're a social species, one designed to live in cooperative communities. Most people find isolation to be emotionally wrenching. Even fake exclusion—like playing a computer game in which people throw a Frisbee back and forth to each other but not to you—has been shown to cause distress.[2] Actual solitary confinement is torture. In prison, it

The exquisite synchrony of marching bands, both musically and in movement, is the kind of coordination that has made humans so successful as a species.

increases the likelihood a person will experience anxiety, depression, and psychosis.[3]

For humans, it's unnatural to be alone. It's always been that way. We were social when *Homo sapiens* came into existence some 300,000 years ago. In fact, we'd already been social for millions of years; the species that would evolve into modern humans was a social one too. Across environments, across continents, across millennia, the presence of other people has been as constant in our lives as oxygen.

As the science of society, **sociology** is the field that takes this fact most seriously.

sociology
the science
of society

SOCIAL FACTS

Sociology is founded on the idea that individuals both influence and are influenced by their communities. Acknowledging this requires a genuine humility. Especially today, and especially in wealthy democracies, we're told to think for ourselves, to do for ourselves, to *be* ourselves. "To thine own self be true," Shakespeare wrote. Or, as we might say today, "You do you." Both phrases evoke the idea that we have an authentic self—one separate from society—and that finding and nurturing that self is essential for a good life.

The truth is less grand but infinitely more beautiful.

It's true that we're born an individual, but we don't remain one. At birth, we join a stream of consciousness hundreds of thousands of years old. We inherit a rich history full of legends, wishes, wisdom, and folly. Though we're all unique, different from all the roughly 108 billion other human consciousnesses that have ever existed on the planet, we're also inevitably and inescapably tied to the other people around us. That's the intriguing paradox that is the premise of sociology: We are individuals, but we are not, have never been, and were never meant to be alone.

Even more humbling, human civilization is indifferent to any one of us. Some people would miss us if we were gone, of course, but social life would otherwise go on unimpeded. There are powerful realities brought into existence by humans, in other words, that are bigger than any individual human. Sociologists call these things **social facts**, products of human interaction with persuasive or coercive power that exist externally to any individual.[4] The phrase was coined in 1895 by Émile (pronounced *eh-meel*) Durkheim (1858–1917), a French social scientist who contributed to the development of sociology.

This book employs an expansive definition of the social fact, encompassing anything produced collectively by people that exerts a force upon us. These range from the trivial to the momentous. That many people around the world traditionally greet each other by shaking hands, for example, is a social fact. Handshakes only exist because humans shake hands. Handshakes also exist independently of you and me. People have been shaking hands for over 2,000 years. Obviously almost everyone who's ever shaken another person's hand is dead by now. And yet, the practice persists.

A French social scientist, Émile Durkheim coined the term "social facts" in 1895.

social facts
products of human interaction with persuasive or coercive power that exist externally to any individual

Handshaking stuck around because it has a persuasive or coercive power. Other people expect to be greeted with a handshake, and doing otherwise can seem strange or rude. Refusing to shake a person's hand might even be interpreted as hostile. So you could decide that you'd rather greet people some other way, but there would be a price to pay. Strained relations, at best. So we keep shaking hands and the behavior is given a life span that exceeds any one of ours.

Because so much of our reality is social, when describing the whole range of social facts, it may be easiest to start by listing what facts are nonsocial. We'd be hard-pressed to change the gravitational pull of the earth, for example. Likewise, the fact of the sun, our solar system, and the universe. But beyond that, things get less clear. In many ways, even nature is a social fact. We're a species that molds nature to suit our own ends. We manicure our backyards, city parks, and college campuses. We build freeways, bridges, and borders between nations that channel the movement of the earth's inhabitants. As a result of agriculture, wheat now covers about 870,000 square miles of the earth's surface.[5] When stay-at-home orders went into effect in response to the Covid-19 pandemic, machines measuring our planet's vibrations registered a sudden stillness.[6] When our natural environment is a product of human interaction with persuasive or coercive power, it can be fairly described as a social fact.

Seen from above, the island of Manhattan is a striking example of how humans cultivate the natural world.

Between nature itself and the handshake are countless other social facts. They include the ways in which we fall in love and build families, our morals and methods of worship, how we play and fight, and so much more. Our nations, economies, and wars are social facts. Our ways of knowing, from medicine to mathematics, are social facts—as is sociology itself, along with all the sciences that humans have invented and developed.

In elaborating on this idea, Durkheim helped invent a new object of inquiry. Geologists studied geological facts, biologists studied biological facts, physicists studied physical facts, and now sociologists studied social facts. If it sounds obvious today, it wasn't then. Durkheim named something that hadn't yet been named. And though social facts depend on humans for their existence, they're as real as any other facts. On this, Durkheim was insistent. Social facts are no less real for being social than rocks are for being geological, cells are for being biological, and fission is for being physical. Social facts are real things and as important to study as any other fact of life. Hence, sociology was born as the science of social facts.

STUDYING SOCIAL FACTS

data
systematically
collected sets
of empirical
observations

At the time, the notion of studying society scientifically was new. Psychologists and biologists studied individuals and their bodies, artists and writers explored the human experience, and philosophers theorized as to what was real and good, but few had thought to put the tools of the scientific method to the task of understanding society itself. In staking a claim on sociology as a science, Durkheim made society into an object of *empirical inquiry*, meaning that it involves looking to the world for evidence with which scientists can test their hunches. Scientists call this evidence **data**, or systematically collected sets of empirical observations.

To collect data, scholars pose **research questions**, queries about the world that can be answered empirically. And they answer those questions with **sociological research methods**, or scientific strategies for collecting empirical data about social facts. In 1895, Durkheim published a book titled *The Rules of Sociological Method*, a manual for how to study society scientifically.[7] His was the second book on the topic. The first—*How to Observe Morals and Manners*—was written almost sixty years earlier by a British sociologist named Harriet Martineau (1802–1876).[8]

Sociological research methods include a wide variety of both qualitative and quantitative strategies for collecting data. **Qualitative research methods** involve careful consideration and discussion of the meaning of nonnumerical data. Qualitative data comes from in-person interviews, images, and text, or through observation. This kind of research is excellent for understanding how people feel, think, and behave.

Quantitative research methods involve examining numerical data with mathematics. This type of research was introduced by another pioneering sociologist, W. E. B. Du Bois (pronounced the American way instead of the French way; that is, *du boyz* instead of *du bwah*). While in graduate school at Harvard, Du Bois (1868–1963) studied at the University of Berlin with social scientists who were inventing *statistics*, a mathematical approach to research that involves collecting, manipulating, and analyzing numerical data. When Du Bois returned to the United States, he was one of only a handful of Americans trained in such methods.

Du Bois recognized the value of quantitative methods because he was trying to communicate facts about Black people to a racist audience. He was born in 1868 to African American parents five years after the end of legal human slavery in the United States. This was not a time of peace and harmony. The country was extending equal protection of the law, citizenship rights, and the right to vote to men of all races—except, in irony most deep, to American Indians—and attempting to reconcile the North and South and adjust to a new economy.[9] These changes were bitterly and violently resisted, especially but not exclusively in the South.

After a visit to the United States in 1834 to observe the local customs, the British sociologist Harriet Martineau wrote the first sociological research methods book.

research questions
queries about the world that can be answered empirically

sociological research methods
scientific strategies for collecting empirical data about social facts

qualitative research methods
tools of sociological inquiry that involve careful consideration and discussion of the meaning of nonnumerical data

quantitative research methods
tools of sociological inquiry that involve examining numerical data with mathematics

W. E. B. Du Bois introduced statistics to American sociology. He used social science to advocate for Black Americans.

sociological sympathy
the skill of understanding others as they understand themselves

research ethics
the set of moral principles that guide empirical inquiry

Du Bois knew that convincing a reluctant majority to understand Black life in the United States would require extremely credible tools. Statistics were a way to ensure that his research would be taken seriously. And it was. Du Bois would become one of the most important Black thinkers in American history, and one of his legacies would be mathematical approaches to data analysis. Thanks in part to him, today's sociologists use ever more sophisticated statistical tools to understand their data.

Du Bois, Durkheim, and Martineau were all insistent that sociological research be systematic and impartial, with the aim of producing accurate findings. Math, though, wasn't the only skill sociologists needed to acquire. Martineau added that studying people in their societies required **sociological sympathy**, the skill of understanding others as they understand themselves. To Martineau, this was important for two reasons.

First, as a type of curiosity, sociological sympathy was an essential tool of data collection. A scholar without it, she argued, is "like one who, without hearing the music, sees a roomful of people begin to dance."[10] Such a person could describe the scene but not fully comprehend its nature. Thus, they might see people moving about in rhythm but miss its role in producing joy or sparking romance.

Second, Martineau argued that only a sociologist with sociological sympathy could be impartial. Only by adopting the point of view of the person being studied are we able to avoid judging them by our own standards. True objectivity, she argued, is not value-neutral but an earnest attempt to understand others' values.

As different research methods are introduced throughout this book, features titled "The Science of Sociology" offer a brief discussion of each method. These are regular reminders that sociology is rooted in the scientific method. They'll also reveal that sociologists are creative and resourceful scientists who've developed a wide range of research methods. For an overview, you can turn to the back of the book and read "A Guide to Sociological Research."

This guide also includes a lengthy discussion of professional **research ethics**, or the set of moral principles that guide empirical inquiry. These principles include *respect* (treating people as autonomous individuals with the right to make informed decisions), *justice* (conducting research that is fair, nondiscriminatory, and nonexploitative), and *beneficence* (doing more good than harm). Practices designed to honor these principles include reporting conflicts of interest, attaining informed consent from research subjects, ensuring confidentiality, and minimizing deception.

THE SCIENCE OF SOCIOLOGY

Sociologists use a wide range of research methods to collect empirical data. They analyze this data with the goal of building sociological theory, then publish these studies as academic articles and books. Thousands of these studies are cited throughout this text, and many can be found in the endnotes referenced at the end of sentences and located at the back of the book. In other words, this book is based on scientific evidence and has been carefully and consistently referenced so that any reader can discover this evidence.

Occasionally the book will discuss a study in some detail. In those cases, features like this one may be included. Together, they introduce thirteen research methods used by sociologists. These features are meant to communicate that sociology is a wide-ranging empirical science that aims to answer research questions in accordance with a moral code.

Please consult "A Guide to Sociological Research" at the back of the book for an extended discussion of sociological research methods, the ethics of scientific inquiry, the process of publishing, and the goal of building sociological theory. ■

One aim of sociological research is to build **sociological theory**, or empirically based explanations and predictions about relationships between social facts. Sociological theories are more than just beliefs; they're conclusions based on the findings of sociological research, some of which spans decades. Theories aim to describe *probabilistic* cause-and-effect relationships, or ones that are likely but not inevitable. To study social facts, then, is to look for **social patterns**: explainable and foreseeable similarities and differences among people influenced by the social conditions in which they live.

Theories start off as sets of related hypotheses and are rigorously tested using both quantitative and qualitative research methods. Theories are always tentative, meaning that scholars are ready to reject or change their theories if the data don't support them. Being willing to change our minds about what we think we know is the core of scientific inquiry, in sociology no less than anywhere else.

Most sociologists also agree that theories are strongest when they're built by many different kinds of scholars asking questions from various **standpoints**, or points of view grounded in lived reality.[11] Standpoint theory was originally developed by women of color, like Chicana sociologist Maxine

sociological theory
empirically based explanations and predictions about relationships between social facts

social patterns
explainable and foreseeable similarities and differences among people influenced by the social conditions in which they live

standpoints
points of view grounded in lived reality

Baca Zinn and Black sociologist Bonnie Thornton Dill. "Lived experience," they write, "creates alternative ways of understanding the social world and the experience of different groups of [people] within it."[12] All standpoints, especially the ones we hear less often, are important for understanding the world. Our personal biographies shape our questions, our research methods, our analysis and insights, and our conclusions. So, if we want sociology to explain the full breadth of social life, everyone has to be involved in its production.

In addition to developing sociological theory, a second aim of sociological research is to support **public sociology**. This involves using sociological theory to make societies better. As the "A Short History of Sociology" unit at the back of the book makes clear, this has always been a central goal of sociology. In the 1800s, Martineau, for example, wrote forcefully about the oppression of women, the enslavement of African Americans, economic inequality, and political disenfranchisement.[13] In *Society in America*, published in 1836, she asked how it was possible that so many U.S. citizens could tolerate these injustices in light of the promise, stated in the Declaration of Independence, that "all men are created equal." Martineau meant for her research to "inform some minds" and "stir up others."[14]

In this sense, sociology is not like other sciences. The power with which sociology is concerned is not geological, chemical, or physical, but social, meaning that sociologists are attentive to the power relationships that exist among us. Sociology doesn't shy away from the hard questions, ones about oppression and exploitation. For this reason, writes the Australian sociologist Raewyn Connell, sociology sometimes "speaks in tones that can offend about power, privilege, and the possibilities of change."[15] It may inform some minds and stir up others. Some may perceive sociology's interest in inequality as evidence of a lack of objectivity. In fact, it is the opposite. Like all social facts, social injustice is real. And sociology is the best intellectual tool we have for alleviating it.

This book takes you on a journey through sociological knowledge and theory. It includes thousands of facts produced by sociologists and describes dozens of research studies in detail. It also introduces you in small doses to sociological research methods. The book also highlights important figures in sociology and offers insight into their standpoints. This will give you a sense of what drives sociologists to ask the questions they do and why diversity is essential to good sociological theory. Hopefully, this will also give you an opportunity to practice your sociological sympathy. Some of the conclusions sociologists draw may not resonate with you. Martineau would recommend that we approach with curiosity if we want to be truly impartial. Always listen for the music.

By the end, you'll have developed a **sociological imagination**.[16] This is the capacity to consider how people's lives—including our own—are shaped by the social facts that surround us. A sociological imagination will help you think even more intelligently about your social worlds, understand how they

public sociology
the work of using sociological theory to make societies better

sociological imagination
the capacity to consider how people's lives—including our own—are shaped by the social facts that surround us

affect your life and the lives of others, and envision different ways of organizing societies, perhaps even better ones. Ultimately, the goal of this book is to help you strengthen your sociological imagination and empower you to understand and influence our shared lives.

We begin right at the center of the paradox that is sociology: the relationship between the individual and society. Letting go of the idea that we're each somehow unaffected by the world around us is an essential first step in developing a sociological imagination. To that end, the next chapter makes an argument that the self is a social fact. Get ready to think about yourself in an entirely new way. ■

COMING UP...

WHAT DOES IT MEAN to say that the self is a social fact? The next chapter suggests that we each develop a sense of self in cooperation with other people, both those we know and those we imagine. We further cultivate that sense of self by thinking frequently about how we want others to see us and working to perfect that self. And we tell stories about our selves in an effort to understand who we are and communicate that to others.

The idea that our self doesn't come spontaneously from somewhere inside of us may be unsettling, but scientists studying the relationship between our psychologies and societies have shown that a sense of self emerges only at the intersection of the two. As I'll emphasize, this doesn't mean that you're not *real*, but it does mean that who you are, and who you will become, is influenced by your social environment. This can be a tough pill to swallow, but I hope the next chapter convinces you that the idea of the social self is not only plausible but more inspirational than the alternative.

Chapter 1 will also introduce you to two research methods, one qualitative and one quantitative.

Welcome to sociology! I'm so glad you're here.

1

THE
SELF

IN THIS **CHAPTER...**

THE PARADOX AT the center of sociology is the fact that although we are individuals, we are not, have never been, and were never meant to be alone. This chapter attempts to resolve that paradox by arguing that our individuality doesn't bubble up from some place deep within us but instead emerges out of interactions with others.

- Humans have the remarkable ability to think about ourselves. That is, we can both do the thinking and be the thing that's being thought about. The sociologist George Herbert Mead captured this by suggesting that we all have an "I" that contemplates a "me." When we see ourselves in a mirror and say, "That's me," our *I* does the recognizing, while our *me* is recognized.

- We're concerned with how others see us, too, and that influences how we see ourselves in turn. Sociologist Charles Horton Cooley theorized that in forming our self-concept, we imagine what other people think about us. He described the self that emerges out of this process as the *looking-glass self*, one that's a consequence of seeing ourselves as we think other people see us.

- We also place ourselves on a life trajectory. We have a sense of where we've been and where we're going. This is our *self-narrative*, a story we tell about the origin and likely future of our selves. Our self-narratives are stories, built only partly on facts and written in collaboration with others.

For all these reasons, our sense of self is a product of human interaction; that is, a social fact.

As you read this chapter, you'll also notice introductions to two research methods:

- The *in-depth interview* is a research method that involves an intimate conversation between the researcher and a research subject.

- The *laboratory experiment* is a research method that involves a test of a hypothesis under carefully controlled conditions.

"Biology gives you a brain. Life turns it into a mind."

—JEFFREY EUGENIDES

One day, a researcher installed a very large mirror in an enclosure containing three Asian elephants: Happy, Patty, and Maxine.[1] The elephants poked and prodded the mirror. They probed underneath, around, and over it. With a little experimentation, they recognized that *they* were the animals in the mirror. They then showed curiosity as to their own appearance. Maxine, for example, was seen opening her mouth to get a good look at her teeth.

This is an example of the mirror test. It's a way to find out whether animals can learn to recognize themselves. Passing the test—being able to tell the difference between another animal and one's own reflection—is taken as strong evidence that a species has the capacity for self-awareness, the ability to be conscious of and able to reflect on one's own existence. To be self-aware is to be a thinking thing that thinks, among other things, about itself.

Though failing the mirror test is not conclusive evidence that an animal *isn't* self-aware, it's surprising how many animals have not yet passed. Sea lions, giant pandas, octopuses, many species of monkeys, and several species of apes have failed the mirror test. Only a handful of animals pass. Seeing themselves in the mirror, magpies will preen. A dolphin will swirl its head and flip upside down. A manta ray will blow bubbles out of curiosity. A chimpanzee, our closest relative, often takes the opportunity to turn around, look over its shoulder, and inspect its rear end.

Like elephants, magpies, and chimpanzees, humans are self-aware. None of us is born this way. Until about four months old, infants are just bundles of perception. They can't differentiate between objects, other people, their environment, and their own bodies. They certainly haven't learned to notice their own existence. Humans won't pass the mirror test until they're between sixteen and twenty-four months old.

Slowly, the brain puts the information together. It notes the synchronized activity in the brain cells that control motion (telling the arm to swing), the

Dolphins, chimpanzees, orcas, and magpies have passed the mirror test, a demonstration of self-awareness. Gorillas have not yet conclusively passed.

ones that process vision (of a flailing fist), and the ones that recognize sensation (when it whacks the side of its crib). Over time, the brain is able to separate the child's body from the other things in its environment. *I did that*, it might understand. *I am a thing.*

I am. This is quite a remarkable thing to think, and this chapter is about what it means for humans to be able to think it. It's about how we become aware of ourselves and others, how those others shape the person we become, and how we maintain a sense of self over a lifetime. Ultimately, this chapter is about how our connections to others make us who we are, ending with the startling idea that we are each a social fact. We start with a careful consideration of what it means to recognize the self.

THE SELF

To think *I am* is to make oneself simultaneously the subject and the object of thought. When we think it, we're both the thing doing the thinking (the subject) and the thing we're thinking about (the object). We can think about ourselves, in other words, the same way that we think about other things. If I scan a typical bathroom, for example, I might see a bathtub, a sink, a towel rack, and myself in the mirror. Among the things I see is *me*, and I can think about myself in the same way that I can think about the fixtures in the room.

In the early 1900s, the sociologist George Herbert Mead (1863–1931) described this dual thinking by differentiating between the "I" and the "me."[2] The *me* is the object of thought: the self we see in the mirror, *our personal person*, the one that is us. As we grow up, the me is the us that we try to get graduated from school and employed in a good job. When one day we see our picture on the wall as Employee of the Month, we say, "That's me!" The me is whom we're proud of being when things go well. It's also whom we're ashamed of when we make decisions that embarrass us.

The *I*, in contrast, is the subject of thought, the person feeling pride or embarrassment. The I is the part of the self that's judging and making judgment calls. It's the part of the self that sets our goals and evaluates our progress. The I is the one that monitors our behavior, trying to ensure that we make the impressions we want to make. It's the part that thinks *Don't mess this up!* during a job interview, *Do they like me?* when we're talking to someone cute, and *What will people think of me?* when we've been caught doing something wrong. Mead described the I as a "running current of awareness," an observer of the me, always watching, planning, and considering.[3]

As an example, think about how people manage their social media accounts. A typical person will have at least one account that's either public or followed by a combination of friends, family, and acquaintances. When they post on it, they'll consider how their followers will perceive the text or images they upload. They ask themselves, in other words, how the post will make them appear to others. The image they choose to present in light of this consideration is their me. And the person doing the considering is their I. They're contemplating: *What do I want others to think of me?* Depending on the desired outcome, the I decides what to post. The me that is then represented is true but also filtered. It's a specific version of you. It's the me your I decides to present to the wider world.

Negotiating the sometimes-treacherous currents of social media requires us to be able to think about other people in complex ways. To do that, we need to develop a **theory of mind**: the recognition that other minds exist, followed by the realization that we can try to imagine others' mental states. We begin developing a theory of mind when we're babies. About the same time that toddlers start to recognize themselves in the mirror, they begin to notice that they're not the only thinking thing in their environment. In other words, they discover not only that *they* exist, but that *other people* exist. Soon a child will be able to imagine what's going on in other people's minds and, against all odds, even feel what other people feel.

By two years old, children are able to express themselves—they know they feel, want, and think—and they're able to imagine that other people also feel, want, and think. Soon they'll be able to be competitive with a sibling who they think has the same wants, know that their caregivers will be pleased if they follow instructions, and learn to play cooperative games like hide-and-seek. All these things require the ability to imagine what's going on in someone else's mind.

We all went through this developmental process, and as we practiced these skills, our theory of mind became quite sophisticated. We practiced gift giving, which requires imagining what someone might like and how an object might fit into their life. We learned to lie, which involves trying to place a false belief

theory of mind
the recognition that other minds exist, followed by the realization that we can try to imagine others' mental states

into the mind of another. By the time we were in elementary school, we could effectively model the collective effort of many brains at once. Participating in a team sport like basketball or playing multiplayer online games, for example, requires us to coordinate our actions with others by simultaneously imagining what *many* other minds are thinking.

Within the first few months of life, our brains were also reaching into the brains of other people, closing the distance between them and us. Our brains do this with *mirror neurons*, cells in our brains that fire in identical ways whether we're observing or performing an action.[4] If I happen to watch you scratch your elbow, for example, the mirror neurons in my brain will light up as if *I* scratched *my* elbow. In fact, a scientist watching my brain would not be able to tell if I had scratched my elbow or you had scratched yours. These brain cells, in other words, don't differentiate between the self and others. Mirror neurons link one brain to another as if they were not two minds but one.

Mirror neurons also respond to emotions. To a mirror neuron, smiling and watching someone else smile are the same. Someone smiles, and our brain smiles with them. So we don't just *understand* that the smiling person is happy, we actually *feel* happy. If your heart has ever been warmed when the couple in a romantic comedy finally admits they're in love, or if you've felt rage tighten your throat in response to someone else's mistreatment, or if you've shared in the joy of a child discovering something new, then you have mirror neurons. My personal weakness is the medal ceremony at the Olympics. How do the happy tears of an athlete I've never met, accepting a medal half a world away, threaten to come streaming out of *my* face? Part of my brain can't tell the difference between someone else's joy and my own. And, so, I am overcome.

Most of us have mirror neuron systems that are just sensitive enough. They allow us to feel what others are feeling without becoming so engrossed in other people's minds that we forget our own. Some people aren't in this "Goldilocks" zone. Their mirror neurons are either too hot or too cold. Some scientists think, for instance, that a cool system helps explain some of the symptoms of autism spectrum disorder.[5] People with autism often struggle to understand what other people are feeling. We take for granted that we tell if someone is happy, sad, or angry. Someone with autism may find this genuinely difficult.

Conversely, some people have mirror neuron systems that are too hot.[6] Interviewed on National Public Radio, a woman named Amanda recalled as a child following a young man around at a Christmas party.[7] "People were hugging him like they hadn't seen him in a while," she said. And every time he got a hug, she would feel as if *she* were getting a hug. "It was like a warm rush up the spine," she said. "And I followed him around, like, the whole entire evening because it was just so nice." It sounds nice, but ultimately her heightened ability to feel what other people are feeling forced Amanda to restrict her contact with others. If people experience pleasure, she experiences pleasure too. But if people get hurt, so does she. Even mundane activities can be extraordinarily uncomfortable. When she watches other people eat, she explained, "It feels like they're shoving food in my mouth." Amanda's mirror neuron system is too hot.

Luckily, most of us have systems that are "just right," and it's a wonderful thing. Scientists and philosophers had long speculated as to the exact mechanism by which humans came to understand and care for one another so intimately. It was a compelling mystery specifically because, in a very real way, we aren't connected at all. We're separate, locked up in our own skulls, inescapably and existentially alone. And yet, the human brain has a way to ease this loneliness. Our biology has provided a way to bring the minds of others tantalizingly close.

Paradoxically, it is out of this closeness that our individuality emerges.

REFLECTING ON THE SELF

In 1902, almost one hundred years before scientists discovered mirror neurons, and eighty years before the first mirror test, the sociologist Charles Horton Cooley (1864–1929) used a different mirror metaphor to explain how humans come to understand themselves, or develop a *self-concept*. This is more than self-awareness, the simple knowledge of our own existence; a self-concept is our understanding of *who* we are based on our personality traits, physical characteristics, ancestry, and biographies. Together with George Herbert Mead—he of the I and the me—Cooley became one of the founders of a field called *social psychology*, the study of the interface between the individual and society. Social psychologists argue that we can't understand either our psychologies or our societies independently of each other. The "mind is social," Cooley insisted, and "society is mental."[8]

Like all scholars, Cooley was motivated to study the relationship between the self and society in part because of his own experiences. He was a shy child and prone to illness, which left him isolated from his peers.[9] He was also intimidated by his high-achieving parents, who had equally high expectations for him. Being socially awkward may have made him hyperaware of the gazes of others, especially if they reflected things he didn't like.

Ultimately, Cooley developed a new theory of the self. Our self-concepts, he argued, could only arise socially, in the presence of other people, through a process in which we choose, interpret, and imagine the views of others. He called this the **looking-glass self**, the self that emerges as a consequence of seeing ourselves as we think other people see us.[10] According to this theory, other people are looking glasses (or mirrors) reflecting a vision from which we form our self-concepts.

Other people are certainly the source of our first ideas about our selves. Before we're even born, our caregivers are busy defining us. To start, they give us our names. We may come into this world as a Charity or a Chardonnay. A Forrest or a Hunter. A Mary or a Jesús. Our parents decide that we're sweet, feisty, or curious long before we could possibly come to those conclusions on our own, and certainly before we have the capacity to challenge them.

looking-glass self
the self that emerges as a consequence of seeing ourselves as we think other people see us

Babies are attributed personality traits and talents, engaged in activities, and given toys. Each of these choices by adults can contribute to the formation of a self.

"He's a kicker," a soccer-loving expectant mom might say proudly as she cringes, smiles, and rubs her belly. "She's the shy one," a dad might tell people about his preschool-age daughter, labeling her with a personality trait that may just be a developmental stage. When parental perceptions stick, kids might grow up to think "I'm sporty" or "I'm an introvert." Our first self is given to us by the people around us.

As we get older, we continue to look to the people around us—our friends, family, and teachers—to inform our self-concept. Some are significant figures, others we encounter only in passing, but anyone can influence how we think about our selves. Mercifully, research shows that we tend to overestimate the extent to which other people like us, so the self-concepts we derive from this process are generally pretty positive.[11]

We also learn to speculate as to what *generalized others* might think of us. These are imagined members of specific social groups. Generalized others represent types of people, with a greater or lesser degree of specificity. We easily divide up the generalized other into categories: teenagers, musicians, NASCAR-lovers, dog people. When we think it's relevant, we tap into our ideas of how an average member of one of these groups might evaluate us. In doing so, we take the perspective of the generalized other. When we look at our behind in the mirror like a chimpanzee, for example, we might be wondering what a generalized other might think of it.

Consider what's going on when people text erotic images to one another. The sociologist Morgan Johnstonbaugh did just this, conducting 101 in-depth interviews with college students (see "The Science of Sociology").[12] In-depth interviews are intimate conversations between a researcher and a *research subject*, a person who agrees to participate in a research project. In interviews, research subjects are offered the opportunity to open up about their personal experiences. Johnstonbaugh asked her interviewees about their motivations and experiences with "sexting," which she defined as the electronic sharing of nude or semi-nude images.

Johnstonbaugh discovered that her female-identified interviewees often sent sexts to their female friends with the express purpose of eliciting positive feedback. "You can't always count on a guy to give you exactly what you want," said one woman. "[Y]ou want someone to be like, I see you, I recognize you for the goddess that you are," she explained. And her female friends were happy to respond that way.

Another interviewee explained why she was happy to see her friends' nudes and respond with support and encouragement. "[G]irls just like don't hear that enough," she told Johnstonbaugh. "[W]e have to struggle already so much in the society as it is [so] women supporting other women and just being like . . . 'you look wonderful and you should know that,' is important." These young women sought the gazes of friends whom they trusted to be complimentary. In doing so, they cultivated looking glasses that would reflect them back as they wanted to see themselves and hoped generalized others would see them that way too.

in-depth interview
a research method that involves an intimate conversation between the researcher and a research subject

THE **SCIENCE** OF SOCIOLOGY

In-depth Interviews

The **in-depth interview** is a research method that involves an intimate conversation between the researcher and a research subject. Interviews are designed to capture the responses of a few people in great depth (a couple dozen, perhaps, or up to several hundred). Interviews tend to be *semi-structured*, meaning that questions are decided ahead of time, but the researcher is allowed to ask different questions depending on the flow of conversation. And the questions are usually *open-ended*. That is, instead of asking questions that can be answered with a yes or no, open-ended questions are designed to elicit lengthy, free-ranging answers. The resulting data are excellent for understanding how people experience their lives and form their opinions.

Researchers generally type out their interviews word for word. The resulting documents are then subjected to **coding**, a process in which segments of text are identified as belonging to relevant categories. These categories, or *codes*, will refer to concrete or abstract features of the conversation that are relevant to the research question. Johnstonbaugh, for example, coded for whether her interviewees said they sent sexts in the hopes of receiving a compliment, a laugh, or an invitation to come over, among other things. After coding, researchers count how frequently certain codes appear and among whom, looking for patterns in how people experience or explain their lives.

In almost all research involving people, sociologists are ethically obligated to protect their research subjects' identities. Usually this means ensuring *confidentiality*. This is a promise that the researcher will not release personal information that can be connected to the research subject, including the fact of their participation. To preserve confidentiality, researchers refrain from releasing the names of people who've participated and keep data in secure locations. After research is completed, they may permanently separate people's real names from the data and destroy any evidence of the connection. When they talk or write about their findings, researchers will also assign *pseudonyms*, or fictitious names, to interviewees. ■

All these reflections are at least somewhat distorted.[13] The looking glass is a bit like a fun house mirror; we need to do quite a bit of guesswork as to whether the reflected image is accurate. Moreover, as we try to guess what other people really think of us, we often add a fair bit of distortion ourselves. Thanks to the inescapable fact of our separateness, we can never truly see what others see, so we use our theory of mind and our mirroring brains to make guesses. In fact, studies show that our self-concepts have more in common with what we *think* other people think of us than what they actually think. These observations led Cooley to summarize his theory this way: "I am not what I think I am. I am not what you think I am. I am what I think you think I am."[14]

We're looking glasses for others too. Other people are trying to discern who they are from us at the same time we're seeing a vision of ourselves. Like any two mirrors that are opposite each other, the result is a recursive set of reflections: mirrors facing each other in perfect symmetry, each reflecting the other reflecting itself, repetitively into the infinite distance. "I imagine your mind," Cooley explained, "and especially what your mind thinks about my mind, and what your mind thinks about what my mind thinks about your mind" and so on.[15] The only way to opt out of the infinity mirror is to opt out of social interaction altogether.

coding
a process in which segments of text are identified as belonging to relevant categories

To see or not to see

Christopher Knight tried to opt out. In 2013, Knight was arrested while raiding a summer camp in central Maine. His mug shot revealed an aging White man with a bald head and scraggly beard wearing the same pair of eyeglasses he'd worn for his senior high school portrait in 1984. He was charged with approximately 1,000 burglaries of camp kitchens and lake cabins in the area.

Knight had lived alone in the woods for a long time. "For how long?" asked the police officer after Knight was arrested. He paused and said that he left the same year the Chernobyl nuclear power plant exploded. That was 1986. "I just walked away," he said.

While he was in jail awaiting trial, Knight reluctantly agreed to be interviewed by a journalist named Michael Finkel. Sitting across from each other, separated by a pane of plastic, the two squared off. Finkel wanted Knight's story to tell us something profound about the human condition. Knight thought this was ridiculous. "Some people want me to be this warm and fuzzy person," he said, annoyed. "All filled with friendly hermit wisdom. Just spouting off fortune-cookie lines from my hermit home."[16]

Knight insisted that there wasn't anything to tell. Out in the woods alone, he said, the human condition didn't reveal itself. It just *went away*. Without other people, he explained, "I lost my identity." His self didn't change, and he certainly didn't become more true to himself, more "authentic" somehow. He continued:

> With no audience, no one to perform for, I was just there. There was no need to define myself; I became irrelevant. . . . I didn't even have a name. I never felt lonely. To put it romantically: I was completely free.[17]

Knight had retreated into a world in which there were no individuals, where neither he nor anyone else existed. Without other people, there were no looking glasses to reflect him. No I and no me. With the exception of his raids of nearby cabins, during which he tried to avoid being caught, he may have even lost the habit of imagining what generalized others might think of him. Why bother? In the woods, without anyone around, and without the anticipation of an encounter, there was no need to define himself. Like a chipmunk, he slept and stayed warm and nibbled on snacks. He existed, but, in a certain way, he had no self-concept. He was, as he put it, "just there," unreflective, unreflected. Without looking glasses to peer into, he disappeared to himself.

Very few of us flee the company of others entirely. Instead, like sexting teenagers, most of us curate our collection of looking glasses. We seek ones that reflect the person we want to be and, to the extent that we can, avoid the rest. Sometimes that means changing who we are so as to give the right impression.[18] Other times, we manage our self-concept strategically. Sometimes people's ideas about us are contradictory, giving us an opportunity

For twenty-seven years, Christopher Knight lived alone in this secret camp in the woods. In the absence of others, he stopped thinking about what others thought of him, and then stopped thinking much about himself at all.

to pick and choose the self we want to embrace. Your mom might say "you're talented" and your dad might say "you're very hardworking" and you might side with one or the other, or both. Often, we simply reject or accept someone's ideas about us. My ex might think I'm a jerk, for example, and I may disagree. Your dog might think you're the best person in the universe, and you might decide that dogs have pretty good judgment.

We may try to pick and choose whose opinions to care about, but this doesn't mean we're immune from caring what others think. It's exactly because we *do* care that we sometimes insist that we do not. And how could we not? Thanks to mirror neurons, we feel other people's emotions as if they were our own. So, if someone looks at us with disgust, disdain, or hatred, their negative perception of us threatens to become part of our self-image. Our mirror neurons can't tell the difference between someone else hating us and us hating ourselves. No wonder we generally avoid people who we think dislike us. From this point of view, that old piece of advice so often given by

self-fulfilling prophecy
a phenomenon in which what people believe is true becomes true, even if it wasn't originally true

laboratory experiment
a research method that involves a test of a hypothesis under carefully controlled conditions

variable
any measurable phenomenon that varies

experimental group
the group in a laboratory experiment that undergoes the experience that researchers believe might influence the dependent variable

control group
the group in a laboratory experiment that does not undergo the experience that researchers believe might influence the dependent variable

causal claims
assertions that an independent variable is directly and specifically responsible for producing a change in a dependent variable

correlational claims
assertions that changes in an independent variable correspond to changes in a dependent variable but not in a way that can be proven causal

adults to teenagers—that we shouldn't care what other people think—sounds pretty unrealistic.

Ultimately, whether we accept or reject someone's opinion of us is influenced by whether we like it, whether it's part of our self-concept already, and whether it's reinforced by other available looking glasses. It also depends on whether we have an intimate relationship with the person, identify with them as a similar kind of person, or see them as someone who can fairly evaluate us.[19] When a person also falls into a group of generalized others that we identify as important, we tend to take their reflections of us more seriously. So, if you're a young woman growing up in Florida, you may find it somewhat easy to ignore what your seventy-two-year-old Minnesotan uncle thinks of you, and a little less easy to ignore what your friends at school think.

Whatever power we exert in shaping others' perceptions, and despite our ability to reject at least some of the ones we don't like, our self is still dependent on those looking glasses. It's hard to imagine we're funny if no one ever laughs at our jokes. But, if they do, we may develop our sense of humor to keep them laughing. In this way, the looking-glass self is a **self-fulfilling prophecy**, a phenomenon in which what people believe is true becomes true, even if it wasn't originally true.[20] Applied to the self, it goes something like this: If enough people consistently reflect us in a certain way, their impressions will shape our impression of ourselves, and we will act accordingly, bringing into existence the self that they originally saw.

In an excellent demonstration of the self-fulfilling prophecy, a group of researchers tested whether wearing cologne changed men's behavior in ways that made them more attractive to women.[21] They did a laboratory experiment, a test of a hypothesis under carefully controlled conditions (see "The Science of Sociology"). They randomly assigned thirty-five men to apply a scented or non-scented body spray, then asked the men how confident they felt about their attractiveness. Men who applied the scented spray reported feeling more confident than those who'd applied the non-scented spray. All the men were then filmed introducing themselves to a hypothetical "attractive woman."

A panel of eight women were then asked to watch the videos and judge the men's attractiveness. They weren't told that the men had been given body spray of any kind and they, of course, could not smell them. Nevertheless, the men who'd been randomly assigned a fragrance were rated as more attractive. The fragrance made the men *feel* more attractive, which gave them a boost in confidence; that confidence made them more attractive to the women observers. The fragrance, in other words, induced a self-fulfilling prophecy. By making the men feel more attractive, it actually made them so. Summarizing the study, the sociologist Bradley Wright explained: "The secret may not be whether a woman thinks a man smells good, but rather whether a man thinks he smells good."[22] To paraphrase Cooley, "I am not as sexy as I think I am. I am not as sexy as you think I am. I am as sexy as I think you think I am."

THE **SCIENCE** OF SOCIOLOGY

Experimental Research in the Laboratory

A **laboratory experiment** is a research method that involves a test of a hypothesis under carefully controlled conditions. In laboratory experiments, researchers bring research subjects into a *lab*, a room specifically designed for experiments. In the lab, researchers attempt to keep the experience of every subject exactly the same, with one exception: the independent variable.

A **variable** is simply any measurable phenomenon that varies. An *independent variable* is one that's hypothesized to influence the dependent variable, or cause an effect. A *dependent variable* is one that's hypothesized to be influenced by the independent variable; it's the phenomenon expected to show an effect. Any other variables that might influence the dependent variable are called *control variables*. They reflect the phenomena that researchers attempt to keep exactly the same, or "hold constant," so that changes in the dependent variable can be attributed to the independent variable specifically.

Experimenters assign research participants to one of two groups. Members of the **experimental group** go through the experience that researchers believe might influence the dependent variable. Members of the **control group** do not go through that experience. After the experiment is over, the researchers look to see whether the independent variable influenced the dependent variable by comparing the data collected from each group.

In the lab study about the effects of body spray, for example, the use of scented or non-scented body spray was the independent variable and women's evaluation of the men's attractiveness was the dependent variable. Other features of the room and the experience were held constant, so every test of the hypothesis proceeded in exactly the same way. The men in the study were randomly assigned to either the experimental or the control group so that each group was about equally handsome on average.

Laboratory experiments are one of the few research methods that allow scientists to make **causal claims**, or assertions that an independent variable is directly and specifically responsible for producing a change in a dependent variable. Almost all other research methods only facilitate **correlational claims**, assertions that changes in an independent variable correspond to changes in a dependent variable but not in a way that can be proven causal. ∎

Our self-concept, then, emerges out of a lifetime of interactions, both real and imagined. Based on these experiences, we come to understand ourselves as a certain kind of person. We're active participants in this process. We have some choices as to what looking glasses to seek out and take most seriously, but we don't develop a self-concept alone. We need others to figure out who we are.

If our self is a product of our interactions with others, though, why do we feel like the same person from day to day? Cooley says that our selves are stable when our circumstances are stable. I'm a college professor, for example, so you'd be right to guess that I enjoy telling other people about ideas. That feels like a fixed thing about me. But is it? Do I keep showing up to teach classes because my self doesn't change? Or does my self stay the same because I keep showing up to teach classes? Does your life stay the same because your personality does? Or is your personality stable because your life stays the same? Cooley believed the latter: Our personalities feel fixed largely because our life circumstances are relatively stable.

We also stabilize our selves by seeking out others who reflect back at us the people we think we are, even at the expense of thinking better of ourselves.[23] In a study of college students living in residence halls, for example, people with strong self-concepts were more likely to want to continue to live with their roommate one year later if their roommate saw them as they saw themselves.[24] Likewise, the most happily married couples are ones who have accurate understandings of each other, not overly romantic ones. We like people who validate our self-concepts, even at the expense of more positive evaluations.

It can be invigorating to shake things up, even if just a little, by taking a vacation, getting a new job, or switching schools. And sometimes we face identity crises that prompt real self-reflection and reinvention, like becoming aware of new facts about our ancestry or beginning to question the gender we were assigned at birth. Outside of these events, however, we rarely change very much. We're attached to our selves. And so are the people around us. If we start acting noticeably differently, it can make others uncomfortable. If the foodie becomes a picky eater overnight, if the football fan loses interest in the game, if the introvert converts to an extrovert, people don't take it in stride. Change, even when it's neither positive nor negative, is disconcerting.

Our selves tend to resist change, too, because our lifetime of formative experiences is a buffer against sudden shifts. Our self-understanding is usually more influential than either our own whims or the whims of others. Even when we go somewhere new or surround ourselves with fresh looking glasses, we know who we are and where we've been. Whether we're in São Paulo, Seoul, or Saskatchewan, we remember who we were back home.

Unless, of course, we don't.

THE STORY OF THE SELF

The role of memory in holding together a sense of self is acutely illustrated by the story of someone whose memory was lost. This is what happened to a twenty-eight-year-old American named David MacLean. One day, he found himself standing in a busy train station in India, and he didn't know who he was. He could remember how to walk, talk, and read. He remembered his email password and the things he learned in school. But he couldn't remember anything about his life or the people he knew. Nor did he know why he was in India. "It was darkness darkness darkness, then snap," he wrote. "Me. Now awake."[25]

The first person to speak to him was a police officer. MacLean explained that he was lost and couldn't remember who he was. The officer replied, kindly: "I am here for you. I have seen this many times before. You foreigners come to my country and do your drugs and get confused. It will be all right, my friend."

MacLean's brain flickered. He had a sudden vision of a dirty mattress in a run-down room and a redheaded girl, he said, "coming toward me twirling little baggies." It was comforting to have a memory, despite the unpleasant conclusion he drew. Although it pained him to recall the drug use, in a way he wished he were still the person he used to be. "A drug addict could cry over his wasted life," he said. "I was worse than a drug addict—I was nothing." The police officer took him to an internet café and he logged into his email, figured out who his parents were, and sent a cry for help.

Later, MacLean would be diagnosed with retrograde amnesia, a loss of the ability to recall anything that happened before an injury or illness. The closest thing most of us will ever experience to retrograde amnesia is the occasional morning when we're woken suddenly out of an especially deep sleep. It can take us a few seconds to remember who we are upon waking. *Just darkness darkness darkness, then snap. Now awake.* It can make us momentarily confused about where we are, what day it is, and what we're supposed to be doing, but it takes our brain only microseconds to reassemble our reality. Then we get up and proceed with our lives.

Imagine if that feeling never left us. That was what MacLean experienced. To have amnesia, he wrote, was to have a pulsing, palpable nothingness inside:

> I could feel the heavy absence in my brain, like a static cloud. I couldn't remember anything past waking up. There was a thick mass of nothing up there. . . . I was alone, alone with no idea how far I was from anyone who knew me. I was alone and empty and terrified.[26]

His memory was gone and, with it, his self-concept.

Remembering our selves

Cases of amnesia like MacLean's show us that our self-concept is reliant on our ability to reassemble our reality, like we do routinely each morning. Our reality is our **self-narrative**, a story we tell about the origin and likely future of our selves.[27] We write it in collaboration with others, though we are its primary author and editor. The non-amnesiac brain remembers its self-narrative. This is how our I recognizes our me every morning. We recall a journey—we note where we've been and where we're going—and then get out of bed and step back on the path.

self-narrative
a story we tell about the origin and likely future of our selves

MacLean's amnesia left him with no such narrative, and he felt this absence acutely. He described himself as a "blank sheet that had just been rolled in the typewriter. No backstory, no motivation, no distinguishing characteristics." He didn't know where he'd been or where he was going and that left him with absolutely no idea as to who he was. He had no narrative.

Someone gave him a cigarette, which he smoked with relish, though he later learned that he'd never smoked a day in his life. Another offered him a glass of Scotch and he recoiled from the taste, only to discover later that he'd been an avid drinker. He leaned heavily on the looking glasses around him for guidance. "All I had to go on for my identity was the reactions of the people around me," he explained. "I assembled a working self out of the behavior of others." And it was a self-fulfilling prophecy: "People treated me a certain way and I became the kind of person who is treated like that."

Like the idea of a drug addict's "wasted life," many of the self-narratives we employ are prepackaged, including familiar characters and plot lines. People rise from "rags to riches" or find themselves "born again."[28] You can too. "Love at first sight" stories send a message about how we find soulmates. "Coming out" stories offer models for how Two-Spirit, LGBTQIA, asexual, or polyamorous people should process and respond to their desires. Attend any Alcoholics Anonymous meeting and you might hear a narrative about "rock bottom," implying a transition between the harmful path that brought the person there and a path of redemption.

We sometimes even nest our narratives in the narratives of others.[29] Those of us whose self-concepts are shaped by the stories we tell about our ancestors, for example, are framing our lives as another chapter in a longer story. We may be a child of immigrants, whose parents braved a new land to give us a better life; a third-generation Louisianan who's carrying on the family tradition of crab fishing; or an adherent of Judaism who's reminded at the annual Passover seder to carry on the legacy of the Jews who came before.

Our self-narrative, then, is built out of a lifetime of experiences and drawn from

When a person imagines themselves to be fulfilling the wildest dreams of their ancestors, they are placing their life story into a larger narrative. This changes the meaning of their personal accomplishments.

prepackaged stories. It's the source of our self-concept and what makes it feel real. Being able to pull events and episodes out of our past to explain our present gives our self-concept a feeling of authenticity. *Look*, we say to others and ourselves, *I was always this way* or *I'm this way because of that* or *I share my story with people like me*. Out of our experiences and cultural narratives, we craft a believable story, one that makes our self feel coherent, stable, and authentic.

But it's never wholly true.

Between fact and fiction

Our self-narrative is not a true story. First, it's not true because most of us forget almost everything that happens to us. Most every conversation, meal, game, and exam are lost to our conscious memory. They're not special enough to merit remembering. Or they were, and they didn't stick anyway.

Second, of the events we do remember, we have considerable leeway in deciding which are plot points, which characters play a starring role, and which story arcs to draw out. Likewise, we can usually discount the things and people in our past that contradict our narrative. In other words, the version of our selves we believe in is probably far more coherent than our actual life history can support. Our self-narrative isn't a faithful account of our life; it's an imaginative one.

Well into my twenties, for example, I told people I grew up on a farm. I described a childhood filled with barbed wire fences, mud pits, and trees to climb. There was an enormous gentle-hearted horse named Jughead, a spotted goat named Joker, and a menagerie of guinea pigs, rabbits, cats and dogs, chickens, and the occasional pair of ducks. We also had a black cow named Valentine that we rode awkwardly; it's very uncomfortable to ride a cow, in case you haven't tried.

I always talked about the farm as if I were describing my life. Then one day it dawned on me that I wasn't. I didn't grow up on a farm. I grew up in the city of San Jose, California, on the border of Milpitas in the left side of a duplex in a crowded multiracial neighborhood. Granted, I spent every summer on the farm with my cousins—the stories were real—but it was *they* who grew up on a farm. Not me.

Those summer months were so memorable, though, and I recalled them with such enthusiasm that I came to *feel like* and *identify as* a farm girl. It became part of my story, even though it wasn't technically accurate. In a way, I was unconsciously telling a lie to get at something that felt true. It's a common type of misrepresentation.

Think about how routinely we're asked to tell the story of our lives. You probably told some version of your self-narrative as part of your college application. In writing it, you may have made an argument about your self. The act of making that argument might have strengthened that self-narrative in your own mind. It may feel more true today than it did the day before you wrote it, especially if you were validated with college admission.

As a child, I spent my summers with my sister, cousins, and a whole host of farm animals. That's me in the middle with Cookie, a Shetland pony. Even though I grew up in San Jose, California, I came to identify as a farm girl.

We tell other kinds of stories in other contexts: with new friends, to therapists, on dates, and in all manner of situations. When we tell these personal stories, we usually do so with a goal other than accuracy.[30] We may be trying to bond with someone, be understood, affirm someone else's experiences, get sympathy, put on a brave face, seem wise, or get a job or a laugh. Each of these goals changes how we draw out the story, what we emphasize and what we leave out. Over time, the real story can get lost in our memory. This makes our autobiographical memories particularly vulnerable to distortion.

In fact, our strongest memories are the ones *most* likely to be untrue. That's because the more often we recall a memory, the less well we remember it. It feels like the opposite must be the case—that recalling memories would keep them fresh in our minds—but that's not how memory works. Instead, each time we recall a memory, we add the recollection to the memory itself. Over time, all the recollections blend in with the original memory, and their content slowly drifts.

To put it metaphorically, if a memory were an oil painting, it wouldn't be finished and hung up on the wall for later reference. Instead, it would stay on the easel. Each time we recalled the memory, we'd paint over it again. The first time, we'd likely repaint it quite faithfully because the original painting would be right there in front of us. It would be easy to copy precisely. But the second time we recalled it, we'd do so just a little less perfectly because, with a layer of paint on top, we wouldn't be able to see it quite as crisply as we did the first time. The third time we recalled it, we'd paint over it again. And so on. Each recollection would mean a new layer of paint. Over time, the content, color, and texture of the painting would inevitably change. The original would get quite lost underneath all those recollections.

Memory distortion is so predictable, and it occurs with such swiftness, that experts recommend trying to avoid recalling memories when accuracy is important. For example, police officers are now advised not to ask eyewitnesses to describe a person they saw committing a crime. Doing so actually reduces the likelihood that they'll be able to accurately pick a guilty person out of a lineup.[31] Recalling the face, even one time, distorts the memory, making it harder for witnesses to recognize the person when they see them again.

Counterintuitively, then, it's our most often recalled memories that are most likely to be untrue. The memories that we most relish, and the ones that most torture us, become the most distorted, because we think about them over and over again until they've taken on a life of their own. To our brain, the last recall is as true as the first.

Meanwhile, some of the memories out of which we build our self-narrative are complete fabrications. Our brain is vulnerable to suggestion. In a famous study, research subjects were asked to look over an advertisement featuring a child shaking hands with Bugs Bunny at Disneyland.[32] Sometime later, a third of the research subjects said they remembered meeting Bugs themselves. This, of course, is impossible; Bugs Bunny belongs to Disney's competitor, Warner Bros. We may resist the idea that this could happen to us, but it almost certainly already has. We all have false memories—probably pretty elaborate ones—and we have no way of knowing which ones they are.

David MacLean's memory of using drugs, for example—the vivid images of a freckled redhead grinning and shaking a small bag of white powder, of shooting drugs into his veins, of a filthy mattress on the floor of a dirty room—were all invented by his brain in response to the policeman's suggestion that he was disoriented because he was high. MacLean wasn't a drug user. His amnesia was a rare side effect of a then-common medicine given to Americans traveling to countries with a risk of malaria. Physicians confirmed that he'd not been taking any illegal drugs. There was no redhead. There never was.

THE SELF AS A SOCIAL FACT

Our brain has a great imagination. It forgets things, it alters memories, it makes stuff up, it merges memories together, it even borrows memories, taking the experiences of others and folding them into our own. Mirror neurons make us especially vulnerable to this. Inside of our head, our brain thinks all of this is real, no matter how warped, twisted, or contrived the memories really are. Maybe there never was a cow named Valentine on my cousins' farm. No amount of digging around in my brain trying to remember her will prove it. And, because of the oil painting effect, the more effort I put into remembering her, the less likely I'll be able to recall her with any clarity at all.

Our sense of self, then, is not true in the normal sense of the word. Instead, it's a messy mix of constantly evolving memories, most of which are semi-true at best, that are passed back and forth between us and the people in our lives who serve as looking glasses.

As we narrate our past, we're also imagining possible future selves.[33] Some of these selves are the selves we think we ought to be, others are who we fear we'll be, and still others are versions of our selves we hope to be. We work these out in collaboration with others too.[34] Our looking glasses affirm or refute possibilities for our coming selves, encouraging us or casting doubt on this version or that. All their feedback shapes who we can imagine being tomorrow and the next day. And the self-fulfilling prophecy plays a role here too.

Our past self, our present self, and our future selves are all, in other words, social facts. From the moment we develop self-awareness, we begin constructing a self-concept out of our interactions with others, committing to memory a narrative about who we are, dismissing and misremembering things inconsistent with our self story, and imagining who we might be in the future. These experiences really do shape who we are, giving our self-concepts an impressive stability most of the time.

The precise nature of our consciousness, then, is a product of human interaction. Had we been born one hundred years ago, on the other side of the world, or into a different family, we'd be different, maybe a lot different than we are today. Of course, this doesn't mean that our self isn't *real*. Quite the contrary. To Durkheim's point, we are real because social facts are real. Surround yourself with different looking glasses, and you might change, but you'll change into a quite different *and equally real* version of yourself. Who will you be tomorrow? It depends. ∎

COMING **UP**...

IN THE INTRODUCTION, this book suggested that we're surrounded by *social* facts. This chapter made an argument that one of those facts is our sense of self. From our earliest moments, we look to others as an important source of self-understanding. And throughout life, we refine our self-concept. We internalize others' gazes but also choose looking glasses that reflect what we want to see. We resist and challenge some people's impressions of us too. But no matter what conclusions we come to, we don't imagine who we are in a social vacuum.

Out of these experiences, we develop a self-narrative. These stories serve a social purpose. They help us communicate to others who we *feel* we are and enable us to craft the kinds of relationships we need and desire. They're also the basis on which we plot our future selves, imagining ourselves on a coherent trajectory.

The next chapter will show that in becoming who we are, we become more than just social. We become *cultural*. Human groups collectively imbue the world around them with symbolic meaning. These meanings are arbitrary; they can be and often are different from group to group. But they're also social facts. So, to get along with others, we must become familiar with the symbolic meanings shared by members of our group and act accordingly.

2

CULTURE &
CONSTRUCTION

IN THIS **CHAPTER**...

THE LAST CHAPTER argued that the self is a social fact developed in concert with the people around us. This chapter explores those people. Its main argument is that all human groups have unique *cultures*, a word we use to describe shared ideas, as well as objects, practices, and bodies that reflect them.

- Humans engage with their natural environment, but they also act in relation to an intricate series of *social constructs*, defined as influential and shared interpretations of reality that vary across cultures.

- We learn these social constructs through *socialization*, a lifelong learning process by which we become members of our cultures and subcultures. Media is a source of this socialization. So are the people around us.

- Socialization is also a force behind what we value. Both our sense of right and wrong, and our rationales for why we believe what we do, have culture as their source. Hence, sociologists warn against *ethnocentrism*, or assuming that one's own culture is superior to the cultures of others.

Two research methods round out this chapter:

- *Social network analysis* involves the mapping of social ties and exchanges between them.
- *Biosocial research methods* investigate relationships between sociological variables and biological ones.

"The easiest way to get brainwashed is to be born."

—ROBERT ANTON WILSON

I n 1893, the U.S. Supreme Court convened to decide a fateful case. Its task: to determine, once and for all, whether the tomato was a fruit or a vegetable. The case was brought by a family with the last name of Nix who had a tomato-importing business. At the time, the law required that taxes be collected on imported vegetables but not fruit. The lawyers for the Nix family argued that the tomato was a fruit and, therefore, exempt from taxation.

Science was on their side. Botanists define fruit according to whether the structure plays a role in plant reproduction. Any plant product with one or more seeds is a fruit, whereas vegetables don't have seeds. All other plant products—stems, roots, leaves, and some seeds themselves—are vegetables. We call children the "fruit of our loins" (and not the "vegetables of our loins") for exactly this reason.

Most of us are not botanists, however; we're people who put food in our mouths. That is, we're generally more interested in how *we* use the parts of plants than in how *plants* use them. In the United States, we tend to divide plant products according to whether they're sweet or savory. If we eat them for dinner, they're vegetables. And if we eat them for dessert, they're fruit.

When the Nix family brought their question to the Court and the botanists made their case about the tomatoes, the justices said, "We don't care," or something to that effect. Here's some of the text of their unanimous opinion:

> Botanically speaking, tomatoes are the fruit of a vine. . . . But in the common language of the people, whether sellers or consumers of provisions, all these are vegetables which are grown in kitchen gardens, and which, whether eaten cooked or raw, are . . . usually served at dinner in, with, or after the soup, fish, or meats which constitute the principal part of the repast, and not, like fruits generally, as dessert.[1]

Tomatoes *are* fruit, in other words, but Americans prefer to think of them as vegetables. So, the Nix family had to pay the tax.

What is the tomato? Yes, it's a reproductive strategy for a plant indigenous to Mexico, but it's more than that to us. It's salsa, spaghetti with meatballs, a

Bloody Mary, a BLT. To the Nix family, the tomato was their livelihood. To the Supreme Court, it was commerce: a product that could be taxed to build roads and bridges. To the chef, it's an ingredient: a source of sauces, carrier of spices, and symbol of summertime. To the heckler, it's used as a classic insult, thrown at an entertainer who's bombing on stage. The tomato is all these things. In this the Supreme Court was right. What really matters to us isn't what the tomato *is*, but what we make of it.

The tomato is also an example of something that makes humans unusual among animals. Thanks to our powerful brains, we don't just encounter the world; we embellish it. We layer an intricate fantasy world onto reality. Just as we see criticism in a tossed tomato, we see love in a golden ring, rage in a middle finger, and friendship in a bracelet made of string. For humans, reality is embroidered with meaning, adorned with significance, and heavy with value.

We pay attention to this fantasy world if we know what's good for us. A red light doesn't mean stop—not *really*—but to ignore one is to risk injury, a fine, or a lawsuit. The lines on the map we call borders aren't natural, but cross one without a country's permission and we can get thrown in jail. We can try to use our middle finger to say "I love you," but it will take quite a bit of explaining. And if we keep putting tomatoes in the fruit salad, we'll stop getting invited to potlucks.

This chapter is about the ideas with which humans elaborate their lives. It's an introduction to **culture**, the word we use to describe differences in groups' shared ideas, as well as the objects, practices, and bodies that reflect those ideas. It's also an exploration of **socialization**, that lifelong learning process by which we become members of our cultures. Through socialization, we become **culturally competent**, able to understand and navigate our cultures with ease. Let's start with social construction.

SOCIAL CONSTRUCTION

By virtue of being different things to different people, the tomato is a **social construct**, an influential and shared interpretation of reality that will vary across time and space.[2] Social constructs emerge out of **social construction**, the process by which we layer objects with ideas, fold concepts into one another, and build connections between them. Generally, members of the same culture share similar social constructs. For this reason, they have staying power; no one person can change them at will. We can try, of course—hence, the tomato going all the way to the Supreme Court—but real change requires a culturewide shift.

Essentially all human communication depends on social constructs, starting with language. Even saying "hello" depends on them. An *h* represents a *huh* sound. Add it to the other line drawings—the swirly *e*, upright *l*s, and self-contained *o*—and you have a collection of letters and series of sounds we recognize as a friendly greeting. Language is merely a very complex and evolving set of social constructs.

But human language is far more expressive than mere letters and sounds. Everything is steeped in meaning. We communicate with cowboy hats, by

culture
differences in groups' shared ideas, as well as the objects, practices, and bodies that reflect those ideas

socialization
the lifelong learning process by which we become members of our cultures

culturally competent
able to understand and navigate our cultures with ease

social construct
an influential and shared interpretation of reality that will vary across time and space

social construction
the process by which we layer objects with ideas, fold concepts into one another, and build connections between them

how we cross our legs, and by whether we own a pit bull or a poodle. We can tell someone we love them with words. Or we can tell them with a thoughtful gift, a home-cooked meal, walks in the park, slow dancing, a hand on the small of the back, long mornings in bed, a "good night" text, or a soft touch. Thanks to social construction, everyday life is exponentially more eloquent than it would be otherwise.

Social constructs are often quite formidable social facts. Consider one of the most essential social constructs in American life: the zinc and copper coins, green pieces of paper, and electronic code we call money. These are mostly worthless in and of themselves, but we've agreed that they stand in for values. Thus, we're able to exchange them for an unimaginably wide range of necessities, luxuries, and experiences.

Money is entirely made up. A fiction. A lie. But it's powerful and coercive. In exchange for it, many of us will strain and sweat, tolerate boredom or disgust, spend our time and energy on strangers, and do things we quite dislike or perhaps even believe immoral. We do this with half or more of our waking lives, often until we're too old to do much of anything at all. Because money is how we survive in the world today, the vast majority of us are forced to do something to make it. And, if we can't make enough, we really do suffer.

As illustrated in Table 2.1, social constructs come in many varieties. Rings, middle fingers, and bracelets made of string—like dollar bills—are a type of social construct called a *signifier*, a thing that stands for something else: in these cases, love, anger, and friendship. Language is made up largely of

TABLE 2.1

Types of Social Constructs

Social Construct	Definition	Examples
Signifiers	things that stand for other things	emojis, a thumbs-up, diamond rings, the Christian cross
Categories	subsets of things that we believe are sufficiently similar to one another to be considered the same	"pets" (a subset of animals), "blue" (a subset of the spectrum), "blouses" (a subset of shirts)
Binaries	categories we see as opposites or otherwise in opposition	good and evil, friends and enemies, legal and illegal
Associations	ideas that have nothing special in common except for the fact that they're connected by a third idea	rainbows and flags (LGBTQIA pride), roses and diamonds (love), red and green (Christmas)
Sequences	ideas arranged into a specific chronological order	outline, draft, edit; hug, kiss, fondle; marry, buy a house, have kids
Hierarchies	ideas placed into ranked relationships	Nordstrom is higher end than Kohl's, mammals are more important than insects, it's better to be young than old

signifiers. An *h* signifies *huh* and the word *hippopotamus* signifies a giant, gregarious, aquatic artiodactyl with stumpy legs and thick skin.

Social constructs also include *categories*, subsets of things that we believe are sufficiently similar to one another to be considered the same, yet different enough from other things to be considered distinct.[3] We put some physically altering substances into the category of "illegal drugs," for example, while others are categorized as "prescriptions." The same chemical substance might be called one or the other depending on how a person attains it and from whom. And sometimes we move substances from one category to the other; marijuana used to be illegal and now is a prescription in many states, whereas heroin used to be a prescription and is now illegal. Still other stimulants and depressants—like coffee, tea, soda, and beer—escape the categories altogether and are simply called "drinks." These categories are socially constructed. We accept them because they're familiar, not because they make sense. Because they're both in the category of "alcohol," for example, we associate beer with wine, though wine has at least as much in common with the grape juice we give to toddlers.

Sometimes categories are explicitly contrasted to one another in the form of *binaries*, categories we see as opposites. We oppose business to pleasure, humans to animals, and married to single. But humans *are* animals and business can be pleasurable; some technically single people are all-but-married and some married people are all-but-single. We socially construct these categories as meaningfully opposed and nonoverlapping, even though life usually fails to obey such simple divisions.

Within categories, ideas become linked by *association*. Associated ideas are ones with nothing particular in common except for the fact that they're

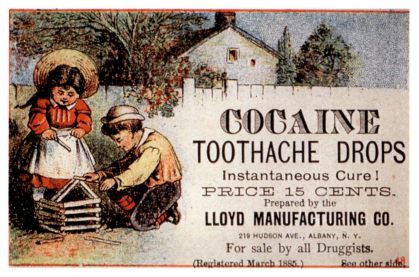

This 1885 advertisement for cocaine recommends it as a cure for children's toothaches. Substances like cocaine, opium, and morphine used to be categorized as medicine but have since been recategorized as illegal drugs.

connected by virtue of a third idea. Pigs and chickens, for instance, have no special relationship in nature, but bacon and eggs come together on our plates because they're linked by the idea of breakfast. We usually wear formal dresses with heels not because we couldn't wear sneakers, but because sneakers don't fall into the category of evening wear and dresses and heels do.

Finally, we socially construct sequences and hierarchies. *Sequences* are ideas arranged into a specific order. *Hierarchies* are ideas placed into ranked relationships. People generally believe, for example, that a "main course" should come after soup or salad and before a sweet dessert. That's a socially constructed sequence. Thanks in part to the Olympic medal ceremony, people also tend to think of gold as better than silver and silver as better than bronze. That's a socially constructed hierarchy.

Taken together, the universe of ideas and their relationships to one another form a **symbolic structure**, a constellation of social constructs connected and opposed to one another in overlapping networks of meaning. Ideas fall into categories, often multiple ones, connecting across and within them to other ideas, which are linked in sequences and ranked in hierarchies, connecting still to other ideas. We call it a structure because it's a complex and relatively rigid network. The meanings it contains allow us to communicate with each other, but the symbolic structure is unyielding, making it difficult to communicate in ways that it doesn't support. In the same way that it's hard to say "vacation" with the word "hippopotamus," in other words, it's hard to say "Great job!" with a thumbs-down.

In the symbolic structure that most of us are probably familiar with, for example, blue-collar work is associated with certain kinds of vehicles, like the pickup truck. Trucks are tied to country music and cowboy hats, associated via the category of rural life, which is opposed in a binary to urban life in cities. People in cities are more likely than people in the country to vote Democratic, the political party signified by the color blue. In that context, to be blue is to be a "lefty." We call our political parties "right" and "left," which implies an opposed binary that makes Republicans and Democrats into moral opponents. And some would say that Republicans, more so than Democrats, value blue-collar work.

Maybe that all sounded familiar, but maybe it didn't. There's no universal symbolic structure. Signifiers, sequences, associations, and other social constructs aren't the same everywhere. That's because the symbolic structure varies by culture.

CULTURE

Culture is a wide-ranging word that sweeps into its definition most of the things about people that vary from place to place. This includes *cultural objects*, like the stop sign. These are natural items given symbolic meaning, or natural resources extracted and molded to serve cultural purposes. It also includes *cultural cognitions*, like the idea that red means stop. These are shared ideas and values. The term also refers to *cultural practices*, like the fact that most of us stop (or almost stop) at stop signs most of the time. Practices

symbolic structure
a constellation of social constructs connected and opposed to one another in overlapping networks of meaning

are habits, routines, and rituals that people frequently perform. And, finally, cultural practices produce *cultural bodies*, culturally influenced shapes and sizes, capacities, and physiological processes. When our foot moves to the brake reflexively when we see a stop sign coming, for example, it's because our body has been culturally conditioned to respond in just that way.

Human beings are not unique in having cultures. *Social learning*—or the transmission of knowledge and practices from one individual to another via observation, instruction, or reward and punishment—has been documented in rats, birds, whales and dolphins, nonhuman primates, and more. Different groups of orcas (also known as killer whales), for example, have different languages. From one group to the next, their sets of calls and whistles are "as different as Greek and Russian."[4] Small pods have distinct dialects. Different groups of orcas also eat different foods, even when they share potential prey. Some groups eat marine mammals like sea lions; others only eat fish. Scientists have observed that the cultural differences are so great that orcas generally won't mate with orcas from other clans.

Though humans are not the only animals to have culture, it's probably fair to say that we're *especially* cultural. For hundreds of thousands of years, we've passed down ideas, behaviors, and objects from one generation to another, relieving each new generation of the need to acquire knowledge from scratch and giving them the opportunity to build on what others have learned. This is true in arenas as wide-ranging as art, mathematics, and human rights. As the German sociologist Karl Mannheim observed: "Strictly speaking it is incorrect to say that the single individual thinks. Rather it is more correct to insist that they participate in thinking further what others have thought before them."[5]

When we speak of culture, then, we're really talking about *cumulative* culture. Those of us alive today are merely at the forefront of hundreds of thousands of generations. We're modifying, advancing, and revolutionizing what we've inherited. Often, we make our societies better; sometimes we make them worse. Human cultures, in other words, evolve, though not always in the direction we desire. They've been doing so, along with human bodies, since the first *Homo sapiens* walked the earth.

Anthropologists call this parallel biological and cultural evolution *dual inheritance theory*.[6] It's the notion that humans are products of the interaction of genetic and cultural evolution. Our genetic evolution influences our cultural evolution, and vice versa. Every human society has specific practices that guide how we accomplish basic biological necessities like eating, reproducing, and staying warm and dry. And, as our cultural practices shift, they put pressure on our genes, newly selecting for some and making others newly disadvantageous.

Cultural innovation, in fact, is probably why humans became suddenly and substantially smarter around 70,000 years ago. The innovation was fire.[7] Cooking made food more digestible, giving humans the ability to consume the extra energy needed to build bigger brains. We call this the cognitive revolution, and it's why we named ourselves *Homo sapiens* (Latin for "wise man"). The practice of cooking, a *cultural* innovation, changed the human body and, thus, the future of our species.

No need to reinvent the wheel. Human culture is cumulative, so each generation inherits the knowledge of their parents, builds upon it, then passes more developed knowledge down to their own children, and so on.

As the art of cooking was passed down across generations of people who spread out across the globe, it also evolved. Human creativity interacted with our diverse environments, producing an incredible range of diets. In Peru, potatoes account for 74 percent of caloric intake; Peruvians cultivate over 3,000 varieties.[8] In Somalia, more than half of calories consumed come from milk, mostly from camels.[9] Traditionally, in Greenland, 75 percent of Inuit calories came from fat harvested from marine mammals. Like orcas, our cuisines vary by clan.[10]

The same variety characterizes our architecture, fashion, rituals, and routines. This cultural diversity makes travel captivating. It can be deliciously energizing, a feast for the senses that inspires us to see our environment anew. Travel can also be quite disorienting. Our cultural competency is compromised; we can't quite be sure what's going on or how to communicate effectively. We call this feeling *culture shock*, and it's a reminder that we aren't born knowing how to get along as a member of a human group. This is something we have to learn from others and it's a lifelong journey, involving adaptation to new, contradictory, and constantly changing cultures. This lifelong journey is called socialization.

SOCIALIZATION

Life is a series of encounters with new and different social environments. We grow up in families, go to a series of schools, encounter various peer groups, try out different hobbies and jobs, and more. Sometimes we move across the country or to another country altogether. All these experiences require us to adapt to subtly or surprisingly different cultural expectations. Socialization is the process by which we become culturally competent in these varying environments.

Through socialization, we learn the beliefs, values, and norms typical of members of the cultures we inhabit. Cultural **beliefs** are ideas about what is true and false. Though we learn many things from direct experience, much of what we think we know has been communicated to us by other people or mass media. If you were under the impression that the tomato is a vegetable,

beliefs
ideas about what is
true and false

for example, it's probably because that's what the people around you call it. If you believe that the earth goes around the sun, it's probably not because you've done the math yourself. And if you think a thumbs-up is a gesture of approval, you probably didn't grow up in the Middle East.

Cultural **values** are notions as to what's right and wrong. Values reflect moral commitments about the way things *should* be. The ideas that we shouldn't cheat, lie, or steal are values. The idea that we should act to protect our natural environment is a value, as is the idea that sexual partners should be monogamous. A belief in private property is a value, too, one that endorses the idea that individuals can rightly own land and that others who don't respect that ownership should be punished. Though we're often deeply committed to our values, we learn these from our culture too.

Finally, cultural **norms** are shared expectations for behavior. This will be discussed in greater detail in Chapter 4, but for now, notice that our customs, practices, gestures, and other ways of acting are tuned to our cultural environment. The precise nature of our table manners, how physically affectionate we are with friends, and whether and how we stand in lines when waiting for a service are cultural. So are the expectations for how we dress and decorate our homes, as well as what careers we pursue and what hobbies we adopt. Some norms apply to all or most of us, while others depend on the mix of identities we carry.

We learn beliefs, values, and norms from *agents of socialization*, channels of influence through which we become socialized. Table 2.2 offers some examples.

values
notions as to what's right and wrong

norms
shared expectations for behavior

TABLE 2.2

Select Agents of Socialization

Families	As the first group to which we belong, families are our first source of socialization. Our family members often have a strong influence on what we grow up to do, believe, and value.
Schools	Our schools teach us reading, writing, and arithmetic, but they also socialize us to listen to authority, follow rules, take turns, and show up on time.
Peers	Our peers can be powerful sources of socialization, shaping what we think is cool, who we think is cute, and how we spend our time.
Religion	For many of us, our religious faith is a source of values, beliefs, and practices; thus, religion socializes us into specific ways of thinking about and being in the world.
Mass media	The mass media often reinforces what we learn elsewhere, but media also teaches us about things few people experience firsthand, like drug dealing, working in an emergency room, or surviving in the wilderness.
Work	To succeed in an occupation, we must adjust to the norms, values, and beliefs typical of people in our profession. We learn most of this on the job.
Military	Individuals who enter the military are subject to assertive and all-encompassing socialization aimed at transitioning them into life as a member of the armed forces.

As we move into and through different social contexts—from our families and our houses of worship, to school and circles of friends, and into various workplaces—we encounter different lessons as to what to think, feel, and do. Some socialization experiences are especially acute. Joining the military, for example, converting to a religion, or entering a strongly rule-bound occupation (like law) may involve substantial *resocialization*, the unlearning of old beliefs, values, and norms in favor of new ones. Meanwhile, mass media both reinforces lessons we learn from specific others and prepares us to encounter cultural contexts with which we have no experience.

Interpersonal and self-socialization

We socialize ourselves and we're socialized by others. **Interpersonal socialization** involves active efforts by others to help us become culturally competent members of our cultures. We're socialized by our family members, friends, teachers, and spiritual leaders, as well as strangers we interact with and people we encounter in the small worlds of hobbies and activities. We call these **subcultures**, subgroups within societies that have distinct cultural ideas, objects, practices, and bodies. From politeness to potty training, through modeling and explicit instruction, others teach us how to get along in a complicated cultural world. Arguably, after keeping us alive, socialization is a parent or guardian's primary job. They and others gently tease, mock, lecture, or encourage us about all manner of cultural expectations.

We also teach ourselves with **self-socialization**, active efforts we make to ensure we're culturally competent members of our cultures. As children, we're

interpersonal socialization
active efforts by others to help us become culturally competent members of our cultures

subcultures
subgroups within societies that have distinct cultural ideas, objects, practices, and bodies

self-socialization
active efforts we make to ensure we're culturally competent members of our cultures

To attend an event like Comic-Con is to enter a subculture of cosplay. New attendees slowly learn the cast of characters, the norms for costuming, and how to interact with fellow cosplayers.

eager copycats, mimicking the things that adults, older siblings, and fellow children do. As we get older, we watch our peers for clues as to how to be liked, envied, or feared. We learn from fictional characters, taking life lessons from the morals of stories. We imagine generalized others and consider how they might evaluate us, changing our clothes, our composure, or our ambitions in response. We attempt to learn skills and information that'll help us get along and bond with other people.

Who are these other people? They are the people who raise us, employ us, laugh with us, and play on our teams. They're our best friends, mentors, rivals, and romantic partners. These are the specific others to whom we have **social ties**, the connections between us and other people. Every two people who're connected represent one social tie. Collectively, social ties add up to **social networks**: webs of ties that link us to each other and, through other people's ties, to people to whom we're not directly linked. About half of our ties also have ties with each other, and almost all will have ties to people to whom we aren't personally connected.[11]

Social ties can be formal or informal and either strong or weak. In most cases, for example, our relationship with our biological mother is a formal tie (she's listed as our parent on our government-issued birth certificate). Our relationships with our friends are informal (voluntary and undocumented). On social media sites like Snapchat or Instagram, we may be friends with or follow people whom we've never met or have met only once. These are probably weak ties. Our ties with our best friends and some family members, though, are probably strong.

Arguably, thanks to **social media**—social networks mediated by the internet—our networks are larger and more extensive than they've ever been. These connections give us impressive reach. The average Facebook user, for example, has 338 friends.[12] If we assume all Facebook users have that many friends (and subtract the number of friends we have in common with our friends), then the average Facebook user has 57,122 friends of friends. That's "one degree of separation," meaning there's only one person between any two people. Add one more degree of separation, and conservatively assume the same amount of friend overlap, and we have 9,653,618 friends of friends of friends. Our social media networks connect us to an extraordinary amount of people, all just a click away.

Our social networks are filled mostly with people like ourselves, thanks to **homophily**, our tendency to connect with others who are similar to us. Because of homophily, people who're tied together in social networks are more homogeneous, or alike, than we would expect by chance alone. But we don't just form ties with people who are already like us; we also socialize each other, leading people who are networked to become even more alike than they were initially.[13] In other words, our ties don't just represent social *connection*: They also enable cultural *contagion*.[14]

In one study, for example, scholars analyzed a social network to demonstrate contagion in levels of exercise. Social network analyses involve the

social ties
the connections between us and other people

social networks
webs of ties that link us to each other and, through other people's ties, to people to whom we're not directly linked

social media
social networks mediated by the internet

homophily
our tendency to connect with others who are similar to us

mapping of social ties and exchanges between individuals or groups (see "The Science of Sociology"). In this case, the scientists used data from an app for runners that logged their miles and shared their mileage with their friends. They found that when a user's friend began running fewer miles, the user would start to reduce their miles too.[15]

Other studies have found similar results.[16] If we tend to our yard, for example, our neighbor will be more likely to tend to theirs. If we sit next to a big eater at a restaurant, we consume more calories. If the people we know are studying hard, experimenting with crime, getting divorced, giving up smoking, or giving to charity, there's a greater likelihood that we will as well.

social network analysis
a research method that involves the mapping of social ties and exchanges between them

THE **SCIENCE** OF SOCIOLOGY

Social Network Analysis

Social network analysis is a research method that involves the mapping of social ties and exchanges between them. The ties can be between people, like those between friends and acquaintances in any given high school. Or they can connect groups or organizations, like the ties between high schools with athletic teams that regularly compete against one another.

Social network analysts map these ties, showing who (or what) is connected to who (or what). This allows them to characterize the nature of the social network. Researchers consider things like network size (how many individuals, groups, or organizations are involved) and network density (the number of ties between the individuals, groups, or organizations). They can also determine the overall shape and character of the collected ties. For example, networks can feature a central figure who ties most people together, two or more prominent cliques that have stronger ties within them than between them, or denser connections in some parts of the network compared with others.

The maps produced by social network analysts are a bird's-eye view of social interaction. Researchers can examine what flows between social ties, including resources like money, information, or contacts. Who lends money to whom? How do ideas get from one part of the network to another? By what pathways do contacts get shared with others in the network? These are the kinds of questions that can be asked of a social network once it's mapped. ■

Influence doesn't just flow through the first degree of separation, though—from us to our tie and back—it goes out about three degrees. In one study, for example, volunteers working for a political campaign went door to door to encourage people to vote; 60 percent of the volunteers' influence was passed on to at least one *other* member of the household, one they never spoke to directly.[17] Likewise, if one of our social ties is happy, our likelihood of being happy increases by 15 percent; when a friend of a friend is happy, by 10 percent; and when a friend of a friend of a friend is happy, by 6 percent.[18]

Social networks influence us because our ties' attitudes and behaviors, especially in the aggregate, socialize us by setting expectations. We're more likely to vote when our friends vote, not out of some neutral commitment to copying others, but because when other people vote, it suggests that voting is the right thing to do. Their decision to vote sets a standard, an expectation that we and others are called to uphold.

By looking at our collective ties, socialization by social network can predict things about us that are otherwise difficult to explain. Take, for example, the lifestyle differences between politi-

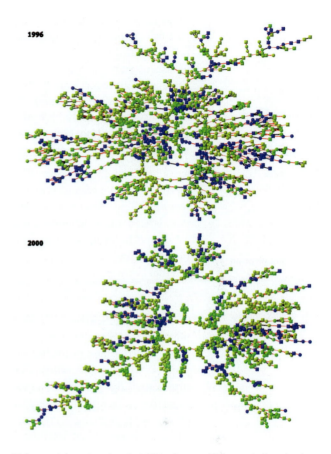

1996

2000

This social network of 1,000-plus residents of Framingham, Massachusetts, shows that happiness spreads between social ties in a network. As a result, happy people (shown in green) tend to be connected to other happy people. Happiness is, in other words, contagious.

cal liberals and conservatives. It makes sense that members of different political parties would differ politically, but we find that they differ in nonpolitical ways too.[19] People who identify as conservative, for instance, are more likely to eat steak than salmon and prefer french fries over a side of brussels sprouts. If they have a salad, they tend to choose iceberg lettuce over romaine and dress it with ranch, not vinaigrette. And they'll probably drink beer with dinner, not wine. People who identify as politically liberal are more likely than conservatives to go the other way. We see these differences even among conservatives and liberals who live in the same town and make the same amount of money.

Why should liberals and conservatives differ in these ways? Because once we cluster together politically, nonpolitical lifestyle preferences spread within that network.[20] Theoretically, the initial entrance of a trend into the network could be random, but pretty soon, it's correlated strongly with network involvement. Then these associations come to symbolize certain political attitudes. Like the tomato, kale isn't just a food item. It's a symbol of urban, monied, hipster, health-consciousness. Once it becomes that, choosing kale over iceberg lettuce sends signals to others, shaping our person-to-person interactions.

Media socialization

mass media
mediated commu-
nication intended
to reach not just
one or a handful of
people but many

media socialization
the process of
learning how to be
culturally compe-
tent through our
exposure to media

Though we've been using symbols to send messages to one another since we started painting on cave walls, truly mass media is rather recent. **Mass media** refers to mediated communication intended to reach not just one or a handful of people but many. In the mid-1400s, a goldsmith in Germany popularized the mechanized printing press. This made texts substantially easier and faster to produce. This would be followed by broadcast radio in the 1920s and television in the 1950s. And starting in the mid-1990s, the internet became a medium of mass culture, a technology with the potential to enable any individual in the world to communicate with any other individual in the world.

Media socialization includes all the cultural competence we gain through our exposure to media, including books, newspapers, magazines, movies, television, video games, music, the whole of the internet, and other widely shared sources. Much of this reaffirms lessons we're getting elsewhere, but some cultural knowledge we absorb almost entirely from media. Few of us have seen more than one or two live marriage proposals, for example, if we've seen any at all, but we've probably seen hundreds of them in ads, commercials, television shows, movies, and on YouTube. We have a good idea of how a marriage proposal is supposed to go—its script, required props, proper locations, and the roles people are supposed to play—thanks primarily to the (mostly fictional) lives we've encountered in pages and on screens.

Likewise, thanks to billboards, advertisements, and magazines that show us certain bodies almost exclusively, we're sometimes painfully familiar with the physical proportions idealized by our culture: six-foot-tall men with six-pack abs and big-busted women with twenty-four-inch waists. Not a lot of people look like that, but we could be forgiven for feeling otherwise. We've also all likely seen thousands of fictional shoot-outs and car chases, hundreds of emergency room crises, and dozens of courtroom trials, even though those things are mercifully rare in most people's daily lives. Heck, thanks to the media, you would probably even have a pretty good idea what to do if you found yourself in possession of a dead body.

The power of the mass media to socialize us, as well as its limits, is illustrated by a story of six brothers and a sister in New York City. As children, they were locked in an apartment with their mother on the sixteenth floor of a housing development.[21] Their father held them captive, teaching them to fear life outside the apartment. Their mother homeschooled them, and they had no internet. For company, they had only their parents, one another, and

Trapped in a small apartment by their father, the Angulo brothers were socially isolated until well into their teens. They socialized themselves by watching Hollywood movies. For their first foray into the outside world, they dressed like the cool criminals from Quentin Tarantino's *Reservoir Dogs*.

about 5,000 films. The siblings watched movies, they said, "all day every day." And when they weren't watching them, they were transcribing the scripts from the videos, making props and costumes out of cardboard and tin cans, and memorizing and reenacting the scenes.

One of the brothers, Mukunda, escaped in 2010. He was fifteen years old. Misunderstanding the real world, he left the house in the middle of the day wearing a creepy homemade mask inspired by the horror movie *Halloween*. He thought it would allow him to go unnoticed. Of course, it did not; it got him arrested. He recalled the scene:

> As the cops approached me and asked me all sorts of questions . . . I was completely catatonic. I had no idea what to say. I didn't know how to speak to a regular person. It was the first time this had ever happened to me in my life.[22]

Mukunda's response was so strange that he was committed to a psychiatric hospital for a week. When he returned home, the "spell was broken."[23] His father gave up control, and slowly all the siblings, ranging from eleven to eighteen, left the apartment. For their first trips outside, they dressed like the men from *Reservoir Dogs*: white shirts, black suits, dark black sunglasses, and all with black hair that fell to their lower backs.

Outside of their odd appearance, their mass media socialization served them pretty well. As Mukunda explained:

> [M]ovies were an escape to me, but they were also an actual guidance to life. They showed me what rivers looked like, what schools looked like, what the countryside looked like. Even animals. Cats, dogs, mice, horses. They even taught me how to talk and how to dress.[24]

The siblings had never eaten at a restaurant, been to the beach, or watched a movie at a theater, but they'd seen actors do these things hundreds of times. They drew on what they knew from media and blended in much better than they would have without the help of films.

Alongside mass media that we merely consume, social media—the kind we both consume and produce—can be a unique source of socialization too. Nonsocial media often features people with lives quite different from our own, but we typically use social media to connect with people similar to us. So, social media can be an important source of socialization.

An in-depth interview study focused on young people who were exploring non-heterosexual identities, for example, found that many went online to learn about the unique values, beliefs, and practices of queer subcultures.[25] Fitting in meant knowing how to dress, what kind of haircut to get, and how to talk and behave. In forums catering to same-sex desire, there are different rules for how to express attraction. So, many of the interviewees joined online forums and networking sites that catered to LGBTQIA people, or followed out celebrities on social media accounts, just to watch how other people went about being queer.

Seeing how LGBTQIA people presented themselves gave these young people clues as to how to look and behave in ways that other queer-identified folks would recognize and accept. One bisexual woman, for instance, sought to learn about "just being an alternative sexuality." Seeing people out and proud clued interviewees into queer language, fashion, and taste. In anticipation of coming out, they were able to gain some cultural competence before jumping into the deep end of queer culture.

In sum, we actively participate in our self-socialization, are socialized by others in our lives, and learn from the mass media. All these sources help us

Queer icons like singer-songwriter and actor Janelle Monáe are cultural touchstones for LGBTQIA youth looking to join queer subcultures.

become fully functioning members of our cultural groups. We don't accept this socialization passively. We say no to certain ideas, values, and expectations. Or we pick and choose among them. We seek out the subcultures we need or want. And we're socialized into many different subcultures simultaneously. Sometimes we even change the cultures of which we're a part. Ultimately, however, we're changed by all these experiences, too, and that change is more than skin deep.

Socialization and the body

Culture isn't just something we learn; it becomes part of our bodies. Culture shapes our muscles and bones, instructs our genetic codes, and exploits our hormones to make us physiologically similar. Culture, in other words, is **embodied**, physically present and detectable in the body itself.[26] It's measurable in the shape, size, and form of our bodies; how our bodies have learned to react to their environments; and the skills we acquire.

embodied
physically present and detectable in the body itself

Consider, first, that we have *cultured physiques*, bodies formed by what we do to and with them. The strength of our skeletons, for example, is dependent in part on whether we participate in high-impact, weight-bearing activities that build bone. In the United States, men are more likely than women to participate in these kinds of activities; consequently, they have up to 30 percent greater bone strength than women. Among ultra-Orthodox Jewish adolescents, this pattern is reversed. Boys in these communities are typically tasked with intense religious study, so they spend much less time exercising than other boys. As a result, their bones never grow as strong as those of their sisters, who have lighter study loads and engage in more activity.[27]

Our cultures shape our bodies in many ways. They influence us to use diet and exercise to change our bodies. They give us ideas and tools with which to adorn them, from fashion to piercings and tattoos. They introduce hazards and risks to which our bodies are sometimes exposed, from war to automobiles to environmental toxins. And they introduce protective elements, too, like seatbelts, fluoride, and medicine. All these things change our bodies, making them as cultural as they are natural.

Second, our cultures influence us to acquire culturally specific skills. These are our *cultured capacities*. Some of us learn to hunt and fish, others to play tennis or soccer, still others to knit or sew. Until about 150 years ago, no human had ever learned to type, and only in the past few decades has any human ever had the capacity to text. These technological and cultural innovations—the typewriter and the cell phone—changed what our bodies would learn to do.

Finally, our bodies are *culturally conditioned*, taught to respond physiologically to a socially constructed reality. Our bodies learn to respond to social cues and stimulate socially appropriate responses. The classic example is Pavlov's dogs. This is the iconic phrase that refers to the physiologist Ivan Pavlov's experiment in which he taught dogs to salivate on cue instead of in response to food. Consider how this works: The mouth of a dog is designed to salivate in the presence of food, but not in response to the ring of a bell. But through classical conditioning, a dog's body can be taught that the bell *means* food, and its body will salivate to the bell just as it would to actual food. It can be trained to respond, in other words, to a social construct, a signifier, as if it were nature itself. Since salivation is not under conscious control, it's not something dogs *decide* to do; it's something their bodies do *to* them.

Human are like this too. Our bodies learn to respond to socially constructed cues, and they do so outside the realm of consciousness or intention. Sociologists examine these physiological responses with biosocial research methods, or ones that document physical responses to social experiences (see "The Science of Sociology"). Biosociologists have found, for example, that levels of testosterone in men, a hormone related to feelings of well-being, tend to rise when men get access to socially constructed signifiers of success. This happens when they drive sports cars and also when they play sports, board games, and video games.[28] Emerging research suggests that women's testosterone levels respond similarly to cues of status and power.

biosocial research methods
tools of sociological inquiry that investigate relationships between sociological variables and biological ones

THE **SCIENCE** OF SOCIOLOGY

Biosocial Research Methods

Our bodies both respond to social interaction and drive us to interact with others in specific ways. To fully understand what happens *between* humans, then, we need to understand what happens *inside of* them. This is the logical result of dual inheritance. Humans have always been both biological and cultural, and it's the interplay between the two that drives us.

Biosocial research methods investigate relationships between sociological variables and biological ones. These include things like hormone levels, brain functioning, and gene expression. Data collection may involve sampling saliva to measure hormone levels, observing brain activity using imaging machines, or identifying patterns in gene expression. This data can be correlated with sociological variables like exposure to harmful experiences (like stress, hunger, and violence) or helpful ones (like success, social support, and security).

Biosocial research is useful because it reveals that social constructs aren't just "in our heads." Our shared ideas—reflected in the symbolic structure—affect our bodies. For example, sociologists using biosocial research methods have tested whether racially discriminatory treatment accelerates the aging process (it does) or whether being misgendered harms peoples' overall health (it does).[29] Biosocial research has shown that social experiences not only affect our bodies in the short term but can also affect us in the long term.

Some of the physical changes caused by those experiences are expressed in our genes and can be passed down to our descendants. The experience of famine, for example, can leave an imprint on a person's genetic code discoverable in the genes of their children and grandchildren.[30] That imprint has been tied to an increased risk for heart disease and diabetes. The societies our grandparents lived in, then, actively affect our lives today. ∎

Some of the things that make us feel good are nonconditioned, like a cool breeze on a hot day. But many are conditioned; we learn to feel good about them, and our bodies cooperate in this feeling. What do we find sexually exciting? What are we scared of? What foods do we crave? These things are cultural. Our bodies are ready to produce culturally relevant sensations and emotions, enabling us to respond to our social environment, whatever its features.

In sum, cultural ideas embellish our environment, layering it with significance. These ideas are the basis of our communication, giving us not just language but a rich network of symbolic meaning. This guides what we believe and value. Culture teaches us how to act. And it seeps into our very bodies, shaping them, providing them with skills, and conditioning them to respond to social constructs. Because cultures vary, we have the potential to encounter many different and sometimes opposing cultural forces. Sometimes those forces are at odds. What happens when people holding opposing value systems disagree?

CULTURE WARS

In 2015, an African lion named Cecil was killed by a hunter in Zimbabwe.[31] The hunter was Walter Palmer, a wealthy American dentist with a lifelong passion for trophy hunting who'd paid $54,000 for the right to kill the animal. With the help of a guide, he attracted the lion with bait, shot it with a crossbow, then tracked the injured animal for two more days, finally killing him with a gun. Palmer and his guide then skinned and beheaded the lion so that Palmer could return to the United States with its skull and coat.

Unfortunately for the dentist, Cecil was one of the most well-known and widely recognized lions in the world. He was a mature male with a pride of twenty-two lionesses and cubs who, unlike many other lions, allowed tourist jeeps to get close. He and his pride had delighted visitors for years. The head of the Safari Operators Association said that his death was nothing less than the "demise of an icon."[32]

Six days after Cecil's death made the news, Palmer was identified as the hunter and the story went viral, spreading across both traditional and social media. The comedian Jimmy Kimmel joined other celebrities in expressing his outrage. He condemned Palmer vigorously on *Jimmy Kimmel Live!*, insulting his masculinity:

> I'm not against hunting if you're hunting to eat or to help keep the animal population healthy or it's part of your culture or something, that's one thing. But if you're some a-hole dentist who wants a lion's head over the fireplace in his mancave so his douchebag buddies can gather around it, drink scotch, and tell him how awesome he is, that's just vomitous.[33]

Kimmel then asked his viewers to donate to a wildlife research group. He became visibly choked up, explaining: "Maybe we can show the world that not all Americans are like this jackhole."

Demonstrations had already begun outside Palmer's dental practice in Minnesota. Some protesters left stuffed animals and paintings of Cecil in remembrance while others chanted and carried signs reading "Walter Palmer kills for fun" and "Scumbag, murderer."[34] Someone spray-painted the phrase "lion killer" across the garage door of Palmer's Florida vacation home. People called for his murder on Twitter. Palmer's profile began disappearing from websites as the dental industry rushed to distance itself from him. Palmer made a statement to the press, saying that he'd legally hunted the lion, and went into hiding.

People sympathetic to trophy hunting came out to defend Palmer and contest the claims made by his critics. They argued that hunting is natural, no less in humans than in other carnivores, and that death is natural too. If an

Responses to Cecil the Lion's death were deeply cultural. Protesters felt in their gut that the killing of Cecil was barbaric. Proponents of trophy hunting felt equally sure that it was natural, even sacred. Both had cultural rationales at the ready to defend their feelings.

animal's pain and suffering is the concern, they suggested that a quick death at the hands of a hunter is preferable to the alternative: a likely slow death from starvation, injuries, or illness, or being eaten alive. At thirteen, Cecil was old for a lion, they rightly observed, and unlikely to live more than a year or two more. Moreover, if one measured the ethics of the kill by suffering, they insisted, trophy hunting is more ethical than eating a hamburger; at least the lion didn't spend his entire abbreviated adult life standing ankle-deep in manure in a stockyard.

The protesters responded by objecting to the comparison between lions and cows, pointing out that lions are an endangered species. Hunters guffawed at this. The money they pay for the right to hunt, they argued, funds conservation efforts. The same man who called Cecil an "icon," in fact, admitted that hunting brings $100 million to Zimbabwe each year, incentivizing the state to protect their big game. Without hunting, there would be less money for conservation. Savannas might be turned into something else that would make money, like strip malls, and then there would be no lions at all.

Few people, you can imagine, changed their minds on the matter.

What *was* Cecil? Was he a symbol of human dominion over all other animals on earth, expendable like the 25 million chickens, turkeys, ducks, pigs, cows, and sheep put through slaughterhouses in America every day? Was he a precious soul, an individual who deserves no more or less respect and care than every other creature on the planet? Was he an economic resource for the national park that brought money to the country of Zimbabwe, both in life and in death? Or was he an opportunity, as Kimmel suggested, for a man to prop up his flagging masculinity? What was Cecil *really*?

For most of us, the answer is in our gut. Kimmel's response, for example, wasn't cerebral; it was emotional. He just *knew* Cecil's death at the hands of Palmer was wrong. He likely responded this way in part because of his own cultural background. Kimmel was born in Brooklyn and grew up in Las Vegas. He'd likely had very little contact with hunters and little or no personal experience with hunting. He may even have grown up around people who taught him to abhor it. He came, in other words, from an American subculture deeply uncomfortable with hunting for pleasure.

Sociologists call this idea—that we're socialized into culturally specific moralities that guide our feelings about right and wrong—the **culture-as-value thesis**.[35] This theory is consistent with the definition of values introduced earlier in this chapter. It posits that the values that are common and widely accepted in our cultural environment tend to become part of our own point of view. When these moral beliefs are violated, it triggers a visceral response. Our brains leap into action, telling us *this is bad*, and our bodies are culturally conditioned to produce a physiological state that makes us feel disgusted. Hence Kimmel's strong reaction to the story.

In contrast, the dentist who killed Cecil grew up in Lisbon, North Dakota, a town with a population that's hovered around 2,000 for the past 100 years. He claims to have learned to shoot at the age of five and describes himself as

culture-as-value thesis
the idea that we're socialized into culturally specific moralities that guide our feelings about right and wrong

a "lifelong hunter." After he killed Cecil, he happily posted a picture of himself with the dead lion on social media. He clearly imagined that many of his friends and family would approve of his kill, thinking it exciting or impressive.

In fact, many of the almost 14 million Americans who identify as hunters did think so. In defending Palmer, these folks described a deep affection for the hunt, calling the practice of stalking and slaying an animal "fulfilling," "enriching," even "spiritual" and "sacred." They have a gut feeling about hunting too. They *love* it. They love it just as much as opponents hate it. Their gut response, like Kimmel's, was more emotional than cerebral.

As the culture clash played out, though, people didn't just express their feelings; they justified them. This is a second role that culture plays in moral battles. Especially when cultures clash, emotional responses require logical arguments. Those rationales are cultural too. Sociologists call this the **culture-as-rationale thesis**, the idea that we're socialized to know a set of culturally specific arguments with which we can justify why we feel something is right or wrong. According to this thesis, our culture offers us a catalog of ideas, a repertoire of rationales that we can draw on to make sense of our gut feelings.[36] Oftentimes the motivation comes first (*I hate this!* or *I love this!*) and the reasoning comes after. When our gut reacts, in other words, we begin searching for culturally familiar rationales to explain our reaction.

The protesters and defenders of Cecil's death drew on culturally available ideas to make arguments intended to be convincing. On both sides, there was creative manipulation of the symbolic structure. Opponents of trophy hunting mobilized the ideas of nonviolence and animal rights. Proponents referenced the inevitability of death and God's conferral of dominion over creation to humans. Both invoked nature conservation, with opponents arguing that hunters were contributing to the extinction of lions, and hunters arguing that they were doing just the opposite.

If we put the culture-as-value and the culture-as-rationale approaches together, we get a pretty good picture of the role culture likely plays in our moral debates.[37] Sociologists disagree about how big a role each plays. Do we feel what is rational or do we rationalize what we feel? Probably a little of both, but research suggests that the latter is more true. We aren't always very thoughtful about why we feel the way we do, but we're very good at coming up with explanations for it.

It was exactly this tendency to react strongly and physically to unfamiliar cultural ideas and norms—especially when they offend our values—that prompted the sociologist Harriet Martineau to ask that we practice sociological sympathy. If you recall from the introduction, this means setting aside our own point of view in favor of trying to understand others as they understand themselves. Sociologists, in other words, warn against **ethnocentrism**, assuming that one's own culture is superior to the cultures of others. This includes the idea that our own culture is normal or good, and that the cultures of others are weird or bad.

In contrast, most sociologists embrace some degree of **cultural relativism**. This is the practice of noting the differences between cultures without passing judgment. Embracing this kind of sociological sympathy doesn't mean we can

culture-as-rationale thesis
the idea that we're socialized to know a set of culturally specific arguments with which we can justify why we feel something is right or wrong

ethnocentrism
the practice of assuming that one's own culture is superior to the cultures of others

cultural relativism
the practice of noting the differences between cultures without passing judgment

never judge other cultures (or, for that matter, our own), but it does mean that we need a reason for criticizing cultural ideas, values, or practices above and beyond the fact that we find them strange or disturbing. Our criticism, in other words, must be based in something other than mere difference.

Each of our reactions to the story about Cecil is genuine. We really do often feel very strongly that how we were raised is right. However, developing a sociological imagination requires that we put aside those reactions—both positive and negative—and put real effort into understanding cultures that are unfamiliar to us, perhaps especially if they offend us. That doesn't mean that we can't judge cultural practices, disagree with their facts, or oppose their values. But it does require that we resist the instinct to be quick to judge and subject our own cultures to an equally critical examination.

CULTURE DURING COVID-19

Before this chapter comes to an end, I feel compelled to introduce one more idea. This idea is related to something with which I'm guessing you have personal experience: culture in times of rapid social change. In such moments—when cultures are disrupted—our relationship to culture is disrupted too.

Consider how, in almost all cases, when we enter a new social environment, we do so as newcomers to a preexisting culture. We may not know exactly what beliefs, values, and norms others share, but established members of the culture do. Accordingly, we can look to them to quickly learn what we need to know to fit in.

Sometimes, however, there are rifts in reality that undo or disrupt a preexisting culture. What we once took for granted is upended. Such sudden changes can leave *everyone* confused as to what is true, right, and normal. New ideas, values, and norms are necessary, and there are no established members of the emerging culture to look to for guidance.

This fairly describes what happened when Covid-19 began spreading through our communities. Rumors of a novel illness trickled in. Concerns about it spreading in the United States were raised. And then, in a matter of days, schools shut down, professional sports canceled their seasons, entertainment venues shuttered, and businesses sent white-collar workers home indefinitely.

Established norms—like shaking hands and hugging goodbye—had to be abandoned. Behaviors that would have been considered odd or disturbing, like wearing a face covering, became common. Crossing the street to avoid someone walking toward us on the sidewalk became right, not rude. New truths were debated, about previously obscure medicines and whether colleges should reopen. House parties were suddenly cast as immoral. Officials' efforts to put new limits on people's behavior prompted cultural clashes between politically left-leaning and politically right-leaning Americans.

This was no ordinary spring.

An essay by the sociologist Ann Swidler is strikingly relevant to this experience. In it, Swidler asked whether people have a different relationship

The Covid-19 pandemic ushered in an "unsettled time." This forced us to invent and adopt new norms, including alternative ways of trick-or-treating on Halloween.

to culture in "settled" and "unsettled" times.[38] Settled times, she suggested, are familiar and stable. The beliefs, values, and norms in place are well established. Things have been as they are for quite a long time, or are changing very slowly, and in bits and pieces. There's reason to expect that tomorrow will be much like today. And so on into the future.

Unsettled times are the opposite of this. They're unfamiliar and unpredictable. Reality has changed, requiring us to reevaluate our beliefs, reconsider our values, and adopt new norms. Today is not at all like our near-past. And we're unsure what the future will bring.

Suddenly, unexpectedly, shockingly, Covid-19 ushered in an unsettled time.

Swidler argued that our relationship to culture is different in settled and unsettled times. During settled times, she wrote, we take for granted that we know what to think, what's right or wrong, and how to act. We have well-worn habits of thought and behavior. And we put relatively little thought into whether we should think or act differently. We are, more or less, on autopilot.

During unsettled times, however, there is no autopilot. We have no settings for our new reality. Many of our old habits may be ineffective, even harmful to ourselves or others. Unsettled times, then, require that we be more thoughtful about what we believe, value, and do. In responding to our new environment, we may find ourselves engaged in deep reflection about the nature of reality, right and wrong, and the best way to interact with others.

This can be a mentally and emotionally demanding set of tasks, requiring us to think hard about things we previously took for granted. And we don't do this work alone. In confusing times, we turn to our social ties. We consider their thoughts and share our ideas with them. We remake culture together. It should be no surprise, then, that varying responses to an unsettled time will cluster within different social networks. During the pandemic, face coverings became a sign of community solidarity on the political left and overreach by local governments on the political right. Attitudes to mask wearing spread through existing social networks, just like attitudes toward kale, brussels sprouts, and salmon tartare.

The global pandemic is an unsettled time. We've all been forced to change. Some of these changes have been quick and are, perhaps, rather superficial, like the temporary moratorium on shaking hands. But others may be more long-lasting and profound. Will Covid-19 change what we value? Who we value? Will it leave a mark on the norms with which we interact? Will isolation leave us feeling differently about our relationships with others? Will the need to sacrifice individual freedoms to protect others change how we think about our role in society? Will the pandemic worsen social divisions, as different responses prompt social conflict? Or will it bring us together in the end?

As I write, it is too early to tell. ∎

COMING **UP...**

CHAPTER 1 ARGUED that humans are social, born into groups of others. This chapter argues that social groups are also cultural. To be cultural is to give the world symbolic significance. We socially construct reality, embellishing it in consequential ways. The symbolic structures we collectively build are powerful social facts, channeling our thoughts, values, and behaviors in predictable ways.

We're socialized into our cultures and subcultures by the people in our social networks, including our families, peers, and coworkers, and by the mass media. This means that people with similar cultural backgrounds come to think and be in the world in parallel ways. We even tend to share the same moral commitments and a common set of ideas with which to defend them. Both our ethical feelings and our ethical arguments, then, are strongly influenced by our socialization.

Sometimes, however, cultures can shift unpredictably, leaving us all collectively confused. Cultures must be reinvented on the fly. In these cases, our cultural awareness is heightened, and we may be more thoughtful about our cultures. Being forced to change can make us more reflective. Covid-19 prompted this kind of reflection by ushering in an unsettled time.

Our selves are social, then, but we're also cultural through and through. The next chapter builds on the first two, exploring a cultural dimension of the self in depth: our identities. None of us is *just* human. We're trans, we're Mormon, we're living with a disability. We're the child of an immigrant or the descendant of an enslaved ancestor. We're White or bisexual, middle-aged or male. Where these identities come from, and what they mean to us, is next.

3

OUR

IDENTITIES

IN THIS **CHAPTER...**

———————————

TO BE HUMAN is to be cultural, and to be cultural is to give the world around us meaning. Part of that process involves giving meaning to one another. *Social identities*—our race and ethnicity, citizenship, gender, sexual orientation, class, age, religion, disability, body size, and more—are culturally influenced social constructs too.

- This chapter shows how we collectively make certain features of humans socially important and carve out subcategories in which to place ourselves. These subcategories are then imbued with meaning (or *stereotypes*) and arrayed in a hierarchy.

- Part of having a social identity is acting in ways that reflect it. Sometimes we enjoy doing so and sometimes we only do so because others expect us to and reward or punish us accordingly.

- We all carry not just one but many social identities, and our lives are shaped by all these identities at once. This fact is referred to as *intersectionality*.

Altogether, sociological observations about identity reflect *social identity theory*: People are inclined to form social groups, incorporate group membership into their identity, take steps to enforce group boundaries, and maximize personal esteem and in-group success.
   Two research methods are helpful for documenting shared cultural beliefs about identities:

- *Content analysis* involves counting and describing patterns or themes in media. Analysis can be quantitative, qualitative, or both.

- *Computational sociology* uses computers to collect, extract, and analyze data. It has become especially useful in the era of *big data*, extremely large and growing repositories of information.

"The Western world is having an identity crisis."

—MARIANNE WILLIAMSON

English offers an elaborate language with which we can express our sexual attraction. We can describe ourselves as heterosexual, homosexual, bisexual, demisexual, pansexual, polysexual, ambisexual, omnisexual, androsexual, gynesexual, skoliosexual, or even asexual. For those who prefer ambiguity, there's queer or fluid. And if we aren't quite sure, there's curious and questioning.

This is new. In the early 1600s, when the Puritans landed on the east coast of what would become the United States, there were exactly zero words for sexual orientation in English.[1] It hadn't occurred to the colonists that people could be categorized according to their sexual desire, so the subcategories of homosexual and heterosexual didn't yet exist.

They realized, of course, that sometimes people had sex with people of the same sex, but it hadn't occurred to them that such activity could reflect an *identity*. Instead, such behavior was lumped together with masturbation, adultery, and oral and anal sex. It was sin, they believed, and something to which everyone was susceptible. Accordingly, while Puritans who felt same-sex desire may have experienced pleasure or shame, they would not have paused to wonder if they were a different kind of person altogether.

It remained this way for another 300 years. What happened next is a matter of economics, urbanization, war, science, politics, and more. It's one of many stories you'll read in this chapter about our **social identities**, the socially constructed categories and subcategories of people in which we place ourselves or are placed by others.[2] Our social identities can be intensely private, deeply personal, and profoundly intimate, but we don't come to them in a vacuum. Just like other parts of human life, our identities are social constructs: Our cultures invent them, provide the subcategories, and give them meaning and value.

Sociologists are particularly interested in social identities that carry substantial social significance and consequence. Not identities like "cat

social identities
the socially constructed categories and subcategories of people in which we place ourselves or are placed by others

people" and "foodies," but ones like race, citizenship, gender, class, age, religion, disability, and body size. These identities *matter*. We read other people's appearances, body language, accents, turns of phrase, and fashion choices for signs of these identities and tend to filter information about people through them.

Our identities are also tethered to unfair advantage and disadvantage. Many identities (such as race) have their origins in efforts to divide and conquer subjugated populations. Others (like thinness) are used to affirm superiority. Some identities are or have been criminalized (like homosexuality) or targeted for genocide (as were the Jews during the Holocaust). White and non-White, male and female, citizen and foreigner, able-bodied and disabled, straight and gay—these are some of the differences on which value is unevenly distributed. Each distinction serves to justify a hierarchy, and they interact to shape our experience in life.

This chapter will explore the process of distinction, and the social construction of identity categories. It will also review how we make identities meaningful, array them into hierarchies, and learn cultural biases. To begin our journey through this material, we start with the idea of forming human groups.

THE LURE OF IDENTITY

In 1939, Germany invaded Poland and declared war on France and the United Kingdom. It was the dawn of World War II. In the next six years, more than 100 million people from more than thirty countries would fight in that war. As many as 60 million people died. This included 6 million Jews, who were imprisoned and then slaughtered in German concentration camps, a gruesome feat accomplished by a murderous dictator with the cooperation of many German soldiers and some civilians.

Henri Tajfel was twenty years old when the war broke out. As a Jew, he was familiar with anti-Semitism. He was born in Poland, where laws limited Jews' opportunities for education, so he enrolled in college in France to study chemistry. Recognizing the threat posed by Germany's leader, Adolf Hitler, Tajfel enlisted in the French army.

After a year of fighting, he was captured by Nazi soldiers. He survived as a prisoner of war only because his religion was never exposed. When he was released at the end of the war, he learned that no one in his family had survived. To ease his own grief, Tajfel took a job helping children who'd been lost or orphaned during the war. When he eventually went back to school, he set chemistry aside to study people.

Like many of his contemporaries, Tajfel struggled to understand how ordinary people could have participated in or tolerated such unimaginable violence. To try to answer this question, he started at the beginning: Where did these identities come from? How do they come to mean so much to us? And what makes them the basis of conflict? Sociologically speaking, these questions were about the process of **distinction**, active efforts to affirm

distinction
active efforts to affirm identity categories and place ourselves and others into their subcategories

identity categories and place ourselves and others into their subcategories. They're also about the desire for **positive distinction**, the claim that members of our own group are superior to members of other groups. This produces **in-group bias**, preferential treatment of members of our own group and mistreatment of others.[3]

One of Tajfel's most famous studies revealed that people need only the smallest reason to form such groups. To demonstrate this, he did an experiment in which he brought sixty-four teenage boys into his laboratory and showed them a series of slides, each displayed for no longer than half a second.[4] On the slides were dots—*lots* of dots—and Tajfel instructed the boys to estimate how many. So, the boys wrote down their best guess for each slide and handed their answers to the experimenters.

Behind closed doors, Tajfel and his collaborators tossed aside the students' estimations and randomly assigned them to one of two groups. Group One was told that they *over*estimated the number of dots on the slides, and Group Two was told that they *under*estimated the number. Neither group was told that their answers were more correct, simply different, and each was told privately, so no student knew which of their peers were in which group.

The task was deliberately designed to have as little significance to the boys as possible. Why would anyone care whether they were an over- or underestimator of dots? It shouldn't matter to them as anything more than a curiosity. And it certainly wasn't a good reason to form groups and decide that their own group was more deserving of a good outcome. Right?

Wrong. Tajfel measured in-group bias by giving each boy the opportunity to give small rewards to their fellow research subjects. Consistent with the hypothesis, the boys penalized the other group and favored their own, people with whom they shared nothing but the outcome of a silly, contrived, and wholly fake exercise involving dots. The fact that people were so quick to form groups and punish outsiders was so surprising, and so haunting in light of the Holocaust, that a new research program emerged.

Many studies later, we have good evidence that humans are partial to

Suzie would later win a Nobel Prize for her Theory of Special Social Relativity.

TABLE 3.I

How to Socially Construct an Identity

Step	Description
1. Invent	Establishing a human feature as a basis of identity.
2. Divide	Deciding what will differentiate people within identity subcategories.
3. Stereotype	Giving identity subcategories different symbolic meanings.
4. Perform	Doing social identities in accordance with stereotypes.
5. Rank	Elevating some identity subcategories over others.

in-group affiliation. We can induce group loyalty by doing something as simple as flipping a coin and putting people into "heads" groups and "tails" groups. Once the group exists, people behave as group members, not simply individuals. *You got tails? Hey, me too!* This is called the **minimal group paradigm**, the tendency of people to form groups and actively distinguish themselves from others for the most trivial of reasons.[5]

Together these observations are called **social identity theory**: People are inclined to form social groups, incorporate group membership into their identity, take steps to enforce group boundaries, and maximize positive distinction and in-group success. This happens in real life as well as the laboratory. Table 3.1 lists five steps by which a human feature becomes a social identity. Categories of identity are invented, and subcategories are carved out. Identities are made meaningful, such that they signify something socially relevant. These identities guide our behavior and we usually act in accordance with them. Finally, identity subcategories are arrayed into a hierarchy. Once social identities are established, they intersect. We each have many social identities and how we experience any one of them is influenced by the others we carry. The remainder of this chapter is dedicated to exploring these things in depth, starting with the invention of identities and a return to sexual orientation.

minimal group paradigm
the tendency of people to form groups and actively distinguish themselves from others for the most trivial of reasons

social identity theory
the idea that people are inclined to form social groups, incorporate group membership into their identity, take steps to enforce group boundaries, and maximize positive distinction and in-group success

STEP 1: INVENT
The Origin of Sexual Identity

We see sexual behavior between individuals of the same sex anywhere we look in nature, and humans are no exception.[6] Because we're cultural creatures, though, how we experience and express same-sex sexual desire depends on where and when we were raised. If we had been born prior to the mid-1900s, for example, we may have recognized such desires but not been able to imagine building an identity, or a life, around them. All that would soon change.

In the 1920s and '30s, a Paris nightclub called Le Monocle was a haven for artists, bohemians, and burlesque dancers. Named after a lesbian fashion of the time — the wearing of monocles — it also hosted a vibrant gay and lesbian nightlife.

Major changes in the organization of everyday life laid the groundwork. First was urbanization: the shrinking of rural populations and the growth of cities.[7] For most of U.S. history, Americans had lived in small towns or in the country, but by 1920 more than half lived in urban locations. These new urban centers provided an unprecedented level of freedom from the surveillance that characterized small communities. This was true especially for men, who were given more freedom than women. In hidden corners of cities, gay subcultures began forming.

Second was industrialization, the shift to an economy based primarily on large-scale mechanized industry.[8] Before the United States industrialized, it was common for people to make their living in family units where they aimed for self-sufficiency. On farms, home was a workplace and family members were the workers. Children were not optional. They grew up more quickly back then and worked on the farm alongside their parents. Heterosexual sex, if not heterosexuality, was a matter of survival.

City life under industrial capitalism was organized differently.[9] People no longer worked as families to produce the food and goods they needed; they worked for money to buy those things and were paid as individuals. It was legal to pay women substantially less than men, so women were still dependent on the family unit. But wages for men were high enough that some could consider building lifestyles around desire instead of reproduction, and they did.

The third factor was World War II, fought between 1939 and 1945. In the United States, one out of every eight males—almost every fit man between eighteen and twenty-six years old—served in the war.[10] As a result, unmarried people on both the front lines and the home front found themselves largely in the company of the same sex. Indulging in homoerotic encounters became easier and more tempting, so much so that one pair of historians called World War II "a nationwide 'coming out' experience."[11]

Living in cities and able to earn an income outside of the heterosexual family, some individuals who experimented with homosexuality during the war decided to organize their lives around their sexual desires when they came home. This was when the idea of the gay *person* burst into daily life. The first openly gay bars in the United States opened in the 1940s and the first gay advocacy organization was founded in 1951. Homosexuality was no longer just something people could *do*, it was something they could *be*. Today we use the term **sexual minorities** to describe people who are gay, lesbian, bisexual, or otherwise non-heterosexual.

The journey from homosexual behavior to sexual identity illustrates the first step in the process of distinction: seeing something as an identity at all. The second step is to socially construct the relevant subcategories; from "heterosexual" and "homosexual," for example, to the abundance of sexual identities we have today. To look at how specific subcategories of identity develop, we'll move from sexual orientation to race and ethnicity.

sexual minorities
people who are gay, lesbian, bisexual, or otherwise non-heterosexual

STEP 2: DIVIDE
Race, Ethnicity, and the Emergence of Subcategories

The racial groups with which we're familiar, whatever they are, are not biological facts.[12] Roughly 85 percent of human genetic variation is found within any group of people we identify as racially alike.[13] Almost all of that variation is contained in sub-Saharan Africa, where the most genetically diverse populations of humans live.[14] This means that there's more genetic difference among Black people than there is between Black people and any other racial subcategory.[15] The same is true for other group comparisons.

Race, though, is a fact. It's a social fact.[16] **Race** is a socially meaningful set of artificial distinctions falsely based on superficial and imagined biological differences. Certain physical features, like eye shape or hair texture, are made to exemplify a racial subcategory and certain characteristics are attributed to people with those physical features. We are then socialized to read people for signs of their race and ignore the diversity within subcategories. As a result, we learn to see races that do not exist in nature.

Instead of being biological, racial subcategories are social constructs; they are products of human invention, not biological evolution. For this reason, the subcategories recognized by different countries vary dramatically. Table 3.2 offers some examples.

In the United States, the most culturally stark distinction is between "Black" and "White," though these subcategories did not exist when English

race
a socially meaningful set of artificial distinctions falsely based on superficial and imagined biological differences

TABLE 3.2

Official Governmental Racial Subcategories in Select Countries

Australia	Brazil	Bulgaria[a]
Aboriginal Torres Strait Islander	White Black Yellow Pardo Indigenous	

South Africa[b]	Guam	United States[c]

Black African
Coloured
Indian or Asian
White
	Chamorro
	Samoan
	Carolinian
	Filipino
	Japanese
	Korean
	Palauan
	Tongan
		White
		Black or African
		  American
		American Indian or
		  Alaska Native
		Asian
		Native Hawaiian or
		  other Pacific Islander

[a]Bulgaria does not recognize any racial groups.
[b]South Africa uses the phrase "population groups."
[c]In the United States, "Hispanic, Latino, or Spanish" is an ethnicity, not a race.

colonizers arrived in 1607.[17] At that time, Africans shared their position at the bottom of the economic ladder with poor Europeans. Both groups were subjected to indentured servitude: bound to a period of enslavement, after which they would be freed.[18] Given their shared class interests, indentured servants of all colors joined together and sometimes rebelled against their so-called masters.

The colonists seized upon color as a way to end these rebellions.[19] In 1705, they introduced the subcategories of White and Black, passing laws that tied rights to skin color. European indentured servants' rights were protected and enhanced, and the potential for Africans to earn their freedom was eliminated. Now Africans could never work hard or long enough to be freed, and their light-skinned former friends were given the right to order, oversee, punish, and capture them.

Race was a way to divide and conquer. Those in the new subcategory of White were given what the sociologist W. E. B. Du Bois called a **psychological wage**, a noneconomic good given to one group as a measure of superiority over other groups.[20] White people's psychological wage—the promise that they had more in common with the White folk at the top of the economic hierarchy than the Black folk at the bottom—motivated them to protect a racial hierarchy that offered them little more than someone to look down on. When slavery was abolished, race lived on.

psychological wage
a noneconomic good given to one group as a measure of superiority over other groups

The U.S. federal government continued to use racial subcategories to further White supremacy. In 1890, the U.S. Census included the subcategories of "mulatto" (defined as three-eighths to five-eighths African ancestry), "quadroon" (one-fourth), and "octoroon" (one-eighth or less). Distinguishing and quantifying multiracial people was an effort to ensure that the line between White and non-White remained strong. In 1930, the government went the other direction, officially defining multiracial people out of existence. Instead of marking all the gradations "in between" Black and White, they counted as Black anyone who had even "one drop" of "Black blood." This is called the **one-drop rule**, the idea that anyone with any trace of Black ancestry should be considered Black. According to the one-drop rule, White people are White, Black people are Black, and multiracial people are Black too.

In 1922 and 1923, the U.S. Supreme Court considered a pair of lawsuits challenging the exclusion of Asians from the subcategory of White.[21] One came from Takao Ozawa, a Japanese man who had lived in the United States for twenty years and started a successful business. The other suit was filed by Bhagat Singh Thind, an immigrant from India who had fought for the United States in World War I. Both men were seeking citizenship, which, in the early 1920s, was only extended to people identified as either White or Black. So, both Ozawa and Thind sued, not on the basis that people of other races should be eligible for citizenship, but on the basis that Japanese and Indian people were White.

Ozawa was up first, arguing that if White was a color, he was it. As evidence he displayed his own skin, which he pointed out was just as light as that of Europeans. The court agreed that his skin was light but insisted that White wasn't a color. Instead, it was a word that meant "Caucasian," which was a reference to people from the Caucasus Mountains, a range in Southern Russia that connects Eastern Europe to West Asia. Japan was in the far east of Asia, nowhere near the West. Therefore, Ozawa was not Caucasian and could not be considered White.

Up next was Thind, who was very pleased with the arguments in the Ozawa case. First, he was from Northern India, far west of Japan and much nearer to the Caucasus Mountains. Second, he was a descendent of genuine Caucasians who had invaded his region of India. His lawyers paraded anthropologists in front of the judges, each of whom argued that people from Thind's region of India were Caucasian and, therefore, White. It seemed like a slam dunk.

The Supreme Court agreed that Thind was Caucasian but argued that no reasonable person would mistake him for White. Reversing their logic from just a few months before, they insisted that White didn't mean Caucasian but was instead an idea based on a "common understanding" among the people. White was, in other words, not a color and not a reference to a geographical place. It was whatever White people wanted it to be.

The very last American to sue to claim a White identity was a woman from Sulphur, Louisiana, by the name of Susie Guillory Phipps. She discovered at the age of forty-three that her birth certificate identified her as "colored," a

one-drop rule
the idea that anyone with any trace of Black ancestry should be considered Black

word that, at the time, cast her as non-White. She protested, spending at least $49,000 on legal fees. Like Ozawa and Thind, she lost. At the time, Louisiana law specified that a person with 1/32nd or more Black ancestry was legally Black. One of Phipps's thirty-two great-great-great grandparents had been identified by the state as Black. She had what someone might describe as one drop of Black blood. It was 1981.

Interestingly, Phipps's argument wasn't based on color, geography, or common understanding. It was based on lifestyle. She claimed that she lived a White life. "I am White," she explained. "I was raised as a White child. I went to White school. I married White twice."[22] No one around her growing up, she claimed, "except the hired hands," were anything but White.[23] By being raised as a White person, going to school alongside White people, and marrying White men, she claimed to have lived in a White way. And that, she insisted, was why she was White.

Because race is a social construction, its logic can always be distorted to include and exclude arbitrarily. More often than not, in U.S. history, this has been done to exclude. But when inclusion is advantageous to certain interests, unwanted assimilation can happen too.

Just four years after the one-drop rule became law, the United States introduced the **blood quantum rule**, a law limiting legal recognition of American Indians to those who have at least a certain level of indigenous ancestry.[24] Unlike the one-drop rule, which pushed people *out* of the subcategory of White, the blood-quantum rule pulled people *into* the subcategory. Why? Because the government had agreed to provide American Indian citizens with services. By artificially shrinking the number of American citizens who could legally identify as American Indian, the government reduced its obligations. To this day, members of tribal nations must have a federally issued card that attests to their "certified degree of Indian blood."

Around the same time, in response to the influx of immigrants from Mexico after a revolution, the United States added "Mexican" to the racial subcategories on the census. It would only appear once. Both Mexican Americans and Mexican nationals were alarmed. They looked at the racial politics of the United States and decided they wanted nothing to do with a racial subcategory all their own. They allied with the Mexican government to get the subcategory removed from the census, arguing that Mexicans were not just White but the "sum and substance of the White race." Under substantial pressure, the United States accepted their logic. That's why "Hispanic, Latino, or Spanish" isn't included as a race even today but is instead listed as an **ethnicity**, an identity based on collective memories of a shared history and distinctive culture.

This brief tour of the history of some U.S. racial and ethnic subcategories reveals that, like the emergence of sexual orientation as an identity, the subcategories within an identity are also socially constructed. In the case of race and ethnicity, the subcategories are products of changing political priorities in a society based on racial and ethnic divides. Gender is another social identity, and it will be used to explore the attribution of meaning.

blood quantum rule
a law limiting legal recognition of American Indians to those who have at least a certain level of documented indigenous ancestry

ethnicity
an identity based on collective memories of a shared history and distinctive culture

STEP 3: STEREOTYPE
Filling Gender Subcategories with Contents

The word **gender** refers to the signifiers of *masculinity* and *femininity*—the ideas, traits, interests, and skills that we associate with being biologically male or female. In the United States, we generally layer gendered signifiers onto **sex**, a reference to physical traits related to sexual reproduction. The words *male* and *female* refer to the two body types, roughly, that human sexual reproduction requires. The subcategories of "men" and "women" are socially constructed identities that conflate maleness with masculinity and femaleness with femininity. The two categories are positioned as opposites, or placed in a **gender binary**. This is the idea that people come in two and only two types, males who are masculine and females who are feminine.

Human variety in bodies is natural. Based on their anatomy, some people are assigned male at birth, some are assigned female at birth, and some are designated as **intersex**—those with physical characteristics typical of both people assigned male and people assigned female at birth. The term **cisgender** is used to refer to people assigned male at birth who identify as men as well as people assigned female at birth who identify as women. In other words, a cisgender person's assigned sex and gender identity align according to cultural norms. People who aren't cisgender may be **transgender**, or trans. The transgender population includes people assigned male at birth who don't identify as men as well as people assigned female at birth who don't identify as women. People (including trans people) can also be **nonbinary** or identify as both man and woman or neither man nor woman. As with other identities, the language we use and subcategories we recognize change over time and are different across cultures.

To ascribe masculinity to people assigned male at birth and femininity to people assigned female at birth is to invoke a **stereotype**, clusters of ideas attached by social convention to people with specific social identities.[25] In the United States, women and girls are stereotyped as warm and expressive, nurturing of others, relationship-oriented, and with limited physical strength and sexual desire.[26] Stereotypes of men and boys portray them as the inverse of this: self-interested and competitive, logical and mathematically inclined, independent, aggressive, physically strong, and intensely sexual.

It's hard to believe, perhaps, but these stereotypes are only about one hundred years old. They emerged out of the same move to city life and wage work that made space for sexual orientation to become an identity. As industrialization took hold of the American economy and people moved off farms and into cities, home was separated from work for the first time. The workplace, newly considered a place for men, was cast as ruthless and competitive; the home, newly seen as a space for women, was cast as a reprieve from the workplace: a place for togetherness, selflessness, care, kindness, and cooperation.

Onto work and home were laid the now-familiar gender stereotypes. Men went to work and earned money, while women stayed home and cared for

---

gender
the ideas, traits, interests, and skills that we associate with being biologically male or female

sex
a reference to physical traits related to sexual reproduction

gender binary
the idea that people come in two and only two types, males who are masculine and females who are feminine

intersex
people with physical characteristics typical of both people assigned male and people assigned female at birth

cisgender
people who are assigned male at birth who identify as men as well as people assigned female at birth who identify as women

transgender
people assigned male at birth who don't identify as men as well as people assigned female at birth who don't identify as women

nonbinary
people who identify as both man and woman or neither man nor woman

stereotype
clusters of ideas attached by social convention to people with specific social identities

Nico Tortorella and Bethany C. Meyers are nonbinary. Both use the personal pronoun they/them/theirs. For their wedding, they wore "genderbending ensembles" that seamlessly invoked both the masculine and the feminine. They hope that their love story will help other nonbinary people "feel less alone" and stand as a testament to "different ways to love."[68]

their husbands and children. If work was competitive and cutthroat, men were too. And if the home was sentimental and sweet, it's because women made it that way. We were suddenly "opposite sexes": distinctly different, with complementary strengths and weaknesses.

These stereotypes are still alive and well in our culture. One way of demonstrating this is with content analysis, a way of carefully documenting the content of media, whether visual, audio, or print (see "The Science of Sociology"). A content analysis of 436 toys for sale on the U.S. Disney Store website, for example, found stereotyping that sent gendered messages about the personalities of boys and girls.[27] Ninety-eight percent of the action figures and 100 percent of the cars and trucks, weapons, and building toys were listed as boy toys, while 97 percent of the dolls and 100 percent of the domestic toys, like play kitchens, were listed as girl toys. The portrayal of boys as busy workers (driving, defending, and building) and girls as happy homemakers (raising children and keeping house) reflects the stereotypes invented during the Industrial Revolution.

content analysis
a research method that involves counting and describing patterns of themes in media

THE **SCIENCE** OF SOCIOLOGY

Content Analyses

Content analysis is a research method that involves counting and describing patterns of themes in media. The media can include print, still images, audio, video, or any other medium that sends messages. One could analyze advertisements, song lyrics, movies, social media updates, podcasts, newspapers, billboards, or even the graphics on clothes people wear.

Researchers decide what content to examine, then decide whether to analyze all of the content or a subset of it. The researchers studying the toys for sale on the Disney website decided to analyze all the toys on the website. In other cases, there may be too much content to analyze (Amazon, for instance, lists over 300,000 toys for sale), in which case researchers will analyze only a sample of it.

To do the analysis, researchers decide on codes to apply, or the features of the content that are relevant to their research question. When analyzing a toy, for example, the researchers coded for whether its colors were bold (masculine) or pastel (feminine) and whether it was a stereotypically masculine or feminine toy (like an action figure or a Barbie doll). Applying the codes to content transforms it into data. Once the coding is completed, the researcher will look for patterns. This might include identifying common words, associations, visual images, sounds, plot devices, or types of people.

Analysis can be quantitative, qualitative, or both. Quantitative content analysis involves counting and correlating codes. Qualitative content analysis involves rich descriptions of specific instances of codes. Using both of them together offers a useful characterization of the content, as researchers can explain both how often certain themes occur and what they are like when they do.

Carefully examining media for persistent themes and messages is an excellent way to show that social constructs are not just in our heads but genuinely present in our culture. When concerned with social identities, content analysis can be used to measure *representation*, whether members of social groups are portrayed, and *misrepresentation*, inaccurate and sometimes harmful representations of social groups. This can reveal what stereotypes are present, how frequently they're communicated, by whom, and in what media. ■

Are these stereotypes accurate? They're not. Scientists have produced thousands of studies comparing men's and women's thoughts, feelings, behavior, intelligence, communication, skills, personalities, physical abilities, and more. Exploiting this abundance of research, scientists perform *meta-analyses*, a method of statistically joining a pool of studies with the aim of aggregating their results to produce a more conclusive finding than any individual study can offer alone. Dozens or hundreds of studies on a single trait can be mathematically combined to determine whether the collected evidence suggests that men and women are different or alike.

In 2015, a team of scholars performed what they called a *meta-synthesis*, a meta-analysis of meta-analyses.[28] They merged 106 meta-analyses representing over 20,000 individual studies involving more than 12 million people. It included over 21,000 measures of 386 traits. The researchers found that the differences between men and women on 85 percent of traits were small to nonexistent, 12 percent were medium, and 3 percent were large. The average difference between men and women—on all traits included—fell into the small category. The bell curve in Figure 3.1 depicts the small difference in levels of self-esteem between men and women, revealing that men's and women's self-esteem levels are much more similar than different.

The results of this meta-synthesis don't support the idea that men and women are exactly the same, but it does offer strong evidence—the strongest scientific evidence currently conceivable—that they're more alike than

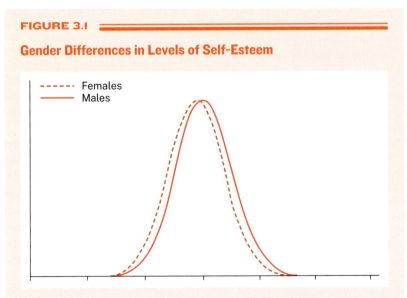

FIGURE 3.1

Gender Differences in Levels of Self-Esteem

- - - - - Females
———— Males

SOURCE: Kristen C. Kling, Janet S. Hyde, Carolin J. Showers, and Brenda N. Buswell, "Gender Differences in Self-Esteem: A Meta-Analysis," *Psychological Bulletin*, 125, no. 4 (1999): 484.

different. The Disney website misrepresents the truth about the relationship between sex and gender. It, along with many other media sources in U.S. society, socially constructs the subcategories of male and female, making them signify caricatures of work and home, respectively.

Depending on what identities we carry, certain stereotypes apply. As individuals living in the world, we have to contend with the fact that others expect us to embody those stereotypes. The expectation that we perform our identities is the subject of the next section, which focuses on age.

STEP 4: PERFORM
Act Your Age

At least some of the differences we see between people are the result of stereotypes. Collectively, we bring stereotypes to life by acting in ways that are consistent with them. None of us perfectly conforms to the stereotypes that apply to us, and many of us feel uncomfortable about conforming, but we all perform our identities at least somewhat. That is, we behave in ways that are consistent with the expectations other people have for members of our social groups. This is described as **doing identity**, or the active performance of social identities.

To elaborate this idea, let's consider age. The sociologist Cheryl Laz wrote that it "seems almost absurd to think about age as anything but a chronological fact and as something every individual simply is."[29] Age, though, is also something we do. There are right ways to be twenty, fifty, or eighty, and we have a specific language with which we admonish people who do their age wrong. Laz explained:

> "Act your age. Stop being so childish," we say to other adults we think are being irresponsible. "Act your age; you're not as young as you used to be," we say to an old person pursuing "youthful" activities. The sanctioned actions vary, but the command "act!" remains the same. When we say "act your age" we press for behavior that conforms to norms.[30]

The social construction of age is part of why the internet found such delight in the modeling of Liu Xianping.[31] At seventy-two years old, Liu began modeling for his granddaughter's boutique, which catered to teen girls. Liu dressed in women's clothes, and specifically in clothes for very young women. He was playing with the performance of both gender and age. The result was a set of delightfully unusual fashion photographs.

The doing of age extends to our appearance, our behavior, and how we spend our time and with whom. When we encounter a person, for example, we look at their face and body to determine how old they are, but we also look at other visual cues too: clothing, hair, makeup, accessories. There's a certain phase of life, for example, in which it's considered socially acceptable to wear a mini-skirt, and it has both a beginning and an end. Likewise, thirty-five-year-old women who dye their hair to hide their gray may be praised for "keeping

doing identity
the active performance of social identities

Liu Xianping's fashion photographs went viral because he posed not just in women's clothes, but in *young* women's clothes. The seventy-three-year-old grandfather was performing both femininity and youth, and in the most delightful way.

themselves up," while sixty-five-year-olds who do so might be criticized as "trying too hard." Middle-aged moms are supposed to have minivans, while middle-aged men are allowed to splurge on a sports car.

Our behavior is expected to change with age too. Eight-year-olds and eighty-year-olds are not supposed to talk explicitly about sex. We're surprised when grandmothers curse and unsurprised when elderly uncles express out-of-date opinions. There's a certain age range when it's acceptable to go out and get irresponsibly drunk several nights each week. But the almost-forty binge drinker might be scolded: "You're not as young as you used to be" and "Don't you think it's time to settle down?"

"Settling down" is a reference to the fact that, as we get older, we are expected to fulfill specific roles in a predictable sequence, like spouse, homeowner, parent and, finally, grandparent. That's why we say things like "they married young" or "he retired late" and why we have labels for people who do things late, early, out of order, or never: "nontraditional student," "teenage mother," "single dad," "spinster."

The fact that we have such sayings in our language reveals that age isn't natural. If it was, we wouldn't have the opportunity to be surprised when ninety-year-olds curse, because they wouldn't. Likewise, if it was natural to go gray at sixty-five—but not one day before—no one would buy dye to hide their gray. And if it was natural for women to have their first child at thirty, we wouldn't have to instruct them to be abstinent or use birth control before then. Aging is natural, but age is socially constructed. It's an identity that's divvied up into sequential life stages onto which stereotypes are heaped.

Aging is also stigmatized. Americans generally consider it better to be young than old. Hence the "over the hill" parties. This is true for sexual orientation, gender, and race and ethnicity too. Some identity subcategories are accorded greater esteem than others. This hierarchy building is the topic of the next section.

STEP 5: RANK
The Building of Body Hierarchies

Prior to around 1900, plumpness was desirable.[32] An ample waistline on a woman was believed to be both beautiful and necessary: evidence that she could make hearty, healthy babies of equal rotundity. Thinness was for preteens. Grown women were supposed to be voluptuous.

Accordingly, women were admired for being buxom. The early advocate for women's rights, Elizabeth Cady Stanton, was praised for being "plump as a partridge," while her counterpart Susan B. Anthony was criticized for being too skinny. Stanton, protective of Anthony, admitted that she was "sharp, angular, [and] cross-grained" on the outside but "broad and generous" on the inside.[33]

Fashion of the time emphasized women's curves, revealing extravagant arcs of flesh. Corsets were used not just to cinch the waist but to squeeze out the breasts and hips. The fashion didn't hide women's girth so much as arrange it in pleasing ways. Upper-class women even padded their bodies underneath their clothes and added bustles to artificially inflate their rear end. They wore "fat suits." On purpose.

On a man, a fat body signified a fat bank account. Only rich men could eat until they were good and stout. Proud of their size, men formed fat men's clubs: networking opportunities for the rich and powerful. They made a good time of it, eating together, hosting competitive weigh-ins, and engaging in contests of strength. Prominent physicians agreed that fat men were the very picture of virility. "Plumpness, roundness, size . . . are rightly believed to indicate well-balanced health," said one.[34] A man without heft was considered insufficiently masculine: soft, resource-poor, sexually feeble.

The story behind how the United States went from a fat-loving to a fat-hating society furthers one of this chapter's central arguments: that the identities that matter to us, and our evaluation of them, is a matter of cultural and historical change. In this case, the change in fat's value occurred in response to a new abundance. Agricultural production more than doubled between 1870 and 1900.[35] Food was plentiful and cheap. This made fat bodies accessible to all, not just the rich.

Rising rates of other types of **consumption**—the use of wages to purchase goods and services—left cultural critics worried that Americans were becoming greedy, materialistic, and immodest. In 1899, in fact, the sociologist Thorstein Veblen coined the phrase **conspicuous consumption** to describe

consumption
the use of wages to purchase goods and services

conspicuous consumption
spending elaborately on items and services with the sole purpose of displaying one's wealth

In the early 1900s, fat men had the reputation of being wealthy, strong, and sexually virile. Proud of their heft, they formed fat men's clubs that celebrated their large bodies.

the phenomenon of spending elaborately on items and services with the sole purpose of displaying one's wealth.[36] All of this undisciplined self-indulgence offended the ideals of self-restraint that characterized much of American history. The rich, in particular—perhaps because they were uniquely positioned to spend lavishly—embodied this new form of moral failing, calling into question their collective character.

Thin bodies were a two-part solution for the rich.[37] First, now that anyone could get fat, the rich needed a new way to create a positive distinction between themselves and the middle and working classes. They used their outsized power to turn the tables on the rest of the population, embracing and valorizing thinness. Then, they turned their thin bodies—accessible to them because they had leisure time and financial resources—into a symbol of their supposedly superior willpower. Regardless of how loosely and flashily they spent their money, their bodies stood as evidence of self-discipline, proof that they were a higher-quality people than the unrestrained masses. In a sudden reversal, thin became good and fat became bad.

Today, to be fat is to carry **stigma**, a personal attribute that is widely devalued by members of one's society. Having aborted a pregnancy can be stigmatizing, for example, as is being unable to afford housing or publicly proclaiming a very unpopular opinion. Some bodies are stigmatized too. People who are missing teeth, for instance, are often discredited, as are people with certain kinds of physical disabilities.

Fat bodies are an example of a stigmatizing physical trait. Content analyses of media show that fat characters are often criticized, made the butt of

stigma
a personal attribute that is widely devalued by members of one's society

jokes, and portrayed as self-hating. They're more likely than thin characters to be presented as unemployed, ugly, unhappy, angry, unintelligent, unlovable, violent, and evil.[38] Media often portray fat people as unhealthy, which is one of the most pernicious lies about fat. A recent meta-analysis of ninety-seven studies with a combined sample of nearly 3 million individuals, published in the *Journal of the American Medical Association*, found that the healthiest people in the United States—the ones *least* likely to get sick or die early—are ones who are defined as "overweight."[39]

The sociologist Patricia Hill Collins would call stigmatizing ideas like these **controlling images**, pervasive negative stereotypes that serve to justify or uphold inequality. She originally discussed the concept when describing stereotypes about Black women, feeling that the word *stereotype* didn't do justice to the degree of harm these representations did to them, nor how damaging stereotypes are to wider debates about public policy. Controlling images, she argued, do more than characterize members of low-status groups one way or another; they do so in distinctly harmful ways, by demeaning, diminishing, or demonizing them. In doing so, she argues, they "make racism, sexism, poverty, and other forms of social injustice appear to be natural, normal, and inevitable parts of everyday life."[40]

Such misrepresentation matters. Asked about a series of trade-offs, almost half of respondents said they'd rather give up a year of their life than be obese.[41] A quarter said they'd rather be infertile, 30 percent said they'd rather get divorced, and 15 percent said they'd rather be depressed or become an alcoholic. These responses reflect **prejudice**, attitudinal bias against individuals based on their membership in a social group. Most people who live in the United States harbor at least some bias against people seen as fat.[42]

In the past few decades—armed with a wide array of research methods—scholars have made impressive strides in understanding prejudice. One of these scholars is the sociologist Cecilia Ridgeway. She grew up in the 1960s, a time when the United States was on the brink of revolutionary changes, and she was inspired to study inequality. She graduated high school at just sixteen years old and ultimately embarked on a career-long research program.[43] She would win lifetime achievement awards for her work on gender inequality and serve a term as the president of the American Sociological Association.

Ridgeway's research has produced robust evidence that highly regarded traits are more often and more easily attributed to people with some identities than others. Identities differ, in other words, in the extent to which they're attributed **status**, high or low esteem. High-status identities are ones for which we have high regard, so people with those identities will be seen as *generally* more valuable than people without those identities. Unless there's a reason to think otherwise, people with high-status identities will be assumed to be better than others in a variety of ways: smarter, nicer, more talented, better looking, more trustworthy and generous, harder working, exceptional parents, more devoted friends, and better in bed. There is status we can earn, like the kind that comes with good deeds, learned skills, and impressive

controlling images
pervasive negative stereotypes that serve to justify or uphold inequality

prejudice
attitudinal bias against individuals based on their membership in a social group

status
high or low esteem

accomplishments, but there's also status that we are simply granted by virtue of who we are.

Above and beyond stereotypes, our thinking about people with different social identities is warped by these ideas. Sociologists call them **status beliefs**, collectively shared ideas about which social groups are more or less deserving of esteem.

Sometimes our status beliefs are attitudes that we hold explicitly. *Explicit attitudes* are beliefs that we choose to have or at least know we have. Other times these attitudes are implicit. *Implicit attitudes* are beliefs that we've absorbed involuntarily and of which we're mostly unaware.[44] We learn implicit attitudes through socialization and our brains retrieve these beliefs automatically, often without our conscious knowledge. While only some of us carry explicitly prejudicial beliefs, it's probably fair to say that we all carry implicit prejudices. In fact, people's explicit and implicit attitudes often diverge; many people committed to fairness nonetheless test positive for implicit bias.[45]

Since our implicit attitudes are not conscious, scholars invented a creative way to detect them. They do so with a form of computer-assisted research, or a set of methods that uses computers to collect data (see "The Science of Sociology"). To test for implicit attitudes, research subjects play a kind of computer game in which they sort low- and high-status ideas and identities. Sometimes they're asked to pair identities and ideas with a similar level of status (like thin with good or fat with bad). Other times, they're asked to pair identities and ideas with inverse levels of status (like thin with bad and fat with good).

We're generally able to match positive ideas with group members we see as highly valued just a hair quicker than we can match them with negative ideas, and vice versa. Longer times mean weaker associations and shorter times mean stronger associations. Computers can measure the speed of our responses with great accuracy, giving us a real, true test of our implicit biases.

In this way, the test gets straight into our brains, able to detect implicit biases that we may not know we have. At the time of this writing, over a million people have taken the implicit attitudes test for preference for fat or thin people: 9 percent showed a preference for fat people, 15 percent little or no preference either way, and 84 percent showed a preference for thin people.[46] (You can test your own implicit biases by going to Harvard's Project Implicit website.)

In sum, prejudice isn't something we're born with; it's something we learn, whether we like it or not. Most Americans have learned to fear fat, both in others and in ourselves, and to dislike or disdain other kinds of people too. Tests of explicit and implicit attitudes also reveal prejudice against people of color, sexual minorities, immigrants, people without advanced education, the rich and the poor, the conventionally unattractive, atheists, Muslims, Jews, and conservative Christians.[47] These are socially constructed hierarchies.

We are carriers of prejudice, but we're also its victims. Some of us carry many stigmatized or otherwise devalued identities, while others of us carry

status beliefs
collectively shared ideas about which social groups are more or less deserving of esteem

computational sociology
a research method that uses computers to extract and analyze data

THE **SCIENCE** OF SOCIOLOGY

Computational Sociology

Computer-assisted research involves a set of methods that uses computers. Computers can detect and record things that human observers generally cannot, like the direction and trajectory of people's gazes, minute differences in the length of time it takes to respond to a prompt, or the brain activity of an individual exposed to different images or sounds.

One form of computer-assisted research is **computational sociology**, a research method that uses computers to extract and analyze data. Computing power has become especially useful in the era of "big data," extremely large and growing sources of information. Google has uploaded, for example, 40 million books to the web, while Twitter users send 500 million tweets every single day. This is easily accessible information, but at a scale unmanageable by humans. Computers, however, can be programmed to do the work in our place.

Sociologists program computers to scour the internet for certain kinds of information, then program them to "read" that information for specific kinds of data and organize it in interpretable ways. For computational sociologists, data can include "digital life" (including social media accounts, discussion boards, streaming sites, search records, and collective projects like Wikipedia), "digital traces" (incomplete records of online activity, including tax data, voter records, death certificates, and data on political contributions), and material that has been "digitalized" (originally nonelectronic information that's been uploaded, like book, newspaper, and photo archives).

Computational sociology is essential for taking advantage of the flood of data made available by the introduction of the internet. Without it, sociologists would be at a loss to contribute valuable knowledge about how life works in the digital age. The ability to program computers, write algorithms, and input massive amounts of data also lets sociologists join other scientists in building sophisticated models and predicting the likely outcomes of interaction on a massive scale. ■

few. The latter are the **status elite**, people who carry many positively regarded social identities. The advantages and disadvantages that come with our positions in social hierarchies will be an ongoing theme of the rest of this book.

The five steps of social identity construction, then, involve choosing a human feature on which to differentiate some people from others, creating

status elite
people who carry many positively regarded social identities

subcategories, and giving those categories symbolic meaning. We are then held accountable to those meanings and pressed to perform our identities. And, finally, identity subcategories are placed in hierarchies, making some more advantageous to carry than others.

Thus far, identities have been discussed in isolation; for example, race and ethnicity separately from sexual orientation. But that's not how we actually experience our identities. Rather, we experience them all at once. This fact is called intersectionality.

INTERSECTIONALITY AND DISABILITY

The social theorist Anna Julia Cooper (1858–1964) was born to an enslaved mother in Raleigh, North Carolina.[48] Her mother, like all enslaved women, lived with the ever-looming possibility of White men's sexual coercion and violence.[49] Though her mother never said so, Cooper believed that her father was the man who enslaved them, or perhaps his brother.[50] Hence, she lived with a visceral understanding that the experience of enslavement was different for women and men. Men were not spared the violence of sexual assault, but women bore its brunt. And while both men and women loved the children in their care, women uniquely carried and birthed the children conceived against their will.

The mother of Black feminism, Anna Julia Cooper wrote the first book dedicated to the unique experiences of Black American women.

Blessedly, the Emancipation Proclamation was signed when Cooper was five years old. At nine, she was granted a scholarship to begin her education. An excellent student, she ultimately enrolled at Oberlin College in 1881—one of the only colleges in the United States to accept Black students—and she opted for the more rigorous four-year "Gentlemen's course" over the lighter two-year "Ladies' course."[51] Eventually, she would become only the fourth American Black woman to earn a PhD, graduating from the Sorbonne in Paris at age sixty-seven.

Cooper's most important contribution to sociology may have been in part inspired by the circumstances of her birth. In a book titled *A Voice from the South*, Cooper argued that understanding the lives of Black women required thinking simultaneously about race and gender.[52] Moreover, she suggested that Black women have unique insights not available to White women or Black men. She insisted on the importance of this point of view and concluded that Black people would never be truly free if Black women and Black men were not raised up in equal measure. This was the first book-length consideration of the lives of Black women, and her insights were so ground-breaking that she is now known as the mother of Black feminism.

Almost exactly one hundred years later, another Black feminist—the law professor Kimberlé Crenshaw—would coin the phrase **intersectionality** to draw attention to the fact that our lives are shaped by multiple interacting identities.[53] She came up with the term in response to a lawsuit against General Motors brought on behalf of five Black women.[54] Their lawyers argued that because the company wasn't hiring Black women, they were unfairly barred from employment at the company. Lawyers for the defense countered that because General Motors hired White women (that is, women) and Black men (that is, Black people), they were clearly not discriminating against either women or Black people. The court agreed. The women lost the case.

Crenshaw used the lawsuit to illustrate the importance of thinking intersectionally. Echoing Cooper, she argued that the lives of Black women are shaped not by race *or* gender but by race *and* gender. This meant that their experiences, and the nature of their disadvantages in American society, were distinct from those of men of the same race and women of other races. General Motors may not have been discriminating against Black people or women, but they absolutely were discriminating against Black women.

Since Crenshaw reintroduced the idea in the early 1990s, scholars have expanded the concept, demonstrating that no single identity truly captures anyone's life experiences. To illustrate, this final section explores some of the experiences of people with disabilities. The experience of impairment is inflected by all of a person's identities, including gender, sexual orientation, body size, and race.

Exactly how an impairment influences our self-concept is often related to gender. Men more so than women are tasked with being strong and independent, so for them, a disability can threaten the gendered expectation that they be able to take care of themselves without help. This was how acquiring a spinal cord injury felt to a twenty-seven-year-old man named Forrest. He lives with his grandmother and depended greatly on both her and his brother to get by. "I can only do so much," he said. "I'm always gonna need help." Isaac, who also lives with a spinal cord injury, described the feeling in relation to his decreased sexual prowess. "You can't throw [a sexual partner] on the table or the stove or the counter. . . . It's just impossible. So that kinda takes some of your manhood too."[55]

For women, a disability can affect their ability to perform physical attractiveness.[56] Stereotypes about people with disabilities portray them as unsexy, even asexual, so women who are visibly impaired may find that their femininity and sexuality become invisible. "Ever since I've been in a wheelchair, I've stopped getting catcalled," one woman observed, speculating that it's because men stopped seeing her as "potentially doable."[57] Another woman agreed: "I am sure that other people see a wheelchair first, me second, and a woman third, if at all."[58]

intersectionality
the recognition that our lives are shaped by multiple interacting identities

Other identities add further twists to the experience of being a wheelchair user. Andrew Gurza, for example, is a gay man with cerebral palsy. He writes about dating at the intersection of sexual orientation, gender, and ability. In one essay, he takes up the issue of the gay bar. All wheelchair users, he explains, will discover that some bars and clubs are inaccessible, but for a gay man wanting to visit a gay space, the options can be especially limited. There aren't that many gay bars to begin with, so if some are eliminated because of accessibility issues, the options may be few and far between, maybe across town, or not where one's friends want to go.

As Gurza points out, this is about more than just the pleasure of "the prowl"; it's about identity. Often a gay bar is the first place that a gay person feels truly safe. It's one of the only places that gay people can be themselves without fear, especially if they live in an otherwise intolerant community. That, Gurza explains, is the "deeper issue": "By not having access to these spaces, I am denied the opportunity to . . . [go] where [gay] sex and sexuality is free and fun."[59]

Gurza struggles not just because he's gay *or* male *or* disabled. It's the specific intersection of the three. Change any one of those qualities and the particular struggles he faces would change.

Kali, a woman with a connective tissue disorder who uses a mechanized wheelchair, sits at the intersection of disability and fat. This, she argues with frustration, is doubly stigmatizing. When thin people use wheelchairs, the assumption is that they require it.[60] Its use is *allowed* by the viewer, while the fat person's use is read as evidence of laziness (a controlling image of fat people). Kali routinely attracts stares and comments. Strangers express disgust, assuming she's fat but otherwise healthy and therefore just extraordinarily lazy. "It makes me so damn mad," she writes, "[to see them] har har over the way I use a scooter because I'm fat."[61] In reality, her joints and ligaments would strain to support her at any weight.

Studies show that fat women like Kali are penalized more than fat men.[62] The sociologist S. Bear Bergman, for example, who's a self-described "gender-jammer" and uses the pronoun "he," sometimes passes for male and sometimes for female.[63] This has allowed Bergman to experience life as both a fat woman and a fat man. As a fat man, he confirms, he's perceived as a "big dude" but "not outside the norm." As a fat woman, though, others perceive him as "revolting." "I am not only unattractively mannish," he writes, "but also grossly fat. . . . G-d help me if I get caught eating (or even shopping [for food]) in public as a woman."[64]

Fat women are stigmatized more heavily than fat men, and fat White women are penalized more than fat women of color.[65] Women perceived to be heterosexual are judged more harshly for being fat than women believed to be non-heterosexual. They, in turn, are also judged less harshly than men perceived to be gay or bisexual, who are held to higher standards than men perceived to be heterosexual. So, as a fat White woman who is read as heterosexual, Kali attracts higher levels of fat stigma than people with a different constellation of identities.

Cara Liebowitz, another White woman who uses a wheelchair, is reasonably thin, so she doesn't deal with the exact same problems faced by Kali. She's in her twenties and conventionally attractive. At worst, she says, people infantilize her and treat her as helpless. "I am the embodiment of innocence," she writes: "eternally fragile and childlike."[66] Consequently, Liebowitz often struggles to get people to take her seriously as a robust adult who should be treated with respect.

Her boyfriend has a very different experience. He's young and fit, too, and he uses a wheelchair as well, but he's Black and male. And that makes all the difference. "[W]hen people look at him," Liebowitz writes, "they assume that his disability resulted from violence." The stereotype of Black men as criminal shapes how people read his use of a wheelchair. "I realized that even though my boyfriend and I share the same disability," Liebowitz explains, "we are having very different experiences in how society sees and treats our bodies. While people often viewed me with pity, they viewed him with distrust and even fear."[67]

We live with many identities. Each interacts with the others we carry, creating constellations that intermix in complicated ways. Understanding any one person's experience will mean seeing the whole person and attending to all their identities as well as their intersections. ■

COMING UP...

GROUP MEMBERSHIP is something that humans crave. We're quick to draw lines between us and them. The groups that emerge as a result of this process—our social identities—are social constructs. We learn to think of ourselves in terms of these constructs. We perform our identities, too, and bring them to life. Our identities become a part of our self-concept, though if we had been born in a different time or place, we would think of ourselves differently.

These identities are often a source of pleasure, pride, and solidarity. But they also grant us different levels of esteem. Stereotypes suggest that we're good and bad at this or that, while status beliefs influence whether we're considered *generally* worthy of esteem. Depending on how our identities intersect, this may bring us advantages or disadvantages.

Our sense of self emerges, then, out of both our engagement with other people and the specific identities made available to us by our cultures. As the next chapter will show, we then bring those identities into interaction with other people. It discusses what sociologists have taught us about how we "do" everyday life. It marvels at the intricacy of it all, while also considering how our identities influence how we act. A chapter about *how* to be ordinary, and *who* can be ordinary, is next.

4

PEOPLE IN
INTERACTION

IN THIS **CHAPTER...**

THIS CHAPTER COVERS the sociological theories that explain the ordinary: routine *social interaction*, or moments we spend with other people. It introduces you to the idea that social interaction is guided by social rules. We follow these rules for a range of reasons; one reason is the threat of *social sanctions*, or reactions by others aimed at promoting conformity. We also learn how to offer *accounts*, or excuses that explain away our rule breaking.

You'll be introduced to the work of three early scholars who developed this area of sociology:

- Herbert Blumer's theory of *symbolic interaction*, the idea that social interaction depends on the social construction of reality.

- Erving Goffman's *dramaturgy*, the practice of looking at social life as a series of performances.

- And Harold Garfinkel's *ethnomethodology*, a type of research aimed at revealing the underlying shared logic that is the foundation for social interaction.

You'll also learn how our social identities shape our social interaction, including where we fit in, what roles we can play, and whether our performances make sense to others. Interactions sometimes involve *interpersonal discrimination*, prejudicial behavior displayed by individuals.

Finally, this chapter introduces you to another sociological research method:

- The *field experiment*, an experimental method that involves a test of a hypothesis outside the laboratory.

"Always remember that you are absolutely unique. Just like everyone else."

—UNKNOWN

One day 262 students walked out of their Introduction to Sociology class at Georgia Southern University and did nothing. Their instructor, the sociologist Nathan Palmer, had asked them to break a *norm*, a shared expectation for behavior. In this case, it was the "norm of activity," the rule that you should do something even when you're not doing anything.[1] Palmer described it this way:

> Think about what people do at an airport while they're waiting for a flight to come in. They don't just stand motionless with no expression on their face. They fidget, they fix their hair, they fix their clothing, they have a cell phone out . . . they're reading a magazine. So, even when we have nothing to do, we have to do something. It's expected of us.[2]

Palmer's students, though, standing outside the student union on a sunny day, didn't do anything. They were "relaxed statues": not frozen but expressionless and still, hands at their sides. If asked what they were doing, they were to respond: "nothing."

The exercise stopped onlookers in their tracks. One student was overheard asking: "What are these people doing?" Recalling the response, a student in Palmer's class said:

> I definitely did not expect that people would take so much notice of us. We were doing something as simple as standing there. If I was texting on the phone or listening to music, no one would have paid attention. But when you're doing something that's outside of the norm, everyone stops and takes notice.

Doing nothing is "outside of the norm," which actually tells us something interesting.[3] It tells us that, far from being automatic, being "normal" is an achievement. It requires extensive knowledge of how other people ordinarily act in all possible circumstances, from the supermarket to the beach to the bowling alley. If we're lucky enough to have that knowledge, being normal also requires the ability to act that way ourselves, for which we need the right resources, information, and skills. Of course, sometimes we do the opposite—we try to make ourselves stand out or seem exceptional—but most of the time we try to blend in.

The sociologist Harvey Sacks described it as "being ordinary."[4] Though being extraordinary usually gets the spotlight, it's ordinariness that makes the world go round. Everyday life, Sacks observed, is dependent on everyone "keeping everything utterly mundane." It requires a certain amount of predictability and an absence of unhelpful surprises: You receive your paychecks, people drive on the right side of the road, your local grocery store has food. Whimsy, quirk, free-spiritedness, strangeness, inventiveness, unruliness, and impulsiveness all have their place, but we need our coffee shop to be open and the buses to run on time. So, all of us are invested in making a lot of life boring and predictable.

Collaboratively producing this normality isn't easy or simple. Normality isn't nothing; it's something. And it's not something we *are*; it's something we *do*. We do it through **social interaction**, moments we share with other people. Social interaction is how we make it possible to buy a candy bar, pass a stranger on the sidewalk, or share an umbrella in the rain. This is easy, right?

social interaction
moments we share with other people

In fact, it's not. Seventy years after the early computer scientist Alan Turing challenged his peers to build a robot that could hold a conversation as well as your average person, we've yet to be able to do it. Today's computers can compose music, write news articles, fly airplanes, play chess, and program themselves, but they fail at basic human interaction.[5]

"Bob was raised in the wilderness by salmon."

Perhaps you've never been impressed by the human ability to simply interact before. You should be. A social interaction is an imaginative, back-and-forth, spontaneous performance requiring ongoing, rapid calculations and an impressive balance between inventiveness and predictability. Interactions are living things. Each one unrolls in real time, invented in the moment by its participants, and every interaction in all of human history has been and always will be unique.

How do we do it?

How do we figure out what's going on? How do we know what to do, wear, and say? How do we know what in the universe of possible actions is allowable? More basically, how do we know how to do anything "right" in a way that others will recognize as normal? That is what this chapter is all about.

PLAYING BY THE RULES

To be "friended" on Facebook is to both receive *and* accept a request to connect on the social media platform. This is one way that Facebook is different than Twitter or TikTok, where we can follow someone who isn't following us back. On Facebook, friendship is reciprocal, meaning that we can only be friends with someone who is also friends with us. This fact encodes a norm into the social media site: the "norm of reciprocity," or the idea that people should act toward one another in parallel ways. Offline, this might mean that if someone says "hi," you acknowledge the greeting and say "hi" in return. If they give you a gift on your birthday, you give them one on theirs. If you vow to "love and cherish," so they vow to you. And so on. On its site, Facebook has made reciprocal friendship compulsory.

A study of twelve-to-thirteen-year-old girls on Facebook found that this norm extended well beyond the act of friending.[6] These girls made reciprocal friendship an art form. If one commented on another's selfie to tell her she was beautiful, the comment would elicit a reciprocal response ("u r gorgeous!"). If a girl posted a picture of her friend edited to include hearts, happy faces, and compliments ("you're the coolest," "I love you!"), the girl featured was expected to do the same. Many girls listed their best friends in their profiles, tagged them as sisters, and posed with them in their profile pictures. If a girl did not respond, such gestures of friendship would usually be quietly retracted.

These practices were how girls maintained and built their friendships. A girl who wanted to make a friend could carefully extend gestures of familiarity and see if her efforts were returned. "So you would comment on someone's photo who you're not really super close with," said Jane, interviewed for a radio program about the topic: "And it's sort of a statement, like, I want to be friends with you, or I want to get to know you, or like, I think you're cool."[7] Conversely, a girl who wanted to move on from a friendship could subtly lower her level of reciprocity. The nature of these interactions also revealed social hierarchies. An extremely popular girl could receive comments and not comment in return. Or, she could respond half-heartedly to a photo that a friend enthusiastically decorated with cute phrases and happy faces.

Anyone watching these carefully crafted interactions could read them for who was friends with whom, which friendships were especially close, who was the most (and the least) popular, and what friendships were forming and which were dissolving. Alert to the audiences to these exchanges, Ella said:

> It's definitely a social obligation because you want to let them know, and also let people who are seeing those [interactions], that I have a close relationship with this person, so close that I can comment on their pictures, like, this is so cute, or, you look so great here.[8]

All of this was useful for knowing how to interact both on- and offline. It revealed both social networks and social hierarchies, giving each girl a sense of where they stood relative to others.

Tween girls have unique cultures, of course, but their social media practices reveal something that is true more generally. Any kind of cooperation depends on establishing some ground rules. If we want to be culturally competent members of our society, we come to know the expectations others have of us. Social interactions, in other words, are guided by **social rules**, culturally specific norms, policies, and laws that guide our behavior. Our social rules are both prescriptive (telling us what to do) and proscriptive (telling us what not to do).

Some norms are only weakly embraced and half-heartedly enforced. Others are strongly embraced and all but compulsory. Loosely enforced norms are called **folkways**.[9] Quite literally, the "ways of the folk." Folkways are often aimed at facilitating everyday social interaction. Norms can also rise to the level of **mores** (pronounced *more-rays*), more tightly enforced norms that carry moral significance. If mores separate right from wrong, folkways separate right from rude.

social rules
culturally specific norms, policies, and laws that guide our behavior

folkways
loosely enforced norms

mores
tightly enforced norms that carry moral significance

To safely hold in-person classes in fall 2020, colleges had to rapidly instill a new set of social norms. Behind this sign's friendly tone is an urgent and downright death-defying campaign to normalize face masks.

At their most extreme, proscriptive norms are described as **taboos**. These are social prohibitions so strong that the thought of violating them can be sickening. Because their violation inspires extremely negative emotions, most of us avoid doing so regardless of whether we expect negative feedback.

Some social rules are made official by organizations and governments. **Policies** are rules that are made and enforced by organizations. **Laws** are rules that are made and enforced by cities, states, or federal governments. These are social rules that are punishable. Many policies and laws are also mores, folkways, or taboos, but not all. Sometimes governments criminalize behavior that most people accept, like jaywalking.

As an example of the whole scope of social rules, consider guidelines as to the proper use of social media more generally. Some are laws for which a person can be prosecuted. For instance, it's illegal to threaten to harm someone or upload child pornography. These are things for which a person could be civilly or criminally charged. Some of the rules for using social media aren't against the law, but they are against company policy. Snapchat has a policy against uploading pictures of people taken without their consent, for example, and Facebook has a rule against most images that include female nipples. (Men are allowed to show all the nipple they want.)

Social media also includes hundreds of ever-evolving folkways. Violations of such rules include posting too often, constantly complaining or "vagueposting," uploading and tagging unflattering pictures of your friends, being overly self-promotional, and liking your own status updates. Some activities on social media are considered not just rude but wrong. They violate mores. This might include online bullying or vicious public attacks, making jokes about harming animals or children, or mocking vulnerable populations.

Finally, some activities on social media may rise to the level of taboo. In 2015, several scandals broke out when women posted images of themselves featuring menstrual blood. A Canadian artist named Rupi Kaur, for example, posted a series of images on Instagram involving artificial blood. The pictures were familiar to anyone who has periods: blood on the floor of the shower, blood in the toilet, blood on an item being thrown in the laundry. Her intention was to destigmatize menstruation. Born in India to Hindu parents, Kaur had been taught that periods were shameful. "And ever since," she wrote, "I have been working so hard to love it. Embrace it. Celebrate it."[10] She wanted to share her struggle and her triumph.

The image that caused the loudest uproar was of Kaur herself from behind, laying on a bed, with menstrual blood seeming to seep through the back of her sweatpants. Instagram deleted the image, claiming that it violated their community standards. Kaur uploaded it again, and it was deleted a second time. The standoff received media attention, triggering both enthusiastic support from people who empathized with Kaur's mission and vicious backlash from people who believed that periods should remain taboo. Her Facebook discussion of Instagram's response was viewed 3 million times in less than a day. Eventually, Instagram apologized, and the image was allowed to remain on its site. The fact that it was scandalous at all, however, suggests that public acknowledgment of menstruation can still cross a line.

Why we follow (and how we break) the rules

Whatever social rules we encounter, we tend to follow them most of the time. We do so for many reasons. We follow them to be courteous, out of habit, for our own convenience, or because we like, enjoy, or endorse them. We also follow rules because breaking them can attract negative attention. **Social sanctions** are reactions by others aimed at promoting conformity. Sanctions can encourage conformity by rewarding it or discourage rule breaking by punishing it. Some sanctioning can be brutal and painful, involving physical or verbal attacks, public shaming, withdrawal of affection, shunning, or the loss of important life opportunities. Much sanctioning, though, is subtle: a raised eyebrow, a mocking or appreciative laugh, or a comment like "Are you sure you want to do that?" or "You look amazing in that!"

social sanctions
reactions by others aimed at promoting conformity

We all participate in promoting conformity, rewarding and punishing others depending on whether they follow the rules. We may gently sanction our friends and family, even if only to cue them in to the risk of being targeted by someone less benevolent than we are. Other times we may be tempted to be mean-spirited in our sanctioning, especially if we're invested in the rule. We may even feel a sense of injustice or unfairness if the rules being broken are ones we genuinely believe in.

We also anticipate receiving social sanctions and act accordingly. When we change our clothes after disliking what we see in the mirror or chastise ourselves for not studying hard enough, we are self-sanctioning. We can be both kind and cruel to ourselves, gently pushing ourselves to follow social rules or hating ourselves for being unable to.

Of course, no one follows the rules all the time. We break them accidentally and on purpose. We break them on principle and for laughs. We break them ironically and to prove a point. Breaking the rules is so commonplace that there's a set of rules to guide rule breaking. In other words, there are rules for breaking rules.

For most social rules—even mores, though rarely taboos—there's a simple way to fend off negative sanctions. It's called an **account**. This is an excuse that explains our rule breaking but also affirms that the rule is good and right.[11] An account consists of two parts: an acknowledgment that the rule is valid and an explanation for why we broke it that resonates with the observer. A good account suggests that we wouldn't break such rules under *other* circumstances, even as we get away with breaking them in *this* circumstance.

account
an excuse that explains our rule breaking but also affirms that the rule is good and right

It goes something like this: "I *wouldn't* have rolled through the stop sign, officer, but our daughter has just been admitted to the ER and we're in a hurry." "I *wouldn't* have gotten drunk last night, honey, but important clients insisted we stay out late." "I *wouldn't* have studied so little for that exam, professor, but I have to work to pay rent." In each of these examples, all the parts are in place: The rule is broken, but the "wouldn't have" affirms its rightness, and an

The fad of wearing ugly Christmas sweaters during the holidays is a built-in account. In fact, the uglier the sweater, the better. Onlookers will simply assume we're in on the joke.

excuse is made that makes sense to the listeners, reassuring them that the rule breaker shares a commitment to the rules.

Notice that offering an account is wholly different from saying nothing at all or rejecting the rule outright. "I know the rules, officer, but I didn't feel like stopping." Or, "What's wrong with getting drunk on a Wednesday night?" Or, "Give me a D if you want; I don't care about school." Each of these responses is entirely possible, but it would cause trouble, start a fight, or attract scorn. In contrast, offering an account usually fends off conflict.

We explicitly reject rules now and then, but it's a lot easier to break them if we affirm them at the same time. Most people let us get away with breaking lots of social rules if we can offer good excuses. In fact, a good account usually works just as well as following the rule in the first place. Still, breaking every social rule all the time would be impractical, impossible even. And people would become tired of our excuses and suspicious of our motivations if we offered hundreds of excuses every day. So, most of us follow most of the rules most of the time.

Of course, there is more than one set of social rules. Rules will vary according to the situation, our role in the social interaction, our identities, and more. A discussion of how we know which set of rules to follow is next.

SYMBOLIC INTERACTIONISM

Herbert Blumer was described by his contemporaries as "larger than life."[12] He was, they recalled, "a big, strong, hearty person." He was a farm boy who grew up in Missouri and dropped out of high school for a time to help his father's carpentry business. He worked odd jobs to get through college before catching the eye of recruiters for the American Professional Football Association (today known as the NFL). At six foot one and 200 pounds, he joined the Chicago (now Arizona) Cardinals in 1925. He played until 1930 and again in 1933.

American football players are known for being larger than life, but great athletes have great minds too. Football requires both physical skill and a clear-eyed understanding of the unfolding drama. Any given play is carefully orchestrated but ultimately unpredictable. Having a sharp and narrow focus on what other players are doing can deliver clues as to what might happen. Did they shift their gaze? Their weight? Noticing such things can make all the difference.

Blumer scored two touchdowns for the Cardinals in his first year on the team. That same year, he started graduate school. He brought to sociology the same keen attention to detail and healthy respect for unpredictability that helped him on the field. His "combination of strength and grace," his colleagues recalled, "set him apart." He was a large man interested in the tiniest details of the smallest interactions. He would name the influential theory he developed **symbolic interactionism**; fundamentally, this is the theory that social interaction depends on the social construction of reality.[13]

symbolic interactionism
the theory that social interaction depends on the social construction of reality

Symbolic interactionism involves three key ideas. First, we don't generally respond to reality itself but to the meaning we give it. Something like a hug, in other words, is never a hug. It's a hello or a goodbye. It's congratulations, comfort, or seduction. It's an effort to avoid a kiss at the end of an evening. Depending on the context, the hug—in all cases, a short embrace—can mean many different things. What it *will* mean depends on the huggers' shared understanding of what is going on.

Second, symbolic interactionism suggests that the meaning of reality doesn't exist prior to human understanding but is produced through social interaction. Only through interaction can shared interpretations emerge, spread from person to person, and evolve. A hug can only be used as a greeting or a form of congratulations, for example, because two people one day hugged for that reason. Then, many people did, and it became a patterned part of the culture.

Finally, symbolic interactionism posits that meaning is negotiated in interaction. When we interact, we're often actively creating or struggling over meaning. Given that the hug can mean so many things, a shared understanding that a hug is neither a greeting nor a congratulations, but seduction, requires action. Our flirtation will fail if the object of our attraction misunderstands the nature of the hug. So, we must do more than offer a hug. We must surround that hug with cues that will give it that particular meaning. To do so, we rely on other signifiers: strong eye contact, generous compliments, or a lingering hand on an elbow.

Symbolic interaction depends on the setting too. If we're in a room with festive decorations, snack foods, cocktails, and clusters of people laughing and

Do you see pain or pleasure? Would it help to know that she just won the lottery? Social context is essential for evaluating even fundamental human experiences like emotion.

talking cheerfully, we can guess we're at a party. If we were to arrive expecting a party, only to see a parent helping a child do their homework at the kitchen table, no amount of double checking the place and time on the party invitation will convince us that a party is going on. The party helps contextualize the hug too. Party hugs are easier to interpret as flirtatious than hospital hugs or graduation ceremony hugs, for instance.

Our behavior is guided by all these signals. We only know how to act when we've read the signs and determined the situation. And others will only understand us if they share the same interpretation of what's going on. Ultimately, successful social interactions depend on everyone involved agreeing and cooperating. We count on others to participate in good faith and often react with confusion or even betrayal when they don't.

In a segment for his late-night talk show, for instance, Jimmy Kimmel exploited the rules of symbolic interaction as they apply to Christmas.[14] Kimmel asked parents to submit videos of their children receiving a "bad gift," so the parents wrapped up and presented their children with items like hammers, batteries, and bananas. Upon opening their presents, the children's faces went from elated to distraught. Some tried to be gracious, but few could hide their disappointment. "I don't like this!" exclaimed a two-year-old, his voice breaking as he examined a mostly empty juice bottle. "Take it back!" yelled a seven-year-old boy who'd received a sweater made for girls (a gift that violated the social rules for doing gender). "She don't want a onion!" explained a three-year-old to her parents when her sister burst into tears.

It might be tempting to describe these kids as ungrateful, but they were responding to more than disappointment at not getting the toy they wanted.

Instead, they were responding to a rip in the fabric of reality. Christmas is a situation: a gift-giving holiday focused on children. Like hugs, gifts are symbols. If it's a good gift, it symbolizes the love between parent and child; if it's a bad gift, it calls that love into question. So, when children received the wrong kind of present, the parents were literally doing Christmas wrong. "We thought really hard about what to get you," said one mom, keeping up the ruse. To which her son replied, "Well, you didn't do a very good job!"

The kids were right about Christmas. They *were* supposed to get something special. When they didn't, they were understandably disoriented. Being given a potato was confusing, even potentially hurtful. Was it punishment? Had they not been good? When others don't cooperate in producing our reality, it feels unfair.

The parents enjoyed the prank more than their children but (usually) gave up the stunt before the threatened meltdowns arrived. How? By stitching reality back together again. They offered their children an account: "I *wouldn't have* given you a bad gift, but I thought it would be fun to tease you a bit." This confirmed the perception of reality that had been disrupted. The kids' anxiety was soothed. They *were* going to get toys. They *were* good. They *did* understand Christmas. And everything that seemed wrong with the world was righted again.

The fragility of social interaction

Appreciating the complexity of basic social interactions suggests, too, that they're delicate. Any given interaction is dependent on everyone acknowledging the situation, recognizing the symbols, playing their roles, and breaking rules only with culturally resonant accounts. It's quite easy, actually, to fail to do any one of these things and dramatically change what's happening.

As an example, consider this true story.[15] A man named Michael, his wife, his daughter, and five friends were sitting around a dinner table in his backyard. They were absorbing the summer evening, talking intimately, and enjoying one another's company. The performance was complete: friends and family, wine and cheese, warm conversation, twinkling lights. It was a dinner party.

Then, the setting was shattered. An unexpected object appeared, and new roles sprung to life. A stranger emerged from the darkness, raised a gun to the head of Michael's wife, and said, "Give me your money or I'm going to start shooting." The dinner party turned into a robbery; the friends and family were no longer guests, they were victims. The situation had changed.

One of the women at the table, however, decided to resist the new setting, and her new role too. She said to the robber: "Why don't you have a glass of wine?" "It was like a switch," Michael recalled. "All of a sudden, the look on the man's face changed." He'd been offered the opportunity to play a different role.

The stranger put the gun in his pocket. He had some wine. And some cheese. Situation restored. After a little while, he said, "I think I've come to the wrong place." The party guests said, "Hey, we understand." They sat together in silence for a few seconds. The stranger asked Michael's wife for a hug (perhaps seeking comfort?) and left with his glass of wine, which he finished and then placed carefully on the sidewalk in front of the house.

As the sudden shift in the scene in Michael's backyard reveals, our social interactions are quite fragile. They rely on nearly 100 percent cooperation. Everyone has to participate competently and consistently and help others if they get off track, or the situation changes. An interaction can go from a party to a robbery in a heartbeat and, in some remarkable cases, back again.

That's how delicate social interactions really are. We're dependent on one another to produce a coherent reality and have the power, if we so choose, to disrupt it. Without collaboration, interaction breaks down. Confusion emerges. Or fear. Or anger. So, when we're with other people, we generally affirm the situation and play our role. We follow the rules that apply. When we break them, we offer good accounts. We push others to do the same. And we do this, another scholar would argue, not only to smooth interactions but to control what others think of us.

DRAMATURGY

The sociologist Erving Goffman was born in Canada in 1922 to a family of Russian immigrants.[16] His family was anxious about their place in their new country and fretted over their reputation in their community. They demanded that Goffman and his siblings keep up appearances: act respectable, be proper, follow etiquette. They thought a lot about themselves, in other words, and about how other people thought of them.

Growing up in such a family, the Goffman children were sensitized from an early age to the fact that people often aim to influence how others see them. One of Goffman's sisters, Francis Bay, grew up to specialize in exactly this. She became an actor, a job in which people work to convince others that they're someone they're not. She played the grandmother in the movie *Happy Gilmore*, among dozens of other roles. Rumor has it that Erving himself was less talented at playing roles. He loved gambling but had a notoriously bad poker face. Poorly suited to pursue a career as a professional gambler, he became a sociologist who studied role play instead. In 1956 he published a book called *The Presentation of Self in Everyday Life*.[17]

Goffman called his approach to understanding social interaction **dramaturgy**, the practice of looking at social life as a series of performances in which we are all actors on metaphorical stages. To perform, we use the roles, scripts, costumes, props, and sets available to us. Consistent with symbolic interactionism, the set is the situation. The roles are the relative positions in a social interaction. The props are symbols. We behave according to the constraints of the situation and role we are expected to play. Others in the scene help us, and we help them in return.

Goffman's work was so influential that some of his ideas are now part of everyday English. He introduced, for example, the idea of **impression management**,

dramaturgy
the practice of looking at social life as a series of performances in which we're actors on metaphorical stages

impression management
efforts to control how we're perceived by others

or efforts to control how we're perceived by others. We don't merely interact "correctly"; we personalize our roles. We make careful choices about *how* to play them: how to appear, what to say, and what to do. We do this with the aim of sending messages about ourselves. Other people are doing the same with us. "We are all just actors," Goffman asserted, "trying to control and manage our public image."[18]

Impression management involves choosing a **face**, a version of ourselves that we want to project in a specific setting, and doing *face-work*, the effort required to establish and maintain our face.[19] Neither the setting nor the role automatically dictates our face. That's up to us. In an office setting, for example, we may want to come across as either a Go Getter or a Team Player. That's our face. And the face-work might involve asking the boss for choice assignments (in the first case) or staying late to help a coworker (in the second).

We're sometimes acutely aware of our performances, but other times we act so convincingly that even we are taken in. A man at a job interview may carefully manage impressions, intending to communicate that he is "hardworking and responsible." But he may be so practiced at doing gender that he doesn't notice that he's also performing "man" (wearing a suit, sitting in a manly way, and speaking with authority). Some of our acts are so habitual that they've come to feel natural.

We're at our most performative when we're **front stage**, a public space in which we are aware of having an audience. Other times we're **back stage**, in private or semiprivate spaces in which we can relax or rehearse. In an office

All of these students are performing "graduate," but each are putting their own spin on the costume. This allows them to manage others' impressions, indicating not only "I am a graduate" but what *kind* of graduate they are.

setting, our interactions with our clients occur on the front stage. Interactions with our coworkers might feel like the back stage (where we might complain about our clients, for example). And being at home with a roommate may feel even more back stage (where we might complain not only about our clients but also about our coworkers).

The children in Kimmel's Christmas prank had a face they intended to project: "good child." And they were prepared to do the face-work necessary: patiently waiting for their gift to be delivered to their laps, "oohs" and "aahs" when the gift was revealed, and gracious "thank yous" and "I love its." Ideally, if the children had gotten a proper gift, their parents would have served as looking glasses, reflecting "good child" back to them.

When the children lost their composure, they couldn't do the face-work and things went awry. They were what Goffman described as *out of face,* acting contradictory to one's desired face or otherwise exposed as in violation of it. When someone *loses face,* they must do extra face-work to *save face,* or recover a face that's been lost. Because losing face is embarrassing and distressing, and emotions are contagious (we often feel upset that others are upset), we sometimes help others save face. In the Christmas prank case, the admission that the gift was bad saved the children's faces because it voided the idea that they were ungrateful.

The tween girls on Facebook were also engaged in impression management. They carefully chose which images of themselves to post, while working hard to make it look as if they put no thought into it whatsoever. They were pretending, in other words, to reveal the back stage when, in fact, they were keenly aware that they were front stage.

To this end, the girls avoided pictures that looked overly posed. They didn't want to look like they were trying too hard. Their chosen face was effortless self-assurance. So, they primarily posted silly pictures, ones in which they adopted goofy poses with friends. They made physical attractiveness look accidental. They'd make a funny face, for example, but take the picture from an angle that flattered their body. Or, they'd post a series of pictures with a friend in which they'd take turns adding the silly. This gave each girl an opportunity to look beautiful, but only because she appeared to forget to consistently pose ridiculously throughout.

Both these examples also offer hints as to the importance of our social identities in shaping social interaction. Age is relevant in the Christmas example, as the holiday is widely understood to be for children. Gender is relevant in the Facebook example, as the impressions these girls wanted to make were gendered. This is a reminder that social identities are social constructs, themselves part of the symbolic structure. Some of the symbols central to social interaction, in other words, are *us.* Our identities shape who can pull off "ordinary," in which situations we seem to fit, what roles others imagine us playing, and how and whether others cooperate with us and help us stay in face. Our discussion of identities in interaction begins by asking who gets to be inside and outside of the norm.

SOCIAL IDENTITIES AND SOCIAL INTERACTIONS

Consider for a moment the ubiquitous symbol that we see on "walk/don't walk" signs. That figure—a stick figure with a round head—is replicated across all kinds of signs: caution, work-in-progress, exit signs, and lots more. Tellingly, it's also the sign used to indicate a men's restroom. That is, the figure on the walk/don't walk sign is also a symbol that means "man." Depending on the situation (that is, looking for a restroom or crossing the street), we read the sign to mean either "man" or "person."

The same can't be said of the symbol for "woman," the stick figure in a skirt. She is rarely seen anywhere other than on a bathroom door. Accordingly, we're not in the habit of reading her as either meaning woman or person. She is always a she. Isn't that curious? Symbols that indicate man can also be used to mean "person," but symbols that indicate woman almost never are.

The sociological way of talking about this is to refer to marked and unmarked identities. Man is (usually but not always) an *unmarked identity*. In the symbolic structure, men are people. They can carry their gender lightly. So lightly that it's sometimes invisible. They're unmarked much of the time, like the stick figure on the walk/don't walk sign.

In contrast, woman is (usually but not always) a *marked identity*. Women are women. They're rarely just people. They're a special kind of people, the female kind. Their gender is usually an important fact about them. So important that it's difficult or impossible for women to carry their identity lightly. It's almost always visible.

Men are unmarked, and women are marked. We can use the word *lion*, for example, to mean all members of the species, but when we use the word *lioness*, we mean only the female members. Similarly, the word *actor* can mean both actors and actresses, but the word *actress* refers only to females in the profession. The same goes for waiters and waitresses. Consider that we have an NBA and a WNBA, but no MNBA. The NBA is just basketball. The WNBA is *women's* basketball. Because men are unmarked, we often address a mixed-gender group as "you guys" but never "you girls." "Guys" means people. "Girls" never does. So, just as with stick figures, "you guys" can mean "hey everybody," but "you girls" can't.

Generally, status-advantaged identities (like "men") remain unmarked, while identities that differ from those (like "women" and "trans men") are marked. In the United States, for instance, we refer to Native Americans, Asian Americans, African Americans, and Hispanic or Latino Americans, but we rarely refer to White Americans or European Americans. White people are just "Americans." Everyone else gets an adjective. We also talk about "marriage" and "*gay* marriage." And "people" and "*disabled* people." To carry a marked identity, then, is to be routinely perceived as a representative of one's group. Judgments about us will be filtered through that identity.

Situations matter, of course. What identities are marked or unmarked will depend on the context. A person with a disability is carrying a marked identity much of the time, but at a retreat specifically dedicated to people with disabilities, it's the able-bodied person who might stand out. In places where men aren't expected, like a gender studies class filled mostly with women, it may be men who are marked, not women. In the Chinatowns of America's largest cities, an Asian person's race isn't notable, but a White person's race may be.

Whether we fit in or stand out in a setting will depend on the intersection of our identities with the situation itself. That said, some of us will have the experience of being marked more often and suffer greater consequences. If people with specific identities tend to dominate higher education, high-powered workplaces, and the halls of political power, for example, it can affect whether people with other identities seem to "belong."

Role play

Our social identities influence how well we fit in various situations. They also influence the roles we can convincingly play. Roles themselves are raced, gendered, and classed, or otherwise associated with certain religions, sexualities, immigration statuses, and other identities. Professional housekeepers who work in homes and businesses, for example, are usually women. But depending on where you live, they may be predominantly African American, Latina, or White. In those same places, most construction workers will likely be the same race as professional housekeepers but a different sex. When we join a new mosque, we'd do a double take if our imam was White, even in a majority-White country. And when we go to a rock show, we'd be surprised to discover that the opening band was a bunch of moms in their sixties.

We learn role-identity associations through socialization, and this has consequences. If you ask elementary-school children to draw a scientist, for example, almost three-quarters will draw a picture of a man, suggesting that men are more strongly associated with science than women.[20] When men are scientists, then, there's a *role-identity match*, a correspondence between the type of person in the role and the role itself, according to the symbolic structure. But when women are scientists, there's a *role-identity mismatch*, a potentially jarring lack of correspondence. This can make it hard for people to see women as scientists, especially non-White women. In one study of 557 female scientists, a quarter of Asian women, a third of White women, and almost half of Black and Latina women reported having been mistaken for an administrative assistant or a member of the custodial staff, sometimes routinely.[21]

interpersonal discrimination
prejudicial behavior displayed by individuals

This is what it's like to be on the receiving end of **interpersonal discrimination**, prejudicial behavior displayed by individuals. If prejudice is an attitude, implicit or explicit, then discrimination involves behaviors that reflect a prejudicial attitude, conscious or unconscious. Interpersonal discrimination ranges from the overt and unambiguous (like hate crimes) to the subtle and ambiguous (like rude treatment). It's also cumulative.[22] It doesn't have to happen to us often to add up. Even occasionally being the victim of discrimination, or being victimized by others at critical life moments, can produce observable and measurable negative consequences for our lives.

A rise in discrimination against Asian Americans during the Covid-19 pandemic is an example. Though the World Health Organization discourages naming novel diseases after a place or a people, then-President Donald Trump began referring to SARS-CoV-2 as the "China virus" in March 2020. That month, implicit association tests began registering a rise in the belief that Asians weren't "real" Americans.[23] As Covid-19 spread across the United States in March, April, and May, more than 2,000 incidents of discrimination against Asians were documented.[24] In 19 percent of cases, the assailants used the term "China virus." In one incident, a White woman rolled down her car window, yelled "Chinese virus," and threw an empty soda can at the victim. In another incident, an Asian woman on a subway platform was yelled at for "creating coronavirus"; the assailant then said that he wanted to "kill Chinese" and suggested he push her onto the tracks. In 32 percent of reports, Chinese people were blamed for Covid-19. Asians experienced this discrimination regardless of their background; only half of the 20 percent of people who were told to "go back to China," for instance, had Chinese ancestry.

Sometimes discrimination is obvious, but not always. Researchers can detect more subtle forms of discrimination with *field experiments*, a type of experiment that involves tests of hypotheses outside the laboratory (see "The Science of Sociology"). Common field experiments involve testing whether social identities like gender, race, or religion influence how likely a person is to land a job interview, get a loan from a bank, or be accepted as a tenant.

In 2020, Americans flooded the streets to protest the rise in hate crimes against Asians. Such discrimination skyrocketed during the Covid-19 pandemic, propelled by racist political rhetoric.

THE **SCIENCE** OF SOCIOLOGY

Field Experiments

The **field experiment** is a research method that involves a test of a hypothesis outside the laboratory. Field experiments occur in natural, real-world settings. They could be done in a classroom, for example, and test whether a new kind of teaching improves student learning. They could occur on the street, testing whether a new siren sound changes drivers' responses to an oncoming ambulance. Or they could occur at a church, testing what kind of message increases the level of donations on any given Sunday.

Like in laboratory experiments, researchers doing field experiments identify an independent variable and a dependent variable. The first is hypothesized to influence the second, or cause an effect. Researchers also identify and hold constant a set of control variables, or ones that might also influence the dependent variable. This way, they can trace any change in the dependent variable to the independent variable only.

Researchers assign research subjects to either the experimental or the control group. Members of the experimental group are exposed to the stimuli that researchers believe might influence the dependent variable. Members of the control group are not exposed. After the research is complete, the data collected from each group can be compared to see whether the independent variable influenced the dependent one.

Many field experiments, for example, test whether people with marked identities are discriminated against when looking for housing, applying for a job, or seeking a loan. Researchers might send out applications from fictional people with either marked or unmarked identities (this is the independent variable). Everything else about the applications will be the same (these are the control variables). Researchers will then measure whether all applicants are received equally favorably (this is the dependent variable).

Field experiments have the advantage of showing that the kinds of things we might document in the lab also happen outside of it. They are genuine real-world scientific experiments, ones from which causal conclusions can be drawn. That makes them powerful tools in the sociologist's methodological toolkit. ■

field experiment
a type of experiment that involves a test of a hypothesis outside the laboratory

In a field experiment about employment discrimination, for example, 6,106 fictional résumés and cover letters were sent to real employers across the United States.[25] This study tested whether an Asperger's diagnosis (a syndrome that can affect interpersonal interaction) or a spinal cord injury (a condition that often affects mobility) influenced employer interest in interviewing applicants for a job. The Asperger's diagnosis and the spinal cord injury were independent variables while employer interest was the dependent variable.

The employers who received the fictional résumés were looking to hire an accountant. A third of the résumés indicated that the job applicant had been diagnosed with Asperger's (this was one experimental group), a third indicated that the applicant lived with a spinal cord injury (this was a second experimental group), and a third did not mention either of these things (this was the control group). Neither Asperger's nor a spinal cord injury would affect a person's performance as an accountant and discrimination against both groups is prohibited under the Americans with Disabilities Act.

Did employers discriminate? Some did. Applicants reporting a spinal cord injury received 27 percent fewer inquiries than ones reporting no disability. And applicants reporting Asperger's received 25 percent fewer inquiries.

Field experiments can provide compelling evidence of real-life discrimination. And, in fact, scholars doing field experiments have documented widespread prejudicial behavior against people with disabilities as well as women, mothers, Muslims, women wearing headscarves, people from poor and working-class backgrounds, sexual minorities, and African, Asian, Hispanic, and Arab Americans. All things being equal, when members of these groups try to get a job, they'll be offered fewer opportunities and lower salaries than their counterparts. When they're looking for a place to live, they are more likely to be told there is no housing available, to be charged higher rents, and to be rejected as a roommate. When they need to get medical care, it will be lower quality. And if they apply for insurance or a loan, they'll be denied or given higher fees or interest rates.[26]

Social scientists also find that the specific intersection of identities we hold can compound or otherwise adjust discriminatory behavior aimed at us. In another field experiment, for example, the sociologist Grace Yukich sent out 1,000 fictional résumés to entry-level job openings in eight cities across the United States.[27] The résumés were identical, except for the applicants' identities, which varied by religion (Muslim, Christian, or no religion noted), gender (male or female), and ethnic background ("White-sounding" or Arabic names).

Yukich collected callbacks. She found that men with Arabic names experienced the most discrimination, especially if they identified as Muslim. These men received about a third as many callbacks as a control group of White, non-Muslim men. In comparison, Muslim-identified women with Arabic names received the same number of callbacks as the control group and were favored over both White Muslim women and non-Muslim women with Arabic names.

Yukich's findings reveal that men very likely bear the brunt of anti-Arab and anti-Muslim discrimination in the job market. Why? Probably because, as content analyses show, U.S. stereotypes about Muslims are gender specific.[28] Men tend to be portrayed as violent terrorists, whereas women tend to be portrayed as passive victims. In light of these stereotypes, employers may be particularly prejudiced against Muslim Arab men, while simultaneously eager to protect and support Muslim Arab women. The symbolic meaning of being female and Muslim Arab and of being male and Muslim Arab is different.

The sociologist David Pedulla has also found that people can react to intersecting marked identities in surprising ways. His research revealed that White employers discriminate against both Black men and gay men in the workplace, but they actually favor Black men who are gay.[29] Why? Possibly because the effeminate stereotype attached to being a gay man cancels out the hypermasculine stereotype attached to being a Black man. Gay Black men are seen as both sufficiently masculine (because they're Black), but not overly so (because they're gay), which means that respondents see them as more like heterosexual White men than either heterosexual Black men or gay White men.

Because we're all socialized into status beliefs, we're all at risk of discriminating, and some conditions make us more likely to do so. In the workplace, ambiguous job qualifications increase the likelihood that employers will rely on status beliefs instead of merit when making hiring decisions; in the absence of good information, we resort to stereotypes.[30] Employees whose workplaces rely on individual discretion rather than bureaucratic procedures also produce more discriminatory outcomes.[31] Clear standards for hiring, promotion, and pay help.

We're also more likely to discriminate when we're tired or busy. If we're overworked, exhausted, or thinking about something else, we have less mental energy to catch ourselves in the act of judging people by their social identities. Discriminatory behavior is also more likely when others around us tolerate or encourage it.[32]

Anyone can be the victim of interpersonal discrimination, but people with low-status identities are far more likely to be subjected to it. The amount and nature of discrimination we encounter depends greatly on how many low-status identities we carry, their intersections, whether our roles and identities match, and the situations in which we find ourselves. All things being equal, some of us will have to work harder than others to reach our full potential. Some of that work can be described as impression management.

Managing others' impressions of our social identities

If we're frequently the target of discriminatory behavior, or if cultural expectations make us seem like a bad fit for a role, we have to do extra work to ensure that we're acknowledged and rewarded. This involves using whatever signifiers are available to balance negative impressions of our identities.[33] In the scientific setting, for example, that may mean that women need to put extra effort into looking like a scientist. They may choose to regularly wear a lab coat, wear glasses instead of contact lenses, introduce themselves with the title of "doctor," and avoid overly casual speech and conversation.

The personal consequences suffered by people who must overperform a role to counter mismatch can range from irritating to life threatening. In the United States, for example, Black men are stereotyped as dangerous, even criminal. That wasn't always the case. Prior to the mid-1800s, it was useful for advocates of slavery to stereotype Black men as childlike and in need of supervision. The idea that they were incapable of running their own households justified enslavement. The idea that Black men were violent and unlawful emerged only after they won their freedom in 1863.

Why? Because the Emancipation Proclamation, which made enslavement unconstitutional, had a loophole. Slavery was illegal *unless* someone was serving a prison sentence for a crime. Eager to continue to exploit Black people's labor, wealthy White Southerners engaged in a systematic effort to convict Black people of crimes.[34] To justify this, they spread the stereotype of Black criminality. Meanwhile, the widespread criminal conviction of Black people that they engineered validated the stereotype further.

Both Black men and women are subject to this stereotype, but it is especially harmful to Black men. This is because they're Black *men*. Contrasted with women, men are also stereotyped as aggressive, violent, and likely to commit crime. For Black men, then, race intersects with gender to supercharge the stereotype.

In the aftermath of the Emancipation Proclamation, this new stereotype had an immediate and devastating effect. In addition to leading to the mass criminalization, imprisonment, and re-enslavement of Black men, it validated *lynching*, or the murder of (mostly) Black men by White mobs, especially by hanging. Lynching was often justified by false accusations that Black men raped White women, a story that drew on the stereotype that Black men were sex criminals. In reality, lynchings were "violent and public acts of terror" intended to traumatize Black people into submission and uphold White supremacy.[35]

Lynching was *not* a response to Black people's criminal activity but a tool of White domination. This was first demonstrated by the sociological theorist Ida B. Wells-Barnett (1862–1931).[36] Born into slavery in Mississippi just months before emancipation, she spent her life working diligently on behalf of Black people's right to be fully free. In her book *Southern Horrors*, for example, she carefully documented how criminal accusations against Black men murdered by lynching were false; instead, lynching was a response by White people to Black people's social and economic uplift. Organized White violence, in other words, was a way to remind Black people that to exercise their rights was to risk death. Her work was awarded a posthumous Pulitzer Prize in 2020.

Sadly, the legacy of this history lives on in the policing of Black men, and Black women too. Some police officers are explicitly anti-Black, but implicit

Ida B. Wells-Barnett was awarded a posthumous Pulitzer Prize in 2020 for bravely investigating and documenting White violence against Black people.

association tests show that *most* police officers—just like the rest of us—have internalized the idea that Black people are violent.[37] This contributes to why young Black men are 2.5 times more likely to die at the hands of police than their White counterparts, even though they're less likely to be engaged in criminal activity when approached.[38] In fact, Black people who die in encounters with police are far more likely than White people who die this way to have been unarmed and nonviolent (see Figure 4.1). In many cases, the *only* thing threatening about a Black man is the combination of his race and gender.

This is part of why the murder of George Floyd sparked nationwide protests in the summer of 2020. Floyd was a Black man who'd been reported to the police for attempting to use a counterfeit $20 bill. In the altercation that followed, a police officer kneeled on Floyd's neck while he begged for his life. He died at the scene. The uprising reflected Black peoples' anguish at the fact that White people are still killing Black people with impunity.

If Black men find themselves in a situation defined as criminal, observers may be quick to slot them into the role of offender. Or, simply bringing a Black male body into a space may be enough to redefine the situation; as we've learned, situations are fragile and symbols are powerful. During the pandemic, we rediscovered that objects can carry different meanings when they adorn a Black body. In our prejudicial symbolic structure, "Black criminal" is a

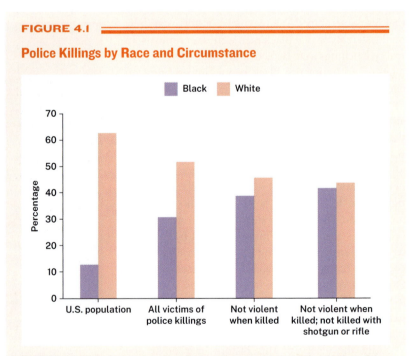

FIGURE 4.1

Police Killings by Race and Circumstance

SOURCE: U.S. Department of Justice, Federal Bureau of Investigation, Uniform Crime Reporting Program Data: Supplementary Homicide Reports, 2012.

role-identity match. So, at a time when public health and city and state ordinances required people to wear face coverings in public, Black men were *still* sometimes viewed suspiciously for wearing one.[39]

Faced with these realities, Black men often learn how to use social constructs to counter others' impressions as a matter of survival. In a revealing essay, the African American journalist Brent Staples described how he lives with the fact that people routinely perceive him as dangerous. "I only needed to turn a corner into a dicey situation, or crowd some frightened, armed person in a foyer somewhere, or make an errant move after being pulled over by a policeman. . . . There is always the possibility of death."[40]

This was not merely hypothetical. Staples once entered a magazine headquarters to deliver a story he'd written as a freelancer, only to have the office manager assume he was a burglar and call security. One time he entered a jewelry store only to have the proprietor immediately excuse herself and return with a growling dog. And when he crossed the street in front of a waiting car at a traffic light, *thunk* went the locks. A Black man had arrived.

Eventually, Staples learned to suppress the anger and frustration this caused. To do otherwise, he said, would have "led to madness." Instead, he changed his own behavior, exploiting the symbolic structure to send messages that countered the ones broadcast by his body. He dressed more professionally more often, even in nonprofessional settings; khakis seemed to ease nerves. And he began whistling classical music when he walked on dark streets late at night. "Virtually everybody seems to sense that a mugger wouldn't be warbling bright, sunny selections from Vivaldi's *Four Seasons*. It is my equivalent of the cowbell that hikers wear . . . in bear country."[41]

Black men face especially perilous consequences for the meanings others attribute to their bodies. Muslim men, poor or working-class White men, and other men of color sometimes face similar consequences. Whomever we are, if we carry a disadvantaged identity, we have to contend with and manage others' impressions. We have to fight being slotted into roles we don't want and fight to be slotted into the ones we do.

When navigating interactions, then, we all must be attentive to the situation we're in and the roles we're expected to play, but we also must consider how our social identities interact with these things and what symbols we have for managing impressions in our favor. There's a lot going on, it turns out, in the most ordinary of interactions. But there's more. Building on the ideas of dramaturgy and symbolic interactionism, another sociologist revealed that the requirements for producing a coherent reality go even deeper.

THE RULES BENEATH THE RULES

When Americans want to suggest that there's more to something than meets the eye, they often turn to the iceberg as a metaphor. Ninety percent of the mass of these giant hunks of ice is hidden beneath the water. So they're much bigger than they appear to be from the surface.

The universe of social rules is bigger than it looks too. Some social rules are "above the waterline," easy for anyone to see, like *don't eat with your mouth open*. Others are hidden well beneath the surface, only visible when we look closely, like *eat at the table, not under it*. For the rules under the waterline, we may have to dive deep, or think hard, but they're there.

There are other rules, though, ones so taken for granted that they largely evade human consciousness. They're beyond and outside of what we normally think of as folkways, mores, policies, and laws, but they're foundational to social interaction nevertheless. They are neither the ice above nor below the waterline. They are, instead, the ocean that floats the iceberg. These are the rules that the sociologist Harold Garfinkel was exploring in the 1960s.

One tool he used to discover these rules was tic-tac-toe.[42] Using the game, he ran an experiment between two students. One was an *accomplice*, a secret partner with Garfinkel. The accomplice would invite the other student to make the first move. After the student penciled an X or O into one of the board's nine boxes, the accomplice would erase it, rewrite it in a different square on the board, make their own move, and then sit back and watch the other student's response.

Two hundred and fifty subjects experienced this violation of the rules of tic-tac-toe. A handful played along, smirking in recognition of the mischievousness. But most subjects—more than three-quarters—reacted strongly and negatively, refusing to play or demanding an explanation. These results, Garfinkel argued, revealed an implicit rule supporting all the other rules of tic-tac-toe, one that most students clung to quite seriously. That rule wasn't *take turns* or *put your X or O in the box*. It was a rule that made all those other rules meaningful. It was *obey the rules*.

When playing a game like tic-tac-toe, we all know that we're supposed to take turns. That's the rule. But turn taking only matters to us if we've *also* accepted that we're supposed to obey the rules. It was exactly this kind of background assumption that Garfinkel found intriguing. He called these assumptions *ethnomethods* and the study of such things **ethnomethodology**, research aimed at revealing the underlying shared logic that is the foundation of social interactions.[43] Ethnomethods, then, are a set of culturally specific background assumptions that we use to make sense of everyday life. They're the water that our iceberg of social rules floats in.

Ethnomethods go far beyond silly games, often applying widely across social life. We are expected, for example, to *act in ways that affirm social identity categories*. That is, when there are social rules that apply specifically to people with our identities, we're held accountable to them. If it didn't matter whether we "do" gender or not, for example, then the rules would be mere curiosities. The ethnomethod is what gives identity-specific social rules their power. Likewise, another rule of tic-tac-toe—*play to win*—is behind a wide array of expectations, including the idea that we should try to get good grades in school, choose a high-paying occupation, and marry someone attractive. *Affirm social identity categories*, *obey the rules*, and *play to win* are part of the

ethnomethodology
research aimed at revealing the underlying shared logic that is the foundation of social interactions

ocean that floats the iceberg: They are the foundation for a whole slew of more specific social rules, thus shaping a wide spectrum of decision making.

In order to make these ethnomethods visible, Garfinkel exploited what he called **breaching**, purposefully breaking a social rule in order to test how others respond. Breaking the rules of tic-tac-toe is a breach. Standing around doing nothing is a breach. Giving a child a potato for Christmas is a breach. Uploading a picture of menstrual blood on social media is a breach.

Some of Garfinkel's most famous breaching experiments involved violating the rules of conversation. Some are simply grammatical, like the subject-verb-object rule. *Subject of the sentence put first we do*, says Yoda, breaking the rule. Lots of conversational rules, though, are not grammatical, like restrictions on allowable topics, turn taking, the amount of time we leave between one person's comment and another's, and how long we can talk without dominating the conversation. All these rules could be summed up with the ethnomethod *cooperate in conversation*. In the United States, this generally means balancing contributions, respecting other people's boundaries, and making other people feel heard.

In an impromptu breaching experiment, one of Garfinkel's students went home to her husband and purposefully thwarted the normal course of conversation by failing to cooperate. "I'm tired," her husband said to her late one night as they watched a movie on TV, an utterance which was almost certainly meant to say: "Let's go to bed soon." But his wife pretended not to understand. Instead of acknowledging the real meaning of the comment, she questioned it. "*How* are you tired? Physically, mentally, or just bored?" "I don't know," the husband responded. "I guess physically, mainly." She probed further: "You mean your muscles ache or your bones?" Her husband balked: "I guess so. Don't be so technical."

After watching the movie for a few more minutes, the husband remarked: "All these old movies have the same kind of old iron bedstead in them." His wife feigned ignorance: "What do you mean? Do you mean *all* old movies, or some of them, or just the ones you have seen?" Her husband became irritated: "What's the matter with you? You know what I mean." She said, "I wish you'd be more specific." The husband raised his voice and repeated himself: "You know what I mean!"[44]

Of course she knew. He meant "lots" of the old movies they'd watched had an old iron bedstead in them, not "all," as he had said. To cooperate in conversation means tolerating some ambiguity, filling in the blanks, and giving the speaker the benefit of the doubt. She was doing it wrong.

When the Georgia Southern University student came across the Introduction to Sociology class doing nothing outside the student union, for example, his question was a philosophical one: "What are these people doing?" He knew exactly what they were doing—they weren't doing anything—but that's not what he meant. He meant "What is going on?" or "What is the meaning of this?" or "What am I missing?" He didn't have any knowledge running in the background with which to make sense of what was(n't) happening. Hence, his confusion.

This shared background knowledge is essential, so we generally aim to develop and maintain the same ethnomethods as the people around us. We put our trust in other people to act on our shared knowledge. And when they don't—when they ask a simple question like "Do you mean *all* old movies?"— we feel not only confused but also betrayed. That's why the student's husband replied with irritation to such innocent-sounding questions. In fact, Garfinkel found that these outsized responses occurred quickly and with surprising frequency. Others count on us to cooperate, to help them communicate; when we don't, we're violating a sacred social pact.

Ethnomethodology, dramaturgy, and symbolic interactionism are all sociological theories of social interaction. In honor of our pro-football-player-turned-sociologist Herbert Blumer, the final section of this chapter applies these ideas to the world of sports.

PUTTING IT ALL TOGETHER: EXPLOITING THE RULES OF THE GAME

In 2010, the Driscoll Middle School football team in Corpus Christi, Texas, got sociological.[45] American football games alternate between time-outs and active play. During time-outs, there's a lot of waiting; during play, there's running, dodging, throwing, and tackling. The time-out is one situation or setting, active play another, and the scripts change. These are the rules.

Driscoll was on offense; they had the ball. To set up their unorthodox play, their coach called for a five-yard penalty and instructed his team to move forward. The center stood up and handed the ball over his shoulder. The quarterback calmly took the ball and walked normally through the defensive line. It appeared that he was just moving up another five yards.

Of course, coaches don't decide penalties, referees do. It made no sense that the coach called to move the ball; it wasn't his role. So the defense was confused. And maybe the play wouldn't have worked if the quarterback and the center hadn't also deviated from their script. Instead of glaring and initiating quick, furtive, and familiar movements—dramaturgical indications that football is being played—they acted nonchalantly, giving the impression that it was still a time-out.

Reading the symbolic messages, the other team interpreted the Driscoll players' behavior as an indication that play hadn't started, but it had. Driscoll had flipped the script, fragile as it was, but they did it as a ploy. As soon as the quarterback was out of reach, they flipped the script back: The quarterback began sprinting toward the end zone. The other team looked around bewildered. Out of face, they looked like chumps. Touchdown, Driscoll. Game tied.

Trick plays aren't against official policy. Moreover, there's nothing in the rulebook that says players have to convey the fact that they're playing with the familiar symbolic interactionist messaging. The center doesn't have to pass the ball quickly, the quarterback doesn't have to run, and no one is required to grimace threateningly at the opposing players. There's nothing in the official rules that says players have to *appear* as if they're playing at all, but it is an informal social rule, maybe even a tightly enforced norm. The quarterback isn't supposed to just get up and walk through the defensive line. When he did, the defense assumed that the coach had been right about the penalty, and it took the defense several seconds to figure out what to do.

The Driscoll team had broken a social rule. They did it brazenly, without offering an account. And they did something that embarrassed the other team— playing them for fools—but did nothing to help them save face. They chest bumped in the end zone instead and piled onto the quarterback in celebration.

Many reacted angrily. Celebrated sports commentator Frank Deford called it "child abuse."[46] "Sure it was legal," he wrote, "but it wasn't fair." It was "a nasty move," said another, and "straight up trickery," equivalent to hitting "below the belt" in boxing.[47] Elsewhere, others called it "poor sportsmanship," accused the team of cheating, and argued that the play disrespected the game.[48] Driscoll didn't violate a formal rule of football, but some observers accused them of violating an ethnomethod: *play fair*.

It's understandable why some people were so upset. What would happen to football, after all, if all the things that are not explicitly prohibited began happening on the field? Social interactions are too fragile to support that level of rule breaking. Without at least some predictability, the game would dissolve into chaos. That's why we're expected to cooperate, to follow most of the rules most of the time. And, we mostly do. ∎

COMING UP...

THIS CHAPTER introduced symbolic interactionism, dramaturgy, and ethnomethodology. These are all sociological theories that explain ordinary social interaction. It introduced you to the idea that social interaction is guided by social rules and enforced with social sanctions, creating patterns in how we interact.

This chapter also considered the role social identities play in shaping interaction. Some of the symbols that are central to social interaction are *us*. When our social identities are attributed meanings that disadvantage us, and others act upon those meanings, we're exposed to interpersonal discrimination. How much discrimination we suffer will depend on the specific intersection of the identities we carry, the settings we find ourselves in, and the roles we choose or are pushed into playing. Some of our impression management, then, is aimed specifically at mediating other people's prejudicial attitudes and discriminatory behavior.

This chapter offered theories that help explain how and why we conform to social rules. The next one does the same for the instances in which we break them. It involves discussions of two kinds of deviance studied by sociologists: *social deviance*, or the violation of norms, and *criminal deviance*, or the breaking of laws. Coming up: how our societies shape our rule breaking and how our rule breaking shapes societies.

5

DEVIANCE &
DEFIANCE

IN THIS **CHAPTER...**

THIS CHAPTER COVERS sociological thinking about *deviance*: behaviors and beliefs that violate social expectations and attract negative sanctions. Using a vivid real-life example, it explains how deviance is socially constructed. It also discusses social reasons for deviant behavior. These suggest that social environments, and not the people in them, are important sources of deviance.

In addition to exploring the causes of deviance, this chapter considers the consequences of deviance. It presents two perspectives on the role that deviance plays in societies:

- One perspective, *structural functionalism*, is traced back to Émile Durkheim, the same sociologist who coined the phrase "social facts." Structural functionalism is the theory that society is a system of necessary, synchronized parts that work together to create social stability.

- The other perspective, *conflict theory*, suggests that societies aren't characterized by shared interests but rather by competing ones. Notably, many of the early sociologists who used a conflict approach were excluded from academia by virtue of their race, gender, or politics.

This chapter also introduces you to two more sociological research methods:

- *Historical sociology* involves collecting and analyzing sources that reveal facts about the evolution of societies.

- *Surveys* involve inviting individuals to complete a questionnaire designed to collect analyzable data.

"The rules!" shouted Ralph. "You're breaking the rules!"

—FROM *LORD OF THE FLIES*, BY WILLIAM GOLDING

In 1940, twelve-year-old Howard Becker taught himself to play piano.[1] By fifteen, he had a regular gig playing in a Chicago strip club. What did musicians play in such a place? Jazz, of course. "My father had a fit," Becker recalled.[2]

At the time, jazz was breaking all the rules. Earlier music had its roots in the military, with perfectly timed beats meant to accompany a march. Jazz shifted the rhythm. It made the music "swing." Jazz broke down racial barriers too. The music was invented and most artfully performed by Black musicians, but it drew both Black and White fans. On stage, in the audience, and on the dance floor, jazz pressed forward the project of racial integration.

When Becker became a sociologist, his time behind the piano would prove intellectually useful. It left him with an insider's view on what sociologists call **deviance**: behaviors and beliefs that violate social expectations and attract negative sanctions. "Most 'deviance theory,'" Becker wrote, "took it for granted that if you did weird things you were a weird person."[3] He didn't think so, and he set out to prove it sociologically.

There was no need to search far and wide for an example. Becker took inspiration from his time playing jazz in strip clubs. Between sets, the musicians often enjoyed a little weed. Accordingly, Becker's first contribution to the sociology of deviance was an article titled "Becoming a Marihuana User."[4] The article, published in the *American Journal of Sociology* in 1953, was the first impartial scientific article about the plant.[5] It wasn't about "marijuana *abuse*," Becker explained, "but of marijuana *use*." His colleagues were as scandalized as his dear old dad.

In the article, he asked: How exactly does a person come to be a marijuana smoker? And he identified three steps. The first is socialization. Through observation and with the help of existing smokers, new smokers learn how to light the plant on fire, inhale, and hold one's breath to give their lungs time to ingest the smoke's chemicals. The second step is to learn to recognize

deviance
behaviors and beliefs that violate social expectations and attract negative sanctions

the drug's effects. People are taught to pinpoint physiological changes and identify them as signs of being high; to differentiate, for instance, between having "the munchies" and merely being hungry. Finally, new smokers have to learn to enjoy the experience. Marijuana use can cause dizziness and confusion. Fellow smokers help new smokers interpret these experiences as positive instead of negative.

Becker's article was revelatory. At the time, people seen as deviant were thought to be biologically sick, psychologically warped, or hopelessly immoral. "[W]hatever the crime may be," said one scholar in 1926, "it ordinarily arises from a deteriorated [human] organism."[6] The cause of crime was simple "biological inferiority." The Italian criminologist Cesare Lombroso, for example, believed that criminal tendencies were embodied, and that criminals could be identified by physical imperfections: large ears, long arms, crooked noses, and prominent cheekbones.[7] Believing that criminality was a human defect, many of these scientists concluded that reducing crime required putting people in prisons, placing them in mental institutions, or even removing parts of the brain.

Becker didn't portray marijuana smokers as sick or bad. Instead, he depicted them as rather normal, even nice. He showed how experienced smokers were often gentle with new ones. They welcomed, taught, and reassured them. This was in stark contrast to the general assumption that people who used marijuana were compulsive addicts who clung together out of desperation. Becker showed otherwise. "It wasn't nutty people who were suffering," he said. "They're having fun."

If the last chapter focused on how and why we obey rules, this one is about breaking them. It centers on two kinds of deviance. One is *social deviance*, or the violation of norms (including mores, folkways, and taboos). The other is *criminal deviance*, or crime, referring specifically to acts that break laws. Social and criminal deviance don't always overlap. Jaywalking is a crime, for example, but it's not considered deviant by most. Conversely, face tattoos might raise some eyebrows, but they aren't illegal. Even though they don't always overlap, social and criminal deviance have a lot in common.

This chapter is premised on the idea that we can't understand deviance by studying individuals alone. We also have to study the societies they live in. Societies, in other words, shape deviance. To that end, this chapter introduces a set of *social* explanations for deviant behavior. It also considers how deviance shapes societies. Collective responses to deviance can bond people together, rip them apart, or force change. Two important sociological perspectives—structural functionalism and conflict theory—will help us understand how.

This chapter begins by showing that deviance is a social construction, meaning that deviance shapes and is shaped by society. To introduce this idea, it draws lessons from one of the more gruesome examples of deviance in modern history. Buckle up, reader, because the plane is going down.

THE SOCIAL CONSTRUCTION OF DEVIANCE

High over the Andes Mountains, the pilots in charge of Uruguayan Air Force Flight 571 made a fatal mistake. They miscalculated their location and descended too soon through the clouds. The passengers joked about the turbulence.

Emergency maneuvers were initiated to avoid the mountain that suddenly loomed. Its black ridge approached, ragged and unyielding. At first impact, the plane clipped its tail cone. Then the right wing was sheared off with such force that it slammed into the back of the plane and ripped off its rear section. The last two rows of seats, and the people in them, gone. A few seconds later, the left wing hit an outcropping. As it severed from the plane, its propeller sliced into the main cabin. Miraculously, the remainder of the plane, now the shape of a bullet, set down on a snowy slope and slid to the bottom of a valley.

The survivors tended to the injured and waited until morning. At daybreak, a man named Nando Parrado stepped outside. Later, he recalled what it was like to reckon with their new reality. "Nothing in this place welcomed human life or even acknowledged its existence," he wrote:

> The cold tormented us. The thin air starved our lungs. The unfiltered sun blinded us and blistered our lips and skin. . . . There was nothing that any living creature could use as food—not a bird, not an insect, not a single blade of grass. A dread began to form in my mind, an unformed thought that I was not yet able to verbalize: *Life is an anomaly here.*[8]

Eight days later, Parrado contemplated his final food ration: a single chocolate-covered peanut. That day, he sucked off the chocolate and put the peanut into his pocket. The next day, he gently divided it, eating half. The third day, he finished the peanut. Over the airplane's still-working radio, the survivors heard that the authorities had called off the search.

Sixteen survivors would spend seventy-two days in that snowy valley. Eventually, Parrado and two others would make an extraordinary trek over the mountains to find rescue. In the meantime, however, they had to eat.

They made the decision delicately. Parrado first shared the idea with a friend. Together, they introduced it to the others. After careful negotiations, the group agreed. The shared nature of their decision didn't make the experience any less wrenching. "It was a horror," Parrado wrote.

To ease the psychic trauma, he drew on the small group's shared Catholicism. In the New Testament, Jesus refers to the bread and wine at the Last Supper table as "my body" and "my blood." Some Christians believe that to take communion is to eat the body of Christ metaphorically; others believe it's the literal consumption of Christ. "The bread is really the Body he gave, and the wine is really the Blood he shed," says Pope Francis, in this tradition.[9] For the survivors, linking cannibalism with communion recast the behavior

The survivors of Flight 571 were rescued after seventy-two days in the frozen Andes mountains. To stay alive, they developed new social rules, ones that made consuming human bodies not only acceptable but mundane.

as an act of faith. Thus, human bodies were moved from the category "not food" to the category "food." Consistent with the theory of symbolic interaction, their unusual situation prompted a shift in the shared meaning they gave to the corpses surrounding them.

In this new situation, and with these new meanings, fresh roles and routines emerged to guide them. The youngest survivors were made responsible for keeping the bodies covered in snow. The people with the strongest stomachs took on the unpleasant task of carving them into edible pieces. Those who planned to embark on a rescue expedition were allowed to eat more than others to grow their strength. The meat was rationed, but the fat, being less desirable, was not. Certain parts of the bodies were off-limits: the genitals, for example. They would eat only one person at a time. No one had to eat their own relatives.

What happened on the top of that mountain, in other words, wasn't a chaotic descent into lawlessness. Like Becker's marijuana smokers, the group built a subculture that was, in fact, quite civilized. It was an orderly renegotiation of a new set of social rules. Insofar as all the survivors cooperated to produce this fragile new reality, cannibalism was no longer taboo.

In fact, the most stunning part of the story of Flight 571 may be the degree to which cannibalism became *routine*. Before long, wrote Parrado, "most of us had grown numb to the horror." Body parts in the process of being consumed, once a hideous reminder of their impossible choice, were now kept at arm's reach for easy access. Discarded bones accumulated, no more remarked upon than piles of laundry. Like a glass of water on a nightstand, someone slept with a severed hand under his pillow in case he woke up hungry.

Revulsion waned, and boredom set in. The diet was bland. They began to seek out new flavors: liver, lungs, heart, brain. Bone marrow became a favorite. Blood clots were a treat for some. Some experimented with eating rotting meat. What had once been unthinkable had become mundane. Eating human bodies was no longer deviant. It was ordinary. *What was deviant had become the norm.*

While cannibalism may seem like a contender for a behavior that is universally condemned, it's not. Forms of the practice are and have been acceptable in some places, at some times, and for certain reasons.[10] Around the world, from New Zealand to Africa to the Americas, certain cannibalistic practices have been allowed. Whether cannibalism is considered deviant, then, will depend on the time, place, and situation.

This is true for deviance more generally. In order for acts, attitudes, or appearances to be considered deviant, they have to be collectively defined as such. This can occur through stigmatization, criminalization, or medicalization. *Stigmatization* is a process by which physical traits or social conditions become widely devalued. Chapter 3 introduced the fat body as an example of a stigmatized trait. *Criminalization* involves collectively defining a trait or condition as criminal. In the United States, for example, drinking alcohol was criminalized in 1920 (and decriminalized in 1933). *Medicalization* involves collectively defining physical traits or social conditions as an illness. Some have argued that the introduction of diagnoses like social anxiety disorder are an example of the medicalization of shyness.[11] In each case, something or someone is defined as deviant by virtue of being socially devalued, classified as criminal, or diagnosed as unhealthy or disordered.

Only one of these processes is necessary to socially construct something as deviant. Cannibalism, for instance, is not formally medicalized in the United States. It's not featured in the American Psychiatric Association's *Diagnostic and Statistical Manual of Mental Disorders*, which lists all professionally recognized mental disorders. Neither is it widely criminalized. In fact, there are no federal laws in the United States against cannibalism, and only one state has a law against it.[12] (What's the story, Idaho?)

It *is* stigmatized, however. Cannibals in pop culture are usually portrayed as vile individuals. In a season of the zombie apocalypse show *The Walking Dead* (2010–), for example, the protagonists battle an enemy group that has taken to slaughtering their fellow survivors. *The Hills Have Eyes* (2006) features a sadistic family of cannibals who torture as well as consume their human prey.

The only horror film to ever win an Oscar for Best Picture, *The Silence of the Lambs* (1991), features a psychologically depraved and manipulative serial killer who eats his victims.

Reflecting this stigma, the survivors of Flight 571 made headlines worldwide after their rescue. The mass media was poised to pounce. A photograph of a half-eaten human leg was printed on the front page of at least two newspapers. Rumors circulated of murder. A furor began to build. The survivors countered with the analogy to communion. Powerfully, the Catholic Church itself made a public statement endorsing the survivors and their decision. As a result, media accounts changed course. They were lucky; their recasting of cannibalism as an act of faith saved them from a lifetime of stigmatization.

Flight 571 is a case study in the social construction of deviance. Its lessons show that (1) deviance is defined through interaction and that such definitions vary across cultures and throughout history. This is because (2) acts, attitudes, or appearances become deviant only through social processes like stigmatization, criminalization, and medicalization. The story of Flight 571 also shows that (3) deviance is subject to the principles of symbolic interaction, which means that symbolic meanings and social rules and roles will change along with the circumstances. And, finally, it illustrates that (4) even especially deviant behavior can come to seem ordinary (and vice versa).

When sociology was new, all these observations about the nature of deviance were quite novel. Up until that time, discussions of deviance focused on the individual: biological explanations maintained that deviance was rooted in the body, while psychological explanations blamed deviance on a troubled mind. Sociologists, in contrast, turned outward, from the individual to society itself, to help explain why people engage in behaviors defined as deviant. We explore five of these theories of deviance in the next section.

HOW SOCIETIES SHAPE DEVIANCE

Had their plane not crashed into the Andes, the survivors of Flight 571 would almost certainly have gone a lifetime without eating human flesh. And it's almost certain that none of them ever ate another human being again. What drove them to cannibalism, in other words, did not come from within. It came from without. It was a matter of circumstance.

Sociological research on deviance considers the "outside" factors that might produce deviance. Several theorists laid the groundwork for studying the contexts and conditions that produce deviant behavior. They focused on blocked opportunities, social networks, the nature of our neighborhoods, the availability of cultural rationales, and the power of language.

Strain Theory: The problem of blocked opportunity

Meyer Schkolnick was a sociologist and an early challenger of the biological model of deviance. In the 1930s, he hypothesized that deviance was not caused by personal inferiority but by something he called "strain": the desire to achieve socially desirable goals alongside an inability to achieve them in traditional ways. As a teenager, he had experienced his own version of strain. He was committed to becoming a magician, to amazing fans with his sleight of hand and showmanship. But he was a Jewish boy growing up in an anti-Semitic society. So he got creative. He changed his name from Meyer Schkolnick to Robert Merton.

strain theory
the idea that deviance is caused by a tension between widely valued goals and people's ability to attain them

This is the origin of **strain theory**, the idea that deviance is caused by a tension between widely valued goals and people's ability to attain them.[13] If people are situated such that they can't live up to social expectations, Merton argued, they may try to achieve them through deviant means. When they do so, they become deviants. Merton's goal was to become an entertainer, but anti-Semitism made it impossible to achieve his goals in a conventional way. So he pretended to be someone else.

Merton thought that people faced with strain would respond in one of five ways (see Figure 5.1). Two types of responses involved obeying the social rules: "conformity" and "ritualism." In both cases, the widely valued goals are pursued in socially sanctioned ways, even though there's little hope of achieving them. Conformists do this earnestly and ritualists do it cynically.

Imagine, for example, you're an eighteen-year-old who wants to afford your own apartment. Living independently is a widely valued goal. As a high school graduate, however, the jobs available to you are mostly in the service industry, none of which pays enough for you to afford a place of your own. So you experience strain: a disconnect between your desire for a widely valued goal and your ability to achieve it.

If you are a ritualist, you'll take a retail job and work it without any hope that it will ever pay enough to get you into an apartment. You'll show up, do your job, and go home to your childhood bedroom. And you'll simply accept the failure to achieve your goal.

If you're a conformist, you'll take the retail job, but you'll do so with hope. You'll show up, do your job, and go home to your childhood bedroom. But unlike the ritualist, you'll do all this believing that hard work will eventually bring you a promotion to assistant manager, then manager, and someday a salary sufficient to pay for that apartment.

FIGURE 5.1

Merton's Deviance Typology

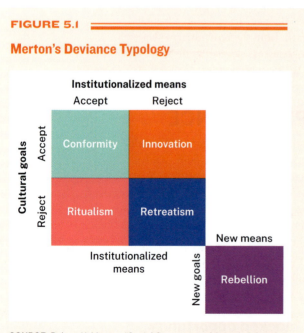

SOURCE: Robert K. Merton, "Social Structure and Anomie," *American Sociological Review* 3, no. 5 (Oct. 1938): 672–682.

Both ritualism and conformity are nondeviant ways of dealing with strain. Merton's other three types of responses, however, include deviance. "Innovation" involves accepting the valued goals but doing something deviant to attain them. If you take the retail job but steal items on the side and sell them to earn extra money, you're an innovator. You're also an innovator if you take the retail job but moonlight as an exotic dancer in the evenings. Absent the ability to earn enough money in a conformist way, you found a deviant way to do it. Some innovative tactics may be criminally deviant (like stealing) and others may be socially deviant (like exotic dancing). (In changing his name, Merton was an innovator too.)

An alternative to innovation is to reject the goals altogether. This is what Merton called "retreatism" and "rebellion." Retreatism is the rejection of valued goals and a decision to opt out of trying to attain them. Rebels also reject valued goals, but instead of simply opting out of society altogether, rebellion involves working to change societies by replacing the existing social goals with different ones.

If your response to being unable to afford your own apartment is to reject it as a valuable goal and join a commune that embraces collective living, you're a retreatist. You've embraced an alternative lifestyle, joining a group of deviants. If your response is to reject the goal, then work to convince everyone *else* that it's not valuable after all, you're a rebel. You're not just opting out of social norms; you're aiming to change them.

Rebellion, retreatism, and innovation are all forms of deviance caused by strain, an inability to achieve socially desirable goals in conformist ways. Identifying this range of possible reactions, Merton located the cause of deviance in the relationship between individuals and society, not within individuals themselves. Hence, strain theory became one of the early sociological contributions to the understanding of crime and deviance. It wouldn't be the last.

Differential Association Theory: The people we know

Also writing in the 1930s, the sociologist Edwin Sutherland explored another social source of deviance: social networks.[14] Using the word *association*, he observed that we all associate with a unique group of people. And using the word *differential*, he noted that these groups differ in terms of how many and what sorts of people they include. Our networks determine what kind of social influence we're under. Hence, Sutherland surmised, our differential associations help predict whether we'll engage in deviance. He called it **differential association theory**. This is the idea that we need to be recruited into and taught criminal behavior by people in our social networks.[15]

According to Sutherland's theory, people are more likely to engage in deviance if they're recruited into a deviant act by someone in their social network. The more people we know, the more likely we are to know people who engage in deviance and the more likely we are to be recruited. If someone has fewer friends, for example, they are more likely to respond to strain

differential association theory
the idea that we need to be recruited into and taught criminal behavior by people in our social networks

by giving up on their goals (or retreating) because no one suggests to them that they could do otherwise. Someone who's friendly with lots of people, however, might know someone who can suggest an alternative way to attain those goals (by innovating).

Once recruited, Sutherland theorized that we need to be taught *how* to engage in deviance. We learn how to break the rules, in other words, the same way we learn how to follow the rules: socialization. We aren't born deviants; we need to be taught. Stealing and selling retail items, for example, is a skill. It helps to know someone who can teach you how to steal without getting caught, how to advertise the goods without attracting police attention, and at what prices items are likely to sell. Exotic dancing is a skill too. It helps to have someone who can teach us how to do deviant things.

Sutherland's research on the role of social networks complemented Merton's strain theory nicely. It offers hypotheses for why only some people who suffer strain end up engaging in deviant behavior. Even if it's logical to engage in deviance, being unsure of how to do it may be a substantial stumbling block. Social networks also help explain why people who *aren't* experiencing strain engage in deviance. Strain can't explain, for instance, why an already-rich person would bother to embezzle money, but networks can.

Sutherland, in fact, was the first person to study the crimes of rich people. He coined the term *white-collar crime* in a book of the same name, published in 1949. This, he wrote, was "crime committed by a person of respectability and high social status in the course of their occupation." These include crimes like

According to differential association theory, we learn how to be deviant from people in our social networks. In the first season of *Breaking Bad*, for example, high school chemistry teacher Walter White knows how to cook meth, but he isn't sure how to sell it. So he asks a former student to teach him.

fraud, bribery, insider trading, embezzlement, and money laundering. Prior to Sutherland, the crimes of rich people received little attention compared with those of the poor and otherwise disadvantaged. This continues to be the case, even though white-collar crime is twice as costly to the American people as street crime.[16]

Merton's strain theory and Sutherland's differential association theory were two of the early contributions to sociological understandings of the cause of deviance. Strain theory points to a gap between the desire to attain a valued goal and the ability to attain it. Differential association theory emphasizes the presence of others who might serve as role models for deviance. A third sociologist turned his attention to the importance of place.

Social Disorganization Theory: The nature of our neighborhoods

The sociologist William Julius Wilson was born in Pennsylvania in 1935.[17] His father was a coal miner who died when Wilson was just twelve years old. His mother, a housekeeper, struggled to support him and his five siblings in a two-room apartment. They avoided going hungry thanks to public assistance and a vegetable garden in the backyard.

Black children who grew up poor in the United States before the Civil Rights Act were unlikely to become Harvard professors. They were even less likely to become president of the American Sociological Association, a member of the National Academy of Sciences, a National Medal of Science winner, and the recipient of forty-five honorary degrees. Wilson is all these things.

Looking back at his life, Wilson credits his admission to college to a church scholarship, the support of an aunt, and the encouragement of teachers at racially diverse, well-performing schools. These modest advantages, he argues, made his success possible.[18] Wilson had to be especially bright and hardworking, but his neighborhood also had functioning schools, a church whose congregants could afford to offer a scholarship, and jobs for his parents. All of this offered him a path forward.

As an adult, Wilson argued that the conditions for similarly situated children had become much, much worse. In comparison, he wrote: "The obstacles those in the inner cities now face are nearly insurmountable."[19] To describe these obstacles, he developed **social disorganization theory**, the idea that deviance is more common in dysfunctional neighborhoods. These are neighborhoods characterized by insecure social networks, family instability, few job opportunities, poor-performing schools, an absence of local organizations, and neglected infrastructure.[20]

Wilson documented neighborhoods like these in the city of Chicago. These were once-vibrant neighborhoods that supported a thriving working class. But they took a turn with the decline of manufacturing industries. When good jobs left, those who could afford to move followed them. Only the poorest remained. This caused a downward spiral. Poor people can't support businesses, so restaurants and grocery stores closed, taking

social disorganization theory
the idea that deviance is more common in dysfunctional neighborhoods

even more jobs. As neighborhoods declined, politicians stopped seeing them as worthy of investment, so residents watched parks, schools, police and fire protection, and other social services deteriorate. By the 1980s, inner cities were plagued by **concentrated poverty**: 40 percent or more of the residents lived below the federal poverty line. These neighborhoods were now seen as ghettos, so no one with any economic means wanted to move in. And the cycle continued.

Such neighborhoods don't offer residents the resources they need to follow social rules, which creates strain. It's hard to work if there are no jobs, to get a church scholarship if parishioners can't fund one, to grow vegetables if you don't have a backyard, or to go to college if your schools don't prepare you. People in disorganized neighborhoods, then, are more likely to engage in deviance, but not because of any individual deficiency. Instead, deviant behaviors are, as Wilson put it, "simply the normal responses of normal people to abnormal social conditions."[21]

This was another important sociological challenge to the idea that deviance is inherent in individuals. Yet another set of scholars would ask a different kind of question. They wondered: If someone is being recruited into deviant behavior, struggling to survive in a disorganized neighborhood, or straining to achieve socially desirable goals, how do they overcome their reluctance to do deviant things?

Neutralization Theory: A culturally credible account

Writing in the 1950s, the sociologists Gresham Sykes and David Matza were struck by the fact that sometimes criminals express feelings of guilt. Many people who choose to break the law feel bad about it, at least a little. Often, they express genuine admiration for law-abiding individuals. And they often hold conventional values, hoping one day to be able to leave their life of crime behind. Why, Sykes and Matza wondered, don't these feelings inhibit their criminal behavior in the first place? Or push them onto the straight and narrow after the fact?

To answer these questions, they developed **neutralization theory**, the idea that deviance is facilitated by the development of culturally resonant rationales for rule breaking.[22] Such justifications allow us to suspend our normal reluctance to engage in deviant acts, thereby "neutralizing" our resistance, guilt, and embarrassment.

Sykes and Matza introduced five types of rationalizations: three denials, a condemnation, and an appeal. Denial of Responsibility is a claim that rule breaking is outside of a rule breaker's control ("it's not my fault"). Denial of Injury is a claim that the rule breaking is allowed because no one is harmed ("no one got hurt"). Denial of the Victim is a claim that any harm that comes is deserved ("they were asking for it"). Condemnation of the Condemners is a rejection of a critic's moral authority to judge the rule breaker ("you're just as bad as me"). And Appeal to Higher Loyalties is the claim that rule breaking is justified in pursuit of a greater good ("I did it for my family").

concentrated poverty
a condition in which 40 percent or more of the residents in an area live below the federal poverty line

neutralization theory
the idea that deviance is facilitated by the development of culturally resonant rationales for rule breaking

Neutralization theory is a distinctly sociological contribution to thinking about deviance for at least two reasons. First, for a rationale to work, it's not enough for it to make sense to the rule breaker; it must also make sense to others. It is, in other words, a shared understanding. Second, we learn these rationales from other rule breakers; we get them from our social ties.

Researchers have found that people justify a wide range of social and criminal deviance, from entering children into beauty pageants to the most serious crimes imaginable, including murder and genocide.[23] A content analysis of online discussions about the legitimacy of music piracy, for example, found that such rationalizations were common. Denials of Injury and Denials of the Victim were especially frequent. "I was under the impression that musicians made most of their earnings via concerts, not from record sales," said one pirate, denying injury by suggesting that piracy doesn't really affect the artist's income. Another denied the victim by saying, "I don't buy hip-hop albums to listen to a guy tell me how many cars he has and how he is throwing bills at strippers."[24] By arguing that the musician was already rich, this person suggests that it's absurd to feel bad for the artist.

Another study—this time of illegal hacking—found frequent Condemnations of the Condemners and Appeals to a Higher Principle.[25] Many of the hackers rationalized their actions by condemning their targets as evil or corrupt. One, for example, hacked into the computers of a weapons manufacturer, arguing that the action was justified given that the company profited from police and military violence. Others appealed to a higher loyalty. A hacker who leaked classified government documents acknowledged breaking the law but argued: "My civil disobedience was for the greater good, for transparency; the government was not being truthful."

Neutralization theory helps sociologists understand how a person might overcome a reluctance to engage in behaviors defined as criminal or deviant. In these cases, individuals use neutralizations to suggest that they're not bad people; rather, they're good people with good reasons for doing bad things. In this way, they resist being defined

As a U.S. Army intelligence analyst, Chelsea Manning leaked thousands of classified documents to Wikileaks. In an op-ed for the *New York Times,* Manning appealed to a higher loyalty, explaining that she acted "out of a love for my country and a sense of duty to others."

as morally bad. Labeling theory, our final sociological theory of deviance, explores what happens to someone who isn't able to avoid being defined this way.

Labeling Theory: The power of language

From time to time, we all deviate from social norms and break laws. We share an unpopular opinion, text while driving, or consume illegal substances. In fact, one poll found that the average person commits seven crimes per week, and that's in addition to all the merely socially unacceptable things we do regularly.[26]

Some of us, however, are defined by our deviant or criminal behavior. Responding to this, another sociological theory considers how people become defined as "deviant." The jazz musician-turned-sociologist Howard Becker called this **labeling**, or the process of assigning a deviant identity to an individual. People can become not just someone who started a fight, for example, but a Bully. Not just someone who once had a problem with drugs, but an Addict. Not just someone who killed someone, but a Murderer. We have many such labels for criminally and socially deviant identities: Delinquent, Gangster, Slut, Deadbeat, Wife Beater, Bum, Cheat. Becker argued that when labels like these are applied to us, they influence our behavior. This is the main premise of **labeling theory**.[27]

Ironically, people who are labeled as deviant or criminal aren't usually very different from people who are not. Those people we consider deviants follow most of the rules most of the time. Even a very ambitious deviant couldn't possibly break them all. At best, they'd be able to boast of "a few deviant details scattered among a vast array of entirely acceptable conduct."[28] Labelers sift through that conduct and pick one action with which to identify a person, often with long-lasting consequences.

One in eight American adults, for example, has been convicted of a felony. Among other crimes, being found guilty of mail fraud, tax evasion, or selling illegal drugs will earn a person the label of Felon. This label is stigmatizing, but it's more than that; it does real harm to a person's life chances. If we've been labeled a Felon, it's legal to deny us housing and employment, the right to vote and serve on juries, educational benefits, and access to social services if we're down on our luck. We may even lose our parental rights. And we'll face these forms of discrimination for life.

Felons are also legally barred from many occupations. If we have a felony record, we're often banned from working for city or state governments; we can't drive city buses, landscape government buildings, or take other public-sector jobs. This means that between 12 and 25 percent of all jobs are unavailable to us, depending on our state.[29] We're also barred from any jobs that involve tending to children, the elderly, or people with disabilities, which means we can't become home health aides, day-care workers, or nurses. In most states, we're automatically disqualified from attaining professional licenses, so we can't drive taxis, work in nail salons or barbershops, or become plumbers or electricians.

labeling
the process of assigning a deviant identity to an individual

labeling theory
a theory about how labels that are applied to us influence our behavior

In addition to being barred from many occupations, felons also face discrimination. In most parts of the United States, it's legal for potential employers to ask whether an applicant has been convicted of a felony and to discriminate against people who report yes. The sociologist Devah Pager did a field experiment in which she sent young Black and White men out to apply for 350 entry-level jobs in Milwaukee, Wisconsin.[30] Each was given a fake résumé; half of these stated that they'd served time for possession of cocaine with intent to distribute. She then collected data on which applicants received interviews. Figure 5.2 shows that applicants with criminal records, whether they were Black or White, were substantially less likely to receive an interview. Because employers favored White candidates over Black candidates, however, a criminal record was especially devastating for Black applicants. In fact, a Black applicant *without* a criminal record had a lower chance of getting an interview than a White applicant *with* one.

FIGURE 5.2

Racial Impact of a Criminal Record on Interview Callbacks

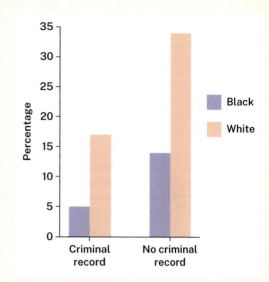

SOURCE: Republished with permission of The University of Chicago Press, from "The Mark of a Criminal Record" by Devah Pager. *The American Journal of Sociology*, 108:5, © 2003; permission conveyed through Copyright Clearance Center, Inc.

Many of us commit felony crimes, but only some of us receive the label of Felon. The label can change our life course. Others may see us as "at risk" for committing further crimes and choose not to befriend, date, or employ us. When these people are our looking glasses, we also may come to see ourselves as defined by our felony conviction.[31] In this way, labeling can be a self-fulfilling prophecy: what is believed to be true about us may become true.

A label, in other words, can be a *cause* of deviance as well as a result. Labeling theorists use the phrase **primary deviance** to describe the instance of deviance that first attracts a label and the phrase **secondary deviance** to describe further instances of deviance prompted by the receipt of that label.[32] At the extreme, a single deviant act can lead to a label that prompts a *deviant career*, a life organized around a deviant identity.[33]

A recent field experiment offered some of the strongest evidence yet that a label can induce deviant behavior.[34] The state of Florida is unusual in giving judges the right to impose sanctions for felony crimes while withholding a formal felony conviction. So some individuals who are found responsible for a felony crime receive the Felon label and others do not. A study of more than 95,000 people who went through this process discovered that, all things being

primary deviance
the instance of deviance that first attracts a deviant label

secondary deviance
further instances of deviance prompted by the receipt of the deviant label

equal, people who received the label of Felon were more likely to be found guilty of a later felony than people who weren't labeled as Felons.

Labels are socially powerful, with real effects on people's lives. If a person responds to strain by engaging in deviance, is recruited into criminal activity, or is pressed into it by a disorganized neighborhood—even if they can justify their actions to themselves and some others—they may be labeled as a deviant type. Such an event can have lifelong consequences, prompting secondary deviance and perhaps escalating into a deviant lifestyle.

Social sources of deviance: A summary

Sociologists have successfully challenged the idea that crime and deviance can be explained solely by individual characteristics. Instead, both crime and deviance are socially constructed categories of behavior, dependent on culture and history and subject to the rules of symbolic interactionism. Deviance has causes—and consequences—that go beyond the individual.

With this in mind, let's briefly return to that cold valley in the Andes and apply these theories. One could argue, for example, that the valley was the ultimate disorganized neighborhood. For the survivors, it failed to provide for even the most basic of human needs. Such abnormal circumstances required an abnormal response. Most critically, the lack of food caused strain. Facing death, they innovated. They found a different way to achieve the goal of survival. It was a deviant way, but it worked.

Parrado was the first to consider cannibalism. He recruited a friend and, together, they convinced the group. To do so, they offered accounts for their deviant behavior that effectively neutralized any lingering objections. The idea that eating the dead was equivalent to taking communion resonated with the group of Catholics.

Still, an ominous label threatened: Cannibal. When they were finally rescued, they came out swinging: *We're not cannibals*, they said. *We're Christians.* By offering a rationale for their rule breaking—*we wouldn't have done this, but we had to survive*—they helped the public understand and accept what they did. The label didn't stick. The public seemed to accept that, at least in this case, their cannibalism was merely the normal response of normal people to abnormal circumstances.

But what if that hadn't happened? What if the international community had decided to make an example of the survivors, to affirm the rule that eating human beings is unacceptable no matter what the circumstances? Or what if some people, upon hearing the story, decided that eating people was a fantastic idea?

If either one of those outcomes had come to pass, the story of Flight 571 would be a different kind of example altogether, one useful for illustrating the next set of sociological insights about deviance: that deviance isn't just an outcome of social forces but is itself a social force. People who engage in deviance can change societies. They can bond a society together or remake it anew.

FUNCTIONS OF DEVIANCE

Émile Durkheim (1858–1917), the sociologist who argued for the power of social facts, was one of the first to engage with the idea of deviance. In 1870, when Durkheim was just twelve years old, France went through its fifth regime change in just over fifty years. It had swung back and forth between two very different kinds of governments: republics and monarchies. In this unstable context, Durkheim's intellectual curiosity was developing. Not surprisingly, when it came time to study society, he turned his attention to the issue of social stability.

The paradigm he developed would become one of the most influential theories in all of sociology. Today we call it **structural functionalism**, or simply "functionalism," the theory that society is a system of necessary, synchronized parts that work together to create social stability.[35] The complementary parts are the "structures" and the stability they produce is the "function." Durkheim likened a healthy society to a healthy human body. Each organ, or part, has a unique and essential role. The heart pumps the blood, the liver cleans it, and the lungs infuse it with oxygen. Working together, our organs keep us healthy, or functional. Lose any one and we die.

Durkheim proposed that the structures of social life are each like a human organ, playing a unique and essential role. The family raises up the next generation, the workplace ensures goods and services for all, and governments provide parks and other public goods. All the parts are interconnected and need one another to do their job. Working together, they keep a society strong. Lose any one and society collapses.

So when Durkheim looked at the social fact of deviance, he did so with an eye toward what makes for a healthy society, asking what role, or function, deviance might play. His first observation was that deviance was an important source of social change. Perfect conformity to every social rule would mean that everyone would act exactly alike for all time. Deviant behavior is proof that social rules can be broken, which also means they can go away.

In the early 1900s, for example, it was essentially required that all American men wear a hat when outside the house. Today, wearing a hat is optional. No one's really sure how this change happened.[36] Some think it was the introduction of the car, which has less headspace than a bus or a train. Others maintain that the hat became unpopular after World War II because it reminded men of a military uniform. Some point to American president John F. Kennedy, who famously went "bareheaded" for his inauguration speech in 1961, inspiring other men to go hatless too.

Whatever the reason, there was a time when going bareheaded was deviant for men. Now it's not. For that, we can thank the people who risked sanctions by leaving their hat at home. Those deviants did something different and, eventually, one by one, they changed society. In this way, Durkheim wrote, deviance is sometimes "an anticipation of future morality." "A step," he wrote enthusiastically, "toward what will be!"[37]

structural functionalism
the theory that society is a system of necessary, synchronized parts that work together to create social stability

This bird's-eye view of a rally in 1927 reveals that less than one hundred years ago, it was considered deviant for men to leave the house without a hat.

collective conscience
a society's shared understanding of right and wrong

Durkheim identified a second function for deviance, one that was quite surprising at the time. While his contemporaries generally believed that deviance was bad, Durkheim argued that a certain amount of bad behavior could be good. Deviance, he maintained, plays a unique role in keeping a society healthy. It nurtures its **collective conscience**, or a society's shared understanding of right and wrong. Durkheim described the collective conscience as "the totality of beliefs and sentiments common to the average citizens of the same society."[38] A healthy body needs a soul.

According to Durkheim, then, deviance serves a very essential function: It gives people an occasion to join together, condemn rule breakers, and hold up the social rule. From the most trivial of rule breaking to the most serious, the collective condemnation of deviance both bonds people together and confirms the bounds of reasonable behavior, strengthening the collective conscience.

In 2019, for example, more than fifty parents were charged in the largest college admissions scandal in American history. A man named William Singer admitted to helping hundreds of wealthy and often famous families cheat to get their kids into college, including Georgetown, Yale, the University of Texas at Austin, UCLA, Stanford, and the University of Southern California (USC).[39] Singer falsified SAT scores, exploited accommodations offered to students with disabilities, and photoshopped the faces of his clients' children onto pictures of high school athletes. For this work, he collected $25 million over seven years. Some kids were complicit in the scheme. Others learned that their parents had bought their way into college the same way the rest of us did: from the splashy headlines.

One of those young people was a first-year student at USC named Olivia Jade Giannulli. As a high school student, Olivia Jade had built a social media following as an "influencer" on YouTube and Instagram. At the time of the scandal, she had more than 3 million followers. She earned money by posting glamorous images and videos of herself and complimenting products sold by companies like Sephora, Dolce & Gabbana, and Amazon.

Olivia Jade's parents—the actress Lori Loughlin (best known for playing Aunt Becky on the sitcom *Full House*) and the fashion designer Mossimo Giannulli (if you've ever shopped at Target, his first name is probably hanging in your closet)—paid Singer half a million dollars to get Olivia Jade and her sister into USC by bribing the crew coach, who pretended to put them on the team. It's unclear whether Olivia Jade was in on the scheme, but she did consent to posing for a picture for Singer that showed her on a rowing machine.

Olivia Jade was a lightning rod for America's outrage over the scandal. She openly admitted to being uninterested in college, proclaiming publicly that she wasn't motivated to study. "I don't know how much of school I'm going to attend," she confessed in a video, "but I do want the experience of, like, game days, partying. . . . I don't really care about school, as you guys all know." It didn't help that her application to trademark her name was returned by the U.S. Patent and Trademark Office because of poor punctuation or that at the very moment the scandal broke, her social media feed located her on a $100 million yacht owned by the chairman of USC's Board of Trustees.

All this made Olivia Jade the perfect target for an American public disgusted by the scandal. Her social media accounts were flooded with criticism. She was called "scum," "idiot," "toxic," and "cheater" and was accused of being entitled and ungrateful. One commenter accused her of taking the opportunity to attend college away from someone more deserving. Others mocked her influencer campaigns, suggesting that she do a tutorial on makeup for mug shots or offer fashion advice for people accompanying their parents to court. Referencing a video she'd posted about decorating her dorm room with free merchandise from Amazon, a commenter suggested she do a how-to video for decorating a prison cell. A final commenter demanded that she make amends by creating a scholarship for less privileged kids.

The scandal, and Olivia Jade's participation in it, was an opportunity for people to openly express their condemnation of the role money plays in college admissions, and the unfair privileges afforded to rich children generally. People born with so many advantages should still make their own way, the commenters suggested. And if they don't, they deserve all the contempt we can heap upon them. This is an example of the process Durkheim described. The scandal gave commenters the opportunity to express their beliefs about right and wrong, and to do so publicly. Such behavior is cathartic in the moment, but it also acts as a warning: Do the wrong thing and the community will be quick to mock and condemn you too.

What happened to Olivia Jade can happen in response to all types of deviance, from the trivial to the most serious. At the extreme, consider some people's reaction to the execution of one of America's most notorious serial killers. Ted Bundy killed at least thirty (and possibly more than a hundred) young women. For these crimes, he was executed by the state of Florida in 1989. Capital punishment is legal murder as a form of punishment, but it also serves as a powerful statement about the crime itself. *This*, the execution says, *is something we do not tolerate.*

The morning of his execution, two thousand people gathered outside the prison to celebrate.[40] "It was almost like a carnival," one witness recalled. The crowd cheered, sang, and chanted "Burn, Bundy, burn!" They held up signs with electrocution puns like "Teddy, you're the toast with the most" and "Tuesday is fry day." Someone set off fireworks. Vendors sold commemorative pins and T-shirts (you can buy reproductions even today). At Florida State University, a fraternity held a cookout and served "Bundy burgers." A strip club hosted a "Bundy Bar-B-Que." A music store had an electric guitar sale with the tagline: "Get 'em while they're hot." When the prison affirmed that Bundy was dead,

A large crowd of onlookers gathered outside Florida State Prison to celebrate Ted Bundy's execution. Their shared condemnation of the serial killer was a moment of collective effervescence.

the crowd outside was elated. Durkheim would have described their shared joy as *collective effervescence,* a strong, unifying emotion experienced communally by a group.

Durkheim felt that moments like these were good for society. He worried, in fact, that without such exhibitions of mass disapproval, a society's collective conscience might be dangerously destabilized. This would result in a condition called **anomie** (pronounced *an-no-me*), widespread normlessness or a weakening of or alienation from social rules.[41] Under conditions of anomie, existing social rules no longer confirm a shared sense of right and wrong, which is disorienting. As Durkheim put it: "No one then knows what is possible and what is impossible, what is just and what is unjust, what constitute legitimate demands and hopes, and which are those that exceed boundaries."[42]

Without a clear sense of what makes life good and meaningful, amorality sets in. If nothing is right or wrong, we might as well do whatever. Vote, or don't. Go to work, or don't. Eat your vegetables, or don't. Why obey the rules, or have any ambition, if there's no guarantee that conformity will bring rewards, and nothing matters anymore anyway? It might seem that people experiencing normlessness would feel free. Durkheim didn't think so. He thought they would feel lost.

Today, studies suggest that feelings of anomie correlate with students' willingness to plagiarize papers and cheat on tests.[43] One such study involved the distribution of a survey, a research method in which respondents are asked to fill out a questionnaire designed to collect analyzable data (see "The Science of Sociology"). In addition to asking the respondents whether they'd ever engaged in academic dishonesty, the survey included a series of questions aimed at measuring each student's level of anomie.[44] On a scale of 1 to 7, for example, students were asked to report whether they "strongly disagreed" or "strongly agreed" with statements like "You sometimes can't help wondering whether anything is worthwhile anymore," "Nowadays, a person has to live pretty much for today and let tomorrow take care of itself," and "Most people don't really care what happens to the next person." Students who agreed with these statements were most likely to admit to cheating. This suggests that a sense of normlessness leaves students with less motivation to uphold norms themselves.

Findings like these confirm that anomie isn't just bad for individuals; it can also harm societies. Anomie is a social crisis. It causes collective confusion, the weakening of social cohesion, and even the functional breakdown of important swaths of life, like education. Durkheim believed that societies characterized by high levels of anomie are in real danger of falling apart. "[If] society lacks the unity based upon the commitment of [the people's] wills to a common objective," he wrote, "then it is no more than a pile of sand that the least jolt or the slightest puff will suffice to scatter."[46] Without us all cooperating to make life meaningful, that is, there's no reason to go on pretending like what we do matters. And if it doesn't matter, why do it at all? Poof, away it goes.

anomie
widespread normlessness or a weakening of or alienation from social rules

THE **SCIENCE** OF SOCIOLOGY

Survey Research

The **survey** is a research method that involves inviting individuals to complete a questionnaire designed to collect analyzable data. Surveys usually include close-ended questions, meaning that respondents are given a predetermined selection of answers from which to choose. If you've ever taken a multiple-choice test, you've answered close-ended questions.

Surveys are designed to collect responses from a large number of respondents, from a few dozen to tens of thousands or more. Scientists will first identify the population of people they want to survey (Native Americans, for example, college students, or Walmart shoppers). Because it often can be expensive and time consuming to study every member of a population, researchers will strategically select a portion of that population. This is called a **sample**: the subset of the population from which data will be collected.

Samples can be designed such that data collected are **generalizable**, or applicable to the whole population from which the sample is drawn, not just to the sample itself. That is, the right sampling strategy can select a subset of the population that's representative of the whole, or likely to deliver data that reflect the full population accurately. If researchers use proper sampling techniques, they can get a remarkably precise picture of even very large populations by surveying just a few thousand.

Responses are combined into a dataset that can be analyzed with *statistics*, a mathematical approach to research that involves collecting and analyzing numerical data. If a sample is representative, the resulting statistics can tell us a *lot* about the kind of people in its sample. If we want to know a series of facts about a population, then, and how those facts are correlated (or related to one another), surveys are the way to go.

Every year, for example, a sample of first-year college students are invited to complete the Freshmen Survey. This research project, conducted by the Higher Education Research Institute at UCLA, documents students' values and goals, academic preparedness, and financial concerns. In 2019, the survey found that 56 percent of students were concerned that they wouldn't be able to afford tuition, and 55 percent would probably work while earning their degree.[45] This is an increase from previous years. Surveys like this allow us to measure whether and how young people are changing. ∎

For functionalists, then, social and criminal deviance is not only useful; it's essential. A shared sense of right and wrong, demonstrated regularly and publicly in rituals of collective condemnation, is what holds us together. Without it, individuals become lost and societies fall apart.

Of course, Olivia Jade might have a thing to say about that. She personally paid the price for whatever collective conscience emerged in the aftermath of the admissions scandal. In fact, a society that relies on demonizing so-called deviants to maintain its norms will have a lot of victims. This led another group of scholars to question some of the assumptions of functionalism and ask the all-important question: For whom, exactly, are these societies functioning?

DEVIANCE, CONFLICT, AND CHANGE

The 1960s challenged many of the premises of functionalist theory. It was a volatile time in American history. The civil rights, Chicano, Latino, and American Indian movements were challenging persistent racial inequality. The gay liberation and women's movements were staking claims on equality for sexual minorities and women. The sexual revolution was saying no to social rules surrounding sexuality. And in the second decade of war with Vietnam, Americans were losing patience with the government.

Conflict seemed to be everywhere. And so was deviance. Activists broke rules: They occupied streets and sidewalks, chanted and sang at the top of their lungs, embraced deviant labels, defied laws, and sometimes engaged in violence. They were rebels in Merton's classic sense of the word. Faced with the strain of oppression, they were fighting to replace the old ways with new ones.

In this environment, sociologists increasingly began criticizing functionalist theories of deviance. For one, functionalism couldn't explain the fact that some Americans were consistently underserved by their society. Poverty, racial inequality, and discrimination against women, for example, suggested that other mechanisms were at play. Moreover, sociologists were becoming less comfortable portraying deviants as either neutral (like men who went without hats) or negative (like Olivia Jade and Bundy). The idea that deviants themselves might be a positive force in society was gaining in popularity.

The truth is that sociological thinkers had long been concerning themselves with these issues, but most of them had been formally excluded from mainstream sociology. One of these people was the sociologist Karl Marx, who we'll learn more about in Chapter 7. His two most famous books—*The Communist Manifesto* (1848) and *Das Kapital* (1867)—were early critiques of capitalism. Considered a radical in his time, Marx was barred from academia and lived half of his adult life in exile from Germany, his country of birth.

Anna Julia Cooper and Ida B. Wells-Barnett—discussed in Chapters 3 and 4, respectively—were also early sociologists whose work questioned the premises

survey
a research method that involves inviting individuals to complete a questionnaire designed to collect analyzable data

sample
the subset of the population from which data will be collected

generalizable
a term used to describe data that are applicable to the whole population from which the sample is drawn, not just to the sample itself

Charlotte Perkins Gilman was an early advocate for the burgeoning discipline of sociology. Many of her works focused on social conflict.

of functionalism. Both Black women, they wrote insightful books about the social forces that constrained African American life. They did so five years before Durkheim published, in 1897, what is still routinely identified as the first book-length sociological study. One of Wells-Barnett's books, *Southern Horrors* (1892), argued that lynching was a tool of White domination, not a response to the criminal activities of the Black population.[47] One of Cooper's, *A Voice from the South*, subtitled *By a Black Woman of the South* (1892), made the case that we can't fully understand Black people's lives without considering Black *women's* lives.[48] She made an intersectional argument a hundred years before the word entered the English language.

Charlotte Perkins Gilman (1860–1935) would write her most enduring short story in the same year that Cooper and Wells-Barnett published their most famous books. *The Yellow Wallpaper* is a fictional essay about the harm sexist societies do to White women. As a White woman herself, she chafed under the expectation that she love men and not women, get married, and find fulfillment in domesticity. Her works exposed both gender and class inequality, criticizing it as illegitimate and unfair. A prolific scholar, she wrote six books of sociology, published in sociological journals, and was a member of the American Sociological Society from its founding in 1905 to her death in 1935.[49] Advocating for the discipline, she wrote: "We must know the mechanisms of a thing if we are to mend it."

While White men were doing sociology from inside the halls of academia, women, people of color, and women of color were doing sociology outside of it, whether by choice or necessity. Political dissidents like Karl Marx were too. And the work they were doing was different. Notably, Durkheim and his colleagues were writing about social *cooperation*, and they would for the next sixty years, whereas Marx, Wells-Barnett, Cooper, and Gilman were writing about social *conflict*.

Ultimately, the uprisings of the 1960s would shift the focus of mainstream sociology to what thinkers outside the mainstream had been concerned with all along. This new paradigm would be called **conflict theory**, the idea that societies aren't characterized by shared interests but competing ones.[50] According to conflict theorists, societies are defined by fights over control of valuable resources like wealth, power, and prestige.

From this perspective, social rules don't reflect widespread agreement about what should or shouldn't be allowed. Instead, they're the result of some people having the power to make certain social rules—rules favorable to them—the ones by which everyone must live. The advantaged, then, have greater power

conflict theory
the idea that societies aren't characterized by shared interests but competing ones

than the disadvantaged to make their own lifestyles the standard for everyone. People who cannot or will not follow these rules will find themselves stigmatized, medicalized, or criminalized.

Conflict theory is particularly concerned with **social inequality**, a condition in which wealth, power, and prestige are most readily available to people with privileged social identities. Today, conflict theories include feminist theory, critical race theory, queer theory, critical disability theory, and postcolonial theory. These are areas of sociology that focus on social inequalities rooted in gender, race, sexuality, disability, and the occupation and exploitation of some nations' peoples by others. Scholars in all these traditions also contribute to critical criminology, research about how policing and punishment reproduce social inequality.

From a conflict theory perspective, social stability isn't a sign that society is functioning well for everyone; it's a sign that those for whom it's not functioning are too weak to fight back. And harmony isn't good, as functionalists argued; it's a sign that those who are benefiting from the status quo have effectively repressed everyone else, leaving them too weak to resist.

When people do resist the status quo, their actions may be cast as deviance. Some deviance, then, is not just deviance but *defiance*. It's deliberately rebellious. It's an effort to change the collective conscience.

When people do fight back, conflict theorists predict that people for whom society is functioning well will resist. In fact, they hypothesize that it's exactly when the powerful are losing their ability to impose their social rules that we should expect to see the strongest efforts to defend them. The final section of this chapter provides a startling example of just this kind of backlash.

Resistance and reaction: A case study

It was the height of the civil rights movement. Black Americans had been fighting for equal treatment since the first of their ancestors had been enslaved in 1619. They won their freedom in 1863, ending 244 years of enslavement, only to face a new kind of inequality: state and local laws that enforced racial segregation. For decades, Black people and their allies had been fighting this new fight.

Their efforts reached a horrifying crescendo in 1968. One of the movement's most inspiring leaders, Martin Luther King Jr., was murdered by a man opposed to racial integration. It was a devastating blow, and activists took to the streets in nearly 200 cities across the United States. These protests lasted for days, sometimes longer. They involved marches, speeches, song, dance and, in about 25 percent of the cities, significant damage to property. King's assassination, in other words, sparked mass deviance—some of it destructive—among Black people who suffered from social inequality in schooling, housing, employment, interactions with police, and more.

Four months after the assassination prompted this period of social unrest, two psychiatrists published an essay in the *Journal of the American Medical Association* with the title "The 'Protest' Psychosis."[51] In it, they argued that

In the 1960s, psychiatrists theorized that Black people protesting racism were mentally unwell.

"recent social-political events" were causing "reactive psychosis" among Black men and women. Protesters, they said, were driven by "paranoid delusions that [they are] being constantly victimized." The article argued that civil rights protesters weren't legitimately oppressed but mentally unwell. The psychiatrists advocated for widespread diagnoses of schizophrenia and the administration of anti-psychotic medication to Black people involved in the civil rights movement. By labeling them as mentally ill, these psychiatrists medicalized their resistance to oppression and cast them as deviants.

A scholar named Jonathan Metzl, both a sociologist and a psychiatrist, wrote about this article and its impact.[52] He used a research method known as historical sociology, which involves collecting and analyzing data that reveal facts about past events (see "The Science of Sociology"). Digging through the archives of state hospitals and analyzing accounts in old newspapers and psychiatry magazines, he found that the article contributed to transforming the stereotype of the schizophrenic person. In the 1950s, psychiatrists primarily saw schizophrenia as a condition affecting bored, middle-class housewives. Beginning in the 1960s, however, the stereotype of a Black male schizophrenic came to replace that idea. Drug advertisements aimed at psychiatrists once featured sad-looking White ladies. Soon, they began featuring angry-looking Black men. In one ad, a "deranged black figure literally shakes his fist" in front of a "burning, urban landscape" meant to indicate a riot.[53]

As a result of the medicalization of protest, the rate at which Black men were institutionalized increased. The patient population of a large mental hospital in Michigan, for example, shifted from mostly White women who were seen as poorly adjusted but nonviolent, to assumed-hostile Black men

historical sociology
a research method that involves collecting and analyzing data that reveal facts about past events, with the aim of enhancing sociological theory

THE **SCIENCE** OF SOCIOLOGY

Historical Sociology

If historians aim to provide as accurate an account of past events as possible, sociologists are interested in using these accounts to test and expand sociological concepts. Accordingly, **historical sociology** involves collecting and analyzing data that reveal facts about past events, with the aim of enhancing sociological theory.

Historians and historical sociologists use the same kind of data: newspapers, artifacts, vintage art and photography, public records, and other material from the era being studied. They may also use oral history interviews with living persons, ones that obtain evidence by interviewing people about their experience of historical events. Sociologists use these data to craft an argument about what happened in the past and what it means for sociological thinking today.

The sociologists Melissa Wilde and Sabrina Danielsen, for example, used historical sociology to explore why many prominent religious groups in the United States began advocating for the legalization of birth control around 1930.[54] They examined the written materials distributed to the congregants of America's twenty-eight largest religious denominations between 1919 and 1934, finding that denominations that advocated for legalization expressed anxiety that immigrants would outbreed White Protestants if birth control wasn't legalized. They also drew on the "social gospel" (the idea that good Christians should try to improve their societies) to justify their advocacy. Their motivation to make birth control more accessible was more related to racist concerns about a shrinking White population than feminist concerns about women's right to planned pregnancies.

Though historical sociology is excellent for explaining why and how a particular historical outcome came about, it's less useful for accounting for how things could have turned out differently. History only goes in one direction, making it impossible to know how easily or with what prompting things could have gone another way. For this reason, some sociologists do comparative research, a method described in the next chapter, with a historical focus. ■

convicted of crimes related to civil unrest, like participation in protests and politically motivated property destruction. Alongside the change in the population, medical records began to reflect the new stereotype. Instead of notes like "can't do her housework" or "she got confused," psychiatrists began writing "paranoid against . . . the police" and "a danger to society."

Through the 1990s, Black men would be diagnosed with paranoid schizophrenia more than any other group and up to seven times as often as White men. A 2005 study found that Black people were still four times more likely to be labeled as schizophrenic than White people, though there is no evidence that they exhibit higher rates of symptoms.[55] Conflict theorists would argue that overdiagnosis is a way for the powerful to maintain control of their societies.

Labeling theory comes into a different focus through the lens of conflict theory. Some kinds of people are more likely to incur damaging labels than others, or labels may be used strategically to stigmatize, medicalize, or criminalize whole groups of people. Other social causes of deviance also seem more ominous from a conflict theory perspective. Differential association theorists sensitive to conflict might ask who is more or less exposed to criminal networks, risking recruitment and socialization. Social disorganization theorists might point out that not everyone is equally likely to live in a disorganized neighborhood and ask why it is that so many of us are more tolerant of some kinds of people living in such conditions. Strain theorists might ask why some people lack the means to achieve socially valued goals. Neutralization theorists might ask whose rationales will be accepted and by whom.

Conflict theorists would argue that this is how our societies are designed to function. They work, in fact, to keep the already marginalized on the margins of society. From this point of view, deviance may not be functional, but it is essential. It's a way, sometimes the only way, for the marginalized and oppressed to fight back against an unfair society. ∎

COMING UP...

SOCIOLOGISTS HAVE shown that social rules don't just determine what is normal; they define the territory of the deviant. This means that nothing is inherently deviant or criminal; it's all dependent on context. In other words, deviance is socially constructed.

Deviance can be prompted by social factors. Whether we engage in a deviant or criminal act is dependent in part on what opportunities we have, who we know, where we live, what excuses we learn, and how our looking glasses reflect us.

Deviance also shapes societies. Structural functionalists have argued that acts of deviance inspire collective condemnation and prevent anomie, playing an important role in social stability. Conflict theorists have argued that deviance is a reaction to strain, disorganized neighborhoods, criminal networks, or stigmatizing and criminalizing labels. Or it's defiance: the decision to fight a system that's harming some people to the benefit of others.

Both functionalist and conflict perspectives will inform the next chapter. Chapter 6 zooms out to explore the "structures" of structural functionalism. And, taking a conflict perspective, it asks just how functional the resulting societies are, and for whom. An introduction to social organizations, social institutions, and the social structure is next.

6

———
———

ORGANIZATIONS
INSTITUTIONS
& STRUCTURES

IN THIS CHAPTER...

THE PREVIOUS TWO chapters were about social interaction, moments in which people act in ways that either conform to or deviate from social rules. This chapter is about social interaction, too, but on a much larger scale. Three concepts are central:

- *Social organizations*, as defined by Max Weber, are formal entities that coordinate collections of people in achieving a stated purpose. A school, for example, is a social organization. Its goal is to organize people in the service of educating children.

- *Social institutions* are widespread and enduring patterns of interaction with which we respond to categories of human need. Schools are part of the social institution of Education. So are bus drivers and crossing guards, Parent Teacher Associations, and companies that make school supplies.

- Finally, the *social structure* is the set of interlocking social institutions in which we live. Other social institutions, like Work and Family, intersect with Education and together they create a structure for our lives.

Large-scale forms of cooperation like these are important to sociologists, in part because they contribute to social inequality.

- The phrase *structural position* refers to the mix of opportunities and constraints offered to us by the social structure.

- Social institutions are often designed to persistently favor some kinds of people over others. When this is the case, the outcome is described as *institutional discrimination*.

- Widespread institutional discrimination produces *social stratification*, a persistent sorting of social groups into enduring hierarchies.

This chapter also introduces a tenth sociological research method:

- *Comparative sociology* involves collecting and analyzing data about two or more cases that can be usefully compared and contrasted.

"Men make their own histories, but they do not make it . . . under circumstances chosen by themselves."

—KARL MARX

Think back to the mischievous middle school football team from Texas, the one that used sociological trickery to score a touchdown. Other than the controversial play, it was a game like any other game happening on thousands of middle school fields across the United States. If we include the cheerleaders, band members, and fans in the stands, there were likely a few hundred people there. The game was a coordinated interaction, and a complex one, but it was also very ordinary. Many games like it had been played before, and many like it will be played in the future.

That game's very ordinariness hints at something much larger. The game had a *history*: countless games going back in time to long before anyone on its field was born. It has a *future*: an unknowable number of games stretching forward in time as football lives on long after everyone alive today is dead.

That game also had a *present*, a vertical line that moved down, connecting the game to the kids playing in peewee leagues, toddlers watching their first football game on TV, and infants dressed in team onesies. That vertical line went up, too, through high school, college, and the pros, involving more and more diverse kinds of people: athletes, coaches, and fans but also recruiters, trainers, managers, team owners, accountants, doctors, souvenir manufacturers, cooks, vendors, janitors, public relations experts, network executives, advertisers, agents, and more.

Sports isn't just whoever shows up to a field on a sunny Saturday. It's an industry enveloping large swaths of society. Nearly 21.5 million kids and teenagers are signed up for at least one school sport each year. Almost every middle school, high school, and college in America fields teams. Hundreds of thousands of people are directly employed by sports-related companies.

If a single game is an impressive display of the human ability to spontaneously produce interaction, then the behemoth that is the sports industry is an example of just how expansive, complex, and layered human interaction can become. These are not the nimble interactions that can go from dinner party to robbery and back again. These are stiff and slow moving, involving the cooperation of sometimes millions of people. This kind of coordination requires more than just an agreement about what is going on; it requires both formal and informal coordination.

In exploring these phenomena, this chapter goes big. Thus far the book has discussed the social nature of our individuality, the power of our imaginations to make life meaningful, the construction of our social identities, the intricacy of our interactions, and the causes and consequences of deviance. Now is the time to add more elaborate webs of relations, ones that involve hundreds, thousands, or even millions of people.

This chapter traces the emergence of the modern era, a time during which human societies became increasingly large and coordination grew increasingly difficult. Organizations, social institutions, and social structures were developed to address this complexity. Today, they enhance our lives, offering a stability and predictability that help us accomplish our goals. They also, however, produce unequal outcomes. In helping some of us more than others, they contribute to large-scale social inequality.

To fully appreciate the significance of this scale of organization, we have to go back to before such coordination was necessary. We begin, then, by remembering the lifestyles of our distant ancestors.

Complexes of gymnasiums, stadiums, and athletic fields on college campuses represent only a fraction of the social and physical infrastructure devoted to sports in America today.

MODERNITY, ITS ORIGINS, AND ITS MUCH-HYPED DEMISE

For 290,000 of the 300,000 years our species of humans has lived on earth, we lived in small kin groups. These were collections of people considered family, more often numbering in the dozens than in the hundreds. Drawing on thousands of years of cumulative knowledge and experience, these groups usually easily attained everything they needed from the wild plants and animals around them.[1] They lived wherever these things were most abundant, setting up camps and moving with the seasons. Foraging groups like these worked only a couple of hours per day, leaving the rest for leisure.[2]

According to anthropologists, foragers were guided by what was understood to be divine will.[3] They obeyed gods, spirits, or the souls of their ancestors. In their daily lives, they deferred to people with *traditional authority*, the kind that comes from custom.[4] They were wedded to tradition and had no narrative of "progress," so they didn't generally seek to change their societies. Today, scholars describe this kind of reasoning as **premodern thought**: a belief in supernatural sources of truth and a commitment to traditional practices.

About 10,000 years ago, this all began to change. Humans invented *agriculture*, the practice of cultivating crops and rearing animals. We slowly gave up our foraging lifestyles in exchange for fields, pastures, and farmhouses. Now we worked from daybreak to nightfall. We plowed land, sowed seeds, delivered water, removed rocks, plucked weeds, shooed vermin, harvested grains, saved seeds, fed animals, fixed fences, and cleaned pens.[5] It was much harder work than foraging, so much so that the archaeological record shows a sudden uptick in bad backs.[6]

Sometimes all this hard work paid off. When it did, farmers could trade their surplus for services and other goods. Humans invented writing to keep track of who owed what to whom. They invented money, a symbolic measure of surplus, to facilitate trade. These inventions freed some people from tending to farms, and they began earning their money as weavers, toolmakers, blacksmiths, and more.[7]

Successful agricultural societies could support larger populations and a more diverse set of occupations. Communities grew. Towns turned into cities, cities into city-states. Over time, upward size pressure—perhaps especially from the threat of war—pushed states to get ever bigger.[8] After hundreds of millennia as happy wanderers, we became residents of **nation-states**: large territories governed by centralized powers that grant or deny citizenship rights. Thus, we arrive at something resembling the societies we have now.

Theorizing modernity

Historians describe this transition to living in larger and more complex societies as a shift from a premodern to a modern era, one dated to just over 500 years ago. As this change occurred, so did ideas about the source

premodern thought
a belief in supernatural sources of truth and a commitment to traditional practices

nation-states
large territories governed by centralized powers that grant or deny citizenship rights

of truth and the goal of our shared existence.[9] Modern thinkers replaced faith and tradition with science and progress.[10] **Modern thought**, then, involves a belief in science as the sole source of truth and the idea that humans can rationally organize societies and improve human life. Modern thinkers are confident they can use logic to design technologically advanced, and ever-advancing, societies.

One of the earliest theorists of the modern era was a sociologist named Max Weber (pronounced *vay-bur* instead of *web-bur*). Born in Germany, Weber (1864–1920) directly experienced a distinct phase of modernization: his country's industrial revolution. By the time Weber was in his mid-thirties, Germany was a world industrial leader. It had built factories, laid railroads, invested in fossil fuels, and developed a highly ordered and competitive economy. Weber introduced the term **rationalization** to describe the process of embracing reason and using it to increase the efficiency and effectiveness of human activities.[11]

Though much of German society was undergoing rationalization, premodern thought prevailed in Weber's childhood home. His mother was deeply religious, a direct descendant of a persecuted religious minority: the French Huguenots. At the dawn of the modern era, members of her faith were slaughtered in a thirty-six-year war prompted by religious intolerance. It was the second most lethal religious war in the history of Europe, costing 3 million lives.

Raised with these stories, and watching his own society change, Weber would become the first sociologist of religion. In the early 1900s, he would write books on Protestantism, Judaism, Hinduism, and Confucianism and develop a research method that sociologists now call comparative sociology (see "The Science of Sociology").[12] Interested in how different faith traditions influenced the development of different societies, he contrasted the economies of Catholic countries like France and Spain with Protestant ones like Germany and the United Kingdom.

This research method has yielded many valuable insights, ones that scholars are still working with today. One among them was rather unexpected. In

America's embrace of atomic power even extended to beauty pageants, with several Las Vegas showgirls winning titles such as Miss A-Bomb and Miss Atomic Blast. These women represented a distinctly modern trust in the capacity of scientists to use great power to do good things.

modern thought
a belief in science as the sole source of truth and the idea that humans can rationally organize societies and improve human life

rationalization
the process of embracing reason and using it to increase the efficiency and effectiveness of human activities

THE SCIENCE OF SOCIOLOGY

Comparative Sociology

Comparative sociology involves collecting and analyzing data about two or more cases that can be usefully compared and contrasted. A **case** is an instance of a thing of interest; it can be a person, a group of people, an organization, an event, or a place. Thus, a researcher conducting a comparative study chooses, researches, and then compares two or more such cases. These inquiries can be small, as in a comparison of two siblings. Or they can be quite large, as in a comparison of three countries. In both instances, the researcher aims for thorough knowledge of each case.

To gather this knowledge, comparative sociologists draw on any source material that may be illuminating. They can do network analyses, in-depth interviews, surveys, content analyses, historical explorations, or laboratory or field experiments. As long as they collect data in the same way for each case, the data can then be examined for similarities and differences. ■

---

comparative sociology
a research method that involves collecting and analyzing data about two or more cases that can be usefully compared and contrasted

case
an instance of a thing of interest; it can be a person, a group of people, an organization, an event, or a place

the face of modernization, religion managed to survive. Instead of bringing about the end of religion, modernity brought us more *organized* religion. In other words, religion itself underwent a process of rationalization. In this context, Weber began to develop a theory to explain this new kind of cooperation: the social organization.

Comparative sociology is excellent for asking whether social forces reliably produce predicted outcomes. If we study only one case, we can identify a trajectory of events, but we can't draw any strong conclusions as to whether, under different conditions, things might have turned out differently. If we study two or more cases, we can measure whether similar social forces produce similar outcomes. We can then develop theories about why and how events unfold as they do. By comparing cases, in other words, sociologists can attempt to identify factors that contribute to how different realities come about.

Comparative research has been extremely useful, for example, for understanding what prompts and what prevents tragedies like ethnic cleansings and civil wars. It's also helped us understand why discontent sometimes prompts political protest or even outright revolution.

The bureaucratic organization

After the widespread adoption of agriculture, human societies grew larger and became increasingly complex. This required new modes of cooperation. We needed to coordinate food production, natural resource extraction, and trade. We needed plans for how to distribute goods and services. We needed codes of conduct, ways of resolving disputes, and rules for punishment. We needed shared ways of reproducing ourselves, both biologically and socially. And we needed processes by which some people could be put in charge.

Social organizations were one solution to these needs. Sociologists define **social organizations** as formal entities that coordinate collections of people in achieving a stated purpose. These include corporations, hospitals, schools, police forces, and social clubs. Social organizations—or just "organizations"—are more planned than routine social interaction. They have clear goals, even "mission statements." They're carefully designed with the intention of meeting their goals (however imperfectly). And they have insiders and outsiders: people who are part of the coordination and people who are not. Organizations also involve **divisions of labor**, complicated tasks broken down into smaller parts and distributed to individuals who specialize in narrow roles.[13]

Highly rationalized organizations are called **bureaucracies**: organizations with formal policies, strict hierarchies, and impersonal relations.[14] Formal policies are written rules that govern conduct. Strict hierarchies grant employees power over one another. And relations are impersonal, meaning that roles can be filled by anyone with the proper qualifications. Ideally, people are treated according to their roles and not their social identities or relationships.

Weber argued that authority isn't *traditional* in bureaucratic organizations, as it was for premodern humans. Instead, it's *rational legal*, derived from logical principles. Authority in these societies comes, then, not from custom ("this is how we do things") but from rationality ("this is the best way to do things"). Thus, modern individuals may not be as quick to subject themselves to the will of elders and ancestors, but they may defer to bureaucrats, legislators, and accountants.

In pop culture, bureaucracies are often mocked as woefully inefficient. In the United States, the classic example is the DMV, or the Department of Motor Vehicles. In the animated movie *Zootopia*, for example, the DMV is run entirely by sloths, an animal most famous for being slooooow. When two characters drop by the DMV on a quick errand, the contrast between their urgency and the sloths' plodding pace is played for laughs.

Ironically, Americans' frustration with the DMV doesn't actually reveal a distaste for bureaucracy. It reveals the opposite. Carefully orchestrated bureaucracies like the DMV only exist because of a modern desire for efficiency. If anything, our frustration only suggests that we want our bureaucracies to be even *more* rationalized and, therefore, more efficient.

More than a hundred years after Weber introduced these ideas, the sociologist George Ritzer argued that rationalization was continuing to escalate.[15] As

social organizations
formal entities that coordinate collections of people in achieving a stated purpose

divisions of labor
complicated tasks broken down into smaller parts and distributed to individuals who specialize in narrow roles

bureaucracies
organizations with formal policies, strict hierarchies, and impersonal relations

The animated movie *Zootopia* satirizes the Department of Motor Vehicles (DMV) by staffing the entire organization with the famously lethargic sloth. The joke's on us, illustrating the frustration of dealing with slow and inefficient bureaucracies.

an example, he pointed to the fast-food restaurant McDonald's. Introduced in 1953, the chain made its name by selling hamburgers extremely efficiently. By 1994 the restaurant's motto was "over 99 billion sold." Today the company operates nearly 38,000 restaurants in 120 countries.

To become the largest fast-food chain in the world, Ritzer argued, McDonald's maximized three features of its organization: efficiency (delivering a product in the shortest time possible), predictability (ensuring that the product tastes the same no matter when or where it's ordered), and calculability (prioritizing quantity over quality). To do this, the company also invested in nonhuman technology. Machines enhance both efficiency (by moving faster with fewer mistakes and no bathroom breaks) and predictability (by ensuring precise measurements and movements). This is a trend that's still escalating today. McDonald's intends to replace its cashiers with computers in all its U.S. locations.

Ritzer argued that just about everything in Western societies has become more like McDonald's. He described this phenomenon as *McDonaldization*, the process by which more and more parts of life are made efficient, predictable, calculable, and controllable by nonhuman technologies. The introduction of standardized testing in education is McDonaldization. So is the Fitbit, a biometric machine designed to guide exercise regimes. Dating websites and apps that rely on algorithms to match users with partners is McDonaldization too.

Both Weber and Ritzer expressed anxiety about the changes that come with modernization. All the way back in 1917, Weber worried that it would cause a "disenchantment of the world." We once implored the gods; now we rely on technocrats, rulebooks, and calculations. We once marveled at the unknown; now we seek to answer every question. We once enjoyed spontaneity; now we try to control everything. Weber saw rationalized bureaucracies as efficient, which was good. But he also worried that they stripped life of things that make it worth living: beauty, astonishment, unpredictability, and creativity.

At least we got flying cars and jet packs! Or maybe not. But we did get modern medicine, communication technologies, space exploration, and virtual reality. Some of the modernist fantasies of TV shows like *The Jetsons*— a 1960s-era cartoon in which a family far in the future lives in the sky with a robot maid—are still far off. But some of the show's predictions, like smart watches and teleconferencing, are here. And others, like holograms and 3D-printed food, are on their way.

Our foraging ancestors hunted. Our farming ancestors raised livestock. Industrial agriculture rationalized the meat industry, making it—some would say—brutally efficient. Soon we'll be eating the products of "cellular agriculture": meat grown in a petri dish. We've come a long way. Have we come so far that we're no longer modern at all?

Are we postmodern?

Some scholars have argued that a "postmodern" age has displaced modernity. This age has its own mode of thinking, one that differs from both premodern and modern thinkers (see Table 6.1). **Postmodern thought** rejects absolute truth (whether supernatural or scientific) in favor of countless partial truths, and it denounces the narrative of progress.[16] Postmodernity is argued to have arrived in the 1980s, though the mode of thought appears in earlier decades.

If both religion and science are premised on the idea that an objective truth can be known, postmodern thinkers doubt the very idea of truth. Such thinkers argue that it doesn't exist or, if it does, we're not able to know it. In which case, the only source of something resembling truth is individual experience, which means there are as many truths as there are individuals. From this perspective, no one's point of view is any more valid than anyone else's.

Taken to its logical conclusion, this assumes that every interpretation of reality is equally correct. And because everyday life is built upon a foundation of shared interpretations, reality itself is fleeting, unstable, and unpredictable. Does red mean stop? Not *really*. Tomorrow we might change our minds, and why not?

postmodern thought
a rejection of absolute truth (whether supernatural or scientific) in favor of countless partial truths, and a denunciation of the narrative of progress

TABLE 6.1

Modes of Thought

	Premodern	Modern	Postmodern
Source of truth	Supernatural	Scientific	Personal experience
Mode of authority	Traditional	Rational legal	No ultimate authority
Nature of identity	Pregiven	Discoverable	Always in flux

A modern thinker might feel the need to know whether the number is a six or a nine, but a postmodern thinker would not. The former believes in one truth; the latter believes in as many truths as there are points of view.

This kind of thinking has changed how some of us think about our selves. The premodern thinker accepted whatever self they were granted at birth. A child born into a family in the 1400s, for example, would carry a family name, be slotted into a gender role, and inherit a class and possibly even a profession. These outcomes would be rigid, and the premodern person would accept this rigidity. They would never think to ask, *Who am I?*

The modern self is a journey and discovering it is a project. Experts can help, as science is the primary source of truth. Thus, the modern individual might seek out therapists or read self-help books. Or they might turn to geneticists who'll read their DNA for hints of their ancestry. Unlike the premodern thinker, the modern one thinks a great deal about questions like *Who am I?* They are seeking not just any identity, but their true identity.

In contrast to the premodern self, the postmodern self isn't inherited by birth. And in contrast to the modern self, it's not something that needs to be discovered. Postmodern selves are merely temporary personal creations.[17] Postmodern thinkers change the nature of their selves at will. They're comfortable with internal inconsistencies. To the postmoderns, identities are experimental, playful. The question they ask themselves is not *Who am I?* but *Who do I want to be today?*

In a postmodern world, for example, a person experiencing same-sex desire might recognize it but feel no need to make it a permanent part of their identity. They're more likely to embrace the idea of being "queer" (non-heterosexual but not in any specific way) or prefer not to label their sexual orientation at all. Likewise, a person might identify as gender fluid, rejecting both the idea of the gender binary and the idea that gender is a stable trait. A postmodern thinker with African ancestry might argue that they're "post-Black," a term that refers to the idea that there are as many ways to be Black as there are Black people making choices about how to be Black on any given day.[18]

If our identities can be fluid, perhaps our organizations can be more fluid too. Modern organizations with their strict hierarchies, rigid divisions of labor, rationalized order, and bureaucratic policies violate postmodern sensibilities. The postmodern thinker is more interested in flexibility than stability. When they can, they may opt out of participating in these organizations or participate in disruptive ways.

A more fluid way of organizing work, for example, is the gig economy. **Gig work** refers to a segment of the labor market in which companies contract with individuals to complete one short-term job at a time. These folks work for companies like Uber, DoorDash, and TaskRabbit.

This is quite postmodern. If a modern worker might become the employee of a single bureaucratic company that pays a salary, gig workers develop at-will relationships with one or more companies and collect one-off fees. They can work any given day, or not. They can work a long day, or a short one. They can Uber one day and TaskRabbit the next. And they can continue all these patterns or discontinue them as they see fit. This is a postmodern way of working, one that fluidly shifts and changes at the whim of the individual.

Is life really postmodern now? Leading sociologists generally say no.[19] Despite signs of postmodern organization, much of our life is still highly rationalized, most of our organizations remain bureaucratic, and divisions of labor still slot us into rather rigid and hierarchical roles. Most of us are not gig workers. And those of us that are still have to go to the DMV. So though postmodernism is an intriguing area of research—and this chapter isn't done with it yet—most sociologists agree that it's premature to say our societies are now wholly postmodern.

In fact, despite the intrigue of postmodern ideas, daily life in the United States is still quite patterned. There are regularities in people's behaviors and interactions that extend even beyond bureaucracies. Sociologists call these patterns social institutions and they are, alongside organizations, another form of social coordination that emerged with the modern era, one that has the potential to incorporate not just hundreds but millions of people.

gig work
a segment of the labor market in which companies contract with individuals to complete one short-term job at a time

THE SOCIAL INSTITUTION

When societies were smaller and life was simpler, all areas of life were overlapping. Members of foraging groups folded their hunting-and-gathering activities into their politics, the education of their youth, their religious practices, and the birthing and raising of babies. Together, they shared responsibility for these things.

Under the more complex conditions of modern societies, however, these different areas of life function as independently organized arenas. Sociologists

social institutions
widespread and
enduring patterns
of interaction with
which we respond
to categories of
human need

came to call these arenas **social institutions**, defined as widespread and enduring patterns of interaction with which we respond to categories of human need.[20] These are collective solutions to personal problems, ones that span whole societies.

Social institutions—or just "institutions"—are really just two things: an *idea* (that's the category of need) and a related set of formal and informal *practices* (these are the patterns of interaction).[21] Consider, for instance, the institution of Education. Most Americans agree that young people should be educated in such a way as to prepare them for citizenship and the workplace. Thus, education is an idea that most Americans share. To this end, there are a set of practices. Some of these are informal, or the stuff of folkways and mores (like back-to-school shopping). Some are formal, made into laws and policies (like the requirement that all children be schooled through at least eighth grade). Altogether, these practices turn the abstract idea of education into concrete interactions.

Several contemporary areas of life are arguably *institutionalized*; that is, sufficiently patterned to qualify as a social institution.[22] We're born into an important one: the Family, an institution that provides interpersonal intimacy, childrearing, and elder care. While we're still children, we're entered into Education, an institution that socializes and trains a next generation of workers. Throughout our lives, we participate in the Economy, an institution that regulates the production and consumption of goods and services. And we're subject to the Law, an institution that sets formal rules, settles disputes, and administers criminal punishment. The nature of the societies we live in is determined by the State, institutionalized patterns of interaction that involve governing a territory and its citizens.

Two additional examples of institutions, Religion and Health, will be discussed in more depth in the following sections. Health is an example of an especially modern institution, while Religion has distinctly postmodern characteristics.

Health: A modern institution

In premodern times, disease and injury were treated with a mixture of magic and medicine. Foraging groups shared knowledge about medicinal plants, and traditional remedies were passed down through generations. Spiritual healers would supplement treatments with calls for supernatural intervention.

Today, the provision of health care is a social institution. The institution rests on the idea that we should be able to live without illness, injury, or pain to the greatest degree possible. And the practices involve formal organizations with rationalized bureaucracies as well as a whole host of informal everyday practices.

The social institution of Health is also distinctly modern. Folk knowledge has been displaced by biometrics, randomized trials, and diagnostic technologies. Treatment plans are rationalized: designed to achieve maximal usefulness for the largest amount of people. Authority is rational-legal, based

In this image, neatly organized shelves of carefully labeled pharmaceuticals are doled out by authorized experts following clear rules. This is what it looks like for medicine to be modern.

on principles believed to produce a correct way of doing things. The explicit goal is to develop increasingly effective treatments for enhancing life and staving off death.

To meet these goals, the institution of Health involves bureaucratic organizations. These include pharmaceutical and health insurance companies alongside hospitals and urgent-care clinics. Professional organizations like the American Medical Association advocate for members of the profession, while others advocate on behalf of patients and other health-care workers. Support groups like Alcoholics Anonymous and companies like Massage Envy are also organizations involved in the institution of Health. So are fitness clubs, public pools, and manufacturers of medical equipment.

Individuals involved in the health-care system play many roles, including patient, doctor, nurse, researcher, administrator, insurance agent, and trainer. These are elaborate and hierarchical divisions of labor. Doctors, for instance, are never *just* doctors. They're pediatricians, gynecologists, radiologists, or neurologists. People in all these roles are expected to perform their duties within their organizations according to rigid rulebooks. People who perform the duties of others or deviate from the rules are negatively sanctioned.

Whatever role we play, we all participate in producing patterns of inter-action that sustain the social institution of Health, both inside and outside of formal organizations. The relevant patterns of interaction, in other words, include all the things we routinely do as individuals. On any given day in America, kids with the flu are being served chicken soup, adults are calling in sick to work, and boxes of tissues are flying off shelves. Regular activities— like eating our vegetables and getting exercise—also contribute to patterns devoted to maintaining our collective health. Some of us seek out alternative and complementary medicines, like acupuncture and chiropractic care.

Health, then, is a distinct social institution. It involves widespread and enduring patterns of interaction. And those patterns add up to a system with the stated goal of keeping us as healthy as we can be. It's imperfect and it doesn't benefit everyone equally. Nonetheless, if we personally want to maximize our health, we'll interact with the institution and become part of its patterns.

Religion: Flirting with postmodernity

Modern thinkers look to science as a source of truth, but that doesn't mean that religion no longer plays a role in our lives. In fact, sociologists have found that people today need faith exactly because rationalization leads to the disenchantment of the world. Religiosity gives life meaning and purpose, something we might crave especially because so much of life is so mind-numbingly bureaucratic.

Much of the way we practice religion today, though, is distinctly modern. Organized religion is a bureaucratic affair. It involves formal doctrine, strict hierarchies of religious authority, and a clear and relatively rigid division of labor. Roles include worshippers, religious leaders, theologians, and armies of different kinds of volunteers. And these individuals are managed by organizations, from houses of worship that serve small communities to the likes of the Roman Catholic Church, which purports to serve over a billion faithful worldwide.

Many religions are also rationalized. Their leaders make measured decisions about how to attract and retain adherents. They consider how to maximize donations and strategically invest and spend organizational funds. They systematically educate and socialize new generations of religious advisers. And they involve divisions of labor that are ultimately impersonal, allowing anyone with the proper qualifications to fill a range of preexisting roles.

Though not every religious person practices their faith in exactly the same way, people who adhere to the same religion tend to engage in similar behaviors and believe in similar things. They congregate in specific places at specific times, practice the same rituals, try to obey the same moral guidelines, and promote the same values. Thus, institutionalized religion produces reliable patterns of interaction.

Religion, then, is a modern social institution, one that tends to our desire to live morally good, meaningful lives. Yet, there are also postmodern elements to how people practice religion today.[23] The number of Americans who identify with organized religion, for example, is shrinking. Three-quarters of Americans between eighteen and twenty-nine now describe themselves as "spiritual but not religious." They embrace a supernatural force in the world but resist identifying with any fixed identity and formal set of practices.

People who identify this way tend to favor a personal relationship with a higher power. They may also develop religious practices unique to them, adopting rituals, symbols, myths, and values from a multitude of faith traditions. Why not? A postmodern thinker is unconcerned with whether their chosen religious practices reflect *Truth* with a capital *T*. They're more interested in listening to their gut and following their heart.

Let's consider two examples. First, we have a self-consciously postmodern religious experiment that calls itself Emerging.[24] Emerging is a group of organizations that reject fixed orthodoxy and aim instead to engage spiritual people in a "conversation." These congregations don't identify a right and wrong way to worship and are open to change. Some leaders host dialogues instead of delivering sermons, rejecting the hierarchy inherent in traditional congregations. Many are interfaith, welcoming people from many different religious backgrounds. This is not "a new religion," writes one advocate, "but, rather, a new way of being religious."[25]

This megachurch in Houston, Texas, draws nearly 50,000 people each week. Held in an arena where the Houston Rockets used to play, the Sunday service is distinctly modern: organized, predictable, high-tech, and efficient.

Second, there is the rise of the megachurch. Defined as churches with 2,000 or more members, megachurches are modern organizations. They're complex and finely tuned machines that produce weekly concert-worthy performances in sometimes stadium-sized venues. People who attend these services often experience *collective effervescence*, powerful emotions that sweep through large groups. Many others watch these services on the web or on television, as most of these churches stream their services on the internet or host television programs. Some are even franchised like McDonald's, with "video venues" in multiple locations screening the day's sermon to hundreds or thousands of people who've congregated in satellite locations. Megachurches undoubtedly deliver meaningful religious experiences to many people. They're also modern institutions: their operations are efficient, the product is predictable, they employ nonhuman technology, and they aim to reach the largest possible audience.

Comparing megachurches with Emerging shows how modern and postmodern elements coexist in contemporary religious practice. Religion continues to operate as a social institution: an idea made concrete with widely followed formal and informal routines. But there are postmodern thinkers who question the validity of notions like "truth" and the right of others to dictate their personal practices.

These are fascinating trends, but unless we find postmodern ways of meeting all our needs, social institutions will persist, and so will their social patterns, divisions of labor, bureaucratic organizations, and hierarchies. Accordingly, while postmodern thinking may have undermined the rigidity of some of our social institutions, they still play a powerful role in our lives. The next two sections expand on this power.

THE INESCAPABILITY OF INSTITUTIONS

We don't opt in or out of social institutions as we please. They offer real solutions to problems that would be difficult for us to solve by ourselves, and provide a framework for achieving our goals. So participation in social institutions is not voluntary; daily life makes them essentially unavoidable. We really have little choice but to take part.

Consider this retelling of a blistering scene from the movie *The Devil Wears Prada*. The actor Meryl Streep plays Miranda Priestly, the silver-haired and sharp-tongued editor of an elite high-fashion magazine. Andy, played by Anne Hathaway, is Priestly's newly hired assistant. A fashion outsider, Andy's only there to pull a paycheck as she pursues a career in journalism, an occupation she considers more important than fashion.

In one scene, Andy makes the mistake of scoffing as Priestly is choosing between two belts with silver buckles, both in a light blue color. "It's a tough call," says one of Priestly's other assistants. "They're *soooo* different." Andy can barely tell the belts apart, prompting the scoff. All eyes turn to her. The gaggle of assistants freeze.

"Something funny?" Priestly asks. Caught off guard, Andy plays dumb, responding, "I'm still learning about this stuff and uh . . ."

Priestly interrupts her. "Thisssss sssstuff?" she responds, drawing out the words threateningly. "Oh, OK. I see. You think this has nothing to do with you." Looking her up and down icily, she says:

> You go to your closet and you select, I don't know, that lumpy blue sweater, for instance, because you're trying to tell the world that you take yourself too seriously to care about what you put on your back. But what you don't know is that that sweater is not just blue, it's not turquoise, it's not lapis, it's actually cerulean.

The sweater is cerulean, Priestly explains, because mega-designer Oscar de la Renta did a collection of gowns in the color and the iconic Yves Saint Laurent followed up with a runway show with cerulean military jackets, after which the color was prominent in the collections of eight additional designers. From there, Priestly continued, speaking to Andy: "It filtered down through the department stores and then trickled down into some tragic Casual Corner where you, no doubt, fished it out of some clearance bin."

With a mocking smile, Priestly concludes:

> That blue represents millions of dollars and countless jobs and it's sort of comical that you think you've made a choice that exempts you from the fashion industry when, in fact, you're wearing a sweater that was selected for you by the people in this room. From a pile of "stuff."

In response to Andy's scoff, Priestly laid bare Andy's powerlessness to escape the institution she disparaged. If Andy thought she was exempt from the system by claiming not to care, she was sorely mistaken. Bargain-bin sweaters don't blink in and out of existence like quantum particles; they're the tail end of an elaborate retail process organized by the Economy. If we're wearing clothes, we're part of it.

We participate in social institutions as a matter of course, then. And few of us ever try to avoid them entirely. If we did, we'd quickly discover that doing so would require almost impossible sacrifices. Christopher Knight, the North Pond Hermit discussed in Chapter 1, is an example of what it might look like. Recall that he lived alone in the woods of Maine for twenty-seven years. No social institutions there, just squirrels. So he didn't make supply runs to Costco. But he did routinely raid campgrounds and cabins. When his camp was discovered, it was filled with useful things: food and clothes, flashlights and batteries, toilet paper and coffee filters, thousands of books, even a television.

Knight was a lone hermit in the woods, but he was still dependent on and accountable to institutions. The glasses he wore for twenty years, for example, were a product of the health-care system. The vacation cabins he raided provided summertime rest and relaxation for families. By virtue of stealing, he may have personally avoided stores, but his actions were dependent on other people's participation in the Economy. And, of course, he ultimately encountered the Law.

It was his participation in these institutions, in fact, that was his undoing. If Knight had truly been outside of society, no one would've ever known he was there. But that would have involved providing for his own needs entirely—a different experiment altogether. So though he made his participation in institutions invisible, he was still very much a part of them.

The most innovative and daring among us may figure out a way to wholly escape a social institution or two—Knight did about as well as he could—but few of us will ever be able to fully do so, and most of us are as embedded as Andy. Institutions are the fabric of contemporary life, and we have little choice but to get dressed.

INSTITUTIONALIZED IDEOLOGIES

ideologies
shared ideas about how human life should be organized

Social institutions are also powerful in that they uphold specific **ideologies**, or shared ideas about how human life should be organized. These are morally charged beliefs about right and wrong ways to respond to human needs and participate in everyday life. They're both prescriptive and proscriptive, telling us what we should and shouldn't do. By participating in social institutions, we're exposed to their ideologies and pressed to behave in ways that uphold them. Often, we do, and rather comfortably, because we've been socialized into them.

As an analogy, consider one of the most famous board games of all time: Monopoly.[26] The game has a set of rules that creates widespread and enduring patterns of interaction. It has rationalized divisions of labor (tenants, landlords). It even has organizations (the prison, the bank). Playing by the rules involves rolling the die, following the path of the board, and taking our victories and defeats as they come, all while trying to win the game by accumulating the most money and bankrupting every other player. Overwhelmingly, we play by these rules simply because we've learned that it's the right way to play.

Any of us could change the rules at any time, but we mostly don't. Not necessarily because we like the rules as they are, but because it simply never occurs to us. As Albert Einstein once quipped: "What does a fish know about the water in which he swims all his life?"[27] Since the fish has never experienced an alternative reality, the saying implies, it never thinks to notice the one it's in. Most of us accept our social institutions as they are, if only because we've never experienced life in any other way.

Faced with someone who wants to change the rules, we may even resist and defend the rules as if they were our own invention. As Harold Garfinkel discovered when he asked unsuspecting students to adjust to violations of the rules of tic-tac-toe: *Changing the rules is against the rules.* But who made up the rules?

Elizabeth Magie did.[28] Growing up during industrialization, she was troubled by the role land ownership played in the rising level of economic inequality. She wanted to draw Americans' attention to landlord-tenant relations, which she saw as draining money from the poor and enriching the already rich. So she invented a game.

Magie's game, which she patented in 1904, came with two sets of rules. One set of rules will be familiar to most people today; it enabled some players to collect land, build houses and hotels, and charge rent, while forcing others into bankruptcy. The other set of rules limited the runaway accumulation of wealth, resulting in a more even distribution of income. It also offered free college instead of prison time and included a public park instead of a parking lot. She named the game played with the first set of rules the Landlord's Game and the game played with the

Today's Monopoly glorifies the amassing of great wealth, but the original version did exactly the opposite. Designed at a time when land ownership was increasing income inequality, the Landlord's Game emphasized the plight of the renter.

second set of rules Prosperity. Magie hoped people would play both games and realize that the latter set of rules was fairer and more humane.

She asked the board game company Parker Brothers to distribute it, but they declined. In the next few decades, though, the Landlord's Game (which ultimately became known by several names, including Business, Finance, Inflation and, finally, Monopoly) became an underground success. People copied down the rules, made their own boards, and used household items as tokens representing each player: coins, jewelry, and, yes, thimbles. Nearly twenty years after Magie invented the games, Parker Brothers decided to release Monopoly but not her companion game, Prosperity.

Most of us don't know that Monopoly was originally part of a game that was supposed to make us feel *bad* for accumulating wealth. We don't know because the rules were written, and then changed, before any of us were born. We have no personal knowledge of the game's origins. Given this, it's easy to play by the Landlord's Game's rules and think *this is the right way to play*.

Likewise, we accept much of the way our health-care system, government, and family life are organized and internalize their ideologies too. As far as we know, things have always been done this way. We would need an occasion, a probing one, to think to question the rules. And a reason, a good one, to want to change them.

Thus, social institutions socialize us into their ideologies. Monopoly, for example, teaches us to play greedily. The game is designed so that to do otherwise is to risk losing. We take someone else's last dollar because we need money to survive our next roll of the die. We may even learn to feel good about taking everyone's money. We may not naturally be brutally competitive, but within the confines of the game, we may act as if we are.

This is not so far from reality. The economic system in which we live—which will be explored in great detail in the next chapter—makes winners and losers of us in real life too. Other social institutions also play a significant role in determining the paths we take. And they do so *jointly*. This fact has inspired sociologists to describe the collection of social institutions in any given society as the *social structure*.

THE SOCIAL STRUCTURE

Though each social institution addresses a distinct arena of life, they are also intertwined. Schools, for example, are part of the social institution of Education, but curriculums are designed to give students the knowledge and skills they'll need as future workers in the Economy. Schools also support the Family by "babysitting" children from morning to early afternoon, allowing parents to work. In working, and thereby earning and spending money to raise their kids, parents expand their state's tax base. This helps the State raise money not only for schools but also Health and the Law. Tax dollars also help schools pay for free or low-cost lunches for students from low-income families, helping supplement children's nutrition and making up for low wages. Everything is interconnected.

Social institutions are also connected by the ideologies they reflect. Often, the same ideologies resonate across most or all of our social institutions. The belief that we should *play to win* is taught to us by games like Monopoly, but that's not the only place we learn it. We're encouraged to get the best possible grades in school and go to the best college we can. Wanting to earn high wages and rise in occupational hierarchies drives much of our economic activity. We're even implicitly encouraged to marry the most attractive spouse and raise the most successful children. Meanwhile, the self-help industry encourages us to try to be our best self. We don't just learn ideologies from one institution at a time. We learn them from many all at once, making their socializing effects all the more powerful.

social structure
the entire set of interlocking social institutions in which we live

Sociologists use the phrase **social structure**—or just "structure"—to describe the entire set of interlocking social institutions in which we live. We call it a structure because together our institutions create a relatively stable framework. This, a structural functionalist might argue, is what makes societies work. Ideally, all a society's social institutions, interlocked and in ideological harmony, provide for all our needs in a predictable and orderly way. The social structure, in other words, is what makes life hum right along.

Functionalists are not wrong to notice this. Social institutions really do address difficult-to-meet needs, however imperfectly. And because they're slow to change, they're helpful for planning for the future. If we want to be a doctor, for instance, there's a framework for doing so. We know we have to go to college and then medical school. It's rational to do this because we can trust that a medical degree will still be a requirement to begin a career in medicine when we finish our schooling eight or so years later. The stability of institutions, and the relationships between them, provides a framework that enables us to make decisions about our future and achieve our goals.

Conflict theorists, however, observe that the social structure isn't equally helpful to everyone. Sometimes the framework that's available is of little use to us. If we want to be a doctor, but we can't afford the cost of tuition or time out of the workforce, we probably won't become one. It won't matter how much medical knowledge and experience we amass on our own, we'll still be a criminal if we practice without a license.

The social structure, then, doesn't merely offer us opportunities; it offers us a specific mix of opportunities and constraints. And not everyone receives the same mix. It depends on whether we live in a rural or urban environment, whether our local schools are high or low performing, and whether we're immigrants or descendants of immigrants. It depends, too, on the amount of money our parents or guardians have when raising us. The features of our lives that determine our mix of opportunities and constraints is described as our **structural position**.

structural position
the features of our lives that determine our mix of opportunities and constraints

The power of position

Our structural position influences all manner of outcomes. Perhaps the most famous demonstration of this comes from Émile Durkheim, the sociologist who brought us functionalism and social facts. In the late 1800s, Durkheim was on a mission to prove that the study of society could offer useful insights that we couldn't get by studying individuals alone. He accomplished this with a book about something previously believed to be purely psychological: death by suicide.[29]

Durkheim observed that people with some kinds of social identities, and in some kinds of societies, are more likely to die by suicide than others. Protestants did so more often than Catholics, for instance, and Scandinavians more often than other Europeans. Were the underlying psychologies of Protestants and Catholics so different? Were Scandinavians biologically unusual? Durkheim wondered whether structural factors could better explain these differences.

He began looking for sociological variables that might increase overall rates of suicide and discovered evidence that both integration (social cohesion) and regulation (social control) were influential. When either is very high or very low, he argued, death by suicide increases. He published his results in 1897 in a book titled *Suicide: A Study in Sociology*.

Durkheim identified four types of suicide that could be attributed to structural factors. First, in *egoistic suicide,* social institutions fail to ensure social cohesion and people are left isolated from their social group (in this case, very low integration predicts suicide). Second, in *altruistic suicide,* people are socialized to identify with the group instead of the self and may choose to sacrifice themselves for it (this is suicide prompted by very high integration). Third, in *fatalistic suicide,* a person's opportunities are blocked by rigid and oppressive institutions, leading them to think that death is the only way out (suicide in response to very high regulation). And, fourth, in *anomic suicide,* institutions fail, resulting in a normlessness that makes a person feel that life is meaningless (suicide in response to very low regulation). In doing this research, Durkheim illustrated the power of structural position, concluding that while our personal qualities and life experiences influence whether we are likely to die by suicide, the kind of society we live in and our social groups matter too.

Today, sociologists are still discovering social causes for outcomes previously believed to be purely psychological. In 2007, for example, a team of sociologists did a similar study. This time, instead of studying the decision to kill oneself, they studied the decision to kill someone else.[30]

As with suicide, rates of murder by serial killer vary. California has almost twice as many per capita as Florida and almost five times as many as Pennsylvania and Ohio. Do some states make serial killing more tempting than others? Perhaps killing is easier in large urban areas that allow for anonymity and offer more potential victims. Perhaps this is especially true if potential victims are made vulnerable by thin social networks; that is, if they are divorced, unemployed, or living alone.

The sociologists found that these structural factors did in fact help to predict the rate of serial killing. Murders were higher in states with a higher percentage of its population living in cities and in states where people were more vulnerable. So we might say that some potentially violent people are "structurally positioned" to kill serially, while others are not.

These two studies—on suicide and serial murder—are evidence that the social structure is a real force. It influences who lives, who dies, and who kills.

Our individual personality traits always matter, as do luck and chance, but the trajectory of our lives also depends on the social structural context in which we begin and move through life. Depending on our structural position, we'll have more and better, or fewer and worse, opportunities (to do both good, bad, and even sad things). The functionalists are right, then, that the social structure offers benefits. But the conflict theorists are right that it doesn't necessarily offer equal benefits to everyone.

Notably, these structural differences don't just affect individuals randomly. The social structure offers certain *kinds* of people more or fewer opportunities than others. Our social identities—our age, race, religion, gender, sexual orientation, disability status, and more—also position us in the social structure. They influence how others see us and whether we inspire support, suspicion, or derision.

STRUCTURAL POSITIONS AND SOCIAL HIERARCHIES

Let's return to the world of sports. In the early 1900s, immigrant Jewish families found themselves isolated in dense, economically strained, urban neighborhoods. Excluded from higher education, they had few opportunities to escape from poverty. One thing they did have? Basketball. Well into the 1930s, Jewish men absolutely dominated on the basketball court.

Why basketball? Unlike other sports, basketball fit the tight spaces and tight budgets faced by inner-city families. Basketball courts are relatively small, and the game requires only a ball and a hoop. "You couldn't play football," said Red Auerbach, a former Jewish player and coach. "They had no fields for baseball. Everything was basketball."[31]

At the time, most colleges did not admit Jews, but they began changing their discriminatory policies when they realized they needed Jewish students if they wanted to field competitive basketball teams. This gave some Jewish men access to higher education and a path out of poverty. Dave Dabrow, a Jewish man who played professional basketball in that era, recalled: "It was absolutely a way out of the ghetto."[32]

After World War II, it became less acceptable in America to be anti-Semitic. At the same time, ethnic differences (whether one was Italian, Irish, or Polish, for example) became less significant than the color of one's skin. Eventually, many Jewish families achieved economic success, allowing them to move out of the inner cities and into the suburbs. This gave them access to other sports and alternative routes to economic success and social esteem.[33] Structurally positioned in ways that offered more paths to prosperity, Jewish boys began making choices from among a wider array of options.

As Jewish families were leaving the inner-city neighborhoods of the Northeast and Midwest, Black folks were moving in. It was part of the Great Migration out of the Jim Crow South. Soon young Black men came to dominate basketball. They did so for the same reasons young Jewish men did. And colleges would eventually cave to the same incentive to relax their discriminatory enrollment practices, making it a way for young Black men to escape disorganized neighborhoods.

In the early 1900s, young Jewish men dominated the sport of basketball. Like many Black men and women today, Jews were growing up in city centers too crowded for baseball, soccer, or football.

Of course, now we use stereotypes of Black people to explain why so many are so good at basketball, but this is an after-the-fact justification. The same was done for Jews. The sports editor of the *New York Daily News* in the 1930s, for example, drew on stereotypes of Jews as untrustworthy, explaining that they were good at basketball because "the game places a premium on an alert, scheming mind, flashy trickiness, artful dodging and general smart aleckness."[34] Moreover, he argued, Jews had the advantage of being short. This gave them "better balance and speed," traits considered at the time to be *the* critical advantage in the game.

At different times, young Jewish and Black men made similar choices because they had similar options. They had, in other words, similar structural positions. It would be correct to argue that they also had similarly *limited* structural positions. Social institutions are often designed such that they persistently favor some kinds of people over others. Sociologists call this **institutional discrimination**. For both Jewish and Black men, basketball seemed like a good option specifically because other good options were closed off. They were targets of institutional discrimination.

The consequence of widespread institutional discrimination is **social stratification**, a persistent sorting of social groups into enduring hierarchies.[35] The United States is a socially stratified society. Some kinds of people are persistently *advantaged*, or well served by our social institutions. Others are *disadvantaged*, neglected or harmed by them.

What this means is that a society doesn't need discriminatory individuals to produce discriminatory outcomes. All it needs is biased bureaucracies and inequitable institutions. If the systems in place predictably advantage some kinds of people and disadvantage others, the systems will produce distinct hierarchies that persist over generations. When sociology was new, this was a whole new way of understanding social inequality. We now recognize that social inequality is caused not only by interpersonal discrimination but also by our social institutions. Exactly how this works will be examined in great depth in the next three chapters. ■

institutional discrimination
widespread and enduring practices that persistently disadvantage some kinds of people while advantaging others

social stratification
a persistent sorting of social groups into enduring hierarchies

COMING UP...

CONTEMPORARY SOCIETIES are more complex than any in human history. They're more highly coordinated, more stiffly bureaucratized, and involve greater divisions of labor. Erected over lifetimes and steeled against change, the resulting institutions can be massive and slow moving. Thus, despite the introduction of postmodern thinking, social life is still structured.

This can be incredibly useful. The social structure meets needs that we would have a very hard time meeting on our own. It also provides the framework within which we make decisions and achieve our goals. The social structure, however, isn't equally useful to everyone. Depending on our structural position, it offers some of us more opportunities than others.

Because our structural positions are partly dependent on our social identities, our societies are not just unequal; they're discriminatory. This is called institutional discrimination. The outcome of this process is enduring social stratification.

The next three chapters build on these observations. Each addresses a different type of social inequality. One will address racial and ethnic inequality. Another will consider gender inequality. First up, though, is economic inequality. Chapter 7 describes how money is distributed in the United States, including *who* happens to have most of it. It considers an early critique of capitalism and tells the story of how capitalism has changed since the dawn of the United States. Finally, it asks you to think about what a fair economic system looks like.

7

ECONOMIC INEQUALITY

IN THIS **CHAPTER...**

THE LAST CHAPTER introduced the idea of *institutional discrimination*, a phenomenon in which social institutions are designed such that they persistently favor some kinds of people over others. This chapter considers how a specific institution — the economy — is designed. Three facts about the U.S. economy are key:

- First, the level of economic inequality — or the distance between the richest and the poorest people — is about as extreme today as it has ever been in American history.

- Second, the economy, as it's currently structured, generally preserves and even strengthens the advantages of the rich, or the *economic elite*.

- Third, the U.S. economy hasn't always been structured this way. The current level of inequality can be traced to decisions made since about 1980.

In exploring these facts, you'll be introduced to the work of Karl Marx, who's famous for an early critique of *free market capitalism*. You'll also learn about another of Max Weber's contributions to sociology: the *Protestant work ethic*, or the idea that one's character can and should be measured by one's dedication to paid work.
    This chapter then asks you to consider four questions:

- How much economic inequality is too much?

- How much poverty is tolerable?

- How much opportunity is enough?

- And what should be done about the fact that the economic elite tend to also hold other high-status identities?

Chapter 7 concludes by considering whether capitalism and its supposed nemesis — *socialism* — are true enemies.

"The law, in its majestic equality, forbids the rich as well as the poor to sleep under bridges."

—ANATOLE FRANCE

When the pandemic arrived in March 2020, Haverford College—a small school in Pennsylvania—shut down campus operations.[1] Administrators told students living in its residence halls to go home. At the time, Professor Anita Isaacs was teaching a class titled "Forced Migration and Refugees." For her students, the course material suddenly hit a little closer to home. Without warning, and against their wishes, they were fleeing for their lives.

When the course reconvened, it did so via videoconference. A student named Isabel joined the class from her family's seaside summer home in Maine. Chace joined from her home in California, one with "sweeping views" overlooking the San Francisco Bay. Tatiana went home to a family in crisis. Her parents' sole source of income—a food truck serving "Latin soul" cuisine—was struggling to survive; she was considering getting a job at a grocery store. Sophie didn't go home at all. Her mother couldn't afford the plane ticket to Russia, so Haverford allowed her to stay on campus. She was one of 135 students who had nowhere to go.

Professor Isaacs and her students saw all of this from their computers. Pixels arranged in tiny boxes revealed who did and didn't have the financial resources to make it safely and comfortably through the crisis. Some students conferenced in from private bedrooms in large, quiet houses; others, from living rooms in crowded apartments. Some sat behind expensive computers surfing on high-speed internet; others froze and pixelated as they tried to participate on their phones. Some could point their computer cameras at their spacious backyards; others' backgrounds were the residence hall furniture familiar to all of them. And some disappeared altogether, faced with crises much larger than a lost semester of effort. "It's as though [we all] had a front-row view on American inequality," Professor Isaacs said.

Chapters 7 through 9 directly address inequality in America. The next chapter will consider the treatment of immigrants and racial and ethnic minorities in schools and on the streets. The chapter after that will focus on gendered oppression at work and at home. This one will address economic inequality, the kind that was on full view in Professor Isaacs's course.

As an introduction to a sociology of economic inequality, this chapter traces the prehistory and near-history of the economic system known as capitalism. It considers who capitalism is designed to advantage and disadvantage. It also asks you to consider what levels of inequality, poverty, and opportunity are compatible with a just society, and to notice how strongly economic inequality correlates with social identities. Some of these themes will be reprised in Chapter 12, which discusses global inequality.

But first, an overview of economic inequality in the United States.

THE NUMBERS

Sociologists use the word **capital** to describe the resources we use to get things we want and need. Such resources can be economic, social, or cultural. The focus of this chapter is **economic capital**, financial resources that are or can be converted into money, including cash, investments, and valuable goods and property. Other forms of capital will be discussed in Chapter 10.

We measure economic capital with two variables: income and wealth. *Income* refers to steady sources of money. These sources include wages or salary as well as regular interest payments, social assistance, pensions, or alimony. *Wealth* refers to money sitting in the bank and ownership of economic assets, minus debts. Assets include investments like stocks and bonds and anything else a person could conceivably sell: property, businesses, cars, boats, or expensive art, for instance.

Income and wealth correlate positively: People with high incomes tend to have high levels of wealth, and people with low incomes tend to have little wealth, no wealth, or negative wealth (they owe more than they own). In part, this is because income can produce wealth (for example, high incomes enable saving), and wealth can also produce income (savings can be invested and earn interest).

Income in America

To describe the financial well-being of the American people, sociologists generally use one of three *measures of central tendency*, or numbers that attempt to describe a population by referring to a midpoint. The *median* is the middle value among a set of numbers arranged from lowest to highest. The *mean* is the sum of all values divided by the number of values (most people know it as an *average*). And the *mode* is the value among a range of values that occurs most often. In short, the median is *middle*, the mean is *mathematical*, and the mode is *most*.

The mean is an intuitive way to measure a population's income because it includes everyone in the math. Including very, very high numbers at the top of the income scale, however, may give the impression that average Americans

capital
the resources we use to get things we want and need

economic capital
financial resources that are or can be converted into money

are doing better financially than they are. In other words, though the mean is a true average, the resulting figure doesn't always describe the financial situation of the typical person very well.

As an illustration, consider the twenty-three workers in Figure 7.1, lined up from left to right according to a hypothetical weekly income. The first ten people earn just $50 a week. The next eight earn $100. Three earn $1,000. And the final two earn an eye-popping $10,000 a week. Our first measure of central tendency, the mode, is $50. More people earn that level of income than any other. Our second, the median, is the middle number: $100, or the income of the twelfth person in the row of twenty-three. Our third, the mean, or mathematical average, is $926 (which is the sum of everyone's weekly income divided by the number of workers).

If you had to pick just one of these numbers to describe this group's income, which would you choose? The mode (far left) can be deceiving because it merely captures what number occurs most often. In this case, it's $50, but more than half the sample earns more than that. The mathematical mean (far right) makes it seem as if the group overall is earning a lot more than they are. The median (in the middle) isn't perfect—it doesn't capture the outliers at the top very well and it ignores the fact that ten people are earning very low incomes—but by virtue of sitting in the middle, the median does a decent job of characterizing the group as a whole.

So what is the median income in the United States? For individuals, it's $35,977 a year.[2] Half of Americans earn more and half earn less. For households—or groups of people living together and sharing resources—it's $68,703 per year.[3] Half of the households in the United States bring in more and half bring in less.

To understand the *distribution* of income, or how it spreads out across Americans, scholars divide U.S. households into fifths: five groups of households ranging from those with the lowest income to those with the highest. Households in the lowest fifth earn a mean of about $15,000 a year, while those in the highest fifth earn about $254,000.[4] That's the difference between earning $1,250 a month and earning over $21,100 a month.

FIGURE 7.1

Illustration of Different Measures of Central Tendency

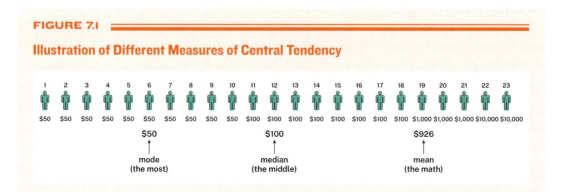

If this sounds like a big difference, the sums at the very top are even more extreme. The highest-earning 10 percent of households make more than $28,500 every month.[5] And the highest-earning 1 percent—with an annual salary of nearly $1,500,000—make about $125,000 a month. A household in the top 1 percent earns more in two weeks than a middle-class household makes all year.

When a resource is distributed unevenly, sociologists describe the distribution as *disproportionate*, which means that something is asymmetrical or unbalanced; literally, out of proportion. How disproportionate is the distribution of income in the United States? Well, of all the income earned by all Americans in any given year, the bottom 90 percent of households share about half of it. The other half goes to the top 10 percent.[6] And nearly half of that half—about 22 percent of all income—goes to the top 1 percent.

Wealth in America

Figure 7.2 shows that wealth is even more unevenly distributed than income.[7] While the richest 1 percent of American households earn almost a quarter of the income, they also control about a third of the wealth. The next richest 9 percent have 38 percent, meaning that the wealthiest 10 percent share 71 percent of all wealth in the United States. The wealthiest of the wealthy—America's 651 billionaires—hold twice the wealth held by the entire bottom half of the U.S. population.[8] Along with the remaining members of the top

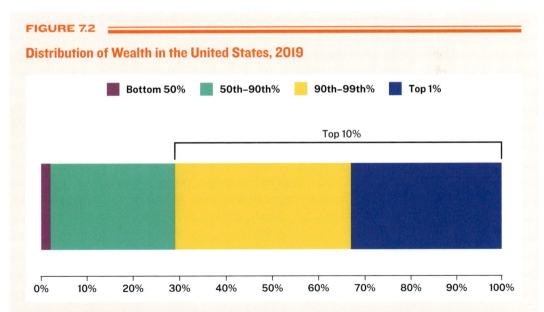

FIGURE 7.2

Distribution of Wealth in the United States, 2019

■ Bottom 50%   ■ 50th–90th%   ■ 90th–99th%   ■ Top 1%

Top 10%

0%   10%   20%   30%   40%   50%   60%   70%   80%   90%   100%

SOURCE: Jesse Bricker, Sarena Goodman, Kevin B. Moore, and Alice Henriques Volz, "Wealth and Income Concentration in the SCF: 1989–2019," FEDS Notes, Board of Governors of the Federal Reserve System, September 28, 2020, https://doi.org/10.17016/2380-7172.2795.

1 percent, billionaires are the **economic elite**, the minority of people who control a disproportionate amount of wealth.

The rest of the wealth—the 29 percent held by the bottom 90 percent of U.S. households—isn't spread out evenly either. Almost all of it belongs to the next richest 40 percent. That means that the poorest 50 percent of Americans have almost no wealth at all or, more commonly, negative wealth. They're in debt.

If you were the median American income earner, personally earning $35,977 a year, how many years would you have to work to earn what the richest households in America have in wealth? If you started at $0, and had no expenses, you'd have to work for 71 years to earn the average wealth of the top 10 percent. To reach the top 1 percent, you'd have to work for 385 years. To reach the top 0.1 percent, you'd have to work for 2,024 years. In other words, you'd have to work from now until the year 4044. And to be as rich as the richest man in America? As of early 2021, that was Elon Musk, the cofounder and CEO of Tesla, who has a net worth of $202 billion. You would have to work 5,614,698 years. That's 28 times longer than the furthest estimates of how long humans have been on this earth.

How did some of us get so rich?

THE PREHISTORY OF ECONOMIC INEQUALITY

The foraging groups in which we lived for the vast majority of human history were surprisingly egalitarian compared with modern human societies.[9] In small groups, decisions could be made more or less democratically, with everyone's input. Leadership was often shared and less materially rewarded. Economic inequality was limited too. Foraging societies were on the move, so a person could only own as much as they could carry.

Not so today.

The seeds of social stratification were planted when humans invented agriculture about 10,000 years ago.[10] Farming could produce large amounts of food, but it was unreliable. Sometimes crops died, or flooded, or were eaten by pests. Sometimes people starved. Foraging groups could simply move along if the weather didn't cooperate or a fungus, insect, or rodent decimated a food supply, but farmers couldn't as easily pick up and go. Farming is more high risk than foraging, even if it also sometimes offers higher rewards.

This uneven mix of bounty and scarcity motivated people to stockpile food, just in case. In the conditions of plenty that the foragers enjoyed, there was no value to having extra food. They simply chose environments in which food was plentiful. But in high-risk conditions like agriculture, surplus is the difference between life and death. Insecurity, then, motivated people to hoard whatever extra they acquired and use it to protect themselves against the possibility of scarcity.

When farmers were able to stockpile food beyond what they needed to survive, even in the medium term, they could trade it to those who needed it. Lucky farmers could sell their surplus for more land and animals. As this process repeated itself over generations, levels of social inequality rose. Whereas graves had once been similar from one to the next, now some people were being buried with signs of wealth. Skeletal remains revealed a rise in health disparities; some people were eating better than others and suffered less from injury and disease. And homes began to diversify in size and differ in the value of their contents.

Over the next several thousand years, various forms of institutionalized economic inequality would take hold in different places and in different times. In *caste systems*, ones found in parts of South Asia, people stayed in whatever stratified layer of society they were born into for a lifetime, passing their status to their children. In the *feudal systems* typical of Europe in the Middle Ages, rich and powerful individuals born into nobility reigned over a peasant class; the peasants worked the noblemen's land and received protection from neighboring armies. Under *enslavement systems*, an economic elite was allowed to legally own a class of humans and exploit them for their labor.

In all these systems, one's place in the economic hierarchy was determined by birth or conquest. In other words, there was little to no **social mobility**, or opportunity to move up or down in the economic hierarchy. Under conditions of low social mobility, it's extraordinarily hard to either lose or gain ground. Under conditions of high social mobility, it's easier to do so.

social mobility
opportunity to move up or down in the economic hierarchy

In most parts of the world, systems with no or very low social mobility were gradually replaced by systems that allowed for greater movement: *class systems*, or ones that sort people into different positions in an economic hierarchy but also allow them to rise or fall. Class-based societies like the United States produce much higher levels of social stratification than were found in foraging societies, but unlike caste and feudal societies and ones based on enslavement, they theoretically allow people to move up and down the economic ladder according to their talent, effort, and luck.

Is that how it works?

THE NEAR HISTORY OF ECONOMIC INEQUALITY

The class system we find in most rich democracies today, including the United States, emerged with industrialization. Beginning in the 1700s, industrialization swept across the Western world, ushering in a modern, rationalized economy that featured things like mechanization, assembly lines, and impersonal relations between workers and employers. Industrialization drew many people out of rural communities, where they mostly worked in small shops and on farms, into cities, where they worked in factories and mines. In return, they received a **wage**, cash payments given to workers in exchange for their labor.

This was the advent of modern **capitalism**, an economic system based on private ownership of the resources used to create wealth and the right of

wage
cash payments given to workers in exchange for their labor

capitalism
an economic system based on private ownership of the resources used to create wealth and the right of individuals to personally profit

German social scientist Karl Marx watched in real time as Europe industrialized. Appalled at the emerging economic inequality, he predicted that workers would revolt against their employers and capitalism would ultimately collapse.

proletariat
a class of people who are employed by others and work for a wage

bourgeoisie
a class of people who employ the workers

means of production
resources that can be used to create wealth

labor
the work people can do with their bodies and minds

individuals to personally profit. Under industrial capitalism, humans began producing, buying, and selling goods and services at rates previously unimaginable. Competition between companies drove innovation that enhanced our leisure, travel, communication, and medical care. Capitalism also facilitated affordable prices, bringing us an unprecedented level of luxury and convenience. By these measures, it raised the standard of living for billions of people.

But there was a dark side to capitalism too. Or so insisted Karl Marx, who would become one of the most notorious social scientists in history.

Living in Europe during the Industrial Revolution, Marx (1818–1883) watched as capitalism changed the lives of the people around him. Specifically, he noted the emergence of two new social and economic classes: the **proletariat**, people employed by others who worked for a wage, and the **bourgeoisie**, the people who employed the workers. The bourgeoisie owned the **means of production**, resources that could be used to create wealth (like land, factories, and money to invest). The proletariat owned only their own **labor**, the work they could do with their bodies and minds. The proletariat, then, sold their labor to the bourgeoisie, who applied it as a means of production.

It was a brave new world, and Marx was worried. With the collaboration and support of another German radical, Friedrich Engels, he argued that the shift to wage labor changed the relationship workers had to their work. First, working for others in large numbers made labor less meaningful to members of the proletariat. Instead of growing crops or crafting useful goods with skills honed over a lifetime, workers were inserted into machines and assembly lines, producing whatever their employers told them to make. So neither the profits nor the products workers created belonged to them. Both belonged to the bourgeoisie. This led workers to feel like their labor wasn't really *theirs* at all. Marx used the word **alienation** to describe this feeling of dissatisfaction and disconnection from the fruits of one's labor.

Second, working for others weakened the proletariat's ability to control their working conditions. The bourgeoisie wanted profits, but this was possible only if they paid workers less than their labor was worth. If an employee's work doubled the value of a product from $1 to $2, for example, the employer had to pay them less than the $1 increase. Otherwise there would be nothing left for expenses and, equally important, their own pockets. Paying workers $0.50 for $1 of work was good for profits; paying them $0.25 was better. It was in the bourgeoisie's interest, then, to pay less and exert more control. The proletariat, on the other hand, wanted more flexibility and higher wages.

Often credited as an early conflict theorist, Marx argued that the interests of the proletariat and the bourgeoisie were directly opposed. In the early years of the Industrial Revolution, capitalism exacerbated class inequality.[11] The rich were getting richer and the poor were getting poorer. Workers protested, but the bourgeoisie used their greater wealth, power, and prestige to ensure that the laws governing workplaces and employment served their own interests.

Observing these dynamics, Marx predicted a **crisis of capitalism**, a coming catastrophic implosion from which capitalism would never recover.[12] First, he argued, the bourgeoisie would set up systems that allowed them to extract wealth from workers' labor. This would shuffle money upward, enriching the bourgeoisie. Second, the proletariat would become increasingly poor and therefore unable to purchase the goods sold by the bourgeoisie. For a while, their ability to buy things might be sustained by loans. But interest on the debt would be just another way for the bourgeoisie to extract money from the proletariat.

Under this form of capitalism, winners take all. So, the number of bourgeoisie would dwindle. A smaller and smaller number of elites would control greater and greater proportions of the total wealth. With no mechanism to interrupt this cycle, the crisis would inevitably come. Large proportions of the proletariat would default on their debt all at once, causing financial institutions to crash. Poor, debt-burdened, alienated, and growing in number, members of the proletariat would develop a **class consciousness**: an understanding that they are members of a group with shared economic interests. The proletariat would then rise up against the bourgeoisie in revolution.

This is Marx's crisis of capitalism. By creating a growing class of workers who reap a shrinking share of the benefits, capitalism gives rise to its own opposition. And by impoverishing the masses to the point that they can't buy its products, capitalism ensures its own demise. Marx predicted that such a crisis would usher in the end of capitalism and the beginning of something new: **socialism**, an economic system based on shared ownership of the resources used to create wealth that is then distributed by governments for the enrichment of all.

Is the crisis of capitalism coming?

THE RISE AND FALL OF CAPITAL IN AMERICA

The period in American history that most resembles Marx's apocalyptic vision of capitalism is described today as the Gilded Age (1870–1900), a period of unusually high economic inequality. By 1890, the 1 percent were so rich that they owned more property than every other American combined. Atop the sky-high hierarchy sat men with names still recognizable today: Carnegie, Vanderbilt, Hearst. In 1916, the oil tycoon John D. Rockefeller would

alienation
the feeling of dissatisfaction and disconnection from the fruits of one's labor

crisis of capitalism
a coming catastrophic implosion from which capitalism would never recover

class consciousness
an understanding that members of a social class share economic interests

socialism
an economic system based on shared ownership of the resources used to create wealth that is then distributed by governments for the enrichment of all

become the world's first billionaire.[13] When he died in 1937, he *personally* owned 1.5 percent of American wealth. That would have been a *proportionate* amount of wealth if there were sixty-six people in America. In fact, there were 128.8 million.

Rockefeller and his fellow capitalists were able to amass such wealth because they were operating under the kind of capitalism that Marx described: **free market capitalism**, a capitalist system with little or no government regulation. Indeed, during the time Rockefeller was earning his fortune, there was very little oversight of companies.[14] Accordingly, many of the most successful capitalists built monopolies, treated workers inhumanely, bribed politicians and law enforcement, and made shady deals with other business owners. The men, women, and children working for these businesses—in their factories and mines, on their railroads, and in their refineries—had few of the labor protections we have today.

Just like Marx predicted, a movement of workers rose up in response. Through the 1800s, workers increasingly formed **labor unions**, associations that organize workers so they can negotiate with their employers as a group instead of as individuals. These labor unions—which were often violently resisted by business owners—advocated for higher wages and overtime pay.[15]

free market capitalism
a capitalist system with little or no government regulation

labor unions
associations that organize workers so they can negotiate with their employers as a group instead of as individuals

Mexican American activist Cesar Chavez worked tirelessly on behalf of farmworkers in the United States, helping them organize for better working conditions and pay.

They also asked for safer workplaces, limits to the workday and workweek, better working conditions, and compensation for workplace injuries. They negotiated for benefits like unemployment insurance, health insurance, and paid sick leave. There's power in numbers, and when workers joined together, their employers were often forced to the bargaining table.

Still, by 1928, the richest 10 percent of Americans were taking home 49 percent of all income.[16] The next year, a mere fifty years after Marx's death, his prediction of catastrophic failure came true. Countries around the globe were slammed by the Great Depression (1929–1939), the most severe economic downturn in the history of the industrialized world. Unregulated, banks had overextended their reserves. Workers could no longer afford to spend and, with no one to buy, factories began slowing production and laying off employees. By 1933, a quarter of the American workforce was unemployed,

WORLD'S HIGHEST STANDARD OF LIVING

There's no way like the American Way

In opposition to the New Deal, business associations erected billboards celebrating the merits of free market capitalism. This photo powerfully illustrates the limitations of this ideology. In it, victims of the 1937 Louisville Flood line up in front of one such billboard, seeking relief.

wages and salaries had fallen by half, and investments had lost three-quarters of their value.

Capitalism was in crisis.

But then something happened that Marx did not predict. Politicians in many countries passed laws to protect the proletariat and rein in the bourgeoisie. In the United States, these policies were collectively described as the New Deal (1933–1936). The deal introduced government regulation to break up monopolies, enforce honest business practices, and protect workers and their right to unionize. Governments also set up systems of *transfer payments,* redistributions of wealth from one social group to another, in order to shuffle some of the money collected by the bourgeoisie back down to the workers.

With these transfer payments, governments provided a **social safety net**, a patchwork of programs intended to ensure that the most economically vulnerable do not go without basic necessities like food, clothing, and shelter. These programs were paid for with taxes. The New Deal made income taxation more *progressive* (as a person's income rises, the rate at which they pay taxes increases) instead of *regressive* (as a person's income rises, the rate at which they pay taxes declines) or *flat* (all levels of income are taxed equally). The top marginal tax rate—that is, the tax paid on additional dollars earned after incomes reach $500,000—was raised to a whopping 94 percent by 1945.

social safety net
a patchwork of programs intended to ensure that the most economically vulnerable do not go without basic necessities like food, clothing, and shelter

That same year, labor union membership peaked; a third of American workers belonged to unions.[17] Unions normalized a **living wage**, an income that allows full-time workers to afford their basic needs.[18] Higher wages at unionized workplaces raised wages elsewhere, too, because employers were forced to compete to attract employees. The highest-earning 1 percent still earned a healthy 11 percent of national after-tax income, but it was substantially less than the 24 percent they took home during the Gilded Age.[19] By the 1960s, the largest private employer in the United States, General Motors, paid their unionized, high school–educated autoworkers the equivalent of over $60,000 a year.[20]

The New Deal made the economy somewhat less beneficial to the rich bourgeoisie and a whole lot more helpful to the working-class proletariat. This was a turn away from a largely free market capitalism to a **welfare capitalism**, a capitalist economic system with some socialist policy aimed at distributing the profits of capitalism more evenly across the population. A large number of financially comfortable workers emerged as a result.

In 1953, a reporter for *Time* magazine marveled at his new country: "Even in the smallest towns and most isolated areas, the U.S. is wearing a very prosperous, middle-class suit of clothes. . . . People are not growing wealthy, but more of them than ever before are getting along."[21] Between the proletariat and the bourgeoisie was a surprising new phenomenon: a *middle* class.

This new middle class was mostly White. Politicians deliberately designed New Deal policies to exclude Black and Hispanic Americans or ensure that they received inferior benefits.[22] Occupations held mostly by Americans of color were exempted from the new minimum wage laws, unemployment insurance, and compensation for workplace injuries. Similarly, the Social Security Act of 1935—a system of financial support for the elderly, poor children, people with disabilities, and the unemployed—was written so that it didn't apply to jobs that employed primarily Black Americans. Labor union contracts, too, locked out women and people of color.

Members of this new, mostly White middle class held **contradictory class locations**, positions in the economy that are in some ways like the proletariat and in other ways like the bourgeoisie.[23] Middle managers in bureaucratic corporations, for example, have a contradictory class location. They don't own the means of production, but they do control the labor of workers who report to them. They enrich the bourgeoisie, who skim profits off the managers' labor, but they also enrich themselves by skimming profits off the labor of the workers below them.

Today, professionals with specialized knowledge are fairly described as occupying a contradictory class location. Engineers, lawyers, and college professors, for example, don't own any means of production; they work for wages like the proletariat. Nor do they directly skim profit off other people's labor. But they can use their specialized knowledge to claim extensive control over their working conditions, something the proletariat cannot do.

In sum, the Great Depression created a crisis of capitalism in countries around the world. In response, many instituted anti-capitalist policies, just like Marx predicted. But in doing so, these countries didn't *kill* capitalism; they *rescued* it. The New Deal spread the wealth just enough to create a large middle class. This changed the class dynamics of the country in a way that Marx did not predict. People in the "middle" could identify with the proletariat, spurring on revolution. Or they could identify with the bourgeoisie, stabilizing capitalism. Largely, they opted to do the latter. A socialist revolution didn't come.

For a little while, then, it seemed like Marx had been wrong.

THE NEW GILDED AGE

Many commentators are describing the United States' current economic condition as the New Gilded Age (approximately 2000–today), a second period of unusually high economic inequality. Table 7.1 shows that even before the Covid-19 pandemic, there were striking similarities between the first Gilded Age and today. In the first Gilded Age, the top 10 percent owned 80 percent of the wealth; today, they own 77 percent. In the first, they took home 49 percent of the income; today, they take home 50 percent.

TABLE 7.1

The First and Second Gilded Age, by the Numbers

	Gilded Age	New Gilded Age
INCOME		
Income earned by the top 0.1%	9%	11%
Income earned by the top 1%	24%	22%
Income earned by the top 10%	49%	50%
WEALTH		
Wealth held by the richest person	1.5%	0.2%
Wealth held by the top 1%	45%	42%
Wealth held by the top 10%	80%	77%
Wealth held by the bottom 90%	20%	23%

SOURCES: Thomas Piketty, *Capital in the Twenty-First Century* (Cambridge, MA: Belknap Press, 2014); Emmanuel Saez, "Striking It Richer: The Evolution of Top Incomes in the United States (Updated with 2018 Estimates)," February 2020, https://eml.berkeley.edu/~saez/saez-UStopincomes-2018.pdf; Emmanuel Saez and Gabriel Zucman, "Wealth Inequality in the United States Since 1913: Evidence from Capitalized Income Tax Data," *Quarterly Journal of Economics* 131, no. 2 (May 2016): 519–578.

A New Gilded Age was not inevitable.[24] Some rich democracies with high levels of economic inequality prior to the Great Depression ultimately returned to those high levels. This includes the United States as well as the United Kingdom, Canada, Ireland, and Australia. But other countries did not, including Germany, Japan, and France. Instead of being unavoidable, today's economy is a predictable outcome of decisions made since 1980.[25]

In the United States, the culprit is decades of politicians who've slowly been unraveling the socialist policies of the New Deal.[26] It started with President Ronald Reagan. By the end of his second term, in 1989, he'd dropped the top marginal tax rate from 70 percent to 28 percent and started shredding the social safety net. Later, President Bill Clinton ended the guarantee of cash support to families living below the poverty line (known as "welfare") and replaced it with a more restrictive program with a five-year lifetime cap, after which recipients are excluded from any further benefits no matter how dire their circumstances. This policy change, known as "welfare reform," pushed some people into low-wage jobs, but it made many of the poorest people even poorer.[27] As a result, child homelessness nearly doubled and the number of children living in *extreme poverty* tripled (poverty is defined as extreme when family members are subsisting on $2.00 a day or less).[28]

Laws protecting unions were rolled back, and the income share going to the top 10 percent rose as union membership dropped.[29] Weak and absent unions also made it harder for workers to respond proactively to new challenges: international trade and the decline of manufacturing in the United States (both discussed in Chapter 12) as well as the shift to a **service and information economy**, or one centered on jobs in which workers provide services (for example, at restaurants, salons, and in retail stores) or work with information (in engineering, technology, and marketing, for instance).

The Great Recession (2007–2009) was an opportunity to consider whether to reorganize the economy to include more socialist policies and strengthen the middle class, as the country did in the 1930s. But President Barack Obama's interventions primarily propped up corporations and did little to help the average American.[30] As the economy recovered, a mostly White economic elite reaped almost all the benefits.[31]

Under the next president, Donald J. Trump, Congress passed a tax bill that reduced taxes, but mostly for the rich (the wealthiest fifth of Americans captured 73 percent of the reduction).[32] The bill also critically undermined the Affordable Care Act, making it much more expensive for Americans to get health care from their government. Over Trump's term, the rich got richer at a faster pace than the rest of the country, and economic inequality widened.[33]

When the pandemic arrived, it devastated some sectors of the economy. People working in entertainment, in the oil and gas industry, and in service jobs (especially leisure, travel, and hospitality) were hit the hardest.[34] By September 2020, 42 percent of U.S. households included a person who had lost their job or took a cut in pay.[35] Low-income earners, young people, and Black and Hispanic workers were more likely to be in these households

service and information economy
an economy centered on jobs in which workers provide services or work with information

than other groups.[36] Meanwhile, the wealth of America's 651 billionaires grew by over $1 trillion.[37]

THE FUTURE OF ECONOMIC INEQUALITY

The fastest-growing jobs in the United States today are at the top and the bottom of the income pay scale.[38] Today the largest private employer isn't General Motors; it's Walmart. In 2018, the company pledged to pay its entry-level workers $11 an hour. If a sales associate or cashier is lucky enough to be working full-time, they'll bring home just over $21,000 a year, about a third of what General Motors workers were making in the 1960s.

Increasingly, low-paying service jobs aren't even jobs; they're gigs. As many as 30 percent of U.S. workers now earn money using apps like Lyft, Grubhub, or TaskRabbit. These workers are mostly under the age of thirty-five and disproportionately women, people of color, and immigrants. Even before the pandemic, the number of gig workers was expected to more than double in the next five years.[39] The pandemic may have accelerated this trend. While the use of lodging and ride-share apps plummeted, this decline was more than balanced by the increase in the number of people using apps to have prepared food, groceries, and other supplies delivered.

The gig economy looks more like the free market economy we had during the Gilded Age than the welfare capitalism that followed the Great Depression.[40] Workers take on piecemeal tasks, work long hours, and have little workplace protections. They don't get paid sick days, overtime, accommodations for disabilities, or compensation if they're hurt on the job.

Altogether, today's workers are putting in as many hours as ever—more even—and working harder, but companies aren't sharing the wealth, and the government is no longer doing much to make them. Figure 7.3 shows that employers stopped sharing almost any increases in profits with the lowest-paid 80 percent of their employees in 1973. Since then, productivity has risen by 72 percent, but wages have only risen by 9 percent.

If wages had kept up with productivity, the federal minimum wage would be over $20 an hour. Instead, it's $7.25. The bourgeoisie have pocketed the difference. As a result, since 1981, incomes among the top 1 percent have grown by 275 percent, whereas the bottom 20 percent have seen their incomes decline.[41]

The result is that most Americans are struggling financially. Nearly half report that they would be unable to pay a $400 fee in an emergency.[42] About 40 percent are living paycheck to paycheck.[43] Their incomes pay for what they need but nothing they want. And they are unable to save for retirement. Because of their uncertain livelihoods, these people have been dubbed the **precariat**, a word referring to a new class of workers who live economically precarious lives.[44] Combining the words *precarious* and *proletariat*,

precariat
a new class of workers who live economically precarious lives

FIGURE 7.3

Disconnect between Productivity and a Typical Worker's Compensation, 1948–2018

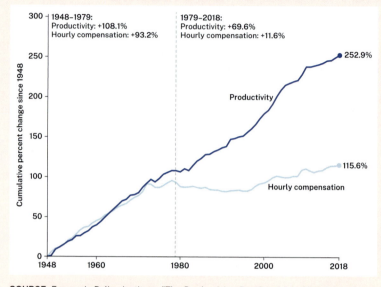

1948–1979:
Productivity: +108.1%
Hourly compensation: +93.2%

1979–2018:
Productivity: +69.6%
Hourly compensation: +11.6%

Productivity — 252.9%

Hourly compensation — 115.6%

Cumulative percent change since 1948

1948   1960   1980   2000   2018

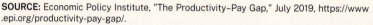

SOURCE: Economic Policy Institute, "The Productivity–Pay Gap," July 2019, https://www.epi.org/productivity-pay-gap/.

the term is meant to draw attention to the economic insecurity faced by so many Americans.

Even college graduates are at risk of becoming members of the precariat. Nearly half of college graduates work in jobs that don't require a college degree.[45] More than half of graduates under twenty-five are unemployed or working fewer hours than they need to make ends meet. Even students who graduate with degrees in science, technology, engineering, and math can find themselves among the precariat. As many as 75 percent of students with these majors end up working in an unrelated field, which means most are finding employment in lower-paying occupations.[46]

As you may know, many of these young people are burdened with high levels of student loan debt. Since 1980, when Reagan began dismantling the social safety net, the cost of college has nearly tripled.[47] More than half of college students now take on debt to get through school, accumulating an average of more than $35,000 in outstanding loans and bills.[48] All of this was a recipe for widespread economic crisis even before the pandemic crashed the global economy.

Marx is on the edge of his seat.

WHEN IS ECONOMIC INEQUALITY UNFAIR?

Is capitalism doomed? It depends. Marx was right that unregulated capitalism worsens economic inequality. High incomes at the top and low ones at the bottom leave the masses too poor to purchase the goods and services produced by their own labor. But Marx didn't predict the rise of welfare capitalism, a capitalist system tempered with socialist and other moderating policies. Whether history will bear out his prediction remains to be seen.

The future of our economies depends on what politicians decide to do. And politicians are supposed to represent our collective interests. It's our job as citizens, then, to have opinions on the kind of economy we want to live in.

In that spirit, this section considers four questions helpful for evaluating our economy. The first three ask you to think about the extent of inequality, the suffering of the most disadvantaged, and the ability to rise and fall in the social strata. Or, to put it more succinctly, whether economic disadvantage in our societies is too extreme, punishing, or unrelenting. The fourth question considers the fact that economic disadvantage correlates with our social identities. Considering these questions together, we can decide whether our economy is just (unequal but fair) or unjust (both unequal and unfair).

Question 1: How much economic inequality is too much?

Research suggests that outside of small communities like those of our foraging ancestors, a perfectly equal society would include a potentially unsustainable number of *free riders*, people who reap the benefits without contributing.[49] A pie split evenly without regard to effort, in other words, fails to motivate anyone to work for their dessert. For better or worse, knowing that our slice might be bigger or smaller is an incentive. If a society's goal is to motivate people to work for the common good, then some economic inequality is necessary.

It's also true that inequality suppresses effort when it's too extreme. Why work harder, or hard at all, if the effort gets you negligible amounts of pie? Winner-take-all economies—ones in which a handful of people get most of the rewards—are just as disincentivizing as ones with no inequality at all.[50]

What does a more equal society, but not a perfectly equal one, look like?

There are many examples of countries that incentivize work without high levels of economic inequality.[51] Among the most equal countries are Iceland, Belgium, and South Korea. But as a working example, consider Denmark. During the first Gilded Age, Denmark's economic inequality was as bad or worse than that of the United States, but today Denmark is the fifteenth most equal country in the world.[52] For comparison, the United States is the ninety-ninth (out of a total of 159).

Denmark's equality is a result of strong laws that protect workers, high tax rates, and generous transfer payments to residents. The top marginal tax rate in Denmark is 56 percent and applies to all income earned over $60,000 (in the United States, it's 37 percent on income over $500,000). The wealth Denmark collects in this way is then redistributed. Some of it goes to the poorest residents, but the state also ensures universal access to health care, a year's worth of paid parental leave for each child, subsidized childcare, free college tuition, student stipends, and other services that equalize opportunity. Most Danes are happy to pay high taxes and receive these benefits.[53] In fact, in 2018, the prime minister had to retract a pledge to lower the top marginal tax rate because the move was politically unpopular.[54]

Would Americans prefer a system like Denmark's?

Actually, yes.

A nationally representative survey of Americans asked respondents to make a guess as to the distribution of wealth in the United States and then describe an ideal distribution of wealth.[55] Figure 7.4 shows the results alongside the actual distribution of wealth. Comparing the top bar to the middle bar reveals that Americans underestimate U.S. wealth inequality dramatically. The average

FIGURE 7.4

The Actual Distribution of Wealth Compared to What Americans Think It Is and Would Like It to Be

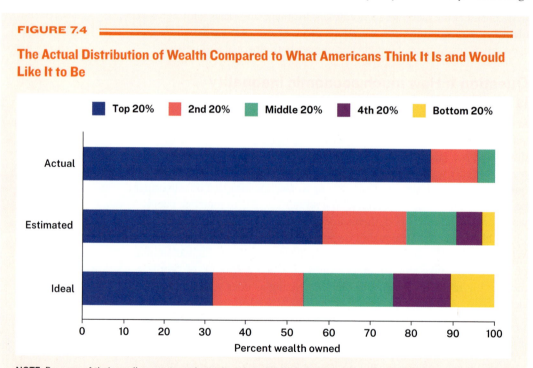

NOTE: Because of their small percentage share of total wealth, both the "4th 20%" value (0.2%) and the "Bottom 20%" value (0.1%) are not visible in the "Actual" distribution.

SOURCE: Republished with permission of SAGE Journals, from "Building a Better America—One Wealth Quintile at a Time" by Michael I. Norton and Dan Ariely. *Perspectives on Psychological Science*, 6:1, pp 9-12. © 2011; permission conveyed through Copyright Clearance Center, Inc.

American guesses that the richest 20 percent of Americans hold around 59 percent of the wealth; in fact, they own nearly 85 percent.

Comparing the middle and the bottom bars reveals the average American's ideal distribution of wealth is even more egalitarian than their estimate. They would prefer that the richest 20 percent hold only about a third of the wealth. Interestingly, all types of people—both the richest and the poorest Americans, men and women, and those on the political right and left—report similar preferences. And, yes, this ideal distribution matches the one seen in Denmark.

Do Americans also say they want a more equal distribution of wealth when they're asked directly? They do. Two-thirds of Americans are dissatisfied with the "way income and wealth are distributed in the U.S."[56] More than 60 percent think that rich people and corporations should pay more in taxes. It makes sense, then, that two-thirds of Americans disapproved of the 2017 bill that cut taxes for both.[57] When it comes to the distribution of wealth and income, most Americans think the country is on the wrong track.

Question 2: How poor is too poor?

Maybe we'd be comfortable with quite substantial levels of inequality if we were all guaranteed a bare minimum of economic resources. Conversely, if those of us at the bottom were truly suffering, we might object to a system with even low levels of overall inequality. Our opinions of an economic system, then, may depend not only on whether it leaves some people worse off than others, but whether it leaves any of us wholly destitute.

How many people in the United States are poor? And how poor are they?

Before the Covid-19 pandemic, 11 percent of Americans lived below the *federal poverty line*, the government's threshold for the minimum level of income needed to provide for basic needs.[58] In 2019, the poverty line for a single person was $12,760 per year. About a third of people who were in poverty—including 3 million children—were in *extreme poverty*, living on less than $2.00 a day.[59] Another 31 percent of Americans were defined as *low income*, or earning less than twice the poverty line.[60] People in low-income households routinely go without essentials: They're unable to pay their rent or mortgage, can't afford their utilities, are going hungry, or are skipping needed dental and medical care. Altogether, about 43 percent of Americans were poor or near poor in 2019. When the pandemic arrived, an economic relief bill called the CARES Act provided Americans with one-time cash payments and increased unemployment benefits for a limited time. Despite these efforts, at least 8 million additional people fell into poverty in 2020.[61]

Even under normal circumstances, two-thirds of Americans will spend at least one year below the federal poverty line.[62] Many will be among the **working poor**, people in the labor force who earn poverty-level wages. One-third of all U.S. jobs pay less than $11.50 an hour.[63] Low wages force many workers to supplement their incomes with government aid. For example, the majority of people who depend on food assistance—70 percent of them—work a full-time job.[64]

working poor
people in the labor force who earn poverty-level wages

People line up in their cars to receive food assistance in Orlando, Florida, in November 2020. More than 8 million additional people fell into poverty as a result of the Covid-19 pandemic.

Compared with other rich democracies, the United States stands out as having particularly high poverty rates.[65] Furthermore, that poverty is deep. Measured by life expectancy, infant mortality, and vulnerability to violence, many of the poor in the United States are experiencing a level of suffering that matches that of people in the poorest countries in the world.[66]

The United Nations has sounded an alarm. In 2018, the Human Rights Council decried five decades of "neglectful" U.S. policy responses to poverty.[67] The report stated that policies seemed "deliberately designed to remove basic protections from the poorest, punish those who are not in employment and make even basic health care into a privilege to be earned rather than a right of citizenship." This, it argued, made the country unique among its peers:

> In practice, the United States is alone among developed countries in insisting that, while human rights are of fundamental importance, they do not include rights that guard against dying of hunger, dying from a lack of access to affordable health care or growing up in a context of total deprivation.

For the United Nations, poverty in the United States isn't just an economic problem; it's a human rights crisis.

Would Americans like to alleviate poverty?

They're not sure.[68] When asked whether government aid to the poor does "more harm than good" or "more good than harm," about half agree to each.[69] This split in opinion is explained by disagreement about *how* the government should help. Americans tend to prefer government-guaranteed work over a social safety net that protects the employed and unemployed alike. The richest Americans are especially likely to oppose social safety net programs.

Americans' veneration of work reflects what the early German sociologist of religion Max Weber called the **Protestant work ethic**.[70] Traced back to an early Protestant sect—and now referred to commonly as just the "work ethic"—this is the idea that one's character can and should be measured by one's dedication to paid work. According to this logic, morally good people are hard workers and people who aren't working hard are morally bad. When people are successful in life, then, it's because they're good. And if people are struggling, it's because they're bad. Research has shown that citizens of Protestant-influenced countries, whether they themselves are Protestant or not, are more likely than citizens of other countries to judge their own worth based on their work.[71]

The United States is a Protestant-influenced country, with about half of Americans identifying with some form of Protestantism.[72] Accordingly, the average American works more hours than residents of similar but less Protestant countries: 345 more hours a year than the Dutch, for example, and 274 more hours than the French.[73] When Americans are out of work, they're also more likely than people in other countries to blame themselves.[74] America is also the home of *prosperity theology*, a branch of Protestant Christianity born in the first Gilded Age that purports that wealth is God's reward for true faith.

The Protestant work ethic gives Americans an almost religious faith in hard work. It also helps explain why Americans are so squeamish about the social safety net. Stereotypes of poor people portray them as lazy, untrustworthy, and greedy cheats with too many children.[75] In turn, many Americans believe that the poor aren't working, don't want to work, or haven't done the work to be worthy of getting work. More than half of Americans believe that transfer payments to people in poverty just encourage them to stay poor.[76] *Why, Americans ask themselves, would we want to give free money to bad people?*

Unfortunately, giving poor adults jobs will not end poverty (see Figure 7.5). Thirteen percent of people in poverty are elderly and 11 percent are living with a disability; another 8 percent of the poor are full-time caregivers and 7 percent are college students.[77] Nearly a quarter—23 percent—are among the working poor; they have a job or even multiple jobs but aren't paid enough to make ends meet. Only 2 percent of poor people don't fall into one of these categories.

Consider Vanessa Solivan, a thirty-three-year-old woman profiled by the sociologist Matthew Desmond.[78] Her husband had passed away, leaving her a

Protestant work ethic
the idea that one's character can and should be measured by one's dedication to paid work

FIGURE 7.5

Americans Living in Poverty, 2018

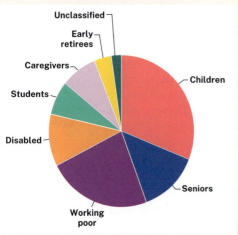

SOURCES: Lauren Bauer, Emily Moss, and Jay Shambaugh, "Who Was Poor in the US in 2018?" Brookings, Dec. 5, https://www.brookings.edu/blog/up-front/2019/12/05/who-was-poor-in-the-u-s-in-2018; Current Population Survey Annual Social and Economic Supplement 2019.

single mother with three children. She moved in with her parents for a while, nursing her father until his death. Recently, she'd been offered a small apartment in public housing. There she cared for her three children: helping with homework, counseling their daily troubles, shuttling them to doctor's appointments, and doling out discipline when necessary. Now her mother was in ill health, so she cared for her too.

Between the responsibilities to her mom and her kids, she was able to work twenty to thirty hours a week. She worked as a home health aide, earning between $10 and $14 an hour, depending on the client. She took care of these elderly and dying people, bathing them, feeding them, keeping them comfortable, and enabling them to stay in their homes in their final years. She liked the work. "I get to help people," she said, "and be around older people and learn a lot of stuff from them."

If she could afford to put her children in day care, she could work more hours. But day care in her state, even for just one child, costs more than she earns.[79] So she works as much as she can and lives frugally. "Vanessa's life revolved around a small routine," Desmond wrote: "drop the kids off at school; work; try finding an apartment that rents for less than $1,000 a month; pick the kids up; feed them; sleep." Her income clocked in at nearly $14,000 below the poverty line for a family of four. At the time Desmond was profiling her, she was trying to save up enough money to "get the kids washcloths and towels." For the working poor, even basic necessities are luxuries.

Poverty in America isn't rare, it isn't comfortable, and it isn't voluntary. People in poverty are not lazy, certainly not any lazier than anyone else. By and large, they're people who are working, who cannot work, or who are doing essential, life-sustaining unpaid work. Accordingly, some people are simply not going to be able to work themselves out of poverty. So no matter how much Americans dislike the idea of taxing and transferring money to poor people, it may be the only viable way to end their suffering. In that case, it's up to us to decide how much deprivation we're comfortable with.

Question 3: How much opportunity is enough?

Even a society with low levels of economic inequality and few people in poverty may not be considered just if it fails to reward merit. Most Americans agree that there should be substantial social mobility.[80] That is, they believe that our economic fates should not be fixed but in flux, with people rising or falling as warranted.

How much mobility is there in the American economy? Figure 7.6 compares people's household incomes at birth (that is, whether they were born into the poorest fifth of households, the richest fifth, or one of the three fifths in between) and their household incomes as adults. The middle column shows the social mobility of people born into the mathematical middle class. From there we see an impressive amount of mobility. A child born into the middle class is about as likely to end up poor as they are to get rich or to land anywhere in between.

The right and left columns reflect the mobility of the poorest and richest Americans. These columns reveal considerably less social mobility: 36 percent of children born into the poorest fifth stay there and only 10 percent make it into the richest fifth. This is also true for those born into

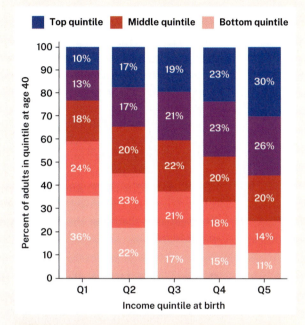

FIGURE 7.6

Social Mobility Matrix Comparing Income at Birth to That at 40 Years Old

NOTE: Fully 36 percent of people born into the poorest fifth of households will still be there at age 40. Only 10 percent will rise to be among the highest-earning households. Similarly, 30 percent of people born into the richest fifth of households will be there at age 40 and only 11 percent will descend into the bottom fifth.

SOURCE: Richard V. Reeves and Isabel Sawhill, "Social Mobility: A Promise That Could Still Be Kept," *Milken Institute Review*, July 15, 2016, https://www.milkenreview.org/articles/social-mobility-a-promise-that-could-still-be-kept.

the top: 30 percent stay rich and only 11 percent end up poor. In both cases, fewer than half of people born either rich or poor will move into or through the middle class.

These data show that class at birth is correlated with life outcomes. Children born at the bottom of the economic hierarchy face what we call a **glass ceiling**, an invisible barrier that restricts upward mobility. It's as if there is an upper limit above which someone born without economic advantage will never rise, no matter their talent, effort, or qualifications. In contrast, children born at the top of the hierarchy are propped up by a **glass floor**, an invisible barrier that restricts downward mobility. No matter how weak their preparation, effort, or talent, their economic advantage ensures that they'll never find themselves at the bottom.

glass ceiling
an invisible barrier that restricts upward mobility

glass floor
an invisible barrier that restricts downward mobility

In international comparison, the glass ceiling and floor in the United States is especially difficult to crack.[81] Despite heralding itself as the "land of opportunity," the United States has lower social mobility than most other high-income nations. For example, in Denmark, parents pass on only about 15 percent of their economic advantage to their children; in the United States, it's 47 percent.[82]

What do Americans think of this?

They're concerned about this aspect of inequality most of all. Only a third agree that the U.S. economic system is "generally fair."[83] Half will say that people are rich because they've had "more advantages than others."[84] A similar proportion say that a person is poor because of "circumstances beyond his or her control." Even among self-identified political conservatives, about two-thirds support policies that ensure equal opportunity.[85]

Generally speaking, social mobility is more important to Americans than either poverty relief or the overall level of inequality. Three-quarters of Americans agree that the American Dream is "being free to accomplish anything with hard work."[86] Americans even express *dislike* for equality if they believe reward is being doled out without regard for merit. Americans are torn about equality, then, but they feel fairly strongly about people getting their just desserts.

Question 4: What should be done about the correlation between money and status?

One last question deserves consideration. Imagine a society with low economic inequality, high levels of mobility, and a social safety net that keeps everyone out of poverty. Now imagine that the inequality that remains aligns with status hierarchies like race and ethnicity, immigration status, gender, and sexual identity. If the economic elite are also disproportionately the status elite, our society is not just.

The economic policies that built a strong middle class after the Great Depression were largely withheld from racial and ethnic minorities. As a result, the "winners" of today's economy are disproportionately White. The median wealth held by White families is $171,000; the median for Asian families is about 10 percent higher. The median held by Black and Hispanic families is $17,600 and $20,700, respectively.[87] White and Asian households, in other words, have about ten times the wealth of Black households and eight times that of Hispanic ones. These are racial **wealth gaps**, differences in the amount of money and economic assets owned by people from different social identity groups.

In addition to wealth gaps, we see **wage gaps**, differences between the hourly earnings of different social identity groups. Figure 7.7, for example, offers an intersectional look at wage gaps in the United States. First, notice that we see gender wage gaps at every educational level, with larger differences among the most highly educated. The more money there is to be made in an

wealth gaps
differences in the amount of money and economic assets owned by people from different social identity groups

wage gaps
differences between the hourly earnings of different social identity groups

FIGURE 7.7

Median Weekly Earnings for Full-Time Workers

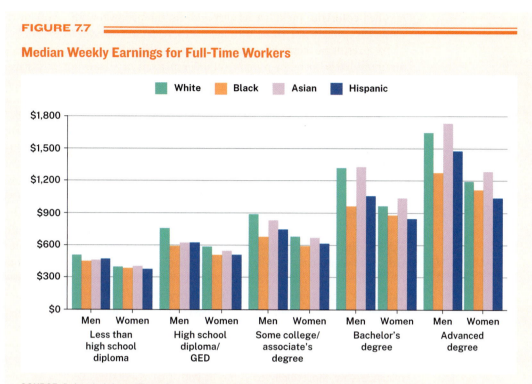

SOURCE: Deborah Ashton, "Does Race or Gender Matter More to Your Paycheck?," *Harvard Business Review*, June 10, 2014, https://hbr.org/2014/06/does-race-or-gender-matter-more-to-your-paycheck.

occupation, the more likely it will be the men who are making it. Across all men and women and all occupations, U.S. women working full-time today make $0.82 for every dollar earned by men working full-time.[88]

Black and Hispanic earners are also paid lower wages than White earners at every educational level, revealing a racial and ethnic wage gap. With the exception of Asian women with a bachelor's degree or more, White women receive more in income than women of other races. White men also receive higher wages than men of other races, with the same exception for Asian men as Asian women. Figure 7.7 doesn't report data for American Indians and Alaska Natives, but their wages are near those of Black Americans.[89] Notice that there is a gender wage gap within racial and ethnic groups too.

As with gender, the differences between the earnings of White, Black, and Hispanic men grow larger as they move up the educational ladder. Black and Hispanic men with a bachelor's degree make about as much as a White man with an associate's degree, for example. Black men and Hispanic women, especially, are left behind, while Asian men catch up and exceed the earnings of White men at the highest educational levels. Within racial groups, people with lighter skin earn higher wages than those with darker skin.[90] This

colorism

prejudice against and discrimination toward people with dark skin compared to those with light skin, regardless of race

is called **colorism**, prejudice against and discrimination toward people with dark skin compared to those with light skin, regardless of race.

As a result of these differences, women and racial and ethnic minorities are more likely to be in poverty. While 9 percent of White Americans live below the federal poverty line, 10 percent of Asian Americans, 15 percent of multiracial Americans, 17 percent of Hispanic Americans, 21 percent of Black Americans, and 24 percent of American Indians and Alaska Natives do.[91] Thirteen percent of women live in poverty, compared with 10 percent of men. A quarter of people with disabilities and 19 percent of noncitizen residents also live in poverty.

Asians are the only racial or ethnic group to earn higher wages than Whites. The sociologists Jennifer Lee and Min Zhou argue that this is because the United States gives priority to very highly educated Asian immigrants from wealthy countries.[92] Lee herself, for example, emigrated with her family from South Korea to the United States when she was a toddler. Her father had been admitted to Temple University, where he would pursue a PhD. Zhou emigrated from China after college, also after being admitted to a PhD program. Neither Lee's family nor Zhou's lived on Easy Street. Everyone worked hard, and often for meager pay, to make ends meet. But by virtue of having college degrees and access to higher education in the United States, both families had a good start.

Compared with immigrants from other racial and ethnic backgrounds, some groups of Asian immigrants—Chinese and South Asian Americans, for instance—are more likely to come in with that good start. Because of this, they also tend to settle in parts of the country with high incomes, excellent job opportunities, and strong education systems. Asian subgroups who are not from wealthy countries, and who have little opportunity to earn immigration with professional-grade skills, have poverty rates at more than twice the American average.[93] These include groups like Cambodian, Laotian, and Hmong Americans. Asians overall are doing very well, then, but Asians whose incomes are in the lower parts of the economic distribution are doing substantially worse than Whites.[94] As a result of this diversity, wealth inequality among Asians is even more extreme than it is among all Americans.[95]

Finally, the glass ceilings faced by racial minorities are especially firm, while the glass floors are particularly soft. A study of 20 million Americans that compared the earnings of parents and their adult children found that Black, Hispanic, American Indian, and Alaska Native children are especially likely to experience downward mobility. The results are displayed in Table 7.2. White children born into the top fifth have a 41 percent chance of staying there and Asian children have a 49 percent chance, but Hispanic, American Indian and Alaska Native, and Black children have only a 31, 23, and 18 percent chance, respectively. The class privilege of Black and Native children born into the upper class is so precarious that those born into the top fifth are only slightly more likely to stay there than they are to fall all the way down to the bottom.

Likewise, upward mobility is much higher among White and Asian children. Among those born into the bottom fifth, 11 percent of Whites and

TABLE 7.2

Social Mobility of Children by Race and Ethnicity

	Chance of staying in the top 5th	Chance of ascending from the bottom 5th to the top 5th
Black Americans	18%	3%
Asian Americans	49%	26%
Hispanic Americans	31%	7%
American Indians and Alaska Natives	23%	3%
White Americans	41%	11%

SOURCE: Raj Chetty, Nathaniel Hendren, Maggie R. Jones, and Sonya R. Porter, "Race and Economic Opportunity in the United States: An Intergenerational Perspective," *Quarterly Journal of Economics* 135, no. 2 (2020): 711–783.

26 percent of Asians will climb to the top. In contrast, only 7 percent of Hispanic children, and 3 percent of American Indian, Alaska Native, and Black children, will rise from the bottom fifth to the top. Differences in family characteristics—variables like parents' marital status and education—explain very little of these gaps, especially for Black children.

These numbers are especially striking for Black men. Among Black Americans, most of the difference between Black and White mobility is due to the lack of upward mobility and likelihood of downward mobility for Black men. Black women, in fact, are about as upwardly mobile as White women, controlling for their class growing up. This is because Black men are facing forms of discrimination different than those faced by Black women, a phenomenon we'll explore in detail in the next chapter. Notably, one of the variables that correlates with better outcomes for Black boys is low levels of racial prejudice among the White people with whom they grow up.

We already know that the Protestant work ethic explains many Americans' tolerance of high levels of poverty and economic inequality. If we already believe that poor people are undeserving, then it's easy to conclude that their poverty is caused by personal failure. In fact, research shows that Americans' tolerance for economic inequality is greater when the people who are disadvantaged are racial or ethnic minorities.[96] Racial prejudice, then, intersects with the Protestant work ethic to leave some of us even less sensitive to the suffering of the poor than we would be otherwise.

Max Weber called this **legitimation**, a process by which a potentially controversial social fact is made acceptable.[97] In this case, linking poverty to bad ethics and ascribing bad ethics to low-status groups makes it seem as if the suffering of the poor is inevitable, or even good. A racialized Protestant work ethic, then, is used not only to *explain* economic inequality but to *legitimate* it.

legitimation
a process by which a potentially controversial social fact is made acceptable

CAPITALISM AND SOCIALISM: ENEMIES OR FRENEMIES?

Our economy is a social institution and, as Marx predicted, Americans are increasingly questioning it. Young people between eighteen and twenty-nine are almost as likely to identify as socialists as they are to identify as capitalists.[98] And 43 percent of Americans now agree that "some form of socialism" might be a "good thing" for the country.[99] The Democratic Socialist Party grew by a third in the aftermath of the 2016 presidential election.[100] The last time this many people were interested in socialism? The first Gilded Age.[101]

Perhaps a new way is on the horizon: neither socialism nor capitalism. Humans have invented many economic systems, and we will invent another. Maybe you will play a part in inventing and implementing something different, something better.

In the meantime, our job as citizens is to decide what we think is fair given the economic systems and mechanisms available. It turns out, much to Marx's surprise, this doesn't require choosing between capitalism and socialism.[102] Some of the most socialist countries in the world, in fact, are in the process of becoming more robustly capitalist. Why? Because they want more money to spread around. As one commentator put it: "They needed to be better capitalists to afford their socialism."[103]

You get to have opinions as to how much economic inequality you think is fair, what depths of poverty are tolerable, how much social mobility is sufficient, and what we should do about the fact that the economic and the status elite overlap so substantially. You also get to decide what socialist policies, if any, should be implemented to bring about an economy that you judge as just.

These protesters hold a sign that ties capitalism to climate disaster. Interest in socialism has soared since the 2016 presidential election, particularly among young people.

What do you think is a fair minimum wage? Should employees be allowed to unionize, and under what conditions? Do you want to help people who cannot or will not work? What should governments do to ensure that poor children can succeed and rich ones can fail?

You may also decide that some public goods—like clean water, shelter, and the internet—should be protected from capitalist forces at all costs. That is, wholly socialized. Many Americans believe that things like the health of the environment (66 percent), the provision of health care (44 percent), and access to higher education (41 percent) should not be left to for-profit companies.[104] You may think that a mostly or wholly socialist economy would be ideal. That's a reasonable opinion to hold too. The truth is that trust in both government and the free market is currently low. Only 32 percent of young Americans trust the federal government to "do the right thing," but an even lower percentage have trust in "Wall Street."[105]

Even if you are an ardent capitalist, you should probably heed Marx's warnings. Perhaps the most surprising lesson of the last 200 years is that while the redistribution of wealth from the rich to the poor is not a capitalist's idea of a good time, these types of policies do appear to save the system from itself, letting it live on another day. ■

COMING UP...

COMPARED WITH similar countries, economic inequality in the United States is especially high, with extensive and punishing levels of poverty, and low social mobility for the rich and the poor. This is because, with the exception of several decades in the mid-1900s, U.S. policies have been protective of rich people's economic privilege. This is a form of institutional discrimination. It ensures that the country remains socially stratified, with its residents occupying a relatively stable class hierarchy.

Most Americans would like more mobility, less inequality, and less poverty, even if they're unsure whether and how to best protect the most vulnerable. Prejudice against racial and ethnic minorities persists, and there's a deep-seated cultural belief that poor people deserve their fate. This dampens some Americans' desire to alleviate poverty.

The next chapter explores institutional discrimination against people of color specifically. It shows how the institution of Education fails students of color, how the institution of Law targets them for punishment, and how these two institutions intersect when policing enters our schools. All these dynamics are possible, in part, because racial and ethnic minorities largely live in different neighborhoods than White people do. A chapter about the unique obstacles faced by people of color is next.

8

———

INSTITUTIONAL
RACISM

IN THIS CHAPTER...

THE LAST CHAPTER argued that the U.S. economy is a social institution that has enriched the wealthy at the expense of the middle and working classes since the 1980s. This chapter explores institutional forms of *racism*, a term that refers to a society's production of unjust outcomes for some racial or ethnic groups. It introduces the following social patterns:

- *Residential segregation* involves the sorting of different kinds of people into separate neighborhoods. Segregation enables the uneven delivery of helpful and harmful goods and services, including environmental toxins and pollutants.

- Residential segregation also contributes to other social patterns, such as inequitable educations. Within any given school, the best educational opportunities are usually reserved for White students, while harsh discipline is doled out disproportionately to Black, Hispanic, and Native students. Meanwhile, schools filled with White students are generally funded better than ones filled with students of color.

- Finally, residential segregation enables police to target racial minority and immigrant neighborhoods. This leads to extremely high rates of imprisonment and deportation among these populations, harming families and communities.

The chapter closes with a big-picture discussion of how institutional discrimination shapes our lives. It argues that advantage and disadvantage are *cross-institutional* (people advantaged by one institution are often advantaged by others, and vice versa), *cumulative* (institutional advantage and disadvantage builds over the life course), and *intergenerational* (children usually inherit advantage or disadvantage from their parents).

You'll also learn about *spatial analysis*, a research method in which data are layered onto a landscape divided into fine-grained segments.

"Not everything that is faced can be changed, but nothing can be changed until it is faced."

—JAMES BALDWIN

In the heart of Los Angeles, amid the tall buildings that populate its skyline, is a neighborhood known as Skid Row. Its residents are America's largest homeless community: about 10,000 people sleeping on sidewalks and in shelters and cheap motels. They're mostly men, mostly Black, and universally economically deprived.

By virtue of having no place to live, the residents of Skid Row face multiple forms of institutional discrimination. Low wages and high rents all but guarantee that there will be a class of people unable to afford shelter, while social services provide housing for only a fraction of the people who need it. Homelessness is inevitable; it's built into the system.

Meanwhile, many of the features of homelessness are criminalized.[1] It's illegal to spend the night on the street or in a public park, even if shelters are full and the money to secure a room is out of reach. It's also illegal to stand or sit on the sidewalk, even during the day. Despite the lack of free public restrooms, it's illegal to urinate or defecate in public. For these folks, there are no legal ways to go about daily life.

Darryl's experience is typical.[2] He found himself on Skid Row in his mid-fifties. He'd struggled to make ends meet, working manual jobs after being released from the military with post-traumatic stress disorder. When one of the stores he worked for closed unexpectedly, he was unable to pay rent for his studio apartment. He turned to the Veterans Administration for help, but all they gave him was a list of last-resort motels. "It hit me like a ton of bricks," Darryl told Forrest Stuart, a sociologist who studied the residents of Skid Row. "I guess that's when it finally sunk in. I was finally at the end of the road. Rock bottom."

Rock bottom, Darryl discovered, wasn't just a metaphor; it was a place. Within weeks of his arrival, Darryl was arrested. He'd been sitting on the sidewalk, resting his feet after a long day pushing a shopping cart filled with goods for sale he'd rescued from dumpsters. A police car pulled up, and

People with no place to live are criminalized by Los Angeles statutes, which make sleeping or even standing on the sidewalk illegal. So, for the residents of Skid Row, it's all but impossible to go a day without the risk of being fined or arrested.

officers jumped out and handcuffed him. A run through their database turned up zero warrants for his arrest. They arrested him anyway. Sitting on the sidewalk is a misdemeanor in Los Angeles.

In the ensuing weeks, Darryl would be detained for loitering while waiting in line for a free sandwich and fined for littering when an officer saw him flick cigarette ash to the ground. When he was unable to pay a $174 fine, financial penalties piled on. Soon he owed over $500. His chances of getting back on his feet got slimmer and slimmer and slimmer.

Laws against loitering, public urination, and other behaviors people like Darryl can't avoid are theoretically neutral; they apply to everyone equally. But structural features of our societies make some people more vulnerable to enforcement efforts. Poor Black men are more likely than other kinds of people to find themselves subjected to these kinds of laws.

This is what the phrase *institutional discrimination* is meant to capture: widespread and enduring practices that persistently disadvantage some kinds of people while advantaging others. Institutional discrimination—both historical and ongoing—is part of how Black men end up on Skid Row. And once they're there, they may become trapped in an unavoidable cycle of further institutional discrimination.

This chapter is about institutional discrimination against racial and ethnic minorities. It's a peek into what sociologists call **racism**, a term that refers to a society's production of unjust outcomes for some racial or ethnic groups. Most scholars agree that racism is not merely prejudicial attitudes or even discriminatory behavior, although it involves these things. Instead, a state of

racism
a term that refers to a society's production of unjust outcomes for some racial or ethnic groups

affairs rises to the level of racism when there's a *social structure*, held in place by the powerful, that maintains racial and ethnic advantage and disadvantage. So while the word *racist* is often used in everyday language to describe attitudes and behavior, sociologists tend to use the word only when social patterns of prejudice and discrimination are also reflected in social institutions.

The institutionalized racism covered in this chapter includes the mechanisms that determine where we live, what kind of school we go to, and how we encounter the criminal justice system. Some kinds of people and not others are routinely subjected to the suspicion of police and immigration enforcement. Some kinds of people and not others are likely to receive substandard educations. And some kinds of people and not others regularly benefit from community goods or are exposed to community harms. This chapter is dedicated to understanding how and why this happens. It begins with a discussion of residential segregation, which some sociologists have described as the "structural linchpin of modern race relations."[3]

RESIDENTIAL SEGREGATION

Across America, people with similar social identities often live together in distinct neighborhoods. There are ethnic enclaves like Little Indias in Southern California, Amish settlements in the Pennsylvanian countryside, and Orthodox Jewish communities in New York City. There are "gayborhoods," too, neighborhoods filled mostly with sexual minorities. And there are rich neighborhoods and poor ones. These are all examples of **residential segregation**, the sorting of different types of people into separate neighborhoods.[4] We find residential segregation all across the country, in the suburbs as well as the cities.[5]

Above all, U.S. neighborhoods are segregated by race and ethnicity. As an example, consider Chicago, Illinois. Map 8.1 shows the distribution of Asian, Black, Hispanic, and White Chicagoans, revealing a pattern of segregation where different groups occupy distinct parts of the city.[6] Segregation between White and Black Chicagoans is the most extreme and the lines between them are especially stark. Two-thirds of Chicago's Black Americans live in neighborhoods that are more than 80 percent Black.[7] Hispanic residents are somewhat less segregated, often living in neighborhoods that divide Black from White parts of the city.

Such racial and ethnic segregation is the norm throughout the United States. And like in Chicago, Black Americans are the most segregated racial group overall.[8] Black people are also the group most likely to experience **hypersegregation**, residential segregation so extreme that many people's daily lives involve little or no contact with people of other races. Black Americans are hypersegregated in Baltimore, Boston, Chicago, Cleveland, Detroit, Kansas City, Milwaukee, New York, Philadelphia, St. Louis, and elsewhere.[9]

Asian and Hispanic Americans are also residentially segregated, though somewhat less than Black Americans.[10] Some of them, though, are more segregated than others. Indian, Filipino, and Vietnamese Americans are

residential segregation
the sorting of different types of people into separate neighborhoods

hypersegregation
residential segregation so extreme that many people's daily lives involve little or no contact with people of other races

more highly segregated than Chinese, Japanese, and Korean Americans, for example.[11] The degree to which Hispanic groups are segregated from Whites correlates strongly with skin color; darker-skinned people of Latin American descent, such as Puerto Ricans, experience stronger isolation.[12] This is evidence of *colorism*, prejudice against and discrimination toward people with dark skin compared to those with light skin.

The least-segregated Americans are American Indians and Alaska Natives, but not necessarily for positive reasons.[13] European colonizers killed 95 percent of the Native population in conflict, with disease, or by driving them off their lands.[14] Those whom the Europeans did not kill, they attempted to assimilate. Native children were taken from their families and "reeducated" into European culture. The U.S. government also encouraged White and Native people to intermarry and have children. The government was trying to ensure that fewer people could fulfill the blood quantum rule that requires a person have at least a certain level of indigenous ancestry in order to qualify for benefits. Today, less than 2 percent of the U.S. population identifies as Native. The minority of American Indians who live on the remaining reservations live in hypersegregated conditions. Off the reservations, however, there are too few American Indians to achieve the same level of concentration as other racial and ethnic minorities.

In 1968, the Fair Housing Act made it illegal to discriminate against renters and buyers because of their race, religion, national origin, or sex. That decade, racial and ethnic residential segregation reached its peak. Its level has remained more or less the same ever since. Only 30 percent of Census tracts are integrated.[15] Segregation among Black Americans remains high and, among Asian and Hispanic Americans, it's on the rise.[16]

How did U.S. cities become segregated? And why do they remain this way?

MAP 8.1

Residential Segregation by Race and Ethnicity in Chicago, Illinois, 2010

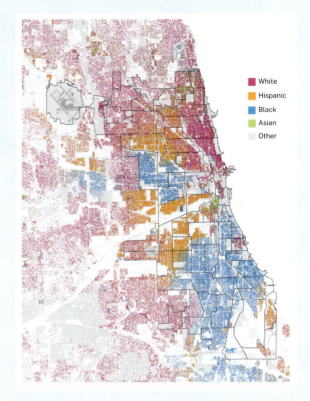

White
Hispanic
Black
Asian
Other

NOTE: Each dot represents twenty-five people.

SOURCE: Bill Rankin, www.radicalcartography.net.

In the late 1800s, children from the Pueblo Indian tribe were taken from their parents and coerced to assimilate into White culture. This so-called reeducation went well beyond new clothes and a haircut. Children were forcibly socialized into European values and punished for speaking their own languages.

Mechanisms of racial and ethnic segregation, past and present

The emancipation of enslaved Black people in the United States prompted a Great Migration. Beginning in the early 1900s, 6 million newly free Black people left Southern plantations for the North. Many of them settled in growing urban centers.

These migrations prompted a flurry of formal laws, organizational policies, and informal practices that ensured that segregation would take hold. Hundreds of cities, for instance, operated as "sundown towns," ones that enforced racial segregation by threatening any non-White person in town after sunset with violence.[17] Elsewhere, neighbors signed "restrictive covenants" in which they agreed among themselves not to sell their homes to non-Whites.[18] The Federal Housing Administration included such covenants, built "Whites-only" suburbs, and put walls or highways between Black and White neighborhoods.[19] With a practice called "steering," real estate agents colluded with neighbors to maintain all-White neighborhoods. Until 1956, the National Association of Real Estate Boards actually *required* real estate agents to show houses in White neighborhoods only to White people.[20]

When these policies and practices failed, racial and ethnic minorities faced **White fight**, organized White resistance to integration.[21] This included protesting integration and advocating for laws that protected or produced segregation. In some cases, White fight was violent. Well into the 1960s, people of color who attempted to move into White neighborhoods were sometimes met with beatings, vandalism, arson, firebombs, and riots. When White fight

White fight
organized White resistance to integration

failed, there was **White flight**, a phenomenon in which White people start leaving a neighborhood when minority residents begin to move in.

Once residential segregation took hold, entrepreneurs and local governments invested in neighborhoods filled mostly with White Americans: businesses were opened, schools were built, and opportunities for leisure arrived. In contrast, neighborhoods filled mostly with racial and ethnic minorities were exploited or neglected. Private banks and government lenders engaged in **redlining**, refusing loans to or steeply overcharging anyone buying in poor and minority neighborhoods.[22] The practice got its name because lenders would literally outline these neighborhoods in red ink. Half the neighborhoods in Chicago were redlined in the 1940s, and a comparison of Maps 8.1 and 8.2 shows that Chicago's historically redlined neighborhoods are occupied primarily by Black residents even today.

By 1968, most practices used to enforce segregation were criminalized, but that doesn't mean they've disappeared. After the foreclosure crisis of 2008—the event that led to the Great Recession—Wells Fargo and Bank of America were sued for illegally burdening people of color with risky home loans. They settled these discrimination lawsuits for a combined $530 million in

MAP 8.2

Chicago Redlining Map from 1939

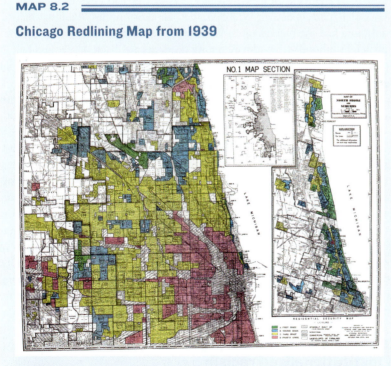

SOURCE: Robert K. Nelson, LaDale Winling, Richard Marciano, Nathan Connolly, et al., "Mapping Inequality," American Panorama, ed. Robert K. Nelson and Edward L. Ayers, accessed April 9, 2021, https://dsl.richmond.edu/panorama/redlining.

fines. In the meantime, twice as many Black families as White families lost their homes. Since 2015, at least twelve banks have been fined for purposefully avoiding or exploiting racial minorities and their neighborhoods.

In 2019, the U.S. government charged Facebook with violating antidiscrimination law. The company was allowing advertisers (including bankers, real estate agents, and landlords) to screen their ads, ensuring that some people would not see them. Advertisers could selectively omit accounts belonging to religious minorities, immigrants, people of color, and people with disabilities. Facebook even allowed advertisers to draw literal red lines around geographic regions they wanted to exclude.

Steering continues as well. In a recent field experiment, research confederates posed as homebuyers. They approached over 8,000 real estate agents in twenty-eight cities.[23] Black and Asian (but not Hispanic) confederates were shown about 20 percent fewer homes than Whites.

We continue to see White fight in the form of NIMBY ("Not In My Back Yard") politics. Across the United States, and in both liberal and conservative communities, residents in predominantly White neighborhoods have opposed affordable housing developments that would likely bring in poor and working-class residents of all races and ethnicities.[24]

When people of color do move in, we still see White flight. Between 2000 and 2010, 12 percent of U.S. Census tracts in the 150 largest cities lost an average of 40 percent of their White population.[25] Los Angeles, Washington, DC, and Atlanta had the highest rates. White people are most likely to flee diversifying neighborhoods when the incoming residents are Black. More than half of White people say they wouldn't move to a neighborhood if its residents were even one-third Black, even if the neighborhood was middle class or wealthy.[26] To a lesser extent, Asian and Hispanic Americans also prefer not to live with Black people, unless their alternative is a 100 percent White neighborhood. In contrast, 85 percent of Black Americans prefer integrated neighborhoods.[27]

As a result of these policies, practices, and preferences, racial and ethnic segregation is alive and well in America today. This is caused by discriminatory behavior as well as legal and not-so-legal mechanisms that preserve neighborhood homogeneity: steering, redlining, and housing policies that disproportionately constrain the choices of people of color.

Residential segregation, however, is about more than a lack of choice. Because it concentrates people of different racial and ethnic backgrounds in certain neighborhoods, just like Skid Row, it makes it easy for cities to produce racially discriminatory outcomes. With residential segregation, it's not necessary to target individual people of color to produce racially discriminatory outcomes. One can target whole neighborhoods.

Residential segregation as a form of institutionalized racism

Residential segregation facilitates the unequal distribution of the benefits and harms of our societies. If different kinds of people live in different neighborhoods, goods and services can be delivered disproportionately to White people. And dangers and vulnerabilities can be delivered disproportionately to people of color.

Low-income neighborhoods and ones filled with racial and ethnic minorities, for example, are more likely than wealthy and White ones to be **resource deserts** (see Table 8.1).[28] These are places that lack beneficial or critical amenities, like a desert lacks water. Some neighborhoods are *service deserts* with less functional utilities, infrastructure, and emergency and non-emergency services. In these places, electricity is less reliable, potholes are filled less often, and firefighters are slower to arrive. Some are *food deserts*, regions lacking access to affordable, healthy food. There are also *health-care deserts*, regions without access to medical care; *green deserts*, neighborhoods without open spaces, parks, or playgrounds; *transit deserts*, neighborhoods without adequate transportation services (including roads, freeways, public transportation, bike lanes, or sidewalks); and *care deserts*, places where there are

resource deserts
places that lack beneficial or critical amenities

TABLE 8.1

Examples of Resource Deserts

Type of Desert	Definition	Example
Care deserts	Regions lacking licensed care facilities for children, the elderly, or people with disabilities	More than half of Americans live in neighborhoods with an insufficient supply of licensed childcare facilities.[29] There are nearly 4,500 children living in Lewis County, WA, for instance, but local childcare providers can only care for about 1,200 kids.[30] Parents who can't find quality childcare are forced to quit their jobs, leave their children in substandard care, or rely on family members.
Food deserts	Regions lacking access to affordable, healthy food	More than 23 million Americans live in food deserts, including 20 percent of rural residents.[31] The city of Camden, NJ, for example, has 75,000 residents but only one grocery store. Most residents — especially those without reliable and efficient transportation — rely on corner stores with high prices and low-quality food.
Green deserts	Regions lacking open spaces, parks, or playgrounds	In Baltimore, predominantly Black neighborhoods have much smaller parks than predominantly White neighborhoods, leading Black residents to suffer more from crowding in green spaces.[32]

TABLE 8.1

Examples of Resource Deserts—cont'd

Type of Desert	Definition	Example
Health-care deserts	Regions lacking sufficient access to medical care	Thirty million Americans would have to drive more than an hour to access emergency care.[33] Residents of Tonopah, NV, for example, saw their hospital close in 2015. Today, their nearest emergency room is 104 miles away.[34]
Service deserts	Regions with less-functional utilities, infrastructure, and emergency and non-emergency services	Three-quarters of towns with populations under 5,000 have all-volunteer fire departments.[35] One of them is Bayliss, CA, an unincorporated farming community several hours north of San Francisco. All its firefighting is provided by volunteers (several of whom are related to me).
Transit deserts	Regions with inadequate transportation services	In an analysis of fifty-two major cities, all had neighborhoods with insufficient public transportation.[36] One of the most underserved cities was Orlando, FL, where 13 percent of residents live in areas without enough public transportation to meet demand.

no nearby day care options for children, elder-care residences, or services for people with disabilities.

During the pandemic, deserts like these contributed to racial and ethnic disparities in death rates by making some populations especially vulnerable to Covid-19. Using a research method called spatial analysis—one in which data are layered onto a landscape divided into fine-grained segments (see "The Science of Sociology")—researchers studying Philadelphia showed that the living conditions common in ZIP codes with higher percentages of Black people increased the likelihood that they would contract the virus.[37] They were vulnerable on their way to work, riding long distances on inefficient public transportation. They were vulnerable at home, where cramped living conditions, often in multigenerational households, ensured close contact with other people at high risk. And if they became sick, they struggled to access timely testing and treatment.

This had deadly consequences. In the first nine months of the pandemic, Black and Hispanic Americans were three times as likely as White Americans to die from Covid-19.[38] American Indians and Alaska Natives were two-and-a-half times more likely to die. The disparity is found among young people too. About half of children and teenagers in the United States are non-White, but

spatial analysis
a research method in which data are layered onto a landscape divided into fine-grained segments

THE SCIENCE OF SOCIOLOGY

Spatial Analysis

All social interaction happens *somewhere*. In the east or the west, close to or far away from landmarks, on this side of the train tracks or the other. And those places have characteristics. They're clean or dirty, loud or quiet, crowded or empty, at high elevation or low. In studying sociology, place matters because every place is a distinct kind of space.

Spatial analysis puts place front and center. It's a research method in which data are layered onto a landscape divided into fine-grained segments. Researchers choose a region to analyze, then divide the region into parts. They may divide it block by block or use ZIP codes or government-determined Census tracts.

Then, for each segment of the region, they gather data on their variables of interest. They might be interested in residents' religiosity, density of housing, or the quality of the water. Whatever variable they choose, they layer the data they collect onto the segments on the map. This allows them to reveal the relationship between the region and the variable, or how levels of religiosity, for example, spread out across a landscape.

Today, sociologists use sophisticated geospatial software — including the same technology that our cell phones use to give us directions when we drive — to make ever more detailed maps. This kind of data allows researchers to find out where variables and features of a region overlap in interesting or troubling ways. Spatial analyses examining racial and ethnic segregation, for instance, are how sociologists have learned that predominantly Black and Hispanic neighborhoods are more likely than predominantly White ones to be resource deserts. It's also how they've determined that people of color are more likely to be exposed to environmental toxins. ∎

the young people who've died of the coronavirus are 83 percent non-White, and especially Black, Hispanic, American Indian, or Alaska Native.[39]

These disparities in infection and death rates are worsened by **environmental racism**, the practice of exposing racial and ethnic minorities to more toxins and pollutants than White people. Residential segregation enables environmental racism by concentrating members of some groups in neighborhoods in which there are environmental hazards.[40] Poor and minority families are more likely to live near industrial mining and agriculture; toxic waste and garbage dumps; power plants; and air, sea, and river ports.[41] These industrial processes

environmental racism
the practice of exposing racial and ethnic minorities to more toxins and pollutants than White people

Poor families and people of color are more likely than their counterparts to live in the shadow of toxic industries — a form of environmental racism that increases one's risk of developing chronic conditions like asthma, diabetes, and cancer.

make the air, soil, and water more dangerous. As a result of this exposure, people of color are more likely than others to give birth to premature babies and develop asthma, lead poisoning, diabetes, cancer, heart disease, and other debilitating and chronic diseases.[42] Many of these conditions, in turn, make us more vulnerable to viruses like Covid-19.

Sociologists have been at the forefront of both documenting and fighting environmental racism since it was first identified in the 1970s. In fact, the first expert witness in an environmental racism lawsuit was an African American sociologist named Robert Bullard. The suit was filed to block a plan to put a garbage dump in a middle-class Black suburb of Houston.

To produce evidence of discrimination, Bullard performed a spatial analysis in which he placed the locations of environmental hazards onto a map depicting segregated neighborhoods. He showed that twelve of the thirteen existing landfills, dumps, and garbage incinerators were in Black or Hispanic neighborhoods.[43] His side won the case, and his path-breaking research documenting environmental racism sparked a movement. Today he is known as the father of environmental justice.

Environmental discrimination is still prevalent throughout America. The water crisis in Flint, Michigan—a city that's 54 percent Black—is a recent example.[44] The crisis began when city officials failed to properly treat the public water supply, in violation of federal law, and aging pipes began leaking lead. Lead exposure can cause anemia, hypertension, and organ damage. It's especially dangerous to children, who may suffer irreversible brain damage. In Flint, up to 12,000 children were exposed to high levels of lead in their drinking water. These children were especially likely to be poor and Black.

Americans are exposed to lead in poor neighborhoods across the United States. Common sources include water from poorly maintained infrastructure, soil contaminated by industrial processes and nearby freeways, and lead-based paint on the walls of low-income housing. Since racial and ethnic minority children are more likely than White children to be poor, and poor children are more likely than middle-class children to live in cheap housing and near industrial and high-traffic areas, children of color are more likely to be exposed to lead.[45]

The environmental conditions of low-income neighborhoods literally cut lives short. Even before the pandemic, Americans in the richest neighborhoods lived an average of thirty-five years longer than those in the poorest.[46] That's the difference between dying at sixty years old and living to ninety-five. Research has found that just a few stops on the L train in Chicago or the subway in New York can separate neighborhoods with life expectancy differences of ten years or more.[47]

This unequal distribution of benefit and harm would be impossible without residential segregation. Under conditions of perfect integration, members of all groups would be equally vulnerable to environmental hazards and harms. Likewise, each would have equal access to services and amenities. And people living in underserved places would have just as much political influence as those living in any other neighborhood. But because our institutions concentrate economic and status disadvantages, it's easy to neglect and harm the least privileged among us.

INEQUITABLE EDUCATIONS

In 1958, a British sociologist named Michael Young coined the word *meritocracy*. He invented the word for the title of his novel, *The Rise of Meritocracy*. It's about a dystopian world in which, despite the abundance and variety of human talents, a person's worth is determined wholly by their performance on a standardized IQ test.[48] In true "modern" fashion, the meritocracy ranked everyone on a simple scale of "better" to "worse," and it did so with brutal efficiency and mathematical confidence. Everyone's humanity, reduced to a number.

Young meant for his book to be a dire warning, but Americans loved the idea. And they have incorporated it into the institution of education perhaps more than any other arena of life. As in Young's novel, a primary job of teachers is to rank their students from best to worst. Schools then aggregate these scores with a similar brutal efficiency, delivering to all students a mathematical measure of their merit: the grade point average, or GPA. Together with scores on standardized tests like the ACT and SAT, our GPAs determine whether we deserve degrees, admission to college or graduate school, and access to opportunities like fellowships, scholarships, and study-abroad programs. Because it's difficult or impossible to opt out of social institutions, we're all but forced to subject ourselves to this relentless ranking.

But it's *fair*, isn't it?

No. Some people find upward social mobility through education. I am one of those people, and you may be too. But to say that *some* people do so doesn't mean that the institution serves *mainly* to create an even playing field for all children. In fact, it mostly does the opposite. The U.S. educational system functions primarily to ensure that privileged children become privileged adults. Some people have greater power to decide what traits are meritorious. And some children have more opportunities than others to develop those traits.

This section discusses some of the ways that our educational opportunities are shaped by race and ethnicity. It considers inequality *between* schools (differences in the quality of education received by students attending different schools) and inequality *within* schools (differences in the educational experiences of children attending the same schools). It then discusses the **achievement gaps** that result, or disparities in the academic accomplishments of different kinds of students.

achievement gaps
disparities in
the academic
accomplishments
of different kinds
of students

Inequality between schools

The educational experiences of American students can vary dramatically. This is because—unlike European and Asian countries—nearly half of school funding in the United States comes from taxes paid by local property owners. The more valuable the property, the higher the taxes, which means that children living in expensive neighborhoods get expensive educations and children living in poor neighborhoods get poor ones. In a notable example, the median property value in Detroit City and Grosse Pointe—two side-by-side school districts in Michigan—are $45,100 and $200,000, respectively, which means that property taxes raise 4.4 times as much money for children attending schools in one district than the other.[49]

Only 18 percent of White students attend high-poverty schools, compared to 30 percent of Asian children and more than 60 percent of Black and Hispanic children.[50] Nationwide, predominantly White school districts receive $23 billion more in funding than ones that are predominantly non-White.[51] This is true even after state and national funding that subsidizes lower-income schools. Charter schools are no better, and possibly worse.[52]

More money means more qualified teachers, smaller class sizes, better supplies and equipment, more field trips, and so on.[53] The teacher and writer Jonathan Kozol famously chronicled the vast differences between well- and poor-financed schools.[54] Some schools, he found, had lively and prepared teachers, sufficient supplies, well-kept grounds, safe playgrounds, opportunities to play sports, up-to-date textbooks, and state-of-the-art technology. Others did not.

Meanwhile, about one in ten families send their children to private schools, a parallel educational system available primarily to the rich.[55] With an average tuition of over $11,000 per year per child, private schools mostly serve families who are financially comfortable. These schools also disproportionately enroll White students.[56] Nearly half of private schools are 90 percent White or more, compared to just a quarter of public schools.[57] And when Black and Hispanic students do attend private schools, they're more likely to attend service-oriented religious schools with lower tuitions than truly elite ones.

Instead of being a great equalizer, the U.S. educational system delivers the most expensive educations to children of wealthy families and the cheapest educations to poor ones. As a social institution, then, Education generally advantages White and wealthy students and disadvantages non-White and poor ones. If that's what education does, it's not because it's broken. It's because it was designed to do just that.

Inequality within schools

Students of color also face several forms of institutionalized racism within schools. To begin, most schools have institutionalized **tracking**, the practice of placing students in different classrooms according to their perceived ability.[58] As early as elementary school, some students will be labeled "gifted," others as "at risk." The former may be put into honors tracks, the latter into remedial education. Low-track classes tend to be of poorer quality, with lower expectations and standards.[59]

tracking
the practice of placing students in different classrooms according to their perceived ability

Immigrants and Black, Hispanic, American Indian, and Alaska Native students are disproportionately likely to be placed in low-track classes.[60] These students are also half as likely as White students to be enrolled in academically rigorous ones.[61] Tracking, in other words, is racialized. In part, this is because many teachers have the same biases as the rest of us.[62] They tend to overestimate the potential of Asian and White students and underestimate the potential of others.[63]

Black and brown children are also subject to more aggressive school discipline.[64] Disciplinary actions are more common in poor and minority schools and, within schools, disproportionately delivered to kids who are American Indian, Alaska Native, Hispanic, and, especially, Black.[65] Fourteen percent of Black students are suspended in any given year, compared with 3 percent of White students and 1 percent of Asian students.[66] Students of color are also more likely than White and Asian students to be given detention, expelled, or otherwise disciplined.

In one experimental study, teachers watched a video of a group of preschool children that included a Black girl, a Black boy, a White girl, and a White boy. Teachers were asked to say which child was most likely to require discipline (though the video didn't reveal any misbehavior by any of them).[67] While the teachers were watching the video, the computer was watching them. A program tracked their eye movements and found that the teachers spent significantly more time watching the Black children, especially the boys. When asked which child was most likely to require discipline, teachers were also most likely to point to the Black boy.

As this experiment suggests, differences in punishment are not explained by different rates of misbehavior. Other research confirms this finding. The state of Texas, for example, followed over 900,000 of its students for six years, starting in seventh grade.[68] Their analysis showed that—independent of all other factors, including behavior—Black, Hispanic, American Indian, and Alaska Native children, and those with disabilities, were punished more often and more aggressively. Nearly three-quarters of students with disabilities were suspended or expelled at least once.

On average, girls are punished less than boys, but the racial disparities are so stark that some girls of color are punished more than some groups of boys. Black girls are especially likely to be subject to school discipline, even more so if they're gender nonconforming.[69] Stereotyped as loud, defiant, and generally unladylike, Black girls receive harsh punishment aimed at getting them to be "good" instead of "ghetto."[70] Black girls who are gender nonconforming or out as non-heterosexual are especially likely to receive this kind of treatment.

This racialized regime of school punishment is now coordinated with police departments.

Policing schools

Since the early 1990s, low-income, predominantly Black and Hispanic schools have increasingly been patrolled by police.[71] These officers subject students to criminal-like surveillance: metal detectors, video cameras, and searches of lockers and backpacks. Instead of the once-dreaded principal's office, teachers now sometimes refer students to police officers. In most states, teachers are even legally required to get police involved under certain circumstances.

adultification
a form of bias in which adult characteristics are attributed to children

This trend reflects the **adultification** of kids of color, a form of bias in which adult characteristics are attributed to children.[72] From the time they're preschoolers, children of color are likely to be treated as if they have malicious intent. This creates routine differences in who's seen as "bad" and who's seen as merely mischievous. The misconduct of White boys is often brushed off as harmless. "Boys will be boys," we say, emphasizing that they're just children. The same behavior from boys of color, however, is often viewed as intentional. Instead of getting the benefit of the doubt, they get swift and unambiguous punishment.

As an example, consider the early life experiences of a Black American teenager named Darius, profiled by the sociologist Victor Rios.[73] Darius grew up in a poor, racially segregated neighborhood in Oakland, California. His school was quick to punish and had close ties with local police.

When Darius was fourteen, he was suspended from school for talking back to his teacher. When he was allowed to return, he told his teacher that he "wanted to do good, or else." He later clarified that he meant that he "wanted to do good, or else I would be very upset at myself." But his teacher didn't give Darius the benefit of the doubt. She interpreted the "or else" as a threat and immediately suspended him again.

Hurt and frustrated, Darius left the school that day and promptly got into a fight with a fellow student. Most kids who get in trouble for fighting will be punished by parents or teachers. Darius wasn't so lucky. He was launched into

For several decades now, police officers have been patrolling school hallways and cafeterias, especially in low-income and minority neighborhoods. This increases the likelihood that students in these schools will be routed out of education and into the criminal justice system.

the juvenile detention system, where he received probation, a period in which a person is subject to surveillance by the criminal justice system on threat of imprisonment.

On yet another day, as Darius walked to school, a neighbor mistook him for someone who'd robbed him. The neighbor called the cops, who pulled up aggressively in an unmarked police car. Darius didn't know that cops had been called and thought someone was trying to run him over. He darted down the street, which prompted the police officer to assume he was guilty. "He thought I was guilty 'cause I was running," Darius recalled, "but I was running 'cause I was scared." Though he was innocent of the robbery, he was now guilty of evading a police officer, another charge. Darius was arrested twice more while on probation, once for allegedly talking back to his probation officer and once for allegedly intimidating a clerk at a shoe store. By this time, Darius's record was expanding and his chance of escaping the adult criminal justice system was shrinking.

The sociologist who profiled Darius was troubled by the swiftness and inflexibility of the punishment Darius received, both from his teachers and the police. Victor Rios had, in fact, grown up in the exact same neighborhood as Darius, and he'd been on a very similar path. Born in Mexico, Rios had immigrated to the United States with his mother at the age of two.[74] At the time he lived there, the neighborhood was so neglected that rats chewed on children in their cribs. When his three-month-old cousin's face was disfigured in this way, Rios dropped out of eighth grade. He wanted to earn money to help his family move somewhere less nightmarish.[75] "I don't want to live like this," he said to his thirteen-year-old self. "I don't want to be poor; I don't want my family to suffer."[76]

When he was fifteen years old, a close encounter with gunfire motivated Rios to get on the straight and narrow. He did so with the help of many kind adults. A teacher helped him find a job, calling dozens of local businesses on his behalf. A police officer let him off with a warning after he, like Darius, was caught fighting. Referring to people like these, Rios remarked:

> I don't think they realize today how important their second chance for me was. At the time it was important for me to hear an adult tell me, listen we know you're a mess up, we know you've been to juvy, we know you're caught up on the streets, we know you're a drop out . . . but we still believe in you. And they gave me that dignity and I ran with it.[77]

These adults, Rios wrote, gave him a "viable choice," a pathway to a label other than Juvenile Delinquent and away from a deviant career. He finished high school, put himself through college, and was admitted to a PhD program. Today he's a professor of sociology at the University of California at Santa Barbara.

Rios returned to the streets of Oakland to study boys like he had once been, and he discovered that the criminalization of children in schools had worsened. Rios was a teenager in the 1990s. That was the first decade after the United States began imposing harsh discipline in schools, dismantling the social safety net, defunding higher education and—as you'll see in the next section of this chapter—ramping up mass incarceration and deportation. It was difficult enough for Rios to transition from juvenile delinquent to college kid. By the time Darius was in school, teachers and police officers were offering even less leniency.

school-to-prison pipeline
a practice of disciplining and punishing children and youth in school that routes them out of education and into the criminal justice system

Now, many poor students of color encounter a **school-to-prison pipeline**, a practice of disciplining and punishing children and youth in school that routes them out of education and into the criminal justice system. Being labeled increases the likelihood that a child will engage in criminal activity, while being pushed out of school exposes students to networks that might introduce them to it. Being suspended just one time doubles the likelihood that a student will drop out of school altogether, which is a primary risk factor for imprisonment as an adult.[78] Unfortunately, all too often, going to school puts students of color at risk of being routed directly into prison.

Achievement gaps

Unequal educational opportunities both within and across schools translate into disparities in academic achievement. Though people of all racial and ethnic backgrounds equally value education, students of color, with the exception of Asians, are less likely to graduate from high school than White students.[79] Only about a third of Black and Hispanic Americans enroll in college before they turn twenty-four. Native populations—Native Hawaiians, American Indians, and Alaska Natives—enroll at even lower rates.

The disparities are even greater when it comes to enrollment at competitive colleges. Dozens of the most prestigious colleges in the United States enroll more students from the 1 percent than they do from the bottom 60 percent combined.[80] A study of Harvard University's admissions discovered that nearly half of White admits were given some kind of priority.[81] They were the child of an employee, had a social tie to a dean, or were a "legacy" (the child or grand-child of an alumnus). In contrast, only 16 percent of Asian, Hispanic, and Black students were granted admission because of a similar priority status. Analysis further showed that three-quarters of those White students would not have earned admission on merit alone. In short, if Harvard actually applied their own criteria fairly, there would be noticeably fewer White students on campus.

By better serving White and wealthy students, the social institution of Education functions as yet another form of legitimation for the status quo. Educational credentials, especially ones from elite schools, justify some people's positions at the top of status and economic hierarchies. Instead of providing an even playing field, then, U.S. education stacks the deck against some children, serves many less well than it should, and preserves the privileges of the highest status among us.

Meritocracy? Not so much. Even the sociologist who coined the term—Michael Young—took advantage of his connections. When he discovered that his own son failed to earn admission to college on merit alone, he made a personal phone call to Oxford University and got him in anyway.[82]

RACE, MIGRATION, AND POLICING

Humans have known about marijuana's pleasurable and medicinal qualities for at least 5,000 years.[83] This is true around the world and in the Americas too. For most of U.S. history, in fact, marijuana was legal, and Americans could freely buy it at pharmacies. They used it to treat headaches, stomachaches, and insomnia. And they used it to get high. In 1843, the *Western Journal of Medicine and Surgery* described marijuana's effects as "of the most cheerful kind."[84]

The first U.S. laws to criminalize the plant were passed in the 1920s in response to anti-immigration sentiment.[85] The sentiment was prompted by an increase in legal immigration to the United States by Mexican citizens fleeing a civil war. Though the vast majority of Mexicans did not use marijuana, anti-immigrant propaganda suggested that they were importing drugs and bringing crime. Though it was known in Africa as *dagga*, in China as *ma*, and in Europe as *hemp*, American authorities adopted the word *marijuana*—a Spanish word—specifically to stigmatize and criminalize Mexican immigrants.

The same propaganda that associated marijuana with Mexico characterized the plant as dangerous. The most infamous example is the 1936 film *Reefer*

The U.S. federal government demonized marijuana, then blamed legal Mexican immigrants for its presence in the United States. The propaganda was a cynical attempt to convince Americans to favor criminalizing the crossing of the border.

Madness, but the effort went all the way to the top of the U.S. federal government. Harry Anslinger, who became the commissioner of the Federal Bureau of Narcotics in 1930, described marijuana as an "evil weed" and argued that it led to murder, suicide, sexual violence, communism, interracial relationships, and "maniacal deeds."[86] Anslinger also blamed marijuana for jazz music, which he said was satanic. In 1937, he wrote an article for the public titled "Marihuana: Assassin of Youth!" (spelled with an *h* to invoke a Spanish accent).[87] That year, nonmedical use of marijuana was criminalized across the United States. Two years later, the United States would also criminalize crossing the border from Mexico.

Fifty years after that, marijuana would play the central role in what President Ronald Reagan would call the "War on Drugs." During the 1980s, politicians voted to raise the combined antidrug funding of the FBI, the Department of Defense, and the Drug Enforcement Administration from $165 million to $2.3 billion a year.[88] In the decades since, the United States has spent more than $1 trillion and made more than 45 million drug arrests.[89] The country's prison population has grown by 1,100 percent.[90]

The majority of people imprisoned for drug crimes are convicted of possession of marijuana. Drug crimes account for two-thirds of the rise in the federal prison population and half the increase in state prisoners.[91] Even today, despite the fact that marijuana has been legalized in many states, despite the 50 percent of Americans who've tried it, despite the 62 percent who now approve of nationwide legalization of recreational use, and despite the 88 percent who approve of medical marijuana, the number of arrests for drug offenses continues to rise.[92] Every twenty seconds, someone is newly arrested for a drug offense.[93] Of these arrests, 85 percent are for marijuana possession with no intent to sell.

The color of incarceration and deportation

As a direct result of the War on Drugs, the United States imprisons more of its population than any other country in the world. It incarcerates four times as many people as Mexico, six times as many as Canada, and nearly

FIGURE 8.1

The U.S. Incarceration Rate in International Perspective

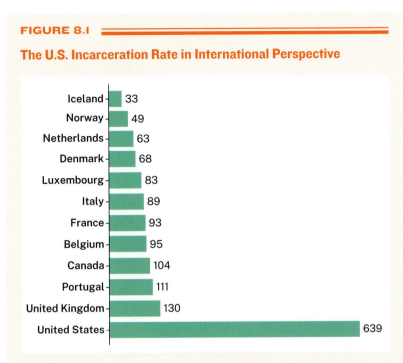

Country	Rate
Iceland	33
Norway	49
Netherlands	63
Denmark	68
Luxembourg	83
Italy	89
France	93
Belgium	95
Canada	104
Portugal	111
United Kingdom	130
United States	639

NOTE: Number of people incarcerated per 100,000 residents.

SOURCE: World Prison Brief, Institute for Crime & Justice Policy Research, 2020, https://www.prisonstudies.org/highest-to-lowest/prison_population_rate (accessed 3/31/2021).

nine times as many as Denmark. As shown in Figure 8.1, when compared with similar rich democracies, the United States is off the charts.[94] All told, in 2019 there were 9 million people in the U.S. correctional system. The rise has inspired some to describe the United States as a country characterized by **mass incarceration**, an extremely high rate of imprisonment in cross-cultural and historical perspective. About one in forty people in the United States is under some form of correctional control.[95]

Factually, the ballooning of the prison population was *not* a reaction to an increase in crime. Rates of crime, including violent crimes like homicide, were falling quickly during these decades.[96] Nor was the rise in incarceration a response to pressure from American citizens. Few considered crime a serious social problem in the 1960s.[97]

Instead, mass incarceration was pushed by politicians with a "tough on crime" agenda. With the help of the media, they convinced Americans that crime, and drug crimes especially, were a substantial threat. Even as the homicide rate fell, media coverage of murder on network news rose by 600 percent, focusing especially on White women victims.[98] By 1990, six in ten Americans were worried that crime was on the rise (it wasn't), and most thought drugs were the greatest danger to youth. The majority of Americans favored harsher criminal punishments and increased spending on law enforcement.

mass incarceration
an extremely high rate of imprisonment in cross-cultural and historical perspective

"In any war," says the legal scholar Michelle Alexander, "you have to have an enemy."[99] And the evidence shows that the enemy in the War on Drugs is Black and Hispanic men.[100] Data show that one in six Hispanic men and one in three Black men go to prison at least once.[101] American Indians and Alaska Natives are also overrepresented.[102] In contrast, one in seventeen White men will spend time in prison. This is startlingly high, higher than the incarceration rate of most other countries, but the numbers for Black and Latino men are truly staggering.

Hispanic Americans are also disproportionately deported. The policing of marijuana continues to be a mechanism by which the federal government targets Hispanic immigrants for deportation. Almost all deportations—97 percent—are carried out against people from Latin America or the Caribbean, and even though half of migrants are women, 90 percent of deportations are of men.[103] Approximately a quarter of these are triggered by arrests for possession of marijuana (less than 1 percent involve someone alleged to be selling drugs).[104]

mass deportation
an extremely high rate of deportation in cross-cultural and historical perspective

Alongside mass incarceration, then, the last several decades of policy have contributed to **mass deportation**, an extremely high rate of deportation in cross-cultural and historical perspective (see Figure 8.2). Presidents George W. Bush and Barack Obama deported more people than every other president in

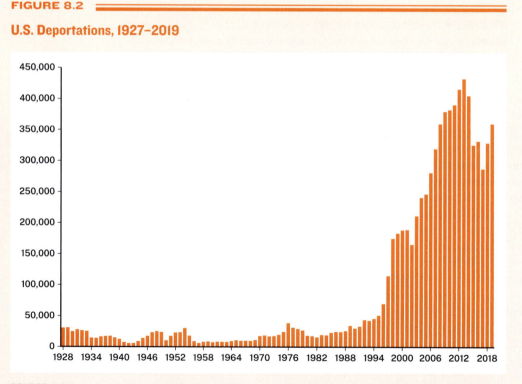

FIGURE 8.2

U.S. Deportations, 1927–2019

SOURCE: U.S. Department of Homeland Security, "2019 Yearbook of Immigration Statistics," Table 39: Aliens Removed or Returned: Fiscal Years 1892 to 2019, https://www.dhs.gov/immigrationstatistics/yearbook/2019.

U.S history combined.[105] President Donald Trump promised to deport as many immigrants as possible, though his rate of deportation was lower than Obama's.[106]

Importantly, drug use is no higher among Black and Hispanic people than it is among White people. According to the National Survey on Drug Use and Health, which queried nearly 70,000 Americans in 2018, 55 percent of White people report having used an illegal drug, compared with 38 percent of Hispanics and 46 percent of Black Americans.[107] Immigrants are half as likely as people born in the United States to have used drugs in the last month.[108] Nor do disadvantaged and immigrant neighborhoods have substantially more drug use than other neighborhoods.[109]

Targeting Black and brown neighborhoods

Instead of reflecting actual rates of drug use, disparate imprisonment and deportation rates are a result of interpersonal and institutional racism. Research on who's pulled over and searched while driving reveals that choices are based on prejudicial stereotypes.[110] A study of almost 100 million U.S. traffic stops, for instance, discovered that the proportion of Black drivers stopped drops substantially after sunset, when officers are unable to discern a driver's race from afar.[111] The same study also found that police have a lower bar for deciding whether to search Black and Hispanic drivers compared with White drivers. In some cities, Black drivers are searched five times as often as White drivers. In other cities, it's Hispanic drivers who are most likely to be searched. In either case, police are *less* likely to find contraband when they search Black or Hispanic drivers than when they search White ones.

The same is true of "stop-and-frisk," a practice in which police temporarily detain someone on the street to question them and search them for drugs, weapons, or other illegal contraband. Police have discretion in deciding whom they stop, needing only to claim "reasonable suspicion." Like most of us, police officers often harbor prejudice against people of color. Stop-and-frisk is also more common in immigrant communities.[112] Notably, when police stop Black and Hispanic men, they find weapons only 1 percent of the time.[113]

Residential segregation concentrates Black and Hispanic Americans in certain neighborhoods, making it easy for police departments to target these populations. And they do. Studies have found that these neighborhoods are more aggressively policed than mostly White neighborhoods regardless of whether they have higher levels of crime.[114] There, a hypervigilant and ever-present police force makes doing everyday things, like driving and walking, a risk factor for encounters with police.

Under these circumstances, people in these neighborhoods who *do* use drugs are likely to be caught. In contrast, people doing drugs in suburban homes, fraternity houses, and private schools will probably go undetected. In this way, the risk of arrest is concentrated among poor people of color.

Their families and neighborhoods suffer.[115] Imprisonment and deportation separate spouses and take parents away from their children. They take earners out of households, further impoverishing their families. Heavy policing makes neighborhoods appear to be "high-crime areas," making entrepreneurs, lenders, and city leaders less likely to want to invest in them. This all intensifies the financial vulnerability of residents and furthers residential segregation, contributing to the cycle that makes institutional discrimination possible in the first place.

DISCRIMINATION AND THE SOCIAL STRUCTURE

Two chapters ago, this book introduced the idea of the *social institution*, widespread and enduring patterns of interaction with which we respond to categories of human need. As helpful as they can be, institutions can also be designed to produce unequal and unjust outcomes. These outcomes are legitimated when they resonate with the symbolic structure, delivering injustice to people whom our societies deem low status. In the examples highlighted in this chapter, the people who are suffering the most are Black, Hispanic, and immigrant men, especially the most economically disadvantaged among them.

The advantage and disadvantage produced by our social institutions is cross-institutional, cumulative, and intergenerational. We see **cross-institutional advantage and disadvantage** when people are positively or negatively served across multiple institutions. Children who grow up in safe and healthy neighborhoods with strong services and amenities, for example, are also likely to get good educations and be relatively free of police oversight. This will help them get good jobs, adequate health care, and access to credit. They'll end up with good social networks and find a good spouse with whom they'll buy a good house in a good neighborhood with good schools, and so on.

Conversely, people who are disadvantaged in one institution usually face disadvantage across the board. They're structurally positioned such that they have fewer opportunities. A person who grows up in a neighborhood characterized by concentrated poverty, underfunded schools, and high levels of policing will face not just one disadvantage but many. Together, these disadvantages can harm the futures of even the brightest and most hardworking children.

The social structure also produces **cumulative advantage and disadvantage**, whereby advantages or disadvantages build over the life course. People who get help from their parents to buy their first house, for example, can rent out a room to a friend, then use their rent money to pay their mortgage, enabling them to buy another house to rent out to still other people, leading to financial advantages in the form of equity that they can use to start their own business.

Alternatively, a person might experience cumulative disadvantage. A person who grows up in a family of modest means may rent instead of own, which makes it difficult to save and increases the likelihood that they'll be unable to pay their bills, leading to a bad credit score that will hinder their ability to afford a reliable car that allows them to remain employed when living in a public transit desert. As people move through life, advantages and disadvantages have a way of snowballing, creating much better or worse opportunities.

Finally, there's **intergenerational advantage and disadvantage**, the kind passed from parents to children. People who were able to buy a home in past

cross-institutional advantage and disadvantage
a phenomenon in which people are positively or negatively served across multiple institutions

cumulative advantage and disadvantage
advantage or disadvantage that builds over the life course

intergenerational advantage and disadvantage
advantage and disadvantage that is passed from parents to children

generations secured economic stability not only for themselves and their (usually) same-race spouses but also their descendants. Over time, homeowners were able to capitalize on tax breaks and inflation, later selling their houses for a profit. They passed these profits on to their kids, who were more likely to be able to buy a home and pass on that advantage to the generation after them, and so on. Figure 8.3 shows, for example, how wealth gaps between Black and White Americans (top) and Hispanic and White Americans (bottom) have tripled in size since U.S. politicians began dismantling the New Deal in 1980.[116]

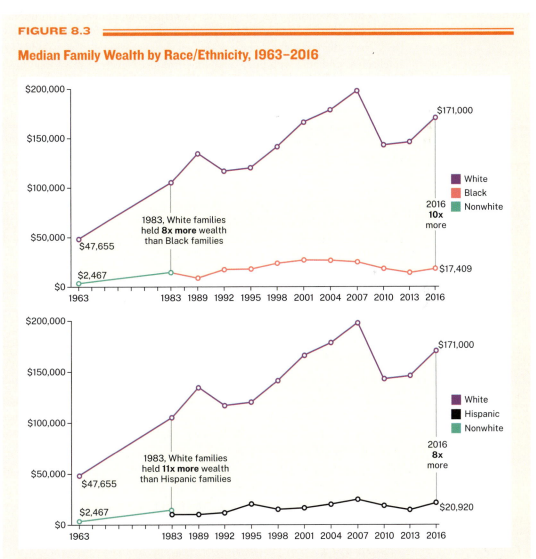

FIGURE 8.3

Median Family Wealth by Race/Ethnicity, 1963–2016

SOURCE: Urban Institute, "Nine Charts about Wealth Inequality in America (Updated)," Oct. 24, 2017, https://apps.urban .org/features/wealth-inequality-charts; Urban Institute calculations from Survey of Financial Characteristics of Consumers 1962, Survey of Changes in Family Finances 1963, and Survey of Consumer Finances 1983–2016.

Of course, there are stories of unlikely success and ones in which people with every advantage fail, but sociological understandings of the world are probabilistic, not deterministic. That is, to study social facts is to look for social patterns, not social laws. Given the mechanisms of social stratification that sociologists have documented, it's probable that a person who's privileged by cross-institutional and cumulative advantage will do nicely in life and that a disadvantaged person will struggle. Same for their children.

When institutional discrimination is so effective that it prevents people from meeting even their basic needs for food, water, shelter, peace of mind, and bodily autonomy, it's referred to as **structural violence**, institutional discrimination that injures the body and mind.[117] A socially stratified society does more than just limit the options of the disadvantaged; it suppresses intellectual potential with poor schooling, produces levels of stress that cause physical and mental illness, and exposes bodies to dangerous environments.

In the context of racism against Black Americans, the civil rights activist Stokely Carmichael explained structural violence this way:

> When White terrorists bomb a Black church and kill five Black children, that is an act of individual racism, widely deplored by most segments of the society. But when in that same city—Birmingham, Alabama—five hundred Black babies die each year because of the lack of proper food, shelter and medical facilities, and thousands more are destroyed and maimed physically, emotionally and intellectually because of conditions of poverty and discrimination in the Black community, that is a function of institutional racism.[118]

Whether it's caused by a knife or neighborhood neglect, by gunshot or solitary confinement, by beatings or through educational deprivation, by a knee to the neck or a lack of healthy food options, it is real harm. And when it causes injury, disease, or death, it's no less violent than an attack.

With these observations in mind, the philosopher Marilyn Frye described oppression as a birdcage. "The experience of oppressed people," she wrote:

> is that the living of one's life is confined and shaped by forces and barriers which are . . . systematically related to each other in such a way as to catch one between and among them and restrict or penalize motion in any direction. It is the experience of being caged in: All avenues, in every direction, are blocked or booby trapped.[119]

In this analogy, each social institution is a wire of a cage. No single wire could trap us in. Not even many wires could. But when so many of the wires are present—when much of the social structure is against us—escape is very difficult. Advantage and disadvantage harmonize across social institutions, over a lifetime, and over generations, creating a cage for some while helping others fly free. ∎

structural violence
institutional discrimination that injures the body and mind

COMING UP...

THE UNITED STATES maintains a system of social stratification based on race, ethnicity, and immigration status. Residential segregation isolates people of color in some parts of cities and concentrates White people in others. This ensures that amenities such as affordable and healthy food, places to play, and social services are easily available only to some. Meanwhile, environmental hazards can be delivered to others.

Residential segregation is also part of how societies deliver substandard educations and criminal punishment specifically to Black, Hispanic, and Native populations. The U.S. system of school funding ensures that schools in low-income neighborhoods, disproportionately filled with students of color, will struggle to deliver high-quality education. Discriminatory policies and practices occur within schools, too, preserving the best educational experiences for White students.

In these same low-income neighborhoods, Black and Hispanic men are more closely surveilled by police. In the past several decades, the policing of marijuana possession, in particular, has led to mass incarceration and deportation. This upends lives, disrupts families, and harms communities, contributing to a cycle of deprivation enabled by residential segregation.

One more chapter addresses the institutionalization of discrimination. This one is about gender. It focuses on how both the family and the workplace are organized in ways that advantage men over women and masculine people over feminine ones. It traces the origins of the ideas that work is a "man's world" and home is a "woman's place." It shows how those ideas still shape men's and women's experiences as employees and family members. And it concludes with an intersectional discussion about the state of "women's liberation." Gendered oppression is next.

9

GENDERED
OPPRESSION

IN THIS **CHAPTER...**

THIS IS THE third of three chapters that address inequality in America. The first looked at economic inequality and the second examined racial and ethnic inequality. This one considers gender inequality:

- *Sexism* is the production of unjust outcomes for people perceived to be biologically female.

- *Androcentrism* is the production of unjust outcomes for people who perform femininity.

Sexism disadvantages women, while androcentrism disadvantages both women and some kinds of men. The most privileged men in American society are generally ones who can and choose to avoid performing femininity, while men who are cast as feminine are seen as lesser men.

All our social institutions are shaped by sexism and androcentrism. This chapter specifically examines the workplace and the family. Because childcare and housework are traditionally cast as "women's work," women do a disproportionate amount of this work, even when they hold full-time jobs. Meanwhile, the workplace is still largely a man's world. Though most people in relationships today want to share paid and unpaid work equally, ideologies and institutional forces press families to make gendered decisions.

For this reason, many sociologists think we're in the midst of a *stalled revolution*, a sweeping change in gender relations that got started but has yet to be fully realized. Because we value masculinity more than femininity, women can embody both. For the same reason, men try *not* to do femininity. While this leaves men less free than women to craft lifestyles that suit them, the options they do have are ones that deliver social and economic rewards.

You'll also learn about *time-use diaries*, a research method in which participants are asked to self-report their activities at regular intervals throughout the day.

"The problem with gender is that it prescribes how we should be rather than recognizing how we are."

—CHIMAMANDA NGOZI ADICHIE

When Max Weber's book on the Protestant work ethic was released in 1905, his wife—a sociologist named Marianne Weber (1870–1954)—was finishing up a book of her own. Marianne's book, *Occupation and Marriage*, would be published the following year.[1] Both important intellectuals of their era, Max and Marianne Weber had different objects of inquiry. He was interested in men at work. She was interested in women at home.

It's easy to imagine why the home so occupied Marianne Weber's intellectual curiosity. Her life was a virtual catalog of women's family obligations.[2] Her mother made the ultimate feminine sacrifice; she died in childbirth when Marianne was just two years old. Her father, unable or unwilling to raise a child alone, sent his daughter to live with female relatives. She grew up with her grandmother and aunt and, as a teenager, became a live-in nanny to another relative, helping to raise her six children. Early in her marriage to Max, Marianne also nursed her husband's severe depression, a condition that left him unable to work for years. Though they would have no children of their own, Marianne raised four of her husband's nieces and nephews after his sister's early death.

Marianne would be widowed when Max died in 1920 at just fifty-six years old. He succumbed to a later wave of the 1918 flu pandemic, joining an estimated 39 million killed by the virus.[3] After his death, Marianne spent the next decade ensuring her husband's legacy, publishing his remaining work and writing his biography.

Such was her life. Yet, Marianne chafed under the domestic work required of women. Wealthy White women like Marianne were excluded from participating in the professions that occupied the men in their lives, leaving them constrained to the domestic realm. Chores and childcare filled her hours—an unrelenting treadmill of feminine responsibility.

It was a life, she complained, "without hope of achievement or intellectual scope."[4] It's not that she didn't value the work of raising children and keeping a home. In fact, as we'll see, she valued it more than most. What she objected to was the idea that women should be limited to those roles.[5] "As a human being," she argued, "[the woman] shares with the man an abundance of talents and abilities that [call her] . . . to participate in every kind of cultural work for which her individual talents fit her."[6] Unfortunately, most of her male contemporaries did not agree.

Her husband was an exception; he encouraged her to pursue her intellectual interests. But in their marriage, and in the outside world, his career took precedence. And Marianne would be one of those extraordinary people who is able to think and write in spite of it all. In fact, she would rise to become one of the most prominent intellectuals of her time, publishing seventeen books and dozens of essays. When the history of sociology was written, Max would be crowned a "founding father" of sociology. Her contributions would go unacknowledged and remain underappreciated to this day.

Marianne and Max Weber both made significant contributions to the study of society. Max was interested in paid work, while Marianne was driven to study family life, especially the unpaid work done almost entirely by women.

This chapter is about Marianne and Max's parallel interests: family and work. It begins with a consideration of the so-called traditional marriage. It considers the extent to which the traditional marriage, and the marriage models that came before and since, reflect *patriarchal* relations, ones that empower men at the expense of women. In order to do this, the chapter also offers an overview of how sociologists think about gender inequality, introducing two related concepts: sexism and androcentrism. It then describes how the diverse families of today attempt to balance work and family.

THE "TRADITIONAL" FAMILY

The oldest model of marital relations is the **patriarch/property marriage**, one in which women and children are owned by men. This form of marriage legally defined women and children as equivalent to any other form of property, like land, animals, or enslaved people. As property, married women couldn't enter into legal contracts, had no rights to their children, and couldn't vote, serve on juries, or run for political office. They couldn't write wills; they were *in* wills. If their husbands died, they were passed on as property to some other man. This type of marriage lasted thousands of years and was practiced in the United States as late as the 1800s.

patriarch/property marriage
a model of marriage in which women and children are owned by men

Early feminists, both Black and White, fought to end the patriarch/property model of marriage. Mississippi was the first U.S. state to begin giving rights to married women. Other states followed.[7] By the time the Industrial Revolution was in full swing, a new kind of marriage had emerged. Today we call it the **breadwinner/homemaker marriage**, a model of marriage that involves a wage-earning spouse supporting a stay-at-home spouse and children.

This was an entirely new way of thinking about the relationship between husband and wife. Before industrialization, on farms, plantations, and among small business owners, the home and work were one. No one "went to work"; they woke up there. The home was a place of work. After industrialization, many people worked in large-scale operations like factories and mines. Urban populations sprung up around them, creating the first large cities. Now there was a "work*place*": a place to go for work.

breadwinner/ homemaker marriage
a model of marriage that involves a wage-earning spouse supporting a stay-at-home spouse and children

The Industrial Revolution forced many men out of the home and into factories and other workplaces. Only then did the home become a "woman's place," one where women alone were responsible for housekeeping, cooking, and caring for children.

Children had worked alongside their parents before industrialization, so it seemed only natural to put the whole family to work in industrial workplaces too. In fact, the first factories employed hardly any men at all.[8] Employers preferred women and children because hiring them weakened the negotiating power of adult male workers. With more laborers competing for the same number of jobs, the bourgeoisie could resist worker demands for higher wages, safer workplaces, and the like.

In response, men organized to limit women's and children's participation in the workforce. Whole industries refused to hire women, claiming the work was too dangerous for them. Others refused to hire married women, on the assumption employment would interfere with their duties at home and undermine husbands' authority. High-status and high-paying occupations, like law and medicine, were made entirely off-limits to women. Organized into labor unions, men collaborated to exclude women and people of color.[9] By 1938, child labor was illegal everywhere (except on farms, where it's still legal today).

With their position strengthened, White working-class men advocated for a **family wage**, an income, paid to a man, that is large enough to support a non-working wife and children. With it came the "stay-at-home" wife, another novel idea that came out of industrialization. The transition neatly divided work and home. Then, once divided, these spaces and their activities were gendered. This is the **ideology of separate spheres**, or the idea that the home is a feminine space best tended by women and work is a masculine space best suited to men. *That* is when the arrangement we tend to refer to today as "traditional" emerged, only about 100 years ago.

The breadwinner/homemaker marriage didn't just place men and women into separate spheres. It also cast them as unequal. This is what Marianne Weber wanted us to understand. It wasn't that caring for a spouse, raising children, keeping a beautiful home, and nursing elders was worthless. Quite the contrary: She believed that these things were incredibly valuable, even priceless. But most men *didn't* value this work. And since they saw women as having lesser value than themselves, it made sense to men to make women do it. These twin phenomena—the devaluation of women and the devaluation of women's work—made the breadwinner/homemaker arrangement keenly unjust.

Marianne's analyses of the family under patriarchy wouldn't pierce mainstream sociology. Perhaps it was because she was a woman, or perhaps it was because she was interested in "women's issues." Even her husband, as supportive as he was, never took gender seriously in his own writings. In fact, in the 1950s, the decade of Marianne's death, the breadwinner/homemaker model of marriage would be in its heyday. Women were no longer property, but they were still held solely responsible for the home half of life. At the time, sociologists who adopted functionalist views of society were ardent supporters of this model.

family wage
an income, paid to a man, that is large enough to support a non-working wife and children

ideology of separate spheres
the idea that the home is a feminine space best tended by women and work is a masculine space best suited to men

THE FATE OF THE BREADWINNER/ HOMEMAKER MARRIAGE

While in graduate school in the 1920s, Talcott Parsons (1902–1979) would encounter Max Weber's sociology. Parsons was so intrigued, so moved by Weber's ideas, that Parsons contacted Marianne Weber—by now a widow— and asked permission to translate one of Max's books into English.[10] A champion of her husband's intellectual legacy, she agreed.

Parsons, however, had no interest in Max's *wife's* ideas. In fact, Parsons strongly disagreed with Marianne Weber's belief that men and women shared the same "talents and abilities." Instead, Parsons argued that men and women were "opposite" sexes: naturally different and with contrasting strengths and weaknesses.[11] Accordingly, he argued that the breadwinner/homemaker marriage was a perfect balance between the masculine and feminine. This balance, he asserted, was essential for functional families and, more broadly, functional societies.

Even in the 1950s, though, real life was failing to live up to this ideal. Only 40 percent of marriages fit the breadwinner/homemaker mold.[12] Many White men were too poor to support a family alone, and men of color were largely denied a family wage. Poor women of all races continued to work, even as the ideology of separate spheres defined their femininity as insufficient and their families as unnatural.

To Parsons, such families were dysfunctional. He regarded homosexuality, failure to marry, not having children, and divisions of labor that defied the separate spheres ideology as threats to individual happiness and social stability.[13] One of his contemporaries, the sociologist and politician Daniel Patrick Moynihan, wrote a widely publicized report for the U.S. government in which he argued that poverty among Black Americans was caused by their failure to adhere to the breadwinner/homemaker model (while downplaying interpersonal and institutional discrimination).[14] Specifically, he blamed the "reversed roles of husband and wife," suggesting that Black women were insufficiently subordinate to their husbands and Black men insufficiently dominant over their wives.

Evidence suggests that Parsons and Moynihan were wrong about breadwinner/homemaker marriages. This family form was not functional; it was failing.[15] Many housewives were bored and depressed. They were self-medicating with booze and sedatives known as "mother's little helpers."[16] When *The Feminine Mystique*, a book about housewives' unhappiness, was published in 1963, it spent six weeks on the *New York Times* bestseller list.[17]

Their husbands were unhappy too. To remain single too long was to be suspected of homosexuality, and "family men" were more likely to be hired and given promotions. To satisfy social expectations, men took on the role of breadwinner young. It was a lot of pressure, and uncomfortable. Many men felt like a bank machine dispensing money to an unhappy wife. Responding to men's unhappiness, a new magazine called *Playboy* launched in 1953. Its first issue was an attack on "gold-digger" women who married for money.[18] The magazine's founder, Hugh Hefner, fed men's fantasies of being perpetually single. He was a millionaire by the end of the decade.

In addition to being boring for women and stressful for men, the breadwinner/homemaker marriage of the 1950s required Americans to ascribe to a set of ideas related to gender and sexuality. For example, the marriage was premised on a gender binary, acknowledging only the presence of men and women. Thus, it wasn't inclusive of people who are nonbinary or gender fluid. It was also **heteronormative**. It promoted heterosexuality as the only or preferred sexual identity, making other sexual desires invisible or casting them as inferior.

The breadwinner/homemaker model was also **mononormative**. It promoted *monogamy*, or the requirement that spouses have sexual relations only with each other.[19] Mononormativity erases other ways of forming sexual and romantic relationships. These include *open relationships* (ones in which partners agree that they are free to have sexual relations with other people) and

heteronormative
promoting hetero-sexuality as the only or preferred sexual identity, making other sexual desires invisible or casting them as inferior

mononormative
promoting mo-nogamy, or the requirement that spouses have sexual relations only with each other

Launched by Hugh Hefner in 1953, *Playboy* magazine fed men's fantasies of a sexy, stress-free bachelor lifestyle. The success of the magazine revealed widespread unhappiness among men, who often carried the heavy burden of being their family's sole breadwinner.

polyamorous relationships (ones in which partners agree that they're free to form relationships with others that are both sexual and romantic).

Finally, the breadwinner/homemaker marriage was **pro-natal**. This model of marriage only reached full completion with the birth of children. Thus, it promoted childbearing and stigmatized childlessness. Children, in turn, heightened the stakes of marriage in specifically gendered ways. Children increased the likelihood that women would feel the need to focus even more intently on the home while increasing the pressure on men to be ever more successful at work.

The breadwinner/homemaker marriage, then, didn't just institutionalize a certain way of being married; it institutionalized the gender binary, monogamy, heterosexuality, and childrearing. None of this was entirely new in the 1950s. But the extreme rigidity of these norms in that decade and the expectation that everyone abide by them *was* new. The whole of society seemed to agree that everyone should fit themselves into a single mold. Politicians, employers, Hollywood producers, and sociologists agreed too. Many people chafed against these constraints, and those who were unable or unwilling to comply found themselves labeled as deviants.

Tragically, Talcott Parsons's own daughter was a victim of this rigid endorsement of the breadwinner/homemaker marriage. Anne Parsons turned twenty in 1950, the decade in which her father was at the height of his intellectual

pro-natal
promoting childbearing and stigmatizing choosing to go child-free

importance. She was a natural thinker who yearned to put her mind to good use. She almost married in college "for security's sake" but couldn't bring herself to do it. "The world seemed so much bigger than split-level houses," she wrote, "and I thought I had better start off to see it."[20] She traveled internationally, pursued her studies, and became a social scientist in her own right. She was especially critical of the profession of psychotherapy, arguing that it was unresponsive to patient diversity.

She loved her work but felt intense anguish over having failed to marry. She criticized herself for not being able to embrace domesticity.[21] And at twenty-five, she figured she was too old. At that "ripe old age," she wrote ruefully, "I found it was already too late: most of my contemporaries were already on the third child." Meanwhile, her career was stifled by a lack of opportunities for women.

When the feminist bestseller *The Feminine Mystique* was released in 1963, she wrote a desperate eight-page letter to its author, Betty Friedan. She felt, she wrote, "cast out" of both the workplace and the home. She confessed to feeling like crying much of the time. She concluded, in rushed and tortured prose: "no matter how I tried, couldn't find any way out." She wrote that letter to Friedan from a psychiatric hospital. Her doctors had diagnosed her as unable to "come to terms with [her] basic feminine instinct." She increasingly lost hope.

Anne Parsons would die by suicide in 1964. She was thirty-three years old. In her last letter to her parents, she reassured them: "it was my life that failed, not your lives."[22]

Her biographer, the sociologist Winifred Brienes, wrote that Anne Parsons "was a prisoner in a culture in which she could not thrive."[23] And her story reminds us that the breadwinner/homemaker model hurt both people who were inside of it and those who were not. That's one reason why the marriage model we call "traditional" today was so short-lived.

In fact, if Anne Parsons had survived just a few more years, she would've been there to see it fall apart. By the early 1970s, American feminists had succeeded in removing gendered language from the marriage contract. It now assigned the same rights and responsibilities to both spouses. This would become the norm. Across much of the world today, in defiance of thousands of years of history, marriage is legally gender neutral.

partnership unions
a relationship model based on love and companionship between equals

Gender-neutral marriage was a step toward institutionalizing **partnership unions**, a relationship model based on love and companionship between equals. The partnership model paved the way not only for gender-egalitarian relationships, but also legal same-sex marriages and ones in which one or both partners change their gender identity. Once the gendered roles of wife and husband were replaced with the idea of partners, it was no longer necessary for spouses to be any particular gender at all.[24]

The capitalist economy's need for workers also contributed to the end of the breadwinner/homemaker marriage.[25] During World War II, women of the middle classes flooded workplaces to fill jobs once restricted to men. Bans on hiring married women fell away. Then, in 1964—the same year that Anne Parsons died—the Civil Rights Act made sex discrimination in the workplace illegal. This didn't end interpersonal discrimination like magic, but it helped ensure that women would begin to be treated more fairly in the workplace.[26]

By the 1980s, abandoning the breadwinner/homemaker marriage was a purely economic decision. Most families could no longer afford to leave an adult out of the workplace. The U.S. government was dismantling the New Deal and wages for the bottom 90 percent of Americans stopped growing. The family wage was a quaint blip in history by then. Women in all but the most economically elite households weren't *choosing* to work; they *had* to.

Today, only the richest and the poorest families are likely to leave one parent at home.[27]

During World War II, while legions of men fought on the front lines, women were recruited into jobs from which they'd previously been excluded. Here a woman assembles a B-52 bomber in a factory in California.

The richest families do so because they can afford it; a parent stays home in nearly half of the wealthiest 5 percent of households.[28] The poorest families do so because they have no other choice. The cost of childcare can easily exceed the entire take-home pay of a low-wage worker.[29] It may seem like a privilege for a rich family to leave a parent at home, or a silver lining for people so poor that they have to, but these marriages are still among the least happy and most likely to end in divorce.[30]

Most Americans, instead, are in partnership unions in which both spouses work.[31] Dual-earner households are now the most common kind. Even among married mixed-sex couples with kids at home, there are twice as many dual-earner partnership unions as there are breadwinner/homemaker marriages.[32] These partnerships are not, however, free of gender. Not even when they involve two partners of the same sex.

Before exploring the gender dynamics of work and family today, it's helpful to introduce a language for talking about gender inequality.

DIMENSIONS OF CONTEMPORARY GENDER INEQUALITY

Sociologists understand gender inequality to involve not one but two central hierarchies. One positions men over women. The other positions some men over other men. Understanding gender inequality, in other words, requires thinking about the relationship between men and women as well as the relationships men have with each other. To grasp how this works, this section introduces two dimensions of gender inequality: sexism and androcentrism.

Men over women

sexism
the production of unjust outcomes for people perceived to be biologically female

The concept with which people are most familiar is **sexism**, a word that refers to the production of unjust outcomes for people perceived to be biologically female. In the United States, men are generally believed to be stronger, braver, more intelligent, more rational, more knowledgeable, and more self-sufficient and independent than women. These characteristics, it's assumed, make men best suited to leadership on the battlefield, in business, in politics, and at home.[33]

Studies find that the average parent, for example, thinks that their son is smarter than their daughter.[34] The average teacher thinks so too. By about age six, so do children. Later in life, laboratory experiments find that art and résumés attributed to men are evaluated more positively than those attributed to women.[35] In one experiment, craft beers supposedly brewed by men were judged to be of higher quality than those supposedly brewed by women.[36] Field experiments outside the laboratory find that employers react more positively to applications submitted by people with men's names rather than women's, even if those applications are identical.[37] Teachers, professors, and graduate advisers do the same.

Partly as a result of this prejudice, men—especially White men from privileged class backgrounds—disproportionately hold the most powerful positions in U.S. society. They are 66 percent of senior-level managers, 74 percent of board members, and 94 percent of the CEOs of S&P 500 companies.[38] More than 73 percent of Congress members are men.[39] Americans have yet to elect a female president. If a patriarchy is a society that vests power in men, the United States is certainly inclined in that direction.

androcentrism
the production of unjust outcomes for people who perform femininity

Coined by the sociologist Charlotte Perkins Gilman, the word **androcentrism** refers to yet another form of gender bias: the production of unjust outcomes for people who perform femininity.[40] If sexism is sex based, androcentrism is gender based. It grants greater reward, respect, value, and power to masculine compared to feminine activities, occupations, and people. So, on average, we're more impressed with athletes than dancers because the former is coded as masculine, even though both do extraordinary things with their bodies. Likewise, we value STEM fields (science, technology, engineering, and mathematics) more than the humanities (history, literature,

Is Misty Copeland an athlete? High-performance activities dominated by women are often defined as something other than sport. In this case, "dance." Dividing athletics in this way enables androcentrism, a form of gender bias in which masculine activities are cordoned off from feminine ones and accorded more prestige and pay.

and art). And we cast football as the main event and high-flying, stunting, tumbling cheerleaders as a sideshow.

Androcentrism is why men are generally taught to avoid being feminine, but women are actually encouraged to be a little masculine. Femininity is devalued, so it lowers men's status when they do it. Accordingly, most men feel pressure to be masculine: to be strong, earn money, like sports, and be unafraid to fight. But they also feel quite a bit of pressure to avoid doing anything deemed feminine: don't cry, eat salads, do yoga, or fall too much in love.

Androcentrism is part of why men were about half as likely as women to wash their hands, avoid crowds, and wear face coverings during the Covid-19 pandemic.[41] To be persnickety about hygiene is coded as feminine. So is fear. According to public health experts, one of the well-worn challenges of fighting pandemics is "mak[ing] sure men don't feel too macho to worry about germs."[42]

Women don't confront such rigid gender rules. They're expected to do femininity, but they're allowed, even encouraged, to do a little bit of masculinity too. Because masculinity is valued, doing it can actually *raise* women's status. That's why we think highly of women who play sports and respect them when they enter male-dominated occupations. Women who do "too much" masculinity are likely to face negative sanctions, but women who do some are generally accorded more respect than women who do none at all. That's androcentrism.

Marianne Weber saw both these dynamics play out in marriage. In a 1912 essay titled "On the Valuation of Housework," she argued that housewives should be paid directly by their husband's employers for the work they do in the home.[43] She rightly observed that his ability to devote himself to working for wages was only possible because he was supported by a wife. If she disappeared, at least some of his energy would need to be redirected to cleaning house, caring for children, running errands, and organizing the family calendar. To stay equally engaged as a worker, he would need to hire a housekeeper, a cook, a nanny, and maybe a secretary—an expensive proposition. Thus, husbands benefited from their wives' efforts, but so did their employers. For one, they got the benefit of their male employees' undivided attention. It was only fair, she concluded, that some of a husband's wage be paid directly to his wife.

If that sounds preposterous, it's partly because of sexism and androcentrism. The idea that work traditionally done by women isn't worth paying for is androcentrism. The assumption that women specifically should be stuck doing the unpaid and undervalued work is sexism. And it's pure patriarchy to think that a man should be paid for his and his wife's combined labor, then given the power to share his income with her as he sees fit. The truth is that homemakers are no more dependent on breadwinners than breadwinners are on homemakers, but patriarchal relations have historically made men's practical dependence on women invisible and women's economic dependence on men inevitable.

Men over men

In placing men above women in a gender hierarchy, sexism promises men unearned advantages, including the support and deference of women. It does not, however, deliver these advantages to all men equally. Instead, in U.S. culture, there's a hierarchy of men, a set of unequal relationships among men in which some enjoy greater male privilege than others. The men who sit atop the hierarchy reap most of the rewards of male privilege.

Two kinds of men are at the greatest risk of falling to the bottom. One group includes men who are deemed insufficiently masculine by the broader culture. These are men who are perceived as gay, weak, effeminate, or dominated by women. These men get called *faggots*, *pussies*, and *cucks*. These are *subordinated masculinities*, men who are seen as lesser based on the androcentric logic that masculine is better than feminine. Because men know that failing to do masculinity may mean losing the respect of other men, and being subordinated as a result, they often follow the narrow rules set out for them.

The second group of men embody *marginalized masculinities*. These men are perceived to be sufficiently masculine but are considered lesser by virtue of another social identity. Working-class men, for example, are stereotyped as overtly sexist and abusive. Likewise, Black and Hispanic men are stereotyped as hypersexual and prone to aggression. In both cases, these men's masculinity is framed as a threat to others.

Typically played by White, conventionally attractive, heterosexual men—like the actor Chris Hemsworth—our action heroes embody hegemonic masculinity and therefore sit at the top of a hierarchy of men.

The gender-related benefits that generally accrue to men, then, come most easily to men who are both sufficiently masculine and members of the economic and status elite. The men at the top of the hierarchy get deference, assistance, and admiration. The men at the bottom experience subordination. They're the sidekick to the superhero. The gay best friend in the heteronormative romantic comedy. The worker to the capitalist. The policed and the punished. And so on.

A sociologist named Raewyn Connell deserves the most credit for developing these ideas.[44] She was drawn to studying masculinity because of her own life experiences, which gave her an especially illuminating point of view, or standpoint. Connell is a trans woman who transitioned later in life. So she spent all of her childhood and most of her adulthood presenting as a boy or man.

This experience left Connell keenly attuned to the pressure that men feel to do masculinity and the consequences of failing to do so. "Having to grapple with contradictions with embodiment in my own life," she explained after transitioning, "would make me sensitive to contradictions in gender constructions in other people's lives."[45] In fact, studies show that while few men feel as uncomfortable with conventional masculinity as Connell perhaps did, most men feel at least a little limited by the social rules that apply to them.[46]

Connell is perhaps most widely known for coining the phrase **hegemonic masculinity**, which refers to the form of masculinity that constitutes the most widely admired and rewarded kind of person in any given culture. Hegemonic masculinities sit atop both hierarchies. Men who embody them, in other

hegemonic masculinity
the form of masculinity that constitutes the most widely admired and rewarded kind of person in any given culture

words, are judged to be superior to women and better than other men. They are our CEOs, our quarterbacks, our adventurers, and our action heroes.

Hegemonic masculinity, then, serves as an anchor for both gender hierarchies. Exalted above all versions of femininity, it validates the idea that men are the better sex. And exalted above all other masculinities, it validates the idea that some men are better than others. It is the measure of all men, the yardstick against which they're encouraged to measure themselves and are judged against, sometimes harshly.

Sexism and androcentrism work together to produce unequal and unjust outcomes for women and many men. This is true in all arenas of life, and it's certainly true both at home and in the workplace.

WORK AND FAMILY TODAY

The sociologist Arlie Hochschild was a teenager in the 1950s.[47] Her father was a diplomat and her mother a homemaker. Well taken care of, Hochschild nonetheless noticed that her mother seemed dissatisfied and so did many of the stay-at-home moms of her friends. Looking back, she wrote:

> I knew that my mother loved my father and he very much loved her. I would overhear them laughing and sensed in their teasing and joking a sensual connection. So, as a child, I concluded that mother wasn't sad about her husband, just about her motherhood.

In contrast, Hochschild noticed that her father would bound off to work every day, "armed with his confidence, clarity, ambition, and joy," to a place she imagined was "serious, interesting, and important." As a girl, she imagined herself someday being a mother but also vowed to attain a "skip-step, happy-whistle career."

And she did. Hochschild would be among the first generation of women to "have it all": a husband, two sons, and a vibrant career. She became a professor at the University of California's flagship campus in Berkeley. Today she boasts eight honorary degrees and countless awards, including five from the American Sociological Association. Her body of work, including eleven books, has sparked multiple academic conferences, newspaper editorials, international lectures, and even theatrical productions. She is, as they say, as big as they come.

Hochschild is perhaps most famous for the idea of the **second shift**. This phrase refers to the unpaid work of housekeeping and childcare that faces family members once they return home from their paid jobs.[48] By the 1980s, very few families left a spouse at home, which meant there was no one to devote time to shopping for supplies, taking care of pets, preparing meals, doing laundry, paying bills, gardening, helping with homework, disciplining, giving kids baths, getting them to bed, and cleaning kitchens, living rooms, bedrooms, and bathrooms. Today people do this work on top of their regular job, making it a second shift.

second shift
the unpaid work of housekeeping and childcare that faces family members once they return home from their paid jobs

In two-parent, dual-earner families, who does the second shift? To answer this question, sociologists have asked research subjects to complete time-use diaries (see "The Science of Sociology"). This is a research method in which participants are asked to record their activities as they go about their day. For any given fifteen-minute interval, and for at least twenty-four full hours, respondents indicate whether they're socializing, sleeping, grooming, working, or studying, etc. A study with a representative sample of participants can paint a fairly accurate picture as to how people spend their time.

time-use diary
a research method in which participants are asked to self-report their activities at regular intervals over at least twenty-four hours

THE **SCIENCE** OF SOCIOLOGY

Time-Use Diaries

How do people use their time? And what is the best way for sociologists to find out? When asked — in surveys, for example, or during in-depth interviews — most people struggle to give accurate answers. Accordingly, the gold standard for studying *time use*, or how people use their time, is the **time-use diary**, a research method in which participants are asked to self-report their activities at regular intervals over at least twenty-four hours. Participants, in other words, are asked to document the day's activities in real time.

Time-use diaries can be recorded on paper, on a computer spreadsheet, or in an app. Participants are asked to record what they're doing (sleeping, working, cleaning, or socializing, for instance) and whether they're multitasking (like cooking dinner while helping a child with homework). Sometimes they're also asked to record where they are, whom they're with, or how they feel about what they're doing.

If researchers collect time-use diaries from a representative sample, the resulting data are a good measure of how whole populations are spending their time. The data also reveal disparities in time use among people with different social identities. Differences in time spent on things like self-care, leisure, and sleep can be a measure of social inequality.

One study using time-use diaries, for example, discovered a gendered division of labor among fifteen-to-seventeen-year-olds.[49] Girls spend an average of forty-three minutes a day on household work; boys spend only twenty-six. Girls also spend more time studying and grooming. Boys make up this difference largely with leisure, spending forty more minutes every day exercising, playing video games, and doing other things for fun. ∎

Time-use diary research finds that women do significantly more of the second shift than men. For example, a recent study using time-use data collected by the Bureau of Labor Statistics found that full-time working women spend 4.9 hours a day on childcare and housework, while full-time working men spend 3.8 hours.[50] Women are doing, then, about an hour more per day. This is equivalent to putting in almost an entire unpaid workday every week.

Women's extra responsibility for the second shift makes it especially difficult for them to live up to the **ideal worker norm**, the idea that an employee should devote themselves to their jobs wholly and without the distraction of family responsibilities. Today's workers are caught trying to be ideal workers without the support that allowed the norm to emerge in the first place.

In short, the breadwinner/homemaker model of marriage involves two people and two jobs: One person does the work at work and another person does the work at home. But most marriages today involve two people and three jobs: Both partners work at work, then they divide the work at home. And single parents? They are one person with two jobs: full responsibility for both the first shift at work and the entire second shift at home. Meanwhile, no matter who we are, our bosses expect us to work as if the *only* job we have is the one we're doing for them.

Under these circumstances, Americans struggle. As one married mother of a toddler put it: "You basically just always feel like you're doing a horrible job at everything. You're not spending as much time with your baby as you want, you're not doing the job you want to be doing at work, you're not seeing your friends hardly ever."[51] Both Work and Family are what we call *greedy*

ideal worker norm
the idea that an employee should devote themselves to their jobs wholly and without the distraction of family responsibilities

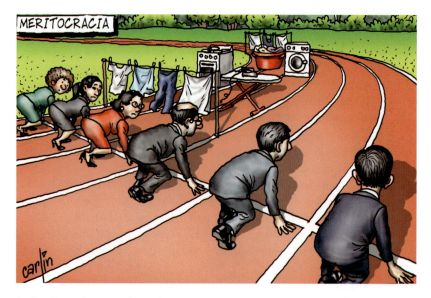

Carlos Tovar Samanez (Carlín) is a Peruvian cartoonist, philosopher, architect and graphic designer. Carlín is currently the daily political cartoonist at *La República*.

institutions, ones that take up a great deal of time and energy. Given time constraints and these demands, it can feel like failure is inevitable.

Faced with this strain, members of families make compromises. The vast majority of both men and women today say that they want a **shared division of labor**, one in which both partners do an equal share of paid and unpaid work. But research shows that most couples adopt a **specialized division of labor**, one in which one partner does more paid work than childcare and housework and the other does the inverse.[52] This is a modified breadwinner/homemaker marriage: Women work and men pitch in at home, but men still focus on breadwinning and women take primary responsibility for the home and the children. Reflecting this, men in mixed-sex marriages are doing about two-thirds of the breadwinning, on average, while women in those marriages are doing about two-thirds of the housework and childcare.[53] People in same-sex marriages are somewhat more egalitarian, but they're still more likely to specialize than share.[54]

U.S. couples continue to specialize when they'd prefer otherwise. Why? Because work and home are still gendered.

The family: "A woman's place"

The idea that we should marry for love is quite new. Prior to industrialization, most people married to help their families survive or thrive. Powerful families used marriage to consolidate wealth and build political alliances. More humble families hoped to join others with land, animals, tools, and labor that complemented their own. People have always fallen in love, but "for most of history," writes the social historian Stephanie Coontz, "it was inconceivable that people would choose their mates on something as fragile and irrational as love."[55] This was true around the world until quite recently.

Love became a reigning reason to marry at the same time that work left the home and care became feminized. In the process, the home became a "sanctuary of domestic love" and women became the bearers of loving kindness.[56] This was the beginning of the *cult of domesticity*, the idea that women could and should wholeheartedly embrace the work of making a loving home.

The decline of the breadwinner/homemaker marriage has chipped away at the idea that women should devote *all* their time to the home, but in one respect—the relationship between mother and child—the cult of domesticity has persisted, even intensified. The dominant parenting ideal in the United States today is the **ideology of intensive motherhood**, the idea that children require concentrated maternal investment.[57] This ideology insists that mothers should give their children close, hands-on attention, that it's normal and good for this to drain most of a mother's time and energy, and that children's needs and interests must take precedence over those of anyone else. The phrase *helicopter parenting*, which entered the English language in 1990, both reflects and mocks this expectation.

Most Americans still believe, at least a little, that children are better cared for by mothers and that fathers are primarily responsible for providing a

shared division of labor
an arrangement in which both partners do an equal share of paid and unpaid work

specialized division of labor
an arrangement in which one partner does more paid work than childcare and housework, and the other does the inverse

ideology of intensive motherhood
the idea that children require concentrated maternal investment

paycheck.[58] From the popularity of "mommy blogs" (but not "daddy blogs") to advertising that targets kid-related products to moms (but not dads), parenting is still gendered female.[59] We talk about "men and women," "he or she," "his and hers," "boys and girls," "Mr. and Mrs.," "king and queen," "brothers and sisters," and "husbands and wives," but when parenting is the topic, we put women first: "mom and dad." Language like this is a subtle reminder that we still consider the family a feminine sphere.

Reflecting androcentrism, the home is also still a devalued sphere. Asked whether he'd be okay if his partner stayed at home, an interviewee named Rich (participating in a study of same-sex couples) replied no.

> Well, I wouldn't like it at all. I don't see how that could be fair, for one person to contribute everything and the other to give little or nothing to the relationship. Plus, what about one's self-respect? I don't see how one could live with oneself by not doing *something* for a living. I would not be comfortable at all telling people that Bill is just a housewife.[60]

Notice that Rich conflates being a stay-at-home parent with "giv[ing] little or nothing to the relationship." And he would find it personally embarrassing to admit that his male partner was "*just* a housewife," using the feminine term to drive home the point.

Such sentiments are common among men and women in mixed-sex relationships too.[61] Rachel, for example, a twenty-seven-year-old living in San Francisco stated: "I see a lot of women who get married and have no job and do absolutely nothing, and that's very sad and I would never want that for myself."[62] Interviewed for a study about the lives of the rich, a family therapist in New York named Susan said that her homemaker clients reported feeling distressed about staying home. "[They] feel so guilty that they're wasting their degrees. . . . They feel so 'less than' . . . that they're not doing anything."[63]

Susan says her clients feel like they're "wasting their degrees." Rachel feels that housewives "do absolutely nothing." In both cases, the language suggests that the work homemakers do doesn't require any skill or knowledge and has no value. Rachel says it would be "sad" for a person to devote their lives to raising their children. Susan refers to "guilt" over a wasted education. And Rich says that homemaking offers no basis for "self-respect." This was exactly the kind of devaluation of housework that Marianne Weber decried in 1906.

Because domestic work is devalued, there's an incentive to try to avoid it. Men typically let women have the kitchen and the baby for the same reason they largely let women have cheerleading and chick flicks. To embrace too much femininity is to lose status. And now that women are increasingly able to have careers—even the skip-step, happy-whistle kind—they also have an incentive to avoid domesticity. As will be clear before the end of the chapter, most American women don't want to be a "housewife" either.

Upon the arrival of a child, however, most women report feeling a great deal of pressure, and often a strong desire, to be an intensive mother. They may be fearful of what will happen if they don't parent intensively. Many also discover that they're pushed away from work. Employers often assume that mothers want to work less, so women sometimes get put on the *mommy track*—a workplace euphemism that refers to employers expecting less from mothers and, in turn, passing them up for raises or promotions—even against their protestations.[64]

Fathers, in contrast, are subjected to the opposite pressures and may prioritize work because they feel it's their responsibility to do so. The people around them, including their wives, may agree.[65] Employers of fathers think so, too, measuring dads against an ideal worker norm. In fact, employers often expect new fathers to work *more* than non-fathers; while the average woman's income falls when she becomes a parent, the average man's income rises.[66]

Men who don't work harder when they become fathers, or who take time off to focus on childrearing, may be penalized in the workplace. A field experiment found that employers were twice as likely to express interest in hiring someone involuntarily unemployed, compared to someone who chose to be a stay-at-home parent.[67] Partly for this reason, men are less likely than women to take parental leave and care for a new baby, even when such leave is available to them.[68]

Above and beyond ideological pressures, structural forces add incentives to specialize rather than share. Workplace policies and U.S. federal and state laws allow employers to deny essential benefits, like health insurance, to employees who don't work full-time. This makes it difficult for more than one parent to deprioritize work. Likewise, the tax code rewards breadwinner/homemaker marriages over partnerships. A married couple with two incomes is generally taxed at a higher rate than a married couple with one income, even if the total income is the same.

These forces press upon same-sex couples, too, who also specialize more often than not. Remember that gender is something we *do*. We perform femininity and masculinity. So, same-sex families are not genderless. Some members of same-sex couples may perform more masculinity or femininity than their partner. This somewhat predicts the division of labor. More masculine partners may specialize in breadwinning and more feminine partners may specialize in housework and childcare.[69]

For many Americans, the Covid-19 pandemic disrupted whatever fragile balance they had managed to achieve. With schools and day-care centers closed to prevent the spread of the virus, parents had to absorb the work normally done by childcare workers and teachers. In response, the amount of time parents spent on education and household tasks ballooned during the pandemic: from 30 hours a week to 59.[70] On average, women married to men did 37 hours of that work, while their husbands did 22.

Sociologists doing in-depth interviews with parents collected the stories behind these statistics. A team led by the sociologist Jessica Calarco, for example, interviewed sixty-five mothers of young children about parenting during the pandemic.[71] One of their interviewees, a computer scientist named Erica, found herself working from home alongside her husband, an office manager.

When schools and day-care centers closed due to the Covid-19 pandemic, the amount of time that parents spent on childcare and housework nearly doubled. Most of that additional work fell to women.

Her one-year-old son was home too; his day care closed indefinitely. They were lucky to be able to work from home, but the situation was unsustainable. A one-year-old needs more supervision than two working adults can provide on their own. Citing that her husband's job was "very demanding," Erica began working only two hours a day.

Without any help from her husband, even those two hours were a strain. Her one-year-old, she sighed, "is into everything."

> He climbs, so you're up and down and up and down, and he's really fast. So, today I was nursing him and trying to read something at the desk, and he swung his leg, and it somehow landed in my tea, and it kicked the teacup over. Tea all over both of us, all over the desk, all over the chair, all over the wall, and then he bit me. . . . I had to get us both cleaned up, clean up everything and then keep nursing him.

Faced with challenges like these, many mothers were forced out of the workplace entirely.[72] In fact, mothers ages twenty-five to forty-four were nearly three times as likely as fathers to report that they weren't working because of childcare demands.

Experts worry that this time spent out of the workforce has already turned the clock back on gender equality.[73] When schools and day cares closed, women largely took on the extra responsibilities, leaving men to earn the bulk of the job experience and capture the majority of raises and promotions. In the aftermath of the pandemic, then, women will be in a worse position relative to men than before, and it's going to be difficult for them to catch back up.

In sum, most families make gendered decisions about how to divide up paid and unpaid work. They do so for both ideological and institutional reasons: the persistence of the ideal worker norm, a commitment to intensive motherhood, and structural incentives to specialize. When the pandemic came, families faced even tougher decisions. These were gendered too.

Work is another social institution that produces gender inequality. Women and men work in different, and differently valued, occupations, and across the board, women are paid less than men. An analysis of workplace dynamics is next.

The workplace: "A man's world"

Today, U.S. women working full-time make $0.82 for every dollar earned by men working full-time.[74] We see similar wage gaps in the overwhelming majority of occupations, even when men and women do the same job and have the same job title.[75] Over the course of a college-educated person's working lifetime, this adds up to an average loss of $461,000 per woman.[76] That's enough money to keep a retiree above today's poverty line until they're 103 years old.

Alongside the gender wage gap, we also see wage gaps between people who are heterosexual and those who are not.[77] Full-time working heterosexual men earn more than gay men. Among women, it's the reverse: Lesbians earn higher wages than both heterosexual women and gay men.

A wage gap based on gender identity emerges, too, with cisgender workers (that is, men who were assigned male at birth and women who were assigned female at birth) earning more than trans workers.[78] People who are trans or gender nonconforming are almost four times as likely as the general population to be living on under $10,000 a year.[79] For trans people of color, these numbers are even more stark. Gender matters here too. People who transition from female to male report no change in their incomes and sometimes even an increase, but people who transition from male to female report a 12 percent decline.[80]

If these seem like a bunch of unrelated data, they're not. There's a clear trend reflecting both sexism and androcentrism. Cisgender men, trans men, and lesbians (who are stereotyped as being somewhat like men) earn more than cisgender women, trans women, and gay men (who are stereotyped as being somewhat like women). The pattern reveals that men and people who perform masculinity attract higher wages than women and people who perform femininity. This results in a **feminization of poverty**, a concentration of women, trans women, and gay, bisexual, and gender-nonconforming men at the bottom of the income scale and a concentration of gender-conforming, heterosexual, cisgender men at the top.

What explains these differences? In the case of cisgender men and women, sociologists have very clear answers.[81] One is related to job experience.

feminization of poverty
a concentration of women, trans women, and gay, bisexual, and gender-nonconforming men at the bottom of the income scale and a concentration of gender-conforming, heterosexual, cisgender men at the top

Because women are more likely than men to take time out of the workforce to care for children, the average woman accumulates less job experience than the average man. Being placed on a mommy track also means fewer opportunities to build their resumes. Differences in career trajectories explain 10 percent of the gender wage gap.

Interpersonal discrimination accounts for 41 percent of the wage gap. Men tend to be favored in both male-dominated and female-dominated occupations. Even a handful of people in a workplace acting in discriminatory ways can prevent women from being promoted, depress their pay, stifle their opportunities, or push them out of promising jobs. As a result, women face a *glass ceiling*, an invisible barrier that restricts upward mobility.[82] Experiencing discrimination at work is the top reason why women decide to leave male-dominated occupations and enter female-dominated ones.[83]

In contrast, men—especially White men—often encounter a **glass escalator**, an invisible ride to the top offered to men in female-dominated occupations.[84] When White men enter feminized occupations, like teaching or nursing, they tend to be promoted much more rapidly than comparable women or men of color. Accordingly, White men tend to be overrepresented in administrative and management roles, even in female-dominated occupations.

The fact that "female-dominated" and "male-dominated" occupations even exist is a result of **job segregation**, or the sorting of people with different social identities into separate occupations. Women are more likely than men to be in caring and helping occupations like teaching, childcare, dental and medical assistance, and nursing. Conversely, men are more likely than women to pursue technical-rational and labor-intensive occupations like construction work and engineering. As a result, the typical man works in a job that's about three-quarters male and the typical woman works in a job that's about two-thirds female.[85] Table 9.1 lists some of the most female-dominated and male-dominated occupations in the United States.

Job segregation is important for the same reason as residential segregation: It enables institutional discrimination. In this case, it's gender discrimination not against women but against jobs women tend to have. Female-dominated occupations pay, on average, less than those filled mostly by men.[86] There is, in other words, an **androcentric pay scale**, a positive correlation between the number of men in an occupation relative to women and the wages paid to employees. Regardless of industry, unionization, physical difficulty, educational requirements, and demand for the work product, people working in female-dominated jobs make between 5 and 21 percent less than people working in male-dominated jobs.[87] Job segregation accounts for 49 percent of the gender wage gap.

On the androcentric pay scale, **care work**—work that involves face-to-face caretaking of the physical, emotional, and educational needs of others—is the least valued. It pays even less than other forms of feminized labor.[88] Childcare workers, for example, earn a median wage of only $11.17 an hour. People who watch cars in parking lots and coats in coatrooms make more money

glass escalator
an invisible ride to the top offered to men in female-dominated occupations

job segregation
the sorting of people with different social identities into separate occupations

androcentric pay scale
a positive correlation between the number of men in an occupation relative to women and the wages paid to employees

care work
work that involves face-to-face caretaking of the physical, emotional, and educational needs of others

TABLE 9.1

Some of the Most Gender-Segregated Occupations

Female-dominated occupations	How female is it?	Male-dominated occupations	How male is it?
Preschool and kindergarten teachers	99%	Brickmasons	99%
Childcare workers	95%	Car mechanics	99%
Dental hygienists	94%	Pest control workers	98%
Speech language pathologists	94%	Electricians	97%
Secretaries and administrative assistants	93%	Roofers	97%
Dieticians and nutritionists	92%	Carpenters	97%
Hairdressers	91%	Firefighters	96%
Home health aides	90%	Construction workers	96%
Maids and housekeepers	88%	Aircraft pilots and flight engineers	94%
Registered nurses	87%	Grounds maintenance workers	94%
Paralegals and legal assistants	86%	Truck drivers	92%
Occupational therapists	86%	Mechanical engineers	91%

SOURCE: U.S. Bureau of Labor Statistics, "Labor Force Statistics from the Current Population Survey," Employed persons by detailed occupation, sex, race, and Hispanic or Latino ethnicity, Jan. 22, 2021, https://www.bls.gov /cps/cpsaat11.htm.

than people who watch over children. Home health aides—workers who care for people who are disabled, sick, or dying—make a median wage of $11.63 an hour. Bellhops, telemarketers, and people who change tires earn more. Nursing assistants, people who help heal people, earn a median of $13.72 an hour. People who fix shoes, bicycles, roofs, and vending machines earn more. And people who teach preschool earn $14.32 an hour, less than file clerks, data-entry workers, and gardeners. The fact that we pay people doing care work so little is a sign that we simply don't value the provision of care.

Notably, it's not that men just happen to choose work that's intrinsically more valuable. Instead, the process works the other way around. When men enter a female-dominated job in sufficient numbers, wages tend to go up. When women enter a male-dominated job, wages tend to go down.[89]

This is what happened, for example, to the job of administrative assistant. In the 1800s, men dominated this occupation.[90] Back then, to be a secretary was to hold a trusted and vital position (the word derives from the Latin word for "secret"). Secretaries were the right-hand men of powerful political leaders and wealthy businessmen. This is why people in high-level positions in the U.S. federal government are still called secretaries, like the secretary of state or the secretary of defense. Secretaries were also apprentices, and many were promoted into the job they'd once supported, becoming leaders and managers themselves.

Women entered the occupation in the 1920s, at which point its prestige and pay declined. Secretaries continued to offer trusted and vital support, but they were no longer regarded with the same reverence, paid high wages, or promoted. Women weren't considered capable of rising above the role of helper, no matter how much they learned about the job in the course of helping someone else do it. In the 1950s, when women came to dominate the job, we started calling secretaries "cute" and "sexy."[91] Today, 88 percent of receptionists are women, as are 93 percent of secretaries and administrative assistants.[92]

Computer programming took the other path, going from female- to male-dominated and rising in prestige and pay in the process. In the 1950s, when computers were introduced, governments and businesses would hire women to operate them. Typing was secretarial work, which was now considered *women's* work; as such, many early programmers were women transferred from the secretarial pool. In 1966, the pioneering programmer Grace Hopper would tell *Cosmopolitan* that working with computers was "just like planning a dinner," explaining: "You have to plan ahead and schedule everything so it's ready when you need it."[93]

In playing to stereotype, Hopper may have encouraged women to become programmers, but she seriously downplayed the difficulty of the work. It was "far harder than today's programming," writes the journalist Clive Thompson:

> It was an uncharted new field, in which you had to do math in binary and hexadecimal formats, and there were no helpful internet forums, no Google to query, for assistance with your bug. It was just your brain in a jar, solving hellish problems.[94]

Under these challenging conditions, women thrived. But as the job increasingly attracted men, some of them actively worked to make the occupation hostile to women. As they did, the stereotype of the computer programmer shifted from detail-oriented mom to awkward man-boy nerd. Today, computer programming is a high-status, well-paying occupation, and four out of five programmers are men.

First, he was a right-hand man, then she was a sexy secretary. First it was "just like planning a dinner," and now he's a computer genius. Occupational trajectories often follow these paths. As jobs feminize or masculinize, prestige and pay follow. This is why the male-dominated jobs in Table 9.1 pay, on average, quite a lot more than the female-dominated ones (unless they are predominantly filled with men of color).

Like residential segregation by race and ethnicity, job segregation by gender is a basis by which other advantages and disadvantages are unequally distributed. In the same way that a house is less valuable when a Black family moves into it, jobs become less valuable when women start doing them. And just as Black families sometimes encounter White flight when they move into a new neighborhood, women entering male-dominated occupations encounter **male flight**, a phenomenon in which men start abandoning an activity when women start adopting it.

The fact that women earn less than men becomes critical when mixed-sex couples struggle to keep up with the second shift. It may make sense for one person to put a little less effort into the

Working for NASA in the 1960s, Melba Roy Mouton used computers to calculate the path of satellites in Earth's orbit. At the time, most computer programmers were women.

workplace. But who? The rational decision is for it to be the person who earns a lower wage. In mixed-sex couples, this is usually the wife. In same-sex couples, it's often the person who's made a more feminine occupational choice. In either case, the decision *seems* gender neutral because it's based on money, not gender. Of course, the institutions themselves were gendered long before the couple sat down to make the decision. In this way, collections of gender-neutral choices nonetheless produce gendered social patterns.

Most people in the United States today desire a partnership union in which spouses or cohabitators see each other as equals and share both domestic responsibilities and paid work. But the mechanisms that characterize gender relations more generally—androcentrism and sexism—still shape modern relationships.

male flight
a phenomenon in which men start abandoning an activity when women start adopting it

THE STATE OF "WOMEN'S LIBERATION"

Women's lives have changed dramatically, and for the better. Women are no longer men's property and no longer their servants. They can work alongside them in any occupation, and they benefit from the smallest wage gap since the dawn of industrialization. Today's marriage contracts state that spouses are equal under the law. Workplace discrimination lawsuits are still being filed, the gender wage gap persists, and the androcentric pay scale holds, but the social institutions of work and family are far more gender egalitarian and inclusive of sexual minorities and people who are gender nonconforming than they have ever been.

Nonetheless, sociologists describe the state of gender inequality in Western countries as a **stalled revolution**, a phrase that refers to a sweeping change in gender relations that started but has yet to be fully realized.[95] On the one hand, women can now embrace valued masculine qualities and spheres of life. So much so, in fact, that today's ideal woman is no longer someone who's 100 percent feminine; she's someone who performs a little bit of masculinity.[96] She likes sports. She plays video games. She's not afraid to get dirty. And she doesn't want a man to pay her bills.

On the other hand, feminists hoped that men would be inspired to embrace feminine qualities and access the feminine spheres of life. On this front, they were disappointed. We revere masculine qualities and domains more than ever, and we dismiss and demean feminine ones still. This has given men little motivation to embrace femininity. Men who enter feminized occupations, adopt feminine leisure pursuits, and do half the housework and childcare attract little praise and sometimes draw criticism. It's no wonder men are reluctant to do it.

The result of the stalled revolution, then, has been paradoxical. Women now have more freedom than men to live their lives as they choose. As long as they do femininity, they're able to mix some masculinity into their personality and make choices that have previously only been available to men. Men today face harsher penalties for not staying in their lane, constraining the options they have as individuals. Men today are less free than women to embrace a mix of masculinity and femininity in their daily lives.

But as the political scientist Heidi Hartmann has said, "Men have more to lose than their chains."[97] Men are less free than women, but they are rewarded for staying in their lane. Men who do masculinity and avoid femininity reap the benefits of persistent patriarchal relations, especially if they have other status advantages. Women, in contrast, face the persistent expectation that they take responsibility for the feminine sphere. This leaves them with at least one foot firmly in the half of life that society devalues. As a group, then, women have less respect and get fewer rewards.

There is, then, a **freedom/power paradox**: Women have more freedom than men but less power, and men have more power than women but less freedom.

Which women benefit from this freedom? Mostly those who are among the economic and status elite. Many of these women have sought to escape the old demands of domesticity and acquire some degree of masculine power. These women manage the work of the second shift partly by hiring

stalled revolution
a sweeping change in gender relations that started but has yet to be fully realized

freedom/power paradox
a situation whereby women have more freedom than men but less power, and men have more power than women but less freedom

help. This is called **domestic outsourcing**, or paying non-family members to do family-related tasks. In place of making a home-cooked meal from scratch, they go to restaurants, order takeout, or get prepped meal kits dropped at their door. In place of household chores, they hire a housekeeper. In place of errands, they task gig workers. To help balance work and family, they drop children off at day care or hire a nanny. Essentially all families do some outsourcing, and some families do a lot of it. Dual-earner professional-class couples with high household incomes are especially likely to outsource family-related tasks.

To be clear, this is not "women's liberation." Domestic outsourcing doesn't raise the value of the feminine sphere, nor does it require men to do their fair share of the unpaid and underappreciated labor in the home. Instead, it displaces that work onto *other women*. And these women are almost always less advantaged than the women whose work they're replacing: 54 percent of domestic workers are a racial or ethnic minority and 32 percent have less than a high school education.[98]

Nearly half of domestic workers are also migrants, and more than a third are non-citizens.[99] These migrants have families, too, ones they leave behind in the care of others. A principal source of these migrant care workers is the Philippines. Two-thirds of Filipinos who migrate to other countries for work are women, and most of them do domestic work. Writing about the Philippines, the sociologist Rhacel Salazar Parreñas explained, "Care is now the country's primary export."[100]

Parreñas migrated from the Philippines with her parents when she was thirteen.[101] Her family experienced what she called "striking downward mobility."[102] Though her parents were professionals back home, in the United States, they only found work in the service industry: her dad as a room service waiter at a hotel and her mother as a housekeeper. She watched as her aunts found work as nannies.

When she became a sociologist, she learned that there was a real need for more research on Filipinos in the United States. At the same time, the number of women who were migrating to support their families was on the rise.[103] So she decided to study the experiences of Filipino migrants and their children.

Her research allowed her to document the toll that parenting across borders takes on both migrants and their children. In an interview with Parreñas, Rosemarie—a Filipina woman who worked as a nanny in Rome—explained:

> The work that I do here is for my family, but . . . sometimes, you feel the separation and you start to cry. . . . If I had wings, I would fly home to my children. Just for a moment, to see my children and take care of their needs, help them, then fly back over here to continue my work.[104]

Parents who support their families through migration face impossible choices. Their children, in turn, feel a mix of gratitude, resentment, and admiration. Most feel deeply loved by their parents but also deep loss.

domestic outsourcing
paying non-family members to do family-related tasks

Migrant domestic workers and their children are part of what sociologists like Parreñas call **global care chains**, a series of nurturing relationships in which the international work of care is displaced onto increasingly disadvantaged paid or unpaid workers. Housekeepers and nannies for class-privileged women in the United States send portions of their meager wages home. They leave their own children in the care of other family members or pay even lower-paid women to look after them. Those caretakers often have their own children who receive, in turn, a little bit less of their own attention. Observing these dynamics, Hochschild has commented that the world has undergone a "global heart transplant," one in which love is pulled from the most vulnerable families in the world and provided to more privileged ones.[105]

Culturally, we have not yet developed a *care work ethic* to match the Protestant work ethic, one that posits that a person's character can and should be measured not only by what one can earn in the marketplace but by one's contribution to the care of others. Until we develop such an ethic, men will continue to avoid both the second shift at home and feminized paid work. When they can, women will do the same. And we will outsource our care work such that it tugs disproportionately at the hearts of some for the benefit of others. ■

COMING UP...

BOTH WORK AND FAMILY are gendered institutions that largely advantage men and masculine people and disadvantage women and feminine people. They do so because they are sexist, meaning that they produce unjust outcomes for people perceived to be biologically female. But they are also androcentric, producing unjust outcomes for anyone who performs femininity.

Patriarchy has loosened. We don't *only* vest power in men. And women have access to some degree of masculine power. But it's mostly status-elite women who've been able to escape devalued "women's work." When they do, they hire less-privileged women to do it. This advantages privileged women at the expense of less-privileged women.

Androcentrism also sets up a hierarchy of men. Because anyone who does femininity accrues less status and pay, men often suffer as a result of androcentrism too. Meanwhile, men who are poor or working class, non-White, or otherwise disadvantaged have less access to the advantages that come with being male.

Gender inequality, then, persists as a social problem, as do the other identity-based hierarchies with which they intersect. These inequalities are maintained not merely by prejudicial ideas and discriminatory individuals but by institutionalized discrimination, the kind baked into our ways of life.

So why don't we change things? The next chapter is about how some people in power resist efforts to make our societies more equal. On to Elite Power.

ELITE POWER

IN THIS CHAPTER...

THE LAST THREE CHAPTERS described ways that social institutions are designed to produce unequal outcomes. This chapter is about the people who have the power to design our societies. These are the *power elite*, a relatively small group of interconnected people who occupy top positions in important social institutions.

Compared with others, the power elite have vast *economic capital*, or money. They also have two other forms of valuable capital:

- *Social capital*, the number of people we know and the resources they can offer us.

- *Cultural capital*, symbolic resources that communicate one's social status.

The power elite use their money, connections, and symbolic resources to attain powerful positions in their societies. They also engage in *social closure*, a process by which advantaged groups preserve opportunities for themselves while restricting them for others. To show how they do this, readers will be introduced to *ethnography*, a research method that involves careful observation of regularly occurring social interaction, often as a participant.

We are often persuaded to accept the power elite's outsized influence on society by *hegemonic ideologies*. These are shared ideas about how human life should be organized that are used to manufacture our consent, or convince us to accept the status quo. As a result of these phenomena, we see *social reproduction*, a process in which society maintains an enduring character from generation to generation.

"All animals are equal. But some animals are more equal than others."

—GEORGE ORWELL

In 2003, a video clip from a scientific experiment went viral.[1] In the segment, two caged monkeys are invited to return rocks handed to them by a researcher. The first monkey passes the rock and receives a tasty cucumber as a reward. Monkeys like cucumbers. Then the second monkey passes the rock and receives a grape. Monkeys *love* grapes. The first monkey observes this and quickly passes another rock to the experimenter. And she receives . . . a cucumber, again.

Visibly upset, the monkey sticks her arm between the bars, cocks her elbow, and throws the cucumber at the researcher. Then, she angrily pounds the table in front of the cage with her palm. Grimacing, she shakes its bars with both hands. She pounds the table some more. She passes the rock a third time, hoping to receive the grape she believes she deserves. She gets a cucumber again and repeats her protest. This is why the video went viral. Her reaction to being treated unfairly is so recognizable—in a way, so humorously *human*—that it's difficult to watch the video and fail to empathize.

Emotional discomfort resulting from witnessing or experiencing an unfair outcome is called *social inequity aversion*. Scientists have found it in a variety of social animals, from monkeys and apes to dogs and birds. We see it in humans too. The last three chapters of this book may even have evoked it in you. When we're confronted with the cold, hard facts about social inequality in our societies today, it's natural to feel upset.

And yet, we don't shake the bars. Not most of us, anyway. We go about our daily lives. Even if we object to certain features of our societies, we may still spend more time climbing hierarchies than trying to pull them down. A surprising number of us even support policies that maintain or exacerbate inequality, even when we're on the losing side. As a result, our socially stratified societies are surprisingly stable. Sociologists call this **social reproduction**, or the process by which society maintains an enduring character from generation to generation.

social reproduction
the process by which society maintains an enduring character from generation to generation

What explains social reproduction? This chapter offers a partial answer. It shows that people who have historically benefited in U.S. society have the greatest access to positions of power. Instead of sharing that power, they try to convince us to accept their hold on it. In this way, they attempt to legitimize the status quo. To begin, the chapter introduces the controversial idea that a small network of people controls most of the levers of power. Then, it reveals how both routine interactions and cultural ideologies are used to justify this state of affairs. Together, these forces persuade many Americans to accept or support social inequality, even when there are good reasons to oppose it.

This will be quite a journey. It starts in the woods of the American Northwest.

ELITE NETWORKS

In a rugged redwood forest, 2,500 men gather for a sixteen-day retreat.[2] They engage in spooky rituals at the foot of a mossy owl shrine, get drunk, and urinate on trees. *Allegedly*, of course. Surrounded by stern signs—No Thru Traffic, No Trespassing, Members and Guests Only—the 2,700-acre property known as the Grove repels the uninvited. Private security officers patrol its boundaries, scanning with binoculars, using infrared sensors at night.

The Grove belongs to a secretive, 150-year-old, all-male organization called the Bohemian Club. Its members are celebrities, Hollywood producers, founders of think tanks and charitable foundations, and CEOs of Fortune 500 companies. At the retreat, they rub elbows with intelligence officials, members of Congress, U.S. presidents, and even foreign leaders. Politicians are prominent because, as one club member asserted, "the campaign trail runs through the club."[3] There they get a concentrated network of campaign donors, media contacts, and high-profile endorsements. "If a person were so inclined," said the sociologist Peter Phillips, "it would be quite possible to build a personal network of corporate America in a matter of a few days."[4]

The Bohemian Grove is a playground for what sociologists call the **power elite**, defined as a relatively small group of interconnected people who occupy top positions in important social institutions.[5] By definition, these people hold positions of power: roles that grant them control over the lives of other people. The sociologist C. Wright Mills called them "the high and mighty."[6] "Insofar as national events are decided," he wrote, "the power elite are those who decide them."

Mills introduced the phrase in 1956 in a book by the same name. It was a scathing and unexpected critique of the state of American democracy. It was also roundly attacked by critics, which suited Mills just fine. A Texan once described as a "burly cowpuncher," he wasn't interested in being liked.[7] "Other men, I suppose," he once wrote, "live for money, women, fun, comradeship. I seem perversely to like trouble better. I seek it out, and if I do not find it, I try to make it up."[8] Before his untimely death of a heart attack at the

power elite
a relatively small group of interconnected people who occupy top positions in important social institutions

age of forty-five, Mills built embattled relationships with colleagues, married four times, and went down in history as the bad boy of sociology.

When *The Power Elite* was published, social scientists generally adopted a **pluralist theory of power**. According to this theory, U.S. politics is characterized by competing groups that work together to achieve their goals.[9] In this vision, politicians work out compromises. Branches of the government are balanced, with the media serving as a watchdog. Businesses compete among themselves. And residents exercise their right to vote, protest, and unionize. Altogether, or so this theory goes, this multitude of players, with a variety of interests, comes to agreement through democratic processes. No one group has an outsized amount of influence on the outcomes.

In contrast, Mills's **elite theory of power** hypothesized that a small group of networked individuals controls the most powerful positions in our social institutions. Like all social networks, those of the power elite are more homogeneous than we would expect by chance alone. So while some members may have been plucked out of poor or working-class neighborhoods via prep schools and elite universities, most are born into the wealthiest households. In other words, the power elite are also the economic and status elite.

pluralist theory of power
the idea that U.S. politics is characterized by competing groups that work together to achieve their goals

elite theory of power
the idea that a small group of networked individuals controls the most powerful positions in our social institutions

Considered the bad boy of sociology, C. Wright Mills published a scathing critique of American democracy in the now infamous book *The Power Elite*.

We all belong to social networks, and often ones that are quite homogeneous, but the networks of the power elite are especially likely to be filled with other elites. This is partly by design.[10] The power elite actively tend their networks. They do so with exclusive organizations like country clubs, business associations, charities, private schools, and secret societies. Membership in these associations can be very expensive. The Bohemian Club's initiation fee, for instance, is reportedly over $33,000, with nearly $8,000 due each year afterward.[11] Some exclusive organizations require that potential new members be sponsored by at least one existing member; you need to be in the network already, in other words, to get into the club.

These associations connect members of the power elite to one another, as well as to the information and opportunities other members control. Members have access to the other members' extended networks, which are filled with additional wealthy and powerful individuals.[12] Sociologists call this **social capital**, defined as the number of people we know and the resources they can offer us. As a member of the Bohemian Club once said: "Other club members are money in the bank when you need to draw out a favor."[13] Whatever is needed—investments, endorsements, introductions—the power elite have it in their network.

These social ties are also a path to positions of power in social institutions. Mills called them "command posts." These include military command (the admirals, generals, and marshals of the U.S. armed forces), high-level politicians (people elected to legislatures and executive branches), and top business executives (people who own and run large businesses), including corporate media producers (people who control our news and entertainment). Later, sociologists would say that Mills missed the emerging role of intellectual elites (scholars in universities and private think tanks who create and disseminate knowledge).[14]

Through their networks, then, members of the power elite come to hold command posts in social institutions. This allows them to exert influence across many social institutions at once.

COORDINATED INSTITUTIONS

Provocatively, Mills argued that the power elite actively conspire to maintain control of their societies. Of all his claims, this may have been the most controversial, and research didn't support it. There's no cabal of elites secretly controlling our society. No secret backroom in the White House, smelling of leather and bourbon, with underground tunnels to the Bohemian Club in San Francisco and the headquarters of America's largest corporations, think tanks, movie studios, and military bases. This is mere conspiracy theory.

But even in the absence of a conspiracy, members of the power elite often have reasons to act in coordinated ways. Consider that business leaders often hold formal positions in one another's organizations. A media executive might sit on the board of a health-care company, for example. A think tank might be advised by the CEO of a technology company. Or a university may have a trustee with ties to a charitable foundation. Mills called these formal connections "interlocks."

Interlocks enhance the likelihood of cooperation. The media executive might give the health-care company he works with positive coverage. The think tank might publish views that reflect well on the technology company's priorities. The charitable foundation might agree to fund a research program at the university, but only one of the foundation's own choosing.

Members of the power elite also often move between social institutions, taking command posts in more than one.[15] A general might leave the military, for example, to work at a private defense contractor. A business executive might leave a corporation to advise the White House. A politician who loses reelection might take a job as a corporate lobbyist. Mills called this the "revolving door," horizontal mobility between command posts in different social institutions.

Rex Tillerson—shown here shaking hands with the president of Russia, Vladimir Putin—is a member of the power elite who has held command posts in more than one social institution. After serving as CEO of ExxonMobil, he walked through the revolving door to serve as secretary of state under Donald J. Trump.

In the years since Mills wrote *The Power Elite*, the revolving door has kept spinning. As an example, consider some of the decisions that contributed to what we now call the opioid epidemic.

Case study: The opioid addiction crisis

In 1996, a pharmaceutical company named Purdue Pharma began marketing a new and more potent version of an opioid painkiller. The brand name was OxyContin. Despite producing no evidence, the company touted the drug as nonaddictive.[16] A Food and Drug Administration examiner—one who would later walk through the revolving door and take a job at Purdue—gave their marketing plan the green light.

Boosted by deceptive and aggressive marketing, opioids would become the most profitable prescription drugs in U.S. history. Between 2006 and 2012, for example (years for which we happen to have excellent data), 76 billion pills were distributed in the United States.[17] That's 233 pills for every American alive today. Small rural communities were especially hard hit by the crisis, leaving some towns devastated by death and addiction.[18] In 2019, an estimated 9.7 million Americans were misusing opioids, and nearly 50,000 people died.[19] The combination of stress, isolation, and limited health care during the Covid-19 pandemic exacerbated this crisis; use of fentanyl—one of the most dangerous opioids—is estimated to have almost doubled.[20]

Blame for this opioid epidemic can't be laid solely at the feet of drug users. Laws passed by the U.S. Congress guide who's allowed to make, distribute, prescribe, and deliver prescription drugs. The Drug Enforcement

Administration (DEA) is tasked with enforcing these laws, as well as setting quotas for drug production, ensuring that the number of pills produced reasonably matches the number that's needed. Everyone involved in the distribution chain—from the manufacturers and the wholesalers to the medical clinics and pharmacies—is required by law to report suspicious activity.

If a Sav-Rite Pharmacy in a town with a population of 401 people orders 2 million pills, for instance—as happened in Kermit, West Virginia, in 2008—it is supposed to be noticed, reported, and investigated. Instead, for over two decades, alarmingly large amounts of drugs were delivered to questionable locations and huge numbers of fraudulent prescriptions were filled.

Why didn't the system protect us?

Records show that many officials at the DEA were trying to preserve friendly relationships with corporations like Purdue. Pharmaceutical companies were routinely hiring DEA employees, bringing them from law enforcement to industry by the dozens, and often quadrupling their salary in the process. Hoping to someday walk through that door, DEA employees were slow to react and gentle in admonishing the industry.[21] They intervened mostly with fines, which amounted to a fraction of the billions the companies were making in profit. Figure 10.1 reveals that at the same time, the DEA was increasing quotas, nearly tripling the availability of opioids like oxycodone and hydrocodone between 2000 and 2015.

When the pharmaceutical industry demanded protection from even the rare intervention by the DEA, politicians delivered. In 2014, they began

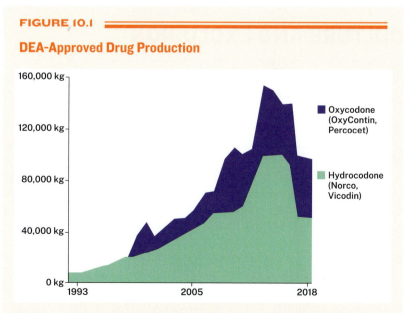

FIGURE 10.1

DEA-Approved Drug Production

Oxycodone (OxyContin, Percocet)

Hydrocodone (Norco, Vicodin)

SOURCE: U.S. Department of Justice, Drug Enforcement Administration, Quotas, Dec. 9, 2020, https://www.deadiversion.usdoj.gov/quotas/index.html.

pushing for a federal law that changed the threshold at which the DEA could freeze suspicious shipments. Under the new law, enforcement agents would have to argue that there was an "immediate threat." This heightened threshold, a top DEA official said, would be "logically impossible" to meet, leaving the drug manufacturers free to distribute without meaningful oversight.[22] Even the fines, in other words, would go away.

Members of the U.S. Congress are America's elected lawmakers, so one might expect that they drafted the law easing the last of the regulations. But no. The first drafts of the law were written by a representative for the pharmaceutical industry. A lawyer for the industry who'd previously worked for the DEA used his "intimate knowledge of the[ir] strategy and how it could be attacked" to write the law.[23] Pharmaceutical companies then spent $102 million lobbying Congress, giving $1.5 million directly to politicians, with especially generous contributions to the bill's most vocal advocates. In 2016, it passed.

In sum, the revolving door gives people with power a reason to cooperate with one another, even if that means failing to protect the public. Meanwhile, by virtue of being a small and homogeneous network, elites are often quite like-minded, whether they're in cahoots or not. Moreover, because elite power networks hold so many potential resources, elites typically try to keep their social ties happy by engaging in mutual back-scratching. This cooperation allows elites to close ranks, ensuring that it's mostly members who have access to the command posts of social institutions. The next section shows how the power elite then use culture to legitimize and maintain their dominance.

CULTURE AND EXCLUSION

As you already know, our positions in the social structure affect our life chances. Did we grow up in a safe and healthy neighborhood? Can we get into an exclusive private school?

Who will we know when it's time to get our first job? Can we marry some-one who's economic and social capital will enhance our own?

At any one of these decision points, doors are opened or closed to us. Sociologists have found that elites use these doors to restrict access to their in-group. Max Weber called it **social closure**, a process by which advantaged groups preserve opportunities for themselves while restricting them for others.[24] Elites maintain their elite status, in other words, in part by controlling access to the opportunities that bestow "eliteness."

Money is one way they do this. Economic capital funds opportunities, like elite educations. Social capital opens doors, too, as members of the Bohemian Club know very well. But there is another kind of capital that matters: **cultural capital**, symbolic resources that communicate one's social status. Neither economic nor social, our cultural capital tells a story about the kind of per-son we are. This partly determines whether we're able to pass through those all-important points of social closure, such as admission to a good school or

social closure
a process by which advantaged groups preserve opportunities for themselves while restricting them for others

cultural capital
symbolic resources that communicate one's social status

elite country club. Like with money, when it comes to cultural capital, it helps to have the valuable kind.

The sociologist credited with this idea is Pierre Bourdieu (pronounced *bord-yoo*, with an emphasis on the second syllable).[25] Bourdieu was born into a humble family in 1930 in a rural part of France. His father never finished high school, working as a sharecropper and then a mail carrier. Bourdieu went to public schools and served in the French army, as all male citizens did at the time. It was a humble and unassuming start for a man who would become one of the most celebrated thinkers of the twentieth century and the most frequently cited scholar in all of social science.[26]

As Bourdieu climbed from the humble countryside to the Parisian intellectual elite, he got a first-hand look at barriers to social mobility. A lack of money, yes. A resource-poor social network, for sure. But there were still other things he needed to successfully climb the social ladder. He learned new ways to dress and talk, so as to blend in. He acquired different hobbies and interests, ones more likely to engage his new peers. He developed a taste for the food, art, and music enjoyed by the upper classes. These things didn't fall under the umbrella of economic or social capital, but they were key to social mobility. So he coined the phrase *cultural capital* and identified three types:

Pierre Bourdieu spent much of his career attempting to understand how the elite maintain their hold on power. In doing so, he introduced new ideas to sociological thinkers—ones like cultural capital—and became one of the most influential thinkers of the twentieth century.

objectified, institutional, and embodied. All three forms of cultural capital are listed in Table 10.1 alongside the other types of capital introduced so far: economic and social.

First, *objectified* cultural capital refers to the symbolic significance of things, or objects, we own. When a friend walks into your room, for example, they learn things about you merely by absorbing the space. Do you have books? What kind? What other possessions are displayed? A stuffed animal tells a story about you. So does a shell from a beach vacation or six empty cans of Mountain Dew. Do you have posters on the walls? They reveal what you think is beautiful, whom you admire, or what you someday hope to possess. What kind of clothes hang in your closet? Are they expensive? Secondhand? Colorful or mostly neutral in tone? All these objects are clues that can signify not only our level of wealth, but also the *kind* of person we are. Anyone walking into that room is judging, even if unconsciously, whether you're the kind of person they might like, look up to, or find intimidating.

Second is *institutional* cultural capital. This refers to the symbolic significance of endorsements from recognized organizations. Think, for instance, about the value of a college degree. It's not just a "piece of paper." It's a nod from an accredited institution that says *We certify that this person is of a certain*

TABLE 10.1

Three Types of Capital

The Term	The Resource	An Illustration
Economic capital	money	If your family has sufficient funds, you can go to an expensive college instead of the most affordable option.
Social capital	social ties	If you know someone who knows the girl you think is cute, you can ask them to introduce you.
Cultural capital	symbolic meaning	If you can present yourself as the "right" kind of person, you may be able to get into an exclusive fraternity or sorority.
Objectified cultural capital	material things	If you decorate your walls with modern art, visitors might think you're a sophisticated person.
Institutional cultural capital	organizational endorsements	If you're chosen for an internship at *Vogue*, the fashion industry will be more likely to consider you an insider.
Embodied cultural capital	the body and its capacities	If you can play golf, you might get an invitation to spend some quality time with the CEO.

quality. People hiring employees trust such institutions to do much of the vetting for them.

Other such institutional nods include trophies, certificates, grants, awards, and scholarships. Getting hired by a respected company benefits a person for the rest of their career; it sits as a line on a résumé indicating that the corporation thought them worthy of employment at their esteemed institution. Positions with known charities or religious organizations suggest that a person plays an important role in their community. Even attractive spouses and accomplished children are a form of institutional cultural capital: the Family kind.

Different kinds of institutional cultural capital may appeal to different kinds of people.

My cousin is a former rodeo queen, winning the title with an encyclopedic knowledge of horses and expert riding skills. Among the country crowd, that made her a minor celebrity and role model. My mother is a hot air balloon pilot authorized by the Federal Aviation Administration to give new balloonists their licenses, and my step-father is the president of the Balloon Federation of America. They're a ballooning power couple admired by their community of hot air balloonists, who trust them to represent and protect their sport. My grandfather was a founding member of his small town's volunteer fire department, later ascending to fire chief and, then, fire commissioner. In town, he was respected as a leader devoted to serving his neighbors. In each of these cases, organizational endorsements generate regard from certain kinds of people, potentially opening doors to new opportunities, connections, or endorsements.

Third, *embodied* cultural capital refers to the symbolic significance of our bodies. This includes how we look, what we know, and what we can do. Recall from Chapter 2 that we *embody* our culture, meaning our cultural experiences are physically present and detectable in the body itself. Our leisure activities, for example, affect the size and shape of our bodies. Access to nutritious food influences how tall we grow as well as the

The actor and humanitarian Angelina Jolie is officially endorsed by the Queen of England! In 2014, she was made an honorary dame (the female equivalent of a knight), thus attaining a coveted form of institutional cultural capital.

quality of our skin, hair, and nails. Our family's income determines whether we get braces and receive professional skin care. These are telltale signs of our backgrounds.

Our bodies also carry *cultured capacities*, specific skills and knowledge useful to the cultural environments in which we live. Because hot air ballooning was the family business, I passively absorbed many of the skills and much of the knowledge I would need if I ever wanted to get a pilot's license myself. In that way, my embodied cultural capital would give me quite an advantage over an aspiring pilot who didn't grow up with the sport. In similar ways, everyone finds themselves embodying the skills and knowledge common to their environments. Whether we learn about hunting or tennis, how to make sushi or fix an engine, or the ins and outs of foreign films or hip hop music, will depend on where and with whom we grow up. This will then determine who will find us impressive and who will find us strange or irrelevant.

We acquire all these forms of cultural capital in the process of growing up and throughout our lives. It's useful to have cultural capital that's well suited to the environments in which we want to be successful. I was the first person in my family to finish college, and I desperately wanted to do well, but knowing a lot about farm animals and hot air balloons didn't help me. So I had to work harder than some to acquire the objects, knowledge, and bodily habits that signaled "serious student who deserves the professor's attention."

When our particular mix of cultural capital matches our social context, we experience what Bourdieu called **fit**. We feel a sense of belonging when we're around people who admire our appearance, skill set, achievements, and material things. When there's a mismatch—when the city kid moves to the countryside, an American moves to Paris, or the daughter of a hot air balloonist becomes a college professor—there's a lack of fit, which causes strain.

Importantly, strain typically hurts people from low-status backgrounds more than it does those from high-status backgrounds. A rich kid who grows

fit
the feeling that our particular mix of cultural capital matches our social context

The hit TV show *Schitt's Creek* finds humor in the Rose family's lack of fit in their new surroundings. After the father's movie rental empire collapses, the Roses are forced to trade their elite lifestyle and Manhattan mansion for a much more humble existence in a small town.

up in Beverly Hills might be as uncomfortable in a low-income neighborhood as a poor kid would be in a private school, but because poor kids don't generally grow up to control the points of social closure, a rich kid's lack of ease in the inner city won't limit his access to prestige, powerful positions, and wealth. The same can't be said of the kid growing up poor. His life chances do, in fact, depend on being able to appear to fit where he really does not. Cultural capital, then, smooths the passage of the already privileged through the points of social closure while weeding out the disadvantaged. This helps ensure that the people who become elite adults are mostly the children of elites themselves.

How do all three of these forms of capital—economic, social, and cultural—combine to produce these outcomes? We can see social closure happen by closely observing interaction in real time. In sociology, this is a research method called ethnography (see "The Science of Sociology"). Two ethnographies, conducted by the sociologist Lauren Rivera, reveal how people make judgments about others' social value. One is an ethnography of an exclusive nightclub, the other a series of elite corporations.

ethnography
a research method that involves careful observation of naturally occurring social interaction, often as a participant

field
the place or places where ethnographers conduct participant observation

THE **SCIENCE** OF SOCIOLOGY

Ethnographic Research

Ethnography, also called *participant observation*, is a research method that involves careful observation of naturally occurring social interaction, often as a participant. Ethnographers spend months or years in the **field**, the place or places where they conduct participant observation. In recent years, for example, ethnographers have studied fashion models, White supremacist groups, truck drivers, and people experiencing homelessness.

Ethnography is an intimate research method in which researchers become part of the daily lives of the people they're studying. For example, the sociologist Karen Ho used ethnography to understand how recent college graduates working in finance are socialized into the culture of Wall Street. To do so, she got hired as an investment banker. She saw her research subjects every workday, traveled with them, and socialized outside of work.

Often, ethnographers attempt to experience for themselves what their research subjects are experiencing. The ethnographer Matthew Desmond, for example, wanted to know what it felt like to do a risky job. So he spent a summer fighting forest fires.

To truly understand, he was committed to feeling the heat of the flames, literally. Likewise, Andrea Boyles began a years-long ethnographic project the day Michael Brown Jr. was killed by police in Ferguson, Missouri. She collected ethnographic data by being a part of the uprisings that ushered in a new era of civil rights activism.

After each visit to the field, ethnographers spend time writing **field notes**, or descriptive accounts of what occurred, alongside tentative sociological observations. These are usually written after leaving the field for the day and may incorporate notes scribbled or dictated while there. Field notes can include observations about everything in the field, including the information collected by all the researcher's senses (sight, sound, smell, etc.) and even maps or social networks. They also include the researcher's reflections on what they witnessed that day and thoughts about what it might mean for future data collection.

Ethnographers are the only social scientists who get in-person, on-the-ground, immersive looks at how social life really works. Ethnography is flexible; researchers can follow new hypotheses as they arise. And it can absorb complexity, enabling scholars to consider large amounts of multifaceted information. Together, these features make it possible for ethnographers to offer truly rich accounts of daily life. ∎

Getting in the door: The nightclub

field notes
descriptive accounts of what occurred in the field, alongside tentative sociological observations

At the nightclub, Rivera watched how people who worked the door evaluated potential patrons. She received permission from the club's manager to hang out with its employees and clients. She also checked coats and worked as a "cigarette girl." And she observed the doormen (they were all men) to get a feel for who was let in and who was turned away—and why. She kept a journal of field notes, recording observations and jotting down theories for later analysis. Over six months, she learned how the club attracted "A-list" clientele and how customers attempted to present themselves as such.

Employees confirmed that the club's business model was centered on exclusivity. "[We] promote to more people than we have the capacity to fit," said the club's head promoter, "[then] we can select . . . and get the best people inside." Referring to economic, social, and cultural capital in a single sentence, he said: "Who is popular or well-known or good-looking or wealthy or anything pretentious, this is where you come."[27]

At the entrance, doormen had to make a snap judgment. Rivera found that they made these decisions by evaluating potential patrons' objectified cultural capital. Generally, doormen said they were quick to let in anyone who was "looking like money." They scrutinized women's handbags and jewelry, men's shoes and watches, and everyone's electronic devices. People wearing clothes

For her ethnography of an exclusive nightclub, the sociologist Lauren Rivera watched as doormen made decisions about whom to let into the club based primarily on the potential patrons' cultural capital, including their clothing, connections, and attitude.

that weren't trendy and expensive, who looked "just average," were turned away. "It's just a vibe you get," said one doorman. "When someone doesn't fit, you can just tell," said another.

It wasn't sufficient, though, for club-goers to be rich; they also had to be "high class," or have the embodied cultural capital associated with the rich. To be effective, expensive clothes and accessories had to be on young, attractive, thin bodies. Moreover, doormen were looking for people who embodied self-assurance, a confidence that they belonged. "It's right off the bat," said a third doorman about how quickly he made his judgments: "It's all their demeanor. As soon as I see you walkin' across the way, where you come in, and I see how you act . . . I can tell if . . . you can come in or not." Eager partygoers who didn't have a high-status "look" would likely wait in vain.

Meanwhile, having gained previous access to the club operated as a form of both social capital and institutional cultural capital. Many of the club's clients were "regulars." They were known by the staff and used the club as a semi-private clubhouse. A doorman observed that many lived in the same expensive apartment complexes. Some were members of rich, famous, or powerful families. "Who's a minister, who's in the government, who's a big business man, who's a big shot," he said, reflecting on what many of his regular clients' fathers did for work.[28] Another doorman observed that regulars had often graduated from elite schools or belonged to the same country clubs.

In sum, to get past the doormen and into this elite party space, it was help-ful to have a high-class attitude and a high-status body adorned with expen-sive and trendy clothes and accessories. It was also useful to be from an elite family, to live in a luxury apartment, and to have Ivy League diplomas and memberships in exclusive clubs. As Bourdieu had argued, Rivera found that all these factors influenced club-goers' value in the eyes of the men in charge.

Making the grade: The professional office

Rivera saw similar processes play out in job interviews at elite investment banks and law and consulting firms. She did nine months of participant observation, attending recruitment events, interacting with candidates, and observing hiring discussions. Her research revealed that new recruits were selected almost exclusively from elite universities, highlighting the importance of having the right institutional cultural capital. After that, however, it was other kinds of cultural capital that mattered most: whether interviewees presented themselves in the right way, enjoyed the right leisure activities, and had the right personal background.

For individuals with the proper credentials, cultural capital was not just *a* criterion for hire; it was *the* criterion. "We are first and foremost looking for cultural compatibility," explained a partner at a law firm. "Someone who . . . will fit in." "In terms of fit," said an employee at a consulting firm, "you want someone that makes you feel comfortable, that you enjoy hanging out with, [and who] can . . . make tough times kind of fun."[29]

Employers wanted coworkers with whom they could build relationships. An attorney compared a job interview to a new romance: "The best way I could describe it is like if you were on a date. You kind of know when there's a match." Another employer explained: "When I'm interviewing, I look for people . . . I'd want to get to know and want to spend time with, even outside of work . . . people I can be buddies with."

In deciding whom to hire, fit was weighed more heavily than grades or work experience. "So you can be the smartest guy ever, but I don't care," admitted a banker. "I need to be comfortable working every day with you, then getting stuck in an airport with you, and then going for a beer after. You need chemistry. Not only that the person is smart, but that you like him."

Rivera observed that the interviewees hired people like themselves because it fluffed their ego to do so. If the person seated across the desk resembled them, it felt good to decide that they were the best person for the job. A banker admitted: "[I] gravitate towards those people that validate [me] the most." Another employee, a graduate of an Ivy League school, said he liked to hire people from similar schools because he knew "how tough it is to get into those places and how hard it is to do well there."

Cultural capital has been shown to be a primary contributor to the *bamboo ceiling*, an invisible barrier to upward mobility faced specifically by Asian Americans. This group is more likely than White Americans to earn college degrees, but they're less likely to be hired, receive raises, and get promotions.[30] At technology companies, for example, Asian Americans are the majority of entry-level workers, but they're only a third as likely as White employees to hold executive jobs.[31]

Cultural capital helps explain why. Stereotypes of Asians portray them as reserved instead of sociable, timid instead of brave, and studious instead of smart. Their Asianness is read as an embodied cue that they're "not management material." An examination of more than 160,000 Harvard applications revealed that this dynamic is at play with college admissions too. While Asian applicants outperform all other racial groups academically, admissions officers systematically rate them low on "personality," decreasing the number of Asian applicants accepted.[32] Whether in hiring or admissions, being Asian is conflated with being un-fun. When looking for someone with whom people will want to be friends, this is considered a serious flaw.

Rivera and others' research underscores that differences in cultural capital determine who's allowed to pass through critical points of social closure. If we have the kind of capital that people on the inside value, then we're more likely to be allowed through. If we don't, then we may wait in line forever.

This process seems rational only because we socially construct the cultural capital specific to elites as a genuine measure of quality. So when opportunities go to people who dress, talk, and look "classy," "sharp," or "smart," it seems only fair. Meanwhile, we're told that the forms of cultural capital common to non-elites signify laziness, a lack of intelligence, or poor taste. The "wrong" posture, accent, or outfit marks a person as not just different but less than. Instead of being recognized as a strategy of exclusion, cultural capital is read as a legitimate way to differentiate the deserving from the undeserving. This allows the power elite to close ranks while simultaneously making it appear as if it's not their intention to do so at all.

SUPPORTING IDEOLOGIES

Cultural capital is one way that elites secure their privileged access to our social institutions' command posts. If we don't have the kind of capital typical of elites, we can be convinced that their hold on power is justified. To stabilize this system even further, however, we need to buy into not just *who* is at the top of the hierarchy, but the hierarchy itself. The cultural force that does this work is called *ideology*. First introduced in Chapter 6, ideologies are morally charged beliefs about right and wrong ways to organize our societies.

The role of ideology was famously articulated by an Italian sociologist named Antonio Gramsci (1891–1937; pronounced *grom-she*), one of the most important conflict theorists in history. His country was taken over in 1922 by the dictator Benito Mussolini, the man who would inspire the word *fascism*. To maintain power, Mussolini portrayed himself as superhuman. He required that journalists write articles that sung his praises. He staged appearances in which he tamed lions, raced cars, and won fights. His government hung posters throughout Italy that glorified him. Later, Adolf Hitler would fashion his own dictatorship after Mussolini's.

Gramsci led an opposition party that resisted Mussolini's rule and called for a return to democracy. In response, Mussolini arrested and imprisoned

The Italian sociologist Antonio Gramsci was imprisoned by the fascist dictator Benito Mussolini for eleven years. During that time, Gramsci secretly wrote political theory about how elites control populations by using persuasion as well as coercion.

Gramsci. During his eleven years as a political prisoner, Gramsci wrote and smuggled out 3,000 pages of sociological thought about political history.[33]

Among his many lasting contributions to sociology was the idea that political leaders can make populations accept their rule with two strategies. One is pure coercion. Leaders can act in overtly oppressive ways. They can beat and tear gas protesters. They can arrest and jail critics, as Mussolini did to Gramsci. They can cow people into submission with soldiers, tanks, and bombs. This is coercion.

Coercion, though, has a cost. Such blatant expressions of power may force a population to submit, but it will almost certainly also spark a simmering resentment. This can incite all-out rebellion. Coercion is risky. It's unstable. For that reason, coercion is usually Plan B.

Plan A is much more subtle: persuasion. People can be coaxed into accepting a state of affairs, even one that does them harm. Gramsci described this as "manufacturing consent," referring to the work needed to convince people to agree to conditions they might otherwise oppose. To describe power maintained primarily by persuasion, Gramsci introduced the phrase **cultural hegemony**. The word *hegemony* comes from the Greek for "authoritative rule." When hegemony is *cultural*, it means that the source of authority isn't fear but agreement. People are motivated to consent to the way things are based on shared cultural values and beliefs.

In contrast to coercion, persuasion is an effective and stable form of power. Cultural hegemony doesn't feel like the exertion of power, not like guns, tanks, and bombs do. Instead, efforts to gain consent often feel like a conversation, even an invitation to adopt a point of view. And when persuasion is most successful, alternative ways of thinking simply disappear.

In everyday life, Americans routinely experience this kind of persuasion in advertising. Forcing people to purchase goods and services is largely illegal, so ads aim to make consumers think that buying them is their own idea. *You don't have to buy this*, the ads say, in so many words, *but you want to, don't you?* Home security companies ask: *Don't you want to be safe?* Beauty product companies ask: *Don't you want to be attractive?* Disneyland asks: *Don't you want to be happy?* Coca-Cola doesn't threaten to break our legs if we don't buy a can; it simply asserts: *Everyone wants a sweet bubbly treat. Don't you?*

In politics, the aim isn't to sell us a soda; it's to sell us on a government's regime. We must be convinced to buy into a particular way of organizing society. The power elite do this by promoting **hegemonic ideologies**. Ideologies are shared ideas about how human life should be organized; ideologies

cultural hegemony
power maintained primarily by persuasion

hegemonic ideologies
shared ideas about how human life should be organized that are used to manufacture our consent to existing social conditions

Since companies like Coca-Cola can't force us to buy their products, their marketing often taps into hegemonic ideologies — like the idea that we all deserve to be happy — to persuade us.

that are hegemonic manufacture our consent to a specific way of thinking or behaving. In other words, when an ideology rationalizes the status quo such that we're persuaded to accept it, it's hegemonic. At their most powerful, these ideologies convince us to accept existing social conditions even when we're directly harmed by them.

You're already familiar with several such ideologies. The Protestant work ethic, for instance, is a hegemonic ideology. It's very common for Americans to judge people's moral worth by how hard they work. And those of us who don't work as hard as we can, even just sometimes, often feel guilty. Many of us believe that we should always be striving to work harder. So Americans work hundreds more hours every year than residents of similar countries.[34]

The ideology of intensive motherhood is also hegemonic. This is the idea that children require near-constant attention from their mothers. Women often struggle to balance their desire to be a good worker with their belief that motherhood should be an all-encompassing occupation. Despite the toll this takes on women's mental and physical health, not to mention the happiness of their marriages, it often goes unquestioned.

Likewise, meritocracy. As the sociologist Michael Young tried in vain to tell us, meritocracy ties our value as human beings to an arbitrary measure of accomplishment. Many of us spend much of our lives trying to live up to these

expectations. If we fail, we may internalize that failure and believe that we, personally, lack value.

In the United States, all these ideologies support the idea of a socially stratified society. The Protestant work ethic is a rationale for both a stingy safety net for the poor and the wealth gap between the rich and the poor. The ideology of intensive motherhood justifies the "mommy track" at work and lets men off the hook when they don't do their fair share of childcare. And meritocracy encourages us to look up to and strive to be like those at the top, while we look down on and stigmatize those at the bottom. In each case, the ideologies work to convince us to accept the society we have, while suppressing thoughts as to whether it's the society we want.

Internalizing ideologies

Richard Scarry's classic children's book *What Do People Do All Day?* introduces young children to hegemonic ideologies about work. Whimsically, Scarry's book teaches children that some kinds of people do grunt work, some do service work, and others rightfully have jobs in which they control and manage everyone else.

We learn these ideologies during the socialization process. It begins when we're babies. Consider one of the most popular English language children's books of all time: Richard Scarry's *What Do People Do All Day?* The book, originally published in 1968, introduces three-to-seven-year-olds to the idea of work with a visit to the (Protestant work ethic–inspired) city of "Busytown." It does this by discussing a series of animals doing various jobs.

The sociologist John Levi Martin did a content analysis of the book, which features 272 characters representing twenty animal species.[35] Certain classes of animals were exclusively or disproportionately portrayed doing certain classes of jobs. Pigs, for example, were usually portrayed doing low-status jobs like ditch digging, street cleaning, or sanitation. Mammals thought to be timid, like rabbits and cats, were usually shown doing female-typed service jobs like administrative assistant, beautician, and flight attendant. Dogs usually did male-typed working-class jobs; they were baggage handlers at airports, truck drivers, and police officers. And the characters with command over others? The managers, CEOs, and mayors? They were represented by apex predators: bears, leopards, and lions.

What does this book teach children about the world? It teaches them not just that there are different jobs, but that certain kinds of people do different kinds of jobs. The slotting of animal species into job categories naturalizes job segregation in real life. Then, when the child sees men and women doing different kinds of work, or people of different racial or ethnic backgrounds slotted into different jobs, these divisions will resonate with what they've already learned.

Moreover, by mapping an animal hierarchy onto an occupational one, it elevates some kinds of jobs—and, by extension, some kinds of people—over others. The lions make the rules, the dogs and rabbits do the work, and the pigs clean up after everyone. The book presents social stratification as natural. In doing so, it contributes to the hegemony of *status beliefs*, our shared ideas about what social groups are more or less deserving of esteem.

From children's books and Hollywood movies to newspapers and advertising, the mass media are places where hegemonic ideologies are shared and affirmed. Who disseminates these ideologies, then? Elites do. The power elite exert substantial control over all media outlets. Five of the ten richest people in the United States own or lead media-related companies. Jeff Bezos owes his fortune to a little company he started called Amazon, which has a streaming service that delivers original movies and TV series. He also used his riches to buy the *Washington Post*. Mark Zuckerberg is the founder and CEO of Facebook; he controls the primary source of news for almost half of American adults. Warren Buffett owns or has owned dozens of newspapers. Larry Page and Sergey Brin cofounded Google; their search engine filters 90 percent of all internet searches, deciding what information we see.

The material released by these outlets presents us with idealized stories, cautionary tales, and moral fables. These socialize us into ideologies that support cultural hegemony. From the media, we learn who's lovable, enviable, and admirable, and who's not. We're instructed as to what the good life looks like, and what should bring us shame. We're told what problems plague our societies, and who's to blame. Like advertisements, these stories use persuasion instead of coercion. The power elite use media to encourage us, subtly and repetitively, to internalize the ideologies that are hegemonic in our societies and reject ones that challenge the status quo.

Of these ideologies, one is of particular interest to sociologists because it's a real obstacle to sociological thinking. It inhibits our ability to think critically about our societies and be imaginative about better ways of doing things. The final section of this chapter is about individualism.

THE CULT OF THE INDIVIDUAL

At one point or another, you've undoubtedly asked yourself this most terrifying question: *What do I want to do with my life?*

Do you want to be an accountant? An actor? A police officer? A politician? Who *are* you? *What* are you? You have one life. How are you going to live it? What are you going to *be*?

Our foraging ancestors did not ask themselves questions like these.[36] They just *lived* their lives. They grew up, found food, had babies, told stories, made art. The end. Blissfully, there was little else to do. Even as recently as the Middle Ages in Europe, there was no existential quest for the unique and authentic self. People's identities were fixed and unyielding. You were born a serf or a prince and that was that.

But not you. You have to decide what to do with your life. This is a stressful decision, if only because there are so many choices. Our social institutions are massive and complex, their divisions of labor intricate and precise. Where in the giant behemoth of our contemporary society do you want to insert yourself?

The early sociologist Émile Durkheim argued that the fact of this choice is the source of an idea that feels timeless to us today: the individual. Whatever we choose to do, we'll be fulfilling a very specific societal need. So, unlike our foraging ancestors, we must figure out what makes us different from other people, what makes us special. This is why the choice is so intimidating. We're called upon to match our unique selves with a predefined social role, and we better hope we get it right.

You've probably been asked "What do you want to be when you grow up?" since you were young enough to appreciate *What Do People Do All Day?*, which eerily reflects Durkheim's most famous work of sociology: *The Division of Labor in Society*. Scarry's children's book begins with the lesson that everyone works: "We all live in Busytown and we are all workers." Then, it introduces children to an astonishing 132 different jobs from which to choose. *What do you want to do with your life, child?*

The book ends with an appreciation of the interdependence inherent in a division of labor. At a party, dozens of animals come together to celebrate their shared productivity. They gather in a house built by construction workers, sit on chairs built by carpenters, wear clothes made by sewing machine operators, and enjoy food grown by farmers and water delivered by plumbers. "My goodness!" writes Scarry in the last sentence of the book, admiring the shared effort of the people of Busytown. "Just look back and think of all the things we can do when we all work together."

Durkheim gave the social cohesion created by this shared effort a name: *organic solidarity*.[37] When everyone needs everyone else to do their part, he posited, we find ways to get along, even if our different roles make us very different indeed. We're individuals, but we find solidarity in knowing that everyone's effort contributes to a collective purpose.

This is different, Durkheim observed, than the social cohesion enjoyed by our foraging ancestors. These groups enjoyed *mechanical solidarity*, the kind of social cohesion that comes from familiarity and similarity. Each person was known to all the others, and they were all quite alike. That functional sameness bound them together. What mattered was how people fit into the group, not what made them stand out. Hence, they never had to ask themselves what *kind* of group member they were.

Over the 10,000 years during which we transitioned from foragers to farmers to wage workers, and as organic solidarity replaced mechanical solidarity, how we differed from others became an important part of our identity. What's important about individuals in modern societies is our uniqueness: what we can uniquely contribute to the common good. This, Durkheim observed, is the origin of **individualism**, the idea that people are independent actors responsible primarily for themselves.

The opposite of individualism is **collectivism**, the idea that people are interdependent actors with responsibilities primarily to the group. Individualism emphasizes autonomy, self-reliance, and uniqueness. In contrast, collectivism emphasizes accountability, interdependence, and conformity.

Individualism is strongest in the West, where it's fairly described as a hegemonic ideology.[38] We can hear the ideology, for example, in common English sayings like "Do what makes you happy" and "It doesn't matter what other people think." The Protestant work ethic, meritocracy, and the ideology of intensive motherhood are all individualistic. According to the Protestant work ethic, an individual's value is determined by their own personal work effort. Meritocracy assumes that individuals have achieved a level of success equal to their personal effort. And the ideology of intensive motherhood demands that each individual child be parented primarily by their own mother.

Corporate slogans invoke individualism too. Ray-Ban incites consumers to "Never hide," Express invites us to "Express yourself," and Reebok encourages

When Covid-19 threatened Japan, the Japanese people adopted widespread mask wearing quickly. Doing so resonated with a collectivist ideology that puts the group before the individual. Not so in the United States, where hegemonic individualism clashed sharply with mask mandates.

us to say "I am what I am." Individualism is in advertising across the consumer landscape, from Loews Hotels ("You first") to L'Oréal ("Because you're worth it") and Nescafé ("It's all about you"). In 2014, Burger King abandoned its forty-year-old slogan "Have it your way," which was already quite individualistic, for an even more individualistic one: "Be your way." Even the U.S. Army, an institution built on conformity and obedience, recently adopted an individualist slogan to attract recruits: "An Army of One."

Individualism has its advantages. It can be pleasurable, even liberating, to discover and express a self that feels authentic. It's good to have the right to consider one's own needs, even in the face of pushback from others. Self-reliance and personal responsibility are empowering ideas, ones that give us control over our lives in meaningful ways. Placing value in uniqueness also encourages us to embrace diversity. Individualism is an important basis of many of the rights-based claims that have challenged inequality across the Western world. If we treat others as individuals, then we can assert that everyone deserves equal treatment, regardless of group membership or social identity.

When individualism is hegemonic, however, it has downsides. During the pandemic, people who were strongly individualistic were less likely than others to comply with requests by governments and scientists to wash their hands, wear masks, and avoid gatherings.[39] Sacrificing one's own comfort for the benefit of others violates a central tenet of individualism. During pandemics, highly individualistic people are also more likely to exhibit **xenophobia**, or prejudice against people defined as foreign.[40] Xenophobic people are less likely to cooperate with others to slow the spread. Partly as a result of these factors, individualistic societies had on average higher rates of infection and death than collectivist ones.[41]

Individualistic thinking can also make it difficult to recognize the *social* forces that shape our lives. As a result, we may be too quick to credit or blame individuals, while ignoring the role of social institutions, social rules, and cultural norms. When this happens, people who bear the brunt of institutional discrimination get more blame than they deserve. We may label them as "criminals," for instance, without considering the social pressures that led them to engage in criminal deviance. We may describe the gender wage gap as an outcome of "personal choice," dismissing the social forces that press men and women into differently valued jobs. Or we may tolerate educational inequality, accepting that people don't want to fund schools in other people's neighborhoods.

As an example of individualistic thinking, consider how people talk about the institutions and the individuals involved in the opioid epidemic.[42] The language we use to describe the drug problem in the United States focuses our attention almost entirely on individuals. There are "drug dealers," "drug abusers," and "drug addicts." When friends and family fail to intervene effectively, they're called "enablers." Corporate executives at Purdue Pharma exploited this language to shift blame away from the company and onto

xenophobia
prejudice against people defined as foreign

Individualism has made it difficult to recognize the role that institutions have played in the opioid epidemic. In this protest, for example, activists are shaming the Sackler family, who owns Purdue Pharma, instead of blaming the Drug Enforcement Agency, Congress, or the pharmaceutical industry writ large.

individuals. In 2001, the then-president encouraged his marketing team to scapegoat people suffering from addiction. "We have to hammer on the abusers in every way possible," he said cynically. "They are the culprits and the problem. They are reckless criminals."[43]

When the pharmaceutical industry, the DEA, and Congress come into view, the story is usually still about individual bad actors: corrupt politicians, unethical regulators, and greedy doctors. The mass media have portrayed the owners and executives of Purdue Pharma, for example, as villains. Perhaps rightly so. But in looking for individuals to blame, our attention is drawn away from the system itself. Blaming individuals—as victims *or* villains—fails to acknowledge that both are part of something larger than themselves.

Couldn't the pharmaceutical industry be described as a *drug dealer*? Did it *abuse* its right to manufacture and distribute drugs? Is the industry *addicted*, unable or unwilling to give up the high profits that opioids deliver? In going easy on the industry and reducing regulations, are the DEA and Congress *enablers*? A laser focus on the culpability of individuals discourages us from even asking these questions. We use words like *dealer, addict,* and *enabler* only when describing people, while institutions get a pass.

Ideologies are powerful. They direct our attention, which is useful. Thinking ideologically can help us see things that we might otherwise miss. Anti-racist and religious ideologies, and feminist, queer, Marxist ones, and more, all help us think about how our societies treat different social groups. Individualism, too, has helped us design societies with greater freedom.

But adhering too closely to any one ideology also limits us. When an ideology is hegemonic, it threatens to narrow our thinking to the point that important realities become invisible. In the West, individualism is powerful enough to sometimes make our social systems invisible. This protects the social structure from critique. It protects the social stratification it produces too. If we don't see it, we can't ask whether we like what we see. Instead, we blame individuals and look only to individuals for solutions. But structural problems aren't solved by punishing or rehabilitating individuals. Social problems—like addiction, inequality, and overwork—need social solutions.

In this way, individualism also protects the power elite. While individual members of the elite may be brought down by scandal, a culturewide lack of attention to social forces helps legitimate the group's hold on power. We mistake their cultural capital for individual merit, attributing their rise to their personal qualities alone without accounting for their social backgrounds. As they pass through points of social closure, we assume it's because they earned these opportunities with individual talent and effort, when that's only part of the story. And when they make decisions that benefit themselves at the expense of others, we feel it's justified to put oneself before the collective. In this way, consent to the elite's hold on power is manufactured, making it far less likely that any one of us will become frustrated enough to shake the bars. ∎

COMING **UP...**

ATOP MODERN COUNTRIES' social institutions sit command posts disproportionately held by people who come from a small and homogeneous group of networked individuals. These individuals have more money than the average person, elite social networks, and the institutional cultural capital needed to gain entrance to elite spaces. They also have the objectified and embodied cultural capital needed to play the part once they do. These individuals share power across institutions and don't necessarily act in everyone's best interests.

The boundaries between the elite and everyone else are hardened by processes of exclusion. If a person doesn't have the capital needed to pass through points of social closure, they're unlikely to fit in among the elite. This means that the poorest Americans, and those with the lowest-status social identities, have the least institutional power. The very people who suffer the most in society, in other words, have the fewest options to make change. Meanwhile, hegemonic ideologies convince many of us that the way things are is the way things should be. And because members of the elite have disproportionate power over the media, they have an outsized influence on how we think.

But this isn't the end of this journey. Writing in the 1950s and dead by 1962, C. Wright Mills didn't anticipate the coming civil rights movement.[44] Nor did he expect the movements on behalf of American Indians, Latinos and Chicanos, and Asian Americans, or the women's movement, the gay liberation movement, or the sexual revolution, all of which were simmering in the decade in which he published his most famous work. Accordingly, he underestimated the power of the people to challenge hegemonic ideologies, work together, and effectively confront the power elite. He was right that forcing the powerful to share their power is difficult. Which is to say, if we want to make our societies better for everyone, we're going to have to fight for it.

IN THIS **CHAPTER...**

THE LAST CHAPTER outlined the strategies elites use to maintain their power in democratic societies. This chapter turns the tables by centering a form of power that non-elites wield in society: *interdependent power*, or the power of noncooperation. When enough of us decide to stop participating in social interactions and institutions, we have a substantial amount of influence over elites.

When people exert their interdependent power, we see the emergence of *social movements*, or persistent and organized collective action meant to promote or oppose social change. To build a social movement, activists need to do the following:

- Grow an *insurgent consciousness*, or the recognition of a shared grievance that can be addressed through collective action.

- Collectively define a state of affairs as harmful and then convince the public that the harm requires a cultural or institutional solution.

- Build *organizational strength*, a combination of strong leadership, human and material resources, social networks, and physical infrastructure.

- Find individuals who have *standing*, or the authority to speak credibly on their topic, and offer resonant *frames*, succinct claims as to the nature of a social fact.

Movement success is never guaranteed, but it's enhanced by favorable political, economic, and cultural conditions. When movements are successful, they're able to generate *social change*, shifts in our shared ideas, interactions, and institutions.

"The most common way people give up their power is by thinking they don't have any."

—ALICE WALKER

Wealthy, high-status, and well-positioned people have more power than their less well-off counterparts, and history shows that elites are often reluctant to use that power to benefit everyone. We should expect, then, that those at the top will resist when challenged from below and prevail when they do. "But not always," the sociologist Frances Fox Piven rightly observes.[1] Sometimes the power elite's resistance fails. And when that happens, people at the bottom succeed in forcing much more powerful individuals to change institutions in ways that benefit the masses. This was the animating question of Piven's career: "Why are people without power able to win anything, ever?"

In fact, the history of the United States includes many examples of people with little power changing their societies. Some of the stories are truly extraordinary. Two hundred and forty-four years after the first Africans were enslaved by British colonists, for example, President Abraham Lincoln signed the Emancipation Proclamation. This escalated a civil war, criminalized the fourth-richest economy in the world (the American South), and made disappear, with a pen stroke, more than $100 billion of elite slaveholders' wealth (in 2020 dollars).[2] It was an unimaginably ambitious goal, and abolitionists made it reality.

Similarly, for its first 144 years the United States did not allow women to vote, serve on juries, give legal testimony, or hold public office. It would take generations of suffragists almost one hundred years to win the vote for White and Black women; even more for the vote to be extended to Native American women and men. This battle included racial betrayals, but also inspired cross-racial alliances. It wasn't easy. It wasn't always pretty. But they did it.

In 1834, a group of teen girls working at a Massachusetts textile mill walked off the job in protest of intolerable working conditions and an impending wage cut. The strike was crushed, but the young women continued to organize and won many concessions in the years to come, helping to start the labor movement. Today, we have them to thank for many things Americans enjoy, like weekends, the minimum wage, the right to unionize, overtime laws, and safety standards. The people sometimes get their way.

This chapter is about the power people have to generate **social change**, shifts in our shared ideas, interactions, and institutions. Social change is prompted by environmental pressures, economic and technological inventions, political and geopolitical forces, cross-cultural contact, and population shifts. It also comes about through **collective action**, the coordinated activities of members of groups with shared goals. Collective action is organized by *activists*, people who participate in collective action in order to influence their societies. When many activists work together over an extended period of time, it's fair to say that they're involved in a **social movement**, persistent, organized collective action meant to promote or oppose social change.[3]

These concepts can help us answer Piven's question: Why are people without power able to win anything, ever? We begin with her case for a people's power.

THE PEOPLE'S POWER

Frances Fox Piven followed an unlikely path into sociology.[4] In 1933, when she was a toddler, her family immigrated to the United States from the Eastern European country of Belarus. She grew up helping them run a deli in Queens, New York. She was accepted to college and worked minimum-wage jobs to supplement a tuition-only scholarship. By the time she entered graduate school, she was a single mother. Coming from such humble beginnings, she dedicated her life and career to understanding and promoting the struggles of everyday people.

Among her many contributions to sociology is an answer to that driving question of how everyday people are able to make change. In her work, she challenges the notion that everyday people are powerless. Elites may have disproportionate access to the power of money, status, and position, she admits, but the masses have another kind of power. When all is said and done, they can always "throw sand in the gears" and bring the machinery of society to a halt.[5] She calls it **interdependent power**, the power of noncooperation.

Interdependent power is rooted in the fundamentally social nature of human life. As this book's tour through symbolic interaction, dramaturgy, and ethnomethodology has shown, everyday life relies on everyone keeping everything rather ordinary. Interaction is spontaneous but heavily guided by social rules. Interaction is also fragile. Remember the dinner party that was interrupted by a would-be robber? As that example showed, interactions are easily disrupted by even a single person's noncooperation.

Social institutions, and the social structure of which they're a part, are dependent on those same predictable interactions. The institution of Religion needs us to turn to faith for guidance, the Law needs us to agree that red

Sidebar definitions

social change
shifts in our shared ideas, interactions, and institutions

collective action
the coordinated activities of members of groups with shared goals

social movement
persistent, organized collective action meant to promote or oppose social change

interdependent power
the power of noncooperation

means stop, and the State needs us to pay our taxes. Without regular worshippers, rule-abiding drivers, and cooperative taxpayers, the ability of these social institutions to function breaks down. However much power the people at the top have as individuals, then, they're absolutely and completely dependent on the masses of people at the bottom.

That dependence gives the masses power. "Social life," writes Piven, "is cooperative life, and in principle, all people who make contributions to these systems of cooperation have potential power over others who depend on them."[6] Even people who have no economic power, no position of power, and a social identity entirely void of prestige have the power to disrupt an interaction. Everyone, no matter how downtrodden, can throw sand. And if enough people decide to do so, to deviate from the norms and social constructs that uphold social institutions, then the elite are in trouble. The whole range of alternative behaviors—from doing nothing to the chaos of mass violence—is a form of power.

To make real social change, of course—to make the consequences of throwing sand accrue to the system and not to the individual—we must act together. One employee who doesn't show up to work gets fired. One tenant who doesn't pay gets evicted. One citizen who refuses to vote goes unheard. But what happens when most or all people do these things? If the whole factory floor stays home, employers don't make money. If the entire city refuses to pay rent, they squeeze the system meant to make them. And if no one votes, politicians can't claim legitimate victories. By breaking the "rules of the game," people who refuse to cooperate challenge the status quo and the elites who benefit from it.

In democratic societies, collective action generally follows a set of social rules. The sociologist Charles Tilly called this the **repertoire of contention**, shared activities widely recognized as expressions of dissatisfaction with social conditions.[7] In most industrialized countries today, this repertoire includes things such as sit-ins, boycotts, strikes, vigils, petitions, rallies, marches, viral hashtags, and even civil unrest. These are all recognizable ways in which individuals and groups can stake a political claim.

Among the tools in the repertoire of contention are many forms of noncooperation. Sit-ins disrupt the use of space, occupying it to make it difficult or impossible to use it for its intended purpose. Marches and rallies often take place in city streets, or even on highways, disrupting traffic and the routine activities that depend on its flow. Strikes shut down workplaces, not only interrupting labor but also potentially critical services like education and health care. Boycotts slow economic activity and threaten companies that depend on a routine inflow of cash. And civil unrest is not only disruptive but potentially destructive, targeting property and at times involving violent conflict.

Sometimes these activities lead to social change. Collective deviance can inflict real pain on social institutions and put real pressure on elites to come to the bargaining table. Using the repertoire of contention, movements can succeed in changing their societies. How do we inspire people to use it?

repertoire of contention
shared activities widely recognized as expressions of dissatisfaction with social conditions

Activists block the road leading to Mount Rushmore in Keystone, South Dakota, to protest a visit from President Donald Trump. Rallies like this one are part of the repertoire of contention.

HARNESSING INTERDEPENDENT POWER

To use our interdependent power, we first have to decide that there's something that needs changing. Socialization into our social institutions can make them feel right, while elites use the media to manufacture consent. If we're struggling in life, we may blame ourselves or the people in our lives rather than cultural or institutional forces. This can make it difficult to recognize that our struggle has a social or political solution.

The process of coming to see a *personal* struggle as an issue of *public* concern involves what sociologists describe as the **social construction of social problems**.[8] The process requires two steps. First, we must define a state of affairs as harmful. Second, we must convincingly claim that the harm requires a cultural or institutional solution instead of a personal or interpersonal one.

Because social problems are socially constructed, perceptions of harm don't always match reality. The sociologist Joel Best, for example, has been appearing on television annually for thirty years to debunk the idea that strangers put poison and razor blades in children's Halloween candy.[9] There's no evidence they do.[10] But parents have been trained for decades to fear "Halloween sadists," and because of this, many carefully examine their children's candy hauls for hazards.

In fact, we are often more or less fearful than is warranted. Most of us fear flying in an airplane more than driving to the airport, for instance, even

social construction of social problems
the process of coming to see a *personal* struggle as an issue of *public* concern

though the car trip is more likely to kill us. We tend to fear violence from strangers more than from people we know, even though the people closest to us are most likely to hurt us. Because harms are socially constructed, it's entirely routine for us to make mistakes in evaluating risk.

Even when harms are widely and fairly understood, we may not consider them *social* problems. Drunk driving, for example, is widely condemned as a bad decision made by an individual—and it is—but it's also a problem related to zoning and public transportation. Because most of our cities separate residential from business districts, then fail to provide convenient late-night bus and train schedules, people going to bars usually *have* to drive. When driving is the only convenient transportation, it enhances the likelihood that individuals, especially those who can't easily afford a ride service like Lyft, will drive drunk. This makes some level of drunk driving all but certain. In other words, drunk driving is a social problem, not just a regrettable choice made by certain individuals.

If activists want to press for social solutions, they have to convince people that the troubling condition is a problem, and a social one at that. This means that activists have to shape our collective conversations (how they do this is covered in a later section). When they shape the conversation successfully, activists can instill an **insurgent consciousness**, a recognition of a shared grievance that can be addressed through collective action. Karl Marx, for example, argued in favor of an insurgent class consciousness that would inspire workers to revolt against the capitalist class. Likewise, the feminists of the 1960s engaged in active *consciousness raising*, efforts by politicized members of a group to help other members recognize that they have shared grievances that are not merely personal. In workshops, the sociologist Victor Rios encourages the Black and Latino boys of Oakland to see their troubles as related to institutional racism, not each one's unique circumstances. He's hoping to raise their consciousness too. Today, some people call it being "woke."

Coming to adopt an insurgent consciousness is often an emotional experience.[11] Sometimes it's sparked by a *moral shock*, an event that shakes us to the core. Such experiences can inspire us to join groups that are trying to make change. We often discover anew the pleasure of bonding with and fighting alongside likeminded others. The emotions that dominate our own lives might need to shift, too—from shame to pride, for instance, as with the gay liberation movement. Using interdependent power requires both intellectual and emotional work. We may need to recognize that the problem is bigger than ourselves, believe there's a better way, feel differently about identities, or replace despair with hope.

Once we're in a community of woke folk, using our interdependent power requires that we realize we have it. Social institutions are hulking and sluggish; they can make us feel helpless. This is useful to elites, who benefit from apathy among the masses. Hegemonic ideologies about who's more valuable in society also make the contributions of everyday people invisible. Our media glamorizes the breadwinner, the corporate executive, and the movie

insurgent consciousness
a recognition of a shared grievance that can be addressed through collective action

As part of the gay liberation movement, LGBTQIA individuals nurtured a shared sense of pride in their identities. Today, queer people and their allies celebrate gay pride across the United States and the world with rainbow flags and joy-filled parades.

star, leaving largely unsung the people on whom they depend: the home-makers, administrative assistants, and makeup artists. If our contributions are devalued, we may not recognize how much we're needed. To use interdependent power, we have to realize that the power elite depend on us, however convincingly they try to persuade us otherwise.

Next, we must get others to work with us. This is the **collective action problem**, the challenge of getting large groups of people to act in coordinated ways.[12] Solving this problem requires leadership, mechanisms of communication, inspiration, and even shifts in the social constructs on which our thinking and interaction depend.[13] It helps to make activism enjoyable. A shared action can be a moment of *collective effervescence*, a mutually emotional experience that leaves a group feeling unified and strong. Being an activist can feel amazing. As the sociologist James Jasper put it, activism involves the "pleasures of conversation, the excitement of interaction, the ability to articulate moral intuitions, [and] a sense of making history."[14] These, alongside the achievement of both big and small goals, are among the "pleasures of participation."

Participation, though, can also carry costs, and it's important to help people withstand them. Throwing sand in the gears is inconvenient for those at the top, but it's inconvenient for those at the bottom too. If incomes

collective action problem
the challenge of getting large groups of people to act in coordinated ways

are compromised, for example, then activists need to help people get by. If goods and services are unavailable, they need to help people go without. And if connections to others are lost, then activists need to provide people with an alternative network. Mutual support to ease the costs of activism is essential.

Finally, we have to overcome mechanisms of social control. Social rules are what Piven calls "instruments of power."[15] They facilitate interaction, she admits, but they're also used by the power elite to preserve the status quo. The more severe consequences of rule breaking—stigma, destitution, social ostracism, and imprisonment—are often imposed by the elite on activists specifically to enforce cooperation. For a social movement to get off the ground, its adherents' desire to fight for change must be stronger than their desire to avoid negative consequences.

What does it look like to successfully overcome these constraints and exert interdependent power?

CASE STUDY: THE MONTGOMERY BUS BOYCOTT

In 1955, laws mandated racial segregation of the buses in the city of Montgomery, Alabama. Black Americans were barred from being hired as drivers, and Black passengers were required to sit in the back of the bus and surrender their seats to White people who wanted them. Then, one day, a seamstress named Rosa Parks refused to give up her seat to a White man.

Her arrest sparked a protest that ended with the Supreme Court ruling that the segregation of public buses was unconstitutional. This decision fueled the desegregation movement across the South. It contributed to a wider social movement that led to the Civil Rights Act, Immigration Act, Voting Rights Act, and Fair Housing Act, all passed during the 1960s.

How did they do it?

First, they had to socially construct the problem. Arguably, the social institution most central to the Montgomery bus boycott was the African American church. Black people were excluded from much of formal political life and from most White religious congregations. This elevated Black churches, as the sociologist Aldon Morris put it, to no less than the "institutional center of the modern civil rights movement."[16]

Churches were not only useful on a practical level; they were inspirational as well. In many of these spaces, Black people learned a *liberation theology*, a movement in Christianity that interprets the gospel of Jesus Christ as a mandate for social justice. On the argument that oppression is a sin against God, congregants came to understand segregation as a problem that demanded a cultural and institutional solution. An insurgent consciousness emerged.

Second, the Black people of Montgomery had to realize that they had power. Rosa Parks was the secretary for the local chapter of the National

Association for the Advancement of Colored People (NAACP). She was not, in other words, just a tired seamstress. She was an activist. Her organization opposed racial segregation, and her action was the first in a carefully planned and orchestrated campaign to end segregation not only in public transportation in Montgomery but everywhere.

Activists like Parks recognized that a recently decided Supreme Court case, *Brown v. Board of Education*, gave them some leverage. The Court had ruled that racially segregated education was unconstitutional. It was the end of "separate but equal." This ruling opened up the possibility of challenging all forms of racial segregation. The people had a precedent.

So why the buses? And why Montgomery? Because there, they surmised, the Black community had substantial interdependent power. Three-quarters of the people who used the city bus system were Black. If they stayed off the buses—if they refused to cooperate—they could financially bankrupt the service.

Next, they had to overcome the collective action problem. The president of the local NAACP chose an inspiring local minster to lead the boycott, a recent graduate of Morehouse College who majored in sociology. His name was Martin Luther King Jr. Under his guidance, the president of the Women's Political Council, Jo Ann Robinson, hand-mimeographed as many as 50,000 fliers describing the boycott. Rosa Parks then tricked the police into arresting her. When the news of the arrest broke, the fliers were distributed to the entire African American community of Montgomery. [17] The flier called attention to Parks's protest and asked every Black resident to protest her arrest by staying off the buses that Monday.

King and his wife, Coretta, were wide awake by 5:30 that morning. "The day for the protest had arrived," King wrote in his book about the boycott, "and we were determined to see the first act of this unfolding drama."[18] He hoped that at least 60 percent of the Black people of Montgomery would stay off the buses.

There was a bus stop just five feet from King's house, serving a route that carried more Black passengers than any other in the city. They waited anxiously for the first bus. "I could hardly believe what I saw," King recalled. The bus was empty. The second bus was empty too. And the third bus was empty except for two White passengers. King was exuberant:

> I jumped in my car and for almost an hour I cruised down every major street and examined every passing bus. During this hour, at the peak of the morning traffic, I saw no more than eight Negro passengers riding the buses. By this time I was jubilant. . . . A miracle had taken place. The once dormant and quiescent Negro community was now fully awake.[19]

That day, 40,000 people boycotted the bus system. The people were using their power.

How long did the boycott last? Three days? Thirty days? Three hundred days? More.

They boycotted for 381 days. For over a year, they biked to work, rode mules, and drove horse-drawn carriages. But mostly they walked. They got up

For more than a year, the Black community boycotted the bus system in Montgomery, Alabama, successfully exerting their interdependent power to bring about the end of racial segregation on buses.

early to get to work, and they got home late. They walked to get groceries, run errands, and visit their friends and relatives. They walked so far and so long that they wore out their footwear, inspiring Black churches all over America to raise money and send shoes to Montgomery.

For people who couldn't as easily stay off the buses—older adults and people with disabilities—the activists set up carpools. People volunteered to drive shifts along the bus routes to make sure that even the people who couldn't walk could participate in the boycott. Three hundred cars were put into service. In solidarity, some White housewives offered their domestic workers rides to and from work, and some taxi drivers charged $0.10 for a ride, the same amount as bus fare.

The cost of the boycott was tired feet and aching bones. It was lost time with loved ones and less leisure. It was the expense of alternative transportation and shoes and clothes worn out on the sidewalks. Black churchgoers, supportive allies, and a small army of volunteers and donors made this possible.

Finally, they had to overcome the mechanisms of social control. Intent on defending the privilege they enjoyed, White elites in Montgomery were determined to make the price of the boycott too high to pay. They pressured insurance companies to cancel policies on cars used to drive the bus routes. They fined taxi drivers for giving discounted rides. The city ordered that buses stop going to Black neighborhoods altogether. King and eighty-nine other leaders of the boycott, including Jo Ann Robinson, were indicted for the crime of interfering with a business.

And there was violence. Boycotters were physically attacked, and King's house was firebombed. Robinson had to duck shattering glass when a large rock was thrown through her front window. Someone poured acid over her car. And Rosa Parks lost her job and received a relentless string of threatening phone calls.

How could a community withstand these attacks? King encouraged them to turn to their faith. He spoke to his supporters in front of what was left of his firebombed home and mandated that they remain peaceful and single-minded: Remember . . . if I am stopped, this movement will not stop, because God is with the movement.[20]

King preached liberation theology.

The community persevered. And perhaps the most inspiring thing about their perseverance is that they didn't know what the future held. They didn't know that after 381 days of walking the U.S. Supreme Court would declare racial segregation on buses unconstitutional. They hoped and prayed that their efforts would be successful, but they persisted on principle, without any guarantee and with no end in sight. "All life is interrelated," King would later say, invoking the power of interdependence.[21] "We are all caught in an inescapable network of mutuality, tied into a single garment of destiny."

Change happens, and when social movements win, it's evidence that everyday people are flexing their interdependent power. What, then, sweeps movements to victory?

HOW MOVEMENTS WIN

Sociologists who study social movements have had a difficult time determining just what makes them successful.[22] There are no guarantees. Certain factors, though, have been identified as helpful: organizational strength, ideas and their spokespersons, and structures of opportunity.

The strength of political organizations

The first factor is **organizational strength**, a combination of strong leadership, human and material resources, social networks, and physical infrastructure.[23] A burgeoning activist group can write a mission statement, build a website, and begin spreading its message through social networks. As the movement grows, organizational strength will include rising numbers of people, material resources like office supplies, physical spaces for organizing, a robust presence on the internet, and alliances with other activist groups, politicians, donors, and others.

A comparison of the gun rights and gun safety movements helps us understand the importance of organizational strength. The National Rifle Association (NRA) is the largest organization on either side. In 2020, it had over 5 million members, chapters in every state, and a $423 million budget. The NRA also has close ties to a $60 billion gun industry, which is the source of much of its funding.[24] And gun rights advocates tend to be especially passionate. Fewer than half of American households contain guns, but of the households that have them, a third have five or more.[25] These are true gun

organizational strength
a combination of strong leadership, human and material resources, social networks, and physical infrastructure

enthusiasts, the kind of people who are willing to show up at rallies, write letters to Congress, and go to the polls.

The gun safety movement, in contrast, consists of a handful of much smaller organizations with fewer ties to local politics and industry, more limited funds, smaller staffs, and less passionate adherents.[26] The gun rights movement out-organizes the gun control movement as a result of this difference in strength. Only 8 percent of Americans think that laws governing gun sales are too strict, but the gun rights movement has been very successful in reducing constraints nonetheless.[27]

The internet has made it significantly easier for movements to build organizational strength. The internet, and especially social media, has enabled activists to build and energize strong **political networks**, webs of ties that link people with similar political goals.[28] This gives social movements greater fundraising opportunities and voice.

The current movement to end sexual violence on college campuses is an impressive example of the use of political networks to launch a movement. It began when Annie Clark and Andrea Pino, both students at the University of North Carolina at Chapel Hill, became friends. In getting to know one another, they discovered that the administration had mishandled both of their reports of sexual assault. With the help and encouragement of women at Yale and Amherst, who they met through an online student-activist

political networks
webs of ties that link people with similar political goals

As students at the University of North Carolina at Chapel Hill, Andrea Pino and Annie Clark plugged into a political network of fellow survivors of sexual assault. Together, they launched a movement aimed at holding colleges accountable for mismanaging reports of sexual violence.

network, they found and interviewed hundreds of other students at their university who'd had similar experiences. In 2013, they collectively reported their college to the Office for Civil Rights for violations of Title IX, a federal law that requires colleges to deliver equivalent educational experiences to men and women.

News spread and survivors of sexual violence at other colleges turned to the women in Chapel Hill for help. In turn, they offered emotional support and assisted them in filing their own reports. As news traveled from school to school, more and more students began sharing their experiences and teaching each other what they'd learned. Two organizations emerged to help students hold their schools accountable—Know Your IX and End Rape on Campus—and formal complaints began flooding into the Office for Civil Rights. As of 2020, 502 schools had been investigated for mishandling reports of sexual violence.[29]

Successful social movements, then, begin with insurgent consciousnesses and can grow into formidable organizations based on social networks that spread far and wide. To make convincing cases for social change, though, activists also need to convince a wider public to offer at least passive support. To garner this support, it's useful to have spokespersons with standing and a compelling frame.

Standing and framing

People who can speak credibly on a topic carry a form of authority called **standing**. People with relevant expertise or experience are sometimes given standing, as are respected celebrities, religious figures, and public intellectuals. Having standing increases the likelihood that a person's point of view will influence an audience. If a social movement has people who can speak powerfully on its behalf, others may listen.

standing
the authority to speak credibly on a particular topic

The survivors of the 2018 mass shooting at Marjory Stoneman Douglas High School in Parkland, Florida, for instance, stood up as representatives of the movement for stronger gun control. In the immediate aftermath, about two dozen survivors committed themselves to fighting gun violence. Given the harrowing experience they'd just endured, it was difficult to argue that they didn't deserve to be heard.

Using the hashtag #neveragain, they began raising awareness, lobbying the Florida legislature, and registering young people to vote. Among other victories, they succeeded in pressing the state of Florida to pass its first gun control measures in more than twenty years. At least nineteen major corporations have since cut ties with the NRA, including Delta and United Airlines, the Best Western hotel chain, and car rental companies Avis, Budget, and Hertz.

Even if a social movement can put forward representatives with standing, they still need to say something engaging. This comes in the form of a compelling and resonant **frame**, a succinct claim as to the nature of a social fact.[30] A frame is an assertion that an event or issue is a case of a particular thing and not a case of something else.

frame
a succinct claim as to the nature of a social fact

Victims of gun violence express their support for one another at the end of the March for Our Lives rally in Washington, DC. These students, including many from Marjory Stoneman Douglas High School in Parkland, Florida, used their standing as victims of a horrific school shooting to push for stronger gun control.

Imagine, for instance, a child falls down a well. If the story receives media attention, then people given standing have some influence over the public's understanding of what the accident was a case of. It could be framed as a case of parental failure. *This accident is proof that people don't know how to parent!* It could be a case of neglected infrastructure. *This accident is proof that we need to invest in public safety!* Or it could be a case of "kids these days." *This accident is proof that today's children have no common sense!* Which frames catch on is a function of what audiences already believe as well as what frames are offered and by whom. Frames accepted by the public affect the *discourse*, or conversation about that topic or event.

Social movements must put forward frames aimed at convincing listeners that a social fact is a particular kind of social problem. If they can do this effectively, then the cause is more likely to gain support. Consider the movement to legalize marijuana. Between 1969 and 2019, the percentage of Americans who supported legalization jumped from 12 to 67 percent, eleven states legalized recreational marijuana, and thirty-three states legalized medical marijuana.[31]

What happened? A new frame had emerged. A content analysis of coverage in the *New York Times* (see Figure 11.1) found that the dominant frame shifted from drug trafficking (that is, "marijuana is criminal") to health ("marijuana is medicine").[32] "Gradually," wrote one commentator, "the stereotypical persona of the marijuana user shifted from the stoned slacker wanting to get high to the aging boomer seeking pain relief."[33] Laws blocking people from using

FIGURE 11.1

Marijuana Coverage in the *New York Times*

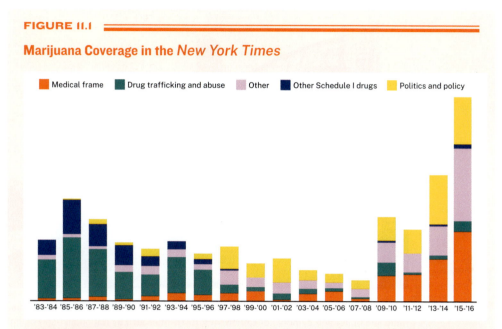

SOURCE: Chart: The Conversation, CC-BY-ND, https://creativecommons.org/licenses/by-nd/2.0/; Data source: Social Science Research (2019), https://theconversation.com/why-do-so-many-americans-now-support-legalizing-marijuana-110593.

marijuana as medicine were framed as social problems, and this opened up some cognitive space for people to change their minds on the issue.

For movement success, it's also helpful for a frame to be resistant to challenge. As social movements grow, they're sometimes met by **countermovements**: persistent, organized collective action meant to resist social movements.[34] Countermovements often introduce **counter frames**, ones meant to challenge an existing social movement's frame.

An excellent example of a frame that proved to be strongly resistant to challenge is Love Wins. This frame gathered support for same-sex marriage in the United States by conflating support for same-sex marriage with support for love. What's the counter frame to love? Love Sucks? Hate Wins? The hashtag didn't give countermovement activists much to work with, and this likely contributed to the movement's success. In 2015, the U.S. Supreme Court ruled that all fifty states had to recognize same-sex marriages.

Black Lives Matter is an example of a frame that has been less successful in fending off counter frames. While the frame does an excellent job of drawing attention to the cause—the loss of Black life in interactions with police—it's also sparked counter frames that resonate powerfully with people less sympathetic to the issue. The slogans All Lives Matter and Blue Lives Matter, for example (the latter referring specifically to police) are used to challenge the Black Lives Matter movement, potentially undermining its effectiveness.

countermovements
persistent, organized collective action meant to resist social movements

counter frames
frames meant to challenge an existing social movement's frame

Some of the rioters who stormed the Capitol on January 6, 2021, invoked Christian nationalism, adding symbols of Christianity to Trump's strictly nationalist campaign: "Keep America Great."

In any given time and place, some frames are picked up by many social movement groups at once. These are called *master frames*, culturally resonant frames that can be used across many different social movement causes.[35] The individual rights frame, for instance, is used widely by many movements, from civil rights to gay rights to gun rights to animal rights. Nationalism, which positions support for an issue as a case of protecting one's nation from perceived outsiders, is another master frame. Nationalist frames are used by anti-immigration activists, those opposed to engagement with a global economy, and groups who advocate for America to be a Christian nation, as well as sovereignty movements intended to free nations from colonial rule. Donald J. Trump's presidential campaign slogans—"Make America Great Again" and "America First"—were nationalist frames.

Especially since the 1960s, visibility has come to be a master frame.[36] Movement goals have traditionally centered on *redistribution*, a more equitable distribution of economic capital and other resources. But they increasingly also demand *recognition*, a more equitable distribution of status across social identities. To be recognized is to have our identity validated and given due respect.

The gay liberation slogan "We're here, we're queer, get used to it," for example, asks that the wider community recognize the presence of non-heterosexual people. More recently, trans and nonbinary people have been fighting for acknowledgement. The hashtag #WontBeErased is used to object to policies that don't recognize the existence of nonbinary people, like gender binary bathrooms and government documents with only two gender categories. Similarly, in 2003 the intersex community declared and commemorated

FIGURE 11.2

New Mentions of "Income Inequality," January 2011–November 2012

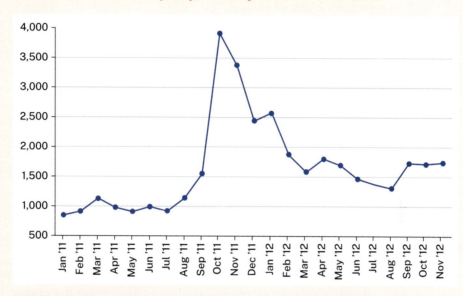

SOURCE: Ruth Milkman, Stephanie Luce, and Penny Lewis, "Changing the Subject: A Bottom Up Account of Occupy Wall Street in New York City," The Murphy Institute, City University of New York, 2013, https://media
.sps.cuny.edu/filestore/1/5/7/1_a05051d2117901d/1571_92f562221b8041e.pdf.

the first Intersex Awareness Day, calling for wider recognition of people with intersex conditions.

Framing may seem to be a matter of mere words, but frames can effectively challenge existing ways of thinking about the world and sometimes pierce powerful hegemonic ideologies. The 2011 Occupy Wall Street movement, for example, introduced the slogan "We are the 99 percent." The phrase identified the majority of Americans as victims of economic inequality, corporate crime, and the revolving door between business and government. Figure 11.2 shows that mentions of "income inequality" in the news spiked during the months Occupy was most active, but the phrase was still being used at nearly five times its pre-Occupy rate even after most activists had gone home. The activists made "the 1 percent" a household phrase, disrupted capitalism's hegemony, and arguably paved the way for Bernie Sanders to excite a new wave of Democratic Socialists during the 2016 and 2020 U.S. presidential primaries.[37]

Opposing social movements often engage in **framing wars**, battles over whether a social fact is a social problem and what kind of problem it is. The abortion debate is an example of just such a battle. Opponents of the right to abortion call themselves "pro-life," a frame that states that abortion is the taking of a life. Their materials include phrases that resonate with this claim, like "abortion stops a beating heart" and "it's not a fetus, it's a baby."

framing wars
battles over whether a social fact is a social problem and what kind of problem it is

In contrast, proponents of the right to abortion describe themselves as "pro-choice," a frame that states that abortion is an exercise of ownership over one's own body. Their materials promote phrases like "my body, my choice" and "keep your laws off my body."

Both sides make a claim as to what abortion is really about: life versus choice. Notice, though, that even as the two sides invoke different ideologies, both are ultimately using the same master frame: individual rights.[38] Pro-life activists describe themselves as being in the "right to life" movement, emphasizing the rights of the developing fetus. Pro-choice activists ground their position in the "right to choose," emphasizing the rights of the pregnant woman. The individual rights frame is a resonant one in the United States, and perhaps the two sides' shared use of it is part of why this particular framing battle is deadlocked. In 2020, 46 percent of Americans considered themselves pro-life and 48 percent considered themselves pro-choice.[39] Only 6 percent of Americans identified as neither.

The social context

A final set of factors key to movement success are external to the movement organization itself: the political, cultural, and economic context. Features of this context offer a blend of opportunities and constraints. To describe this, sociologists use the phrase *opportunity structure*. This section describes and gives some examples of political, cultural, and economic opportunity structures.

Political Opportunities and Constraints

The **political opportunity structure** includes strengths and weaknesses in the existing political system that shape the options available to social movement actors.[40] Movements are aided, for example, by being in countries that tolerate at least some degree of activism. The United States fashions itself a democracy, which means that it's responsive to its citizens, at least in theory. Strong support for free speech and other democratic values makes it easy to frame protest as a genuinely American thing to do.

Other countries with more authoritarian regimes are much less tolerant of activism, with leaders willing to intimidate, imprison, or murder challengers, as was the case for Antonio Gramsci in Mussolini's Italy. The people of Hong Kong, for example, have been fighting to maintain their democratic norms in the face of an increasingly intolerant China. Under an agreement between them, Hong Kong is guaranteed the right to determine its own political system. China, however, has been moving to undermine this freedom, passing an "extradition law" that gives them the power to arrest political dissidents. This has made political protest much riskier in Hong Kong than it is in the United States.

There are other forms of political opportunity too. The last chapter discussed how elites are often in cahoots, whether intentionally or incidentally. When political elites are unified in their opposition to social movements, success can be very difficult. But disagreements among elites—or *inter-elite competition*—presents an opportunity.[41] Activists can appeal to whichever

political opportunity structure
the strengths and weaknesses in the existing political system that shape the options available to social movement actors

For years, activists in Hong Kong have protested against China's efforts to erode their democracy. Since 2019, the Chinese government has escalated attacks on these protests, making it much more dangerous to engage in activism.

elites happen to agree with them. And conversely, elites can point to like-minded activist groups to give their own aspirations a veneer of righteousness.

The incredibly fast rise of the Tea Party, a political movement favoring low taxes and decreased government spending, is an example. The Tea Party was introduced in 2009, and just two years later, there were sixty Tea Party members in Congress. By 2013 about 10 percent of Americans identified with the movement. In part, the Tea Party's rise can be explained by divisions among Republican politicians.[42] Most notably, David Koch—the eleventh richest person in America with a net worth of $50.5 billion when he died in 2019—wanted to push the Republican Party further to the right.[43] He saw an opportunity with the Tea Party and funneled an unknown amount of money to their politicians. Media elites with influence over political programming at Fox News also embraced the Tea Party, giving them valuable coverage.

Elite opinions matter, but public opinion matters too. Politicians are at least somewhat accountable to the people they represent. Once public opinion supports a change, it's harder for even the most elite to resist it. For example, the United States is the only rich democracy without a national health care system that covers all its citizens. Yet, two-thirds of Americans—including 85 percent of Democrats and 73 percent of Independents—support the idea of government-provided health care.[44] This made it politically risky for

Republicans to advocate for the repeal of the Affordable Care Act (a government initiative to help people pay for private health insurance), while giving Democrats an incentive to support it.

Cultural Opportunities and Constraints

cultural opportunity structure
cultural ideas, objects, practices, or bodies that create or constrain activist strategies

Social movement success also depends on the **cultural opportunity structure**: cultural ideas, objects, practices, or bodies that create or constrain activist strategies.[45] Culture constrains what positions activists can successfully take up. Sometimes, for example, the symbolic structure simply doesn't have a place for a movement. A group of U.S. environmentalists who oppose immigration fall into this category.[46] They believe that higher populations lead to overcrowding and water shortages, while urban sprawl means lost farmland and animal habitat. Accordingly, they argue, strict limits on immigration are necessary to protect the health of the environment.

Anti-immigration environmentalists, however, have largely failed to gather a following, despite the fact that many Americans favor reducing immigration and many favor protecting the environment. The problem is that few Americans favor both. In the symbolic structure, pro-environment and anti-immigrant attitudes are squarely placed on opposing sides of a socially constructed binary: Democrat and Republican. The case that we should restrict immigration to protect the environment can't gain traction on either side. Environmentalists usually see people who are anti-immigration as political opponents, and vice versa.

The cultural opportunity structure is also dependent on the media elite, who can choose to ignore social movements, portray them negatively, or elevate them. In 2016, for example, the professional football player Colin Kaepernick began kneeling during the National Anthem. He did so in solidarity with Black Lives Matter and Say Her Name, the movements against state and vigilante violence against Black Americans. By 2017, his football career was over, but some elites in the culture industry have lionized him. *GQ* magazine made him their Citizen of the Year, and *Sports Illustrated* gave him a Legacy Award. In 2018, Nike chose him to star in a new ad campaign with the slogan: "Believe in something, even if it means sacrificing everything." And Harvard University gave him a medal named after the sociologist W. E. B. Du Bois. The positive treatment by cultural powerhouses has drawn real attention to the movements he represents.

critical event
a sudden and dramatic occurrence that motivates non-activists to become politically active

Sometimes current events present unexpected cultural opportunities that activists can use to rally support. Sociologists call these **critical events**, sudden and dramatic occurrences that motivate nonactivists to become politically active.[47] Nuclear accidents, terrorist attacks, or stunning celebrity confessions are examples of critical events. Sometimes such events change the direction of history.

A tragic example is the murder of Vincent Chin in 1982. On the night of his bachelor party, two White men who worked in a nearby automobile factory confronted him at a bar. At the time, the U.S. auto industry was struggling in the face of competition from Japan, and autoworkers were losing their jobs. When they saw Chin, they assumed he was Japanese. As the fight began, one said: "It's because of you little motherfuckers that we're out of work."[48] They beat Chin to the brink of death with a baseball bat. He died four days later.

Above and beyond the fact that it was a hate crime, Chin's murder got the attention of Asian Americans for two unsettling reasons. First, Chin wasn't Japanese. He was Chinese. He was, in other words, a Chinese man who was murdered for being Japanese. This was a wake-up call to a diverse community of people from Asia who didn't always think of themselves as belonging in the same category. The term *Asian* had only been around for about a decade; at the time, people identified as Samoan, Vietnamese, Filipino, Cambodian, Malaysian, Indonesian, Laotian, Korean, Taiwanese, Singaporean, and Thai, but not Asian.

Chin's murder sent a message that while they didn't see themselves as the same, other Americans did. And they realized they might need to join forces to protect themselves.

Second, the two men who murdered Chin were found guilty, but not of murder. They were found guilty of the lesser charge of manslaughter, the crime of killing a person by accident. They spent three years on probation and paid a $3,000 fine. Neither spent a day in prison. "These weren't the kind of men you send to jail," wrote the judge who sentenced them, as if their brutal attack didn't reflect on the kind of men they were. This outcome sent a message that Asian lives were of little value.

Chin's murder was a tragedy. It was also a critical event. It mobilized a community, made a new social identity meaningful, and created a much larger constituency for activism.

The murder of George Floyd by a Minneapolis police officer in 2020 was a critical event, too, one equally tragic and powerful. Thanks to the bravery of Darnella Frazier, a seventeen-year-old Black woman who filmed the event, the whole world would witness Floyd's death. He cried out "I can't

The murder of George Floyd by a Minneapolis police officer in May 2020 was a critical event that inspired unprecedented levels of social movement participation.

breathe" over twenty times, begged for his life, called for his dead mother, and told his children he loved them—for an agonizing eight minutes—while a police officer casually kneeled on his neck.

Frazier's video sparked protests in over 2,000 cities and towns in more than sixty countries. As many as 26 million Americans attended these protests, or 10 percent of the U.S. population, which is an unprecedented level of social movement participation.[49] In contrast, the civil rights marches of the 1960s involved only hundreds of thousands of people. The Floyd protesters were also more diverse than those from the civil rights era; about half of participants were White.[50]

The protests may have inspired elites, or given them some cover, to come out in support of Black Lives Matter. The National Football League, National Basketball Association, and Major League Baseball all eased its rules on players making political statements on the field or court. NASCAR banned the Confederate flag at its events. The response to the protests, however, wasn't only symbolic. Minneapolis pledged to rebuild its police department. New York passed a law to make police disciplinary records more transparent. And half of the country's largest police departments changed their policies on the use of chokeholds. The sociologist Douglas McAdam commented:

> It looks, for all the world, like these protests are achieving what very few do: setting in motion a period of significant, sustained, and widespread social, political change. We appear to be experiencing a social change tipping point—that is as rare in society as it is potentially consequential.[51]

George Floyd's death was a powerful catalyst, in large part because Frazier uploaded the video of his death to the internet, where it was able to spread via social media. Since the widespread adoption of the internet in the mid-1990s, and especially since the introduction of social media in the early 2000s, activists have used online spaces to initiate collective action.

An especially clever example of this can be attributed to a group of teenagers and K-pop fans on TikTok. Opposed to the 2020 reelection of Donald Trump—or merely enticed at the idea of pranking him—they encouraged one another to reserve free tickets to a campaign rally in Tulsa, Oklahoma. "It spread mostly through Alt TikTok," said Elijah Daniel, who helped spread the word. "We kept it on the quiet side where people do pranks and a lot of activism."[52] He added that Alt TikTok and K-pop Twitter know how to coordinate with one another and exploit algorithms to get views. Their aim was to artificially inflate the number of anticipated attendees. It worked. Before the rally, a Trump campaign spokesman bragged that over 1 million tickets had been requested. Just over 6,000 people showed up.

Of course, the internet isn't just a tool for embarrassing politicians. Activists can use it to spark insurgent consciousnesses and reframe personal troubles as social problems.[53] Prompted by revelations of the sexually predatory behavior of movie producer Harvey Weinstein and comedian Bill Cosby, as well as the confirmation of Brett Kavanaugh to the Supreme Court after hearings into a history of alleged rape, the actress Alyssa Milano invited people on Twitter to echo the activist Tarana Burke and say #metoo. The hashtag was a way for people to tell the world that they, too, had survived sexual abuse or assault. On Twitter, half a million people responded within twenty-four hours.[54] On Facebook, the hashtag was used in 12 million posts and comments.[55] It was a new way to "come out" and make what felt personal a very public and political issue.

The internet is no substitute for face-to-face interaction, but it does have some advantages.[56] It enables people to enter activist spaces with very low cost and risk. People with limited leisure time due to caregiving or work responsibilities can participate at least a little bit online, as can people with physical disabilities or those who live far from centers of activism, in rural areas and on remote reservations. For people for whom activism is risky—like feminists in orthodox religious communities or sexual minorities in small towns—the internet offers the opportunity to share ideas with some safety. The internet can also bring otherwise geographically dispersed minorities together, like individuals advocating for people with rare diseases.

Online activities like these are often derisively called *slacktivism*, a critical word for supposedly lazy forms of activism. But participating in such viral moments can make a difference. In this case, the Weinstein scandal prompted the Alianza Nacional de Campesinas—a national organization of female farmworkers—to write an open letter in solidarity with the women in Hollywood. By bridging the economic and cultural chasms between movie stars and farmworkers, the letter captured the spirit of the #MeToo movement. Soon the hashtag #allwomen was trending and the focus turned toward women in all

Mily Treviño-Sauceda and Mónica Ramírez cofounded a national organization of women farmworkers with the primary goal of ending workplace exploitation and sexual harassment.

kinds of occupations and in countries around the world.[57] Sexual minorities, trans women, and cisgender men also used the hashtags to draw attention to their abuse.

In response, the *New York Times* collaborated with the National Women's Law Center to start a fund to offer free legal support for low-income people facing sexual harassment and violence at work. Celebrities used the 2018 Grammys as a platform to raise people's consciousness. Within months the fund had raised $22 million and 780 attorneys had volunteered to work for free.[58] A hashtag born online can be a springboard for concrete change.

Economic Opportunities and Constraints

economic opportunity structure
the role of money in enabling or limiting a movement's operations and influence

A final part of the recipe for successful activism is the **economic opportunity structure**, a phrase that refers to the role of money in enabling or limiting a movement's operations and influence. For one, consider a movement's base. Movements supported by the poor and working class will have weaker fundraising, all else being equal, than movements supported by the middle and upper classes. Adherents of the anti-vaccination movement, for instance, often live in some of the richest neighborhoods in the country.[59] In contrast, supporters of Fight for 15, the movement to raise the minimum wage to $15 an hour, disproportionately come from the poorest-paid rungs of society. These differences will have financial consequences for building organizational strength.

Many social movements target industries. Ones that are economically vulnerable may cooperate with activists; ones that aren't may not. Consider a group of animal rights activists who opposed Sweden's fur garment industry. The activists were positioned well in light of the cultural opportunity structure—most Swedes like animals, especially furry ones, and so they were easily persuaded to oppose the raising of animals for the harvesting of their coats—but the industry was resilient to attacks because of the economic opportunity structure. The fur breeders sell most of their garments abroad. Because most of their buyers were outside the country, a Swedish boycott had little effect.

interest convergence
the alignment of the interests of activists and elites

Economic interests can also be an opportunity for activists. **Interest convergence** occurs when the interests of activists and elites align.[60] Some hopes for immigration reform—citizenship for the children of immigrants (called "Dreamers"), amnesty for the undocumented, a stronger embrace of refugees, and easier paths to immigration for all—rest on interest convergence.[61] If business elites believe that more welcoming immigration policies will provide them with a pool of employees, they might be willing to support such policies alongside pro-immigration activists.

Economic inequality itself also shapes the options of activists. The richest people in society will inevitably have more money than the poorest to spend on issues they care about, and greater inequality exacerbates this difference. Some of the wealthiest people in America—Bill Gates, Mark Zuckerberg, Warren Buffett, Elon Musk, and Larry Ellison—have pledged to donate more than half of their fortunes between now and their death. Between the five of them, they'll deliver at least $295 billion to causes of their choice. That's nice, but should *any* five people really have that much power to decide which social problems deserve attention? In contrast, other Americans, and especially those of us with little money to spare, are less able to support the causes we care about. Because of economic inequality, rich people have more say as to which social movements are financially supported.

Economic, cultural, and political opportunity structures shape the likelihood that a movement will be successful. Internal factors like the passion of supporters, organizational strength, political networks, and the resonance of frames and counter frames matter too. And all things being equal, critical moments and other unpredictable events can help or hinder a social movement. Just as the boycotters in Montgomery didn't know what future their efforts would bring, it's impossible to know ahead of time whether an insurgent consciousness will turn into a social movement that changes its society. The only way to find out is to try. ∎

COMING UP...

WHEN THE BRITISH sociologist Harriet Martineau visited the United States in the early 1800s, she observed that the new country was a contradiction: simultaneously an aristocracy ruled by the power elite and a democracy extended to the people.[62] Throughout U.S. history, people have used the country's democratic principles to flex their interdependent power and challenge its aristocracy. Because the whole range of social life is dependent on cooperation, any individual can muck things up. And many individuals, working together, can do truly extraordinary things. This is the stuff of social movements.

Harnessing interdependent power depends on the ability to think sociologically — that is, being able to see personal troubles as related to the social organization of the world around us. It requires an insurgent consciousness and a belief that there's power in numbers. To use it, we have to decide it's worth it and overcome mechanisms of social control. And we have to convince others to do so too.

Our most successful social movements build organizational strength. They combine strong and inspirational leadership with resources, both human and otherwise, and they nurture political networks and build infrastructure. They also tap into our symbolic structure and develop frames that resonate with large numbers of people. They capture both hearts and minds. If luck holds — if the political, cultural, and economic opportunity structures are in their favor — then they may be able to accomplish their goals.

Anything is possible. In fact, some argue that the United States is in a new era of heightened activism right now. Today's political discontent is not only national but global. The next chapter addresses globalization and the activists who are working across borders to solve the world's biggest social problem.

12

OUR FUTURE
ON EARTH

IN THIS CHAPTER...

THOUGH WE OFTEN think of the world as a *nation-state system*, one consisting only of sovereign, self-contained territories, we actually live in a *world system*, a planet with a global market organized by a capitalist economy. In a world system, people are highly interconnected. This chapter is about the expansion and intensification of that interconnectedness across nation-states. We call this *globalization*.

Globalization has produced:

- *Cultural hybridization*, the production of ideas, objects, practices, and bodies influenced by two or more cultures.

- *Transnational organizations*, companies that cross borders, governments that make alliances, and activists who organize across countries.

- *Global commodity chains*, a transnational economic process that involves extracting natural resources, transforming them into goods, and marketing and distributing them to consumers.

Our world system is disproportionately controlled by a *global power elite*, a relatively small group of interconnected people who occupy top positions in globally important social institutions. And this system produces *global inequality*, a relatively stable system of world social stratification characterized by a mix of poor, rich, and middle-income countries.

Globalization has also enabled *transnational social movements*, ones that coordinate activism across more than one country. These movements encourage people to engage in collective action that transcends borders. This chapter will use global climate activism as an example of a transnational social movement.

"Change is coming, whether you like it or not."

—GRETA THUNBERG

In the mid-1300s, the Black Death crept along the Silk Road.[1] The disease slowly traversed the ancient 7,000-mile network of trade routes linking the Chinese and Roman Empires. Over the four-year outbreak, the Black Death would become the most fatal pandemic in recorded human history, killing at least 75 million people in Asia, Africa, Europe, and beyond.

Nearly 700 years later, a novel coronavirus would also spread across the globe. But this time, it would only take a matter of months, not years. On the very last day of 2019, China announced it was in the midst of an outbreak caused by an unfamiliar pathogen. Eight days later, scientists reported that the cause was a virus never before detected in people. The first known victim of Covid-19 died the next day.

Three days later, Thailand reported the first known case outside China. Three days after that, Japan. Three days more, South Korea. By the end of January, the virus had jumped continents, with known cases in Australia, Germany, and the United States. On January 30, the World Health Organization declared the pandemic a global emergency. As of this writing, the novel coronavirus is believed to have spread to every country on earth, except for twelve isolated island nations.[2]

This chapter is about the global connectedness that made both of these pandemics possible. Though we're citizens of distinct nation-states—large territories governed by centralized powers that grant or deny citizenship rights (more colloquially, countries)—our economies, cultures, identities, and institutions transcend national borders. The reach of the Black Death shows that such connections aren't new, but the extent of our connectedness has rapidly increased in recent years. In French, this escalation is called *mondialisation*; in Spanish, *globalización*; and in German, *globalisierung*. In English, we call it **globalization**: the social processes that are expanding and intensifying connections across nation-states.[3]

globalization
the social processes that are expanding and intensifying connections across nation-states

Globalization helps explain why the spread of the coronavirus so aggressively outpaced that of the Black Death. The global movement of people and products is greater today, and the speed by which they can move is unparalleled in history. This allowed Covid-19 to go farther and faster than any pandemic before.

Since the 1990s, some scholars have argued that we're in a state of "hyperglobalization."[4] The internet went live in the mid-1990s; nearly half of the human population is now online. World trade has accelerated. Today, much of our clothes, furniture, food, and medicine come to us from far away. Increasingly, humans travel abroad. Prior to the pandemic, over 1 billion people were vacationing in another country every year.

This chapter is about how globalization has changed life on earth. Nothing has escaped this process, not our media, communication, culture, politics, or economics. Not even our self-concepts, and certainly not our health. Globalization has also introduced new forces of inequality, requiring a wider lens to understand social stratification. And it's changed the nature of social movements. These changes are the subject of this book's final chapter. To understand them, it will focus on a specific global challenge: the climate crisis.

LIVING IN A GLOBALIZING HUMAN SOCIETY

There are about 195 nation-states on the planet, depending on how you count them, but the distance between us is shrinking. In some ways, though not all, national borders are now permeable. Several intertwined but distinct threads are useful for understanding how.

The most familiar thread is mass and social media. Today, we can access foreign films on Netflix or follow Twitch channels streamed from other countries. We can download music from almost any corner of the globe. And we can follow Facebook, TikTok, and Instagram users on every continent, giving us unprecedented access to the lives of people around the world.

This access has accelerated the sharing of cultures across societies. Globalization incites **cultural hybridization**, the production of ideas, objects, practices, and bodies influenced by two or more cultures.[5] So-called creole languages like Hawaiian Pidgin and Jamaican Patois, for example, arise when people who speak different tongues come into extended contact and learn to communicate. Trendy "fusion" restaurants, like New York's Asia de Cuba or London's Chino Latino, are examples of cultural hybridization, producing new tastes. New music genres often arise from cultural contact too. K-pop, for example, traces back to an American missionary who taught U.S. and British folk songs to Korean schoolboys. As cultures come into contact, hybrid cultural forms are born.

Our politics have globalized too. Nation-states still control foreign and domestic policy, but they face competition from organizations. **Transnational organizations** are ones that operate in more than one country. Transnational

cultural hybridization
the production of ideas, objects, practices, and bodies influenced by two or more cultures

transnational organizations
organizations that operate in more than one country

The South Korean boy band BTS has been at the forefront of a dramatic increase in U.S. consumption of Korean culture. But the cultural exchange goes both ways, as K-pop is traced directly to schoolchildren who learned American and British folk songs from an American missionary.

governmental organizations include the United Nations (193 members) and the European Union (27 members).[6] Transnational *nongovernmental* organizations include associations with charitable goals (like the Red Cross), ones dedicated to social justice (like Amnesty International), professional organizations (like the International Council of Nurses), and interest organizations (like the International Quidditch Association).

Some transnational organizations are economic.[7] Beginning in the 1400s, European empires engaged in **colonialism**, a practice in which countries claim control over territories, the people in them, and their natural resources, then exploit them for economic gain (see Map 12.1). Britain alone invaded 90 percent of then-existing countries. At its peak in the early 1900s, its empire controlled 23 percent of the world population. The United States is one of its rebel colonies and later became a colonizer itself. France, Belgium, Germany, Portugal, and the Netherlands had extensive colonial empires too. Most of Africa, Polynesia, Asia, and Australia were colonized. During this period, resources were extracted from their lands and exported to enrich empires.

About one hundred years later, the international community condemns such behavior, but economic relations between countries are as strong as ever. Now they're controlled by international agreements decided by the world's most powerful countries, most of which were colonial powers. Instead of outright exploitation, countries agree on treaties and trade deals and form transnational organizations like the World Bank, the World Trade Organization, and the International Monetary Fund. These organizations now enforce a global version of capitalism.

colonialism
a practice in which countries claim control over territories, the people in them, and their natural resources, then exploit them for economic gain

MAP 12.1

A Map of European Colonialism

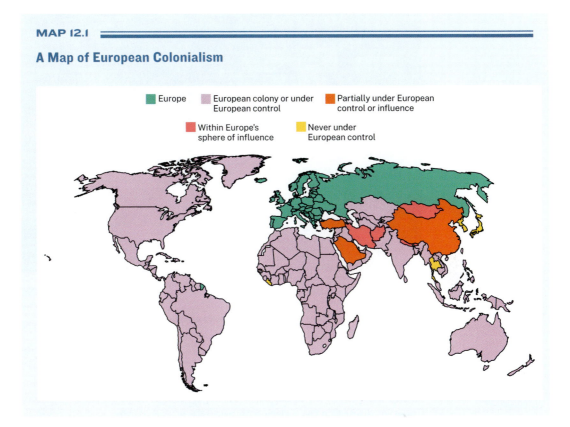

■ Europe   ■ European colony or under European control   ■ Partially under European control or influence

■ Within Europe's sphere of influence   ■ Never under European control

World capitalism supports *transnational corporations*, ones that do business in multiple countries. About 43,000 such companies exist, and together they control two-thirds of all world trade. These businesses take advantage of the same resources exploited by colonizing countries (human and natural) and the ease of international transportation (enabled by fossil fuels, the internet, and related technologies).

The richest and most powerful transnational corporations are disproportionately based in the richest countries. So, that's where most of the spoils of global capitalism go. In 2018, the 500 largest and richest transnational corporations took home more than a third of total global profits, to the tune of nearly $33 trillion.[8] This is an astronomical sum of money. If you spent a dollar a second, it would take you more than a million years to spend it.

Some of these companies are so rich that they've displaced countries as the dominant economic actors on the planet. Today, more than 75 percent of the 200 highest-revenue-generating entities on earth are corporations. In 2019, for example, Apple produced more wealth than the entire country of Australia. Microsoft produced nearly twice as much as Sweden.

These corporations become rich, in part, by designing extremely profitable **global commodity chains**, a transnational economic process that involves

global commodity chains

a transnational economic process that involves extracting natural resources, transforming them into goods, and marketing and distributing them to consumers

At the beginning of the Covid-19 pandemic, workers in this garment factory in Kenya quickly pivoted to making PPE. Their work added 30,000 face masks to the supply daily, compensating for critical breakdowns in global supply chains.

extracting natural resources, transforming them into goods, and marketing and distributing them to consumers. Thanks to Covid-19, much of the world became hyperaware of the global commodity chains for PPE, or personal protective equipment, in 2020. Most PPE is produced via a global commodity chain, meaning that the sourcing of materials, manufacturing, and distribution are spread across multiple countries. When the pandemic hit, 95 percent of the surgical masks used by the United States each year were processed through global supply chains like these. This quickly became a problem. If work in even one of the countries involved was disrupted, the chain would break.

A Canadian company called Medicom Inc., for example, was sourcing the fabric for surgical masks in Europe, then sending the fabric to China for manufacturing, then shipping the completed masks to Japan and the United States for distribution to buyers.[9] When factories in China were shut down in response to the virus, the entire commodity chain collapsed temporarily. This exacerbated an already dangerous shortage of supplies, and nation-states found themselves dependent on other virus-threatened countries for dwindling stocks.

The crisis in PPE reveals that nation-states are vulnerable to the operations of transnational corporations. Another force is challenging the nation-state from within. **Global cities** are urban areas that act as key hubs in the world economy.[10] They're often more linked to other global cities than they are to the countries in which they sit. Cities like Tokyo, Sydney, and São Paulo are centers of world finance, home to transnational corporations, and the source of much cultural power.

What happens in these cities often has global implications. The San Francisco Bay Area, for example, is home to many of the companies that

global cities
urban areas that act as key hubs in the world economy

shape the nature of life online: Facebook, Netflix, Google, and Twitter, among others. Similarly, the global Great Recession was triggered primarily by a series of banks headquartered in just one city: New York.

This suggests that the world is no longer a **nation-state system**, one consisting only of sovereign, self-contained territories. Instead, we live in a **world system**, one characterized by a global market organized by a capitalist economy.[11] Nation-states, in other words, no longer have economies of their own but are part of one world economy. This means that there aren't just rich people and poor people, but rich countries and poor countries.

GLOBAL INEQUALITY

The first person to articulate the global nature of capitalism was a sociologist named Oliver C. Cox (1901–1974). Cox was born on the Caribbean island of Trinidad and immigrated to the United States as a teenager in 1919. He finished high school, then attended community college, completing his education with a PhD from the University of Chicago. During this time, he contracted polio and became a wheelchair user.

As an immigrant, Cox was struck by the amount of racism he encountered in the United States. Carrying African ancestry, he was accustomed to being discriminated against in Trinidad, where there was a bias against dark skin. American racism, however, was more virulent. He set out to understand why.

Ultimately, in a book titled *The Foundations of Capitalism* (1959), Cox concluded that racism in the United States could only be understood if we acknowledged its origins in a world economic system.[12] The very idea of race as a social identity, he noted, was invented to justify the economic exploitation of poor people by colonizers. Recall from Chapter 3 that the distinction between Black and White was invented by elite European men tasked with colonizing the Americas for the purpose of enriching Europeans. Faced with unrest among their labor force, the colonizers aimed to divide and conquer the poor. Newly called "White" people were given the psychological wage of being supposedly superior to newly called "Black" people. This distinction was then institutionalized in the permanent enslavement of Black people and their descendants. This incentivized the **global slave trade**: the practice of kidnapping human beings, transporting them around the world, and selling them for profit.

Later, Cox's argument would be further developed by a next generation of world system theorists, the most famous of whom is the sociologist Immanuel Wallerstein (1930–2019). Wallerstein was born in the global city of New York, after his Polish parents moved from Spain to Germany and then to the United States.[13] He became interested in international affairs as a teenager in the 1940s, during which he followed India's efforts to throw off colonial rule. During his college years, he would study in England, Brussels, France, and Mexico, and he would serve in the U.S. Army during the Korean War. As a professor, he would teach in Canada, China, Tanzania, Italy, and the

Netherlands. Eventually, he would lead both the U.S. African Studies Association and the International Sociological Association.

Safe to say, Wallerstein made the world his intellectual playground. Building on Cox, he became one of our greatest theorists of global inequality, showing that global capitalism has produced a relatively stable system of social stratification. Global economic inequality, in fact, is even greater than the economic inequality we see in the United States today. The richest 1 percent of U.S. households control more than a third of the country's wealth. Globally, the richest 1 percent controls nearly half of all wealth on earth.[14]

The world's wealth is not distributed evenly across countries, and neither is global poverty. More than three-quarters of the residents of Madagascar and the Democratic Republic of Congo live in *extreme poverty*, defined by the United Nations as living on less than $1.90 a day.[15] Half of Zambia and Sierra Leone also live in extreme poverty, as do more than a third of people in Kenya, Liberia, and Guinea. In the Americas, Haiti and Honduras stand out, at 16 and 24 percent of residents, respectively. In Asia, India and Laos are the poorest countries, with more than 20 percent of people living under these conditions.

The world system

Instead of merely noting each country's level of wealth, Wallerstein argued that we should describe them according to their relationship to the world economy. For instance, Wallerstein asked us to think of poor countries as not merely poor, but *peripheral*. Peripheral countries in the world economy—including those in many previously colonized regions—are the home of the world's working poor. The world's richest and most powerful people are unlikely to live there. Peripheral countries contribute mostly natural resources and physical labor to the world economy.

Likewise, Wallerstein asked us to think of rich countries as not just rich, but *core* to the world economy. Core countries include Japan, the United States and Canada, the nation-states of Western Europe, and other advanced industrialized nation-states. These countries are home to most of the world's economic capital. They control most of the transnational governmental organizations and are host to the richest transnational corporations (the 500 largest are headquartered in just thirty-four countries). Core countries also have the most powerful militaries.

The world's richest people also disproportionately live in core countries. There are around 175,000 people in the world worth $50 million or more, and nearly all of them live in just twenty nation-states.[16] Half live in the United States. In global perspective, these aren't the 1 percent; they're the 0.001 percent. Many are at the helm of powerful organizations that control the world system, whether in global cities, rich corporations, or core countries. These are the **global power elite**, a relatively small group of interconnected people who occupy top positions in globally important social institutions.[17]

Finally, Wallerstein labeled middle-income countries as *semi-peripheral*. Countries like Russia and South Africa are in the semi-periphery, as are some

global power elite
a relatively small group of interconnected people who occupy top positions in globally important social institutions

countries in Asia and Latin America, like South Korea and Mexico. These kinds of countries exploit the periphery when they can, struggle to avoid falling into it, and try to compete with richer countries.

And what of the individuals who live in these countries? Unlike transnational organizations, individuals have limited mobility. The core countries have decided that corporations should be mostly free to cross borders to find cheap labor, take advantage of lax environmental laws, and seek the lowest taxes and most lucrative markets for their products. However, the same freedoms are not extended to people. Instead, immigration laws restrict workers' rights to cross borders. Unlike corporations, people do not have the run of the globe.

Case study: Big Oil and the people of Guyana

As an example of these dynamics, consider Standard Oil, a company started in the Gilded Age by John D. Rockefeller, the world's first billionaire. Over the years, Standard Oil transformed, dividing and rebranding, often in response to crackdowns on its illegal business practices. Today its principal descendant is ExxonMobil, a U.S.-based transnational corporation operating in fifty-one countries on six continents. It discovers, extracts, transports, refines, and markets oil and gas. This has made it the eighth most profitable company in the world, with more than $290 billion in revenue in 2019. If it were a country, it would be the fiftieth richest in the world, between Peru and New Zealand.[18]

ExxonMobil is based in Texas, but it drills for oil and gas in many peripheral and semi-peripheral countries. It exports these products around the world and brings the profits home to many people in the United States. Currently, it's exploring for or extracting oil and gas in forty-one different countries, most of which have smaller annual revenues than the corporation itself.

In 2018, the company announced the discovery of one of the largest oil reserves in the world. They found it off the coast of Guyana, a small Caribbean nation. Guyana's original inhabitants were a semi-nomadic foraging population, and many of the current residents still live off the land. The indigenous population endured 350 years of colonial rule by the Dutch and then the British. Starting in 1616, these powers used the land to grow tobacco and sugarcane, importing enslaved Africans and Indian indentured servants when European diseases began killing the indigenous population. Guyana's two largest racial groups today are descendants of colonial-era Africans and Indians.

Guyana freed itself from colonial rule in 1966, just over fifty years ago. But, like many previously colonized countries, colonial rule left this newly independent country in the periphery of the world economy. In 2018, the annual revenue of the entire country amounted to just 1 percent of that of ExxonMobil. Comparatively, then, ExxonMobil had vastly more resources than Guyana to put into oil exploration and extraction. This made Guyana dependent on the company, or a company like it, to tap its own natural resources.

So Guyana made a deal. The contract it signed with ExxonMobil allows the company to recover 100 percent of its investment and operating costs. It then

Guyana is a small Caribbean country on the North Atlantic coast of South America. A recent oil discovery offshore catapulted the country into the top tier of global oil producers, but ExxonMobil will capture most of the revenue.

splits the remaining revenue roughly fifty-fifty. This means ExxonMobil will not, in the end, have spent a penny of its own money finding and exporting Guyana's oil, but it will still capture half the profits. It will also do so tax free, as the contract specifies that Guyana will pay ExxonMobil's taxes.

In Guyana, almost 40 percent of people live in poverty; 19 percent in extreme poverty.[19] The contract with ExxonMobil will bring billions of dollars into the country, and it may be used to help its people. But the company will also make billions of dollars. Accordingly, the discovery of oil in Guyana will contribute to the same two-sided outcome we've seen in the world system more broadly: Guyana's natural resources will enrich it, but they will also enrich ExxonMobil.

Is global capitalism sustainable?

Some predict a global crisis of capitalism.[20] Workers in all parts of the world are protesting. An anti-globalization movement has emerged. We're seeing a rise in nationalist leaders who pit their countries' interests against the world's.[21] The United Kingdom's vote to leave the European Union, known as "Brexit," was this kind of statement. It's possible that a global capitalism, if unregulated and unresponsive to the people, will implode from within, just as Karl Marx predicted.

There is, however, an even more urgent crisis upon us. And Marx foresaw this crisis too.[22]

Recall that Marx argued that proletariat workers under capitalism would experience *alienation*, a feeling of dissatisfaction or disconnection from the fruits of their labor. Marx believed that capitalism also alienated workers from nature. In the industrialized cities of his era, people no longer put their fingers in soil, tended to delicate green sprouts, or put their hands reassuringly on their animals. They now spent their days in mechanized factories and purchased what they'd previously made from the land. Nature seemed remote.

Among the bourgeoisie, Marx observed an even more worrisome form of alienation. Casting themselves as separate from and superior to nature, capitalists seemed to view nature as just another resource to exploit for economic gain. Achieving economic growth, then, took precedence over caring for the earth.

Marx described this alienation from nature as a "rift," an unnatural crack that would open between people and their environment. He also predicted that this rift would lead to ecological catastrophe. And he was right.

THE BIGGEST PROBLEM IN THE WORLD

The planet has entered a new geological epoch called the Anthropocene, a period in which human activities are changing the earth's geology.[23] One of these changes is to the earth's atmosphere. Current agricultural and industrial practices—especially the burning of fossil fuels—are releasing historically unprecedented levels of methane, ozone, nitrous oxide, chlorofluorocarbons, and especially carbon dioxide, or CO_2. These are described as greenhouse gases because they intensify the earth's natural *greenhouse effect*, the process by which the planet traps some of the heat from the sun.

The warming process began with industrialization in the 1700s, but fully half of the excess greenhouse gases have been released in just the last thirty years, after the onset of hyperglobalization.[24] As a result of these activities, the planet is currently 1.8 degrees Fahrenheit hotter than it was prior to industrialization.[25] This global warming is a result of *anthropogenic*, or human-caused, climate change. The earth is now a social fact.

Collectively, core countries have released the majority of greenhouse gases (see Figure 12.1). The forty-two richest countries are responsible for 76 percent of all emissions of CO_2 (the main cause of warming) since 1850.[26] Combined, the United States and the European Union have released nearly half of the total. But the United States is the primary culprit. It's home to only 4 percent of the world's population but has released 25 percent of excess greenhouse gases.

In contrast, peripheral countries have released negligible amounts. Some developing countries, like China, are a significant threat to the climate today but still bear substantially less historical responsibility. Altogether, the 154 least industrialized countries in the world have contributed only 24 percent of all emissions. On average, in other words, each of these countries is responsible for only *one-sixteenth of one percent* of the total.

FIGURE 12.1

Who Has Contributed Most to Global CO_2 Emissions?

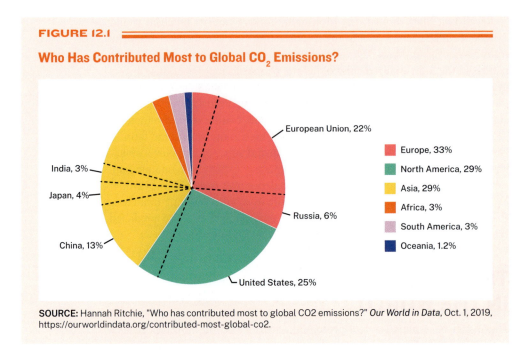

SOURCE: Hannah Ritchie, "Who has contributed most to global CO2 emissions?" *Our World in Data*, Oct. 1, 2019, https://ourworldindata.org/contributed-most-global-co2.

If we shift our lens from countries to corporations, we learn that fully half of all emissions can be traced to just twenty fossil fuel companies.[27] ExxonMobil is the second-largest emitter in the world, outpaced only by Chevron and followed by British Petroleum, ConocoPhillips, and Shell. In a field of 43,000 transnational corporations and millions of small businesses worldwide, these five entities alone are responsible for 12.5 percent of all industrial CO_2 emissions since 1854. Only ninety corporations, all in either fossil fuels or cement manufacturing, are responsible for two-thirds.

The harm of the climate crisis

At current levels, we're on track to reach 2.7 degrees of warming as early as 2030. This is contributing to rising sea levels, acidification of the ocean, desert expansion, extinction of species, and extreme weather. In 2018, the UN Intergovernmental Panel on Climate Change urged us to do everything in our power to limit warming to 2.7 degrees.[28] To achieve this, global emissions need to be substantially reduced starting immediately and reach zero by 2050.

Failure to do this is harming life on earth.[29] Species are disappearing, and ecosystems are becoming unstable, leading to the rise of dangerous disease vectors (like mosquitoes) and the disappearance of insects upon which agriculture depends (like honeybees). A warming planet harbors more pathogens, while forest loss increases the likelihood that humans will encounter them. HIV, Ebola, and Covid-19 were all results of this process. There will be more, and more frequent, epidemics and pandemics.

As countries struggle to adapt to climate change, global economic crises will escalate.[30] Rising seas, creeping deserts, and water and food shortages are forcing human migrations that nation-states are not prepared to absorb.[31] Countries are hardening their borders. Hate groups and authoritarian governments are on the rise. Terrorism is escalating. Peace is increasingly precarious.

Despite bearing almost no responsibility for the current crisis, peripheral and semi-peripheral countries will bear the brunt of these harms.[32] They're island nations, in the arctic or near the equator, or on parts of the planet prone to floods or drought. Already, people in the least industrialized countries are dying from climate disasters at five and a half times the global average.[33]

Thus far, the hardest-hit countries are Honduras in Central America, Myanmar in Southeast Asia, and the Caribbean island of Haiti.[34] Puerto Rico, a U.S. colony, has also suffered terribly. In the long run, the countries that face the starkest risk include Canada, Scandinavia, most of South and Central America, nearly all of Africa, and much of the Middle East.

Because many of these countries are peripheral to the world economy, they can't afford to maintain systems of sea walls, build hurricane-resistant infrastructure, or repair cities buckled by thawing permafrost. Human-caused climate change, then, is *institutionalized global environmental racism*. Those least responsible for the emissions of greenhouse gases—disproportionately poor, previously colonized, non-White, and indigenous—will pay the steepest price.

Women will also be on the front lines.[35] Women in core countries do most of the extra work involved in "greening" households: recycling, designing sustainable diets, choosing local produce, and reducing home energy use. On the periphery and semi-periphery, women are having to walk farther and work

Prolonged drought, exacerbated by the climate crisis, sparked a civil war in Syria that has lasted more than a decade. The result has been a refugee crisis of catastrophic proportions, affecting over 13 million people.

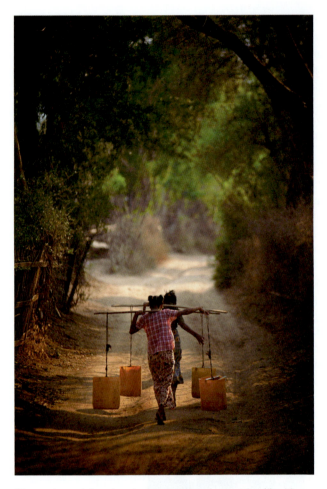

Women in peripheral and semi-peripheral countries like Myanmar often have to walk long distances to collect water for their families. The climate crisis has made it increasingly difficult to find water, adding to the burden placed on women.

harder to do everyday tasks, like collecting water. Women around the world are also more vulnerable than men to the physical risks and interpersonal violence that accompany extreme weather events.[36] As the primary caregivers of children, they're more likely to sacrifice themselves trying to save others. Because of the feminization of poverty, women are more likely than men to be vulnerable based on class as well.

Ironically, the country of Guyana, ExxonMobil's new partner in fossil fuel extraction, is among the countries most vulnerable to rising sea levels. Guyana sits on the Atlantic Ocean along the northern coast of South America. Ninety percent of its residents live in a low-lying strip of land along the ocean, much of which is already a full meter below sea level. This coast is also home to three-quarters of the country's economic activities and almost all its agriculture. The climate crisis is already bringing stronger hurricanes, worse drought, more severe flooding, more infectious disease, and saltwater intrusion into the water used for drinking and farming.[37]

In 2005, the country suffered the worst natural disaster in its history.[38] That January, the skies dumped forty-four inches of rain. Climate change was already raising sea levels, and this extreme weather combined with an extra high tide to flood the homes of more than half the country's people. The water took over six weeks to recede. It flooded people's homes and possessions, polluted their drinking water, killed their animals, destroyed their crops, and poisoned their land with sewage and salt.

Since 2005, the climate crisis has made life in Guyana increasingly perilous, especially for farmers. Rosamund Benn, a thirty-year veteran farmer interviewed about her experiences, reports more flooding, heavier rains, and longer periods of drought. "What we are seeing now is that you can no longer predict the weather," she explained. Unusually heavy rains were now common; it rained both during the rainy season and outside of it; and, between the rain showers, the sun shined hotter than ever.[39]

In response, farming has become both a more difficult and less secure lifestyle. Now Benn digs wells and drainage ditches to control the flow of water, constructs shades to protect plants from the sun, and builds planter boxes to elevate her crops and protect them from floods. Some farmers have simply yielded pastures and farmland to the rising seas. "You have to plant whenever the weather gives you a chance to do so," explained a farmer named Jacinta Gonsalves. "[And] when you lose a crop, your expenses are still there," adds Vilma de Silva. "So whatever is left on the farm [you] have to make do with."[40] Despite working harder, their crops are less productive, and they lose more plants and animals to weather every year.

Guyanese farmers are using their knowledge and skills to innovate in the face of increasingly uncertain natural conditions. But unless we collectively decide to address the climate crisis, the challenges will just become ever more difficult to overcome. So what can we do?

How to stop climate change

The good news is that we know how to protect Guyana, its most vulnerable residents, and the rest of the planet from the severest effects of the climate crisis. To stop and even reverse the runaway greenhouse effect, we need to emit fewer gases and absorb more. We have the knowledge and technology to do this. [41]

We emit less by quickly switching to renewable energies such as solar, wind, and nuclear. These sources of energy are already as cheap or cheaper than fossil fuels. We also need to reduce energy consumption. This will involve choosing lighter cars and smaller homes, buying local produce, and making other modest changes in our lifestyles. According to one estimate, we'd be a full third of the way toward zero net emissions if the richest 10 percent of the world population (which includes most Americans) just "cut their use of energy to the same level as affluent, comfortable Europe."[42]

We absorb more by pulling greenhouse gases out of the atmosphere. One way to do this is with "capture" technologies, artificial means of absorbing harmful gases. These techniques are yet unproven on a large scale. But we can also absorb greenhouse gases by protecting and revitalizing nature. We can preserve and restore forests and wetlands, fill our cities with plants and flowers, and engage in more sustainable farming practices. These are all ways that the earth naturally stores CO_2.

Individuals can make some of these changes on their own, but individuals alone cannot solve the climate crisis. Businesses and governments are of central importance. Companies need to develop sustainable business plans that involve conserving energy and reducing emissions, and they need to sell environmentally friendly products so consumers can buy them. Governments need to establish standards for companies, reward green innovation, and hold themselves accountable for protecting the environment too.

In some ways, it's that simple. We know how to fix the problem, we have the technology, and we have the ability to coordinate a collective response.

We also have the money. A trillion dollars are spent on this planet *every day*. Straightforwardly, most of this is spent by people and entities in the richest countries. Some of that money needs to go to the poorest countries. A worldwide fix, then, will require transnational socialist policies that pull some of the money global capitalism has sent to the top back down to the bottom. In any case, failing to pay for it now will only translate into much greater costs later, when we're spending not only on managing greenhouse gases but responding to ever more extreme climate threats and economic collapses.[43]

The truth is, we're quite capable of fixing this problem. We don't even have to do *everything* in our power to limit warming to 2.7 degrees; we only have to do *enough*. If enough of our powerful nation-states and corporations make real strides in reducing and absorbing at least some kinds of emissions, we will meet our goal.

Why on earth have we not done this already?

THE CAMPAIGN TO DENY CLIMATE CHANGE

The basic principles of the greenhouse effect were established in the mid-1800s.[44] By 1908, the idea had reached a popular audience with *Worlds in the Making*, a book that described a coming atmospheric "hot-house."[45] By the 1930s, scientists had documented warming in the North Atlantic. Over the next several decades, more scientists got involved, the level of funding increased, the tools of research got better, and computer modeling was invented.

By the 1960s, scientists were confident that humans were causing the planet to warm. U.S. President Lyndon Johnson expressed his concern to Congress in 1965.[46] An energized environmental movement emerged alongside these revelations. The first Earth Day was celebrated in 1970, followed by the first international conference focused on the health of the planet two years later. By 1980, Congress had passed fifteen major laws protecting the environment, and the United States had started three new environmental agencies.

Running for U.S. president in 1988, George H. W. Bush promised to use the "White House effect" to battle the "greenhouse effect." He rallied the country to respond to the crisis with these words:

> Some say these problems are too big. That it's impossible for an individual, or even a nation as great as ours, to solve the problem of global warming or the loss of forests or the deterioration of our oceans. My response is simple. It can be done. And we must do it.[47]

By now, the totality of the evidence for human-caused climate change was "one of the most beautiful, sturdy, and complex ever assembled."[48] Arguably, it was nothing short of "the best documented event" in human history. With science, politics, and public opinion all aligned, it was time to start a meaningful response.

The fossil fuel industry recognized this as an existential threat.

On April 20, 1970, New Yorkers came together to celebrate the first Earth Day. They donned face masks not to protect themselves from a contagious virus but to draw attention to air pollution.

The corporate climate countermovement

Scientists working for fossil fuel companies, including ExxonMobil, had confirmed the research on climate change as early as the 1970s. A meaningful response to the climate crisis, however, would require burning less coal, gas, and oil. This the fossil fuel companies were not willing to do. With trillions of dollars in future profits at stake, they formed a countermovement dedicated to sowing misinformation in order to stop, slow, and undo efforts to address the climate crisis. They formed alliances with industries that depended on fossil fuels and members of the global power elite committed to free market capitalism.[49] They had two related goals: to prevent politicians from passing laws regulating the use of fossil fuels and to confuse the public so that they wouldn't demand such laws.

As one of its first moves, the countermovement hired the man at the center of the tobacco industry's campaign to deny that smoking caused cancer. ExxonMobil also hired an advertising team to help them engage in a "concentrated PR effort."[50] The countermovement framed climate change as a disputed scientific theory and efforts to stop or slow it as a threat to economic prosperity.

Just as C. Wright Mills's elite theory of power predicts, the countermovement also exploited their social capital. They met with powerful figures in their networks and sat on corporate boards across industries. They paid a small army to lobby U.S. politicians, donated money to political campaigns, and sabotaged international agreements.[51] They also spun the revolving door between government and industry.[52] Members of the countermovement sat on White House advisory boards, joined presidential cabinets, and were tapped to head environmental agencies. Across administrations, these individuals whispered in the ears of policymakers, edited and deleted scientific papers, and reported back to the fossil fuel industry.

To suppress public outcry, the countermovement made skepticism about climate change culturally hegemonic. They influenced school curricula, ran television ads, bought editorials in leading newspapers, and hired scientists to appear on talk shows.[53] They paid authors to write over 100 books denouncing the science of climate change.[54] The countermovement also got standing in the news media by successfully bullying journalists into covering "both sides" as if the science was truly uncertain. They offered to pay scientists to write misleading or downright deceptive research articles (including at least one sociologist, who refused).[55]

By 1990, the countermovement was described as a "controlling influence in the White House."[56] And just two years after President Bush's inspirational speech, he reversed his position, referring to "scientific uncertainty" and opposing a plan to regulate emissions. He defended his newfound skepticism with a report written by the ex-tobacco man hired by the countermovement.

To put it starkly: Corporations funded a think tank that hired a propagandist to convince the U.S. president to delay a response to the climate crisis.

This is just a slice of a complicated story in which a relatively small group of well-networked members of the global power elite spent tens of billions of dollars to stop a bipartisan effort to address the climate crisis. Suffice to say, the effort was enormously successful. No consequential U.S. policies to address climate change have been passed into law and no binding international agreements have been established. Meanwhile, we've released higher levels of greenhouse gases into the earth's atmosphere almost every consecutive year.

Everyday Americans on the right and the left

The countermovement also succeeded in making what was once a happily bipartisan issue into one of the most politicized in the United States.[57] The countermovement blocked both left- and right-leaning Americans from developing an insurgent consciousness. On the right, Americans largely accepted the countermovement's false claims that the science was uncertain. Even today, only 21 percent of conservative Republicans agree that the climate crisis is human-caused.[58] Disavowal is especially strong among conservative White men, who are four times more likely than the general public to deny climate change.[59] Research suggests that caring for the earth has been cast as feminine, leading people who adopt androcentrism (prejudice against femininity) to stigmatize environmentalism.[60]

In contrast, 86 percent of liberal Democrats believe in human-caused climate change. Women, people with low incomes, and Black and Hispanic Americans are more likely than their counterparts to believe that climate change is caused by humans.[61] Yet, these groups, too, have remained largely quiet on the issue. Interview-based research suggests that this passivity is largely due to feelings of hopelessness.[62] Durkheim might have described it as *anomie*, that deeply uncomfortable sense that what used to matter doesn't matter anymore. For believers, climate change is a slow-motion human-caused disaster of planetary proportions, and the response is a global shrug.

How does a person make sense of that? "It's a little helpless feeling," explained a worried dad living in Washington State, "like what can you possibly do as one person?"[63] A neighbor echoed his sentiment: "The real problem I see is the big corporations. . . . What can I do about that?" When asked to choose one word to describe how they feel about the climate crisis, interviewees in one study used words like *catastrophic* and *apocalyptic*, alongside ones like *impending*, *inevitable*, and *terrified*.[64]

People also recognize that our social institutions, which we can't readily escape, make it nearly impossible to opt out of contributing to the climate crisis.[65] A Coloradan who admitted he didn't do as much as he could to prevent climate change explained:

> This isn't being hypocritical; it's being an American. No, I'm serious. I mean, we live in a society that makes it next to impossible to do the right thing as far as the environment is concerned. We have to drive. We're pinched for time, so we need modern labor-saving conveniences. . . . I have responsibilities to my family that keep me from rejecting the modern lifestyle, even though this lifestyle has considerable ecological implications.[66]

A school counselor expressed a similar feeling of inevitability and sadness: "I'm starting to feel that maybe we're not going to be able to stop what's going on right now. So, I'm scared, and I feel sad because I feel like the earth is hurting."[67] To think too often about the changing climate is to sink into a depression. And if there's nothing to be done, why go there?

The sociologist Kari Marie Norgaard theorizes that these reactions aren't merely psychological but sociological.[68] Drawing on symbolic interactionism, she suggests that the behavior called for by the enormity and immediacy of the crisis doesn't "fit" with our everyday social contexts. We're allowed to yell and scream at a political rally or confess our fears in whispers to our closest friends and lovers, but talking all the time about an impending apocalypse is simply off-script in most circumstances. As one of the interviewees from Washington put it, climate change is "a topic that nobody wants to talk about."[69] "Only in certain settings. Only with certain groups," said another. Moreover, social rules require that we stay positive, control emotional outbursts, and refrain from bullying others into sharing our points of view.

On the political left, then, we see daily inattention. This is demanded by social rules, but it's also part of an effort to avoid full-blown anomie. On the political right, we see outright denial that the climate crisis is real or human-caused. Between these poles, there's been little demand to respond to climate change. So, until recently, no mass protests have emerged to hold politicians' feet to the fire.

But all is not lost. Globalization has something to offer even the little people. It enables new ways of communicating insurgent ideas and new ways of organizing to exert interdependent power. And we should not underestimate this power. After all, there is no reason why social movements can't reach the same scale as the social institutions they seek to change.[70] Globalization can just as well come from the bottom up as it can from the top down. Indeed, while there may be 2,208 billionaires in the world, the rest of us actually number in the billions.

TRANSNATIONAL SOCIAL MOVEMENTS

Our politics, economics, communications, and cultures have all gone global; so, too, has our activism. Globalization allows us to feel connected to the art and entertainment of other places, to foreign cities, and to people who live in faraway places. New translation technologies break down language barriers. Increasing numbers of people are also migrating from one country to another, often creating transnational loyalties.

Such experiences may inspire us to connect to a **global imagined community**, a socially constructed in-group based on a shared planet.[71] This is an understanding that we're first and foremost earthlings; our in-group is the human race. This may be easier for the youngest generations, who, by virtue of being native to globalizing technologies, have had the opportunity to think of themselves in this way from the beginning.

Activists who adopt a global consciousness must frame social problems in ways that resonate with people all over the world. Often this means connecting global concerns with local ones in a phenomenon described as *glocal*, meaning both global and local.[72] Master frames that cast wide symbolic nets are especially useful. Similar but not identical struggles can be understood as a matter of "rights," "choice," or "freedom from violence." This may tie people together for a common cause.

The internet then gives transnational activists the ability to share their frames across borders. Unlike earlier forms of mass media, the internet isn't completely controlled by elites. We don't just consume information, in other words; we also produce it. We can post status updates, join discussion boards, upload videos, and make memes. This means that we have a voice that others might hear, one that can reach thousands or tens of thousands or more. And if social influence can spread through networks, then our new social networks are like a megaphone. A megaphone for each one of us. With hashtags.

We have never been better equipped to wrest the power of cultural hegemony away from the people who use it to maintain the status quo. Our shared voices undercut the ability of elites to manufacture consent: to convince us that the state of affairs most beneficial to them is most beneficial to everyone, even when it's not. When we can talk to one another directly, we can discover our common causes.

This is breathing new life into another kind of transnational organization: the *transnational social movement*, one that coordinates activism across more

global imagined community
a socially constructed in-group based on a shared planet

than one country.[73] Brought together by social media, people across the globe can join coordinated campaigns. And with half a million more people getting internet access every day, participants are increasingly from peripheral and semi-peripheral countries.

Together, these global activists are developing a new transnational *repertoire of contention*, or those shared activities widely recognized as expressions of dissatisfaction with social conditions. Media campaigns that cross borders with viral hashtags and global petition campaigns are in this repertoire. Activists have also learned to hold protests alongside meetings held by transnational governmental organizations to divert international attention. One of the most successful tools is the multi-site protest. This is a coordinated action, perhaps a march or sit-in, held in many countries on the same day and with the same message. Simultaneous protests like these have arguably been the largest collective action events in world history.

Globalization also provides workarounds for restrictive opportunity structures that limit activism in one's own country.[74] Activists can go around the nation-state, for example, by appealing to global cities, transnational organizations, international treaties, and other countries with power. A demand refused outright in one country might find more reception in another, allowing activists to pressure a foreign country to pressure a transnational governmental organization to pressure their own country to make the change they desire. This is a type of "boomerang" politics in which activists strategically throw their goal out to a non-national entity in the hopes it will come back home. A world system multiplies the possible routes to exerting this kind of pressure.

In 2019, feminist activists in Chile wore blindfolds to draw attention to sexual assault as "the violence you don't see." Video of the protest went viral. Here, women in Colombia reenact the spectacle.

It's hard to imagine a task more daunting than changing the world. And yet, it does happen. New norms can emerge on a global scale, reach a tipping point, and cascade across continents. In regard to the climate, some of us are already hard at work to make that happen.

GLOBAL CLIMATE ACTIVISM

As of this writing, none of the twenty highest-emitting countries has a plan to meet the United Nations' directive to limit global warming to no more than 2.7 degrees of warming. India is on track for 3.6. Mexico, Canada, Australia, Brazil, and the European Union are taking us to 5.4 degrees. South Korea, South Africa, Japan, Indonesia, and China are sending us even higher. The United States is in the category of worst offenders. With Russia, Saudi Arabia, and Turkey, it has us on a path to exceed substantially more than 7.2 degrees of warming by 2050.

The world's most polluting corporations aren't responding with urgency either. In 2018, the world's twenty-four largest fossil fuel companies spent 1 percent of their research and development dollars on renewable energy.[75] ExxonMobil devoted approximately one-fifth of 1 percent. Instead, these companies invested more than $50 billion in new oil, gas, and coal projects, like the one in Guyana. These investment patterns aren't compatible with a future in which the earth avoids warming over 2.7 degrees. Meanwhile, nation-states currently give fossil fuel companies an estimated $5.2 trillion in subsidies annually, making fossil fuels more profitable than they would be in a truly free market.[76]

Given these facts, it appears the only solution to the climate crisis is a transnational social movement in which people around the world harness their interdependent power to bend the will of the global power elite.[77] Luckily, in the most powerful nation on earth, concern about climate change is rising. Today, 62 percent of Americans say they believe human-caused change is occurring, up 15 percentage points from five years ago.[78] People are also taking the issue more seriously: 29 percent report being "alarmed" about our warming planet (up 15 percentage points).[79] Even larger percentages now believe that the climate crisis will harm the world's poor, future generations, and other life on earth. Concern is highest among Democrats, but the trend is found even among Republicans.

Among the most activated are young people. American teenagers are 13 percentage points more likely than the average American to believe in human-caused climate change; a full 86 percent say so.[80] More than half also say this makes them angry or afraid. Young people are developing insurgent consciousnesses. Fully 88 percent of teens believe there's "still time" to act to prevent the worst, but many don't trust either Republicans or Democrats to do what's necessary.

So, what are they doing about it? They're engaging in activism. One in four teenagers has walked out of school, attended a rally or protest, or written a politician to express their concern.[81] The young people, especially, are woke.

And so, we are seeing a global insurgency led by a diverse group of young people around the world.

An icon of this movement is the Swedish teenager Greta Thunberg. When she was just fifteen years old, Thunberg was dismayed to learn about the climate crisis. Around the same time, she watched as students in Parkland, Florida, walked out of classes to protest gun violence after the massacre at their high school. Inspired, her first act of protest against inaction on the climate crisis was to refuse to go to school. She sat in front of the Swedish Parliament with a sign that read "School Strike for Climate."

Thunberg has Asperger's Syndrome, which she describes as a "superpower." One of its advantages may be a freedom from the desire to obey social rules that leads many people to censor themselves. Asperger's, in other words, has given Thunberg a useful bluntness. The flier she handed out on the first day of her protest read: "I am doing this because you adults are shitting on my future."[82]

That day, Thunberg used social media to publicize her protest, posting about it on Instagram and Twitter. This attracted the attention of adult climate activists. They shared her protest with sympathetic audiences and, within days, Thunberg had attracted the attention of the mass media. The gatekeepers to this larger audience decided to give her standing. She framed her protest like this:

> Why should I be studying for a future that soon will be no more when no one is doing anything whatsoever to save that future? And what's the point of learning facts in the school system when the most important facts given by the finest science of that same school system clearly means nothing to our politicians and our society?[83]

When she was fifteen years old, Swedish activist Greta Thunberg skipped school to sit in front of the country's parliament with a sign that read "School Strike for Climate."

Framed in such stark terms, Thunberg's protest went viral. Other students joined her on the street. Then, students started protesting elsewhere in Sweden; then, in other countries and soon around the world. Today, Thunberg leads a social movement organization that encourages students to skip school every Friday in response to failure to meaningfully address the climate crisis.

Thunberg was not the first young person to demand to be heard. By the time she joined the fight, many young activists were already building organizational strength.[84] Her action, then, connected her to already-existing youth-led climate activist organizations, including Extinction Rebellion, Sunrise, Zero Hour, Uplift, SustainUS, and U.S. Youth Climate Strike. Their global political network allowed them to take advantage of the public's reaction to Thunberg's brutal honesty.

Some of these activists frame the crisis as an "economic opportunity" and advocate for capitalism-friendly reforms, like more investment in renewable energy.[85] Others are demanding more radical changes. Some argue that global capitalism is incompatible with a just and sustainable earth. These activists describe climate change as "climate injustice" and call for a redistribution of global wealth. Young activists are also framing inaction in moral terms. As a spokesperson for the more radical wing, Thunberg describes inaction as "evil" and a "betrayal" of future generations.[86] She describes adults as "thieves" who've stolen young people's futures. Activists like her suggest that, in failing to act, the power elite are deviants.

In fact, most of the truly global changes in history have been driven not by geopolitical or economic interests but emotions.[87] In this way, powerful social movements are often led by people calling on others to do the *right* thing. Sociologists call these *moral entrepreneurs*, activists who attempt to reshape our understanding of right and wrong. In pointing not just to the social problem of climate change, but deception and negligence on the part of global elites, these young activists are reframing "business as usual" as immoral.

The global climate strike of 2019

The climate activists' biggest action yet occurred on September 20, 2019. They organized a protest at the same time as an international event they knew would attract global attention: the UN Climate Action Summit in New York. Using websites and social media indifferent to international borders, they publicized their action and asked people around the world to join them in a school walkout. What happened next was extraordinary.

The day of the protest, the sun first rose in the Pacific Islands, where students in almost all the island nations participated: Fiji, Samoa, Vanuatu, Tuvalu, Tonga, and more. In the Solomon Islands, students wore traditional grass skirts and gathered at the ocean's edge. Students in the Republic of Kiribati chanted: "We are not sinking, we are fighting."[88]

The protest spread east to Bangladesh, Japan, South Korea, Hong Kong, Indonesia, the Philippines, Taiwan, and Thailand, where students staged a die-in at the nation's environment ministry. A teenager's sign read: "The planet is getting hotter than my imaginary boyfriend."[89]

Moving west, protesters came out in Turkey, Lebanon, and Israel. In India, a girl in a school uniform held a sign: "Be a part of the solution, not part of the pollution."[90] In Afghanistan, a group of young women led a march in Kabul carrying a banner reading "Fridays for Future," a slogan that had originated 2,830 miles away. In Pakistan, protesters marched through a heat wave.

Protests occurred across Africa in Ghana, Burundi, Uganda, Tanzania, Senegal, and South Africa. In Kenya, students covered themselves in single-use plastic bottles. "No leader should forfeit the future of younger generations," insisted a youth activist in Nigeria.[91] "There is no Planet B," proclaimed one in Uganda, echoing what has become a global rallying cry.

Most European countries were represented. "Make love, not CO_2," read a sign held by a protester in Austria.[92] In Finland, a man dressed as Santa Claus held a sign saying "My house is on fire."[93] Germany may have had the biggest march, with more than 1.4 million people participating.

Across the Atlantic, a young Guyanese woman named Suphane Dash-Alleyne was in New York as a delegate to the UN Youth Climate Summit. She protested there with 250,000 other young people. "We as Guyanese youths have the responsibility to ensure our voices are heard," she said, "as climate change will drastically affect our future in this beautiful land we call our home."[94] Elsewhere in the United States, another 800 separate protests were held. In Washington, DC, the median age was just twenty-two years old.[95] In Canada, students followed Thailand with their own die-in.[96] Students also protested in Central and South America: Brazil, Paraguay, Chile, Colombia, El Salvador, Peru, and Grenada. In Mexico, they chanted "Se ve, se siente, la tierra está caliente."[97] *You see it, you feel it. The earth is getting hotter.*

According to conservative estimates, more than 4 million people in over 150 countries took to the streets.[98] If that's true, more than three-quarters of the world's countries were represented. Consistent with the idea that global social movements must also be "glocal," the focus of the protests varied by country. In the Solomon Islands, they called attention to rising sea levels; in South Africa, toxic waste; in India, air pollution; and in Australia, the death of the Great Barrier Reef. The young activists had found a message that resonated with people across cultures, borders, and economic conditions. Everyone needs to protect the land they live on.

The work of these activists might be turning the tide. Several notable things occurred in the days surrounding the protest. Media coverage of the climate crisis surged, reaching an audience of over 1 billion.[99] More people searched the internet for "climate change" that day than any other day in history. Jeff Bezos, the founder of Amazon and one of the richest men in the world, committed his company to net zero emissions by 2040, ahead of the 2050 deadline set by the UN. On the day of the protest, Germany's chancellor announced that the country would earmark another 50 billion euros for curbing their own contributions to the crisis. And the day after the protest, sixteen children

On September 20, 2019, over 4 million young people in more than 150 countries joined together to protest global inaction in the face of the climate crisis.

and teenagers from twelve countries filed a landmark complaint to the United Nations, arguing that inaction on climate is in violation of its Convention on the Rights of the Child. This is a treaty, ratified by 140 countries, binding each by law to act with the well-being of children in mind.

These successes are proof of some of the new opportunities globalization presents to activists. Germany is a country. The United Nations is a transnational governmental organization. The media is a global social institution. And Amazon is the world's ninth-largest transnational corporation. Only one of these victories involved a nation-state. The rest were global actors.

These successes reveal something else too: The power elite is divided.[100] An elite coalition has risen up in the United States in response to the one formed by fossil fuel–related industries and free market capitalists.[101] This coalition includes elites in the media, higher education, left-leaning charitable foundations, and top corporate law firms. Social network research reveals that the conservative countermovement still has a strong hold on the revolving door between business and politics.[102] But this new coalition of elites potentially has greater influence with the mass media, contacts with celebrities, and connections to higher education.

There are signs that some elites are starting to respond to activists. The Rockefeller family, for example, the descendants of the man who started what is now ExxonMobil, recently described the company's behavior as "morally reprehensible." They've announced that they'll no longer invest their $4.2 billion charitable fund in fossil fuel companies. The British Royal Family, the pension manager of Japan, and the World Council of Churches have made similar decisions. This is called *disinvestment*, and college students were the first to launch such campaigns, leading nearly 150 colleges and universities to divest from fossil fuel companies. Today, a combined 1,000 institutions of all kinds have committed to divesting $6.25 trillion.[103]

These examples—and there are more—make clear that the groundswell of activism from below is finding common cause with sympathetic actors at the top. Levers are being pulled, pressure is being applied, and some people who have the power to stop climate change are actually doing something about it. That is real cause for optimism.

THE END?

As far as we know, humans have always understood danger. Tigers, lightning storms, and angry enemies are dangerous and best avoided. But the idea of *risk* is relatively new in the history of human cultural evolution.[104] To wrap one's head around risk requires that we be able to think about probability. Not just *Is that dangerous or not?* But *How dangerous is it? What's the chance that I'll be harmed? And am I willing to take that chance?*

Words referring to the concept of risk first appeared in reference to colonial exploration. They originated in Spanish or Portuguese with the idea of "daring" and were used to describe the possibility of death when sailing into uncharted waters.[105] Was the prospect of discovery worth it? These calculations required people to consider the likelihood that a decision made now might bring them harm later.

Notably, for these explorers, sailing into uncharted waters was optional. It was a choice they made or was made for them. The risk, in other words, was introduced by them or their fellow humans and not an intrinsic part of life on earth, like tigers. Since then, we've introduced more and more unnatural risks into our daily lives: fast cars, synthetic drugs, extreme sports, and such. And thinking about risk has become second nature. We now calculate it as a matter of course. We decide whether to skip this year's flu shot, whether to Lyft or walk home after dark, whether to eat the expired cottage cheese.

To describe this change, a German sociologist named Ulrich Beck introduced the idea of a **risk society**, one organized around the self-conscious production, distribution, and management of risk.[106] This makes for a new kind of social organization, one that creates not only social "goods" but also social "bads." Risk societies, then, involve a new form of advantage and

risk society
a society organized around the self-conscious production, distribution, and management of risk

disadvantage. Who gets to enjoy the goods? And who is forced to dodge the bads? Middle-class families enjoy pristine fruits and vegetables, for example, while migrant farmworkers risk absorbing pesticides through their skin and lungs. Residents enjoy the lights of downtown Charleston, West Virginia, while coal miners risk contracting the disease known as "black lung." White families settle in safe neighborhoods, while people of color face over-policing in neighborhoods with concentrated poverty. Today, the most valuable luxury of all is knowing that you're relatively safe from the very real dangers that abound.

Now, Beck says, we live in a *world risk society*, one in which some nation-states export risks and others absorb them.[107] Core countries now pay those in the periphery and semi-periphery to store their contaminated waste. Core countries' corporations hire low-wage workers in peripheral countries to dig precious metals out of their lands for jewelry and cell phones. Core countries' militaries stock weapons of mass destruction in the name of deterrence but strong-arm other countries into remaining defenseless.

What's different now is that human-made risks are threatening us all. The bads can no longer be doled out only to the people with the least power to resist. So much harm has been done that there may be no safe neighborhood, no safe nation, nowhere safe at all anymore. This is the essence of the climate crisis. We will either transform the systems that are causing the crisis, or they will die with us.

Indeed, a crisis as vast and threatening as climate change may be the only thing big enough to dislodge the hegemonic ideologies that have brought us here. In this way, this dark moment in world history may have a silver lining. Faced with an all-encompassing disaster, we'll need to think more imaginatively than we thought possible. And we'll have to find within us a power we

By suggesting that despair can trigger action, this mural evokes emancipatory capitalism. Credited to Banksy, the street art popped up overnight at the end of two weeks of protests by the global environmental movement known as Extinction Rebellion.

didn't think we had. To capture this perilous moment, Beck offered the idea of *emancipatory catastrophism*.[108] This is a phenomenon in which the likely impact of a looming disaster is so unfathomably awful that it dislodges previously intractable identities, beliefs, and practices.

We got a taste of this in 2020 when a novel coronavirus did something few people thought possible: It forced the world's richest nation-states to put their economies on hold. Life changed, and in ways that were previously inconceivable. The potential catastrophic loss of life forced us to rapidly adapt to radically new norms, while the resulting economic crisis revealed the financial precarity suffered by so many. It'll take a decade to know whether this has sufficiently unsettled elites and invigorated activists, and whether this will finally lead us to change our social institutions.

If we find emancipation in this climate catastrophe, it will be because of collective action. Both the pandemic and the climate crisis are critical events, but such moments do not, in themselves, change the world for the better. People do. People must come to a shared understanding of what the threat means and how to address it. Old norms, values, and ideologies will need to be replaced by new ones. Our institutions will need to be destroyed and rebuilt. And new ideas about justice will need to be developed and shared.

In short, to save the planet, new worlds will need to be imagined and a world's worth of people will need to be inspired. ∎

COMING UP...

TODAY'S GLOBAL power elite control a world system that is facing a planetary climate crisis. Both the origins of and solutions to this crisis are social. Industrialization sparked it. Globalization escalated it. And hyperglobalization put it into overdrive. The crisis is not natural but human-made. Like other social "bads," climate change is hurting the least privileged among us the most, especially those living in the periphery of the global economy.

Encouragingly, young climate activists have built a transnational social movement. A new global repertoire of contention has emerged. These activists are targeting not only nation-states but also transnational corporations, transnational organizations, and global cities. They demand that we see ourselves as a *global imagined community*, members of an in-group that cares not only for our friends and neighbors but all humans. Public opinion polls are shifting; we may save the planet after all.

What's next? With a few concluding thoughts, I ask you to contemplate all you've learned during this introduction to sociology. Not just facts and figures or phrases and terms. No, you've learned something much more valuable. A new way to think. A new window on the world. A sociological superpower, no less. You've come this far; come on one last journey.

THE SOCIOLOGICAL IMAGINATION

You might chuckle to learn that the worst grade on my college transcript is the one I received in Introduction to Sociology. I took the class in my first year. At the time, I didn't know what to expect. But as the course proceeded, I grew resentful and frustrated. I resisted learning the material. The bad grade was fair.

As a child, I'd been taught to be independent and self-reliant. I was offended by the sociological idea that my thoughts were strongly influenced by the people around me, instead of mine and mine alone. I was alarmed by the possibility that my values weren't carefully reasoned and right but largely reflective of my cultural experiences. I was intimidated by the notion that a massive global social structure shaped my life chances—had, in fact, *already* shaped them. My emotions got the best of me, and I argued with the professor on the essay exams. I didn't want to give her the answers I knew she was asking for.

I suppose that, at the time, what I wanted and needed most was control over my life. I was the first person in my family to go to college, and I wasn't confident I would make it to graduation. I feared failure. And there was a pandemic then too. Today, HIV is a chronic but treatable illness. When I started college, it was a death sentence. It appeared to have a fatality rate of 100 percent. Everyone who was infected died. By my sophomore year, AIDS was the leading cause of death in America. There is still no vaccine.

I wanted a guarantee that if I studied hard enough, I wouldn't fail. And if I followed the rules for "safe sex," I wouldn't die.

Sociology said: *Well . . . maybe.*

Sociology doesn't grant us control over our lives. It acknowledges that we're individuals with free will, but it never lets us forget that we're part of something bigger than ourselves. Instead of being independent of social forces, as I wanted to be, we're buffeted by them. We're socialized into cultures we don't choose, interact according to a culture's social rules, and live in a social structure that presses us onto its preferred paths. Sociology tells us that we can try to change our societies but makes no guarantees that we'll succeed. We can do everything right and still get a bad grade. Sex can only be "safer." Danger lurks, and sometimes it sneaks up on us.

This is not *good* news. And when I was in Introduction to Sociology, I didn't want to hear it. I majored in philosophy. Philosophy promised me that an independent thinker with a strong work ethic could discover truth with a capital *T*. I was reassured by its overconfidence.

In my senior year of college, though, I set aside my first impression and took an upper-division course called the Sociology of AIDS. That changed my life. The instructor—his name is Matthew Mutchler—taught us about the social factors that contributed to HIV infection; the uneven toll it took on gay men, people of color, and the poor; the unprecedented effort to normalize condom use; and the activism that led an unresponsive U.S. government to step up and save lives.

What I learned in that class, in other words, was that sociology's lessons can be unsettling, but they're also vital. There was no way to understand the AIDS pandemic without sociology. And there was no way to protect the vulnerable, change social practices, or force government accountability without sociological thinking. I was converted. I later pursued a PhD in sociology and became a scholar who primarily studies sexuality.

The promise of sociological thinking, combined with the sometimes dreadful things we learn, inspired the sociologist C. Wright Mills to write: "In many ways, it is a terrible lesson; in many ways a magnificent one."[1] Sociology lays bare the injustices in our society. It shatters the illusion that we, as individuals, have control. And it reveals a brutal truth: There's little one person can do about any of this. These are deeply uncomfortable realities.

But sociology also gives us the intellectual tools to imagine something better. By revealing that our societies are socially constructed, sociology frees our minds. In parsing the dynamics of social interaction, it gives us clues as to how to change social norms. And in mapping our social institutions, it offers us guidance for how to remake them. Perhaps most importantly, sociology shows us that we have great power when we cooperate. When we build social movements, we succeed in pressing the elites to respond to demands from below. Not always, but sometimes.

You are now in possession of these intellectual tools. It was Mills who called it the *sociological imagination*. This is the capacity to consider how people's lives—including our own—are shaped by the social facts that surround us. To use a sociological imagination is to acknowledge the things beyond our control: where we're born on the globe, when we're born in the span of time, where in the social structure we land, what identities we carry, and more. It also encompasses the ability to see that our "private troubles," as Mills called them, are often linked to "public issues." To think sociologically is to comprehend the abstract stuff of society and link it to the concrete stuff of everyday life. To see how social constructs, norms, networks, organizations, and institutions translate into laughter, tears, transcendence, pain, hate, and love. And vice versa.

When I was growing up, I experienced the HIV pandemic as a private trouble. Sex was death. Condoms were weird. The virus couldn't be passed through routine contact with others and safer sex offered good protection, thank goodness. But broken condoms, unfaithful partners, or unwise decisions could be fatal. Sex was an option rife with risk. As of today, over 32 million people have died from AIDS-related illnesses.

A public health campaign of unprecedented proportions, led by gay men, made wearing condoms the norm.[2] Meanwhile, the same men organized a social movement to demand that governments respond meaningfully to the pandemic.[3] Activists fought to reduce the stigma of a diagnosis and reduce fear of people who tested positive for the virus. That younger U.S. generations can grow up without the same fear of AIDS is due in large part to these efforts. Meanwhile, transnational social movements to advocate for people with HIV and protect others from infection are ongoing.[4] Rates of HIV remain at epidemic levels in countries peripheral to the world economy, especially in parts of Africa.

We've each experienced the Covid-19 pandemic as a private trouble too. We've worried for ourselves and our friends and family. We've grieved for victims. We've suffered stay-at-home orders. We've lost or fretted about losing income. And weighed whether to go to school.

But, like AIDS, Covid-19 is also a social issue. Our level of risk has been influenced by all manner of social factors, from the seriousness with which the people around us practice physical distancing, to the environmental quality of our neighborhoods, to the decisions made by powerful political elites. Our suffering is shaped by the actions of others, sometimes for better and sometimes for worse. This is true not only because we're all vulnerable physically, but because the environment through which the virus spreads is a social as well as natural one.

If that sounds right to you, it's because you've developed a sociological imagination. And that is awesome. Truly, it is. To be able to think sociologically is a fantastic power. Without it, we can only view our private troubles as personal failures. We're unable to link the individual experience with the social one. We can't be thoughtful about our societies or imagine ways of designing them differently. We can't see interdependent power and the promise of collective action.

You can do all these things now.

It's ironic, really. When I first took Introduction to Sociology and resisted learning how to think sociologically, I wasn't maintaining control over my life. I was ceding it. Acknowledging social facts makes us more free, not less, because it gives us a truer picture of the context in which we make decisions and some ability to wrest control over that context. "Freedom is not merely the opportunity to do as one pleases," wrote Mills. In fact, there's no environment—social or otherwise—in which we face no constraints. "Neither," he said, "is it merely the opportunity to choose between set alternatives." Others, after all, have decided what those alternatives will be. "Freedom is . . . the chance to formulate the available choices, to argue over them," Mills concluded, "and *then*, the opportunity to choose."[5]

Freedom is the right to be part of the conversation, to have some say in the design of the societies we live in. That requires a sociological imagination. Thank you for taking the time to develop one. I hope you cherish it. It *is* magnificent. I hope you use it to inspire others; please, share it widely. I hope you find a way to work together to mend this imperfect world. Because goodness knows we need your help. Your future is a social fact. Go get it.

APPENDIX A

A SHORT HISTORY OF SOCIOLOGY

"To understand a science, it is necessary to know its history."

—AUGUSTE COMTE

A French intellectual by the name of Auguste Comte is often given credit for being the first sociologist. He was born in the aftermath of the Enlightenment, a time in which the rise of scientific thinking undermined the dominance of religious authority (see Chapter 6). Embracing this profound ideological shift, Comte argued that science could replace religion as the arbiter of good public policy. Reason, he argued, would allow political leaders to throw off tradition and think critically about which policies worked and which did not. He advocated, that is, for a science of society based on **positivism**, a philosophical theory stating that scientific tools give us the capacity to accurately measure a true, objective reality. In 1838, he named the new field "sociology."[1]

Not coincidentally, Comte also coined the word *altruism*, the term we now use to refer to selfless kindness. And the scholars who pursued and developed Comte's new science largely agreed that their goal was to use sociology to make societies better.[2] The early European sociologists with the most lasting effects on sociology certainly worked in this tradition. Harriett Martineau, Karl Marx, Émile Durkheim, and Marianne and Max Weber were among them.

positivism
a philosophical theory stating that scientific tools give us the capacity to accurately measure a true, objective reality

SOCIOLOGY'S EUROPEAN FOUNDATIONS

Harriett Martineau (1802–1876) was born into a financially comfortable family in England. She was educated in the domestic arts and raised to be a properly feminine Victorian lady.[3] When her father's textile business failed, however, the family allowed her to begin earning an income by writing. This, she said, was a blessing for her life. She would become a prolific, profitable, and celebrated writer.

Martineau would use her skills and renown to advocate for democracy. She wrote in favor of economic justice, the abolition of slavery, and equality for women. Enamored with Auguste Comte's ideas regarding a science of society, she would be the first to translate his works from French to English. As discussed in the introduction, she also wrote the first book on sociological research methods (*How to Observe Morals and Manners*, 1838) and a three-volume analysis of the United States (*Society in America*, 1837). Altogether, Martineau would write thousands of articles and over twenty books, many of which were incisive works of sociology.

Émile (pronounced *eh-meel*) Durkheim (1858–1917) was born in France at a time of political and economic instability. The country had undergone five regime changes in as many decades, oscillating between republican and monarchical rule. Meanwhile, industrialization was uprooting traditional ways of life. The France in which Durkheim grew up, then, was defined by a period of momentous political changes and was actively struggling with large-scale economic ones.

In this context, Durkheim made many foundational contributions to sociological thinking. He developed a theory of social stability called *structural functionalism* (see the discussion on pages 131–137). This is the idea that society is a system of necessary, synchronized parts that work together to create social stability.[4] Social stability in modern societies, he argued, was founded on *organic solidarity,* a kind of stability rooted in the interdependence created by a division of labor in which people take on complementary social roles. This was in contrast with the social solidarity produced in foraging societies: *mechanical solidarity,* or the kind based on people living parallel and thus very similar daily lives (see pages 280–281 for more). Durkheim also introduced the idea of a *collective conscience*, or the "beliefs and sentiments common to the average citizens of the same society."[5] When the collective conscience broke down, he observed, citizens would experience *anomie*, or a collective confusion caused by the weakening of shared social rules.

In a life that overlapped with Durkheim's, the German intellectual Karl Marx (1818–1883) would make history as a tireless advocate for the working class. With Friedrich Engels, his close collaborator, Marx delivered a scathing critique of capitalism (discussed on pages 178–179).[6] They described a capitalist class (the *bourgeoisie*, or owners and employers) that was pitted against a working class (the *proletariat*, or wage workers). Inevitably, they argued, this irresolvable clash of interests would lead to a *crisis of capitalism*, a coming catastrophic implosion from which capitalism would never recover. These arguments are why Marx is often described as one of the founders of *conflict theory*, an alternative to structural functionalism that posits that societies are characterized by competing interests instead of shared ones (see pages 137–142).

Another German sociologist, Max Weber (pronounced *vay-bur* instead of *web-bur*; 1864–1920), appreciated Marx's insights but also challenged his overriding concern with class conflict.[7] Weber found inspiration in the study of religion. He was descended from a persecuted religious minority, the Huguenots. His ancestors had suffered at the hands of French Lutherans and Catholics during the second most lethal religious war in the history of Europe. In the late 1500s, 3 million people died as the Roman Catholics and Huguenots faced off in thirty-six years of warfare.

Weber's mother kept this memory alive in his household. Perhaps not surprisingly, then, Weber would become the first sociologist of religion, writing books in the early 1900s on Protestantism, Judaism, Hinduism, and Confucianism. Based on his comparative research on world religions, he developed the concept of the *Protestant work ethic*, the idea that one's character can and should be measured by one's dedication to paid work (described on page 191). If Marx is now famous for arguing that material concerns (that is, money and things) drove societies, Weber added that cultural ideas, like those associated with religion, could have powerful effects too. This claim—that social identities like religious faith could be the basis for prestige or stigma—paved the way for later theory about status beliefs and inequalities related to things like race, disability, immigration status, and sexual identity (as discussed throughout but especially in Chapter 3 and Chapters 7 through 9).

Weber is also famous for being one of the first theorists of *modernity*, an era—starting just over 500 years ago—characterized by a belief in science as the sole source of truth, alongside the idea that humans can rationally organize societies and improve human life. In describing this era, he introduced the idea of *rationalization*, the process of embracing reason and using it to increase the efficiency and effectiveness of human activities. This, he argued, led to the emergence of *bureaucracies*, organizations with formal policies, strict hierarchies, and impersonal relations.

Max Weber was married to the sociologist Marianne Weber (1870–1954), who studied the family. She saw marriage as a source of gendered oppression, arguing that the domestic work women were required to perform was unfairly undervalued and that requiring women to do it reflected an undervaluing of women (see pages 230–233).[8] This made marriage not only constraining for women (in that they were expected to perform specific tasks) but also disempowering (in that the tasks themselves were seen as unproductive). Radical for her time, she advocated for clear recognition and reward for women's work in the form of a wage. A wage, she wrote, would ensure that a woman would no longer be forced to beg her husband for spending money, giving her "some free scope for structuring her personal life."[9]

This brief discussion of these important early sociologists shows that, from the beginning, the field was exploring questions related to human welfare. Social stability, fair politics, economic justice, physical and mental health, and race and gender equality were all topics that inspired the founders of the discipline. This would be true, too, as sociology hopped the pond and established itself in the United States.

SOCIOLOGY ARRIVES IN AMERICA

The first American sociologists were children during the Reconstruction Era. This was the immediate aftermath of the Civil War (1861–1865), during which time Americans continued to fight over whether Black Americans would be truly and equally incorporated into the Union.[10] These early American sociologists would live through the first Gilded Age and make their most lasting marks on American society as it transitioned into the Progressive Era of the early 1900s. This was a period of widespread social activism and political reform driven by concern for the well-being of everyday people.

One of these sociologists was Jane Addams (1860–1935), a woman born into a wealthy family in Illinois who devoted her life to helping the disadvantaged and promoting world peace.[11] She taught classes at the University of Chicago, influenced its male faculty, and published in the first volume of its flagship journal, the *American Journal of Sociology*. Addams is perhaps most famous, however, for cofounding Hull House in Chicago in 1889, one of the most prominent anti-poverty organizations in American history. At its height, the "house" included twelve buildings, covered half a city block, and supported a neighborhood playground and a camp in Wisconsin. The organization ran a kindergarten and nursery, provided adult education classes, and helped immigrants and the poor understand their civil rights and responsibilities. It also included a gymnasium and free spaces for community activism to thrive. Hull House associates successfully campaigned to remove juveniles from the adult court system, improved sanitation for the poor, passed legislation on behalf of workers, advocated for women's suffrage, and built playgrounds for children.

In addition to cofounding Hull House, Addams cofounded the American Civil Liberties Union (ACLU), the Women's International League for Peace and Freedom, and the National Child Labor Committee. She was also an early member of the National Association for the Advancement of Colored People (NAACP). In 1931, she became the first American woman to win a Nobel Peace Prize. Today she is recognized as the founder of **social work**, a skilled profession aimed at helping people in need.

The sociologists Charlotte Perkins Gilman (1860–1935), Anna Julia Cooper (1858–1964), and Ida B. Wells-Barnett (1862–1931) were also powerful public figures during this time, all publishing their most striking and influential works in 1892. Gilman is most famous for her fictional short story "The Yellow Wallpaper," and her criticism of patriarchal marriage. Cooper wrote *A Voice from the South: By a Black Woman of the South*, the first book about intersectionality. And Ida B. Wells-Barnett wrote the first evidence-based account of the terrorism known as lynching in *Southern Horrors*, a book for which she won a posthumous Pulitzer Prize in 2020. Each of these women was articulating conflict

social work
a skilled profession aimed at helping people in need

theories of American society long before conflict theory became a mainstream approach to sociology.

The sociologist W. E. B. Du Bois (pronounced *du boyz*; 1868–1963) was a contemporary of these women, writing his first influential work in 1899. This book, *The Philadelphia Negro*, was an exhaustive analysis of Black American life in the city. His approach was unusual for the time, involving the use of many different research methodologies to capture as accurate an understanding of their lives as possible. He performed in-depth interviews with 2,500 households, examined archival documents, and conducted surveys (having brought the science of statistics home to the United States after studying abroad in Europe, as discussed on pages 7–8).

Du Bois argued that the primary causes of Black Philadelphians' struggles were interpersonal and institutional racism (discussed in Chapters 4 and 8, respectively). To prove it, he compared his Black subjects with Philadelphia's European immigrants. He found that when both groups had similar access to good jobs and affordable rents, their outcomes were similar, and when they did not have similar opportunities, their outcomes were not similar. That is, Black Americans performed just as well as Europeans when the conditions were conducive to success. Du Bois was motivated to develop sociology's research methodologies in part because he believed that only irrefutable scientific analysis would convince a racist public that Black Americans' struggles were rooted in discrimination rather than inferiority.[12]

Du Bois would live an extraordinary life in the service of Black Americans. He would cofound the NAACP and write over thirty books, including the now-iconic *The Souls of Black Folk* (1903), a personal and intimate portrayal of the Black experience. As a tribute to his tremendous accomplishment and as an acknowledgement of his important contributions to sociology, the American Sociological Association Career of Distinguished Scholarship Award—the most prestigious prize given to professional sociologists today—is named after him.

From Addams to Du Bois, these early sociologists practice what is now called **public sociology**, the work of using sociological theory to make societies better. As sociology evolved alongside higher education, tension arose between sociologists with an outward orientation—ones we now call *public sociologists*—and those with an inward one. That is, many sociologists continued to see everyday people as an important audience for their work, while others primarily spoke to and wrote for other sociologists. These debates are ongoing.

public sociology
the work of using sociological theory to make societies better

A BIGGER AND BROADER SOCIOLOGY

Beginning in the 1870s, American universities expanded their mandate. Previously designed to communicate *existing* knowledge, they increasingly aimed to develop *new* knowledge.[13] This led to the growth of PhD programs, which teach new scientists how to make original scientific contributions to their fields. As sociology began to get a foothold in the new universities, the world's first sociology textbook was published. *Introduction to a Science of Society* was written in 1890 by a sociologist named Albion Small (1854–1926).[14] He was an impassioned advocate for sociology, and his enthusiasm inspired the president of the (freshly founded) University of Chicago to hire Small in 1892 as the first U.S. sociology professor. That same year, he started the first department of sociology (three years before Durkheim would establish the first European department). Shortly after, Small would launch the *American Journal of Sociology*, a place for sociologists to publish their original research— another historical first. By 1905, there was also a professional society, known today as the American Sociological Association (ASA).

As the discipline grew in scope and influence, it diversified. Sociologists began developing a wide range of both qualitative and quantitative research methods to study the social world (see Appendix B for an overview). Building on the foundational work of W. E. B. Du Bois, sociologists developed increasingly sophisticated techniques for collecting and analyzing quantitative data. They began using statistics to accurately describe large-scale phenomena, like the prevalence of poverty, the frequency of divorce, and correlations between the two. Sociologists at Columbia University, where the second department of sociology was formed, were especially committed to building a social science that mirrored the natural sciences. Echoing Comte, the department's founder encouraged his students to make sociology "an exact, quantitative science."[15]

Qualitative methods evolved similarly. University of Chicago sociologists, for example, adapted what is today called *ethnography*, a research method that involves careful observation of naturally occurring social interaction, often as a participant (as introduced on pages 271–272). Originally designed to allow anthropologists to immerse themselves in indigenous cultures, sociologists began using similar methods to study the many subcultures of the city of Chicago. This was the origin of an emerging "urban sociology" at a time when the city as we know it today was still quite new.

The sociologist Robert Park (1864–1944) was a central pioneer in developing this approach to sociological research. "You have been told to go grubbing in the library," he once suggested to a group of sociology students, somewhat disparagingly.[16] That was fine, he admitted, but he also encouraged his students to "go get the seat of your pants dirty":

> Go and sit in the lounges of luxury hotels and on the doorsteps of the flophouses; sit on the Gold Coast settees and on the slum shakedowns; sit in the orchestra hall and in the Star and Garter burlesque.[17]

microsociology
intricate studies of everyday interaction

macrosociology
elaborate studies of large-scale social trends

Along with other qualitative methods like in-depth interviews and content analysis (see discussions on pages 20–21 and 73, respectively), getting one's "pants dirty" remains an important way in which sociologists learn about the world.

Sociology would also expand to include intricate studies of everyday interaction, called **microsociology**; elaborate studies of large-scale social trends, called **macrosociology**; and everything in between. Many of the early sociologists studied society-wide phenomenon (like Marx's analysis of the economy, Durkheim's concern with political stability, and Marianne Weber's criticism of the systematic oppression of women). Sociologists of the mid-1900s began to study the small scale too: the stuff of everyday interaction (Chapter 4 is an overview). Reflecting Harriett Martineau's idea of sociological sympathy, these sociologists studied people's shared understanding of their social worlds. This is a distinctly anti-positivist approach because it assumes that the meaning of things is not "out there" but rather is dependent on the people involved. We talk about this today when we refer to *social constructs*, or influential and shared interpretations of reality that vary across cultures (see pages 37–40).

Microsociologists like George Herbert Mead (1863–1931) and Charles Horton Cooley (1864–1929) concerned themselves with a sociology of the self (introduced on pages 15–26). Mead introduced the idea that humans have the capacity to be both the subject and object of thinking, or to be an "I" that contemplates a "me." And Cooley is the source of the concept of the *looking glass self*, or the self that emerges as a consequence of seeing ourselves as we think other people see us.

Turning to the study of small group interaction, Herbert Blumer (1900–1987) developed *symbolic interactionism*, a theory that social interaction depends on the social construction of reality. Symbolic interactionists argue that we don't generally respond to reality itself but to the meanings that emerge out of interaction. Also working in this tradition was Erving Goffman (1922–1982), who developed *dramaturgy*, the practice of looking at social life as a series of performances in which we're actors on metaphorical stages. There was also Harold Garfinkel (1917–2011), who did a deep dive into the underlying shared logic that is the foundation of social interaction, known as *ethnomethodology*. Symbolic interactionist approaches joined other major paradigms in sociology—notably structural functionalism and conflict theory (see Table 1)—and they remain a central theme of sociological inquiry to this day.

TABLE 1

Three Influential Paradigms in Sociology

Paradigm	Summary
Structural functionalism	Societies are systems of necessary, synchronized parts that work together to create social stability.
Conflict theory	Societies are characterized by competing interests and defined by fights over control of valuable resources like wealth, power, and prestige.
Symbolic interactionism	Social interaction depends on the social construction of reality. We respond to symbolic meanings produced in the process of human interaction.

By the 1930s, sociology was so diverse as to be difficult to describe.[18] It was large- and small-scale, qualitative and quantitative, positivist and non-positivist. And sociologists were still debating whether their research should be "pure" or "practical." That is, primarily focused on developing a science of society or primarily aimed at solving social problems.

In the 1950s, sociology underwent a notable shift in orientation. World War II had pressed American scientists, policy makers, and funders to focus on efficiency, and both the tools and orientations developed during the war were now part of civilian life. Computers were introduced, and sociologists began to turn toward positivist approaches and quantitative methods. Meanwhile, a post-war concern for social stability—echoing Durkheim—was one of the reigning sentiments of the era. The 1950s were unusual in emphasizing conformity to social norms. It's not surprising, then, that it would also be the heyday of structural functionalism, embodied most clearly by Talcott Parsons (1902–1979) (see pages 233–237 and his views on marriage as an example).

Functionalism would soon suffer an intellectual blow, however. The 1960s brought a raft of social movements—ones on behalf of women and indigenous populations and sexual, racial, and ethnic minorities, and on issues like sexual freedom and world peace. Suddenly the idea that societies naturally functioned smoothly and with widespread consensus seemed faulty. This was when conflict theory rose to prominence in sociology, becoming one of its dominant paradigms (as discussed on pages 137–142). Karl Marx, who'd previously been only reluctantly embraced by the field, was recast as an early conflict theorist, and a prophetic one.

With its origins in the Progressive Era, sociology could boast almost one hundred years of studying social problems like racism, sexism, poverty, and crime. This made it well suited to understanding the upheavals of the 1960s. Indeed, sociology expanded nationally in these years and rose in prominence. Between 1960 and 1970, membership in the American Sociological Association would double, rising to more than 14,000 professional sociologists.[19]

Perhaps more than any other discipline, sociology informed the student activists driving the era's radicalism.[20] Contemporary scholars like C. Wright Mills (1916–1962), who published *The Power Elite* in 1956 (see pages 261–263), were suddenly hyper-relevant. Sociology students—like the inestimable Martin Luther King Jr.—were also overrepresented among activists. Many would later become influential sociology professors.

Sociology itself was also informed by these movements.[21] The field began to confront racism and sexism within its own ranks. It started the slow process of acknowledging its erasure of the contributions of non-White and non-male sociologists, many of whom did sociology outside of universities primarily because they were not allowed to practice it within them. This prompted a revision of the history of sociology, leading the discipline to recognize the contributions of early sociological thinkers who had been previously overlooked or excluded.

Women and racial and ethnic minorities also started to become sociologists in greater numbers. The Association of Black Sociologists and the Sociologists for Women in Society were both founded in 1970. Today more than half of sociology PhDs are earned by women, and more than a third are earned by people of color.[22]

As sociologists themselves diversified, so did their sociological theories. Conflict theory expanded well beyond class to include critical disability studies, critical race theory, queer theory, feminist theory, postcolonial studies, and more. In the 1990s, the legal scholar Kimberlé Crenshaw (1959–) introduced the idea of *intersectionality*, the recognition that our lives are shaped by multiple interacting identities (as introduced on pages 82–85). Many sociologists, especially Black feminist scholars like Patricia Hill Collins (1948–), were instrumental in further developing this idea, and it's a central organizing concept in much sociological research today.

In the aftermath of the social movements of the 1960s, sociology was a diversifying field. It was attuned to the power of social identities. And it had embraced the importance of thinking intersectionally. In this context, many sociologists came to embrace *standpoint theory*, developed in 1989 by the sociologist Dorothy Smith (1926–). This theory claims that our understanding of the world is shaped by our social position. Who we are, in other words, matters for what research questions we think are interesting, what methods we believe will answer them, and what findings we'll discover in our data.

Interestingly, standpoint theory challenges Auguste Comte's foundational vision for a positivist sociology. Standpoint theory posits that what we see depends on who we are. Accordingly, combined with the belief in the necessity of using a wide range of research methods, standpoint theory suggests that sociology is at its best when many different kinds of people with many different standpoints use many different types of research methods. Only with such a kaleidoscope of knowledge can we understand anything in its true complexity. Sociologists today capture this diversity more than ever before.

Today, about 30,000 students graduate from college with a degree in sociology every year. Sociology students go on to work in a wide range of fields. Learning how to think critically about social constructs, interaction, group dynamics, and organizations is useful in many, many occupations. Sociology helps people who go into counseling, social work, religious leadership, and health professions. Understanding the context in which people encounter and overcome problems is the first step in knowing how to help them.

Sociology majors also go into marketing and public relations. Appreciating the power of social symbols is helpful for persuading potential customers. Sociology majors become journalists, as thinking sociologically is a critical tool for reporting on society. They become lawyers and politicians and use the law to advocate for a more just society. And they become teachers who help young people learn about the worlds they live in.

Sociology majors become researchers, policy analysts, politicians, and activists too. A sociology degree is an advantage in any job that involves thinking about how to collect and analyze data, design and evaluate social systems, or make a pitch for a better society. Sociologists are insightful artists, filmmakers, novelists, actors, and writers. Because sociology is the science of society, sociology majors can offer genuinely informed and sophisticated commentary on the social world.

We need sociologists now more than ever. Our societies are increasingly complex; our challenges as momentous as any. If humans are going to continue to thrive, we'll need people with **sociological imaginations**, or the capacity to consider how people's lives—including our own—are shaped by the social facts that surround us. Professional sociologists serve as beacons of the sociological imagination, but every sociological thinker has the ability to shine a light on our shared struggles. Now that includes you. Together, we'll continue to imagine a brighter reality.

sociological imagination
the capacity to consider how people's lives — including our own — are shaped by the social facts that surround us

APPENDIX B

A GUIDE TO SOCIOLOGICAL RESEARCH

"Research is formalized curiosity. It is poking and prying with a purpose."

—ZORA NEALE HURSTON

Sociology is a *social* science, one that concerns people, their relationships, and their societies. This means that sociologists are committed to producing knowledge about human life that's grounded in scientific inquiry. Ultimately, science is about observation, which means sociology is committed to **empirical inquiry**, or looking to the world for evidence with which it can test its claims. Sociologists pose **research questions**, or queries about the world that can be answered empirically. Next, they gather **data**, or systematically collected sets of empirical observations. Then, they examine those data in an effort to answer their research question.

This appendix offers an overview of the sociological research methods introduced throughout this book and discusses the advantages of having many different approaches to answering questions. It also describes the process by which sociologists pursue and publish research, including a consideration of how they do this ethically. Finally, it explores one of the primary goals of research: the building of **sociological theory**, or empirically based explanations and predictions about relationships between social facts.

SOCIOLOGICAL RESEARCH METHODS

One of the things that sets sociology apart from other social sciences is the wide range of research methods used by sociologists. **Sociological research methods** are scientific strategies for collecting empirical data about social facts. Table 1 describes all the methods introduced in this book and

empirical inquiry
a form of investigation that involves looking to the world for evidence

research questions
queries about the world that can be answered empirically

data
systematically collected sets of empirical observations

sociological theory
empirically based explanations and predictions about relationships between social facts

sociological research methods
scientific strategies for collecting empirical data about social facts

TABLE I

Descriptions of Select Sociological Research Methods

Research method	Description	Page
Biosocial research	Investigating the relationships between sociological variables and biological ones	52
Comparative methods	Collecting and analyzing data about two or more cases that can be usefully contrasted	150
Computational sociology	Extracting and analyzing data using computers	81
Content analysis	Counting and describing patterns of themes in media	73
Ethnography	Carefully observing naturally occurring social interaction, often as a participant	271
Field experiments	Testing a hypothesis under carefully controlled but otherwise naturally occurring conditions	104
Historical sociology	Collecting and analyzing data that reveal facts about past events	141
In-depth interviews	Conducting intimate conversations with respondents	20
Laboratory experiments	Testing a hypothesis in a neutral setting under carefully controlled conditions	25
Social network analysis	Mapping social ties and exchanges between them	46
Spatial analysis	Layering data on a landscape divided into fine-grained segments	211
Standardized surveys	Using a questionnaire designed to elicit analyzable data	136
Time-use diaries	Having participants self-report their activities at regular intervals over at least twenty-four hours	243

directs you to where they're discussed in-depth. The list captures many of the research strategies used by sociologists, but not all of them.

Some research methods rely heavily on sociologists' interpersonal skills. In-depth interviews involve intimate conversations between researchers and respondents. The researcher must be able to pose useful questions, listen very carefully to answers, and respond in productive ways. Likewise, ethnography requires sociologists to carefully observe naturally occurring interaction and sometimes participate too. Ethnographers need to be able to build relationships, spend lots of time with others, and pay close attention to the setting. Because they involve careful consideration and discussion of the meaning of nonnumerical data, in-depth interviews and ethnographies are considered **qualitative research methods**.

Other research methods rely heavily on mathematical and computer skills. There is an art and a science to writing a good survey, but once data are collected, the work is primarily statistical. Social scientists have developed computer programs that allow sociologists to use advanced math to make sense of survey data, as well as ones with which sociologists can build maps and model social ties. Sociologists who do social network analysis often rely on computers to characterize the shape and structure of people's connections. Those who use spatial analysis look at how individuals and social conditions are arrayed in space, whether and where they overlap, and for whom. Because these methods involve examining numerical data with mathematics, they are generally described as **quantitative research methods**.

All these methods involve humans as *research subjects*, or participants. Research involving data collected from people is called **human subjects research**. Some sociological research doesn't directly involve research subjects. Instead, it measures and summarizes patterns in artifacts produced by people. These artifacts can include media like books or songs as well as more ambient material like billboards or clothing logos. Content analysis can be either quantitative or qualitative. Historical sociologists often do a form of content analysis on documents from the past.

These research methods often find **correlations**, or observed relationships between variables. Correlations can be *positive*, meaning that as one variable changes, the other changes in the same direction. Or they can be *negative*, meaning that as one variable changes, the other changes in the other direction. For example, there's a positive correlation between age and wealth. The older a person is, the more wealth they have likely accumulated. Age and wealth go "up" together. There's a negative correlation, however, between age and health. The older a person is, the poorer their health is likely to be. As age goes "up," health goes "down."

But are these causal relationships? We see **causation** when a change in one variable produces a change in the other. The correlation between age and health is causal; aging is a source of declining health. The correlation between age and wealth is not causal. Getting older does not cause money in the bank to multiply. In this case, the correlational relationship is **spurious**, or caused by a third variable. In this case, time. Both aging and wealth acquisition are a function of how long we've been alive.

Sometimes sociologists are interested in offering evidence that the correlations they discover are causal. They do this with experiments. All experiments aim to isolate the potential influence of an *independent variable* (the cause) on a *dependent variable* (one that might register an effect). Sociologists do laboratory experiments, ones that take place in environments specifically designed for research. But they especially appreciate field experiments because these test hypotheses outside the laboratory under real-world conditions.

Finally, sociologists look to the body as a source of data. Biosocial research methods are tools of sociological inquiry that investigate relationships

qualitative research methods
tools of sociological inquiry that involve careful consideration and discussion of the meaning of nonnumerical data

quantitative research methods
tools of sociological inquiry that involve examining numerical data with mathematics

human subjects research
research involving data collected from people

correlation
an observed relationship between variables

causation
a statistical relationship in which a change in one variable produces a change in the other

spurious
a statistical relationship between two variables that appears because both correlate with a third variable

between social variables and biological ones. These include body shape and size; the condition of people's skin, hair, and teeth; biometrics like hormone levels, gene expression, and brain functioning; and health indicators like blood pressure, premature birth, or cancer rates. Sociologists who use biosocial research methods are able to show how the body facilitates social interaction (for example, by producing emotional states that are appropriate to the social situations we find ourselves in) and registers inequality (by measuring the harm done to the health of victims of discrimination, for instance).

All these research methods produce valuable information. We learn what ideas are circulating in our cultures. We learn how people think and feel, why they make the choices they do, and how they interact with others. We also learn what kind of experiences people are likely to have, given their social identities and structural positions. With all of this, we can draw useful conclusions about how the world works and how we might change our societies for the better.

WHY SO MANY METHODS?

Sociologists use a wide range of methods because no one method can answer every type of research question. Each method has its advantages and its limitations. Which method a sociologist chooses will depend on the question they want to answer. Table 2 lists a select strength and weakness for each research method discussed in this book.

Surveys, for example, are great at answering "who" and "what" questions. Who goes to college? What do they major in? Who majors in what? Surveys,

TABLE 2

Select Strengths and Weaknesses of Sociological Research Methods

Research method	Example strength	Example weakness
Biosocial research	Shows that social facts have physical effects on our bodies	Threatens to oversimplify how social facts shape experience and behavior
Comparative methods	Enables researchers to test whether social forces produce predicted outcomes across cases	Involves too few cases to conclude whether even consistently observed outcomes would reliably occur
Computational sociology	Allows us to collect and analyze large amounts of data beyond what humans can manage	Relying on computers sometimes results in miscoding that can produce biased results
Content analysis	Documents that social constructs are not just in our heads but are genuinely present in our culture	Cannot be used to infer what content creators intended or what audiences take away

TABLE 2

Select Strengths and Weaknesses of Sociological Research Methods—cont'd

Research method	Example strength	Example weakness
Ethnography	Allows in-person, on-the-ground, immersive looks at how social life really works	Findings can only shed light on the dynamics of the field site(s) under study
Field experiments	Enables researchers to make causal claims that apply to everyday life	Can't reveal the processes by which one variable causes another
Historical sociology	Facilitates a sociological analysis of why and how particular historical events occurred	Does little to help us understand how easily events could have turned out differently
In-depth interviews	Provides an understanding of how people experience and think about their lives	Assumes that people's interpretations of their own lives are reliable
Laboratory experiments	Enables researchers to make causal claims	Does not guarantee that findings will replicate outside of a carefully controlled laboratory setting
Social network analysis	Offers a bird's-eye view of social interaction by capturing the structure, characteristics, and central players of a social network	Fails to capture the micro-level interactions on which social ties depend
Spatial analysis	Provides a unique perspective on how variables are distributed across a landscape	Offers little information on why variables are distributed the way they are
Standardized surveys	Collects data that are generalizable, or attributable more generally to the whole population from which the sample is drawn	Cannot be used to infer why variables correlate with one another, or how they came to do so
Time-use diaries	Provides fine-grained data about how people use their time	Reveals nothing about why daily tasks are divided the way they are

though, aren't very good for answering "why" questions. For that, a sociologist might use in-depth interviews, asking people to explain why they decided to go to college (or not) and why they chose the major they did. As a complement to both surveys and interviews, ethnography is often better at answering "how" questions. How do majors get recruited by departments? How does a student's major shape the rest of their college experience?

In addition to answering different kinds of questions, different research methods also tap into different *levels of analysis*, a way of referring to the focus of the investigation. For instance, biosocial methods show us what's going on inside the body. Interviews help us understand what's going on in the mind. Social network analysis and ethnography help us see what's happening at the level of the group. Content analysis can describe the cultural environment. Surveys can represent entire populations. Historical analysis can explain how we got here. And comparative analysis can reveal alternative paths. The body is one "level," the group another, the population a third, and so on.

As an example of the way multiple studies using different methods can help scholars get a fuller picture of reality, consider how six studies about sex on college campuses came together to build researcher confidence that hooking up, or casual sexual activity, had become common among college students. For the first research project, seventy-two Stanford University students engaged in a collective ethnography project.[1] Each spent ninety minutes at a college party carefully observing their peers' interaction. Their shared field notes were then used as data for a paper about a form of dancing at college parties commonly known as *grinding*. Among their observations was the fact that grinding was a central activity at college parties, and that it often led to hooking up.

If grinding is a central activity at college parties, and grinding leads to hooking up, does that mean that students go to college parties *specifically* to hook up? Two sociologists at the University of Illinois at Chicago decided to ask them. Eighty-seven students were interviewed in-depth. Many of these students confirmed that hooking up went, as one put it, "hand in hand with the parties."[2] Another described casual sexual activity as part of the "true college experience." The researchers concluded that "hooking up as part of an alcohol-fueled party scene" was considered by many students to be a routine and expected part of college life.

But is it like that everywhere? Or just at Stanford and the University of Illinois? Another set of sociologists used data from a survey to see if the qualitative findings of the ethnography and the interview study were **generalizable**, or attributable to the whole population from which the sample was drawn. Attributable, that is, to college students more generally. These sociologists collected and analyzed surveys from over 20,000 students attending twenty-one different colleges.[3] They found that about 70 percent of students reported hooking up at least once by their senior year, and most of those hookups had involved quite a lot of alcohol (an average of about five and a half drinks).

The survey found that this was common at all the colleges they studied except one: a college with no residence halls. These quantitative data suggest that "hookup cultures" are relatively widespread on college campuses, but not all of them. This built researcher confidence that hooking up had become a norm, while also pointing to a kind of student who may not be having the so-called true college experience.

The answers produced by one method can often prompt research that uses another. For example, survey data suggested that hooking up negatively correlated with student well-being. That is, students who hooked up more than their peers reported being less happy.[4] Why would this be?

generalizable
a term used to describe data that are applicable to the whole population from which the sample is drawn, not just to the sample itself

To help answer this question, two scholars did a content analysis of the written responses of 343 students who were asked to describe an "ideal" hookup and an "actual" one.[5] They found that more than half of hookups were failing to live up to students' expectations. Their sexual experiences were shorter, less pleasurable, and less meaningful than they wanted them to be. In yet another study, this one based on 111 in-depth interviews, both male and female students confessed that they often had romantic feelings for their partner but felt pressure to hide their emotions.[6] Women also expressed frustration about a lack of sexual pleasure and the risk of sexual violence.

Using survey data, scholars discovered a correlation between hooking up and emotional distress. Content analysis revealed discrepancies between what students wished for and what they got. And interviews gave students an opportunity to elaborate on their disappointment. Together, these studies (and many more) suggest that hookup culture is making it hard for students to form romantic relationships and, in the meantime, isn't always delivering the hot sex it promises. Using more than one research method, or *mixed methods*, to help sociologists get answers to research questions is sometimes called *triangulation*, or the strategy of seeking an answer to a question from multiple angles.

PURSUING AND PUBLISHING SOCIOLOGICAL RESEARCH

Whatever research method a sociologist chooses, the process of pursuing a project—summarized in Table 3—is similar. The researcher is first struck with

TABLE 3

The Ten Steps of Sociological Research

(1) Choose a topic or theory to investigate.
(2) Conduct a review of the existing academic literature.
(3) Write a research question.
(4) Design a methodology.
(5) Operationalize the variables.
(6) Ensure that the research design is ethical.
(7) Collect the data.
(8) Evaluate the data for quality.
(9) Analyze the data.
(10) Write a report for publication.

curiosity. They choose either a topic they find interesting (like baseball or parenting) or a theory they'd like to test (like symbolic interactionism or the elite theory of power). Second, they read the existing **academic literature**, the empirical and theoretical writing that scholars have previously produced. With this in mind, the scholar asks: Is there a need for further description or theoretical development?

If the answer is yes, then the sociologist will design a research project. This involves drafting a precise research question and choosing a method that will answer it. The researcher must also carefully define the relevant variables and figure out how to measure them systematically. Sociologists describe this as *operationalization*, a process by which researchers define their variables and decide how to measure them.

Sometimes operationalization is straightforward. It's easy, for example, to define and measure age. Our age is the amount of time since we were born. We can measure it with days, months, or years. Other variables are more difficult to operationalize. What counts, for instance, as a hookup? Is grinding at a party a hookup? Is kissing after spending some time together a hookup? If two people have been going home together after every party all semester, are those hookups? Answering these kinds of questions so that something like "number of hookups" can be measured is exactly what we mean by operationalization.

Once the research project has been designed and the variables have been operationalized, the researcher will consider the ethics of their project. **Research ethics** are a set of moral principles that guide empirical inquiry. Most fundamentally, this involves minimizing the risk to participants. Once a project is deemed ethical, the researcher proceeds with the plan, staying aware of the possibility that unexpected ethical issues may arise and need attention. (Research ethics are discussed in much more detail in the next section.)

When data are in hand, the sociologist must evaluate it for its quality. A researcher conducting a survey will need to check to ensure that their questions weren't widely misunderstood, and their questionnaires were filled out in good faith. A researcher performing a content analysis will have to check that their word searches returned the kind of data they were looking for. A researcher using biosocial research methods will have to be on the alert for equipment or human errors in recording biometric data. A sociologist conducting an experiment will need to be on the lookout for any unexpected interference in their data collection.

Only then, when the data have been evaluated for quality, can researchers get down to the business of analysis. This is the process by which scholars assess their data in light of their research question. If the research is quantitative, this will involve statistics. If it's qualitative, it might include the counting and correlating of common themes. The analysis produces what are described as the *findings* or *results*.

Finally, scholars must publish their work in the form of an article or book. Research articles are submitted to academic journals whose editors solicit feedback from other researchers with related expertise; this process is known as **peer review**. If the article is deemed to be methodologically sound and theoretically interesting or descriptively important, it may be published. Books are submitted to academic publishers, including university presses, who subject the work to the same rigorous evaluation. Some research is never published, but most research projects—sometimes after extensive revisions suggested by peer reviewers—eventually find a home and become part of the academic literature.

DOING RESEARCH ETHICALLY

Sociologists are committed to doing ethical research. Fundamentally, this means pursuing projects that will benefit society and ensuring that those benefits substantially outweigh the risk of harm to research subjects. Central to minimizing the risk of harm is ensuring that all research subjects are consenting participants with a clear understanding of what their participation entails. This is called **informed consent**, and it's obtained with a *consent form*, a document that explains the study and the potential participants' rights. Deception is allowed only when it's absolutely necessary to the study design and when the risk of harm is very low. Researchers who use deception *debrief* subjects afterward, or tell them the true purpose of the study.

Informed consent is especially important if participation may trigger emotional distress. Sociologists are concerned with social problems, so the topics they study can be upsetting. Especially if a study has the potential to cause psychological harm, the subjects' well-being is placed front and center. Often, in an abundance of caution, researchers include referrals to local mental health counselors and crisis hotlines on the consent form.

Almost universally, researchers are required to protect subjects' **confidentiality**, or keep private both their participation in and specific contributions to the study. In confidential research, the fact that a subject consented to participate should never be made public, nor should anyone who reads the findings be able to figure out whom they are based upon. Sociologists use a variety of strategies—including private research spaces, secure files, and pseudonyms for names and places—to ensure they keep the identities of their participants secret. When confidentiality will not be protected, like with some historical research in which who says what really matters, sociologists are explicit about this. They'll also give the participant some control over their data, including how and where it will appear and what will happen to it after the research is done.

Sociologists are extra vigilant about following these ethical guidelines when **vulnerable populations** are being studied. These are groups that are at relatively high risk of being harmed if they are included as research subjects. Risk is high, for example, when a person carries a stigmatized identity or label, if they're under someone else's control, or if there's a reason to believe that informed consent can't be guaranteed. Children are generally considered a vulnerable population. Undocumented immigrants are also vulnerable, as they're targets of law enforcement; imprisoned people are vulnerable, too, as they can be punished or rewarded by guards and parole boards. People with cognitive disabilities or mental health conditions must also be treated with extra care.

Sociologists get help with these ethical requirements from **institutional review boards**. These are panels of professionals that evaluate research proposals to ensure they comply with the moral principles outlined in codes of ethics. All disciplines have associations that publish codes of ethics, and all scientists doing human subjects research are expected to show that they're complying with those codes before proceeding with their projects. Doing otherwise is itself considered unethical by most. Getting approval, however, is the bare minimum expected from sociologists. They're expected to remain vigilant even of risks that review boards don't identify and minimize harm accordingly.

Finally, sociologists are expected to maintain **professional ethics**, a set of moral principles that guide sociologists' everyday activities. They're required to be transparent about any conflicts of interest that might bias their research. They're expected to give credit to others when they borrow their ideas. They are absolutely prohibited from plagiarizing others' work or lying about their own. And they're expected to be good colleagues to their peers and good mentors to their undergraduate and graduate students, treating them fairly and with respect.

BUILDING SOCIOLOGICAL THEORY

Ultimately, sociologists' primary goals are to describe and theorize. To describe human life is to depict its objective truths as accurately as possible. To theorize it is to explain what we see and predict what we might see next. If description reveals social patterns, in other words, theory tries to explain *why* and *how* we see the social patterns we do.

Theory is quite an abstract idea, so let's use a *very* simple but also usefully concrete example. Consider your average American living room. Alongside other objects, a living room will probably include a couch and maybe several chairs, end tables, a television, and some decorations. If we did a content analysis of living rooms, it would likely reveal some social patterns regarding their contents. Televisions and couches would probably be nearly universal and bookshelves and decorations somewhat common. Things like beds, bathtubs, and workbenches would be comparatively rare. That's description.

Once we know *what* is in living rooms, we can begin to theorize *why* we see those things and not others. We might theorize that living rooms are more likely to have TVs than desks because the room has a purpose: leisure. And we might theorize that there are often many places to sit instead of just one because it's a place for family and friends to gather. It is, in other words, a shared space for relaxation. *That* is why TVs, couches, chairs, and decorations are so frequently observed, and beds, bathtubs, and workbenches (almost) never. That's a theory.

institutional review boards
panels of professionals at colleges that evaluate research proposals to ensure they comply with the moral principles outlined in codes of ethics

professional ethics
a set of moral principles that guide sociologists' everyday activities

Once sociologists have a theory, they want to test it. Each research method is a different kind of test. A nationally representative survey can tell us how well our preliminary descriptive study of living rooms matches reality. Because such data are generalizable, our results will allow us to estimate how much seating is in the average living room, how rare it is to see a bed in one, and whether there are differences in living room contents by class, region, or social identity. In-depth interviews can reveal why people chose to include these items in their living rooms and whether we're right to guess that people design the room for shared relaxation.

Finally, ethnographers can be sent out to sit in actual living rooms for days, weeks, or months at a time. Their results will reveal how people *really* use their living rooms. Perhaps both the content analyses and the interviewees' visions are misleading, and the most common activity in living rooms is eating dinner alone in front of the TV. Leisure, yes. Shared leisure, no.

If this were the finding, then we'd want to revise our theory. Perhaps it's not that the living room is a shared space for relaxation; perhaps it's a room that we *imagine* or *wish* to be a shared space for relaxation. This finding prompts new questions: Why? Where did this idea come from? And is it this way everywhere? A content analysis of living rooms in children's books, sitcoms, and design magazines might give us a hint as to why people aspire to design their living rooms for family gatherings and parties. This is certainly how living rooms are portrayed in pop culture.

Moreover, such collective leisure is often featured as a source of happiness. A historical sociologist might seek to discover where this idea came from, mapping the transition from the homes of rural homesteaders before urbanization (during which beds, bathtubs, and workbenches were likely quite common in living rooms), to tenement apartments in densely packed cities (where dedicated rooms for leisure were likely rare except among the wealthy), and through to 1950s suburbia (where a growing middle class could expand into single-family homes and a new gadget called the television would be introduced).

Good sociological theory, then, is built upon good description. It's subsequently tested and refined using multiple methods. Ideally, the resulting theory is generalizable, meaning it can be used to explain not only the subjects studied, but others like them.

Of course, the living room is an oversimplified example. In reality, sociologists study an expansive range of complicated phenomena. And they've been building theory for almost 200 years. Yet, there is still more to understand.

There will *always* be more to understand. This is, first, because all science is a process by which we get ever closer to the truth but never quite arrive. Sociology is no different. Sociologists are always eager to refine their theories, making them incrementally more accurate as more research is completed. So sociologists know that the theory they build, no matter how strong, will inevitably have to be revised.

Second, societies evolve. So, what sociologists are attempting to describe and theorize is always changing. Living rooms were invented, and someday they'll go away. The process of aging is increasingly aided by technology, improving health outcomes. Economies are changing, potentially disrupting the relationship between money and time. Hookup culture dominated U.S. colleges, until Covid-19 forced campuses to shut down. There's always a tomorrow, sometimes a surprising one, and it will require new description and new theory. So as long as there are people to study, there will be sociology to do.

KEY MOMENTS
IN THE HISTORY OF SOCIOLOGY

1838	Auguste Comte coins the word *sociology*.
	The first book on sociological research methods—Harriett Martineau's *How to Observe Morals and Manners*—is released in the United Kingdom.
1848	*The Communist Manifesto*, by Karl Marx with Friedrich Engels, becomes available in Germany.
1867	Marx publishes his infamous criticism of free market capitalism, *Capital: A Critique of Political Economy*.
1889	The American sociologist Jane Addams co-opens Hull House, an anti-poverty organization; she will later be credited with founding the profession of social work.
1890	The first sociology textbook—*Introduction to a Science of Society* by Albion Small—is published.
1892	At the University of Chicago, Small becomes the first U.S. professor of sociology. That year, he founds the first department of sociology anywhere in the world.
	Ida B. Wells-Barnett's *Southern Horrors*, the first evidence-based account of lynching, is released.

Anna Julia Cooper publishes one of the earliest works of intersectionality, *A Voice from the South: By a Black Woman of the South*, in which she articulates the need for a Black feminism.

1893 An early work of structural functionalism, *The Division of Labor in Society* by Émile Durkheim, is released in France.

1895 Durkheim argues in favor of studying "social facts" in *The Rules of Sociological Method: And Selected Texts on Sociology and Its Methodology*.

The first academic journal devoted to sociological research — the *American Journal of Sociology* — is established.

The American Sociological Society — today known as the American Sociological Association — is founded at Johns Hopkins University.

1897 Émile Durkheim describes "anomie" in his book *Suicide: A Study in Sociology*.

1898 Charlotte Perkins Gilman publishes *Women and Economics*, the first of many book-length sociological analyses.

1899 Using a mix of research methods, W. E. B. Du Bois publishes *The Philadelphia Negro*, a meticulous account of the role of racism in shaping Black American life.

1902 In *Human Nature and the Social Order*, Charles Horton Cooley introduces the idea of the looking-glass self.

1903 *The Souls of Black Folk*, Du Bois's personal and intimate portrayal of the Black experience, is released.

1905 The German sociologist Max Weber introduces the term *work ethic* in his book *The Protestant Ethic and the Spirit of Capitalism*.

1906 Also in Germany, *Occupation and Marriage*, the first of Marianne Weber's many works on the sociology of the family, is published.

1909 Du Bois and Wells-Barnett, among others, form the National Association for the Advancement of Colored People (NAACP).

1931	Jane Addams becomes the first American woman to win a Nobel Peace Prize.
1934	In a book titled *Mind, Self, and Society*, George Herbert Mead introduces the distinction between the "I" and the "me."
1937	Herbert Blumer coins the term *symbolic interactionism*.
	Talcott Parsons releases his most famous book, *The Structure of Social Action*.
1950	A now-classic study of American character — *The Lonely Crowd* by David Riesman, Nathan Glazer, and Reuel Denney — becomes the first book of sociology to sell more than a million copies.
1956	In *The Presentation of Self in Everyday Life*, Erving Goffman offers his influential theory of human interaction, known as dramaturgy.
	C. Wright Mills shocks America with the publication of *The Power Elite*.
1959	Mills coins the phrase *sociological imagination* in a book of the same title.
1967	Harold Garfinkel's *Studies in Ethnomethodology* reveals the underlying shared logics that support social interaction.
1970	The Association of Black Sociologists and the Sociologists for Women in Society are founded.
1972	In *Sex, Gender and Society*, Ann Oakley argues in favor of a social constructionist understanding of gender.
1974	Immanuel Wallerstein, the sociologist of globalization, releases *The Modern World-System*.
1978	William Julius Wilson's *The Declining Significance of Race* is published.
1979	French sociologist Pierre Bourdieu introduces the idea of cultural capital in *Distinction: A Social Critique of the Judgement of Taste*.

1989	Arlie Hochschild's *The Second Shift: Working Parents and the Revolution at Home* reveals what it's like for women to try to "have it all."
1993	Douglas Massey and Nancy Denton describe racial and ethnic residential segregation in *American Apartheid: Segregation and the Making of the Underclass*.
1995	The American Sociological Association celebrates its 100th birthday.
2004	For the first time in its history, the theme for the American Sociological Association annual conference is "public sociology"; the meeting attracts over 5,000 sociologists, breaking attendance records.
2015	The American Sociological Association files an amicus curiae brief with the Supreme Court citing research showing conclusively that "children raised by same-sex parents fare just as well as children of different-sex parents."
	Aldon Morris's book *The Scholar Denied* shakes the foundations of professional sociology by reclaiming the contributions of W. E. B. Du Bois and exposing those who wished to erase them.
2017	*Evicted: Poverty and Profit in the American City*, by sociologist Matthew Desmond, wins the Pulitzer Prize for general nonfiction.
2020	Ida B. Wells-Barnett is awarded a posthumous Pulitzer Prize for *Southern Horrors: Lynch Law in All Its Phases*, her 1892 book on the murder of Black Americans during the Reconstruction Era.
	Sociologists Tressie McMillan Cottom and Forrest Stuart win MacArthur "genius" grants.
2021	Amanda Gorman—sociology major and America's first National Youth Poet Laureate—attracts international acclaim after reading her poem "The Hill We Climb" at President Joseph R. Biden's inauguration.
	Sociologist Alondra Nelson is tapped by President Biden to be the deputy director for science and society in the Office of Science and Technology Policy.

GLOSSARY

A

academic literature: the existing body of empirical and theoretical publications written by scholars

account: an excuse that explains our rule breaking but also affirms that the rule is good and right

achievement gaps: disparities in the academic accomplishments of different kinds of students

adultification: a form of bias in which adult characteristics are attributed to children

alienation: the feeling of dissatisfaction and disconnection from the fruits of one's labor

androcentric pay scale: a positive correlation between the number of men in an occupation relative to women and the wages paid to employees

androcentrism: the production of unjust outcomes for people who perform femininity

anomie: widespread normlessness or a weakening of or alienation from social rules

B

back stage: private or semiprivate spaces in which we can relax or rehearse

beliefs: ideas about what is true and false

biosocial research methods: tools of sociological inquiry that investigate relationships between sociological variables and biological ones

blood quantum rule: a law limiting legal recognition of American Indians to those who have at least a certain level of documented indigenous ancestry

bourgeoisie: a class of people who employ the workers

breaching: purposefully breaking a social rule in order to test how others respond

breadwinner/homemaker marriage: a model of marriage that involves a wage-earning spouse supporting a stay-at-home spouse and children

bureaucracies: organizations with formal policies, strict hierarchies, and impersonal relations

C

capital: the resources we use to get things we want and need

capitalism: an economic system based on private ownership of the resources used to create wealth and the right of individuals to personally profit

care work: work that involves face-to-face caretaking of the physical, emotional, and educational needs of others

case: an instance of a thing of interest; it can be a person, a group of people, an organization, an event, or a place

causal claims: assertions that an independent variable is directly and specifically responsible for producing a change in a dependent variable

causation: a statistical relationship in which a change in one variable produces a change in the other

cisgender: people who are assigned male at birth who identify as men as well as people assigned female at birth who identify as women

class consciousness: an understanding that members of a social class share economic interests

coding: a process in which segments of text are identified as belonging to relevant categories

collective action: the coordinated activities of members of groups with shared goals

collective action problem: the challenge of getting large groups of people to act in coordinated ways

collective conscience: a society's shared understanding of right and wrong

collectivism: the idea that people are interdependent actors with responsibilities primarily to the group

colonialism: a practice in which countries claim control over territories, the people in them, and their natural resources, then exploit them for economic gain

colorism: prejudice against and discrimination toward people with dark skin compared to those with light skin, regardless of race

comparative sociology: a research method that involves collecting and analyzing data about two or more cases that can be usefully compared and contrasted

computational sociology: a research method that uses computers to extract and analyze data

concentrated poverty: a condition in which 40 percent or more of the residents in an area live below the federal poverty line

confidentiality: a guarantee that a research subject's participation in and contributions to a research study will be known only to the researchers

conflict theory: the idea that societies aren't characterized by shared interests but competing ones

conspicuous consumption: spending elaborately on items and services with the sole purpose of displaying one's wealth

consumption: the use of wages to purchase goods and services

content analysis: a research method that involves counting and describing patterns of themes in media

contradictory class locations: positions in the economy that are in some ways like the proletariat and in other ways like the bourgeoisie

control group: the group in a laboratory experiment that does not undergo the experience that researchers believe might influence the dependent variable

controlling images: pervasive negative stereotypes that serve to justify or uphold inequality

correlation: an observed relationship between variables

correlational claims: assertions that changes in an independent variable correspond to changes in a dependent variable but not in a way that can be proven causal

counter frames: frames meant to challenge an existing social movement's frame

countermovements: persistent, organized collective action meant to resist social movements

crisis of capitalism: a coming catastrophic implosion from which capitalism would never recover

critical event: a sudden and dramatic occurrence that motivates nonactivists to become politically active

cross-institutional advantage and disadvantage: a phenomenon in which people are positively or negatively served across multiple institutions

cultural capital: symbolic resources that communicate one's social status

cultural hegemony: power maintained primarily by persuasion

cultural hybridization: the production of ideas, objects, practices, and bodies influenced by two or more cultures

culturally competent: able to understand and navigate our cultures with ease

cultural opportunity structure: cultural ideas, objects, practices, or bodies that create or constrain activist strategies

cultural relativism: the practice of noting the differences between cultures without passing judgment

culture: differences in groups' shared ideas, as well as the objects, practices, and bodies that reflect those ideas

culture-as-rationale thesis: the idea that we're socialized to know a set of culturally specific arguments with which we can justify why we feel something is right or wrong

culture-as-value thesis: the idea that we're socialized into culturally specific moralities that guide our feelings about right and wrong

cumulative advantage and disadvantage: advantage or disadvantage that builds over the life course

D

data: systematically collected sets of empirical observations

deviance: behaviors and beliefs that violate social expectations and attract negative sanctions

differential association theory: the idea that we need to be recruited into and taught criminal behavior by people in our social networks

distinction: active efforts to affirm identity categories and place ourselves and others into their subcategories

divisions of labor: complicated tasks broken down into smaller parts and distributed to individuals who specialize in narrow roles

doing identity: the active performance of social identities

domestic outsourcing: paying non-family members to do family-related tasks

dramaturgy: the practice of looking at social life as a series of performances in which we're actors on metaphorical stages

E

economic capital: financial resources that are or can be converted into money

economic elite: the minority of people who control a disproportionate amount of wealth

economic opportunity structure: the role of money in enabling or limiting a movement's operations and influence

elite theory of power: the idea that a small group of networked individuals controls the most powerful positions in our social institutions

embodied: physically present and detectable in the body itself

empirical inquiry: a form of investigation that involves looking to the world for evidence

environmental racism: the practice of exposing racial and ethnic minorities to more toxins and pollutants than White people

ethnicity: an identity based on collective memories of a shared history and distinctive culture

ethnocentrism: the practice of assuming that one's own culture is superior to the cultures of others

ethnography: a research method that involves careful observation of naturally occurring social interaction, often as a participant

ethnomethodology: research aimed at revealing the underlying shared logic that is the foundation of social interactions

experimental group: the group in a laboratory experiment that undergoes the experience that researchers believe might influence the dependent variable

F

face: a version of ourselves that we want to project in a specific setting

family wage: an income, paid to a man, that is large enough to support a non-working wife and children

feminization of poverty: a concentration of women, trans women, and gay, bisexual, and gender-nonconforming men at the bottom of the income scale and a concentration of gender-conforming, heterosexual, cisgender men at the top

field: the place or places where ethnographers conduct participant observation

field experiment: a type of experiment that involves a test of a hypothesis outside the laboratory

field notes: descriptive accounts of what occurred in the field, alongside tentative sociological observations

fit: the feeling that our particular mix of cultural capital matches our social context

folkways: loosely enforced norms

frame: a succinct claim as to the nature of a social fact

framing wars: battles over whether a social fact is a social problem and what kind of problem it is

freedom/power paradox: a situation whereby women have more freedom than men but less power, and men have more power than women but less freedom

free market capitalism: a capitalist system with little or no government regulation

front stage: a public space in which we are aware of having an audience

G

gender: the ideas, traits, interests, and skills that we associate with being biologically male or female

gender binary: the idea that people come in two and only two types, males who are masculine and females who are feminine

generalizable: a term used to describe data that are applicable to the whole population from which the sample is drawn, not just to the sample itself

gig work: a segment of the labor market in which companies contract with individuals to complete one short-term job at a time

glass ceiling: an invisible barrier that restricts upward mobility

glass escalator: an invisible ride to the top offered to men in female-dominated occupations

glass floor: an invisible barrier that restricts downward mobility

global care chains: a series of nurturing relationships in which the international work of care is displaced onto increasingly disadvantaged paid or unpaid workers

global cities: urban areas that act as key hubs in the world economy

global commodity chains: a transnational economic process that involves extracting natural resources, transforming them into goods, and marketing and distributing them to consumers

global imagined community: a socially constructed in-group based on a shared planet

globalization: the social processes that are expanding and intensifying connections across nation-states

global power elite: a relatively small group of interconnected people who occupy top positions in globally important social institutions

global slave trade: the practice of kidnapping human beings, transporting them around the world, and selling them for profit

H

hegemonic ideologies: shared ideas about how human life should be organized that are used to manufacture our consent to existing social conditions

hegemonic masculinity: the form of masculinity that constitutes the most widely admired and rewarded kind of person in any given culture

heteronormative: promoting heterosexuality as the only or preferred sexual identity, making other sexual desires invisible or casting them as inferior

historical sociology: a research method that involves collecting and analyzing data that reveal facts about past events, with the aim of enhancing sociological theory

homophily: our tendency to connect with others who are similar to us

human subjects research: research involving data collected from people

hypersegregation: residential segregation so extreme that many people's daily lives involve little or no contact with people of other races

I

ideal worker norm: the idea that an employee should devote themselves to their jobs wholly and without the distraction of family responsibilities

ideologies: shared ideas about how human life should be organized

ideology of intensive motherhood: the idea that children require concentrated maternal investment

ideology of separate spheres: the idea that the home is a feminine space best tended by women and work is a masculine space best suited to men

impression management: efforts to control how we're perceived by others

in-depth interview: a research method that involves an intimate conversation between the researcher and a research subject

individualism: the idea that people are independent actors responsible primarily for themselves

informed consent: a clear understanding on behalf of a research subject of what their participation in a research study entails

in-group bias: preferential treatment of members of our own group and mistreatment of others

institutional discrimination: widespread and enduring practices that persistently disadvantage some kinds of people while advantaging others

institutional review boards: panels of professionals at colleges that evaluate research proposals to ensure they comply with the moral principles outlined in codes of ethics

insurgent consciousness: a recognition of a shared grievance that can be addressed through collective action

interdependent power: the power of noncooperation

interest convergence: the alignment of the interests of activists and elites

intergenerational advantage and disadvantage: advantage and disadvantage that is passed from parents to children

interpersonal discrimination: prejudicial behavior displayed by individuals

interpersonal socialization: active efforts by others to help us become culturally competent members of our cultures

intersectionality: the recognition that our lives are shaped by multiple interacting identities

intersex: people with physical characteristics typical of both people assigned male and people assigned female at birth

J

job segregation: the sorting of people with different social identities into separate occupations

L

labeling: the process of assigning a deviant identity to an individual

labeling theory: a theory about how labels that are applied to us influence our behavior

labor: the work people can do with their bodies and minds

laboratory experiment: a research method that involves a test of a hypothesis under carefully controlled conditions

labor unions: associations that organize workers so they can negotiate with their employers as a group instead of as individuals

laws: rules that are made and enforced by cities, states, or federal governments

legitimation: a process by which a potentially controversial social fact is made acceptable

living wage: an income that allows full-time workers to afford their basic needs

looking-glass self: the self that emerges as a consequence of seeing ourselves as we think other people see us

M

macrosociology: elaborate studies of large-scale social trends

male flight: a phenomenon in which men start abandoning an activity when women start adopting it

mass deportation: an extremely high rate of deportation in cross-cultural and historical perspective

mass incarceration: an extremely high rate of imprisonment in cross-cultural and historical perspective

mass media: mediated communication intended to reach not just one or a handful of people but many

means of production: resources that can be used to create wealth

media socialization: the process of learning how to be culturally competent through our exposure to media

microsociology: intricate studies of everyday interaction

minimal group paradigm: the tendency of people to form groups and actively distinguish themselves from others for the most trivial of reasons

modern thought: a belief in science as the sole source of truth and the idea that humans can rationally organize societies and improve human life

mononormative: promoting monogamy, or the requirement that spouses have sexual relations only with each other

mores: tightly enforced norms that carry moral significance

N

nation-states: large territories governed by centralized powers that grant or deny citizenship rights

nation-state system: a world society consisting of only sovereign, self-contained territories

neutralization theory: the idea that deviance is facilitated by the development of culturally resonant rationales for rule breaking

nonbinary: people who identify as both man and woman or neither man nor woman

norms: shared expectations for behavior

O

one-drop rule: the idea that anyone with any trace of Black ancestry should be considered Black

organizational strength: a combination of strong leadership, human and material resources, social networks, and physical infrastructure

P

partnership unions: a relationship model based on love and companionship between equals

patriarch/property marriage: a model of marriage in which women and children are owned by men

peer review: a step in the publication process in which editors solicit feedback on a scholar's work from other researchers with related expertise

pluralist theory of power: the idea that U.S. politics is characterized by competing groups that work together to achieve their goals

policies: rules that are made and enforced by organizations

political networks: webs of ties that link people with similar political goals

political opportunity structure: the strengths and weaknesses in the existing political system that shape the options available to social movement actors

positive distinction: the claim that members of our own group are superior to members of other groups

positivism: a philosophical theory stating that scientific tools give us the capacity to accurately measure a true, objective reality

postmodern thought: a rejection of absolute truth (whether supernatural or scientific) in favor of countless partial truths, and a denunciation of the narrative of progress

power elite: a relatively small group of interconnected people who occupy top positions in important social institutions

precariat: a new class of workers who live economically precarious lives

prejudice: attitudinal bias against individuals based on their membership in a social group

premodern thought: a belief in supernatural sources of truth and a commitment to traditional practices

primary deviance: the instance of deviance that first attracts a deviant label

professional ethics: a set of moral principles that guide sociologists' everyday activities

proletariat: a class of people who are employed by others and work for a wage

pro-natal: promoting childbearing and stigmatizing choosing to go child-free

Protestant work ethic: the idea that one's character can and should be measured by one's dedication to paid work

psychological wage: a noneconomic good given to one group as a measure of superiority over other groups

public sociology: the work of using sociological theory to make societies better

Q

qualitative research methods: tools of sociological inquiry that involve careful consideration and discussion of the meaning of nonnumerical data

quantitative research methods: tools of sociological inquiry that involve examining numerical data with mathematics

R

race: a socially meaningful set of artificial distinctions falsely based on superficial and imagined biological differences

racism: a term that refers to a society's production of unjust outcomes for some racial or ethnic groups

rationalization: the process of embracing reason and using it to increase the efficiency and effectiveness of human activities

redlining: a practice of refusing loans to or steeply overcharging anyone buying in poor and minority neighborhoods

repertoire of contention: shared activities widely recognized as expressions of dissatisfaction with social conditions

research ethics: the set of moral principles that guide empirical inquiry

research questions: queries about the world that can be answered empirically

residential segregation: the sorting of different types of people into separate neighborhoods

resource deserts: places that lack beneficial or critical amenities

risk society: a society organized around the self-conscious production, distribution, and management of risk

S

sample: the subset of the population from which data will be collected

school-to-prison pipeline: a practice of disciplining and punishing children and youth in school that routes them out of education and into the criminal justice system

secondary deviance: further instances of deviance prompted by the receipt of the deviant label

second shift: the unpaid work of housekeeping and childcare that faces family members once they return home from their paid jobs

self-fulfilling prophecy: a phenomenon in which what people believe is true becomes true, even if it wasn't originally true

self-narrative: a story we tell about the origin and likely future of our selves

self-socialization: active efforts we make to ensure we're culturally competent members of our cultures

service and information economy: an economy centered on jobs in which workers provide services or work with information

sex: a reference to physical traits related to sexual reproduction

sexism: the production of unjust outcomes for people perceived to be biologically female

sexual minorities: people who are gay, lesbian, bisexual, or otherwise non-heterosexual

shared division of labor: an arrangement in which both partners do an equal share of paid and unpaid work

social capital: the number of people we know and the resources they can offer us

social change: shifts in our shared ideas, interactions, and institutions

social closure: a process by which advantaged groups preserve opportunities for themselves while restricting them for others

social construct: an influential and shared interpretation of reality that will vary across time and space

social construction: the process by which we layer objects with ideas, fold concepts into one another, and build connections between them

social construction of social problems: the process of coming to see a personal struggle as an issue of public concern

social disorganization theory: the idea that deviance is more common in dysfunctional neighborhoods

social facts: products of human interaction with persuasive or coercive power that exist externally to any individual

social identities: the socially constructed categories and subcategories of people in which we place ourselves or are placed by others

social identity theory: the idea that people are inclined to form social groups, incorporate group membership into their identity, take steps to enforce group boundaries, and maximize positive distinction and in-group success

social inequality: a condition in which wealth, power, and prestige are most readily available to people with privileged social identities

social institutions: widespread and enduring patterns of interaction with which we respond to categories of human need

social interaction: moments we share with other people

socialism: an economic system based on shared ownership of the resources used to create wealth that is then distributed by governments for the enrichment of all

socialization: the lifelong learning process by which we become members of our cultures

social media: social networks mediated by the internet

social mobility: opportunity to move up or down in the economic hierarchy

social movement: persistent, organized collective action meant to promote or oppose social change

social network analysis: a research method that involves the mapping of social ties and exchanges between them

social networks: webs of ties that link us to each other and, through other people's ties, to people to whom we're not directly linked

social organizations: formal entities that coordinate collections of people in achieving a stated purpose

social patterns: explainable and foreseeable similarities and differences among people influenced by the social conditions in which they live

social reproduction: the process by which society maintains an enduring character from generation to generation

social rules: culturally specific norms, policies, and laws that guide our behavior

social safety net: a patchwork of programs intended to ensure that the most economically vulnerable do not go without basic necessities like food, clothing, and shelter

social sanctions: reactions by others aimed at promoting conformity

social stratification: a persistent sorting of social groups into enduring hierarchies

social structure: the entire set of interlocking social institutions in which we live

social ties: the connections between us and other people

social work: a skilled profession aimed at helping people in need

sociological imagination: the capacity to consider how people's lives—including our own—are shaped by the social facts that surround us

sociological research methods: scientific strategies for collecting empirical data about social facts

sociological sympathy: the skill of understanding others as they understand themselves

sociological theory: empirically based explanations and predictions about relationships between social facts

sociology: the science of society

spatial analysis: a research method in which data are layered onto a landscape divided into fine-grained segments

specialized division of labor: an arrangement in which one partner does more paid work than childcare and housework, and the other does the inverse

spurious: a statistical relationship between two variables that appears because both correlate with a third variable

stalled revolution: a sweeping change in gender relations that started but has yet to be fully realized

standing: the authority to speak credibly on a particular topic

standpoints: points of view grounded in lived reality

status: high or low esteem

status beliefs: collectively shared ideas about which social groups are more or less deserving of esteem

status elite: people who carry many positively regarded social identities

stereotype: clusters of ideas attached by social convention to people with specific social identities

stigma: a personal attribute that is widely devalued by members of one's society

strain theory: the idea that deviance is caused by a tension between widely valued goals and people's ability to attain them

structural functionalism: the theory that society is a system of necessary, synchronized parts that work together to create social stability

structural position: the features of our lives that determine our mix of opportunities and constraints

structural violence: institutional discrimination that injures the body and mind

subcultures: subgroups within societies that have distinct cultural ideas, objects, practices, and bodies

survey: a research method that involves inviting individuals to complete a questionnaire designed to collect analyzable data

symbolic interactionism: the theory that social interaction depends on the social construction of reality

symbolic structure: a constellation of social constructs connected and opposed to one another in overlapping networks of meaning

T

taboos: social prohibitions so strong that the thought of violating them can be sickening

theory of mind: the recognition that other minds exist, followed by the realization that we can try to imagine others' mental states

time-use diary: a research method in which participants are asked to self-report their activities at regular intervals over at least twenty-four hours

tracking: the practice of placing students in different classrooms according to their perceived ability

transgender: people assigned male at birth who don't identify as men as well as people assigned female at birth who don't identify as women

transnational organizations: organizations that operate in more than one country

V

values: notions as to what's right and wrong

variable: any measurable phenomenon that varies

vulnerable populations: groups that are at high risk of being harmed if they are included as research subjects

W

wage: cash payments given to workers in exchange for their labor

wage gaps: differences between the hourly earnings of different social identity groups

wealth gaps: differences in the amount of money and economic assets owned by people from different social identity groups

welfare capitalism: a capitalist economic system with some socialist policy aimed at distributing the profits of capitalism more evenly across the population

White fight: organized White resistance to integration

White flight: a phenomenon in which White people start leaving a neighborhood when minority residents begin to move in

working poor: people in the labor force who earn poverty-level wages

world system: a global market organized by a capitalist economy

X

xenophobia: prejudice against people defined as foreign

ENDNOTES

INTRODUCTION

1. Yuval Noah Harari, "What Explains the Rise of Humans?," filmed June 2015 at TEDGlobal London, video, 17:00, https://www.ted.com/talks/yuval_noah_harari_what _explains_the_rise_of_humans?language=en.

2. Chris H. J. Hartgerink, Ilja van Beest, Jelte M. Wicherts, and Kipling D. Williams, "The Ordinal Effects of Ostracism: A Meta-Analysis of 120 Cyberball Studies," *PLOS ONE* 10, no. 5 (May 2015), https://doi.org/10.1371/journal .pone.0127002.

3. Fatos Kaba et al., "Solitary Confinement and Risk of Self-Harm among Jail Inmates," *American Journal of Public Health* 104, no. 3 (March 2014): 442–447.

4. Émile Durkheim, *The Rules of Sociological Method: And Selected Texts on Sociology and Its Methodology* (New York: Free Press, 2014 [1895]).

5. Yuval Noah Harari, *Sapiens: A Brief History of Humankind* (New York: HarperCollins, 2015).

6. Thomas Lecocq, Stephen P. Hicks, Koen Van Noten, Kasper van Wijk, et al., "Global Quieting of High-Frequency Seismic Noise Due to COVID-19 Pandemic Lockdown Measures," *Science* 369, no. 6509 (September 2020): 1338–1343.

7. Durkheim, *The Rules of Sociological Method*.

8. Harriet Martineau, *How to Observe Morals and Manners* (London: Charles Knight and Co., 1838).

9. W. E. B. Du Bois, *Black Reconstruction in America: An Essay Toward a History of the Part Which Black Folk Played in the Attempt to Reconstruct Democracy in America, 1860–1880* (New York: Harcourt, Brace, 1935).

10. As quoted on page 34 of Patricia Madoo Lengermann and Jill Niebrugge-Brantley, *The Women Founders: Sociology and Social Theory, 1830–1930* (Long Grove, IL: Waveland Press, 1998).

11. Patricia Hill Collins, *Black Feminist Thought* (New York: Routledge, 2000); Maxine Baca Zinn and Ruth Enid Zambrana, "Chicanas/Latinas Advance Intersectional Thought and Practice," *Gender & Society* 33, no. 5 (October 2019): 677–701; Martin Nakata, "An Indigenous Standpoint Theory," in *Disciplining the Savages: Savaging the Disciplines* (Canberra, A.C.T.: Aboriginal Studies Press, 2007): 213–217.

12. Maxine Baca Zinn and Bonnie Thornton Dill, "Theorizing Difference from Multiracial Feminism," *Feminist Studies* 22, no. 2 (1996): 328.

13. Martineau, *How to Observe Morals and Manners*, 27.

14. Ibid, 23.

15. Raewyn Connell, "In Praise of Sociology," *Canadian Review of Sociology* 54, no. 3 (August 2017): 283.

16. C. Wright Mills, *The Sociological Imagination* (New York: Oxford University Press, 1959).

CHAPTER I

1. Joshua M. Plotnik, Frans B. M. de Waal, and Diana Reiss, "Self-recognition in an Asian Elephant," *Proceedings of the National Academy of Sciences* 103 (November 2006): 17053–17057.

2. George H. Mead, *Mind, Self, and Society* (Chicago, IL: University of Chicago Press, 1934).

3. George H. Mead, "The Social Self," *The Journal of Philosophy, Psychology and Scientific Methods* 10 (1913): 374–380.

4. Marco Iacoboni, *Mirroring People: The Science of Empathy and How We Connect with Others* (New York: Picador, 2008).

5. Jillian M. Saffin and Hassaan Tohid, "Walk like Me, Talk like Me: The Connection Between Mirror Neurons and Autism Spectrum Disorder," *Neurosciences Journal* 21, no. 2 (2016): 108–119.

6. Michael J. Banissy, Roi Cohen Kadosh, Gerrit W. Maus, Vincent Walsh, and Jamie Ward, "Prevalence, Characteristics, and a Neurocognitive Model of Mirror-Touch Synaesthesia," *Experimental Brain Research* 198, no. 2 (2009): 261–272.

7. Alix Spiegel and Lulu Miller, interview with Geoff Brumfiel and Amanda, *Invisibilia*, NPR, January 30, 2015, podcast, 33:47, https://www.npr.org/2015/01/30/382453493 /mirror-touch.

8. Arthur Evans Wood, "Charles Horton Cooley: An Appreciation," *American Journal of Sociology* 35, no. 5 (1930): 707–717.

9. "Charles Horton Cooley," *American Sociological Association*, accessed January 21, 2017, http://www.asanet.org/about /presidents/Charles_Cooley.cfm; Edward Clarence Jandy, *Charles Horton Cooley: His Life and His Social Theory* (New York: Dryden Press, 1942).

10. Charles Horton Cooley, *Human Nature and the Social Order* (New York: Scribner's, 1902).

11. Richard B. Felson, "The (Somewhat) Social Self: How Others Affect Self-Appraisals," in *Psychological Perspectives on the Self*, vol. 4, ed. Jerry M. Suls (New York and London: Taylor and Francis, 2014), 1–26.

12. Morgan Johnstonbaugh, "Sexting with Friends: Gender, Technology, and the Evolution of Interaction Rituals," paper in progress.

13. J. Sidney Shrauger and Thomas J. Schoeneman, "Symbolic Interactionist View of Self-Concept: Through the Looking Glass Darkly," *Psychological Bulletin* 86, no. 3 (1979): 549–573.

14. Charles Horton Cooley, *Human Nature and the Social Order*.

15. Ibid.

16. Michael Finkel, "The Strange and Curious Tale of the Last True Hermit," *GQ*, August 4, 2014.

17. Ibid.

18. Thomas J. Scheff, "Looking-Glass Self: Goffman as Symbolic Interactionist," *Symbolic Interaction* 28, no. 2 (2005): 147–166.

19. John C. Turner, *Social Influence* (Milton Keynes: Open University Press, 1991).

20. Robert K. Merton, "The Self-Fulfilling Prophecy," *Antioch Review* 8, no. 2 (1948): 193–210.

21. S. Craig Roberts, A. C. Little, A. Lyndon, J. Roberts, J. Havlicek, and R. L. Wright, "Manipulation of Body Odour Alters Men's Self-Confidence and Judgements of Their Visual Attractiveness by Women," *International Journal of Cosmetic Science* 31 (2009): 47–54, http://www.scraigroberts.com/uploads/1/5/0/4/15042548/2009_ijcs.pdf.

22. Bradley Wright, "Cologne and Self-Fulfilling Prophesies," *Everyday Sociology Blog*, W. W. Norton, January 15, 2009, https://www.everydaysociologyblog.com/2009/01/cologne-and-self-fulfilling-prophesies.html.

23. William B. Swann Jr., Brett W. Pelham, and Douglas S. Krull, "Agreeable Fancy or Disagreeable Truth? How People Reconcile Their Self-enhancement and Self-verification Needs," *Journal of Personality and Social Psychology* 57, no. 5 (1989): 782–791.

24. William B. Swann Jr. and Brett W. Pelham, "Who Wants Out When the Going Gets Good? Psychological Investment and Preference for Self-verifying College Roommates," *Self and Identity* 1 (2002): 219–233.

25. David Stuart MacLean, *The Answer to the Riddle Is Me: A Memoir of Amnesia* (New York: Houghton Mifflin Harcourt, 2014).

26. Ibid.

27. Martin Conway and C.W. Pleydell-Pearce, "The Construction of Autobiographical Memories in the Self-Memory System," *Psychological Review* 107, no. 2 (2000): 261–288; Matthew D. Grilli and Mieke Verfaellie, "Supporting the Self-Concept with Memory: Insight from Amnesia," *Social Cognitive and Affective Neuroscience* 10, no. 12 (2015): 1684–1692.

28. Dan P. McAdams, *The Redemptive Self: Stories Americans Live By* (New York: Oxford University Press, 2013).

29. Kenneth J. Gergen and Mary M. Gergen, "Narrative and the Self as Relationship," *Advances in Experimental Social Psychology* 21 (1988): 17–56.

30. Elizabeth J. Marsh, "Retelling Is Not the Same as Recalling: Implications for Memory," *Current Directions in Psychological Science* 16, no. 1 (2007): 16–20.

31. Christian A. Meissner and John C. Brigham, "A Meta-Analysis of the Verbal Overshadowing Effect in Face Identification," *Applied Cognitive Psychology* 15, no. 6 (2001): 603–616.

32. Kathryn A. Braun, Rhiannon Ellis, and Elizabeth F. Loftus, "Make My Memory: How Advertising Can Change Our Memories of the Past," *Psychology & Marketing* 19, no. 1 (January 2002): 1–23, https://staff.washington.edu/eloftus/Articles/BraunPsychMarket02.pdf.

33. Hazel Markus and Paula Nurius, "Possible Selves," *American Psychologist* 41 (1986): 954–969.

34. Sheila K. Marshall, Richard A. Young, José F. Domene, and Anat Zaidman-Zait, "Adolescent Possible Selves as Jointly Constructed in Parent-Adolescent Career Conversations and Related Activities," *Identity* 8 (2008): 185–204.

CHAPTER 2

1. Nix v. Hedden, 149 U.S. 304 (1893).

2. Peter L. Berger and Thomas Luckmann, *The Social Construction of Reality: A Treatise in the Sociology of Knowledge* (New York: Doubleday, 1966).

3. Eviatar Zerubavel, "Lumping and Splitting: Notes on Social Classification," *Sociological Forum* 11, no. 3 (1996): 421–433.

4. Lisa Stiffler, "Understanding Orca Culture," *Smithsonian Magazine*, August 2011, https://www.smithsonianmag.com/science-nature/understanding-orca-culture-12494696/.

5. Karl Mannheim, *Ideology and Utopia: Collected Works Volume One* (New York: Routledge, 1936). Edited for inclusivity, p. 3.

6. Robert A. Paul, *Mixed Messages: Cultural and Genetic Inheritance in the Constitution of Human Society* (Chicago: Chicago University Press, 2015).

7. Richard Wrangham, *Catching Fire: How Cooking Made Us Human* (New York: Basic Books, 2009).

8. Peter J. Keane, Robert H. Booth, and Nilda Beltran, *Appropriate Technique Development and Manufacture of Low-Cost Potato-Based Food Products in Developing Countries*, International Potato Center, 1986; Stephan Guyenet, "Potatoes and Human Health, Part III," *Whole Health Source*, October 2, 2010, http://wholehealthsource.blogspot.com/2010/10/potatoes-and-human-health-part-iii.html.

9. "What the World Eats," *National Geographic*, http://www.nationalgeographic.com/what-the-world-eats/; "Gateway to Dairy Production and Products," Food and Agriculture Organization of the United Nations, http://www.fao.org/agriculture/dairy-gateway/milk-production/dairy-animals/camels/en/#.V5FHbvkrKM8.

10. Patricia Gadsby and Leon Steele, "The Inuit Paradox," *Discover*, January 19, 2004, http://discovermagazine.com/2004/oct/inuit-paradox.

11. Nicholas A. Christakis and James H. Fowler, *Connected: The Surprising Power of Our Social Networks and How They Shape Our Lives* (New York: Little, Brown, 2009).

12. Aaron Smith, "What People Like and Dislike about Facebook," Pew Research Center, February 3, 2014, http://www.pewresearch.org/fact-tank/2014/02/03/6-new-facts-about-facebook/.

13. Kyle Puetz, "Consumer Culture, Taste Preferences, and Social Network Formation," *Sociology Compass* 9, issue 6 (2015): 438–449, https://doi.org/10.1111/soc4.12265.

14. Noah E. Friedkin and Karen S. Cook, "Peer Group Influence," *Sociological Methods & Research* 19, no. 1 (1990): 122–143; Robert B. Cialdini and Melanie R. Trost, "Social Influence: Social Norms, Conformity and Compliance" in *The Handbook of Social Psychology*, 4th ed., eds. Daniel Todd Gilbert, Susan T. Fiske, and Gardner Lindzey (Boston: McGraw-Hill, 1998), 151–192.

15. Sinan Aral and Christos Nicolaides, "Exercise Contagion in a Global Social Network," *Nature Communications* 8 (2017), https://doi.org/10.1038/ncomms14753.

16. Christakis and Fowler, *Connected*.

17. David W. Nickerson, "Is Voting Contagious? Evidence from Two Field Experiments," *American Political Science Review* 102, no. 1 (February 2008): 49–57, https://doi.org/10.1017/S0003055408080039.

18. Christakis and Fowler, *Connected*, 30.

19. Claude S. Fischer and Greggor Mattson, "Is America Fragmenting?" *Annual Review of Sociology* 35 (2009): 435–455, https://doi.org/10.1146/annurev-soc-070308-115909.

20. Christakis and Fowler, *Connected*.

21. *The Wolfpack*, directed by Crystal Moselle (New York: Magnolia Pictures, Kotva Films, and Verisimilitude, 2015).

22. Mukunda Angulo, "How My Imagination Set Me Free," video, 16:27, YouTube, posted by TEDx Talks, January 28, 2016, https://www.youtube.com/watch?v+ECCQ7DyA5M0.

23. Gail Deutsch and Alexa Valiente, "How 'The Wolfpack' Brothers Changed after Spending Years Locked in NYC Apartment," *ABC News*, June 17, 2015, https://abcnews.go.com/Entertainment/wolfpack-brothers-changed-spending-years-locked-nyc-apartment/story?id+31807232.

24. Angulo, "Imagination."

25. Jesse Fox and Rachel Ralston, "Queer Identity Online: Informal Learning and Teaching Experiences of LGBTQ Individuals on Social Media," *Computers in Human Behavior* 65 (December 2016): 635–642, https://doi.org/10.1016/j.chb.2016.06.009.

26. Pierre Bourdieu, *The Logic of Practice* (Stanford, CA: Stanford University Press, 1990 [1980]).

27. Anne Fausto-Sterling, "The Bare Bones of Sex: Part I—Sex and Gender," *Signs* 30, no. 2 (2005): 1491–1527.

28. Rebecca M. Jordan-Young and Katrina Karkazis, *Testosterone: An Unauthorized Biography* (Cambridge, MA: Harvard University Press, 2019).

29. Chloe Grace Hart, Aliya Saperstein, Devon Magliozzi, and Laurel Westbrook, "Gender and Health: Beyond Binary Categorical Measurement," *Journal of Health and Social Behavior* 60, no. 1 (January 30, 2019): 101–118, https://doi.org/10.1177/0022146519825749; Brennan J. Miller, Will Kalhoff, Joshua Pollock, and Matthew A. Pfeiffer, "Persistent Identity Threats: Emotional and Neurological Responses," *Social Psychology Quarterly* 82, no. 1 (March 14, 2019): 98–111, https://doi.org/10.1177/0190272518812081; Michael J. McFarland, John Taylor, Cheryl A. S. McFarland, and Katherine L. Friedman, "Perceived Unfair Treatment by Police, Race, and Telomere Length: A Nashville Community-Based Sample of Black and White Men," *Journal of Health and Social Behavior* 59, no. 4 (November 12, 2018): 585–600, https://doi.org/10.1177/0022146518811144; Ronald L. Simons et al., "Testing Life Course Models Whereby Juvenile and Adult Adversity Combine to Influence Speed of Biological Aging," *Journal of Health and Social Behavior* 60, no. 3 (August 14, 2019): 291–308, https://doi.org/10.1177/0022146519859896.

30. Marcus E. Pembrey et al., "Sex-Specific, Male-Line Transgenerational Responses in Humans," *European Journal of Human Genetics* 14 (2006): 159–66.

31. Christina Capecchi and Katie Rogers, "Killer of Cecil the Lion Finds Out That He Is a Target Now, of Internet Vigilantism," *New York Times*, July 29, 2015, http://www.nytimes.com/2015/07/30/us/cecil-the-lion-walter-palmer.html.

32. Desmond Kwande and Alexander Smith, "Cecil the Lion: Zimbabwe Safari Operator Says Animal Was 'Murdered'," *NBC News*, August 5, 2015, http://www.nbcnews.com/news/world/cecil-lion-zimbabwe-safari-operator-says-animal-was-murdered-n404336.

33. *Jimmy Kimmel Live!*, directed by Andy Fisher, featuring Jimmy Kimmel, aired July 29, 2015, on ABC.

34. Paul Walsh and Brandon Stahl, "U.S. Agencies Step Up in Case of Twin Cities Dentist Who Killed Cecil the Lion," *StarTribune*, July 30, 2015, http://www.startribune.com/police-poised-for-protest-at-shuttered-dentist-office-of-twin-cities-hunter-who-killed-lion/319428081/.

35. Clifford Geertz, *The Interpretation of Cultures* (New York: Basic Books, 1973).

36. Ann Swidler, "Culture in Action: Symbols and Strategies," *American Sociological Review* 51, no. 2 (April 1986): 273–286, https://doi.org/10.2307/2095521.

37. Stephen Vaisey, "Motivation and Justification: A Dual-Process Model of Culture in Action," *American Journal of Sociology* 114, no. 6 (May 2009): 1675–1715, https://doi.org/10.1086/597179.

38. Swidler, "Culture," 273–286.

CHAPTER 3

1. Francis J. Bremer and Tom Webster, eds., *Puritans and Puritanism in Europe and America: A Comprehensive Encyclopedia*, vol. 2 (Santa Barbara, CA: ABC-CLIO, 2006).

2. Henri Tajfel, *Human Groups and Social Categories: Studies in Social Psychology* (Cambridge: Cambridge University Press, 1981); Peggy A. Thoits and Lauren K. Virshup, Me's and We's: Forms and Functions of Social Identities, in *Self and Identity: Fundamental Issues*, eds. R. D. Ashmore and L. Jussim (New York: Oxford University Press, 1997).

3. Henri Tajfel, ed., *Differentiation between Social Groups: Studies in the Social Psychology of Intergroup Relations* (London: Academic Press, 1978).

4. Henri Tajfel, M. G. Billig, R. P. Bundy, and Claude Flament, "Social Categorization and Intergroup Behaviour," *European Journal of Social Psychology* 1, no. 2 (1971): 149–178, https://doi.org/10.1002/EJSP.2420030103.

5. Miles Hewstone, Mark Rubin, and Hazel Willis, "Intergroup Bias," *Annual Review of Psychology* 53 (2002): 575–604, https://doi.org/10.1146/annurev.psych.53.100901.135109.

6. Joan Roughgarden, *Evolution's Rainbow: Diversity, Gender, and Sexuality in Nature and People* (Oakland, CA: University of California Press, 2009).

7. George Chauncey, *Gay New York: Gender, Urban Culture, and the Making of the Gay Male World: 1890–1940* (New York: Basic Books, 1994); John D'Emilio and Estelle B. Freedman, *Intimate Matters: A History of Sexuality in America* (New York: Harper & Row, 1988); Joy Hakim, *War, Peace, and All*

That Jazz: 1918–1945 (New York: Oxford University Press, 1995).

8. John D'Emilio, "Capitalism and Gay Identity," in *The Lesbian and Gay Studies Reader*, eds. Henry Abelove, Michèle Aina Barale, and David Halperin (New York: Routledge, 1993): 467–476.

9. Stephanie Coontz, *The Way We Never Were: American Families and the Nostalgia Trap* (New York: Basic Books, 1992).

10. United States Selective Service System, *Selective Service and Victory* (Washington, DC: Government Printing Office, 1948): 91.

11. D'Emilio and Freedman, *Intimate Matters*.

12. American Association of Physical Anthropologists, "AAPA Statement on Biological Aspects of Race," *American Journal of Physical Anthropology* 101 (1996): 569–570.

13. Ryan A. Brown and George J. Armelagos, "Apportionment of Racial Diversity: A Review," *Evolutionary Anthropology* 10 (2001): 34–40, https://doi.org/10.1002/1520-6505 (2001)10:13.0.CO;2-P; Richard C. Lewontin, "Confusions about Human Races," *Race and Genomics*, June 7, 2006, http://raceandgenomics.ssrc.org/Lewontin/.

14. Felicia Gomez, Jibril Hirbo, and Sarah A. Tishkoff, "Genetic Variation and Adaptation in Africa: Implications for Human Evolution and Disease," *Cold Spring Harbor Perspectives in Biology* (2014): 1–21, https://doi.org/10.1101/cshperspect .a008524.

15. Ning Yu et al., "Larger Genetic Differences within Africans Than Between Africans and Eurasians," *GENETICS* 161, no. 1 (2002): 269–274, https://www.genetics.org /content/161/1/269.

16. Michael Omi and Howard Winant, *Racial Formation in the United States* (New York: Routledge, 1994).

17. Nell Irvin Painter, *The History of White People* (New York: W. W. Norton, 2010).

18. Lerone Bennett Jr., *The Shaping of Black America* (Chicago: Johnson Publishing, 1975); Edmund S. Morgan, *American Slavery, American Freedom* (New York: W. W. Norton, 1975).

19. William J. Cooper Jr., *Liberty and Slavery: Southern Politics to 1860* (Columbia, SC: University of South Carolina Press, 2001).

20. W. E. B. Du Bois, *Black Reconstruction in America* (Oxford: Oxford University Press, 2014).

21. Ian Haney López, *White by Law* (New York: New York University Press, 1996).

22. Associated Press, "Slave Descendant Fights Race Listing," *New York Times*, September 15, 1982.

23. Art Harris, "Louisiana Court Sees No Shades of Gray in Woman's Request," *Washington Post*, May 21, 1983, https://www.washingtonpost.com/archive/politics /1983/05/21/louisiana-court-sees-no-shades-of-gray -in-womans-request/ddb0f1df-ba5d-4141-9aa0 -6347e60ce52d/.

24. Paul Spruhan, "A Legal History of Blood Quantum in Federal Indian Law to 1935," *South Dakota Law Review* 51, no. 1 (2006), https://papers.ssrn.com/sol3/papers .cfm?abstract_id+955032.

25. Walter Lippmann, *Public Opinion* (San Diego: Harcourt, Brace, 1922).

26. Elizabeth L. Haines, Kay Deaux, and Nicole Lofaro, "The Times They Are a-Changing . . . or Are They Not? A Comparison of Gender Stereotypes, 1983–2014," *Psychology of Women Quarterly* 40, no. 3 (2016): 353–363, https://doi.org/10.1177/0361684316634081.

27. Carol J. Auster and Claire S. Mansbach, "The Gender Marketing of Toys: An Analysis of Color and Type of Toy on the Disney Store Website," *Sex Roles* 67 (2012): 375–388, https://doi.org/10.1007/s11199-012-0177-8.

28. Ethan Zell, Zlatan Krizan, and Sabrina R. Teeter, "Evaluating Gender Similarities and Differences Using Metasynthesis," *American Psychologist* 70, no. 1 (2015): 10–20, https://doi .org/10.1037/a0038208.

29. Cheryl Laz, "Act Your Age," *Sociological Forum* 13 (1998): 85, https://doi.org/10.1023/A:1022160015408.

30. Ibid.

31. Ellie Krupnick, "Chinese Grandfather, Liu Xianping, Models Women's Clothing for Granddaughter's Boutique, Yuekou," *Huffington Post*, November 20, 2012, https://www .huffingtonpost.com/2012/11/20/chinese-grandfather-liu -xianping-models-womens-clothing_n_2164197.html.

32. Peter N. Stearns, *Fat History: Bodies and Beauty in the Modern West* (New York: New York University Press, 1997).

33. Amy Erdman Farrell, *Fat Shame: Stigma and the Fat Body in American Culture* (New York: New York University Press, 2011).

34. Stearns, *Fat History*.

35. Giovanni Federico, "The Growth of World Agricultural Production, 1800–1938," *Research in Economic History* 22 (2004): 125–181, https://doi.org/10.1016/S0363 -3268(04)22003-1.

36. Thorstein Veblen, *The Theory of the Leisure Class* (New York: Macmillan 1899).

37. Harvey A. Levenstein, *Paradox of Plenty: A Social History of Eating in Modern America* (New York: Oxford University Press, 1993).

38. Farrell, *Fat Shame*.

39. Katherine M. Flegal, Brian K. Kit, Heather Orpana, and Barry I. Graubard, "Association of All-Cause Mortality with Overweight and Obesity Using Standard Body Mass Index Categories: A Systematic Review and Meta-analysis," *Journal of the American Medical Association* 309, no. 1 (2013): 71–82, https://doi.org/10.1001/jama.2012.113905; Abigail C. Saguy, *What's Wrong with Fat?* (New York: Oxford University Press, 2013).

40. Patricia Hill Collins, *Black Feminist Thought: Knowledge, Consciousness, and the Politics of Empowerment* (New York: Routledge, 2008): 69.

41. Marlene B. Schwartz, Lenny R. Vartanian, Brian A. Nosek, and Kelly D. Brownell, "The Influence of One's Own Body Weight on Implicit and Explicit Anti-fat Bias," *Obesity* 14, no. 3 (2006): 440–447, https://doi.org/10.1038/oby.2006.58.

42. Rheanna N. Ata and J. Kevin Thompson, "Weight Bias in the Media: A Review of Recent Research," *Obesity Facts* 3, no. 1 (2010): 41–46; Rebecca M. Puhl and Chelsea A. Heuer, "The Stigma of Obesity: A Review and Update,"

Obesity 17, no. 5 (2009): 941–964, https://doi.org/10.1038/oby.2008.636.

43. Shelley J. Correll and Kathryne M. Young, "Meet the 2013 ASA President: Cecilia Ridgeway," *American Sociological Association*, http://www.asanet.org/cecilia-ridgeway.

44. Cheryl Staats, "State of the Science: Implicit Bias Review 2014," Kirwan Institute for the Study of Race and Ethnicity, http://kirwaninstitute.osu.edu/wp-content/uploads/2014/03/2014-implicit-bias.pdf.

45. Wilhelm Hofmann et al., "A Meta-Analysis on the Correlation between the Implicit Association Test and Explicit Self-Report Measures," *Personality and Social Psychology Bulletin* 31, no. 10 (2005): 1369–1385, https://doi.org/10.1177/0146167205275613.

46. Harvard University, "Project Implicit," accessed November 10, 2020, https://implicit.harvard.edu/implicit; Schwartz, Vartanian, Nosek, and Brownell, "Body Weight and Anti-Fat Bias," 440–447.

47. William J. Hall et al., "Implicit Racial/Ethnic Bias among Health Care Professionals and Its Influence on Health Care Outcomes: A Systematic Review," *American Journal of Public Health* 105, no. 12 (2015): 60–76, https://doi.org/10.2105/AJPH.2015.302903; Janice A. Sabin, Rachel G. Riskind, and Brian A. Nosek, "Health Care Providers' Implicit and Explicit Attitudes Toward Lesbian Women and Gay Men," *American Journal of Public Health* 105, no. 9 (2015): 1831–1841, https://doi.org/10.2105/AJPH.2015.302631; Elizabeth R. Peterson, Christine M. Rubie-Davies, Danny Osborne, and Chris G. Sibley, "Teachers' Explicit Expectations and Implicit Prejudiced Attitudes to Educational Achievement: Relations with Student Achievement and the Ethnic Achievement Gap," *Learning and Instruction* 42 (2016): 123–140, https://doi.org/10.1016/j.learninstruc.2016.01.010; Penny Edgell, Douglas Hartmann, Evan Stewart, and Joseph Gerteis, "Atheists and Other Cultural Outsiders: Moral Boundaries and the Non-Religious in the United States," *Social Forces* 95, no. 2 (2016): 607–638, https://doi.org/10.1093/sf/sow063; James E. Driskell and Brian Mullen, "Status, Expectations, and Behavior: A Meta-Analytic Review and Test of the Theory," *Personal and Social Psychology Bulletin* 16, no. 3 (1990): 541–553, https://doi.org/10.1177/0146167290163012; Will Kalkhoff and Shane R. Thye, "Expectation States Theory and Research: New Observations From Meta-Analysis," *Sociological Methods & Research* 35, no. 2 (2006): 219–249, https://doi.org/10.1177/0049124106290311; Cecilia L. Ridgeway, "Understanding the Nature of Status Inequality: Why Is It Everywhere? Why Does It Matter?" Mayhew Lecture, University of South Carolina (2018): 1–24; Amy J. Cuddy, Susan T. Fiske, and Peter Glick, "The BIAS Map: Behaviors from Intergroup Affect and Stereotypes," *Journal of Personality and Social Psychology* 92, no. 4 (2007): 631–648, https://doi.org/10.1037/0022-3514.92.4.631; Susan T. Fiske, Amy J. Cuddy, Peter Glick, and Jun Xu, "A Model of (Often Mixed) Stereotype Content: Competence and Warmth Respectively Follow from Perceived Status and Competition," *Journal of Personality and Social Psychology* 82, no. 6 (2002): 878–902, https://doi.org/10.1037/0022-3514.82.6.878; Schwartz, Vartanian, Nosek, and Brownell, "Body Weight and Anti-Fat Bias,"

440–447; Brian A. Nosek et al., "Pervasiveness and Correlates of Implicit Attitudes and Stereotypes," *European Review of Social Psychology* 18, no. 1 (2007): 1–53, https://doi.org/10.1080/10463280701489053; Laurie A. Rudman, Joshua Feinberg, and Kimberly Fairchild, "Minority Members' Implicit Attitudes: Automatic Ingroup Bias as a Function of Group Status," *Social Cognition* 20, no. 4 (2002): 294–320, https://doi.org/10.1521/soco.20.4.294.19908; Tiffani "Tie" S. Wang-Jones et al., "Development of Gender Identity Implicit Association Tests to Assess Attitudes Toward Transmen and Transwomen," *Psychology of Sexual Orientation and Gender Diversity* 4, no. 2 (2017): 169–183, https://doi.org/10.1037/sgd0000218; Rudman, Feinberg, and Fairchild, "Minority Members' Implicit Attitudes"; William A. Cunningham, John B. Nezlek, and Mahzarin R. Banaji, "Implicit and Explicit Ethnocentrism: Revisiting the Ideologies of Prejudice," *Personality and Social Psychology Bulletin* 30, no. 10 (2004): 1332–1346, https://doi.org/10.1177/0146167204264654.

48. Patricia Madoo Lengermann and Gillian Niebrugge, *The Women Founders: Sociology and Social Theory 1830–1930* (Long Grove, IL: Waveland Press, 2006).

49. Rachel A. Feinstein, *When Rape Was Legal: The Untold History of Sexual Violence during Slavery* (New York: Routledge, 2018).

50. Archives of the Episcopal Church, "The Church Awakens: African Americans and the Struggle for Justice" (online exhibit), "Anna Julia Haywood Cooper, 1858–1964," accessed November 10, 2020, https://episcopalarchives.org/church-awakens/exhibits/show/leadership/lay/cooper.

51. Episcopal Archives, "Anna Julia Hayward Cooper."

52. Anna J. Cooper, *A Voice From the South* (Xenia, OH: The Aldine Printing Company, 1892).

53. Kimberlé Crenshaw, "Mapping the Margins: Intersectionality, Identity Politics, and Violence against Women of Color," *Stanford Law Review* 43, no. 6 (1991): 1241–1299, https://doi.org/10.2307/1229039; Gloria Anzaldúa, *Borderlands/La Frontera: The New Mestiza* (San Francisco: Aunt Lute Books, 1987); Patricia Hill Collins, *Black Feminist Thought: Knowledge, Consciousness, and the Politics of Empowerment* (New York: Routledge, 1991); Angela Y. Davis, *Women, Race and Class* (New York: Random House, 1983); Trinh T. Minh-ha, *Woman, Native, Other: Writing Postcoloniality and Feminism* (Bloomington, IN: Indiana University Press, 1989); Cherríe Moraga and Gloria Anzaldúa, eds., *This Bridge Called My Back: Writings by Radical Women of Color* (New York: Kitchen Table, 1981).

54. Kimberlé Crenshaw, "Demarginalizing the Intersection of Race and Sex: A Black Feminist Critique of Antidiscrimination Doctrine, Feminist Theory and Antiracist Politics," *University of Chicago Legal Forum* 1, no. 8 (1989): 139–167, https://philpapers.org/archive/CREDTI.pdf.

55. R. Noam Ostrander, "When Identities Collide: Masculinity, Disability, and Race," *Disability & Society* 23, no. 6 (2008): 585–597, https://doi.org/10.1080/09687590802328451.

56. Tom Shakespeare, Kath Gillespie-Sells, and Dominic Davies, *The Sexual Politics of Disability: Untold Desires*. (London: Cassell, 1996).

57. Fem Korsten, "Grappling with My Sexuality Now That I'm in a Wheelchair," 2012, on the xoJane UK website, accessed January 29, 2017, http://www.xojane.co.uk/issues /disability-sexuality-street-harassment (site discontinued).

58. Shakespeare, Gillespie-Sells, and Davies, *Sexual Politics of Disability.*

59. Andrew Gurza, "Opening the Door to the Deliciously Disabled: The Importance of Having Accessibility in Sexual Spaces," updated February 2, 2016, http://www .huffingtonpost.com/andrew-morrisongurza/opening-the -door-to-the-d_1_b_6868040.html.

60. All Dolled Down, "The Intersectionality of Thin Privilege and Disability," Tumblr, 2012, http://alldolleddown.tumblr .com/post/27362249503/the-intersectionality-of-thin -privilege-and-disability.

61. Kali, "About," *Brilliant Mind Broken Body* (blog), 2009, accessed January 29, 2017, https://brilliantmindbrokenbody .wordpress.com/about/.

62. Abigail C. Saguy, "Why Fat Is a Feminist Issue," *Sex Roles* 68, no. 9 (2012): 600–607, https://doi.org/10.1007 /s11199-011-0084-4.

63. S. Bear Bergman, "About," on S. Bear Bergman's website, accessed November 10, 2020, http://www.sbearbergman .com/about/.

64. S. Bear Bergman, "Part-Time Fatso," in *The Fat Studies Reader*, eds. Esther Rothblum and Sondra Solovay (New York: New York University Press, 2009), 139–142.

65. Janna Fikkan and Esther D. Rothblum, "Is Fat a Feminist Issue? Exploring the Gendered Nature of Weight Bias," *Sex Roles* 66, no. 9 (2012): 575–592, https://doi.org/10.1007 /s11199-011-0022-5; Saguy, "Why Fat Is a Feminist Issue," 600–607.

66. Cara Liebowitz, "At the Intersection of White Privilege and Disability," *The Body Is Not an Apology*, 2015, https://thebodyisnotanapology.com/magazine/at-the -intersection-of-White-privilege-and-disability/.

67. Ibid.

68. Nico Tortorella and Bethany C. Meyers, "Inside Nico Tortorella and Bethany Meyers' Private, Epic Wedding," *Them*, March 17, 2018, https://www.them.us/story /inside-nico-tortorella-and-bethany-meyers-private -epic-wedding.

CHAPTER 4

1. Nathan Palmer, "Doing Nothing," March 2, 2011, YouTube video, 4:54, https://www.youtube.com /watch?v=kgso3Y-l0h8.

2. Erving Goffman, *Behavior in Public Places* (New York: Free Press, 2008 [1963]).

3. John Maxwell Atkinson and John Heritage, eds., *Structures of Social Action: Studies in Conversation Analysis* (Cambridge, MA: Cambridge University Press, 1985).

4. Atkinson and Heritage, *Structures of Social Action*, 419.

5. Séverin Lemaignan, Mathieu Warnier, E. Akin Sisbot, Rachid Alami, "Human-Robot Interaction: Tackling the AI Challenges," *Artificial Intelligence* (2014).

6. Erin Deann Martin, "Tweens, Sexualization, and Cyborg-Subjectivity: New Zealand Girls Negotiate Friendship and Identity on Facebook" (master's thesis, University of Canterbury, Department of Sociology and Anthropology, 2014).

7. "Status Update," *This American Life*, WBEZ and PRX, November 27, 2015, https://www.thisamericanlife.org /573/status-update.

8. "Status Update."

9. William Graham Sumner, *Folkways: A Study of the Sociological Importance of Usages, Manners, Customs, Mores, and Morals*, ed. Albert Galloway Keller (New York: Cosimo Classics, 2007 [1906]).

10. Mallika Rao, "About That Period That Broke the Internet," *Huffington Post*, May 6, 2015, https://www.huffpost.com /entry/rupi-kaur-instagram-period-photo-series_n_7213662.

11. Marvin B. Scott and Stanford M. Lyman, "Accounts," *American Sociological Review* 33, no. 1 (1968): 46–62, https://doi.org/10.2307/2092239.

12. "Herbert Blumer, Sociology: Berkeley," Calisphere, University of California, 1987, accessed November 16, 2020, http://texts.cdlib.org/view?docId=hb6z09p0jh&doc .view=frames&chunk.id=div00005&toc.depth=1&toc.id=.

13. Herbert Blumer, *Symbolic Interactionism: Perspective and Method* (Berkeley: University of California Press, 1986).

14. Jimmy Kimmel Live, "YouTube Challenge—I Gave My Kids a Terrible Present," December 12, 2011, YouTube video, 5:09, https://www.youtube.com/watch?v=q4a9CKgLprQ.

15. Alix Spiegel, "Flip the Script," *Invisibilia*, NPR, July 15, 2016, https://www.npr.org/programs/invisibilia/485603559 /flip-the-script.

16. Michael Delaney, "Erving Goffman's Early Years: Recollections of Family and Friends," *Erving Goffman Archives*, accessed November 16, 2020, http://cdclv.unlv.edu/ega/articles /delaney_eg_early-bio_07_11.pdf; Dmitri N. Shalin, "Interfacing Biography, Theory and History: The Case of Erving Goffman," *Symbolic Interaction* 37, no. 1 (2013): 2–40.

17. Erving Goffman, *The Presentation of Self in Everyday Life* (New York: Doubleday, 1956).

18. Ibid.

19. Erving Goffman, "On Face-Work: An Analysis of Ritual Elements in Social Interaction," *Psychiatry* 18, no. 3 (1955): 213–231, https://doi.org/10.1080/00332747 .1955.11023008.

20. David I. Miller, Kyle M. Nolla, Alice H. Eagly, and David H. Uttal, "The Development of Children's Gender-Science Stereotypes: A Meta-Analysis of 5 Decades of U.S. Draw-A-Scientist Studies," *Child Development* 89, no. 6 (2018): 1943–1955, https://doi.org/10.1111/cdev.13039.

21. Joan C. Williams, Katherine W. Phillips, and Erika V. Hall, "Tools for Change: Boosting the Retention of Women in the STEM Pipeline," *Journal of Research in Gender Studies* 6, no. 1 (2016): 11–75.

22. Devah Pager and Hana Shepherd, "The Sociology of Discrimination: Racial Discrimination in Employment, Housing, Credit, and Consumer Markets," *Annual Review of Sociology* 34 (2008): 181–209, https://doi.org/10.1146 /annurev.soc.33.040406.131740.

23. Sean Darling-Hammond S, Eli K. Michaels, and Amani M. Allen et al., "After 'The China Virus' Went Viral: Racially Charged Coronavirus Coverage and

Trends in Bias Against Asian Americans," *Health Education & Behavior* 47, no. 6 (2020): 870–879, https://doi.org/10.1177/1090198120957949.

24. Melissa Borja et al., "Anti-Chinese Rhetoric Tied to Racism against Asian Americans Stop AAPI Hate Report," Chinese for Affirmative Action and Asian Pacific Policy and Planning Council, June 17, 2020, http://www.asianpacificpolicyandplanningcouncil.org/wp-content/uploads/Anti-China_Rhetoric_Report_6_17_20.pdf.sss.

25. Mason Ameri et al., "The Disability Employment Puzzle: A Field Experiment on Employer Hiring Behavior," *ILR Review* 71, no. 2 (2018): 329–364, https://doi.org/10.1177/0019793917717474.

26. Michael Ewens, Bryan Tomlin, and Liang Choon Wang, "Statistical Discrimination or Prejudice? A Large Sample Field Experiment," *Review of Economics and Statistics* 96, no. 1 (2014): 119–134, https://doi.org/10.1162/REST_a_00365; Shelley J. Correll, Stephen Benard, and In Paik, "Getting a Job: Is There a Motherhood Penalty?" *American Journal of Sociology* 112, no. 5 (2007): 1297–1339, https://doi.org/10.1086/511799; Katrin Auspurg, Andreas Schneck, and Thomas Hinz, "Closed Doors Everywhere? A Meta-Analysis of Field Experiments on Ethnic Discrimination in Rental Housing Markets," *Journal of Ethnic and Migration Studies* 45, no. 1 (2018): 95–114, https://doi.org/10.1080/1369183X.2018.1489223; Lincoln Quillian, Devah Pager, Ole Hexel, and Arnfinn H. Midtbøen, "Meta-Analysis of Field Experiments Shows No Change in Racial Discrimination in Hiring over Time," *Proceedings of the National Academy of Sciences* 114, no. 41 (2017): 10870–10875, https://doi.org/10.1073/pnas.1706255114; Emma Mishel, "Discrimination against Queer Women in the U.S. Workforce: A Résumé Audit Study," *Socius: Sociological Research for a Dynamic World* (2016): 1–13, https://doi.org/10.1177/2378023115621316; Hua Sun and Lei Gao, "Lending Practices to Same-Sex Borrowers," *Proceedings of the National Academic of Sciences* 116, no. 19 (2019): 9293–9302, https://doi.org/10.1073/pnas.1903592116; Michael Wallace, Bradley R. E. Wright, and Allen Hyde, "Religious Affiliation and Hiring Discrimination in the American South: A Field Experiment," *Social Currents* 1, no. 2 (2014): 189–207, https://doi.org/10.1177/2329496514524541; Kyla Thomas, "The Labor Market Value of Taste: An Experimental Study of Class Bias in U.S. Employment," *Sociological Science* 5, no. 24 (2018): 562–595, https://doi.org/10.15195/v5.a24; Lisa Rice and Erich Schwartz Jr., "Discrimination When Buying a Car: How the Color of Your Skin Can Affect Your Car-Shopping Experience," National Fair Housing Alliance, 2018, https://nationalfairhousing.org/wp-content/uploads/2018/01/Discrimination-When-Buying-a-Car-FINAL-1-11-2018.pdf; Mason Ameri et al., "The Disability Employment Puzzle"; Margery Austin Turner et al., "Housing Discrimination against Racial and Ethnic Minorities 2012: Executive Summary," U.S. Department of Housing and Urban Development, 2013, https://www.huduser.gov/portal/Publications/pdf/HUD-514_HDS2012_execsumm.pdf; S. Michael Gaddis and Raj Ghoshal, "Searching for a Roommate: A Correspondence Audit Examining Racial/Ethnic and Immigrant Discrimination among Millennials," *Socius*, January 2020, https://doi.org/10.1177/2378023120972287.

27. Grace Yukich, "Muslims Need Not Apply?: Religious, Ethnic, and Gender Discrimination in the U.S. Labor Market,"

Quinnipiac University draft paper, 2018, https://amc.sas.upenn.edu/sites/www.sas.upenn.edu.andrea-mitchell-center/files/Yukich%20-%20Muslims%20Need%20Not%20Apply.pdf.

28. Lila Abu-Lughod, *Do Muslim Women Need Saving?* (Cambridge, MA: Harvard University Press, 2013); Sue Malvern and Gabriel Koureas, "Terrorist Transgressions: Exploring the Gendered Representations of the Terrorist," *Historical Social Research* 39, no. 3 (2014): 67–81, https://www.jstor.org/stable/24146114.

29. David S. Pedulla, "The Positive Consequences of Negative Stereotypes: Race, Sexual Orientation, and the Job Application Process," *Social Psychology Quarterly* 77, no. 1 (2014): 75–94, https://doi.org/10.1177/0190272513506229.

30. John F. Dovidio and Samuel L. Gaertner, "Aversive Racism and Selective Decisions: 1989 and 1999," *Psychological Science* 11, no. 4 (2000): 315–319, https://doi.org/10.1111/1467-9280.00262; Monica Biernat and Diana Kobrynowicz, "Gender- and Race-Based Standards of Competence: Lower Minimum Standards but Higher Ability Standards for Devalued Groups," *Journal of Personality and Social Psychology* 72, no. 3 (1997): 544–557, https://doi.org/10.1037/0022-3514.72.3.544.

31. Brent R. Moulton, "A Reexamination of the Federal-Private Wage Differential in the United States," *Journal of Labor Economics* 8, no. 2 (1990): 270–293, https://doi.org/10.1086/298223; Barbara F. Reskin, "The Proximate Causes of Employment Discrimination," *Contemporary Sociology* 29, no. 2 (2000): 319–328, https://doi.org/10.2307/2654387.

32. Victor Ray, "A Theory of Racialized Organizations," *American Sociological Review* 84, no. 1 (2019): 26–53, https://doi.org/10.1177/0003122418822335.

33. Joan C. Williams, "Double Jeopardy? An Empirical Study with Implications for the Debates over Implicit Bias and Intersectionality," *Harvard Journal of Law & Gender* 37 (2014): 185–242, https://repository.uchastings.edu/faculty_scholarship/1278.

34. Khalil Gibran Muhammad, *The Condemnation of Blackness: Race, Crime, and the Making of Modern Urban America* (Cambridge, MA: Harvard University Press, 2019).

35. Equal Justice Initiative, "Lynching in America: Confronting the Legacy of Racial Terror," Equal Justice Initiative, 2017, https://lynchinginamerica.eji.org/report/.

36. Ida B. Wells-Barnett, *Southern Horrors: Lynch Law in All Its Phases* (New York, 1892; Project Gutenberg, 2005), https://www.gutenberg.org/files/14975/14975-h/14975-h.htm.

37. Katherine B. Spencer, Amanda K. Charbonneau, and Jack Glaser, "Implicit Bias and Policing," *Social and Personality Psychology Compass* 10, no. 1 (2016): 50–63, https://doi.org/10.1111/spc3.12210.

38. Frank Edwards, Hedwig Lee, and Michael Esposito, "Risk of Being Killed by Police Use of Force in the United States by Age, Race-Ethnicity, and Sex," *Proceedings of the National Academy of Sciences* 116, no. 34 (2019): 16793–16798, https://doi.org/10.1073/pnas.1821204116.

39. Tracy Jan, "Two Black Men Say They Were Kicked Out of Walmart for Wearing Protective Masks. Others Worry It Will Happen to Them," *Washington Post*, April 9, 2020,

https://www.washingtonpost.com/business/2020/04/09/masks-racial-profiling-walmart-coronavirus/.

40. Brent Staples, "Just Walk On By: Black Men and Public Space," 1986, https://www.ohlone.edu/sites/default/files/documents/imported/justwalkonbyblackmenandpublicspace.pdf.

41. Ibid.

42. Harold Garfinkel, *Studies in Ethnomethodology* (Upper Saddle River, NJ: Prentice Hall, 1967).

43. Garfinkel, *Ethnomethodology*.

44. Harold Garfinkel, "Studies of the Routine Grounds of Everyday Activities," *Social Problems* 11, no. 3 (1964): 225–250.

45. Jay Livingston, "The Sneakiest Sneak," *Montclaire SocioBlog*, December 16, 2010, http://montclairsoci.blogspot.com/2010/12/sneakiest-sneak.html.

46. Frank Deford, "Trickery on the Football Field: Like Child Abuse?," *Morning Edition*, NPR, November 17, 2010, http://www.npr.org/2010/11/16/131358322/trickery-on-the-football-field-like-child-abuse.

47. hearit, "The Truth about the Nasty Driscoll Middle School Football Game Trick Play," Wacktrap.com, accessed November 16, 2020, http://www.wacktrap.com/sports/sports-types/team-sports/football/truth-about-nasty-driscoll-middle-school-football-game-tric.

48. Cindy Boren, "Driscoll Middle School Trick Play: 'A Really Slow Quarterback Sneak,'" *Washington Post*, November 9, 2010, http://voices.washingtonpost.com/early-lead/2010/11/driscoll_middle_school_trick_p.html; "Best trick play ever," Colorado4x4.org Forums, January 2, 2011, http://www.colorado4x4.org/vbb/archive/index.php/t-177496.html.

CHAPTER 5

1. Adam Gopnik, "The Outside Game," *New Yorker*, January 5, 2015, https://www.newyorker.com/magazine/2015/01/12/outside-game.

2. Carrie Golus, "Who's the Deviant Here?," *The University of Chicago Magazine*, July–August 2015, https://mag.uchicago.edu/law-policy-society/whos-deviant-here.

3. Gopnik, "The Outside Game."

4. Howard S. Becker, "Becoming a Marihuana User," *American Journal of Sociology* 59, no. 3 (1953): 235–242, https://doi.org/10.1086/221326.

5. Golus, "Who's the Deviant Here?"

6. E. A. Hooten, quoted on page 38 of Ronald L. Akers, *Criminological Theories: Introduction and Evaluation* (London: Routledge, 1999).

7. Mary Gibson, *Born to Crime: Cesare Lombroso and the Origins of Biological Criminology* (Westport, CT: Praeger, 2002).

8. Nando Parrado and Vince Rause, *Miracle in the Andes: 72 Days on the Mountain and My Long Trek Home* (New York: Three Rivers Press, 2006).

9. "Pope: The Eucharist Is Jesus Who Gives Himself Entirely to Us," *AsiaNews.it*, August 16, 2015, http://www.asianews.it/news-en/Pope:-The-Eucharist-is-Jesus-who-gives-himself-entirely-to-us-35052.html.

10. Ann Gibbons, "Archaeologists Rediscover Cannibals," *Science* 277, no. 5326 (1997): 635–637, https://doi.org/10.1126/science.277.5326.635.

11. Susie Scott, "The Medicalisation of Shyness: From Social Misfits to Social Fitness," *Sociology of Health & Illness* 28 no. 2 (April 2006): 133–153, https://doi.org/10.1111/j.1467-9566.2006.00485.x.

12. "Cannibalism," Legal Information Institute, accessed November 28, 2020, https://www.law.cornell.edu/wex/cannibalism.

13. Robert King Merton and Robert C. Merton, *Social Theory and Social Structure* (New York: Free Press, 1968).

14. Edwin H. Sutherland, *White Collar Crime* (New York: Holt, Rinehart & Winston, 1949).

15. Sutherland, *White Collar Crime*.

16. Mark A. Cohen, "Economic Costs of White-Collar Versus Street Crime," in *The Oxford Handbook of White-Collar Crime*, eds. Shanna R. Van Slyke, Michael L. Benson, and Francis T. Cullen (Oxford: Oxford University Press, 2016).

17. "William Julius Wilson: The American Underclass: Inner-City Ghettos and the Norms of Citizenship," American RadioWorks (blog), APM, accessed November 28, 2020, http://americanradioworks.publicradio.org/features/blackspeech/wjwilson.html.

18. "William Julius Wilson 1935–," *Encyclopedia.com*, accessed November 28, 2020, http://www.encyclopedia.com/people/history/panama-history-biographies/william-julius-wilson.

19. Gretchen Reynolds, "The Rising Significance of Race," *Chicago Magazine* (1992): 80.

20. Clifford Shaw and Henry D. McKay, *Juvenile Delinquency and Urban Areas* (Chicago: University of Chicago Press, 1942); Edwin Hardin Sutherland, Donald Ray Cressey, and David F. Luckenbill, *Principles of Criminology* (Boston: General Hall, 1992); Robert J. Sampson and William Julius Wilson, "Toward a Theory of Race, Crime, and Urban Inequality," in *Crime and Inequality*, eds. John Hagan and Ruth D. Peterson (Stanford, CA: Stanford University Press, 1995); Richard A. Cloward and Lloyd E. Ohlin, *Delinquency and Opportunity: A Theory of Delinquent Gangs* (Glencoe, IL: Free Press, 1960).

21. Ronald L. Akers, *Criminological Theories: Introduction and Evaluation* (London: Routledge, 1999): 116.

22. Gresham M. Sykes and David Matza, "Techniques of Neutralization: A Theory of Delinquency," *American Sociological Review* 22, no. 6 (1957): 664–670, https://doi.org/10.2307/2089195.

23. Shadd Maruna and Heith Copes, "Excuses, Excuses: What Have We Learned From Five Decades of Neutralization Research?," *Crime and Justice* 32 (2005): 221–320, https://doi.org/10.1086/655355; Alexander Alvarez, "Adjusting to Genocide: The Techniques of Neutralization and the Holocaust," *Social Science History* 21 (1997): 139–178, https://doi.org/10.2307/1171272; Martha Heltsley and Thomas C. Calhoun, "The Good Mother: Neutralization Techniques Used by Pageant Mothers," *Deviant Behavior* 24 (2003): 81–100, https://doi.org/10.1080/01639620390117202; Ken Levi, "Becoming a Hit Man: Neutralization in a Very Deviant Career," *Urban Life* 10, no. 1 (1981): 47–63, https://doi.org/10.1177/089124168101000103.

24. Steven Caldwell Brown, "Where Do Beliefs about Music Piracy Come From and How Are They Shared? An Ethnographic Study," *International Journal of Cyber Criminology* 10, no. 1 (2016): 21–39, https://doi.org/10.5281/zenodo.58518.

25. Kimberly A. DeTardo-Bora, Erica N. Clark, and Bill Gardner, "'I Did What I Believe Is Right': A Study of Neutralizations among Anonymous Operation Participants," *Journal of Qualitative Criminal Justice & Criminology* 8, no. 1 (2019): 129–155, https://doi.org/10.21428/88de04a1.5c02a7d3.

26. "How we all break the law every day," *Telegraph*, September 22, 2008, http://www.telegraph.co.uk/news/uknews/law-and-order/3044794/How-we-all-break-the-law-every-day.html.

27. Howard S. Becker, *Outsiders* (New York: Free Press, 1973 [1963]); David Matza, *Becoming Deviant* (Englewood Cliffs, NJ: Prentice Hall, 1969).

28. Kai T. Erikson, *Wayward Puritans: A Study in the Sociology of Deviance* (New York: Pearson College Division, 2004).

29. Michael B. Sauter, "Public Sector Jobs: States Where the Most People Work for the Government," *USA Today*, June 1, 2018, https://www.usatoday.com/story/money/economy/2018/06/01/states-where-the-most-people-work-for-government/35302753/.

30. Devah Pager, "The Mark of a Criminal Record," *American Journal of Sociology* 108, no. 5 (2003): 937–975, https://doi.org/10.1086/374403.

31. Ross L. Matsueda, "Reflected Appraisals, Parental Labeling, and Delinquency: Specifying a Symbolic Interactionist Theory," *American Journal of Sociology* 97, no. 6 (1992): 1577–1611, https://www.jstor.org/stable/2781549.

32. Edwin McCarthy Lemert, *Social Pathology: A Systematic Approach to the Theory of Sociopathic Behavior* (New York: McGraw-Hill, 1951).

33. William J. Chambliss, "The Saints and the Roughnecks," *Society* 11 (1973): 24–31, https://doi.org/10.1007/BF03181016.

34. Ted Chiricos, Kelle Barrick, William D. Bales, and Stephanie Bontrager, "The Labeling of Convicted Felons and Its Consequences for Recidivism," *Criminology* 45, no. 3 (2007): 547–581, https://doi.org/10.1111/j.1745-9125.2007.00089.x.

35. Émile Durkheim, *The Division of Labor in Society* (New York: Free Press, 1997 [1893]).

36. Matt Pomroy, "Why Did Men Stop Wearing Hats?," *Esquire Middle East*, May 15, 2020, http://www.esquireme.com/style/why-did-men-stop-wearing-hats.

37. Émile Durkheim, *The Rules of Sociological Method* (New York: Free Press, 2014 [1895]).

38. Durkheim, *The Division of Labor in Society*.

39. Tom Winter and Minyvonne Burke, "College Cheating Ringleader Says He Helped More Than 750 families with Admissions Scheme," *NBC News*, March 13, 2019, https://www.nbcnews.com/news/us-news/college-cheating-mastermind-says-he-helped-nearly-800-families-admissions-n982666.

40. "Conversations with a Killer: The Ted Bundy Tapes," IMDB, January 24, 2019, https://www.imdb.com/title/tt9425132/; Laura Parker, "2,000 Cheer Execution of Killer Bundy," *Washington Post*, January 25, 1989, https://www.washingtonpost.com/archive/politics/1989/01/25/2000-cheer-execution-of-killer-bundy/203569fd-4a76-4cd5-97ea-0d1fa2a99554/?noredirect=on&utm_term=.b695421505ef.

41. Émile Durkheim, *On Suicide* (London: Penguin Books Limited, 1952 [1897]).

42. Durkheim, *On Suicide*.

43. Albert Caruana, B. Ramaseshan, and Michael T. Ewing, "The Effect of Anomie on Academic Dishonesty among University Students," *The International Journal of Educational Management* 14, no. 1 (2000): 23–30; Lisa R. Muftić, "Advancing Institutional Anomie Theory: A Microlevel Examination Connecting Culture, Institutions, and Deviance," *International Journal of Offender Therapy and Comparative Criminology* 50, no. 6 (2006): 630–653, https://doi.org/10.1177/0306624X06287284; Hilal Bashir and Kundan Singh, "The Investigation of the Relationship between Anomie and Academic Dishonesty of College Students," *IAHRW International Journal of Social Sciences Review* 6, no. 1 (2018): 5–8.

44. Caruana, Ramaseshan, and Ewing, "The Effect of Anomie on Academic Dishonesty."

45. Ellen Bara Stolzenberg et al., *The American Freshman: National Norms Fall 2019* (Los Angeles: Higher Education Research Institute, 2020), https://www.heri.ucla.edu/monographs/TheAmericanFreshman2019.pdf.

46. Émile Durkheim, *Moral Education* (New York: Free Press, 1973 [1925]).

47. Paula Giddings, *Ida: A Sword Among Lions: Ida. B. Bells and the Campaign Against Lynching* (New York: Amistad, 2008); Ida B. Wells-Barnett, *Southern Horrors: Lynch Law in All Its Phases* (New York: 1892); S. Mintz and S. McNeil, Digital History (online edition, 2018), accessed November 28, 2020, https://www.digitalhistory.uh.edu/disp_textbook.cfm?smtid=3&psid=3614.

48. Vivian M. May, *Anna Julia Cooper, Visionary Black Feminist: A Critical Introduction* (London: Routledge, 2007); Anna Julia Cooper, *A Voice from the South* (Xenia, OH: 1892; Documenting the American South, University of North Carolina at Chapel Hill, online edition, 2000), accessed November 28, 2020, https://docsouth.unc.edu/church/cooper/cooper.html.

49. Patricia Madoo Lengermann and Gillian Niebrugge, *The Women Founders: Sociology and Social Theory 1830–1930* (Long Grove, IL: Waveland Press, 2006).

50. Randall Collins, *Conflict Sociology* (New York: Academic Press, 1975).

51. Walter Bromberg and Franck Simon, "The 'Protest' Psychosis: A Special Type of Reactive Psychosis," *Archives of General Psychiatry* 19, no. 2 (1968): 155–160, https://doi.org/10.1001/archpsyc.1968.01740080027005.

52. Jonathan M. Metzl, *The Protest Psychosis: How Schizophrenia Became a Black Disease* (Boston: Beacon Press, 2011).

53. Arturo Baiocchi, "The Racialization of Mental Illness," *Sociological Images* (blog), May 23, 2011, https://thesocietypages.org/socimages/2011/05/23/the-racialization-of-mental-illness/comment-page-1/.

54. Melissa J. Wilde and Sabrina Danielsen, "Fewer and Better Children: Race, Class, Religion, and Birth Control Reform in America," *American Journal of Sociology* 119,

no. 6 (2014):1710-1760, https://doi.org/10.1086/674007.

55. Shankar Vedantam, "Racial Disparities Found in Pinpointing Mental Illness," *Washington Post*, June 28, 2005, http://www.washingtonpost.com/wp-dyn/content/article/2005/06/27/AR2005062701496.html.

CHAPTER 6

1. Richard B. Lee, *The Dobu Ju/'hoansi* (Boston, MA: Cengage Learning, 2012).

2. Richard B. Lee and Irven DeVore, eds., *Man the Hunter* (London, UK: Aldine Publishing Company, 1968).

3. David Riches, "Hunting and Gathering Societies," in *Encyclopedia of Social and Cultural Anthropology*, eds. Alan Barnard and Jonathan Spencer (New York: Routledge, 2009).

4. Max Weber, "Die drei reinen Typen der legitimen Herrschaft" ("The Three Types of Legitimate Rule"), *Preussische Jahrbücher* 187 (1922): 1–2.

5. Carles Boix, "Origins and Persistence of Economic Inequality," *Annual Review of Political Science* 13 (2010): 489–516, https://doi.org/10.1146/annurev.polisci.12.031607.094915; "A Deep Divide between Rich and Poor Dates Back Millennia," Archaeology, Nature.com, November 15, 2017, https://www.nature.com/articles/d41586-017-06050-0.

6. Yuval Noah Harari, *Sapiens: A Brief History of Humankind* (New York: Harper Perennial, 2018).

7. Michael Mann, *The Sources of Social Power* (Cambridge: Cambridge University Press, 2012).

8. Charles Tilly, *Coercion, Capital and European States, A.D. 990–1990* (Hoboken, NJ: Wiley-Blackwell, 1992).

9. Stephen Kalberg, ed., *Max Weber: Readings and Commentary on Modernity* (Hoboken, NJ: Wiley-Blackwell, 2005).

10. Anthony Giddens, *The Consequences of Modernity* (Stanford, CA: Stanford University Press, 1991).

11. Max Weber, *The Protestant Ethic and the Spirit of Capitalism* (New York: Routledge, 2001 [1905]).

12. Stephen Kalberg, *Max Weber's Comparative-Historical Sociology* (Chicago: University of Chicago Press, 1994).

13. Émile Durkheim, *The Division of Labor in Society* (New York: Free Press, 1997 [1893]).

14. Max Weber, "Bureaucracy," in *Weber's Rationalism and Modern Society: New Translations on Politics, Bureaucracy, and Social Stratification*, eds. Tony Waters and Dagmar Waters (New York: Palgrave Macmillan US, 2015).

15. George Ritzer, *The McDonaldization of Society* (Thousand Oaks, CA: Sage Publishing, 2007).

16. Jean Baudrillard, *Simulacra and Simulation* (Ann Arbor, MI: University of Michigan Press, 1994); Jean-François Lyotard, *The Postmodern Condition: A Report on Knowledge* (Minneapolis, MN: University of Minnesota Press, 1984); Zygmunt Bauman, *Liquid Modernity* (Cambridge, UK: Polity, 2000).

17. Zygmunt Bauman, "From Pilgrim to Tourist—or a Short History of Identity," in *Questions of Cultural Identity*, eds. Stuart Hall and Paul du Gay (Thousand Oaks, CA: Sage Publications, 2011).

18. Touré, *Who's Afraid of Post-Blackness: What It Means to be Black Now* (New York: Atria Books, 2012).

19. Ulrich Beck, Anthony Giddens and Scott Lash, *Reflexive Modernization: Politics, Tradition and Aesthetics in the Modern Social Order* (Oxford: Blackwell, 1994).

20. Jonathan H. Turner, *Human Institutions: A Theory of Societal Evolution* (Lanham, MD: Rowman & Littlefield, 2004); Anthony Giddens, *The Constitution of Society* (Oakland, CA: University of California Press, 1986); John W. Mohr and Harrison C. White, "How to Model an Institution," *Theory and Society* 37, no. 5 (2008): 485–512, https://doi.org/10.1007/s11186-008-9066-0; Peter L. Berger and Thomas Luckmann, *The Social Construction of Reality: A Treatise in the Sociology of Knowledge* (New York: Anchor, 1967).

21. William Graham Sumner, *Folkways: A Study of Mores, Manners, Customs and Morals* (New York: Cosimo Classics, 2007).

22. Examples borrowed from Turner, *Human Institutions*.

23. David Lyon, *Jesus in Disneyland: Religion in Postmodern Times* (Cambridge, UK: Polity, 2000).

24. Eddie Gibbs and Ryan K. Bolger, *Emerging Churches: Creating Christian Community in Postmodern Cultures* (Ada, MI: Baker Academic, 2005); Jason Wollschleger, "Off the Map? Locating the Emerging Church: A Comparative Case Study of Congregations in the Pacific Northwest," *Review of Religious Research* 54, no. 1 (2012): 69–91, https://doi.org/10.1007/s13644-011-0042-1.

25. Philip Clayton, "Letting Doubters in the Door," *Los Angeles Times*, March 25, 2012, https://www.latimes.com/opinion/la-xpm-2012-mar-25-la-oe-clayton-emergingchurch-20120325-story.html.

26. Example borrowed from Allan G. Johnson, *The Gender Knot: Unraveling Our Patriarchal Legacy* (Philadelphia: Temple University Press, 2014).

27. Albert Einstein, *Out of My Later Years* (New York: Citadel Press, 1956 [1950]), 5.

28. Tristan Donovan, "The Original Monopoly Was Deeply Anti-Landlord," *VICE*, May 23, 2017, https://www.vice.com/en_us/article/evgknn/the-secret-anti-landlord-origin-of-monopoly; Edward J. Dodson, "How Henry George's Principles Were Corrupted into the Game Called Monopoly," HenryGeorge.org, December 2011, http://www.henrygeorge.org/dodson_on_monopoly.htm.

29. John A. Spaulding, George Simpson, and Émile Durkheim, *Suicide: A Study in Sociology* (New York: Free Press, 2010 [1897]).

30. James DeFronzo, Ashley Ditta, Lance Hannon, and Jane Prochnow, "Male Serial Homicide: The Influence of Cultural and Structural Variables," *Homicide Studies* 11, no. 1 (2007): 3–14, https://doi.org/10.1177/1088767906297434.

31. Michel Martin, "New Documentary Explores History of Jews and Basketball," *Tell Me More*, NPR, February 4, 2010, https://www.npr.org/templates/story/story.php?storyId=123368994.

32. Jon Entine, "The 'Scheming, Flashy Trickiness' of Basketball's Media Darlings, The Philadelphia 'Hebrews'–Err . . . Sixers," *Jewish Magazine*, July 2001, http://www.jewishmag.com/45mag/basketball/basketball.htm.

33. Karen Brodkin, *How Jews Became White Folks and What That Says About Race in America* (New Brunswick, NJ: Rutgers University Press, 1998).

34. Len Canter, "Basketball: The Jewish Game . . . A to Z," *Chutzpah*, 2010: 47.

35. Douglas S. Massey, *Categorically Unequal: The American Stratification System* (New York: Russell Sage Foundation, 2008).

CHAPTER 7

1. Nicholas Casey, "College Made Them Feel Equal. The Virus Exposed How Unequal Their Lives Are," *New York Times*, April 4, 2020, https://www.nytimes.com/2020/04/04/us/politics/coronavirus-zoom-college-classes.html.

2. U.S. Census Bureau, "Real Median Personal Income in the United States," FRED, Federal Reserve Bank of St. Louis, September 16, 2020, https://fred.stlouisfed.org/series/MEPAINUSA672N.

3. Jessica Semega, Melissa Kollar, Emily A. Shrider, and John F. Creamer, "Income and Poverty in the United States: 2019," U.S. Department of Commerce, U.S. Census Bureau, September 2020, https://www.census.gov/content/dam/Census/library/publications/2020/demo/p60-270.pdf.

4. U.S. Census Bureau, "Historical Income Tables: Households," accessed November 18, 2020, https://www.census.gov/data/tables/time-series/demo/income-poverty/historical-income-households.html.

5. Adrian Dungan, "Individual Income Tax Shares, 2015," *Statistics of Income Bulletin*, Internal Revenue Service, Winter 2018, https://www.irs.gov/pub/irs-soi/soi-a-ints-id1801.pdf.

6. Emmanuel Saez, "Striking It Richer: The Evolution of Top Incomes in the United States (Updated with 2018 Estimates)," Department of Economics, University of California, Berkeley, February 2020, https://eml.berkeley.edu/~saez/saez-UStopincomes-2018.pdf.

7. Jonathan Eggleston and Robert Munk, "Net Worth of Households: 2015," U.S. Department of Commerce, U.S. Census Bureau, May 2019, https://www.census.gov/content/dam/Census/library/publications/2019/demo/P70BR-164.pdf; Chuck Collins and Josh Hoxie, "Billionaire Bonanza: The Forbes 400 and the Rest Of Us," Institute for Policy Studies, November 2017, https://ips-dc.org/wp-content/uploads/2017/11/BILLIONAIRE-BONANZA-2017-FinalV.pdf; Estelle Sommeiller and Mark Price, "The New Gilded Age: Income Inequality in the U.S. by State, Metropolitan Area, and County," Economic Policy Institute, July 19, 2018, https://www.epi.org/publication/the-new-gilded-age-income-inequality-in-the-u-s-by-state-metropolitan-area-and-county/; Thomas Piketty, *Capital in the Twenty-First Century* (Cambridge, MA: Belknap Press, 2014).

8. Chuck Collins, "Updates: Billionaire Wealth, U.S. Job Losses and Pandemic Profiteers," Inequality.org, Dec. 9, 2020, https://inequality.org/great-divide/updates-billionaire-pandemic/.

9. Christopher Boehm, *Hierarchy in the Forest: The Evolution of Egalitarian Behavior* (Cambridge, MA: Harvard University Press, 2001); John M. Gowdy, ed., *Limited Wants, Unlimited Means: A Reader on Hunter-Gatherer Economics and the Environment* (St. Louis, MO: Island Press, 1998).

10. Carles Boix, "Origins and Persistence of Economic Inequality," *Annual Review of Political Science* 13 (2010): 489–516, https://doi.org/10.1146/annurev.polisci.12.031607.094915.

11. Charles H. Feinstein, "Pessimism Perpetuated: Real Wages and the Standard of Living in Britain during and after the Industrial Revolution," *Journal of Economic History* 58, no. 3 (1998): 625–658, https://doi.org/10.1017/S0022050700021100.

12. Karl Marx, *Capital: A Critique of Political Economy, Vol. 3* (New York: Penguin Classics, 1993 [1894]).

13. Daniel Okrent, *Great Fortune: The Epic of Rockefeller Center* (New York: Viking Press, 2003).

14. David Bunting, *The Rise of Large American Corporations, 1889–1919* (New York: Garland Press, 1987).

15. Graham Adams, *The Age of Industrial Violence, 1910–1915* (New York: Columbia University Press, 1966).

16. Emmanuel Saez, "Striking It Richer: The Evolution of Top Incomes in the United States (Updated with 2012 Preliminary Estimates)," Department of Economics, University of California, Berkeley, September 3, 2013, https://eml.berkeley.edu/~saez/saez-UStopincomes-2012.pdf.

17. Gerald Mayer, "Union Membership Trends in the United States," Congressional Research Service, August 31, 2004, August_2004_Union_Membership_Trends_in_the_United_States.pdf.

18. Bruce Western and Jake Rosenfeld, "Unions, Norms, and the Rise in U.S. Wage Inequality," *American Sociological Review* 76, no. 4 (2011): 513–537, https://doi.org/10.1177/0003122411414817.

19. Saez, "Striking It Richer."

20. John Barnard, *American Vanguard: The United Auto Workers during the Reuther Years, 1935–1970* (Detroit, MI: Wayne State University Press, 2005).

21. Paul Krugman, *The Conscience of a Liberal* (New York: W. W. Norton, 2009), 37.

22. Jill Quadagno, *The Color of Welfare: How Racism Undermined the War on Poverty* (New York: Oxford University Press, 1996); Cybelle Fox, *Three Worlds of Relief: Race, Immigration, and the American Welfare State from the Progressive Era to the New Deal* (Princeton, NJ: Princeton University Press, 2012); Ira Katznelson, *When Affirmative Action Was White: An Untold History of Racial Inequality in Twentieth-Century America* (New York: W. W. Norton, 2006); Ira Katznelson, *Fear Itself: The New Deal and the Origins of Our Time* (New York: Liveright, 2013).

23. Erik Olin Wright, "Class Boundaries in Advanced Capitalist Societies," Institute for Research on Poverty, July–August 1976, https://www.ssc.wisc.edu/~wright/Published%20writing/ClassBoundaries.pdf.

24. Max Roser and Esteban Ortiz-Ospina, "Income Inequality," OurWorldInData.org, December 2013, https://ourworldindata.org/income-inequality.

25. Lane Kenworthy, "Why the Surge in Income Inequality?," *Contemporary Sociology* 46, no. 1 (2017): 1–9, https://doi.org/10.1177/0094306116681789.

26. Emmanuel Saez, "Striking It Richer: The Evolution of Top Incomes in the United States," in *Inequality in the 21st Century*, eds. David B. Grusky and Jasmine Hill (New York: Routledge, 2017); Steve Fraser and Gary Gerstle, *The Rise and Fall of the New Deal Order, 1930–1980* (Princeton, NJ: Princeton University Press, 1990).

27. Danilo Trisi and Arloc Sherman, "Incomes Fell for Poorest Children of Single Mothers in Welfare Law's First Decade," Center on Budget and Policy Priorities, August 11, 2016, https://www.cbpp.org/research/family-income-support/incomes-fell-for-poorest-children-of-single-mothers-in-welfare-laws.

28. H. Luke Shaefer and Kathryn Edin, "Welfare Reform and the Families It Left Behind," *Pathways*, Winter 2018, https://static1.squarespace.com/static/551caca4e4b0a26ceeee87c5/t/5a5e48e171c10b3c917591f7/1516128483955/Shaefer-Edin-NEW.pdf; H. Luke Shaefer and Kathryn J. Edin, "What Is the Evidence of Worsening Conditions among America's Poorest Families with Children?" (blog), TwoDollarsADay.com, December 7, 2016, http://www.twodollarsaday.com/blog/2016/9/5/what-ts-the-evidence-of-worsening-conditions-among-americas-poorest-families-with-children.

29. Western and Rosenfeld, "Unions, Norms, and the Rise in U.S. Wage Inequality."

30. Timothy Smeeding, "Income, Wealth, and Debt and the Great Recession," Russell Sage Foundation and Stanford Center on Poverty and Inequality, October 2012, https://inequality.stanford.edu/sites/default/files/IncomeWealthDebt_fact_sheet.pdf; Fabian T. Pfeffer, Sheldon Danziger, and Robert F. Schoeni, "Wealth Disparities before and after the Great Recession," *Annals of the American Academy of Political and Social Science* 650, no. 1 (2013); 98–123, https://doi.org/10.1177/0002716213497452.

31. Edward N. Wolff, "Household Wealth Trends in the United States, 1962 to 2016: Has Middle Class Wealth Recovered?," National Bureau of Economic Research Working Paper Series, November 2017, http://www.nber.org/papers/w24085.

32. "The Final Trump-GOP Tax Bill: National & 50-State Analysis," Institute on Taxation and Economic Policy, December 2017, https://itep.org/wp-content/uploads/Trump-GOP-Final-Bill-Report.pdf.

33. Jeanna Smialek, "Even as Americans Grew Richer, Inequality Persisted," *New York Times*, Sept. 28, 2020, https://www.nytimes.com/2020/09/28/business/economy/coronavirus-pandemic-income-inequality.html.

34. Kenneth Terrell, "8 Occupations Hit Hardest by the Pandemic in 2020," AARP, Jan. 11, 2021, https://www.aarp.org/work/job-search/info-2020/job-losses-during-covid.html.

35. Ibid.

36. Kim Parker, Rachel Minkin, and Jesse Bennett, "Economic Fallout From COVID-19 Continues To Hit Lower-Income Americans the Hardest," *Pew Research Center*, Sept. 24, 2020, https://www.pewsocialtrends.org/2020/09/24/economic-fallout-from-covid-19-continues-to-hit-lower-income-americans-the-hardest/.

37. Collins, "Updates: Billionaire Wealth, U.S. Job Losses and Pandemic Profiteers."

38. David Autor, "Work of the Past, Work of the Future," National Bureau of Economic Research Working Paper Series, February 2019, https://www.nber.org/papers/w25588.

39. "How Many Gig Workers Are There?," Gig Economy Data Hub, accessed November 18, 2020, https://www.gigeconomydata.org/basics/how-many-gig-workers-are-there.

40. Alexandra J. Ravenelle, *Hustle and Gig: Struggling and Surviving in the Sharing Economy* (Oakland, CA: University of California Press, 2019), 6.

41. Thomas Piketty, Emmanuel Saez, and Gabriel Zucman, "Distribution National Accounts: Methods and Estimates for the United States," *Quarterly Journal of Economics* 133, no. 2 (2018): 553–609, https://doi.org/10.1093/qje/qjx043.

42. "Report on the Economic Well-Being of U.S. Households in 2014," Board of Governors of the Federal Reserve System, May 2015, https://www.federalreserve.gov/econresdata/2014-report-economic-well-being-us-households201505.pdf; "Nearly 60% of Americans Can't Afford Common Unexpected Expenses," Bankrate.com, January 12, 2017, https://www.bankrate.com/pdfs/pr/20170112-january-money-pulse.pdf.

43. Angela Rachidi, "The Working Class and the Federal Government's Social Safety Net," American Enterprise Institute, January 2018, https://www.aei.org/wp-content/uploads/2018/01/The-Working-Class-and-the-Federal-Governments-Social-Safety-Net.pdf?x88519.

44. Guy Standing, *The Precariat: The New Dangerous Class* (London, UK: Bloomsbury, 2011).

45. Susan Adams, "Half of College Grads Are Working Jobs That Don't Require a Degree," *Forbes*, May 28, 2013, https://www.forbes.com/sites/susanadams/2013/05/28/half-of-college-grads-are-working-jobs-that-dont-require-a-degree/?sh=1256e2ae6d7a.

46. National Science Board, "Science and Engineering Indicators 2014," NSF.gov, 2014, https://www.nsf.gov/statistics/seind14/; Janelle Jones and John Schmitt, "A College Degree Is No Guarantee," Center for Economic and Policy Research, May 2014, https://cepr.net/documents/black-coll-grads-2014-05.pdf.

47. "Table 330.10: Average Undergraduate Tuition and Fees and Room and Board Rates Charged for Full-Time Students in Degree-Granting Postsecondary Institutions, by Level and Control of Institution: Selected Years, 1963–64 through 2016–17," National Center for Education Statistics, accessed November 18, 2020, https://nces.ed.gov/programs/digest/d17/tables/dt17_330.10.asp.

48. Matt Tatham, "Student Loan Debt Climbs to $1.4 Trillion in 2019," Experian.com, July 24, 2019, https://www.experian.com/blogs/ask-experian/state-of-student-loan-debt/.

49. Mancur Olson, *The Logic of Collective Acton: Public Goods and the Theory of Groups* (Cambridge, MA: Harvard University Press, 1971).

50. Richard B. Freeman and Alexander M. Gelber, "Prize Structure and Information in Tournaments: Experimental Evidence," *American Economic Journal: Applied Economics* 2, no. 1 (2010): 149–164, https://doi.org/10.1257/app.2.1.149.

51. Lane Kentworthy, "Economic Growth," *The Good Society*, January 2020, https://lanekenworthy.net/economic-growth/; "Level of GDP Per Capita and Productivity," Organisation for Economic Co-operation and Development, accessed

November 18, 2020, https://stats.oecd.org/index.aspx?DataSetCode=PDB_LV.

52. "GINI Index (World Bank Estimate)–Country Ranking," IndexMundi.com, accessed November 18, 2020, https://www.indexmundi.com/facts/indicators/SI.POV.GINI/rankings.

53. David Kestenbaum, "Denmark Thrives Despite High Taxes," *Planet Money*, NPR, January 29, 2010, https://www.npr.org/templates/story/story.php?storyId=123126942.

54. Michael Barrett, "Tax Cut Plans Scrapped by Danish Government," *The Local*, January 9, 2018, https://www.thelocal.dk/20180109/tax-cut-plans-scrapped-by-danish-government.

55. Michael I. Norton and Dan Ariely, "Building a Better America–One Wealth Quintile at a Time," *Perspectives on Psychological Science* 6, no. 1 (2011): 9–12, https://doi.org/10.1177/1745691610393524.

56. Isabel V. Sawhill and Christopher Pulliam, "Americans Want the Wealthy and Corporations to Pay More Taxes, but Are Elected Officials Listening?," (blog), Brookings, March 14, 2019, https://www.brookings.edu/blog/upfront/2019/03/14/americans-want-the-wealthy-and-corporations-to-pay-more-taxes-but-are-elected-officials-listening/.

57. "Voters Like High School Gun Protesters; Don't Like NRA," Public Policy Polling, March 27, 2018, https://www.publicpolicypolling.com/polls/voters-like-high-school-gun-protesters-dont-like-nra/.

58. Jessica Semega, Melissa Kollar, Emily Shrider, and John Creamer, "Income and Poverty in the United States: 2019," U.S. Department of Commerce, U.S. Census Bureau, September 2020, https://www.census.gov/content/dam/Census/library/publications/2020/demo/p60-270.pdf.

59. Kathryn J. Edin and H. Luke Shaefer, *$2.00 a Day: Living on Almost Nothing in America* (Boston, MA: Mariner Books, 2016).

60. Rachidi, "The Working Class and the Federal Government's Social Safety Net."

61. Zachary Parolin et al., "Monthly Poverty Rates in the United States during the COVID-19 Pandemic," Working Paper, Center on Poverty & Social Policy, School of Social Work, Columbia University, October 15, 2020, https://static1.squarespace.com/static/5743308460b5e922a25a6dc7/t/5f87c59e4cd0011fabd38973/1602733471158/COVID-Projecting-Poverty-Monthly-CPSP-2020.pdf.

62. Mark R. Rank and Thomas A. Hirschl, "The Likelihood of Experience Relative Poverty over the Life Course," *PLOS ONE* 10, no. 7 (2015): 1–11, https://doi.org/10.1371/journal.pone.0133513.

63. Mark R. Rank, "Rethinking American Poverty," *Contexts* 10, no. 2 (2011): 16–21, https://doi.org/10.1177/1536504211408794.

64. "Federal Social Safety Net Programs: Millions of Full-Time Workers Rely on Federal Health Care and Food Assistance Programs," United States Government Accountability Office, October 2020, https://www.gao.gov/assets/720/710203.pdf.

65. "Poverty Rate," Organisation for Economic Co-operation and Development, accessed November 18, 2020, https://data.oecd.org/inequality/poverty-rate.htm.

66. H. Luke Shaefer, Pinghui Wu, and Kathryn Edin, "Can Poverty in America Be Compared to Conditions in the World's Poorest Countries?," *American Journal of Medical Research* 4, no. 1 (2017).

67. "Report of the Special Rapporteur on Extreme Poverty and Human Rights on His Mission to the United States of America," Human Rights Council Thirty-eighth Session, United Nations General Assembly, May 4, 2018, http://undocs.org/A/HRC/38/33/ADD.1.

68. Christopher Howard, Amirio Freeman, April Wilson, and Eboni Brown, "Poverty," *Public Opinion Quarterly* 81, no. 3 (2017): 769–789, https://doi.org/10.1093/poq/nfx022.

69. "Most Republicans Say the Rich Work Harder than Others, Most Democrats Say They Had More Advantages," U.S. Politics & Policy, Pew Research Center, January 22, 2014, https://www.people-press.org/2014/01/23/most-see-inequality-growing-but-partisans-differ-over-solutions/poverty-3/.

70. Max Weber, *The Protestant Ethic and the Spirit of Capitalism* (Milton Park, UK: Taylor & Francis, 2013 [1905]).

71. André van Hoorn and Robbert Maseland, "Does a Protestant Work Ethic Exist? Evidence from the Well-Being Effect of Unemployment," *Journal of Economic Behavior & Organization* 91 (2013): 1–12, https://doi.org/10.1016/j.jebo.2013.03.038.

72. "Religious Landscape Study," Religion & Public Life, Pew Research Center, http://www.pewforum.org/religious-landscape-study/.

73. "Hours Worked" (Indicator), Organisation for Economic Co-operation and Development, accessed December 14, 2020, https://data.oecd.org/emp/hours-worked.htm.

74. Ofer Sharone, "Why Do Unemployed Americans Blame Themselves While Israelis Blame the System?," *Social Forces* 91, no. 4 (2013); 1429–1450, https://doi.org/10.1093/sf/sot050.

75. Michael Katz, *The Undeserving Poor: America's Enduring Confrontation with Poverty: Fully Updated and Revised* (New York: Oxford University Press, 2013).

76. Thomas Suh Lauder and David Lauter, "Views on Poverty: 1985 and Today," *Los Angeles Times*, August 14, 2016, https://www.latimes.com/projects/la-na-pol-poverty-poll-interactive/.

77. Lauren Bauer, Emily Moss, and Jay Shambaugh, "Who Was Poor in the US in 2018?" (blog), Brookings, December 5, 2019, https://www.brookings.edu/blog/up-front/2019/12/05/who-was-poor-in-the-u-s-in-2018/.

78. Matthew Desmond, "Americans Want to Believe Jobs Are the Solution to Poverty. They're Not.," *New York Times*, September 11, 2018, https://www.nytimes.com/2018/09/11/magazine/americans-jobs-poverty-homeless.html.

79. "The US and the High Price of Child Care: An Examination of a Broken System," ChildCareAware of America, accessed November 23, 2020, https://www.childcareaware.org/our-issues/research/the-us-and-the-high-price-of-child-care-2019/.

80. Paul Bloom, "People Don't Actually Want Equality," *Atlantic*, October 22, 2015, https://www.theatlantic.com/science/archive/2015/10/people-dont-actually-want-equality/411784/.

81. Miles Corak, Matthew J. Lindquist, and Bhashkar Mazumder, "A Comparison of Upward and Downward Intergenerational Mobility in Canada, Sweden and the United States," *Labor Economics* 30, no. C (2014): 185–200, https://doi.org/10.1016/j.labeco.2014.03.013; Raj Chetty et al., "The Fading American Dream: Trends in Absolute Income Mobility Since 1940," *Science* 356, no. 6336 (2017): 398–406, https://doi.org/10.1126/science.aal4617.

82. Miles Corak, "Inequality from Generation to Generation: The United States in Comparison," Institute for the Study of Labor (IZA), May 2016, http://ftp.iza.org/dp9929.pdf.

83. Shai Davidai and Thomas Gilovich, "Building a More Mobile America—One Income Quintile at a Time," *Perspectives on Psychological Science* 10, no. 1 (2015): 60–71, https://doi.org/10.1177/1745691614562005.

84. "Most Republicans Say the Rich Work Harder than Others."

85. Christopher Ellis and James A. Stimson, *Ideology in America* (New York: Cambridge University Press, 2012).

86. "Findings from a National Survey & Focus Groups on Economic Mobility," Economic Mobility Project, Pew Charitable Trusts, Greenberg Quinlan Rosner Research, and Public Opinion Strategies, March 2009, https://www.pewtrusts.org/-/media/legacy/uploadedfiles/wwwpewtrustsorg/reports/economic_mobility/emp20200920survey20on20economic20mobility20for20print2031209pdf.pdf.

87. "Recent Trends in Wealth-Holding by Race and Ethnicity: Evidence from the Survey of Consumer Finances, Accessible Data," Board of Governors of the Federal Reserve System, September 27, 2017, https://www.federalreserve.gov/econres/notes/feds-notes/recent-trends-in-wealth-holding-by-race-and-ethnicity-evidence-from-the-survey-of-consumer-finances-accessible-20170927.htm#figure1.

88. U.S. Bureau of Labor Statistics, "Highlights of Women's Earnings in 2019," BLS Reports, Dec 2020, https://www.bls.gov/opub/reports/womens-earnings/2019/home.htm.

89. Cynthia Hess and Jessica Milli, "The Status of Women in Washington: Forging Pathways to Leadership and Economic Opportunity," Institute for Women's Policy Research, February 2015, https://wawomensfdn.org/wp-content/uploads/2020/07/ReportStatusofWomeninWA.pdf.

90. Margaret Hunter, "The Persistent Problem of Colorism: Skin Tone, Status, and Inequality," *Sociology Compass* 1, no. 1 (2007): 237–254, https://doi.org/10.1111/j.1751-9020.2007.00006.x.

91. Kaiser Family Foundation, "Poverty Rate by Race and Ethnicity," Jan. 15, 2021, https://www.kff.org/other/state-indicator/poverty-rate-by-raceethnicity/.

92. Jennifer Lee and Min Zhou, *The Asian American Achievement Paradox* (New York: Russell Sage Foundation, 2015).

93. Gustavo López, Neil G. Ruiz, and Eileen Patten, "Key Facts about Asian Americans, a Diverse and Growing Population," Pew Research Center, September 8, 2017, http://www.pewresearch.org/fact-tank/2017/09/08/key-factsabout-asian-americans/.

94. Mary Dorinda Allard, "Asians in the U.S. Labor Force: Profile of a Diverse Population," Monthly Labor Review, November 2011, https://www.bls.gov/opub/mlr/2011/11/art1full.pdf.

95. Christian E. Weller and Jeffrey Thompson, "Wealth Inequality Among Asian Americans Greater than Among Whites," Center for American Progress, December 20, 2016, https://www.americanprogress.org/issues/race/reports/2016/12/20/295359/wealth-inequality-among-asianamericans-greater-than-among-Whites/.

96. Victor Ray, "A Theory of Racialized Organizations," *American Sociological* 84, no. 1 (2019): 26–53, https://doi.org/10.1177/0003122418822335.

97. Cathryn Johnson, Timothy J. Dowd, and Cecilia L. Ridgeway, "Legitimacy as a Social Process," *Annual Review of Sociology* 32 (2006): 53–78, https://doi.org/10.1146/annurev.soc.32.061604.123101.

98. Harvard Kennedy School Institute of Politics, Harvard Youth Poll, 39th Edition, April 23, 2020, https://iop.harvard.edu/youth-poll/spring-2020-poll.

99. Mohamed Younis, "Four in 10 Americans Embrace Some Form of Socialism," Gallup.com, May 20, 2019, https://news.gallup.com/poll/257639/four-americans-embrace-form-socialism.aspx.

100. David Duhalde, "DSA, YDS Membership Grew Fast, Still Growing," Democratic Socialists of America, November 8, 2016, https://www.dsausa.org/dsa_yds_membership_grew_fast_still_growing.

101. Michael Tomasky, "What Are Capitalists Thinking?," *New York Times*, August 5, 2018, https://www.nytimes.com/2018/08/05/opinion/what-are-capitalists-thinking.html?nytapp=true.

102. Gøsta Esping-Andersen, *The Three Worlds of Welfare Capitalism* (Princeton, NJ: Princeton University Press, 1990); Peter B. Evans, *Embedded Autonomy: States and Industrial Transformation* (Princeton, NJ: Princeton University Press, 1995).

103. Will Wilkinson, "The Freedom Lover's Case for the Welfare State," Vox, September 1, 2016, https://www.vox.com/2016/9/1/12732168/economic-freedom-score-america-welfare-state.

104. Younis, "Four in 10 Americans Embrace Some Form of Socialism."

105. Harvard Kennedy School Institute of Politics, Harvard Youth Poll.

CHAPTER 8

1. The National Coalition for the Homeless and The National Law Center on Homelessness & Poverty, "A Dream Denied: The Criminalization of Homelessness in U.S. Cities," January 2006, http://www.nationalhomeless.org/publications/crimreport/report.pdf; Randall Amster, *Lost in Space: The Criminalization, Globalization, and Urban Ecology of Homelessness* (El Paso, TX: LFB Scholarly Publishing, 2008).

2. Forrest Stuart, *Down, Out, and Under Arrest: Policing and Everyday Life in Skid Row* (Chicago: University of Chicago Press, 2016).

3. Thomas F. Pettigrew, "Racial Change and Social Policy," *Annals of the American Academy of Political and Social Science* 441 (1979): 114–131, http://www.jstor.org/stable/1043297.

4. Douglas S. Massey and Nancy A. Denton, *American Apartheid: Segregation and the Making of the Underclass* (Cambridge, MA: Harvard University Press, 1993).

5. Douglas S. Massey, "Still the Linchpin: Segregation and Stratification in the USA," *Race and Social Problems* 12 (2020): 1–12, https://doi.org/10.1007/s12552-019-09280-1.

6. Robert J. Sampson, *Great American City: Chicago and the Enduring Neighborhood Effect* (Chicago: University of Chicago Press, 2012).

7. Steve Bogira, "Separate, Unequal, and Ignored," *Chicago Reader*, February 10, 2011, https://www.chicagoreader.com /chicago/chicago-politics-segregation-african-american -black-white-hispanic-latino-population-census-community /Content?oid=3221712.

8. Maria Krysan and Kyle Crowder, *Cycle of Segregation: Social Processes and Residential Stratification* (New York: Russell Sage Foundation, 2017).

9. Douglas S. Massey, "Residential Segregation Is the Linchpin of Racial Stratification," *City & Community* 15, no. 1 (2016): 4–7, https://doi.org/10.1111/cico.12145.

10. John Iceland and Rima Wilkes, "Does Socioeconomic Status Matter? Race, Class, and Residential Segregation," *Social Problems* 53, no. 2 (2006): 248–273, https://doi .org/10.1525/sp.2006.53.2.248.

11. John R. Logan and Richard D. Alba, "Locational Returns to Human Capital: Minority Access to Suburban Community Resources," *Demography* 30, no. 2 (1993): 243–268.

12. Marta Tienda and Norma Fuentes, "Hispanics in Metropolitan America: New Realities and Old Debates," *Annual Review of Sociology* 40, no. 1 (2014): 499–520, https://doi.org/10.1146/annurev-soc-071913-043315.

13. Roxanne Dunbar-Ortiz, *An Indigenous Peoples' History of the United States* (Boston, MA: Beacon Press, 2015).

14. Russell Thornton, *American Indian Holocaust and Survival: A Population History Since 1492* (Norman, OK: University of Oklahoma Press, 1990).

15. Ingrid Gould Ellen, Keren Horn, and Katharine O'Regan, "Pathways to Integration: Examining Changes in the Prevalence of Racially Integrated Neighborhoods," Furman Center for Real Estate & Urban Policy, May 2012, https://furmancenter.org/files/publications/Pathways_to _Integration_May_2012_2.pdf.

16. Camille Zubrinsky Charles, "The Dynamics of Racial Residential Segregation," *Annual Review of Sociology* 29 (2003): 167–207.

17. James W. Loewen, *Sundown Towns: A Hidden Dimension of American Racism* (New York: The New Press, 2005).

18. Daniel C. Vock, J. Brian Charles, and Mike Maciag, "How Housing Policies Keep White Neighborhoods So White (and Black Neighborhoods So Black)," Governing.com, January 23, 2019, https://www.governing.com/topics /health-human-services/gov-segregation-housing.html.

19. Richard Rothstein, *The Color of Law: A Forgotten History of How Our Government Segregated America* (New York: Liveright, 2017).

20. Diana M. Pearce, "Gatekeepers and Homeseekers: Institutional Patterns in Racial Steering," *Social Problems* 26, no. 3 (1979): 325–342, https://doi.org/10.2307/800457.

21. Matthew Desmond and Mustafa Emirbayer, *Race in America* (New York: W. W. Norton, 2015).

22. Rothstein, *The Color of Law*.

23. Margery Austin Turner et al., "Housing Discrimination Against Racial and Ethnic Minorities 2012: Executive Summary," Office of Policy Development and Research, U.S. Department of Housing and Urban Development, June 2013, https://www.huduser.gov/portal/Publications /pdf/HUD-514_HDS2012_execsumm.pdf.

24. Danielle McLean, "Both Liberals and Conservatives Are NIMBYs, Especially if They Own Their Home," ThinkProgress.org, August 21, 2018, https://thinkprogress.org /research-finds-both-liberals-and-conservatives-are-nimbys -especially-if-they-own-their-home-de0ed22f4054/.

25. Samuel H. Kye, "The Persistence of White Flight in Middle-Class Suburbia," *Social Science Research* 72 (2018): 38–52, https://doi.org/10.1016/j.ssresearch .2018.02.005.

26. Sapna Swaroop and Maria Krysan, "The Determinants of Neighborhood Satisfaction: Racial Proxy Revisited," *Demography* 48, no. 3 (2011): 1203–1229, https://doi .org/10.1007/s13524-011-0047-y; Maria Krysan, Mick P. Couper, Reynolds Farley, and Tyrone A. Forman, "Does Race Matter in Neighborhood Preferences? Results from a Video Experiment," *American Journal of Sociology* 115, no. 2 (2009): 527–559, https://doi.org/10.1086/599248.

27. Camille Zubrinsky Charles, "The Dynamics of Racial Residential Segregation," *Annual Review of Sociology* 29 (2003): 167–207.

28. Renee E. Walker, Christopher R. Keane, and Jessica G. Burke, "Disparities and Access to Healthy Food in the United States: A Review of Food Deserts Literature," *Health & Place* 16 (2010): 876–884, https://doi.org /10.1016/j.healthplace.2010.04.013; "Milwaukee story," ChildCareDeserts.org, 2018, https://childcaredeserts.org /index.html; Joan A. Casey et al., "Race, Ethnicity, Income Concentration and 10-Year Change in Urban Greenness in the United States," *International Journal of Environmental Research and Public Health* 14, no. 12 (2017): 1546, https://doi.org/10.3390/ijerph14121546; Roberto M. Fernandez and Celina Su, "Space in the Study of Labor Markets," *Annual Review of Sociology* 30 (2004): 545–569, https://doi.org/10.1146/annurev.soc.29.010202.100034; Ming Wen et al., "Spatial Disparities in the Distribution of Parks and Green Spaces in the USA," *Annals of Behavioral Medicine* 45, no. 1 (2013): S18–S27, https://doi.org/10.1007/s12160-012-9426-x; Darrell J. Gaskin, Gniesha Y. Dinwiddie, Kitty S. Chan, and Rachael R. McCleary, "Residential Segregation and the Availability of Primary Care Physicians," *Health Services Research* 47, no. 6 (2012): 2353–2376, https://doi.org/10.1111/j .1475-6773.2012.01417.x; Rasheed Malik, Katie Hamm, Mayram Adamu, and Taryn Morrissey, "Child Care Deserts: An Analysis of Child Care Centers by ZIP Code in 8 States," Center for American Progress, October 27, 2016, https://www.americanprogress.org/issues/early-childhood /reports/2016/10/27/225703/child-care-deserts/; William Julius Wilson, *The Truly Disadvantaged: The Inner City, the Underclass, and Public Policy* (Chicago: University of Chicago Press, 1987).

29. Steven Jessen-Howard and Simon Workman, "Early Learning in the United States: 2019," Center for American Progress, September 2019, https://www.americanprogress.org/issues/early-childhood/reports/2019/09/16/474487/early-learning-united-states-2019/.

30. Celene Fitzgerald, "'A Childcare Desert': Centralia Gets Update on United Learning Center," *Daily Chronicle*, October 14, 2020, http://www.chronline.com/news/a-childcare-desert-centralia-gets-update-on-united-learning-center/article_6fa4304a-0e71-11eb-aa44-1756882b71a4.html.

31. Sarah Treuhaft and Allison Karpyn, "The Grocery Gap: Who Has Access to Healthy Food and Why It Matters," Policy Link, The Food Trust, 2010, https://www.policylink.org/sites/default/files/FINALGroceryGap.pdf.

32. Christopher G. Boone, Geoffrey L. Buckley, J. Morgan Grove, and Chona Sister, "Parks and People: An Environmental Justice Inquiry in Baltimore, Maryland," *Annals of the Association of American Geographers* 99, no. 4 (2009): 767–787, https://doi.org/10.1080/00045600903102949.

33. Brendan G. Carr et al., "Disparities in Access to Trauma Care in the United States: A Population-Based Analysis," *Injury* 48, no. 2 (2017): 332–338, https://doi.org/10.1016/j.injury.2017.01.008.

34. Caitlin Ostroff and Ciara Bri'd Frisbie, "Millions of Americans Live Nowhere Near a Hospital, Jeopardizing Their Lives," CNN, August 3, 2017, https://www.cnn.com/2017/08/03/health/hospital-deserts/index.html.

35. Angelo Verzoni, "Shrinking Resources, Growing Concern," *NFPA Journal*, July–August 2017, https://www.nfpa.org/News-and-Research/Publications-and-media/NFPA-Journal/2017/July-August-2017/Features/Rural.

36. Junfeng Jiao and Chris Bischak, "People Are Stranded in 'Transit Deserts' in Dozens of US Cities," *The Conversation*, March 14, 2018, https://theconversation.com/people-are-stranded-in-transit-deserts-in-dozens-of-us-cities-92722.

37. Sharrelle Barber et al., "COVID-19 in Context: Racism, Segregation, and Racial Inequalities in Philadelphia," Drexel University Urban Health Collaborative, June 2020, https://drexel.edu/uhc/resources/briefs/Covid-19%20in%20Context/.

38. Centers for Disease Control and Prevention, "Health Disparities: Race and Hispanic Origin," January 6, 2021, https://www.cdc.gov/nchs/nvss/vsrr/covid19/health_disparities.htm.

39. Danae Bixler et al., "SARS-CoV-2–Associated Deaths Among Persons Aged <21 Years — United States, February 12–July 31," Centers for Disease Control and Prevention, *Morbidity and Mortality Weekly Report*, September 18, 2020, https://www.cdc.gov/mmwr/volumes/69/wr/mm6937e4.htm?s_cid=mm6937e4_w.

40. Mercedes A. Bravo, Rebecca Anthopolos, Michelle L. Bell, and Marie Lynn Miranda, "Racial Isolation and Exposure to Airborne Particular Matter and Ozone in Understudied US Populations: Environmental Justice Applications of Downscaled Numerical Model Output," *Environmental International* 92–93 (2016): 247–255, https://doi.org/10.1016/j.envint.2016.04.008.

41. Michelle L. Bell and Keita Ebisu, "Environmental Inequality in Exposures to Airbone Particulate Matter Components in the United States," *Environmental Health Perspectives* 120, no. 12 (2012): 1699–1704, https://doi.org/10.1289/ehp.1205201; Ihab Mikati et al., "Disparities in Distribution of Particulate Matter Emission Sources by Race and Poverty Status," *American Journal of Public Health* 108, no. 4 (2018): 480–485, https://doi.org/10.2105/AJPH.2017.304297.

42. Michael R. Kramer and Carol R. Hogue, "Is Segregation Bad For Your Health?," *Epidemiologic Reviews* 31 (2009): 178–194, https://doi.org/10.1093/epirev/mxp001.

43. Robert D. Bullard, "Solid Waste Sites and the Black Houston Community," *Sociological Inquiry* 53, no. 2–3 (1983): 273–288, https://doi.org/10.1111/j.1475-682X.1983.tb00037.x.

44. Carla Campbell, Rachael Greenberg, Deepa Mankikar, and Ronald D. Ross, "A Case Study of Environmental Injustice: The Failure in Flint," *International Journal of Environmental Research and Public Health* 13, no. 10 (2016): 951, https://doi.org/10.3390/ijerph13100951.

45. Brandi M. White, Heather Shaw Bonilha, and Charles Ellis Jr., "Racial/Ethnic Differences in Childhood Blood Lead Levels Among Children <72 Months of Age in the United States: A Systematic Review of the Literature," *Journal of Racial and Ethnic Health Disparities* 3 (2016): 145–153, https://doi.org/10.1007/s40615-015-0124-9.

46. David A. Ansell, *The Death Gap: How Inequality Kills* (Chicago: University of Chicago Press, 2017).

47. "Mapping Life Expectancy," VCU Center on Society and Health, Virginia Commonwealth University, September 26, 2016, https://societyhealth.vcu.edu/work/the-projects/mapping-life-expectancy.html.

48. Michael Young, *The Rise of the Meritocracy 1870–2033* (New York: Penguin Books, 1962).

49. Cory Turner, "The 50 Most Segregating School Borders In America," *nprEd*, NPR, August 23, 2016, https://www.npr.org/sections/ed/2016/08/23/490513305/the-50-most-segregating-school-borders-in-america.

50. Gary Orfield and Chungmei Lee, "Why Segregation Matters: Poverty and Educational Inequality," The Civil Rights Project, Harvard University, January 2005, https://civilrightsproject.ucla.edu/research/k-12-education/integration-and-diversity/why-segregation-matters-poverty-and-educational-inequality/orfield-why-segregation-matters-2005.pdf.

51. Cory Turner et al., "Why America's Schools Have a Money Problem," *Morning Edition*, NPR, April 18, 2016, https://www.npr.org/2016/04/18/474256366/why-americas-schools-have-a-money-problem; EdBuild, "$23 Billion," EdBuild.org, February 2019, https://edbuild.org/content/23-billion/full-report.pdf.

52. Ron Zimmer et al., "Charter Schools in Eight States: Effects on Achievement, Attainment, Integration, and Competition," RAND Corporation, 2009, https://www.rand.org/pubs/monographs/MG869.html; Erica Frankenberg, Genevieve Siegel-Hawley, and Jia Wang, "Choice Without Equity: Charter School Segregation and the Need for Civil Rights Standards," The Civil Rights

Project/Proyecto Derechos Civiles at UCLA, 2010, https://www.civilrightsproject.ucla.edu/research/k-12-education/integration-and-diversity/choice-without-equity-2009-report/frankenberg-choices-without-equity-2010.pdf; Ivan Moreno, "US Charter Schools Put Growing Numbers in Racial Isolation," Associated Press, December 3, 2017, https://apnews.com/article/e9c25534dfd44851a5e56bd57454b4f5; John R. Logan and Julia Burdick-Will, "School Segregation, Charter Schools, and Access to Quality Education," *Journal of Urban Affairs* 38, no. 3 (2015): 323–343, https://doi.org/10.1111/juaf.12246.

53. Eve L. Ewing, *Ghosts in the Schoolyard: Racism and School Closings on Chicago's South Side* (Chicago: University of Chicago Press, 2018); Prudence L. Carter and Kevin G. Welner, eds., *Closing the Opportunity Gap: What America Must Do to Give Every Child an Even Chance* (New York: Oxford University Press, 2013); Greg J. Duncan and Richard J. Murnane, eds., *Whither Opportunity? Rising Inequality, Schools, and Children's Life Chances* (New York: Russell Sage, 2011).

54. Jonathan Kozol, *Savage Inequalities: Children in America's Schools* (New York: Crown Publishers, 2012).

55. Richard J. Murnane, Sean F. Reardon, Preeya P. Mbekeani, and Anne Lamb, "Who Goes to Private School?," EducationNext.org, July 17, 2018, https://www.educationnext.org/who-goes-private-school-long-term-enrollment-trends-family-income/.

56. "Status and Trends in the Education of Racial and Ethnic Groups," National Center for Education Statistics, U.S. Department of Education, February 2019, https://nces.ed.gov/programs/raceindicators/indicator_rbb.asp.

57. Steve Suitts, "Race and Ethnicity in a New Era of Public Funding of Private Schools: Private School Enrollment in the South and the Nation" (Atlanta, GA: Southern Education Foundation, 2016).

58. Maureen T. Hallinan, "Tracking: From Theory to Practice," *Sociology of Education* 67, no. 2 (1994): 79–84, https://doi.org/10.2307/2112697.

59. Carol C. Burris, Kevin G. Welner, and Jennifer Brezoza, "Universal Access to a Quality Education: Research and Recommendations for the Elimination of Curricular Stratification," National Education Policy Center, December 14, 2009, https://nepc.colorado.edu/publication/universal-access.

60. Amanda E. Lewis and John B. Diamond, *Despite the Best Intentions: How Racial Inequality Thrives in Good Schools* (New York: Oxford University Press, 2015).

61. Christine Nord et al., "America's High School Graduates: Results from the 2009 NAEP High School Transcript Study," National Center for Education Statistics, April 2011, https://nces.ed.gov/nationsreportcard/pubs/studies/2011462.aspx.

62. Sabine Glock and Julia Karbach, "Preservice Teacher's Implicit Attitudes Toward Racial Minority Students: Evidence from Three Implicit Measures," *Studies in Educational Evaluation* 45 (2015): 55–61, https://doi.org/10.1016/j.stueduc.2015.03.006; William B. Lacy and Ernest Middleton, "Are Educators Racially Prejudiced?:

A Cross-Occupational Comparison of Attitudes," *Sociological Focus* 14, no. 1 (1981): 87–95, https://doi.org/10.1080/00380237.1981.10570384.

63. Jessika H. Bottiani, Catherine P. Bradshaw, and Tamar Mendelson, "Inequality in Black and White High School Students' Perceptions of School Support: An Examination of Race in Context," *Journal of Youth and Adolescence* 45 (2016): 1176–1191, https://doi.org/10.1007/s10964-015-0411-0; Walter S. Gilliam et al., "Do Early Educators' Implicit Biases Regarding Sex and Race Relate to Behavior Expectations and Recommendations of Preschool Expulsions and Suspensions?," Yale University Child Study Center, September 28, 2016, https://medicine.yale.edu/childstudy/zigler/publications/Preschool%20Implicit%20Bias%20Policy%20Brief_final_9_26_276766_5379_v1.pdf.

64. Russell J. Skiba, Kavitha Mediratta, and M. Karega Rausch, eds., *Inequality in School Discipline: Research and Practice to Reduce Disparities* (London: Palgrave Macmillan, 2016).

65. Russell J. Skiba et al., "Race Is Not Neutral: A National Investigation of African American and Latino Disproportionality in School Discipline," *School Psychology Review* 40, no. 1 (2011): 85–107, https://doi.org/10.1080/02796015.2011.12087730.

66. "Status and Trends in the Education of Racial and Ethnic Groups 2018," National Center for Education Statistics and American Institute for Research, U.S. Department of Education, February 2019, https://nces.ed.gov/pubs2019/2019038.pdf.

67. Gilliam et al., "Early Educators' Implicit Biases."

68. Skiba et al., "Race Is Not Neutral."

69. Skiba, Mediratta, and Rausch, *Inequality in School Discipline*.

70. Nikki Jones, *Between Good and Ghetto: African American Girls and Inner-City Violence* (New Brunswick, NJ: Rutgers University Press, 2009).

71. Victor M. Rios, *Punished: Policing the Lives of Black and Latino Boys* (New York: NYU Press, 2011).

72. Ann Arnett Ferguson, *Bad Boys: Public Schools in the Making of Black Masculinity* (Ann Arbor, MI: University of Michigan Press, 2000).

73. Victor M. Rios, *Human Targets: Schools, Police, and the Criminalization of Latino Youth* (Chicago: University of Chicago Press, 2017).

74. *PBS NewsHour*, "One Man's Journey From Gang Member to Academia," February 1, 2012, YouTube video, 9:31, https://www.youtube.com/watch?v=ReQar2BTlKY.

75. Jesse Kapukui, "Professor, Award Winning Author Speaks at 'We the Future Social Justiece Conference,'" *Oak Leaf News*, April 17, 2019, https://www.theoakleafnews.com/news/2019/04/17/award-winning-author-professor-speaks-at-we-the-future-social-justice-conference/.

76. Victor M. Rios, *Street Life: Poverty, Gangs, and a Ph.D.* (Scotts Valley, CA: CreateSpace Independent Publishing Platform, 2011).

77. *PBS NewsHour*, "One Man's Journey."

78. "Highlights from the U.S. PIAAC Survey of Incarcerated Adults: Their Skills, Work Experience, Education, and Training," Educational Testing Service, Westat, and

National Center for Education Statistics, U.S. Department of Education, November 2016, https://nces.ed.gov/pubs2016/2016040.pdf.

79. Lorelle L. Espinosa, Jonathan M. Turk, Morgan Taylor, and Hollie M. Chessman, "Race and Ethnicity in Higher Education: A Status Report," American Council on Education, 2019, https://www.equityinhighered.org/wp-content/uploads/2019/02/REHE-Exec-Summary-FINAL.pdf.

80. Raj Chetty et al., "Mobility Report Cards: The Role of Colleges in Intergenerational Mobility," National Bureau of Economic Research, July 2017, https://opportunityinsights.org/wp-content/uploads/2018/03/coll_mrc_paper.pdf.

81. Peter Arcidiacono, Josh Kinsler, and Tyler Ransom, "Legacy and Athlete Preferences at Harvard," June 3, 2020, http://public.econ.duke.edu/~psarcidi/legacyathlete.pdf.

82. Robert Booth, "Toby Young: Social Media Self-Obsessive Still Battling with Father's Shadow," Guardian, January 5, 2018, https://www.theguardian.com/media/2018/jan/05/why-impulsive-vain-toby-young-wants-us-to-take-him-seriously.

83. Eric Schlosser, "Reefer Madness," Atlantic, August 1994, https://www.theatlantic.com/magazine/archive/1994/08/reefer-madness/303476/.

84. "The Indian Hemp," The Western Journal of Medicine and Surgery, May 1843.

85. Isaac Campos, Home Grown: Marijuana and the Origins of Mexico's War on Drugs (Chapel Hill, NC: University of North Carolina Press, 2012).

86. As quoted in Rudolph J. Gerber, Legalizing Marijuana: Drug Policy Reform and Prohibition Politics (Westport, CT: Greenwood Publishing Group, 2009), 9; Laura L. Finley, Hawking Hits on the Information Highway: The Challenge of Online Drug Sales for Law Enforcement (New York: Peter Lang, 2008), 28; Jack Herer, Jeannie Herer, and Leslie Cabarga, The Emperor Wears No Clothes: The Authoritative Historical Record of Cannabis and the Conspiracy Against Marijuana (London: Knockabout Comics, 1994), 29.

87. H. J. Anslinger, "Marijuana—Assassin of Youth," U.S. Commissioner of Narcotics, The American Magazine, July 1937, https://web.archive.org/web/20040404113055/http://cannabis.net/assassin-of-youth.html.

88. Michelle Alexander, The New Jim Crow: Mass Incarceration in the Age of Colorblindness (New York: The New Press, 2010).

89. Eugene Jarecki, "The House I Live In," Independent Lens, April 8, 2013, https://www.pbs.org/independentlens/films/house-i-live-in/.

90. Marc Mauer and Ryan S. King, "A 25-Year Quagmire: The War on Drugs and Its Impact on American Society," The Sentencing Project, September 2007, https://www.sentencingproject.org/wp-content/uploads/2016/01/A-25-Year-Quagmire-The-War-On-Drugs-and-Its-Impact-on-American-Society.pdf.

91. Marc Mauer, Race to Incarcerate (New York: The New Press, 2006).

92. Andrew Daniller, "Two-Thirds of Americans Support Marijuana Legalization," Pew Research Center, November 14, 2019, https://www.pewresearch.org/fact-tank/2019/11/14/americans-support-marijuana-legalization/.

93. Suchitra Rajagopalan, "New FBI Report: Every 20 Seconds, Someone Is Arrested for a Drug Law Violation in the U.S.," DrugPolicy.org, September 24, 2018, https://drugpolicy.org/blog/new-fbi-report-every-20-seconds-someone-arrested-drug-law-violation-us.

94. Prison Policy Initiative, PrisonPolicy.org, accessed December 2, 2020, https://www.prisonpolicy.org/.

95. Laura M. Maruschak and Todd D. Minton, "Correctional Populations in the United States, 2017–2018," U.S. Department of Justice, Bureau of Justice Statistics, August 2020, https://www.bjs.gov/content/pub/pdf/cpus1718.pdf.

96. Alexander, The New Jim Crow.

97. Francis T. Cullen, Bonnie S. Fisher, and Brandon K. Applegate, "Public Opinion about Punishment and Corrections," Crime and Justice 27 (2000): 1–79. https://scholarcommons.sc.edu/cgi/viewcontent.cgi?article=1011&context=crim_facpub.

98. Barry Glassner, The Culture of Fear: Why Americans Are Afraid of the Wrong Things (New York: Basic Books, 2010).

99. Quoted in Eugene Jarecki, "The House I Live In," Independent Lens, April 8, 2013, https://www.pbs.org/independentlens/films/house-i-live-in/.

100. Drug Policy Alliance, "The Drug War, Mass Incarceration and Race," DrugPolicy.org, January 2018, http://www.drugpolicy.org/sites/default/files/drug-war-mass-incarceration-and-race_01_18_0.pdf.

101. The Sentencing Project, "Criminal Justice Facts," SentencingProject.org, accessed December 2, 2020, https://www.sentencingproject.org/criminal-justice-facts/.

102. Roxanne Daniel, "Since You Asked: What Data Exists about Native American People in the Criminal Justice System?," PrisonPolicy.org, April 22, 2020, https://www.prisonpolicy.org/blog/2020/04/22/native/.

103. Tanya Golash-Boza, "The Deportation Crisis for Latino Immigrant Men and Their Families," Scholars Strategy Network, April 2014, https://scholars.org/sites/scholars/files/ssn_key_findings_golash-boza_on_latino_men_and_the_deportation_crisis_1.pdf.

104. Human Rights Watch, "A Price Too High: US Families Torn Apart by Deportations for Drug Offenses," HRW.org, June 16, 2015, https://www.hrw.org/report/2015/06/16/price-too-high/us-families-torn-apart-deportations-drug-offenses.

105. Golash-Boza, "Deportation Crisis."

106. TRAC Immigration, "Tracking Over 2 Million ICE Arrests: A First Look," Trac.syr.edu, September 25, 2018, https://trac.syr.edu/immigration/reports/529/.

107. Substance Abuse and Mental Health Services Administration, "Results from the 2019 National Survey on Drug Use and Health: Detailed Tables," National Survey on Drug Use and Health, 2020, https://www.samhsa.gov/data/sites/default/files/reports/rpt29394/NSDUHDetailedTabs2019/NSDUHDetTabsSect1pe2019.htm.

108. Education Development Center, "FAQ: Connecting Across Cultures," IDHDP.com, accessed December 2, 2020, https://idhdp.com/media/531220/faq2_rwj.pdf.

109. Leonard Saxe et al., "The Visibility of Illicit Drugs: Implications for Community-Based Drug Control

Strategies," *American Journal of Public Health* 91, no. 12 (2001): 1987–94, https://doi.org/10.2105/ajph.91.12.1987.

110. Emma Pierson et al., "A Large-Scale Analysis of Racial Disparities in Police Stops Across the United States," *Nature Human Behaviour* 4 (2020): 736–745, https://doi.org/10.1038/s41562-020-0858-1; Frank R. Baumgartner, Derek A. Epp, Kelsey Shoub, *Suspect Citizens: What 20 Million Traffic Stops Tell Us About Policing and Race* (Cambridge: Cambridge University Press, 2018).

111. Pierson et al., "A Large-Scale Analysis of Racial Disparities in Police Stops Across the United States."

112. Garth Davies and Jeffrey Fagan, "Crime and Enforcement in Immigrant Neighborhoods: Evidence from New York City," Columbia Public Law Research Paper No. 12–292 (2012), https://scholarship.law.columbia.edu/cgi/viewcontent.cgi?article=2725&context=faculty_scholarship.

113. *David Floyd, Lalit Clarkson, Deon Dennis, and David Ourlicht v. The City of New York*, 08 Civ. 1034 (SAS) (2013), https://ccrjustice.org/sites/default/files/assets/files/Floyd-Liability-Opinion-8-12-13.pdf.

114. Alexander, *The New Jim Crow.*

115. Ingrid Gould Ellen and Justin Peter Steil, *The Dream Revisited: Contemporary Debates About Housing, Segregation, and Opportunity* (New York: Columbia University Press, 2019).

116. Christopher E. Herbert, Daniel T. McCue, and Rocio Sanchez-Moyano, "Is Homeownership Still an Effective Means of Building Wealth for Low-Income and Minority Households? (Was It Ever?)," Joint Center for Housing Studies, Harvard University, September 2013, http://www.jchs.harvard.edu/sites/default/files/hbtl-06.pdf; New Jersey Institute for Social Justice, "Becoming the United States of Opportunity: The Economic Equity and Growth Case for Apprenticeships," NJISJ.org, September 6, 2018, https://d3n8a8pro7vhmx.cloudfront.net/njisj/pages/1164/attachments/original/1536250817/Becoming_the_United_States_of_Opportunity_LR_Version.pdf?1536250817.

117. James Gilligan, *Violence: Reflections on a National Epidemic* (New York: First Vintage Books, 1996); Johan Galtung, "Violence, Peace, and Peace Research," *Journal of Peace Research* 6, no. 3 (1969): 167–191.

118. National Humanities Center, "Stokely Carmichael: Toward Black Liberation," *The Massachusetts Review*, Autumn 1966, http://nationalhumanitiescenter.org/pds/maai3/segregation/text8/carmichael.pdf.

119. Marilyn Frye, "Oppression," in Marilyn Frye, *Politics of Reality: Essays in Feminist Theory* (Berkeley, CA: Crossing Press, 1983).

CHAPTER 9

1. Marianne Weber, *Beruf und Ehe: Die Beteiligung Der Frau an Der Wissenschaft: Zwei Vorträge* (Berlin-Schöneberg, DE: Buchverlag der Hilfe, 1906).

2. Christopher T. Conner, Nicholas M. Baxter, and David R. Dickens, eds., *Forgotten Founders and Other Neglected Social Theorists* (Lanham, MD: Lexington Books, 2019).

3. Robert Barro, Jose Ursua, and Joanna Weng, "Coronavirus and the Lessons We Can Learn from the 1918–1920 Great Influenza Pandemic," World Economic Forum, March 23, 2020, https://www.weforum.org/agenda/2020/03/coronavirus-great-influenza-pandemic-covid19-prepared-outbreak/.

4. Quoted in Conner, Baxter, and Dickens, *Forgotten Founders,* 46.

5. Marianne Weber, "On the Valuation of Housework," in Elizabeth Kirchen, trans., *Selections from Marianne Weber's Reflections on Women and Women's Issues* (Unpublished manuscript, 1988 [1912]), 42–58.

6. Quoted in Patricia Madoo Lengermann and Gillian Niebrugge, *The Women Founders: Sociology and Social Theory 1830–1930* (Long Grove, IL: Waveland Press, 2006), 207.

7. B. Zorina Khan, *The Democratization of Invention: Patents and Copyrights in American Economic Development, 1790–1920* (New York: Cambridge University Press, 2005).

8. Claudia Goldin, *Understanding the Gender Gap: An Economic History of American Women* (New York: Oxford University Press, 1992).

9. Philip S. Foner, *Women and the American Labor Movement: From Colonial Times to the Eve of World War I* (New York: Free Press, 1979).

10. Uta Gerhardt, "Much More than a Mere Translation: Talcott Parsons's Translation into English of Max Weber's "Die protestantische Ethik und der Geist des Kapitalismus": An Essay in Intellectual History," *The Canadian Journal of Sociology* 32, no. 1 (2007): 41–62, https://doi.org/10.2307/20460615.

11. Talcott Parsons and Robert F. Bales, *Family, Socialization and Interaction Process* (New York: Free Press, 1955).

12. Stephanie Coontz, *The Way We Never Were: American Families and the Nostalgia Trap* (New York: Basic Books, 1993).

13. Jeffrey P. Dennis, *The Myth of the Queer Criminal* (Milton Park, UK: Taylor & Francis, 2017).

14. Daniel Patrick Moynihan, "The Negro Family: The Case for National Action," Washington, DC: Office of Policy Planning and Research, 1965.

15. Coontz, *The Way We Never Were.*

16. Stephanie Coontz, *A Strange Stirring: The Feminine Mystique and American Women at the Dawn of the 1960s* (New York: Basic Books, 2012); Coontz, *The Way We Never Were.*

17. Betty Friedan, *The Feminine Mystique* (New York: W. W. Norton, 2001); Coontz, *A Strange Stirring.*

18. Barbara Ehrenreich, *The Hearts of Men: American Dreams and the Flight from Commitment* (New York: Anchor Books, 1983).

19. Mimi Schippers, *Beyond Monogamy: Polyamory and the Future of Polyqueer Sexualities* (New York: NYU Press, 2016).

20. Anne Parsons, "Letter to Betty Friedan after reading *The Feminine Mystique*," 1963, quoted in Winifred Breines, "Alone in the 1950s: Anne Parsons and the Feminine Mystique," *Theory and Society* 15, no. 6 (1986): 805–843, https://doi.org/10.1007/BF00160775.

21. Anne Parsons, "Diary of a Mental Patient," 1963, quoted in Breines, "Alone in the 1950s," 816.

22. Anne Parsons, "Letter to Parents," 1963, quoted in Breines, "Alone in the 1950s," 838.

23. Breines, "Alone in the 1950s," 830.

24. Myra Marx Ferree, "The Gay Wedding Backlash," *Newsday*, May 23, 2004.

25. Goldin, *Understanding the Gender Gap.*

26. Jo Freeman, *We Will Be Heard: Women's Struggles for Political Power in the United States* (Lanham, MD: Rowman & Littlefield, 2008).

27. David Cotter, Paula England, and Joan Hermsen, "Moms and Jobs: Trends in Mothers' Employment and Which Mothers Stay Home," Council on Contemporary Families, May 10, 2007, https://contemporaryfamilies.org/wp -content/uploads/2013/10/2007_Briefing_Cotter_Moms -and-jobs.pdf.

28. Cotter, England, and Hermsen, "Moms and Jobs."

29. ChildCare Aware of America, "The US and the High Price of Child Care: An Examination of a Broken System," accessed December 7, 2020, https://usa.childcareaware .org/advocacy-public-policy/resources/research/costofcare/.

30. Daniel L. Carlson, Sarah Hanson, and Andrea Fitzroy, "The Division of Childcare, Sexual Intimacy, and Relationship Quality in Couples," *Sociology Faculty Publications* 4 (2015).

31. U.S. Bureau of Labor Statistics, "Percentage of Employed Women Working Full Time Little Changed over Past 5 Decades," *The Economics Daily*, December 1, 2017, https://www.bls.gov/opub/ted/2017/percentage-of -employed-women-working-full-time-little-changed -over-past-5-decades.htm.

32. U.S. Bureau of Labor Statistics, "Employment Characteris- tics of Families Summary—2019," April 21, 2020, https://www.bls.gov/news.release/famee.nr0.htm.

33. Janet Swim, Eugene Borgida, Geoffrey Maruyama, and David G. Myers, "Joan McKay versus John McKay: Do Gender Stereotypes Bias Evaluations?," *Psychological Bulletin* 105, no. 3 (1989): 409–429, https://doi.org/10.1037 /0033-2909.105.3.409; Pamela Paxton, Sheri Kunovich, and Melanie M. Hughes, "Gender in Politics," *Annual Review of Sociology* 33 (2007): 263–284, https://doi.org/10.1146 /annurev.soc.33.040406.131651; Corinne A. Moss-Racusin et al., "Science Faculty's Subtle Gender Biases Favor Male Students," *Proceedings of the National Academy of Sciences* 109, no. 41 (2012): 16474–16479, https://doi.org/10.1073 /pnas.1211286109.

34. Lin Bian, Sarah-Jane Leslie, and Andrei Cimpian, "Gender Stereotypes About Intellectual Ability Emerge Early and Influence Children's Interests," *Science* 355, no. 6323 (2017): 389–391, https://doi.org/10.1126/science.aah6524; Aaron Lecklider, *Inventing the Egghead: The Battle over Brainpower in American Culture* (Philadelphia: University of Pennsylvania Press, 2013); Adrian Furnham, Emma Reeves, and Salima Budhani, "Parents Think Their Sons Are Brighter Than Their Daughters: Sex Differences in Parental Self-Estimations and Estimations of Their Children's Multiple Intelligences," *Journal of Genetic Psychology* 163, no. 1 (2002): 24–39, https://doi.org /10.1080/00221320209597966; Sarah-Jane Leslie, Andrei Cimpian, Meredith Meyer, and Edward Freeland, "Expectations of Brilliance Underlie Gender Distributions

across Academic Disciplines," *Science* 347, no. 6219 (2015): 262–265, https://doi.org/10.1126/science.1261375; Penelope Espinoza, Ana B. Arēas da Luz Fontes, and Clarissa J. Arms-Chavez, "Attributional Gender Bias: Teacher's Ability and Effort Explanations for Students' Math Performance," *Social Psychology of Education* 17 (2014): 105–126, https://doi.org/10.1007/s11218-013 -9226-6.

35. Swim et al., "Joan McKay"; Renée B. Adams, Roman Kräussl, Marco A. Navone, and Patrick Verwijmeren, "Is Gender in the Eye of the Beholder? Identifying Cultural Attitudes with Art Auction Prices," CFS Working Paper Series No. 595 (December 6, 2017), http://dx.doi .org/10.2139/ssrn.3083500.

36. Elise Tak, Shelley J. Correll, and Sarah A. Soule, "Gender Inequality in Product Markets: When and How Status Beliefs Transfer to Products," *Social Forces* 98, no. 2 (2019): 548–577, https://doi.org/10.1093/sf/soy125.

37. Moss-Racusin et al., "Science Faculty's Subtle Gender Biases."

38. "Women CEOs of the S&P 500," Catalyst, December 2, 2020, https://www.catalyst.org/research/women-ceos -of-the-sp-500/; "Women on Corporate Boards: Quick Take," Catalyst, March 13, 2020, https://www.catalyst.org /research/women-on-corporate-boards/; "Women in Management: Quick Take," Catalyst, August 11, 2020, https://www.catalyst.org/research/women-in-management/.

39. Center for American Women and Politics, "Women in Elective Office 2021," https://cawp.rutgers.edu/women -elective-office-2021.

40. Charlotte Perkins Gilman, *The Man-Made World: or, Our Androcentric Culture* (New York: Charlton Press, 1911).

41. Kelly R. Moran and Sara Y. Del Valle, "A Meta-Analysis of the Association between Gender and Protective Behaviors in Response to Respiratory Epidemics and Pandemics," *PLoS One* 11, no. 10 (2016): e0164541, https://doi.org/10.1371 /journal.pone.0164541.

42. Alyson Krueger, "Where Women Are Ahead of Men: Hand Washing," *New York Times*, March 17, 2020, https://www .nytimes.com/2020/03/17/us/women-men-hand-washing -coronavirus.html.

43. Weber, "On the Valuation of Housework."

44. R. W. Connell, *Masculinities* (Cambridge, UK: Polity Press, 1995); R. W. Connell, *Gender and Power: Society, the Person, and Sexual Politics* (Stanford, CA: Stanford University Press, 1987).

45. Sveva Magaraggia, "Gender in Theory and Practice: An Interview with Raewyn Connell," *Feminist Review* 102 (2012): 119.

46. Connell, *Gender and Power*; R. W. Connell and James Messerschmidt, "Hegemonic Masculinity: Rethinking the Concept," *Gender & Society* 19, no. 6 (2005): 829–59.

47. Arlie Russell Hochschild, *The Commercialization of Intimate Life: Notes from Home and Work* (Oakland, CA: University of California Press, 2003).

48. Arlie Hochschild and Anne Machung, *The Second Shift: Working Families and the Revolution at Home* (New York: Penguin Publishing Group, 2012).

49. Vanessa R. Wight, Joseph Price, Suzanne M. Bianchi, and Bijou R. Hunt, "The Time Use of Teenagers," *Social Science Research* 38, no. 4 (2009): 792–809, https://doi.org/10.1016/j.ssresearch.2009.05.009.

50. Cynthia Hess, Tanima Ahmed, and Jeff Hayes, "Providing Unpaid Household and Care Work in the United States: Uncovering Inequality," Institute for Women's Policy Research, January 2020, https://iwpr.org/wp-content/uploads/2020/01/IWPR-Providing-Unpaid-Household-and-Care-Work-in-the-United-States-Uncovering-Inequality.pdf.

51. Claire Cain Miller, "Stressed, Tired, Rushed: A Portrait of the Modern Family," *New York Times*, November 4, 2015, https://www.nytimes.com/2015/11/05/upshot/stressed-tired-rushed-a-portrait-of-the-modern-family.html.

52. Kathleen Gerson, *The Unfinished Revolution: Coming of Age in a New Era of Gender, Work, and Family* (New York: Oxford University Press, 2011).

53. U.S. Bureau of Labor Statistics, "American Time Use Survey—2019 Results," June 25, 2020, https://www.bls.gov/news.release/atus.nr0.htm.

54. Nicole Civettini, "Gender Display, Time Availability, and Relative Resources: Applicability to Housework Contributions of Members of Same-Sex Couples," *International Social Science Review* 91, no. 1 (2015), https://digitalcommons.northgeorgia.edu/cgi/viewcontent.cgi?article=1112&context=issr; Michael J. Smart, Anne Brown, and Brian D. Taylor, "Sex or Sexuality? Analyzing the Division of Labor and Travel in Gay, Lesbian, and Straight Households," *Travel Behaviour and Society* 6 (2017): 75–82, https://doi.org/10.1016/j.tbs.2016.07.001; Maura Kelly and Elizabeth Hauck, "Doing Housework, Redoing Gender: Queer Couples Negotiate the Household Division of Labor," *Journal of GLBT Family Studies* 11, no. 5 (2015): 438– 464, https://doi.org/10.1080/1550428X.2015.1006750; Timothy J. Biblarz and Evren Savci, "Lesbian, Gay, Bisexual, and Transgender Families," *Journal of Marriage and Family* 72, no. 3 (2010): 480–497, https://doi.org/10.1111/j.1741-3737.2010.00714.x.

55. Stephanie Coontz, *Marriage, a History: How Love Conquered Marriage* (New York: Penguin Books, 2006), 15.

56. Coontz, *Marriage, a History*.

57. Sharon Hays, *The Cultural Contradictions of Motherhood* (New Haven, CT: Yale University Press, 1996); Patrick Ishizuka "Social Class, Gender, and Contemporary Parenting Standards in the United States: Evidence from a National Survey Experiment," *Social Forces* 98, no. 1 (September 2019): 31-58, https://doi.org/10.1093/sf/soy107.

58. Kathryn Edin and Timothy J. Nelson, *Doing the Best I Can: Fatherhood in the Inner City* (Oakland, CA: University of California Press, 2013).

59. Rachel M. Schmitz, "Constructing Men as Fathers: A Content Analysis of Formulations of Fatherhood in Parenting Magazines," *Journal of Men's Studies* 24, no. 1 (2016): 3–23, https://doi.org/10.1177/1060826515624381.

60. Christopher Carrington, *No Place Like Home: Relationships and Family Life Among Lesbians and Gay Men* (Chicago: University of Chicago Press, 2002).

61. Ann Crittenden, *The Price of Motherhood: Why the Most Important Job in the World Is Still the Least Valued* (London: Picador, 2010); Judith Warner, "The Opt-Out Generation Wants Back In," *New York Times Magazine*, August 7, 2013, https://www.nytimes.com/2013/08/11/magazine/the-opt-out-generation-wants-back-in.html; Neil Chethik, *VoiceMale: What Husbands Really Think About Their Marriages, Their Wives, Sex, Housework, and Commitment* (New York: Simon & Schuster, 2008); Susan Walzer, *Thinking about the Baby: Gender and Transitions into Parenthood* (Philadelphia: Temple University Press, 1998).

62. Ellen Lamont, *The Mating Game: How Gender Still Shapes How We Date* (Oakland, CA: University of California Press, 2020).

63. Allison J. Pugh, *The Tumbleweed Society: Working and Caring in an Age of Insecurity* (New York: Oxford University Press, 2015).

64. Kevin T. Leicht, "Broken Down by Race and Gender? Sociological Explanations of New Sources of Earnings Inequality," *Annual Review of Sociology* 34 (2008): 237–255, https://doi.org/10.1146/annurev.soc.34.040507.134627.

65. A. W. Geiger, Gretchen Livingston, and Kristen Bialik, "6 Facts about U.S. Moms," Pew Research Center, May 8, 2019, https://www.pewresearch.org/fact-tank/2019/05/08/facts-about-u-s-mothers/.

66. Rebecca Glauber, "Race and Gender in Families and at Work: The Fatherhood Wage Premium," *Gender and Society* 22, no. 1 (2008): 8–30, https://doi.org/10.1177/0891243207311593.

67. Katherine Weisshaar, "From Opt Out to Blocked Out: The Challenges for Labor Market Re-entry after Family-Related Employment Lapses," *American Sociological Review* 83, no. 1 (2018): 34–60, https://doi.org/10.1177/0003122417752355.

68. Brad Harrington, Tina Lawler McHugh, and Jennifer Sabatini Fraone, "Expanded Paid Parental Leave: Measuring the Impact of Leave on Work & Family," Boston College Center for Work & Family, 2019, https://www.bc.edu/content/dam/files/centers/cwf/research/publications/researchreports/Expanded%20Paid%20Parental%20Leave-%20Study%20Findings%20FINAL%2010-31-19.pdf.

69. Nicole Civettini, "Housework as Non-Normative Gender Display Among Lesbians and Gay Men," *Sex Roles* 74 (2016): 206–219, https://doi.org/10.1007/s11199-015-0559-9.

70. Matt Krentz, Emily Kos, Anna Green, and Jennifer Garcia-Alonso, "Easing the COVID-19 Burden on Working Parents," Boston Consulting Group, May 21, 2020, https://www.bcg.com/publications/2020/helping-working-parents-ease-the-burden-of-covid-19.

71. Jessica M. Calarco, Elizabeth Anderson, Emily V. Meanwell, and Amelia Knopf, "'Let's Not Pretend It's Fun': How COVID-19-Related School and Childcare Closures Are Damaging Mother's Well-Being," SocArXiv Papers, November 2020, https://doi.org/10.31235/osf.io/jyvk4.

72. Misty L. Heggeness and Jason M. Fields, "Parents Juggle Work and Child Care During Pandemic," U.S. Census Bureau, August 18, 2020, https://www.census.gov/library

/stories/2020/08/parents-juggle-work-and-child-care
-during-pandemic.html.

73. Francesca Donner, "How Women Are Getting Squeezed by the Pandemic," *New York Times*, May 20, 2020, https://www.nytimes.com/2020/05/20/us/women-economy-jobs-coronavirus-gender.html?action=click&module =RelatedLinks&pgtype=Article.

74. U.S. Bureau of Labor Statistics, "Highlights of Women's Earnings in 2019," BLS Reports, December 2020, https://www.bls.gov/opub/reports/womens-earnings /2019/home.htm.

75. Francine D. Blau and Lawrence M. Kahn, "The Gender Wage Gap: Extent, Trends, and Explanations," National Bureau of Economic Research, January 2016, https://www .nber.org/system/files/working_papers/w21913/w21913 .pdf; "Women Had Higher Median Earnings Than Men in Relatively Few Occupations in 2018," *TED: The Economics Daily*, U.S. Bureau of Labor Statistics, March 22, 2019, https://www.bls.gov/opub/ted/2019/women-had-higher -median-earnings-than-men-in-relatively-few-occupations -in-2018.htm#:~:text=In%202018%2C%20women%20 who%20were,for%20both%20women%20and%20men.

76. "Education and Lifetime Earnings," Research, Statistics & Policy Analysis, Social Security, accessed December 7, 2020, https://www.ssa.gov/policy/docs/research-summaries /education-earnings.html.

77. Marieka Klawitter, "Meta-Analysis of the Effects of Sexual Orientation on Earnings," *Industrial Relations* 54, no. 1 (2015): 4–32, https://doi.org/10.1111/irel.12075.

78. Kristen Schilt, *Just One of the Guys?: Transgender Men and the Persistence of Gender Inequality* (Chicago: University of Chicago Press, 2010).

79. Center for American Progress and Movement Advancement Project, "Paying an Unfair Price: The Financial Penalty for Being Transgender in America," LGBTMap.org, February 2015, https://www.lgbtmap.org/file/paying-an-unfair-price -transgender.pdf.

80. Kristen Schilt and Matthew Wiswall, "Before and After: Gender Transitions, Human Capital, and Workplace Experiences," *B.E. Journal of Economic Analysis & Policy* 8, no. 1 (2008), https://doi.org/10.2202/1935-1682.1862; Lydia Geijtenbeek and Erik Plug, "Is There a Penalty for Registered Women? Is There a Premium for Registered Men? Evidence from a Sample of Transsexual Workers," *European Economic Review* 109 (2018): 334–347, https://doi.org/10.1016/j.euroecorev.2017.12.006.

81. Francine D. Blau and Lawrence M. Kahn, "The Gender Pay Gap: Have Women Gone as Far as They Can?," *Academy of Management Perspectives* 21, no. 1 (2007): 7–23, https://doi.org/10.5465/amp.2007.24286161.

82. Nancy M. Carter and Christine Silva, "Pipeline's Broken Promise," Catalyst, 2010, https://www.catalyst.org /wp-content/uploads/2019/01/Pipelines_Broken _Promise_Final_021710.pdf; David A. Cotter, Joan M. Hermsen, Seth Ovadia, and Reeve Vanneman, "The Glass Ceiling Effect," *Social Forces* 80, no. 2 (2001): 655–681, https://doi.org/10.1353/sof.2001.0091.

83. Sylvia Ann Hewlett and Carolyn Buck Luce, "Off-Ramps and On-Ramps: Keeping Talented Women on the Road to Success," *Harvard Business Review*, March 2005, https://hbr .org/2005/03/off-ramps-and-on-ramps-keeping-talented -women-on-the-road-to-success; Carter and Silva, "Pipeline's Broken Promise."

84. Christine L. Williams, "The Glass Escalator: Hidden Advantages for Men in the 'Female' Professions," *Social Problems* 39, no. 3 (1992): 253–267, https://doi.org /10.2307/3096961; Adia Harvey Wingfield, "Racializing the Glass Escalator: Reconsidering Men's Experiences with Women's Work," *Gender & Society* 23, no. 1 (2009): 5–26, https://doi.org/10.1177/0891243208323054.

85. Philip N. Cohen, "The Persistence of Workplace Gender Segregation in the US," *Sociology Compass* 7, no. 11 (2013): 889–899, https://doi.org/10.1111/soc4.12083.

86. Elyse Shaw, Ariane Hegewisch, Emma Williams-Baron, and Barbara Gault, "Undervalued and Underpaid in America: Women in Low-Wage, Female-Dominated Jobs," Institute for Women's Policy Research, 2016, https://iwpr.org /wp-content/uploads/2020/09/D508-Undervalued-and -Underpaid.pdf.

87. Philip N. Cohen and Matt L. Huffman, "Individuals, Jobs, and Labor Markets: The Devaluation of Women's Work," *American Sociological Review* 68 (2003): 443–463, https://doi.org/10.2307/1519732.

88. "May 2019 National Occupational Employment and Wage Estimates," U.S. Bureau of Labor Statistics, May 2019, https://www.bls.gov/oes/current/oes_nat.htm#00-0000.

89. Asaf Levanon, Paula England, and Paul Allison, "Occupa-tional Feminization and Pay: Assessing Casual Dynamics Using 1950–2000 U.S. Census Data," *Social Forces* 88, no. 2 (2009): 865–891, https://doi.org/10.1353/sof.0.0264.

90. Margery W. Davies, *Woman's Place Is at the Typewriter* (Philadelphia: Temple University Press, 1984).

91. "Sexy Secretary, 1800–2000," Google Books Ngram Viewer, accessed December 7, 2020, https://books.google .com/ngrams/graph?content=sexy+secretary&year _start=1800&year_end=2000&corpus=15&smoothing =3&share=&direct_url=t1%3B%2Csexy%20secretary %3B%2Cc0.

92. "Household Data: Annual Averages," U.S. Bureau of Labor Statistics, 2019, https://www.bls.gov/cps/cpsaat11.htm.

93. Lois Mandel, "The Computer Girls," *Cosmopolitan*, April 1967, in Elaine Burke, "The Computer Girls: 1967 Cosmo Article Highlights Women in Technology," *Silicon Republic*, August 18, 2015, https://www.siliconrepublic.com/people /women-in-technology-the-computer-girls-cosmopolitan.

94. Clive Thompson, "The Secret History of Women in Coding," *New York Times*, February 13, 2019, https://www .nytimes.com/2019/02/13/magazine/women-coding -computer-programming.html.

95. Arlie Hochschild and Anne Machung, *The Second Shift: Work-ing Parents and the Revolution at Home* (New York: Viking Penguin, 1989); Paula England, "The Gender Revolution: Uneven and Stalled," *Gender & Society* 24, no. 2 (2010): 149–166, https://doi.org/10.1177/0891243210361475.

96. Jean M. Twenge, "Changes in Masculine and Feminine Traits over Time: A Meta-Analysis," *Sex Roles* 36 (1997); 305–325, https://doi.org/10.1007/BF02766650.

97. Heidi I. Hartmann, "The Unhappy Marriage of Marxism and Feminism: Towards a More Progressive Union," *Capital & Class* 3, no. 2 (1979): 1–33, https://doi.org/10.1177/030981687900800102.

98. Linda Burnham and Nik Theodore, "Home Economics: The Invisible and Unregulated World of Domestic Work," National Domestic Workers Alliance, 2012, https://idwfed.org/en/resources/home-economics-the-invisible-and-unregulated-world-of-domestic-work/@@display-file/attachment_1.

99. Burnham and Theodore, "Home Economics."

100. Rhacel Salazar Parreñas, "The Care Crisis in the Philippines: Children and Transnational Families in the New Global Economy," in *Global Woman: Nannies, Maids, and Sex Workers in the New Economy*, eds. Barbara Ehrenreich and Arlie Russell Hochschild (New York: Henry Holt and Company, 2004).

101. Personal communication.

102. Personal communication.

103. Nicola Piper, "Gender and Migration," Policy Analysis and Research Programme of the Global Commission on International Migration, September 2005, http://incedes.org.gt/Master/pipersesentacuatro.pdf.

104. Rhacel Salazar Parreñas, *Servants of Globalization: Women, Migration, and Domestic Work* (Stanford, CA: Stanford University Press, 2001).

105. Ehrenreich and Hochschild, *Global Woman*.

CHAPTER 10

1. Sarah F. Brosnan and Frans B. M. de Waal, "Monkeys Reject Unequal Pay," *Nature* 425 (2003): 297–299, https://doi.org/10.1038/nature01963; vladimerk1, "Capuchin Monkey Fairness Experiment," YouTube video, 0:57, April 13, 2012, https://www.youtube.com/watch?v=-KSryJXDpZo, from Frans B. M. de Waal, "Moral Behavior in Animals," TEDxPeachtree, TED.com, November 2011, https://www.ted.com/talks/frans_de_waal_moral_behavior_in_animals/up-next.

2. Adair Lara, "The Chosen Few: S.F.'s Exclusive Clubs Carry on Traditions of Fellowship, Culture—and Discrimination," *San Francisco Chronicle*, July 28, 2004, https://www.sfgate.com/news/article/THE-CHOSEN-FEW-S-F-s-exclusive-clubs-carry-on-2740755.php; G. William Domhoff, *The Bohemian Grove and Other Retreats: A Study in Ruling-Class Cohesiveness* (New York: Harper & Row, 1975); Peter Martin Phillips, *A Relative Advantage: Sociology of the San Francisco Bohemian Club* (Davis, CA: University of California, Davis Press, 2017); "Compiled by DuPre Jones," *New York Times*, October 28, 1973, https://www.nytimes.com/1973/10/28/archives/the-sayings-of-secretary-henry-language-negotiation-humility-the.html?mcubz=2; Brenden Gallagher, "25 Outrageously Expensive Social Clubs in America," *Complex*, May 8, 2014, https://www.complex.com/pop-culture/2014/05/25-outrageously-expensive-social-clubs-in-america/; Alex Shoumatoff, "Bohemian Tragedy," *Vanity Fair*, May 2009, https://www.vanityfair.com/culture/2009/05/bohemian-grove200905.

3. Diana Kendall, *Members Only: Elite Clubs and the Process of Exclusion* (Lanham, MD: Rowman & Littlefield, 2008).

4. Peter Martin Phillips, "A Relative Advantage: Sociology of the San Francisco Bohemian Club," PhD diss., University of California, Davis, 1994, https://sonoma-dspace.calstate.edu/bitstream/handle/10211.3/143729/phillips_relative.pdf?sequence=1.

5. G. William Domhoff, *Who Rules America? Triumph of the Corporate Rich* (New York: McGraw-Hill, 2014).

6. C. Wright Mills, *The Power Elite* (New York: Oxford University Press, 1959).

7. John B. Judis, "The Spiritual Wobbly," *New York Times*, July 9, 2000, http://www.nytimes.com/books/00/07/09/reviews/000709.09judist.html?mcubz=2.

8. C. Wright Mills, "Growing Up in Texas," https://archive.nytimes.com/www.nytimes.com/books/first/m/mills-writings.html, in *Letters and Autobiographic Writings*, eds. Kathryn Mills and Pamela Mills (Oakland, CA: University of California Press, 2000).

9. Robert A. Dahl, *Who Governs?: Democracy and Power in an American City* (New Haven, CT: Yale University Press, 2005); Joseph A. Schumpeter, *Capitalism, Socialism, and Democracy* (New York: Harper Perennial Modern Classics, 2008); John Kenneth Galbraith, *American Capitalism: The Concept of Countervailing Power* (Boston, MA: Houghton Mifflin Harcourt, 1952).

10. G. William Domhoff, "Social Clubs, Policy-Planning Groups, and Corporations: A Network Study of Ruling-Class Cohesiveness," *Insurgent Sociologist* 5, no. 3 (1975): 171–184, https://doi.org/10.1177/089692057500500310; Michael Useem, *The Inner Circle: Large Corporations and the Rise of Business Political Activity in the U.S. and U.K.* (New York: Oxford University Press, 1986); Kendall, *Members Only*; Sidney Verba, Kay Lehman Schlozman, and Henry E. Brady, *Voice and Equality: Civic Voluntarism in American Politics* (Cambridge, MA: Harvard University Press, 1995).

11. In 2020 numbers; according to 2014 numbers: $30,000 with $7,200 due each year afterward, adjusted for inflation, in Gallagher, "25 Outrageously Expensive Social Clubs in America."

12. Nicholas A. Christakis and James H. Fowler, *Connected: The Surprising Power of Our Social Networks and How They Shape Our Lives* (New York: Little, Brown and Company, 2009).

13. Kendall, *Members Only*, 3.

14. William Davies, "Elite Power under Advanced Neoliberalism," *Theory, Culture & Society* 34, no. 5–6 (2017): 227–250, https://doi.org/10.1177/0263276417715072; Janine R. Wedel, "From Power Elites to Influence Elites: Resetting Elite Studies for the 21st Century," *Theory, Culture & Society* 34, no. 5–6 (2017): 153–178, https://doi.org/10.1177/0263276417715311.

15. Gerald F. Davis, Mina Yoo, Wayne E. Baker, "The Small World of the American Corporate Elite, 1982–2001," *Strategic Organization* 1, no. 3 (2003): 301–326, https://doi.org/10.1177/14761270030013002.

16. Art Van Zee, "The Promotion and Marketing of OxyContin: Commercial Triumph, Public Health Tragedy," *American Journal of Public Health* 99, no. 2 (2009): 221–227, https://doi.org/10.2105/AJPH.2007.131714.

17. Scott Higham, Sari Horwitz, and Steven Rich, "76 Billion Opioid Pills: Newly Released Federal Data Unmasks the Epidemic," *Washington Post*, July 16, 2019, https://www.washingtonpost.com/investigations/76-billion-opioid-pills-newly-released-federal-data-unmasks-the-epidemic/2019/07/16/5f29fd62-a73e-11e9-86dd-d7f0e60391e9_story.html.

18. Laura C. Palombi et al., "A Scoping Review of Opioid Misuse in the Rural United States," *Annals of Epidemiology* 28, no. 9 (2018): 641–652, https://doi.org/10.1016/j.annepidem.2018.05.008.

19. "Key Substance Use and Mental Health Indicators in the United States: Results from the 2019 National Survey on Drug Use and Health," Center for Behavioral Health Statistics and Quality, Substance Abuse and Mental Health Services Administration Center for Behavioral Health Statistics and Quality, Substance Abuse and Mental Health Services Administration (SAMHSA), 2020, https://www.samhsa.gov/data/sites/default/files/reports/rpt29393/2019NSDUHFFRPDFWHTML/2019NSDUHFFR090120.htm; "Overdose Death Rates," National Institute on Drug Abuse, Jan. 29, 2021, https://www.drugabuse.gov/drug-topics/trends-statistics/overdose-death-rates; "Opioid Overdose: Drug Overdose Deaths," Centers for Disease Control and Prevention, accessed March 19, 2020, https://www.cdc.gov/drugoverdose/data/statedeaths.html.

20. Danielle F. Haley and Richard Saitz, "The Opioid Epidemic During the COVID-19 Pandemic," *Journal of the American Medical Association* 324, no. 16 (2020): 1615–1617.

21. Bill Whitaker, "Ex-DEA Agent: Opioid Crisis Fueled by Drug Industry and Congress," *60 Minutes*, CBS News, October 15, 2017, https://www.cbsnews.com/news/ex-dea-agent-opioid-crisis-fueled-by-drug-industry-and-congress/.

22. Scott Higham and Lenny Bernstein, "The Drug Industry's Triumph Over the DEA," *Washington Post*, October 15, 2017, https://www.washingtonpost.com/graphics/2017/investigations/dea-drug-industry-congress/.

23. Higham and Bernstein, "The Drug Industry's Triumph."

24. Max Weber, *Economy and Society: An Outline of Interpretive Sociology* (Oakland, CA: University of California Press, 1922).

25. Pierre Bourdieu, *Distinction: A Social Critique of the Judgment of Taste* (Cambridge, MA: Harvard University Press, 1984).

26. Etienne Ollion, "Death Is Not the End: The Rise and Rise of Pierre Boudieu in US Sociology," *OUPblog* (blog), Oxford University Press, July 31, 2015, https://blog.oup.com/2015/07/pierre-bourdieu-us-sociology/.

27. Lauren A. Rivera, "Status Distinctions in Interaction: Social Selection and Exclusion at an Elite Nightclub," *Qualitative Sociology* 33 (2010): 229–255, https://doi.org/10.1007/s11133-010-9152-2.

28. Rivera, "Status Distinctions," 236.

29. Lauren A. Rivera, "Hiring as Cultural Matching: The Case of Elite Professional Service Firms," *American Sociological Review* 77, no. 6 (2012): 999–1022, https://doi.org/10.1177/0003122412463213.

30. "Purpose & Progress: 2017 Environmental, Social and Governance Report," Goldman Sachs, 2017, https://www.goldmansachs.com/citizenship/sustainability-reporting/esg-content/esg-report-2017.pdf; "Federal Equal Opportunity Recruitment Program (FEORP) Report to Congress Fiscal Year 2016," United States Office of Personnel Management, February 2018, https://www.opm.gov/policy-data-oversight/diversity-and-inclusion/reports/feorp-2016.pdf.

31. Buck Gee and Denise Peck, "The Illusion of Asian Success: Scant Progress for Minorities in Cracking the Glass Ceiling from 2007–2015," Ascend Pan-Asian Leaders, accessed December 8, 2020, https://cdn.ymaws.com/www.ascendleadership.org/resource/resmgr/research/TheIllusionofAsianSuccess.pdf.

32. Wesley Yang, "Harvard Is Wrong That Asians Have Terrible Personalities," *New York Times*, June 25, 2018, https://www.nytimes.com/2018/06/25/opinion/harvard-asian-american-racism.html.

33. Antonio Gramsci, *Prison Notebooks: Volume I* (New York: Columbia University Press, 1992).

34. "Average Annual Hours Actually Worked per Worker," Organisation for Economic Co-operation and Development, accessed December 8, 2020, https://stats.oecd.org/Index.aspx?DataSetCode=ANHRS.

35. John Levi Martin, "What Do Animals Do All Day?: The Division of Labor, Class Bodies, and Totemic Thinking in the Popular Imagination," *Poetics* 27 (2000): 195–231.

36. Anthony Giddens, *Modernity and Self-Identity: Self and Society in the Late Modern Age* (Stanford, CA: Stanford University Press, 1991); Zygmunt Bauman, *Liquid Modernity* (Cambridge, UK: Polity, 2000).

37. Émile Durkheim, *The Division of Labor in Society* (New York: Free Press, 1997 [1893]).

38. Richard E. Nisbett, *The Geography of Thought* (New York: Free Press, 2003); Henri C. Santos, Michael E. W. Varnum, and Ignor Grossmann, "Global Increases in Individualism," *Psychological Science* 28, no. 9 (2017): 1228–1239, https://doi.org/10.1177/0956797617700622; Beth Morling and Marika Lamoreaux, "Measuring Culture Outside the Head: A Meta-Analysis of Individualism—Collectivism in Cultural Products," *Personality and Social Psychology Review* 12, no. 3 (2008): 199–221, https://doi.org/10.1177/1088868308318260.

39. University of Kent, "Collectivism Drives Efforts to Reduce the Spread of COVID-19," *ScienceDaily*, June 29, 2020, www.sciencedaily.com/releases/2020/06/200629120140.htm.

40. Heejung S. Kim, David K. Sherman, and John A. Updegraff, "Fear of Ebola: The Influence of Collectivism on Xenophobic Threat Responses," *Psychological Science* 27, no. 7 (2016): 935–944, https://doi.org/10.1177/0956797616642596.

41. Gregory D. Webster et al., "Culture, COVID-19, and Collectivism: A Paradox of American Exceptionalism?," PsyArXiv, November 28, 2020, https://doi.org/10.31234/osf.io/hqcs6.

42. Fiona Webster, Kathleen Rice, and Abhimanyu Sud, "A Critical Content Analysis of Media Reporting on Opioids: The Social Construction of an Epidemic," *Social Science & Medicine* 244 (2020): 112642, https://doi.org/10.1016/j.socscimed.2019.112642.

43. German Lopez, "The Case for Prosecuting the Sacklers and Other Opioid Executives," *Vox*, updated October 10, 2019, https://www.vox.com/policy-and-politics/2019/10/10/20881636/sacklers-purdue-opioid-epidemic-prison-prosecution-criminal-investigation.

44. G. William Domhoff, "Mills's *The Power Elite* 50 Years Later," *Contemporary Sociology* 35, no. 6 (2006): 547–550, https://doi.org/10.1177/009430610603500602.

CHAPTER II

1. Frances Fox Piven, "Can Power from Below Change the World?," *American Sociological Review* 73, no. 1 (2008): 1–14, https://doi.org/10.1177/000312240807300101.

2. In 1860, just before the Civil War, the nearly 4 million enslaved people are estimated to have been worth $3.5 billion. Ta-Nehisi Coates, "Slavery Made America," *Atlantic*, June 24, 2014, https://www.theatlantic.com/business/archive/2014/06/slavery-made-america/373288/.

3. Doug McAdam and David A. Snow, *Social Movements: Readings on Their Emergence, Mobilization, and Dynamics* (Los Angeles, CA: Roxbury Publishing Company, 1997).

4. Abby Margulies, "Frances Fox Piven: The Weight of the Poor," *Guernica*, September 15, 2011, https://www.guernicamag.com/west_piven_interview_9_15_11/.

5. Frances Fox Piven, "Throw Sand in the Gears of Everything," *Nation*, January 18, 2017, https://www.thenation.com/article/archive/throw-sand-in-the-gears-of-everything/.

6. Piven, "Can Power from Below Change the World?"

7. Charles Tilly, *From Mobilization to Revolution* (Reading, MA: Addison-Wesley, 1978).

8. Joel Best, *Social Problems* (New York: W. W. Norton, 2016).

9. Matthew Zuras, "The Poisoned Candy Expert Is Pretty Sure No One's Trying to Kill Your Kids on Halloween," *Vice*, October 27, 2016, https://www.vice.com/en/article/gvmav4/the-poisoned-candy-expert-is-pretty-sure-no-ones-trying-to-kill-your-kids-on-halloween.

10. Joel Best, "Halloween Sadism," JoelBest.net, accessed December 9, 2020, https://www.joelbest.net/halloween-sadism.

11. Deborah B. Gould, *Moving Politics: Emotion and ACT UP's Fight Against AIDS* (Chicago, IL: University of Chicago Press, 2009).

12. Mancur Olson, *The Logic of Collective Action: Public Goods and the Theory of Groups* (Cambridge, MA: Harvard University Press, 1971).

13. Neil Smelser, *Theory of Collective Behavior* (New York: Free Press, 1962).

14. James M. Jasper, "Emotions and Social Movements: Twenty Years of Theory and Research," *Annual Review of Sociology* 37, no. 1 (2011): 285–303, https://doi.org/10.1146/annurev-soc-081309-150015.

15. Piven, "Can Power from Below Change the World?"

16. Aldon D. Morris, *The Origins of the Civil Rights Movements* (New York: Free Press, 1986).

17. Jo Ann Robinson, "Don't Ride the Bus," Women's Political Council, December 1, 1955, https://web.archive.org/web/20150402155441/http://mlk-kpp01.stanford.edu/index.php/encyclopedia/documentsentry/leaflet_dont_ride_the_bus_come_to_a_mass_meeting_on_5_december/.

18. Martin Luther King, Jr., *Stride Toward Freedom: The Montgomery Story* (Boston, MA: Beacon Press, 2010).

19. Ibid., 53–54.

20. Martin Luther King, Jr., Speech after King's house was firebombed, Jan. 30, 1956, as quoted in King, *Stride Toward Freedom: The Montgomery Story*: 138.

21. Martin Luther King, Jr., "A Christmas Sermon on Peace," December 25, 1967, YouTube video, 29:52, https://www.youtube.com/watch?v=1jeyIAH3bUI.

22. Lorenzo Bosi, Marco Giugni, and Katrin Uba, *The Consequences of Social Movements* (Cambridge, UK: Cambridge University Press, 2016).

23. John D. McCarthy and Mayer N. Zald, "Resource Mobilization and Social Movements: A Partial Theory," *American Journal of Sociology* 82, no. 6 (1977): 1212–1241, https://www.jstor.org/stable/2777934.

24. "Firearm and Ammunition Industry Economic Impact Report 2020," National Shooting Sports Foundation, The Firearm Industry Trade Association, 2020, https://d3aya7xwz8momx.cloudfront.net/wp-content/uploads/2020/04/2020-Economic-Impact.pdf.

25. "Majority of Gun Owners Own Multiple Guns," Social & Demographic Trends, Pew Research Center, June 20, 2017, https://www.pewsocialtrends.org/2017/06/22/americas-complex-relationship-with-guns/psdt_2017-06-22-guns-00-10/.

26. Robert J. Spitzer, *Gun Control: A Documentary and Reference Guide* (Westport, CT: Greenwood Publishing Group, 2009).

27. "Guns," In Depth: Topics A to Z, Gallup, accessed December 9, 2020, https://news.gallup.com/poll/1645/guns.aspx.

28. Mario Diani and Doug McAdam, *Social Movements and Networks: Relational Approaches to Collective Action* (New York: Oxford University Press, 2003).

29. "Title IX: Tracking Sexual Assault Investigations," *Chronicle of Higher Education*, accessed December 9, 2020, http://projects.chronicle.com/titleix/.

30. Robert D. Benford and David A. Snow, "Framing Processes and Social Movements: An Overview and Assessment," *Annual Review of Sociology* 26, no. 1 (2000): 611–639, https://doi.org/10.1146/annurev.soc.26.1.611.

31. Andrew Daniller, "Two-Thirds of Americans Support Marijuana Legalization," Pew Research Center, November 14, 2019, https://www.pewresearch.org/fact-tank/2019/11/14/americans-support-marijuana-legalization/.

32. Jacob Felson, Amy Adamczyk, and Chistopher Thomas, "How and Why Have Attitudes About Cannabis Legalization Changed So Much?," *Social Science Research* 78 (2019): 12–27, https://doi.org/10.1016/j.ssresearch.2018.12.011.

33. Amy Adamczyk and Christopher Thomas, "This Is the Surprising Reason Why Americans Have Dramatically Shifted Their Views on Legalizing Pot," *MarketWatch*, February 23, 2019, https://www.marketwatch.com/story/this-is-the-surprising-reason-why-americans-have

-dramatically-shifted-their-views-on-legalizing-pot
-2019-02-05.

34. Tahi L. Mottl, "The Analysis of Countermovements,"
Social Problems 27, no. 5 (1980): 620–635, https://doi
.org/10.2307/800200.

35. Benford and Snow, "Framing Processes and Social
Movements."

36. Nancy Fraser, "Rethinking Recognition," *New Left Review*,
May/June 2000, https://newleftreview.org/issues/ii3/articles
/nancy-fraser-rethinking-recognition.

37. Heather Gautney, *Crashing the Party: From the Bernie Sanders
Campaign to a Progressive Movement* (New York: Verso Books,
2018); Ruth Milkman, Stephanie Luce, and Penny Lewis,
"Changing the Subject: A Bottom-Up Account of Occupy
Wall Street in New York City," Joseph S. Murphy Institute,
The City University of New York, 2013, https://media
.sps.cuny.edu/filestore/1/5/7/1_a05051d2117901d
/1571_92f562221b8041e.pdf.

38. Pamela E. Oliver and Hank Johnson, "What a Good
Idea! Ideologies and Frames in Social Movement
Research," *Mobilization: An International Quarterly* 5,
no. 1 (2000): 37–54, https://doi.org/10.17813/maiq.5.1
.g54k222086346251.

39. Lydia Saad, "Americans' Abortion Views Steady in Past
Year," Politics, Gallup, June 29, 2020, https://news.gallup
.com/poll/313094/americans-abortion-views-steady
-past-year.aspx.

40. Doug McAdam, *Political Process and the Development of Black
Insurgency, 1930–1970* (Chicago, IL: University of Chicago
Press, 1999).

41. Jenny Irons, "Political Elites and the Culture of Social
Movements," *Social Compass* 3, no. 3 (2009): 459–474,
https://doi.org/10.1111/j.1751-9020.2009.00214.x.

42. Theda Skocpol and Vanessa Williamson, *The Tea Party and
the Remaking of Republican Conservatism* (New York: Oxford
University Press, 2016).

43. "#11 David Koch, Deceased," *Forbes*, March 4, 2019,
https://www.forbes.com/profile/david-koch/?sh
=15672b62659b.

44. Lunna Lopes, Liz Hamel, Audrey Kearney, and Mollyann
Brodie, "KFF Health Tracking Poll – January 2020: Medicare-
for-all, Public Option, Health Care Legislation and Court
Actions," KFF.org, January 30, 2020, https://www.kff.org
/health-reform/poll-finding/kff-health-tracking-poll
-january-2020/.

45. Doug McAdam, "Culture and Social Movements," in *Culture
and Politics*, eds. Lane Crothers and Charles Lockhart
(New York: Palgrave Macmillan, 2000); William A. Gamson
and David S. Meyer, "Framing Political Opportunity,"
in *Comparative Perspectives on Social Movements: Political
Opportunities, Mobilizing Structures, and Cultural Framings*,
eds. Doug McAdam, John D. McCarthy, Mayer N. Zald
(New York: Cambridge University Press, 1996); Francesca
Polletta, "Culture In and Outside Institutions," *Research in
Social Movements, Conflicts and Change* 25 (2004): 161–183,
https://doi.org/10.1016/S0163-786X(04)25007-8.

46. Leslie King, "Charting a Discursive Field: Environmentalists
for U.S. Population Stabilization," *Sociological Inquiry* 77,

no. 3 (2007): 301–325, https://doi.org/10.1111/j.1475
-682X.2007.00195.x.

47. Karl-Dieter Opp, *Theories of Political Protest and Social
Movements: A Multidisciplinary Introduction, Critique, and
Synthesis* (London, UK: Routledge, 2009).

48. Frances Kai-Hwa Wang, "Who Is Vincent Chin? The
History and Relevance of a 1982 Killing," NBC News,
June 15, 2017, https://www.nbcnews.com/news
/asian-america/who-vincent-chin-history-relevance
-1982-killing-n771291.

49. Larry Buchanan, Quoctrung Bui, and Jugal K. Patel, "Black
Lives Matter May Be the Largest Movement in U.S. History,"
New York Times, July 3, 2020, https://www.nytimes.com
/interactive/2020/07/03/us/george-floyd-protests-crowd
-size.html.

50. Melissa Chan, "These Black Lives Matter Protesters Had
No Idea How One Arrest Could Alter Their Lives," *Time*,
August 19, 2020, https://time.com/5880229/arrests
-black-lives-matter-protests-impact/.

51. Buchanan, Bui, and Patel, "Black Lives Matter May Be the
Largest Movement in U.S. History."

52. Taylor Lorenz, Kellen Browning, and Sheera Frenkel,
"TikTok Teens and K-Pop Stans Say They Sank Trump
Rally," *New York Times*, Nov. 6, 2020, https://www.nytimes
.com/2020/06/21/style/tiktok-trump-rally-tulsa.html.

53. Dustin Kidd and Keith McIntosh, "Social Media and Social
Movements," *Sociology Compass* 10, no. 9 (2016): 785–794,
https://doi.org/10.1111/soc4.12399.

54. Natalie Jarvey, "Sexual Assault Movement #MeToo Reaches
Nearly 500,000 Tweets," *Hollywood Reporter*, October 16,
2017, https://www.hollywoodreporter.com/news/metoo
-sexual-assault-movement-reaches-500000-tweets
-1049235.

55. CBS/AP, "More Than 12M 'Me Too' Facebook Posts,
Comments, Reactions in 24 Hours," CBS News, October
17, 2017, https://www.cbsnews.com/news/metoo-more
-than-12-million-facebook-posts-comments-reactions
-24-hours/.

56. Kidd and McIntosh, "Social Media and Social Movements."

57. CBS/AP, "More than 12M 'Me Too' Facebook Posts."

58. Joanna Walters, "#MeToo a Revolution That Can't Be
Stopped, says Time's Up Co-founder," *Guardian*,
October 21, 2018, https://www.theguardian.com
/world/2018/oct/21/metoo-revolution-times-up-roberta
-kaplan.

59. Y. Tony Yang, Paul L. Delamater, Timothy F. Leslie, and
Michelle M. Mello, "Sociodemographic Predictors of
Vaccination Exemptions on the Basis of Personal Belief in
California," *American Journal of Public Health* 106 (2016):
172–177, https://doi.org/10.2105/AJPH.2015.302926.

60. Derrick A. Bell, "Who's Afraid of Critical Race Theory?,"
University of Illinois Law Review 893 (1995): 893–910.

61. Steven W. Bender, "Faces of Immigration Reform,"
Florida International University Law Review 519 (2011):
251–267.

62. Harriet Martineau, *Society in America* (London, UK:
Routledge, 1981).

CHAPTER 12

1. "Black Death: How Can We Learn from the Spread of Disease along the Silk Roads?," UNESCO, March 31, 2020, https://en.unesco.org/news/black-death-how-can-we-learn-spread-disease-along-silk-roads.

2. Kaia Hubbard, "Places Without Reported COVID-19 Cases," *US NEWS,* February 22, 2021, https://www.usnews.com/news/best-countries/slideshows/countries-without-reported-covid-19-cases?slide=16.

3. Manfred B. Steger, *Globalization: A Very Short Introduction* (New York: Oxford University Press, 2013).

4. Dani Rodrik, *The Globalization Paradox: Democracy and the Future of the World Economy* (New York: W. W. Norton, 2011).

5. Jan Nederveen Pieterse, "Globalization as Hybridization," *International Sociology* 9, no. 2 (1994): 161–184, https://doi.org/10.1177/026858094009002003.

6. Saskia Sassen, *Losing Control? Sovereignty in an Age of Globalization* (New York: Columbia University Press, 1996).

7. William I. Robinson, *Global Capitalism and the Crisis of Humanity* (New York: Cambridge University Press, 2014).

8. "Global 500: 2019," *Fortune,* accessed December 9, 2020, https://fortune.com/global500/2019/.

9. Cyn-Young Park et al., "Global Shortage of Personal Protective Equipment amid COVID-19: Supply Chains, Bottlenecks, and Policy Implications," ADB (Asian Development Bank) Briefs, April 2020, https://www.adb.org/sites/default/files/publication/579121/ppe-covid-19-supply-chains-bottlenecks-policy.pdf.

10. Saskia Sassen, *The Global City: New York, London, Tokyo* (Princeton, NJ: Princeton University Press, 2001).

11. Immanuel Maurice Wallerstein, *Worlds-Systems Analysis: An Introduction* (Durham, NC: Duke University Press, 2004).

12. Oliver C. Cox, *The Foundations of Capitalism* (London, UK: Peter Owen, 1959).

13. Alan Sica, "Immanuel Wallerstein," in *Social Thought: From the Enlightenment to the Present* (Boulder, CO: Westview Press, 2005); Immanuel Wallerstein, *The Essential Wallerstein* (New York: The New Press, 2000); Immanuel Wallerstein, "Curriculum Vitae," IWallerstein.com, April 2009, https://iwallerstein.com/wp-content/uploads/docs/iwallerstein-cv-eng-09.pdf.

14. Anthony Shorrocks, James Davies, and Rodrigo Lluberas, "Research Institute: Global Wealth Report 2020," Credit Suisse, October 2020, https://www.credit-suisse.com/about-us/en/reports-research/global-wealth-report.html.

15. Max Roser and Esteban Ortiz-Ospina, "Global Extreme Poverty," Our World in Data, March 27, 2017, https://ourworldindata.org/extreme-poverty.

16. Shorrocks, Davies, and Lluberas, "Research Institute: Global Wealth Report 2020."

17. Peter Phillips, *Giants: The Global Power Elite* (New York: Seven Stories Press, 2018).

18. "Annual Reports," Corporate.ExxonMobile.com, 2020, https://corporate.exxonmobil.com/investors/annual-report#Ourcompetitiveadvantages.

19. Richa Sekhani, "Poverty Facts: Almost 4 in 10 Guyanese Cannot Afford Basic Costs of Living," Guyana Budget & Policy Institute, August 2017, https://gbpi.institute/2017/08/27/poverty-facts-almost-4-in-10-guyanese-cannot-afford-basic-costs-of-living/.

20. Roy Kwon, Ellen Reese, and Kadambari Anantram, "Core-Periphery Divisions among Labor Activists at the World Social Forum," *Mobilization: An International Journal* 13, no. 4 (2008): 411–430, https://doi.org/10.17813/maiq.13.4.2107l2l1086467q5.

21. Florian Bieber, "Is Nationalism on the Rise? Assessing Global Trends," *Ethnopolitics* 17, no. 5 (2018): 519–540, https://doi.org/10.1080/17449057.2018.1532633.

22. John Bellamy Foster, *The Vulnerable Planet: A Short Economic History of the Environment* (New York: Monthly Review Press, 1994).

23. Owen Gaffney and Will Steffen, "The Anthropocene Equation," *Anthropocene Review* 4, no. 1 (2017): 53–61, https://doi.org/10.1177/2053019616688022.

24. Richard Heede, "Tracing Anthropogenic Carbon Dioxide and Methane Emissions to Fossil Fuel and Cement Producers, 1854–2010," *Climatic Change* 122 (2014): 229–241, https://doi.org/10.1007/s10584-013-0986-y.

25. "Global Warming of 1.5 °C," IPCC (The Intergovernmental Panel on Climate Change), accessed December 9, 2020, https://www.ipcc.ch/sr15/.

26. Kevin A. Baumert, Timothy Herzog, and Jonathan Pershing, "Navigating the Numbers: Greenhouse Gas Data and International Climate Policy," World Resources Institute, 2005, http://pdf.wri.org/navigating_numbers.pdf.

27. Heede, "Tracing Anthropogenic Carbon Dioxide."

28. "Global Warming of 1.5 °C," IPCC.

29. David Wallace-Wells, *The Uninhabitable Earth: Life After Warming* (New York: Tim Duggan Books, 2019); Elizabeth Kolbert, *The Sixth Extinction: An Unnatural History* (London, UK: Picador, 2015); "Global Warming of 1.5 °C," IPCC; Sonia Shah, "Think Exotic Animals Are to Blame for the Coronavirus? Think Again," *Nation,* February 18, 2020, https://www.thenation.com/article/environment/coronavirus-habitat-loss/.

30. Stephane Hallegatte et al., "Shock Waves: Managing the Impacts of Climate Change on Poverty," World Bank Group, 2016, https://openknowledge.worldbank.org/bitstream/handle/10986/22787/9781464806735.pdf.

31. Kanta Kumari Rigaud et al., "Groundswell: Preparing for Internal Climate Migration," World Bank Group, 2018, https://openknowledge.worldbank.org/handle/10986/29461.

32. J. Timmons Roberts and Bradley C. Parks, *A Climate of Injustice: Global Inequality, North-South Politics, and Climate Policy* (Cambridge, MA: MIT Press, 2006).

33. David Ciplet et al., "A Burden to Share? Addressing Unequal Climate Impacts in the Least Developed Countries," International Institute for Environment and Development, November 2013, https://pubs.iied.org/pdfs/17181IIED.pdf.

34. David Eckstein, Marie-Lena Hutfils, and Maik Winges, "Global Climate Risk Index 2019: Who Suffers Most from Extreme Weather Events? Weather-related Loss Events in

2017 and 1998 to 2017," Germanwatch, December 2018, https://germanwatch.org/sites/germanwatch.org/files /Global%20Climate%20Risk%20Index%202019_2.pdf.

35. Sherilyn MacGregor, "A Stranger Silence Still: The Need for Feminist Social Research on Climate Change," *Sociological Review* 57, no. 2 (2009): 124–140, https://doi.org/10.1111 /j.1467-954X.2010.01889.x.

36. Laura A. McKinney and Gregory M. Fulkerson, "Gender Inequality and Climate Justice: A Cross-National Analysis," *Social Justice Research* 28, no. 3 (2015): 293–317, https://doi .org/10.1007/s11211-015-0241-y.

37. Patrick R. Saunders-Hastings, Nadine Overhoff, and Raywat Deonandan, "Likely Health Impacts of Climate Change in Guyana: A Systematic Review," *Journal of Health and Medical Sciences* 1, no. 1 (2018): 42–49, https://doi.org/10.31014 /aior.1994.01.01.6.

38. Joe Mozingo, "In Guyana, Losing Out to Nature," *Washington Post*, March 6, 2005, https://www.washingtonpost .com/archive/politics/2005/03/06/in-guyana-losing-out -to-nature/4ff056bf-7dab-49be-b66c-ea89b1306425/.

39. Johann Earle, "Guyana's Women Farmers Adapt to Worsening Flooding," Thomson Reuters Foundation, August 29, 2011, https://news.trust.org/item/20110829153000-zvf48.

40. Ibid.

41. Stephen Pacala and Robert Socolow, "Stabilization Wedges, Solving the Climate Problem for the Next 50 years with Current Technologies," *Science* 305, no. 5686 (2004): 968–972, https://doi.org/10.1126/science.1100103. See also newclimateeconomy.report, exponentialroadmap.org, and nature.org.

42. John Lanchester, "Two New Books Dramatically Capture the Climate Change Crisis," *New York Times*, April 12, 2019, https://www.nytimes.com/2019/04/12/books/review /david-wallace-wells-uninhabitable-earth-nathaniel-rich -losing-earth.html.

43. Rachel Warren et al., "Risks Associated with Global Warming of 1.5°C or 2°C," Tyndall Centre for Climate Change Research, May 2018, https://tyndall.ac.uk/sites/default /files/publications/briefing_note_risks_warren_r1-1.pdf; "The Costs of Climate Inaction," *Nature* 561 (2018): 433, https://doi.org/10.1038/d41586-018-06827-x; Stephane Hallegatte, Jun Rentschler, and Julie Rozenberg, "Lifelines: The Resilient Infrastructure Opportunity," World Bank Group, 2019, https://openknowledge.worldbank.org /handle/10986/31805.

44. Raymond P. Sorenson, "Eunice Foote's Pioneering Research on CO$_2$ and Climate Warning," AAPG Databases, Inc. Search and Discovery, January 31, 2011, http://www .searchanddiscovery.com/pdfz/documents/2011 /70092sorenson/ndx_sorenson.pdf.html.

45. Svante Arrhenius, *Worlds in the Making: The Evolution of the Universe* (New York: Harper & Brothers Publishers, 1908).

46. Lyndon Baines Johnson, *Public Papers of the Presidents of the United States, Lyndon B. Johnson, January 1 to May 31, 1965* (Washinton DC: U.S. Government Printing Office, 1966).

47. George H. W. Bush, "Road to the White House 1988: Bush Campaign Speech," CSPAN, https://www.c-span.org /video/?4248-1/bush-campaign-speech.

48. Bruno Latour, "Waiting for Gaia. Composing the Common World Through Arts and Politics," lecture at French Institute, London, November 2011, http://www.bruno-latour.fr /sites/default/files/124-GAIA-LONDON-SPEAP_0.pdf.

49. James Everett Hein and J. Craig Jenkins, "Why Does the United States Lack a Global Warming Policy? The Corporate Inner Circle versus Public Interest Sector Elites," *Environmental Politics* 26, no. 1 (2017): 97–117, https://doi.org/10.1080/09644016.2016.1244966; Aaron M. McCright and Riley E. Dunlap, "Challenging Global Warming as a Social Problem: An Analysis of the Conservative Movement's Counter-claims," *Social Problems* 47, no. 4 (2000): 499–522, https://doi .org/10.2307/3097132; Aaron M. McCright and Riley E. Dunlap, "Defeating Kyoto: The Conservative Movement's Impact on U.S. Climate Change Policy," *Social Problems* 50, no. 3 (2003): 348–373, https://doi.org/10.1525/sp .2003.50.3.348; Robert J. Antonio and Robert J. Brulle, "The Unbearable Lightness of Politics: Climate Change Denial and Political Polarization," *Sociological Quarterly* 52, no. 2 (2011): 195–202, https://doi.org/10.1111/j.1533 -8525.2011.01199.x.

50. *Inside Climate News*, "PR Plan for Exxon's CO2 Research (1980)," Oct. 22, 2015, https://insideclimatenews.org /documents/pr-plan-exxons-co2-research-1980/

51. Jason M. Breslow, "Robert Brulle: Inside the Climate Change 'Countermovement,'" *Frontline*, PBS, October 23, 2012, https://www.pbs.org/wgbh/frontline/article/robert-brulle -inside-the-climate-change-countermovement/.

52. Justin Farrell, "Network Structure and Influence of the Climate Change Counter-Movement," *Nature Climate Change* 6 (2016): 370–374.

53. Katie Worth, "Democrats Condemn Climate Change Skeptics for Targeting Teachers," *Frontline*, PBS, April 12, 2017, https://www.pbs.org/wgbh/frontline/article/democrats -condemn-climate-change-skeptics-for-targeting-teachers/; Katie Jennings, Dino Grandoni, and Susanne Rust, "How Exxon Went from Leader to Skeptic on Climate Change Research," *Los Angeles Times*, October 23, 2015, https://graphics.latimes.com/exxon-research/; Meagan Clark, "Exxon Mobil Acknowledges Climate Change Risk to Business for First Time," *International Business Times*, April 1, 2014, https://www.ibtimes.com/exxon-mobil -acknowledges-climate-change-risk-business-first-time -1565836.

54. Riley E. Dunlap and Peter J. Jacques, "Climate Change Denial Books and Conservative Think Tanks: Exploring the Connection," *American Behavioral Scientist* 57, no. 6 (2013): 699–731, https://doi.org/10.1177/0002764213477096.

55. Steve Coll, *Private Empires: ExxonMobil and American Power* (New York: Penguin Books, 2013).

56. Naomi Oreskes and Erik M. Conway, *Merchants of Doubt: How a Handful of Scientists Obscured the Truth on Issues from Tobacco Smoke to Global Warming* (London, UK: Bloomsbury Publishing, 2010).

57. Aaron M. McCright and Riley E. Dunlap, "The Politicization of Climate Change and Polarization in the American Public's Views of Global Warming, 2001–2010," *Sociological Quarterly* 52, no. 2 (2011): 155–194, https://doi.org

/10.1111/j.1533-8525.2011.01198.x; Antonio and Brulle, "The Unbearable Lightness of Politics."

58. Anthony Leiserowitz, Edward Maibach, Seth Rosenthal, and John Kotcher, "Politics & Global Warming: April 2019," Yale Program on Climate Change Communication and George Mason University Center for Climate Change Communication, April 2019, https://climatecommunication.yale.edu/wp-content/uploads/2019/05/Politics-Global-Warming-April-2019b.pdf.

59. Aaron M. McCright and Riley E. Dunlap, "Cool Dudes: The Denial of Climate Change among Conservative White Males in the United States," *Global Environmental Change* 21, no. 4 (2011): 1163–1172, https://doi.org/10.1016/j.gloenvcha.2011.06.003.

60. Aaron R. Brough et al., "Is Eco-Friendly Unmanly? The Green-Feminine Stereotype and Its Effect on Sustainable Consumption," *Journal of Consumer Research* 43, no. 4 (2016): 567–582, https://doi.org/10.1093/jcr/ucw044.

61. Troy Elias et al., "Understanding Climate Change Perceptions and Attitudes across Racial/Ethnic Groups," *Howard Journal of Communications* 30, no. 1 (2019): 38–56, https://doi.org/10.1080/10646175.2018.1439420; Aaron M. McCright, "The Effects of Gender on Climate Change Knowledge and Concern in the American Public," *Population and Environment* 32 (2010): 66–87, https://doi.org/10.1007/s11111-010-0113-1.

62. Kari Marie Norgaard, *Living in Denial: Climate Change, Emotions, and Everyday Life* (Cambridge, MA: MIT Press, 2011).

63. Emily Huddart Kennedy and Jennifer E. Givens, "Eco-habitus or Eco-powerlessness? Examining Environmental Concern across Social Class," *Social Perspectives* 62, no. 3 (2019): 646–647, https://doi.org/10.1177/0731121419836966.

64. Robin J. Kemkes and Sean Akerman, "Contending with the Nature of Climate Change: Phenomenological Interpretations from Northern Wisconsin," *Emotion, Space and Society* 33 (2019), https://doi.org/10.1016/j.emospa.2019.100614.

65. John Urry, *Climate Change and Society* (Cambridge, UK: Polity, 2011).

66. Michael Carolan, "Sociological Ambivalence and Climate Change," *Local Environment* 15, no. 4 (2010): 309–321, https://doi.org/10.1080/13549831003677662.

67. Kennedy and Givens, "Eco-habitus or Eco-powerlessness?"

68. Norgaard, *Living in Denial.*

69. Kemkes and Akerman, "Contending with the Nature of Climate Change."

70. Boaventura de Sousa Santos, "Globalizations," *Theory, Culture & Society* 23 (2006): 393–399, https://doi.org/10.1177/026327640602300268.

71. Benedict Anderson, *Imagined Communities: Reflections on the Origin and Spread of Nationalism* (London: Verso, 1983); Katrina Running, "World Citizenship and Concern for Global Warming: Building the Case for a Strong International Civil Society," *Social Forces* 92, no. 1 (2013): 377–399, https://doi.org/10.1093/sf/sot077.

72. Roland Robertson, "Globalisation or Glocalisation?," *Futures* 1, no. 1 (1994): 33–52, https://doi.org/10.1080/13216597.1994.9751780.

73. Paul Almeida and Chris Chase-Dunn, "Globalization and Social Movements," *Annual Review of Sociology* 44 (2018): 189–211, https://doi.org/10.1146/annurev-soc-073117-041307.

74. Donatella Della Porta and Sidney Tarrow, *Transnational Protest & Global Activism* (Lanham, MD: Rowman & Littlefield Publishers, 2004); Margaret E. Keck and Kathryn Sikkink, *Activists beyond Borders: Advocacy Networks in International Politics* (Ithaca, NY: Cornell University Press, 1998).

75. Luke Fletcher, Tom Crocker, James Smyth, and Kane Marcell, "Beyond the Cycle: Which Oil and Gas Companies Are Ready for the Low-Carbon Transition?," CDP Worldwide, Disclosure Insight Action, 2018, https://6fefcbb86e61af1b2fc4-c70d8ead6ced550b4d987d7c03fcdd1d.ssl.cf3.rackcdn.com/cms/reports/documents/000/003/858/original/CDP_Oil_and_Gas_Executive_Summary_2018.pdf?1541783367.

76. Clayton Coleman and Emma Dietz, "Fact Sheet: Fossil Fuel Subsidies: A Closer Look at Tax Breaks and Societal Costs," Environmental and Energy Study Institute (EESI), July 29, 2019, https://www.eesi.org/papers/view/fact-sheet-fossil-fuel-subsidies-a-closer-look-at-tax-breaks-and-societal-costs.

77. David Ciplet, J. Timmons Roberts, and Mizan R. Khan, *Power in a Warming World: The New Global Politics of Climate Change and the Remaking of Environmental Inequality* (Cambridge, MA: MIT Press, 2015); Anthony Giddens, *The Politics of Climate Change* (Cambridge, UK: Polity, 2011).

78. Abel Gustafson, Parrish Bergquist, Anthony Leiserowitz, and Edward Mailbach, "A Growing Majority of Americans Think Global Warming is Happening and Are Worried," Yale Program on Climate Change Communication, February 21, 2019, https://climatecommunication.yale.edu/publications/a-growing-majority-of-americans-think-global-warming-is-happening-and-are-worried/.

79. Abel Gustafson, Anthony Leiserowitz, and Edward Mailbach, "Americans Are Increasingly 'Alarmed' About Global Warming," Yale Program on Climate Change Communication, February 12, 2019, https://climatecommunication.yale.edu/publications/americans-are-increasingly-alarmed-about-global-warming/.

80. "Washington Post-Kaiser Family Foundation Climate Change Survey, July 9–Aug. 5, 2019," *Washington Post*, December 9, 2019, https://www.washingtonpost.com/context/washington-post-kaiser-family-foundation-climate-change-survey-july-9-aug-5-2019/601ed8ff-a7c6-4839-b57e-3f5eaa8ed09f/.

81. "Washington Post-Kaiser Family Foundation Climate Change Survey."

82. David Crouch, "The Swedish 15-year-old Who's Cutting Class to Fight the Climate Crisis," *Guardian*, September 1, 2018, https://www.theguardian.com/science/2018/sep/01/swedish-15-year-old-cutting-class-to-fight-the-climate-crisis.

83. Greta Thunberg, "The Disarming Case to Act Right Now on Climate Change," TEDxStockholm, November 2018, https://www.ted.com/talks/greta_thunberg_the_disarming_case_to_act_right_now_on_climate#t-115737.

84. Riley E. Dunlap and Robert J. Brulle, *Climate Change and Society: Sociological Perspectives* (New York: Oxford University Press, 2015).

85. Beth Schaefer Caniglia, Robert J. Brulle, and Andrew Szasz, "Civil Society, Social Movements, and Climate Change," in *Climate Change and Society: Sociological Perspectives*, eds. Riley E. Dunlap and Robert J. Brulle (New York: Oxford University Press, 2015).

86. NPR Staff, "Transcript: Greta Thunberg's Speech At The U.N. Climate Action Summit," NPR, September 23, 2019, https://www.npr.org/2019/09/23/763452863 /transcript-greta-thunbergs-speech-at-the-u-n-climate -action-summit.

87. Jeff Goodwin, James M. Jasper, and Francesca Polletta, (eds.), *Passionate Politics: Emotions and Social Movements* (Chicago: University of Chicago Press, 2001).

88. Sandra Laville and Jonathan Watts, "Across the Globe, Millions Join Biggest Climate Protest Ever," *Guardian*, September 20, 2019, https://www.theguardian.com /environment/2019/sep/21/across-the-globe-millions -join-biggest-climate-protest-ever.

89. Gabriella Borter, Katharine Houreld, and Jake Spring, "Inspired by Greta Thunberg, Worldwide Protest Demands Climate Action," Reuters.com, September 19, 2019, https://www.reuters.com/article/us-climate-change-strike /inspired-by-greta-thunberg-worldwide-protest-demands -climate-action-idUSKBN1W507I; Eliza Barclay and Brian Resnick, "How Big Was the Global Climate Strike? 4 Million People, Activists Estimate," *Vox*, September 22, 2019, https://www.vox.com/energy-and-environment /2019/9/20/20876143/climate-strike-2019-september-20 -crowd-estimate.

90. Scott Neuman and Bill Chappell, "Young People Lead Millions To Protest Global Inaction on Climate Change," NPR, September 20, 2019, https://www.npr.org/2019 /09/20/762629200/mass-protests-in-australia-kick-off -global-climate-strike-ahead-of-u-n-summit.

91. Laville and Watts, "Across the Globe, Millions Join Biggest Climate Protest Ever."

92. Borter, Houreld, and Spring, "Inspired by Greta Thunberg."

93. Neuman and Chappell, "Young People Lead Millions To Protest Global Inaction."

94. "Environmental Activist to Represent Guyana at Inaugural UN Youth Climate Summit," Kaieteur News, September 20, 2019, https://www.kaieteurnewsonline.com/2019/09/20 /environmental-activist-to-represent-guyana-at-inaugural -un-youth-climate-summit/.

95. Dana R. Fisher, "The Young Climate Strikers Marching This Week Are All Fired Up and Ready to Vote," *Washington Post*, September 28, 2019, https://www.washingtonpost.com /politics/2019/09/28/young-climate-strikers-marching-this -week-are-all-fired-up-ready-vote/.

96. "Climate Strike 'Die-In' Held in Vancouver as Part of Worldwide Demonstrations," *CBC News*, September 20, 2019, https://www.cbc.ca/news/canada/british-columbia /climate-strike-vancouver-art-gallery-1.5291054.

97. Laville and Watts, "Across the Globe, Millions Join Biggest Climate Protest Ever."

98. Laville and Watts, "Across the Globe, Millions Join Biggest Climate Protest Ever"; Barclay and Resnick, "How Big Was the Global Climate Strike?"; Borter, Houreld, and Spring, "Inspired by Greta Thunberg"; Cecilia Rodriguez, "Biggest-Ever Climate Protest In Photos: Greta Thunberg And The World's Youth Demand Action," *Forbes*, September 21, 2019, https://www.forbes.com/sites/ceciliarodriguez/2019 /09/21/biggest-ever-climate-protest-in-photos-greta -thunberg-and-the-worlds-youth-demand-action /?sh=1d3b185fab4d.

99. Mark Hertsgaard and Kyle Pope, "A New Beginning for Climate Reporting," *Columbia Journalism Review*, September 16, 2019, https://www.cjr.org/covering _climate_now/climate-crisis-new-beginning.php; Ted MacDonald, "Mixed Coverage of New UN Climate Report Underscores Need for the Covering Climate Now Journalism Initiative," Media Matters, October 2, 2019, https://www.mediamatters.org/broadcast-networks /mixed-coverage-new-un-climate-report-underscores -need-covering-climate-now.

100. Simone Pulver, "Organising Business: Industry NGOs in the Climate Debates," in *The Business of Climate Change: Corporate Responses to Kyoto*, eds. Kathryn Begg, Frans van der Woerd, and David Levy (London: Routledge, 2005).

101. Hein and Jenkins, "Why Does the United States Lack a Global Warming Policy?"

102. Ciplet, Roberts, and Khan, *Power in a Warming World*.

103. "The Global Fossil Fuel Divestment and Clean Energy Investment Movement: 2018 Report," Arabella Advisors, 2018, https://www.arabellaadvisors.com/wp-content /uploads/2018/09/Global-Divestment-Report-2018.pdf.

104. Anthony Giddens, *Runaway World: How Globalization Is Reshaping Our Lives* (London: Routledge, 2002).

105. Anthony Giddens, "Lecture 2–Risk–Hong Kong," *BBC Reith Lectures 1999*, accessed December 14, 2020, http://news.bbc.co.uk/hi/english/static/events/reith_99 /week2/week2.htm.

106. Ulrich Beck, Mark Ritter, and Brian Wynne, *Risk Society: Towards a New Modernity* (New York: Sage Publications, 1992).

107. Ulrich Beck, *World Risk Society* (Cambridge, MA: Polity, 1999).

108. Ulrich Beck, *The Metamorphosis of the World: How Climate Change Is Transforming Our Concept of the World* (Hoboken, NJ: Wiley, 2016).

CONCLUSION

1. C. Wright Mills, *The Sociological Imagination* (New York: Oxford University Press, 1959).

2. Susan Kippax, R. W. Connell, G. W. Dowsett, and June Crawford, *Sustaining Safe Sex: Gay Communities Respond to AIDS* (London: Falmer Press, 1993).

3. Steven Epstein, *Impure Science: AIDS, Activism, and the Politics of Knowledge* (Berkeley: University of California Press, 1998).

4. Tony Barnett and Alan Whiteside, *AIDS in the Twenty-First Century: Disease and Globalization* (New York: Palgrave Macmillan, 2002).

5. C. Wright Mills, *The Power Elite* (New York: Oxford University Press, 1956).

APPENDIX A

1. Auguste Comte, *The Positive Philosophy of Auguste Comte*, ed. Harriet Martineau (London: J. Chapman, 1853).

2. Craig Calhoun, ed., *Sociology in America: A History* (Chicago: University of Chicago Press, 2007); Mary Romero, "Sociology Engaged in Social Justice," *American Sociological Review* 85, no. 1 (2020):1–30.

3. Diana Postlethwaite, "Mothering and Mesmerism in the Life of Harriet Martineau," *Signs* 14, no. 3 (1989): 583–609.

4. Émile Durkheim, *The Division of Labor in Society* (New York: Free Press, 1997 [1893]).

5. Durkheim, *The Division of Labor in Society*.

6. Karl Marx, *The Communist Manifesto* (New York: Norton Critical Edition, Second Edition, 2012 [1848]); Karl Marx, *Capital: A Critique of Political Economy* (New York: Penguin Classics, 1990 [1867]).

7. Max Weber, "Class, Status, Party" from *Economy and Society: An Outline of Interpretive Sociology* (Berkeley, CA: University of California Press, 1922).

8. "Selections from Marianne Weber's *Reflections on Women and Women's Issues*," Elizabeth Kirchen, trans. (unpublished manuscript, 1988 [1912]); Marianne Weber and Craig R. Bermingham, "Authority and Autonomy in Marriage," *Sociological Theory* 21, no. 2 (2003 [1912]): 85–102; Marianne Weber, *Marriage, Motherhood, and the Law* (Ehefrau und Mutter in der Rechtsentwicklung) (Tübingen: J. C. B. Mohr, 1907).

9. Quoted in Patricia Madoo Lengermann and Gillian Niebrugge, *The Women Founders: Sociology and Social Theory 1830–1930* (Long Grove, IL: Waveland Press, 2006).

10. W. E. B. Du Bois, *Black Reconstruction in America: An Essay Toward a History of the Part Which Black Folk Played in the Attempt to Reconstruct Democracy in America, 1860–1880* (New York: Harcourt, Brace, 1935).

11. Mary Deegan, *Jane Addams and the Men of the Chicago School, 1892–1918* (New Brunswick, NJ: Transaction Books, 1988); Lengermann and Niebrugge, *The Women Founders*.

12. Aldon Morris, *The Scholar Denied: W. E. B. Du Bois and the Birth of Modern Sociology* (Berkeley, CA: University of California Press, 2017).

13. Calhoun, ed., *Sociology in America*.

14. Thomas W. Goodspeed, "Albion Woodbury Small," *American Journal of Sociology* 32, no.1 (1926): 1–14.

15. Craig Calhoun and Jonathan VanAntwerpen, "Orthodoxy, Heterodoxy, and Hierarchy: 'Mainstream' Sociology and Its Challengers," in Calhoun, ed., *Sociology in America*.

16. Quoted in John C. McKinney, *Constructive Typology and Social Theory* (New York: Meredith Publishing Company, 1966): 71.

17. Ibid.

18. Calhoun and VanAntwerpen, "Orthodoxy, Heterodoxy, and Hierarchy."

19. Immanuel Wallerstein, "The Culture of Sociology in Disarray: The Impact of 1968 on U.S. Sociologists," in Calhoun, ed., *Sociology in America*.

20. Craig Calhoun, "Introduction," in Calhoun, ed., *Sociology in America*.

21. Patricia Hill Collins, "Pushing the Boundaries or Business as Usual?: Race, Class, and Gender Studies and Sociological Inquiry," in Calhoun, ed., *Sociology in America*; Myra Marx Ferree, Shamus Rahman Khan, and Shauna A. Morimoto, "Assessing the Feminist Revolution: The Presence and Absence of Gender in Theory and Practice," in Calhoun, ed., *Sociology in America*; Barbara Laslett, "Feminist Sociology in the Twentieth-Century United States: Life Stories in Historical Context," in Calhoun, ed., *Sociology in America*.

22. American Sociological Association, "Doctorate Recipients in Sociology, by Gender and Race/Ethnicity," https://www.asanet.org/research-and-publications/research-sociology/trends/doctorate-recipients-sociology-gender-and-raceethnicity.

APPENDIX B

1. Shelly Ronen, "Grinding on the Dance Floor: Gendered Scripts and Sexualized Dancing at College Parties," *Gender and Society* 2, no. 3 (2010): 355–77, https://doi.org/10.1177/0891243210369894.

2. Rachel Allison and Barbara J. Risman, "'It Goes Hand in Hand with the Parties': Race, Class, and Residence in College Student Negotiations of Hooking Up," *Sociological Perspectives* 57, no. 1 (2014):102–23, http://www.jstor.org/stable/44289988.

3. Jessie Ford, Paula England, and Jonathan Bearak, "The American College Hookup Scene: Findings from the Online College Social Life Survey," American Sociological Association Annual Meeting, Chicago, August 22–25, 2015.

4. Merlina Bersamin et al., "Risky Business: Is There an Association between Casual Sex and Mental Health among Emerging Adults?" *Journal of Sex Research* 51, no. 1 (2013): 43–51.

5. Jessica M. W. Kratzer and Jennifer Stevens Aubrey, "Is the Actual Ideal?: A Content Analysis of College Students' Descriptions of Ideal and Actual Hookups," *Sexuality & Culture* 20, no. 2 (2015): 236–54.

6. Donna Freitas, *The End of Sex: How Hookup Culture Is Leaving a Generation Unhappy, Sexually Unfulfilled, and Confused About Intimacy* (New York: Basic Books, 2013).

CREDITS

FRONT MATTER
P. **v**: Babs Evangelista.

INTRODUCTION
P. **4**: ZUMA Press Inc/Alamy Stock Photo; **p. 5**: Pictorial Press Ltd/Alamy Stock Photo; **p. 6**: Carol M. Highsmith Archive, Library of Congress, Prints and Photographs Division; **p. 7**: Chronicle/Alamy Stock Photo; **p. 8**: Library of Congress, LC-DIG-ppmsca-38818.

CHAPTER 1
Excerpts from Morgan Johnstonbaugh, "Sexting with Friends: Gender, Technology, and the Evolution of Interaction Rituals." Paper in progress; **p. 15**: Xavier Hubert-Brierre; **p. 19**: Lauren Lee/Stocksy; **p. 23**: Molloy/Portland Press Herald via Getty Images; **p. 28**: Brandan "BMike" Odums; **p. 30**: Lisa Wade.

CHAPTER 2
P. **39**: Gado Images/Alamy Stock Photo; **p. 42**: Panther Media GmbH/Alamy Stock Photo; **p. 44**: Andre Luiz Moreira/Shutterstock; **p. 47**: Fowler James H, Christakis Nicholas A. Dynamic spread of happiness in a large social network: longitudinal analysis over 20 years in the Framingham Heart Study BMJ 2008; 337 :a2338. doi: https://doi.org/10.1136/bmj.a2338; **p. 49**: Larry Busacca/Getty Images; **p. 50**: UPI/Alamy Stock Photo; **p. 54**: REUTERS/Alamy Stock Photo; **p. 58**: Onfokus/Getty Images.

CHAPTER 3
P. **64**: Betsy Streeter via CartoonStock, Ltd.; **p. 66**: Paul Thompson/FPG/Getty Images; **p. 72**: Victoria Matthews; **p. 76**: STR/AFP via Getty Images; **p. 78**: Transcendental Graphics/Getty Images; **p. 83**: Library of Congress, LC-DIG-bellcm-15413.

CHAPTER 4
P. **89**: Drew Dernavich via Cartoon Collections; **p. 91**: Lisa Wade; **p. 94**: Svetikd/Getty Images; **p. 96**: Constantine Johnny/Getty Images; **p. 99**: Yakoniva/Alamy Stock Photo; **p. 103**: San Francisco Chronicle/Hearst Newspapers via Getty Images; **p. 107**: Everett Collection Historical/Alamy Stock Photo.

CHAPTER 5
P. **119**: Rolls Press/Popperfoto via Getty Images/Getty Images; **p. 124**: AA Film Archive/Alamy Stock Photo; **p. 127**: Shawn Thew/EPA-EFE/Shutterstock; **p. 132**: Everett Collection Historical/Alamy Stock Photo; **p. 134**: AP Photo/Mark Foley; **p. 138**: Pictorial Press Ltf/Alamy Stock Photo; **p. 140**: AP Photo/Ashley Landis.

CHAPTER 6
P. **147**: Robert Quinlan/Alamy Stock Photo; **p. 149**: Prismatic Pictures/BridgemanImages;**p.152**:©WaltDisneyCo./Courtesy Everett/Everett Collection; **p. 154**: Christophe Boisson/Shutterstock; **p. 157**: SofikoS/Shutterstock; **p. 159**: Julian J Rossig/iStock/Getty Images; **p. 163**: Courtesy of Thomas Forsyth/LandlordsGame.Info; **p. 167**: WS Collection/Alamy Stock Photo.

CHAPTER 7
P. **178**: ITAR-TASS News Agency/Alamy Stock Photo; **p. 180**: Arthur Schatz/The LIFE Picture Collection via Getty Images; **p. 181**: Shawshots/Alamy Stock Photo; **p. 190**: Paul Hennessy/SOPA Images/LightRocket via Getty Images; **p. 198**: Skully/Alamy Stock Photo.

CHAPTER 8
P. **203**: Apu Gomes/AFP via Getty Images; **p. 205**: Bill Rankin, www.radicalcartography.net; **p. 206**: Everett Collection/Bridgeman Images; **p. 207**: Robert K. Nelson, LaDale Winling, Richard Marciano, Nathan Connolly, et al., "Mapping Inequality," American Panorama, ed. Robert K. Nelson and Edward L. Ayers, accessed April 9, 2021, https://dsl.richmond.edu/panorama/redlining/#loc=9/41.944/-88.301&city=chicago-il; **p. 212**: Daniel Melling; **p. 217**: Melissa Golden/Redux; **p. 220**: Mccool/Alamy Stock Photo.

CHAPTER 9
P. **231**: The History Collection/Alamy Stock Photo; **p. 232**: The History Collection/Alamy Stock Photo; **p. 235**: PA Images/Alamy Stock Photo; **p. 237**: Gado Images/Alamy Stock Photo; **p. 239**: MasterClass/MEGA/Newscom; **p. 241**: Album/Alamy Stock Photo; **p. 244**: Carlos Tovar Samanez (Carlín) is a peruvian cartoonist, philosopher, architect and graphic designer. Carlín is currently the daily political cartoonist at La República.; **p. 248**: Barry Anson/Alamy Stock Photo; **p. 253**: NASA/Science Source.

CHAPTER 10
P. **262**: Gjon Mili/The LIFE Picture Collection via Getty Images; **p. 264**: ITAR-TASS News Agency/ Alamy Stock Photo; **p.267**: Lartige Christophe/SIPA/Newscom; **p. 269**: REUTERS/Alamy Stock Photo; **p. 270**: ©CBC/Courtesy Everett Collection; **p. 273**: Myron Standret/Alamy Stock Photo; **p. 276**: Archivo GBB/Alamy Stock Photo; **p. 277**: August Snow/Alamy Stock Photo; **p. 278**: Sasha Levitt; **p. 281**: ZUMA Press, Inc./Alamy Stock Photo; **p. 283**: AP Photo/Eugene Hoshiko.

CHAPTER 11
P. **291**: Andrew Caballero-Reynolds/AFP via Getty Images; **p. 293**: Agustin Paullier/AFP via Getty Images; **p. 296**: Don

Cravens/The LIFE Images Collection via Getty Images/Getty Images; **p. 298:** Thomas Patterson/The New York Times/Redux; **p. 300:** Abaca Press/Alamy Stock Photo; **p. 302:** Lev Radin/Shutterstock; **p. 305:** Lam Yik Fei/The New York Times/Redux; **p. 307:** ZUMA Press Inc/Alamy Stock Photo; **p. 309:** Art Streiber/August.

CHAPTER 12
P. 316: Image Press Agency/Alamy Stock Photo; **p. 318:** Luis Tato/AFP via Getty Images; **p. 322:** Adriana Loureiro Fernandez/The New York Times/Redux; **p. 325:** Orlok/Shutterstock; **p. 326:** J Marshall - Tribaleye Images/Alamy Stock Photo; **p. 329:** Santi Visalli/Getty Images; **p. 333:** Sebastian Barros/Shutterstock; **p. 335:** Jasper Chamber/Alamy Stock Photo; **p. 338:** Dan Kitwood/Getty Images; **p. 341:** Jamie Lorriman/Alamy Stock Photo.

INDEX

Italic locators signify illustrations; bold locators signal definitions of terms.

distinction, 63–65, **63**, *64*, 67–70, *68*, 275
distribution of income, 174–75
distribution of wealth, 175–76, *175*, 188–89, *188*
Division of Labor in Society, The (Durkheim), 280
divisions of labor, **151**
doing identity, **75**
domestic outsourcing, **255**
dramaturgy, **98**
drug use, 219–20, *220*, 223, 300–301, *301*
dual inheritance theory, 41
Du Bois, W. E. B., 7–8, *8*, 68, 306
Durkheim, Émile, 5
  on anomie, 135, 331
  on empirical inquiry, 7, 8
  on functions of deviance, 131–32, 134, 135, 138
  on individualism, 280
  social change and, 138
  on social facts, 5, 6, 32
  on structural position, 165–66

E
economic capital, **173**, 266, *268*
economic elite, **176**
  crime and, 124–25
  fatness and, 78
  gender inequality and, 254–55
  Great Recession and, 184
  social networks and, 262
  See also economic inequality; elite power
economic inequality, 172–99
  alternatives to, 187–89, *188*
  American history of, 179–83, *180*, *181*, *182*, 184, 237
  consumption and, 78
  Covid-19 pandemic and, 172, 184–85
  future of, 185–86, *186*
  globalization and, 317, 319–23, 328
  income and, 173–75, *174*
  New Gilded Age, 183–85, *183*
  prehistory of, 176–77
  race origins and, 68
  social change and, 303, 310–11
  socialism and, 179, 198–99
  social mobility and, 192–94, *193*, 196–97, *197*
  status hierarchies and, 194–97
  wealth and, 175–76, *175*, 188–89, *188*, 194, 225, *225*
  See also poverty
economic opportunity structure, 310–11, **310**

economy
  ideologies and, 163–64, *163*
  as social institution, 156, 164
  See also economic inequality
education
  as agent of socialization, *43*
  economic inequality and, 186
  institutional racism and, 213–19
  as social institution, 156
Einstein, Albert, 162
elite power, 261–84
  climate crisis and, 329–30
  cultural capital and, 266–75
  ideologies and, 275–79, *277*
  inter-elite competition and, 304–5, 338–39
  opioid crisis and, 264–66, *265*, 282–83
  social capital and, 262–63
  social change and, 296, 304–5, 310, 336, 338–39
  social closure and, 266–67
  social institutions and, 263–66
elite theory of power, **262**
Ellison, Larry, 310
emancipation from slavery, 107, 206, 288
emancipatory catastrophism, 341
embodied cultural capital, 269
embodiment, **51**, 269
Emerging, 159, 160
emotions
  mirror neurons and, 17, 23–24
  social change and, 336
empirical inquiry, 7, 8
employment. *See* work
Engels, Friedrich, 178
enslavement systems, 177
environmental movement, 306
  See also climate crisis
environmental racism, 211–13, **211**, *212*, 325
ethics. *See* research ethics
ethnicity, **70**
ethnocentrism, **56**
ethnography, 271–72, **271**
ethnomethodology, 110–12, **110**, 113
Eugenides, Jeffrey, 14
experimental group, **24**, 25, 104
explicit attitudes, 80
Extinction Rebellion, *340*
extreme poverty, 184, 189, 320
ExxonMobil, 321–22, 324, 329, 334

F
face, **99**, 100, 112, 113
Facebook. *See* social media
face-work, 99, 100

Fair Housing Act (1968), 205
false memories, 31
family
  as agent of socialization, *43*
  as social institution, 156
  See also marriage
family wage, **233**, 234, 237
fascism, 275–76
fatness, 77–79, *78*, 84
federal poverty line, 189
female workforce participation, 232, 234, 236–37, *237*, 248
Feminine Mystique, The (Friedan), 234, 236
femininity, 71
  See also gender
feminism, 236, 292
feminization of poverty, **249**, 326
feudal systems, 177
field, **271**
field experiments, 103, **104**
field notes, **272**
Fight for 15, 310
Finkel, Michael, 22
fit, 270–71, **270**, 274
flat taxation, 181
Flint water crisis, 212
Floyd, George, 108, 307–8, *307*
folkways, **91**, 92
food deserts, 209, *209*
fossil fuel industry, 321–22, 328–30, 334, 339
Foundations of Capitalism, The (Cox), 319
frames, 299–304, **299**, *301*, 335–36
framing wars, 303–4, **303**
France, Anatole, 172
Frazier, Darnella, 307
freedom/power paradox, 254–55, **254**
free market capitalism, **180**, 187
free riders, 187
Friedan, Betty, 234, 236
front stage, 99–100, **99**
functionalism, 131–35, 137–38, 165

G
Garfinkel, Harold, 110, 112, 162
Gates, Bill, 310
gay liberation movement, *293*, 302
gender
  economic inequality and, 194–95
  intersectionality and, 82–83, 105–6
  marked vs. unmarked identities and, 101
  postmodern thought on, 155
  poverty and, 196

inter-elite competition, 304–5, 338–39
interest convergence, **310**
intergenerational advantage and
	disadvantage, 224–25, *224*, *225*
internet. *See* social media
interpersonal discrimination, 102–6,
	102, 107–9, 250
interpersonal socialization, **44**
intersectionality, 82–85, **83**, 138
	interpersonal discrimination and,
		105–6
	wage gaps and, 194–95, *195*
	intersex people, **71**, 302–3
Isaacs, Anita, 172

J

Jasper, James, 293
Jetsons, The, 153
Jewish Americans, 167, *167*
job segregation, **250**, *251*, 278–79
Johnson, Lyndon B., 328
Johnstonbaugh, Morgan, 19–20
Jolie, Angelina, 269
justice, 8

K

Kaepernick, Colin, 306
Kapital, Das (Marx), 137
Kaur, Rupi, 92
Kavanaugh, Brett, 308–9
Kennedy, John F., 131
Kimmel, Jimmy, 54, 96, 100
King, Coretta Scott, 295
King, Martin Luther, Jr., 139, 295,
	296, 297
Knight, Christopher, 21, 22, 161–62
Koch, David, 305
Kozol, Jonathan, 214

L

labeling, **128**
labeling theory, 128–30, **128**
labor, **178**
laboratory experiments, **24**, 25
labor unions, **180**, 181–82, 184,
	288–89
language, 37–39, 41
laws, **92**, 117, 156
Laz, Cheryl, 75
Lee, Jennifer, 196
legitimation, **197**
LGBTQIA people
	economic inequality and, 249
	heteronormativity and, 234
	insurgent consciousness and, 293
	intersectionality and, 106
	marriage and, 236, 246, 247, 301
	media socialization and, 50, *50*

postmodern thought and, 154–55
self-narrative and, 28
social change and, 293, 302–3
social identities and, 62, 65–67, *66*
stereotypes and, 106
liberation theology, 294, 297
Liebowitz, Cara, 85
life expectancy, 213
Liu Xianping, 75, *76*
lived experience. *See* standpoint theory
Lombroso, Cesare, 117
looking-glass self, 18–21, **18**, 22–23,
	28, 129
losing face, 100
low income, 189
lying, theory of mind and, 16–17
lynching, 107

M

MacLean, David, 27, 28, 31
Magie, Elizabeth, 163
male flight, **253**
Mannheim, Karl, 41
Manning, Chelsea, *127*
marginalized masculinities, 240
marijuana
	criminalization of, 219–20, *220*
	legalization of, 300–301, *301*
marked identities, 101–2, 104
marriage, 231–37
	breadwinner/homemaker model,
		232–36, *232*, **232**, 244, 245,
		247, 253
	Covid-19 pandemic and, 247–49,
		248
	partnership union model, 236, 253
	patriarch/property model, 231–32
	shared division of labor model, 245
	specialized division of labor model,
		245, 247
Martin, John Levi, 278
Martineau, Harriet, 7, *7*, 8, 10, 56
Marx, Karl, 137, 146, *178*
	on alienation, 178, 323
	conflict theory and, 138, 179
	on crisis of capitalism, 181, 183
	on free market capitalism, 180, 187
	future of economic inequality and,
		186
	on insurgent consciousness, 292
	theory of, 178–79
masculinity, **71**, 240–42, *241*, 254
	See also gender
mass deportation, 222–23, *222*, **222**
mass incarceration, 220–22, *221*, **221**
mass media, **48**
	climate crisis and, 330, 339
	content analyses, 72, 73

elite power and, 279, 305, 306
fatness and, 79
gender stereotypes and, 72, 75
hegemonic ideologies and, 279, 283
social change and, 339
socialization and, *43*, 48–51, *49*
master frames, 302, *302*
Matza, David, 126
McDonaldization, 152
Mead, George Herbert, 15, 18
mean, 173–74, *174*
means of production, **178**
measures of central tendency, 173–74,
	174
mechanical solidarity, 280
media. *See* mass media; social media
median, 173, 174, *174*
media socialization, *43*, 48–51, **48**, *49*
medicalization, 88–94, 140–42
megachurches, *159*, 160
memory, self and, 26–27, 29–31
men. *See* gender; gender inequality;
	masculinity
menstruation, 92–93
meritocracy, 213, 219, 277–78, 281
Merton, Robert K., 121–23, *122*, 137
meta-analyses, 74
meta-synthesis, 74–75
#MeToo movement, 308–10, *309*
Metzl, Jonathan, 140
Meyers, Bethany C., 72
middle class, 182, 183
Milano, Alyssa, 309
military, *43*
Mills, C. Wright, 261–62, *262*, 263,
	329, 344, 345–46
minimal group paradigm, **65**
mirror neurons, 17–18, 23–24
mirror test, 14, *15*
mode, 173, 174, *174*
modern thought, 148–55, **149**, *153*,
	154
mommy track, 247
Monáe, Janelle, *50*
money, 38
monogamy, 234–35
mononormativity, 234–35, **234**
Monopoly, 162–64, *163*
Montgomery bus boycott, 294–97, *296*
moral entrepreneurs, 336
moral shocks, 292
mores, **91**, 92
Morris, Aldon, 294
Mouton, Melba Ray, *253*
Moynihan, Patrick, 234
multiracial people, 69
multi-site protests, 333, 336–37
Musk, Elon, 310

rationalizations, 126–28
rational legal authority, 151
Reagan, Ronald, 184, 186, 220
rebellion, 123
reciprocity, norm of, 90
recognition, 302
redistribution, 302
redlining, *207*, **207**, 208
Reefer Madness, 219–20
regressive taxation, 181
religion
    as agent of socialization, *43*
    modern thought and, 150, 158
    postmodern thought and, 158–61
    premodern thought and, 149
    as social institution, 158–60, *159*
    work ethic and, 191
repertoires of contention, **290**, 333
research ethics, **8**
research questions, **7**
research subjects, 20
residential segregation, 204–13, *204*,
    204
    environmental racism and, 211–13,
        212
    mechanisms of, 206–8, *207*
    policing and, 223–24
    resource deserts and, 209–11,
        209–10
resource deserts, 209–11, *209–10*,
    209
respect, 8
restrictive covenants, 206
retreatism, 123, 124
retrograde amnesia, 27, 28
rich people. *See* economic elite;
    economic inequality
Ridgeway, Cecilia, 79
Rios, Victor, 216–18, 292
risk society, 339–40, **339**
ritualists, 122
Ritzer, George, 151–52
Rivera, Lauren, 271, 272–74, 275
Robinson, Jo Ann, 295, 296
Rockefeller, John D., 179–80, 321
Rules of Sociological Method, The
    (Durkheim), 7

S

Sacks, Harvey, 89
safety net. *See* social safety net
same-sex marriage, 236, 246, 247,
    301
samples, 73, 136, **137**
sanctions, 93
Sanders, Bernie, 303
saving face, 100
Say Her Name, 306

Scarry, Richard, 278–79, *278*, 280
Schitt's Creek, 270
schizophrenia, 139–42
school discipline, 215–16
schools. *See* education
school-to-prison pipeline, **218**
science, modern thought and, 149,
    154
science of sociology. *See* sociological
    research methods
secondary deviance, **129**
second shift, 242–45, **242**, *244*,
    254–55
self, 15–32
    I vs. me, 15–16
    looking-glass self, 18–21, 22–23,
        28, 129
    memory and, 26–27
    postmodern thought on, 154–55
    self-concept, 18–24, 26
    self-fulfilling prophecy and, 24,
        28
    self-narrative, 27–31
    as social fact, 31–32
    social psychology on, 18–20
    stabilization of, 26
    theory of mind and, 16–17
self-awareness, 14–15, *15*
self-concept, 18–24, 26
self-fulfilling prophecy, **24**, 28
self-narrative, 27–31, **27**
self-sanctioning, 93
self-socialization, 44–45, **44**
semi-peripheral countries, 320–21,
    323, 325
separate spheres, ideology of, **233**
sequences, *38*, 40
service and information economy,
    184
service deserts, 209, *210*
sexism, **238**, 240
    See also gender inequality
sexting, 19–20
sexual assault, activism on, 298–99,
    298, 308–10, @INTX2:*309*, *333*
sexual minorities, **67**
    See also LGBTQIA people
sexual orientation. *See* LGBTQIA
    people
shared division of labor, **245**
signifiers, *38*
Silence of the Lambs, The, 121
Singer, William, 132–33
slacktivism, 309
slavery
    economic inequality and, 177
    emancipation, 107, 206, 288
    global slave trade, 319

intersectionality and, 82
race origins and, 68
social capital, 262–63, **263**, 266, *268*,
    329–30
social change, 288–311, **289**
    climate crisis and, 328–32, 334–39,
        335, *338*, 340–41
    collective action problem and,
        293–94, 295
    conflict theory on, 138–39
    countermovements and, 301,
        328–30
    deviance and, 131, *132*, 137–42
    elite power and, 296, 304–5, 310,
        336, 338–39
    insurgent consciousness and,
        292–93, 330
    interdependent power and, 289–90,
        295, 297
    labor unions and, 180
    liberation theology and, 294, 297
    opportunity structures and, 304–11,
        333
    organizational strength and, 297–99,
        298
    protest and, 139–40, *140*
    repertoires of contention and, 290,
        333
    social construction of social
        problems and, 291–92
    sociological imagination and, 344
    standing/framing and, 299–304,
        300, *301*, *302*, 335–36
    transnational social movements,
        332–39, *333*, *335*, *338*
social closure, **266**
social construction, 37–40, *37*, 67–70,
    76, 95
    See also social constructs
social construction of social problems,
    291–92, **291**
social constructs, **37**, 52–53
    types of, *38*, 39–40
    See also social construction
social context
    cultural capital and, 269–71
    marked vs. unmarked identities
        and, 102
    social interaction and, 95–97, *96*
social deviance, 117
social disorganization theory, 125–26,
    125
social facts, 5–6, *5*, *6*
    climate crisis and, 323
    scientific study of, 6–11
    self as, 31–32
    social constructs as, 38
    sociological imagination and, 345

social identities, 62–85
  construction overview, *65*, 81–82
  critical events and, 307
  deviance and, 128–30
  distinction and, 63–65, *64*, 67–70, 68, 275
  division stage, 67–71
  ethnomethodology and, 110
  individualism and, 280–81
  invention stage, 65–67
  marked vs. unmarked, 101–2, 104
  performing, 75–77
  ranking, 77–82
  role identities, 102
  social interaction and, 100–109
  See also gender; intersectionality; race; status hierarchies
social identity theory, **65**
social inequality, **139**
  conflict theory on, 139, 165, 166, 179
  individualism and, 282
  See also economic inequality; gender inequality; institutional racism; racism; status hierarchies
social inequity aversion, 260
social institutions, 155–60, **156**
  cultural capital and, 267–68
  elite power and, 263–66
  ideologies and, 162–64
  individualism and, 283
  inescapability of, 160–62
  institutional racism and, 224
  social change and, 289–90
social interaction, 89–113, **89**
  deviance and, 121
  fragility of, 97–98, 108, 289
  impression management and, 98–100, *99*, 106–7, 109
  interpersonal discrimination and, 102–6, 107–9, 250
  social change and, 289–90
  social context and, 95–97, *96*
  social identities and, 100–109
  social rules and, 88–94
socialism, **179**, 198–99, 303
socialization, **37**, 42–53
  agents of, 43–44, *43*
  body and, 48, 51–53
  culture and, 42–44, 55–56
  deviance and, 116–17, 124
  hegemonic ideologies and, 278–79
  interpersonal, 44
  interpersonal discrimination and, 106
  mass media and, *43*, 48–51, *49*
  self-socialization, 44–45

social institutions and, 164
social networks and, 45–48, *47*
social learning, 41
social media, **45**
  impression management on, 100
  institutional racism and, 208
  social change and, 308–10, *309*, 332–33, 335
  social rules and, 90–91, 92–93
  socialization and, 45, 50
  transnational social movements and, 332–33, *333*, 335, *335*, 336, *338*
social mobility, **177**, 192–94, *193*, 196–97, *197*, 214
social movements, **289**
social network analysis, 45–46, **46**
social networks, **45**
  Covid-19 pandemic and, 58–59
  deviance and, 123–25
  elite power and, 261–62
  norms and, 91
  social change and, 298–99, *298*, 336
  socialization and, 45–48, *47*
social organizations, 146–47, *146*, 151–52, **151**
social patterns, **9**
social psychology, 18–20
social reproduction, 260–61, **260**
social rules, 88–94, **91**
  breaking, 93–94, *94*, 110, 111, 112–13, 126–28
  deviance and, 119–20
  ethnomethodology and, 110–12, 113
  ideologies and, 162
  social change and, 294, 331, 335
  status hierarchies and, 138–39
  See also deviance
social safety net, **181**, 186, 191
social sanctions, **93**
Social Security Act (1935), 182
social stratification, **168**, 177
  See also status hierarchies
social structure, 164–68, **164**, 204, 224–26
  See also institutional discrimination
social ties, **45**, 46, 58
Society in America (Martineau), 10
socioeconomic status. *See* economic inequality; poverty
sociological imagination, 10–11, **10**, 343–46
sociological research methods, **7**, 9
  biosocial research methods, 52–53
  comparative sociology, 149, 150
  computational sociology, 80, 81
  content analyses, 72, 73
  ethnography, 271–72

field experiments, 103, 104
historical sociology, 140, 141
in-depth interviews, 20–21
laboratory experiments, 24, 25
meta-analyses, 74
meta-synthesis, 74–75
social network analysis, 45–46
spatial analysis, 210, 211, 212
surveys, 136, 137
time-use diary, 243–44, **243**
sociological sympathy, **8**, 56–57
sociological theory, 9–10, **9**
sociology, **4**
  origins of, 6, 7
Solivan, Vanessa, 191–92
Southern Horrors (Wells-Barnett), 107, 138
spatial analysis, 210, **210**, 211, 212
specialized division of labor, **245**, 247
stalled revolution, 253–56, **254**
standardized tests, 213
standing, 299–304, **299**, *300*, 335
standpoint theory, 9–10, **9**
Stanton, Elizabeth Cady, 77
Staples, Brent, 109
state as social institution, 156
  See also nation-states
statistics, 7–8
status, 79–80, **79**
status beliefs, **80**, 279
status elite, **81**, 254–55, 262
  See also elite power; status hierarchies
status hierarchies, 77–82
  acceptance of, 260–61
  economic inequality and, 194–97
  hegemonic ideologies and, 278–79
  impression management and, 106–7, 109
  interpersonal discrimination and, 102–6, 107–9, 250
  marked vs. unmarked identities and, 101, 102, 104
  masculinity and, 240–42, *241*
  norms and, 91
  poverty and, 196
  social rules and, 138–39
  social stratification and, 168
  social structure and, 224–26
  stigma and, 77, 78–79, 84
  See also economic inequality; institutional racism; social inequality
steering, 206, 208
stereotypes, **71**, 83
  gender and, 71–72, 74–75, *74*, 238–39